516

CALGARY PUBLIC LIBRARY
BOYS' & GIRLS' DEPT.

CALGARY PUBLIC LIBRARY

D1071123

j
028.
5
DAR
1982

Darton, F. J. Harvey.
   Children's books in England : five centuries of social
life / F.J. Harvey Darton. -- 3rd ed. / revised by Brian
Alderson. --   Cambridge ₍Cambridgeshire₎ ; New York
: Cambridge University Press, 1982.
   xviii, 398 p. : ill. ; 26 cm.

   Includes index.
   Bibliography: p. 362-371.
   LC: 81006161   ISBN: 0521240204 : $24.95

CALGARY PUBLIC LIBRARY
BOYS' & GIRLS' DEPT.

   1. Children's literature, English -- History and
criticism.   2. Children's literature, English -- Bibliography.
                                          (See next card)
                  516

   5268 CPLA   0100 83JAN26 95432668
   PRODUCED IN CANADA BY UTLAS   PRODUIT AU CANADA PAR UTLAS

Children's Books in England

CHILDREN'S BOOKS IN ENGLAND

Five Centuries of Social Life

F. J. HARVEY DARTON

THIRD EDITION
REVISED BY BRIAN ALDERSON

CAMBRIDGE UNIVERSITY PRESS

CAMBRIDGE
LONDON   NEW YORK   NEW ROCHELLE
MELBOURNE   SYDNEY

Published by the Press Syndicate of the University of Cambridge
The Pitt Building, Trumpington Street, Cambridge CB2 IRP
32 East 57th Street, New York, NY 10022, USA
296 Beaconsfield Parade, Middle Park, Melbourne 3206, Australia

© Cambridge University Press 1958, 1982

First published 1932
Second edition 1958
Reprinted 1960
Third edition 1982

Printed in Great Britain at the University Press, Cambridge

Library of Congress catalogue card number: 81-6161

British Library Cataloguing in Publication Data
Darton, F.J. Harvey
Children's books in England. – 3rd ed.
1. Children's literature
I. Title   II.Alderson, Brian
028. 5'09   Z1037

ISBN 0 521 24020 4

Contents

Preface to the First Edition

The story of English children's books has not yet, so far as I know, been written as a continuous whole, or as a minor chapter in the history of English social life, which is what the present volume is meant to furnish. It has in fact been told only once with any completeness, in Mrs Field's *The Child and His Book* (1891). That, however, has no closely sustained argument – I speak without prejudice, because I was a member of the firm which published it – and virtually stops short with the accession of Victoria; thereby omitting, as other works have, the period when children's books in the modern sense really 'grew up'.

A working definition of the subject is given in Chapter 1. The main object of it is to make clear that this is not meant to be a collection of queer facts or antiquarian scraps, but a record of what certain human beings meant to write, and of their reasons for writing, if they can be discovered. It may seem that here and there too much stress is laid upon commercial and bibliographical details. Their intrusion, if it is an intrusion, is deliberate. They often show, as no reference to current philosophies or 'schools of thought' can show, what was the actual determining cause, what the practical human circumstances, of a book's first appearance. It is more important, from the point of view of English social history, to know what Lamb the writer said to Godwin the book-merchant about the 'tone' of his books, than to appreciate and love the Essays of Elia. But not many children's books give the historian such a choice of emphasis. Ninety per cent were written to pay their way, and the author's and publisher's ways.

Some provision is made for the book collector's point of view; not so much for the psychologist's, or the educational historian's. Little is said about the aesthetic merits of children's books. The limitations of space exclude those general subjects. There is really only one 'text' in these pages, and that is, that children's books were always the scene of a battle between instruction and amusement, between restraint and freedom, between hesitant morality and spontaneous happiness. That conflict is not confined to the nursery. Even within that narrow space it is not yet decided, but liberty began to gain ground in the reign of Victoria. Changes in perspective in this regard came very slowly, and I have not ventured to trace events much beyond 1901.

I have not given a full bibliography. It is impossible. I must refer those who want more detailed information to that provided in the *Cambridge History of*

English Literature (vol. XI), the bibliographies in which are at present being revised for separate re-issue in a compendious form.* But even a list of principal works by principal authors in this connection would present almost insuperable practical difficulties. Here, for the convenience of readers who may wish to pursue special points, a compromise has been made. The authority for minor facts, if unusual, has been mentioned in the text. At the end of each chapter are given the titles of the chief works dealing with particular persons or subjects, though these references, on the one hand, are not meant to be exhaustive, and, on the other, do not include obvious authorities on a large scale, such as (for instance) standard biographies of Bunyan or Lamb. It would have overloaded the book to give references for every small detail, or to justify historical generalizations which are based upon ordinary reading. Much of what may seem new here and there is drawn from the children's books themselves: I have taken no such material at second-hand. I have had access to hundreds of them. My own large collection, unhappily, went to America in the stress of the Peace, but I retained a very full catalogue of it which I have used freely. It is hoped that the Index will make reference to particular authors, books, and a few special subjects reasonably easy. For the convenience of bibliographers, the first-edition dates, when known, are there given under title-entries.

Finally, I do not apologize for using portmanteau phrases like 'adult books', 'juvenile library', and so on. I know they are not the purest English, but they are good sense, and more convenient than 'books meant to be read by adult persons', or other long correctnesses.

I have received many kindnesses from collectors and others, acknowledged in the text upon occasion, but particularly from Mr F. G. Green, F.S.A., of Messrs Dean and Son, Ltd, Mr Morley Kennerley, Dr N. M. Penzer, Mr R. M. J. Knaster, and Mr Wilbur Macey Stone (of New York). Help has also come from the catalogues of and correspondence with Messrs Birrell and Garnett, Ltd (London) and Mr Arthur Rogers (Newcastle-on-Tyne). I am indebted to the Editor and Proprietors of the *Cornhill Magazine* for leave to reprint part of Chapters VII, XIII and XIV; to the Syndics of the Cambridge University Press for permission to repeat some phrases and quotations from my chapter (vol. XI, Chap. XV) in the *Cambridge History of English Literature*; and, for similar courtesy, to the Editor and Proprietors of the tenth edition of the *Encyclopaedia Britannica*. The illustrations are from sources acknowledged on pp. 372–3.

F.J.H.D.

September 1932

---

* [Now the *New Cambridge Bibliography of English Literature (N.C.B.E.L.)* listed on p.363.]

Preface to the Third Edition
by Brian Alderson

I

'It is probably safe to say that Darton will never be supplanted' wrote Kathleen
Lines in her Introduction to the second edition of *Children's Books in England* in
1958. Now, at the start of a third edition, within touch of the fiftieth
anniversary of the book's first appearance, the only change that I would wish to
make to that judgment is to delete the word 'probably'. *Children's Books in
England* is unsupplantable, for it is rooted in an experience and a quality of
mind that are beyond the attainment of more recent generations.

Kathleen Lines was right too in her perception of the elements that came
together to make this such an exceptional book. Most obviously there is Harvey
Darton's lineage: great-great-grandson of the founder of an historic children's
publishing-house – an inheritance that could not help but give him a sure insight
into the commercial decisions that so often determine the character of children's
books at any one time. And this, of course, was supported by his own practical
knowledge of the day-to-day work of a publisher – and one, moreover, still in
touch with the trade procedures of the nineteenth rather than the twentieth
century.

Alongside these inherited advantages, however, Harvey Darton also possessed a natural affection for English literature – when 'English literature' was not
the cramped, syllabus-ridden thing that it subsequently became. So far as he
was concerned, the reading of books was one means towards the rounding-out of
a man's character: a dialogue with the past that heightened one's sense of the
present. Thus he was able to bring to his reading of children's books a rich
understanding of larger literary and historical themes.

This fullness of understanding manifests itself in many ways in the following
pages. It is there in the easy movement of the author's mind through a multitude
of off-hand references – from Chaucer and Shakespeare to his beloved Lamb
and Dickens. It is there in the respect with which he treats all authors who are
seeking, to the best of whatever their limited ability, to express themselves. (So
far as children's books are concerned this respect is unusual at any time. In 1932
it was truly remarkable, since not even today's minimal progress had been made
in literary circles towards seeing children's books as having any cultural
significance beyond quaintness.)

Above all, though, Darton's understanding is to be seen in the style with which he carried out what was, in effect, the first assault on his subject. Here is no arid text-book, systematically plodding through phases and categories, but a continuously lively and often witty response to the human and literary factors in a 'record of lesser history'. Kathleen Lines, again, wisely remarks on the soundness of his judgment about what makes a good children's book:

He disclaims having much to say about 'aesthetic' qualities, but his own high standards are implicit all the time and occasionally clearly stated as, for example, when he gives a quotation from Mrs Barbauld and says, 'language like that, so simple, yet almost majestic, is worth giving to children'.

And indeed, not only is *Children's Books in England* more replete with such judgments than its author gives himself credit for, but it is also packed with tiny summaries and comments which bespeak a degree of thought on the subject unmatched by any later historians. When, to take a couple of points at random, he touches on the labelling of Romances, which 'was all that mattered to seller or buyer' (p. 82), or on the 'loving fidelity of youth' to particular texts, which renders all others unpalatable, he is summing up perfectly certain features about the way people read books that are too often overlooked by purely 'literary' historians.

2

Part of the reason for the maturity of Darton's judgments lies in the simple fact that *Children's Books in England* was written towards the end of a life devoted to the topics that figure in, and around the edges of, its text, and perhaps this Preface is as good a place as any to outline the career of its author.

Frederick Joseph Harvey Darton was born on September 22, 1878, the son of Joseph William Darton, who was at that time partner with William Wells Gardner in a publishing house that made a speciality of the publishing of children's books. (The complications of the Darton firms are summarized in Appendix 2, but it must be added here that Joseph William was directly linked through his father, John Maw Darton, to the famous Darton publishing houses, the first of which commenced independent business in 1787.) 'Fred', as he was known in the family, was sent to school at Dover College and from there he went to St John's College, Oxford, graduating B.A. in Classics in 1899. He immediately went in to the Wells Gardner, Darton firm, becoming a director in 1904 (when the business became a limited company), and remaining with it until 1928 when it was sold to Love and Malcomson of Redhill.

During this period he had good opportunity to experience all the disciplines of a complex job – even in a small house, much of whose business was in less weighty publishing. He necessarily had to learn all the financial and administrative pecularities of a trade notorious for its persistent under-capitalization, but persistently manufacturing a considerable quantity of diverse products each year – each of which possessed separate individual characteristics and had to make its way in the world beset by much competition. At the same time he was busily engaged in the more 'literary' side of publishing: editing manuscripts (it seems as though he was responsible for commissioning *Martin Hyde* from John Masefield as early as 1906), editing, or helping to edit, the firm's magazines – especially *Chatterbox* and *The Prize*★ – and contributing books to the list on his own account. A bibliography of his published books, many done for Wells Gardner, Darton before 1928, is given in Appendix 3 and among these will be found a number of re-tellings of stories from fable and romance – honest workmanship, often glossily produced in a style undoubtedly influenced by the *Colour Fairy Books* of Andrew Lang. (At least two of these titles remained in print to the 1950s, but my own favourite, *The Merry Tales of the Wise Men of Gotham* (1907), amusingly illustrated in colour by Gordon Browne, seems to have been less successful.)

As well as writing these children's books for the firm, and editing such adult works as his *Life* of Mrs Sherwood, Harvey Darton wrote a novel (part of which deals with the trials of a young man born into the household of a small, inglorious publisher) and was also doing general journalism, especially reviewing for the *Daily News*. The Literary Editor of that paper, Bertram Christian, in his supplement to *The Times*'s obituary of Darton, wrote glowingly of his ability to cope with 'anything (except science) from metaphysics to one of those treatises with which American Universities used then to deluge us on laundry work or the care of poultry'. Apparently Darton also won at least twice (under a pseudonym) the old *Westminster*'s annual competition for 'the best review of the best book of the year'. He also contributed two brief monographs on Arnold Bennett and J. M. Barrie to a series of such studies that Christian was editing.

Indeed, the craft of the writer seems to have figured more prominently among Darton's enthusiasms than that of the publisher, and once he was released from his business duties it was to writing that he turned for his chief occupation. Already, as well as the journalism, the editorial work, and the children's books, he had written two broadly historical studies of southern England: *The Marches of Wessex* (1922) and *A Parcel of Kent* (1924), and the impulse behind much of his subsequent work came from his profound feeling for English traditions and a concern to preserve an awareness of their rich idiosyncrasies. All his life he had walked the English countryside, developing a keen sense of the relationship that subsists between man and the landscape in which he lives (to say nothing of a keen connoisseurship of such lesser matters as farm cider and table-skittles). Now, despite personal troubles – some of which may perhaps be glimpsed behind the facade of his second novel – he set about developing some individual themes.

Unsurprisingly, Kent and Dorset (a place returned to 'like reading an old book which is still alive') were the centres from which he conducted his activities. Never deeply rooted in any domestic base he had often spent time out of London, and, for a year or two after 1928, he seems to have lodged at Sutton

---

★   His own account of this editorial experience is given here in Appendix 4.

Valence, near Maidstone. It was here that he probably wrote *From Surtees to Sassoon*, a book which seeks to celebrate the Englishness of certain English writers with an almost Elgarian plangency; and it was here that, in 1931, he prepared the first draft of *Children's Books in England*. (According to a note in his own hand, the book was 'Written at Sutton Valence, 1931-2; rewritten at Dulwich [at his mother's house] 1932. Printed and published at Cambridge in 7 weeks' – a rather speedier time-scale than its 1982 revision.)

After the publication of *Children's Books in England*, Darton moved to Cerne Abbas in Dorset where his last topographical books were written: *English Fabric* (1934) and *Alibi Pilgrimage* (1936). It is not hard to discern in both of these the author's continuing passion for knowing his subject not just from behind a desk but 'as a healthy person using his proper legs'. Ironically though, according to *The Times*'s obituary notice, Harvey Darton's death on July 26, 1936 – at the early age of fifty-seven – was brought about by heart strain 'largely caused by his long walks through his beloved Dorset'.

Of the five main books that he wrote during his final years, *Children's Books in England* must have been the most demanding on his stamina – being not only a long book, but also one requiring the painstaking accumulation and organization of data from a variety of often obscure, and not always reliable sources. He had, however, been laying the foundations of the scholarship in the book for many years. His early writing for children had directed his attention to materials related to legend and romance. His work in publishing had stimulated his inclinations towards an historical understanding of the trade. His love of books in themselves caused him to recognize the often unnoticed significance of both the contents and the appearance of children's books. And his activity as a collector had caused him to pursue his investigations with the skill of a bibliographer as well as a literary historian. Indeed, the need to organize both his facts and his ideas about children's books had been given added impetus through his work as a contributor to the *Cambridge History of English Literature*, and elsewhere (see his Preface above, p. viii), and through his work as a Section Organizer and cataloguer for the Leipzig Exhibition (see below p. 366). Already in these works he can be seen refining the position which he was to expand upon so successfully in the big book of 1932.

In critical terms, the publication of *Children's Books in England* on November 25, 1932 was a great success. Reviewers welcomed the book warmly – but not without indulging in that bane of all discussion of children's books: sentimental reflections on their own youth – and the *Times* obituarist was later to sum up these attitudes in his praise of the book for its learning and its vivacity. However, as Kathleen Lines records in her Introduction to the second edition:

In the spring of 1933 the author, who had been so appreciative of the physical appearance of the book ('though it seems impertinent to admire the Press I am gloriously amazed – I don't know which to be most grateful for, the noble type, the noble binding . . . the product is astonishing in its complete fineness') writes sadly to his publishers – 'I received duly the dismal account for *Children's Books*. I can only say I am very sorry that the Press have been so let in by it.'

The book – ahead of its time in treating so apparently trivial a subject with such attention – sold slowly, and (astonishing though it may seem now) the last of its 1,500 copies did not sell out until 1945 and it then took a further thirteen years before the second edition brought the original text back into print. From 1958 onwards, however, the book has held an honoured place in a world where the study and discussion of children's books has reached proportions which were surely undreamed of by the author, pioneering his way through many a bibliographical thicket in the quiet lamp-light of a Wealden inn.

3

So far as I can reconstruct it, the manner in which *Children's Books in England* was composed in 1931–2 helps to explain both the book's strengths and its weaknesses. As has been said, Harvey Darton, by the time of his retirement, possessed a secure idea of his main thesis, together with a mass of facts which he had garnered himself. (Many of these stemmed direct from his own collection of early children's books, but, as he says in his Preface, this went to America 'in the stress of the Peace' and he had to rely on the detailed catalogue which he made of it before its emigration.) With these facts to hand – and with many more in his head – he was able to write the book with concentrated energy, and it is this which gives it the homogeneity of style and viewpoint that are its personality. It is very much a unity; a book to be read for all that its author has to say and not just an assemblage of facts for the mining activities of reference librarians and students.

Given such a character, the book has proved a difficult one to edit. For, despite the accuracy of its judgments and the exactness of its perceptions, it frequently goes astray in matters of detail, and, in so far as the details are often carefully dove-tailed into the larger structure, their alteration has had to be managed with as much tact as possible. At first, when the new edition was mooted, it was thought that changes (as with the second edition) might be imposed upon a photographic reprint of the original work. As checking proceeded, though, it swiftly became obvious that a large number of modifications would have to be made and the book as it now appears is not altogether the work that proceeded from Harvey Darton's hands fifty years ago. The present reader therefore needs some indication of the nature of the changes that have been made.

1. *Minor amendments in the text.* The ambition of the editor has been to check every fact. This, alas, has not been possible – partly for the very good reason that Darton was writing a book for readers, not researchers, and, as he says: 'It would have overloaded the book to give references for every small detail, or to justify historical generalizations which are based upon ordinary reading.' However, at least three-quarters of his references, quotations, and examples have been traced and his text checked against them. Wherever there has been a

slip in transcription, or wherever later research has revealed more information, corrections have been silently made.

2. *More extensive alterations to the text.* In a number of instances (e.g. his discussion of the Newbery fable books) Darton's notes seem to have let him down, while in others (e.g. Cundall's activities as a publisher) modern scholarship has made more facts available. Consequently, more radical changes to his text have been necessary. On several of these occasions, in order to preserve the flow of an argument, it has seemed better to rewrite passages than to supply laborious or pedantic notes. Wherever possible, though, Harvey Darton's own words have been retained, albeit within altered paragraphs, and an explanation has been incorporated in the Editor's Notes at the end of the book.

3. *Editor's Notes.* With some reluctance these Notes have been admitted – initially to allow for explanations of textual changes, as outlined above, but finally to allow also a variety of additional comments, largely arising from the progress of our knowledge of early children's books. Thus the reader will find here a miscellany of editorial asides, further references and fuller elucidation, carried out with some attempt at catching the informal quality of the author's own discussions.

4. *Footnotes.* Here and there a new (usually bibliographical) comment seemed appropriate, but hardly warranted a place in the Editor's Notes. On these occasions a footnote has been given enclosed in brackets.

5. *Appendixes.* Again, without any wish to convert *Children's Books in England* into an academic tome, it has nonetheless seemed helpful to provide some Appendixes of supplementary information which would have clogged up the main text and would have been out of proportion in the Editor's Notes. Most of these are self-explanatory, but the most ambitious of them, the additional 'chapter' on late-Victorian books, requires some fuller justification. It has been written from a sense that – as he was drawing to the end of his book – Darton hastened his footsteps and did not dwell on what was almost his own period with quite the same fullness that he devoted to earlier times. To some extent this is obviously a matter of perspective – in 1932 he was still too close to events to see all their ramifications – and to some extent it may have been due to a fear that his book was becoming too long. Nevertheless, it does seem important that certain other aspects of Victorian writing for children and of the Victorian book-trade should find a place in *Children's Books in England* and, in consequence, the present editor has added a group of by no means exhaustive comments on topics and writers that are not otherwise substantially discussed.

6. *Illustrations.* When Harvey Darton originally planned the book he hoped that it might be fully illustrated, but this unfortunately did not prove possible. With great generosity the publishers have now permitted a large extension to the number of illustrations in the 1932 and 1958 editions and these have been chosen to assist further the up-dating and clarification of the text. Most of Darton's own choice of pictures has been retained, with his captions worked in

as far as possible. For the rest, the aim has been either to choose material directly related to points in the text, or to employ the illustration as a means of providing additional facts (e.g. the Boreman picture, fig. 19). In both cases, extended captions may have been given by the editor to fill out information. Illustrations are the actual size of the original, except where stated.

7. *Book Lists*. These have proved to be in many ways the most taxing items to deal with. The chief reason for this is the extent to which Darton has used his Book Lists to supplement or comment on his preceding text. Under these circumstances, it was thought best to retain his semi-formal lists largely as he left them, making only a few deletions, additions or corrections. At the same time a further semi-formal listing of later material has been tacked on below Darton's entries, and this follows his policy of providing a few useful general references to works of largely bibliographical or biographical interest, related to the subject of the chapter. A more formal, systematic bibliography of works applying to the history of English children's books *in toto* has been given at the end of the book, replacing Darton's little list at the end of Chapter 1.

8. *Dates*. Anyone who has paid the least attention to the history or bibliography of early children's books will know that the establishing of exact dates for many of these obscure or ephemeral publications is not easily achieved. With many undated works circumstantial evidence, or the unreliable evidence of advertisements, must be used. Here, and with many dated works, it may also transpire that earlier publication occurred either in magazines or in advance of the printed date. (A book – like Carroll's *Through the Looking-Glass* – appearing in November 1871, but dated 1872, could be sold for two Christmas seasons as a new book instead of one.)

Harvey Darton tended to adopt a 'degressive' stance towards this matter – as also towards the inclusion of publishers' names. Where the book warranted it he gave full details, but on other occasions he supplied only the 'official' date of publication in book form, as far as this could be ascertained – and only rarely is a distinction made between dated books and undated ones, whose year of publication is nonetheless known. This can lead to typographic formulae out of place in a discursive study.

This method has been broadly followed in the new edition. Wherever possible an exact year of publication has been given, with evidence mentioned in problematic cases, or with notes on earlier appearance attached to prominent ones. Where a date is only conjectural it has been queried (1823?) if the year is likely to be correct, or given a *circa* prefix (*c.* 1823) if it is more uncertain. Without doubt the extension of scholarship into the field of popular publishing, as instanced in the growth of Victorian studies, or the massive labours attending the compilation of the eighteenth-century *Short-Title Catalogue*, will lead to a much more reliable foundation of fact before long.

9. *'Now'*. From time to time Darton refers to events in the immediate present of 1932. These remarks have mostly been allowed to stand unaltered, since they give a flavour which is an essential part of his whole approach to his subject. In

some cases, however, a qualifying note or footnote has been added to comment on the present of 1979-80. Here as elsewhere every effort has been made to respect Darton's attitude towards 'children's books in England' and to catch something of his vivacity, if not his learning.

10. *Index and comparative paging.* The book has been re-indexed broadly in conformity with the pattern established for the 1932 edition, as is noted on p. 376.

Because of its position as a leading work on its subject, *Children's Books in England* has frequently been cited in other works, often by page rather than chapter and section numbers. Users of the present edition may therefore like to know that there is a fairly close correspondence between the paging of the 1932 and 1982 editions. The increased number of words to a page in the present edition tends to be counterbalanced by the increased number of illustrations, so that only towards the end of the book (from Chapter x) do the 1982 page numbers lag from five to ten pages behind those of 1932.

B. A.

August 1980

Acknowledgments

Like Harvey Darton before me, I have received many kindnesses from friends, collectors and librarians in working on *Children's Books in England*. I should especially like to thank Iain Bain for advice about Bewick; Gerry and Muriel Bell for hospitable conversations on a variety of topics; Tim Darton for biographical information; Jane Gardner for help in the British Museum; Derek Gibbons, who can perhaps stand for a host of booksellers whose catalogues and opinions are so stimulating; Jill Grey for supplying bibliographical details about the Kilners and others; Victor Neuburg for discussions about chapbooks; Iona and Peter Opie, and Fernand and Anne Renier, who rescued me with information that seemed beyond my discovery elsewhere; and Justin Schiller for his very practical friendship and hospitality.

Harvey Darton clearly relied for much of his basic research on the collection of children's books housed in our national library at the British Museum. While one must regret that, in the fifty years since his book was published, the authorities in charge of these holdings have shown little interest in this part of their collection I must nonetheless thank the helpful officials in the Reading Room who have permitted work to be undertaken there and have endeavoured to find books misplaced or lost since 1932. Much help has also been received from the Victoria and Albert Museum Library, and especially from Ann Hobbs and Irene Whalley; from its associated Museum of Childhood at Bethnal Green; from the London Library – that wonderful institution; from the University Library, Cambridge, and the Bodleian Library, Oxford; and from the public libraries at Birmingham and Wandsworth, especially from Nikki Rathbone and Ferelith Aglen.

Abroad, I owe thanks to the Toronto Public Library, who enabled me to spend time working in the peerless Osborne Collection, where I was much helped by the former librarian, Judith St John, and the present librarian, Margaret Maloney. I gained much from visits to the Darton Collection at the Teachers College of Columbia University, and the Pierpont Morgan Library, New York, where Gerald Gottlieb introduced me to a veritable Aladdin's Cave of treasures. I am also most grateful to the authorities at the Polytechnic of North London who gave me leave of absence to undertake this and other work, and to my colleagues at the School of Librarianship there, especially Eleanor

Von Schweinitz and Bob Barker, who have shown so much tolerance for my abstracted behaviour.

Finally, and above all, thanks to my wife Valerie for her support during all stages of this work, for her help in research, and for the many hours spent toiling over the new index; to two of my sons, William and John, for their good-hearted drudgery in matters of typing and pasting; and to my friends Pat Garrett, Marjorie Moon and Lawrence Darton, whose hospitality, ready help and constant enthusiasm have buoyed me up through many despairing moments.

B.A.

CHAPTER I

An Introductory Survey

I

By 'children's books' I mean printed works produced ostensibly to give children spontaneous pleasure, and not primarily to teach them, nor solely to make them good, nor to keep them *profitably* quiet. I shall therefore exclude from this history, as a general rule, all schoolbooks, all purely moral or didactic treatises, all reflective or adult-minded descriptions of child-life, and almost all alphabets, primers, and spelling-books; though some works in each category will be mentioned because they purposely gave much latitude to amusement, or because they contained elements which have passed into a less austere legacy. The definition is given as a broad principle liable to perpetual exception.

Roughly speaking, under its terms, there were no children's books in England before the seventeenth century, and very few even then. There were plenty of schoolbooks and guides to conduct, but none which would openly allow a child to enjoy himself with no thought of duty nor fear of wrong. Children's books did not stand out by themselves as a clear but subordinate branch of English literature until the middle of the eighteenth century. Today, in the statistics[1] of printed matter, they are second only to works of fiction. To put it commercially, it is less than two centuries since they became a definite object of the activities of the book-trade; that is to say, since authors first wrote them, and merchants first produced them, *habitually*, in quantities and with a frequency which implied that they were meant for a known, considerable, permanent class of readers ready to receive them. Because an arbitrary date is a convenience, and for no other reason, I will say that that commencement took place in 1744, when John Newbery, the most authentic founder of this traffic in minor literature, published his first children's book.

It is worth while to quote some particulars of this engaging work which is by way of being a 'key' publication. It was called *A Little Pretty Pocket-Book*.[2] The frontispiece shows a mother or a governess teaching a boy and girl. Underneath is the inscription 'Delectando monemus. Instruction with Delight.' The expanded title, as given in the first advertisement for the book in the *Penny London Morning Advertiser* of June 18, 1744, states that the *Pocket-Book* was intended for the Instruction and Amusement of Little Master Tommy and Pretty Miss Polly; with an agreeable Letter to read from *Jack the Giant-Killer*, as also a Ball and a Pincushion, the use of which will infallibly make Tommy a good Boy, and Polly a good Girl . . . Price of the Book alone, *6d.*, with Ball or Pincushion, *8d.*

I

The great I Play.

CRICKET.

THIS Leſſon obſerve,
　When you play at *Cricket*,
Catch *All* fairly out,
　Or bowl down the *Wicket*.

MORAL.

This Maxim regard,
　Now you're in your Prime;
Look ere 'tis too late;
　By the Fore-lock take *Time*.
　　　C 3　　　　STOOL-

1. Eighteenth-century cricket with a moral of 'insecure relevance' from the 1767 edition of *A Little Pretty Pocket-Book*.

It was published at the sign of the Bible and Crown, near Devereux Court, London, close to the Grecian Coffee House, one of Oliver Goldsmith's haunts. John Newbery in 1744 had just come to London from Reading, where he had been an assistant and partner of William Carnan, printer and bookseller. He had also had business connections with Collins, the Salisbury bookseller. In London, besides the Bible and Crown, he set up an establishment at the Golden Ball, close to the Royal Exchange, probably for the sake of the sea-borne and eastern counties trade, which came by road through Whitechapel and by river up to London Bridge. In 1745, however, he transferred the whole of his business to the more famous address, 'the *Bible and Sun*, near the Chapter House, in St Paul's Church-Yard'. Here his successors remained as publishers almost to the reign of George V.

These facts have some importance in a small historical way. More to the immediate purpose are a few further details of the *Pocket-Book's* contents. The most significant point is that Newbery deliberately set out to provide amusement, and was not afraid to say so. Fifty years before he might not have ventured to such lengths, and he would hardly have said anything about the good looks of Miss Polly, whatever her excellence. He certainly puts instruction before amusement; but his ideas of both instruction and amusement differed greatly from those exhibited by his few and intermittent predecessors in this style of publishing, which he was to make peculiarly his own. In fact, after some preliminary remarks meant for parents, instruction is dragged in only by the scruff. Most of the book is taken up with pictures of children playing games, and little rhymes not very securely relevant to them.*

The pedagogue is mollified by the heading of each pastime, which is, with no relevance at all, a letter of the alphabet – 'The Great A Play', 'The Great B Play', and so on. There are also 'Little a [b, etc.] Plays', with rhymes not more congruous. For instance, 'Little s' stands at the head of

> Here's great K, and L,
> Pray Dame can you tell,
> Who put the Pig-Hog
> Down into the Well?

and 'Little t' is

> So great O, and P,
> Pray what do you see?
> *A naughty Boy whipt*;
> But that is not me.

These are accompanied by small blocks, respectively, of a well and of a boy being birched upon an extensive bare rump. Such blocks had done duty in more than one *abecedarium* of a generation earlier.

It might have been expected that with such careless treatment of instruction itself Newbery would have indulged his fancy over Jack the Giant-Killer. But the moralists of the preceding ages had banished Jack from the nursery (a feat often attempted), and they had also been very suspicious of any recommendation to play at ball. Newbery compromised ingeniously with their point of view. The 'letter' from Jack was simply an instruction in the proper use of the ball and pincushion. Each object had one side red, the other black. Every good deed done by Tommy and Polly was to be marked by sticking a pin into the red half, every ill deed by one in the black. And Jack had another function. Towards the end of the *Pocket-Book* four fables are given, and he is introduced as the author of the rhymed morals attached to them. Thus all trace of the brutal and licentious giganticide is whitewashed, though his familiar name is used as an attraction. He is turned into an agent of conscious virtue.

But it was not enough to offer a giant as a bait. Two other 'letters' appear in

---

* It may be of interest to mention the games. They aré Chuck-Farthing; Kite-Flying; Maypole Dancing; Taw (marbles); Hoop and Hide (Hide and Seek); Thread the Needle (a chase-game); Fishing; Blindman's Buff; Shuttle-Cock; King (of the Castle) I am; Peg Farthing (driving a coin out of a circle with a pegtop); Knock-out and Span (marbles); Hop, Step and Jump; 'Boys and Girls come out to Play'; 'I sent a letter to my Love'; Pitch and Hussle; Cricket (with two stumps and a curved-club bat); Stool-Ball (here a sort of rounders); Swimming; Base Ball (rounders as now played); Trap-Ball; Tip-Cat; Fives; Leap-Frog; Birds'-Nesting (reprobated); Train-Banding; 'All the Birds in the Air' (a mimicry game); Hop-Hat; Shooting; Hop-Scotch; Riding; and 'Who will play at my Squares?' (which looks like a card-game but is probably a concealed advertisement for Newbery's educational *Sett of Fifty-six Squares*).

the volume. They display the earthly reward of eminence in book-learning. The well-schooled, satisfactory boy is shown as eventually riding in a coach and six, the good girl as being given a fine gold watch.

There is some probability that Newbery wrote the *Pocket-Book* himself. It is of a piece with the known character of the man, 'Jack Whirler', of Johnson's *Idler* (no. 19). He was a kind of business bumble-bee, though a worker too. In the *Pocket-Book's* address to parents he shows admiration of Locke on Education, but almost in the same breath gives advice which is pure Rousseau: and one of his most characteristic productions, *The Twelfth-Day Gift* (1767), has a frontispiece which might almost serve as his coat-of-arms. It shows two men carrying, on a sort of stretcher, a monstrous fine cake. Underneath is the motto 'Trade and Plumb-cake for ever, Huzza!'

It is no good pretending that John Newbery was consistent, or had any reasoned theory of infant psychology, or was an apostle of this or that school of educational thought. He was simply an active and benevolent tradesman, who was the first to see that, in his line of business, children's books deserved special attention and development. He produced almost nothing original that has passed into the nursery library to live for ever. Even his most famous juvenile

Trade & Plumb-cake for ever Huzza!

2. The copperplate frontispiece to *The Twelfth-Day Gift* (1770). The scene is evidently 'Ludgate Street' (the present Ludgate Hill) with St Paul's in the background. Newbery's premises stood at the top left-hand corner. The first edition of the *Gift* was published by John Newbery in 1767, but it may have been preceded by an edition in 1764. Original size of engraving and caption 4 by 2½ in.

publication, *Goody Two-Shoes*, is utterly dead. His personality and his friendships – what he was and what he did, in fact – have endured longer than any of
his wares. He prospered, and his books proved by success that they met a want.

They will come up for closer examination in due course. Here I would only
dwell on the features just selected from the *Little Pretty Pocket-Book*: the claim
to provide amusement with instruction, the use of the alphabet both as a form of
amusement and, by its mere presence, as an instrument of education, the bold
introduction of the unedifying name of the Giant-Killer, the inclusion of fables,
and the various small commercial touches which made it clear, as indeed the
very form of the stout little book does, that the producer had a social rather than
a scholastic or religious market quite plainly in view. Those little details all
suggest various things that must have been in some sort of existence already.
What was the social – or the mercantile – inheritance of which Newbery, not a
real creator nor a daring innovator, was able to take advantage immediately he
set out to make his fortune as a London bookseller? What was the nature of any
children's books which existed before his time, why at that particular time was
their development brought, as if by an abrupt miracle, into touch with that of
'adult' English literature – in fact, why and how, such as they were, were they
themselves ever composed and published at all?

Most of the answer lies in the Newbery slogan, as it might be called today –
'Trade and Plumb-cake for ever'. That would not have been a natural war-cry
for a middle-class commercial man in England before about the reign of George
II. It was natural for at least a century afterwards. And children's books, written
as such, have been in England almost entirely a product of the large domesti-
cated middle-class, which began to exist, free of civil war, not wildly excited
about religion nor very heedful of political arts, but increasingly conscious and
desirous of freedom, under the Hanoverian dynasty. There lies nearly all the
rest of the answer. The reading habit had come into middling social life, and the
English novel was born. The microcosm of children was to receive the reflection
of this slow great change in the English character. Internal peace, increasing
trade at home and abroad, wider literacy in all but the lowest classes, made such
an opportunity for a quick brain as had not existed hitherto; and Newbery
possessed the business intuition and the vague idealism to seize it.

2

But what were the precise materials which, in that fortunate conjunction,
Newbery combined and used? It is clear that he found already in his lumber
room or property store several things that are still known in nurseries: the
Pocket-Book, even in its own period, is evidently both ancient and modern.
Consider the features already outlined. How many of them legitimately belong
to 'children's books', in a long view, and to what extent need their historical
nature be examined here? They can be regarded for the moment as separate
abstractions.

(*a*) *The fable* was explicitly present in Newbery's compilation. In one form or another, it is still in every nursery library,[3] and, however you define a children's book, no one will seriously deny Aesop the right of entry. In England anyone who could read and get hold of a book was likely to meet him, as soon as Caxton had put him into the best English. Fables, likewise, have always been the oral possession of the illiterate. They have, moreover, been a common vehicle of education, and have assumed other forms also. It is obvious that their development into a 'children's book' in the more restricted sense ought to be scrutinized. On the other hand, the study of the fable as such, and of the book or person called Aesop in particular, is a special branch of learning, and would be entirely out of place here.

(*b*) *Romance*, in a semi-literary sense is present only by implication. Jack the Giant-Killer was said to have been in the employ of King Arthur, of whom other publications show that Newbery was aware. Jack, however, is really a figure of folk-lore. Newbery did not know the then uninvented word 'folk-lore'. Moreover, he seems not to have touched the chief subjects of the Middle Age Romances. Nevertheless, children read versions of them in his day, as other evidence proves. Jack may therefore be taken in this connection, as a sign-post to a subject which, since children certainly read those Romances now also, it is necessary to explore slightly. But the only question is how the tales of Bevis, St George and the rest became children's books, before or after Newbery's time; not who first wrote them, nor when, nor why.

(*c*) *Conduct and education* are inherent in the *Pocket-Book* from the title-page onwards. The words cover aspects of juvenile life which are separable only in logic, not completely in practice. In fact, the confusion between 'instruction' and 'amusement', and the struggle about them in the minds of purveyors of both (in Newbery's, for instance), are to no small extent the real subject of this book. But treatises on the way to behave and schoolbooks, are only relevant here if and when they influenced more genuine children's books, or contained border-line material for them, like the genial alphabet in the *Pocket-Book* itself, or made references to them, usually of a derogatory nature, but useful as evidence of what was really read.

These three elements in Newbery's first juvenile publication, then, will have to be exhibited, with some notice of the condition in which he found them, and how they came to be available to him and to children. They were all in print at least two centuries before 1744. A fourth element, by far the most important, was actually much later than they in reaching type. This is the *Fairy-tale*, for which Jack's person may be said to stand here, rather clumsily. Whether as literature or folk-lore, the Fairy-Tale appeared but scrappily between the covers of printed books before 1744, and for a long while afterwards. In Newbery's day it was not high in the favour of the judicious. That very fact must be investigated, because, with the kindred Nursery Rhyme, the Cabinet of the Fairies is both the corner- and the coping-stone of any child's library. But nothing whatever need be said here about anthropology or the distribution of folk-lore. It does not concern us to know whether or not Cinderella was a native of Borrioboola-Gha, on the left bank of the Niger. It is much more to the point to discover why the contemporaries of Mrs Jellyby encouraged such an alien in England, and what, even earlier, Newbery knew about glass slippers and fairy godmothers.

Two further considerations arise out of the *Pocket-Book*. Newbery was at pains to placate a public opinion which demanded a 'moral': why? The reason is to be discovered in the Puritans' concern for children seventy years or more before he went to Devereux Court. Their attempts to write for children, whether one calls the result 'children's books' or not, had a lasting influence on those books both in England and in America. They are usually displayed as examples of exactly what should not be offered to young minds. But justice demands rather closer inquiry into both motives and products; and Bunyan cannot be ignored, even if *The Pilgrim's Progress* was not meant for children.

The other significant phenomenon is the cheap price of this well-printed, compact little volume, and the apparent ease with which a young man from Berkshire became important in the multifarious book-trade of England. Though newspapers were increasing in number, and even spreading 'literary intelligence', the distribution of popular booklets was not by any means automatic: at least, not very clearly so. The machinery which lay to Newbery's hand is very well worth close inspection. Children's books, of sorts – not the fully developed sort – were in circulation before ever he made a business of them.

3

What this amounts to is not a contradiction of the statement that children's books began to be published in 1744. It merely means that 1744 is a date comparable to the 1066 of the older histories. There is written history and even a kind of archaeology about the period before Newbery the Conqueror. It is summarized in the next few chapters. Its value is precisely the value of pre-Norman adult history. It is the chronicle of the English people in their capacity of parents, guardians and educators of children; with this reservation, that in these pages the child at leisure is to be considered as their preoccupation, and their care for its routine of intellectual discipline very largely (though not entirely) set aside. It is in their human aspect that I wish to see those who wrote children's books; as kind people inspired more by love and happiness than by purpose, though happiness was often enough seen as duty and duty uncompromisingly said to be happiness.

It is, in fact, just by reason of his human personality that Newbery stands out. There were woven into the experience of his time all those earlier strands which can be classified and picked out separately in a retrospect. But they too were always part of the fabric of everyday life rather than neat categories of evolution. I do not want to forget that, nor to label past things 'quaint' because we have forgotten their ordinary touch and feel, and even their faint fragrance. If 1744 is as it were a line drawn, it is only an imaginary one, though the air is clearer this side of it. Another, as will be seen, could be drawn as truthfully and usefully at the year 1865. But people still living today were children in 1865, and never saw the line and are unaware of it now. There will be plenty of evidence of continuity before and after Little Master Tommy and Pretty Miss Polly had their agreeable letter from Jack the Giant-Killer.

4

So much for preconceptions which it is hoped to avoid and by-ways which it would be tiresome and needless to enter. There is one other notable thing in that eighteenth-century emergence of the children's book-trade, and that is that the three most famous wares in its market, as well as in our market today, were not children's books at all: *The Pilgrim's Progress*, *Gulliver's Travels* and *Robinson Crusoe*. It would be stupid to let any definition crowd them out, especially as editions of them have always been prepared specially for children. But the fact remains that they, and a few lesser works, were created for adults and simply annexed by children – and by young children at that.

There is room for endless discussion on that subject; but not here. It raises the question, what *constitutes* a children's book – not whether this or that volume is a book written for children and read by them, but what qualities such a book does possess if it is read and should possess if it is purposely written. That is a matter for psychologists, empirical and theoretical alike: not for the historian of books which have existed and of the people who wrote them.

With that, it is time to consider the juvenile literature of days when there were not so many things to think about even as in 1744.

[The 'Brief Book List' appended to this chapter in the first edition contained general works on English children's books. It has been transferred to the General Book List on pp. 362–71 where the items which were here listed are marked with an asterisk.]

CHAPTER II

The Legacy of the Middle Ages:
(i) Fables

I

Of all printed matter which could be adapted for the use of children when Newbery set up in business, 'Aesop' was the most obvious item. The fables had been in English print ever since Caxton finished his translation from the French on March 26, 1484, 'in the first year of the reign of King Richard the Third'. He did not mean this text, any more than he meant *Reynard the Fox* (1481), for children. He did not know that even as he worked at his press a sad story for later children was in the making; for in March, 1484, the two little princes lay in the Tower, and neither the boy Edward V nor his uncle Richard III had been crowned or proclaimed king. Caxton simply printed good literature for plain Englishmen to read, as he had seen ordinary people reading on the Continent. He chose fables 'for to shewe al maner of folk what maner of thyng they ought to ensyewe and folowe. And also what maner of thyng they must and ought to leve and flee, for fable is as moche to seye in poeterye as wordes in theologye.' No one has ever achieved a straightforward purpose in better English. Caxton's *Aesop*, with infinitely little modernization, is the best text for children today.

If Caxton had lived from 1822 to 1891, instead of in the corresponding years four centuries earlier, he would have seen the publication of, among others, the following illustrated editions of 'Aesop', done in a spirit which children would appreciate: 1848, illustrated by Tenniel; 1857, by C. H. Bennett; 1860, by Harrison Weir; 1867 by Thomas Dalziel and others; 1869, by Ernest Griset; 1883, by Randolph Caldecott; 1887, by Walter Crane. His successors would have known the volumes adorned in 1909 by E. J. Detmold and in 1912 by Arthur Rackham. These were all new editions. No strict canon was observed in the texts, though Tenniel was given a fresh translation, by Thomas James, and Harrison Weir later did a fresh set of illustrations (engraved by John Greenaway) for a text 'literally translated from the Greek' by the Rev. George Fyler Townsend M.A. (1867). There were also probably current, up to the middle of the nineteenth century, reprints or surviving copies of the texts by Ogilby, L'Estrange, Croxall (with its engraved pictures, or with Bewick's more handsome copies) and Jefferys Taylor. The Victorian child and its successors had a rich inheritance. How and why did it accumulate thus?

There were two lines of descent for *Aesop* in England, until it became definitely a 'family' book and so a children's book. One was through the schools, the other through fashionable society. The school versions (apart from Greek and Latin texts meant for instruction in grammar and syntax) were for teaching English as well as the nearly dead languages, and it is possible to see 'the painefull schoolemaster' trying to get humanity into his task. The freest early translation, in fact, was by a pedagogue, who was also a poet. Robert Henryson put *Aesop* into brave verse, not unworthy to be compared (as it can be in the fable of the Cock and Fox) with Chaucer's. He died early in the sixteenth century, but his version was not printed till much later: *The Morall Fabillis of Esope the Phrygian, Compylit in Eloquent, and Ornate Scottis Meter, be Maister Robert Henrisone, Scholemaister of Dunfermeling . . . Edinburgh,* 1570.*

English school versions began to grow numerous in the latter half of that century. The compulsory use of our native tongue in the more numerous and no longer ecclesiastical schools had a rapid humanizing effect, and, though the fables were as a rule used only as a vehicle for teaching both Latin and English, they took on something of local colour and something of each translator's personality; one sees behind them, often, a man speaking to children, as well as a pedagogue teaching pupils.

One of the first of these versions is certainly a humane document; and so, by a happy chance, is the actual copy of it preserved in the British Museum Library. It was published in 1585. The title must be reproduced literally. It runs:

Æsopz Fablz in tru Ortŏgraphy with Grammar-notz. Her-yntoo ar also jooined the short sentencez of the wýz Cato . . . transláted oyt-of Latin in-too English By William Byllokar.

William Byllokar, in fact, was an early spelling reformer. He was also a moralist, for his 'life' of 'Aesop' dwells on the fabulist's excellence 'when he toucheth mortal discipline or fashion of life'.

As a translator he is a very little more ornate than Caxton. But in simplicity, in truth of aim, his English is almost startlingly removed from the contemporary literary style – of the *Arcadia*, or *Jack Wilton*, for instance. It is plain English, once more. Bullokar veritably wrote with a human young reader in his mind. Maybe he was, in our cant phrase, a crank. But he had a crank's honourable earnestness, downrightly expressed.

And the British Museum copy of his book was once owned by just such a reader as he sought. It belonged at different times to four people who wrote their names in it. Two of them were perhaps grown-up, to judge by their script. But the only dated entry is a piece of life, and is in a distinctly juvenile hand: 'James Dodson is my name and with my pen i write the same and write the same and if my pen had beene a litle beter I would mend† every Letter 1690.' Nearly two and a half centuries ago, that is to say, that very volume had had a hundred years' use as a human possession.

---

*   The at present unique copy of this is in the British Museum, the gift of the great collector, Mr S. R. Christie-Miller, of Britwell Court.

†   [Possibly 'mind'.]

There is a personal touch also in the next outstanding school version, 'printed by I. D. for Thomas Man, and are to be sold by Thomas Pavier, 1624'.* It was a famous schoolmaster, John Brinsley, who here translated *Esop's Fables* 'both Grammatically, and also in propriety of our English phrase'. He did it for grammar-school use, for scholars of from seven to fifteen. By seven years of age they were to have learned 'the Abcie and Primer' – before going to the grammar school – and by fifteen they were to be ready for the university.

Brinsley's educational theories are developed fully in his *Ludus Literarius, or the Grammar School* (1612): they are for the most part irrelevant here. He himself was born about 1565, and went to Christ's, Cambridge, in 1580. He eventually became headmaster of Ashby-de-la-Zouch School, founded probably, in Henry VIII's reign. Here, according to one of his pupils, he showed himself 'a strict puritan' and later, indeed, was ejected on account of his Puritan opinions.

He explained that the 'painefull schoolemaster' (his own phrase) must not treat the fables only as a lesson in accidence. The boys must be able to furnish a digest, to show that they understood the meaning ('morals' are provided) and must know it as a *story*. There are excellent textual notes on points of detail, and it is in one of these that Brinsley peeps out individually. The daw in borrowed plumes – it was a jay in Bullokar – is here turned into a 'Cornish chough'. Brinsley, fortunate man, must have seen one, and passed on the knowledge to schoolboys. He was not a prattling Holofernes, but a man who had had a young mind and seen English country sights. That is an advance towards the making of a genuine children's book, 'in propriety of our English phrase', to use Brinsley's own words.

2

Let us leave the schoolroom at that. *Aesop* was to become also the prey of literary hacks. But he was at least perceived by them to be worth reading for pleasure. The mid-seventeenth century gave 'the Phrygian' a new air; or, more accurately, airs and graces. The first 'polite' edition – meant for children as well as grown ups – set a fashion in England before La Fontaine appeared in France. It came out in the year of Cromwell's 'crowning mercy', 1651, and was by one of those bizarre figures of the Commonwealth and Restoration periods who really ought to have lived for Dickens to see: John Ogilby,[1] a first-rate road-recorder, a good cosmographer, editor–publisher of some fine illustrated books, a lottery-manager, trooper in Ireland, dancing-master, authority on coronation ceremonies, and poet bad enough for special derision at the hands of Dryden and Pope.

* Pavier of the falsely dated 'Pied Bull' quartos of Shakespeare.

His view was that the school versions, 'read and familiar with children', were utterly unworthy. He obtained for his own text the commendation of the aged James Shirley and the imprisoned Sir William D'Avenant, and dedicated the first edition, not without the customary fulsomeness, to Lord Winchelsea and Lord Beauchamp: *The Fables of Aesop, Paraphras'd in Verse, and adorn'd with Sculpture* (1651). A second edition, dedicated to Lord Ossory, appeared in 1665, and when the sheets for this were destroyed in the Great Fire he set about producing a new volume: *Aesopic's: or a Second Collection of Fables Paraphras'd in Verse* (1668). He obtained a Royal Proclamation (in common form) against infringement of his copyright, and for the last two books he got Hollar, Stoop and Francis Barlow to prepare etchings – very good ones, which illustrate the text, nor merely decorate it, in spite of their gelid semi-classical style. The publisher of the 1651 and 1665 editions was Andrew Crooke, who that same year issued Hobbes' *Leviathan*, the penultimate chapter of which was not sympathetic to fables; but Crooke was daringly catholic in his output, and it would be interesting to know more of him. He produced cheap books as well as these sumptuous *Aesops*. But it is plain that Ogilby wished to bestow upon two clearly envisaged publics – the young and the elegant – what a tradesman in books today would call a high-class or fine art production; and he certainly succeeded though his English was not so good as its embellishments.

The 1665 and 1668 volumes had an odd sequel on their fashionable side. One of their chief illustrators, Francis Barlow, did a version of his own, which was published in 1666 (etched title-page dated 1665) and which had printed texts in French and Latin, by Robert Codrington M.A., and a rhymed English version on the etched plates by Tho. Philipott Esq. Most of this edition, however, was also destroyed in the Fire and in 1687 Barlow published an improved edition, where, for the English, he procured the services of one whom he proclaimed a notable colleague: 'The Ingenious Mrs A. Behn has been so obliging as to perform the English Poetry, which in short comprehends the Sense of the Fable and Moral: Whereof to say much were needless, since it may sufficiently recommend it self to all Persons of Understanding.' Aphra Behn, the incomparable Astraea! She was near her end. She was to produce the moral *Oroonoko* the next year, and die unhappily in 1689. She could gleek upon occasion, but in her *Aesop* she was to reduce the sonorous, the swoln Ogilby to an elegant neatness. Here is her *Fox and Grapes:*

> The Fox who longd for grapes, beholds with paine
> The tempting Clusters were too high to gaine,
> Grieu'd in his heart he forc'd a careles smile,
> And cryd, they'r sharpe and hardly worth my toyle.

> MORALL
> Young Debauchees to Beauty thus ingrate,
> That vertue blast they can not violate.

That *may* conceivably be a moral, just as 'smile' and 'toyle' may rhyme. But a version like that is as far from Ogilby as from Brinsley and Caxton. It is the apotheosis (or even the apocolocyntosis[2]) of the Phrygian slave in a Palladian Temple of the Muses. It was certainly not for 'al maner of folk', much less for children.

It ought almost to have killed any just appreciation of *Aesop*. But it is clear that a good version was still wanted. The school-texts remained too popular. As early as 1660, Hoole, in his *New Discovery of the Old Art of Teaching School*, had attacked them as 'a mere rhapsody of fragments'. Almost the same words were used by the next eminent literary (as opposed to scholastic) translator, with the same ostensible desire to give children something better: 'This Rhapsody of Fables', he wrote, 'is a Book Universally Read and Taught in All our Schools; but almost at such a Rate as we teach Pyes and Parrots, that Pronounce the Words without so much as Guessing at the Meaning of them.' He therefore made an enormous treasury of fables which were definitely meant to be read by children outside school; though his edition was not, in a commercial sense, anything like a children's book, a familiar and manageable companion for leisure hours. It was a handsome and expensive 'gift-book', in today's phrase.

This new arrival was one of the liveliest figures in the seventeenth-century welter, Roger L'Estrange, perhaps the most prolific of all the partisan pamphleteers of that vituperative age, and a patriarch (not exactly venerable) in the history of English journalism. At the Revolution of 1688 he lost the office of Licenser of the Press, which he had held since 1663 and had used with much agility of mind and wit, but with very little impartiality. He was in financial straits, and when six booksellers asked him to do a complete *Aesop*, he accepted, and went into the business thoroughly, and, it is fair to believe, conscientiously. He got £300 for the job, and the result came out in 1692 as *The Fables of Aesop and other Eminent Mythologists: with Morals and Reflections*. It is said to be the largest collection of fables in the English language. It contains five hundred, not only drawn from old writers like Phaedrus, Avian, and others, but including such recent work as La Fontaine's. The really significant thing, however, is the fact that the booksellers saw a clear and profitable opening for an edition suited to the general reader, and especially the young reader; to which must be added, as an historical portent in this survey, the point of view L'Estrange himself took.

He had some idea at first of weaving all the fables into a continuous narrative, a sort of *Reynard the Fox*. It would have suited his political mind, but it was either too difficult or, after 1688, too dangerous. Then he thought of making a plain new translation from the Oxford and Cambridge Latin texts. 'But upon jumbling matters and thoughts together, and laying one thing by another' – a pleasant revelation of his method – he concluded that a mere fresh textual translation would not satisfy his own standard of what a fable should accomplish: 'an emblem without a key to it is no more than a tale of a tub', and the 'morals' in the existing versions were so 'insipid and flat' as to be 'rather

a

3. In the etchings for his *Fables* of 1666, Francis Barlow produced a series of images which inspired, directly or indirectly, a chain of imitations that stretched over more than two centuries. Here the transmission of one illustration can be seen through a variety of editions and, incidentally, through a variety of technical processes:

(a) Barlow's etching of *The Dog and the Shadow* in 1666. Original size 6½ by 6½ in.

(b) A relief engraving, probably on soft metal, and probably by Elisha Kirkall, for Croxall's *Fables* of 1722.

(c) Thomas Bewick's wood engraving for the *Fables* that he illustrated for Saint (Newcastle, 1784). Taken from a late printing of the blocks in Pearson's edition of 1871.

(d) An unacknowledged copy, reversed, of Barlow's original etching appearing in an early-twentieth-century *Aesop*.

dangerous than profitable'.* Finally he decided that the only way to meet the trade requirements and to carry out his own ideals was to work on the most comprehensive scale – to collect and retranslate all available fables, to rewrite the 'morals', and to add to them persuasive 'Reflexions' at large.

L'Estrange had not been nicknamed 'Dog Towzer' for nothing, though he received the label for other qualities than his terrier-like pugnacity. King Charles's Head would come in. But in spite of his obvious prejudices, the book was a very thorough performance, and deserved to be used, as it was, by most

* It is to be hoped he was not thinking of Mrs Behn; for she had written a whole panegyrical poem about him, asserting that his works were, like himself, 'eminently great'.

later compilers and editors. L'Estrange took it seriously and sincerely. He had a certain psychology of childhood in his outlook, though its philosophy is not original, obviously enough. He said that the young mind is 'blank paper, ready indifferently for any impression' (practically Locke's own words), and the wise parent or guardian must write good sentiments upon it. 'It may be laid down in the first place, for an universal rule, never to suffer children to learn any thing, (now seeing and hearing, with them, is learning) but what they may be the better for all their lives after.' (L'Estrange also made it clear that they would not be the better for imbibing the sour milk of Puritanism.) But he did not claim that the impressions made on the pure surface must be entirely arbitrary. The pupil must be a willing party to his own character-moulding, because 'I suppose that the delight and genius of children lies much toward the hearing, learning, and telling of little stories'. That discovery alone – made use of by Shakespeare in *The Winter's Tale*, but not explicitly formulated, I think, before L'Estrange – would have made this *Aesop* remarkable. It was an opinion genuinely held by him, and his text brings it out almost unconsciously. His style has not the 'uncouth' simplicity of Caxton, but it shows that he was not thinking in words only: in his own phrase, he was, like a child, 'seeing and hearing'.

In *The Fox and the Grapes* his mind is evident. He had a picture in it. It was not a theatrical scene nor a condescension, but a lively reality such as a simple reader would construct in all seriousness. The average English child would be aware that in England, at least, foxes and grapes are incompatible. So L'Estrange puts it thus (italics mine):

There was a time when a Fox would have ventured as far for a bunch of grapes as for a shoulder of mutton, and *it was a Fox of those days, and that palate,* that stood gaping under a vine, and licking his lips at a most delicious cluster of grapes that he had spied out there. He fetched a hundred and a hundred leaps at it, till at last, when he was as weary as a dog, and found that there was no good to be done, 'Hang 'em' (says he), 'they are as sour as crabs'; and so away he went, turning off the disappointment with a jest.

The narrative is wordy compared with Caxton's or Bullokar's, but it has the right touch of truth and humour, and puts the fable in its proper period – the eternal days of 'once upon a time'. One feels, too, that the man who made the translation enjoyed it himself. It was quite a different man who 'reflected' upon it and dragged in politics. But that duality is a common feature in children's books, and this great edition really was meant for children.

3

But in one of the most valuable points – a matter to which Newbery gave special attention – none of these 'full dress' editions was adapted to children's personal use, any more than the schoolbooks were. Yet it was in a school volume that this particular advance was first made. It consists in the provision of *suitable* illustrations. The large drawings in the folios were all very well as works of art, but they were cold and lacking in intimacy for the youngest readers. There was nothing lovable about them. Even the ugly woodcuts in the little Puritan didactic volumes of the period – to be dealt with later – had a more direct kind of naturalness. The right type of thing appeared in an almost unknown and evidently unsuccessful English and Latin text of 1703, possibly devised by John Locke. It contains seventy-five nicely cut little 'sculptures', engravings of animals, each an inch or so square. They are the oldest – and among the best – specimens I have found of the small blocks, superior to the crude chapbook illustrations, which passed from children's book to children's book and publisher to publisher for a hundred years and more, vanishing, early in the nineteenth century, with the alphabetical 'battledore'. They were used as a rule to decorate alphabets.

The importance of illustrations, however, was not yet fully realized, or rather, the theory of a 'children's book' had not yet become clear and logical. L'Estrange had tried, with some success, to see the child's standpoint, but he could not get away from the fact that fables are almost inevitably a vehicle of emphatic morals; while to a schoolmaster pictures could be no more than a most useful engine of education. Locke's famous pronouncement on fables, in fact, gives the two points of view as one argument: though it should be remembered that he was writing as a private tutor moulding one child, not as a schoolmaster handling many together.

The passage (§ 148) from *Some Thoughts Concerning Education* (1693; in the 1705 edition this had become §156) had better be quoted in full. As soon as a child knows the alphabet, says Locke, he should be led to read for pleasure, though not, in so doing, to 'fill his head with perfectly useless trumpery':

To this purpose I think *Aesop's Fables* the best, which being stories apt to delight and entertain a child, may yet afford useful reflections to a grown man. And if his memory retain them all his life after, he will not repent to find them there, amongst his manly thoughts and serious business. If his *Aesop* has pictures in it, it will entertain him much the better, and encourage him to read when it carries the increase of knowledge with it. For such visible objects children hear talked of in vain, and without any satisfaction, whilst they have no ideas of them; those ideas being not to be had from sounds, but from the things themselves, or their pictures. And therefore I think, as soon as he begins to spell, as many pictures of animals should be got him as can be found, with the printed names to them, which at the same time will invite him to read, and afford him matter of enquiry and knowledge. *Raynard the Fox* is another book, I think, may be made use of to the same purpose. And if those about him will talk to him often about the stories he has read, and hear him tell them, it will, besides other advantages, add incouragement and delight to his reading, when he finds there is some use and pleasure in it. These baits seem wholly neglected in the ordinary method: And 'tis usually long before learners find any use or pleasure in reading, which may tempt them to it, and so take books only for fashionable amusements, or impertinent troubles, good for nothing.

The admirable good sense of that judgment is not really more than a summing-up of what was gradually happening to the text of 'Aesop', with no regard for fashionable versions but also with very little recognition of any virtue in free imagination. It is to be regretted, from a literary standpoint, that Locke, with

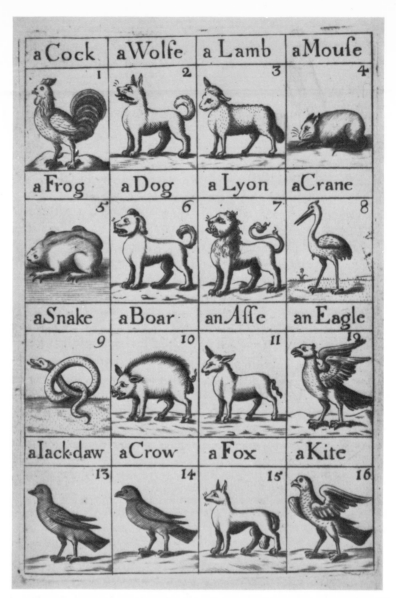

a Cock	a Wolfe	a Lamb	a Moufe
1	2	3	4
a Frog	a Dog	a Lyon	a Crane
5	6	7	8
a Snake	a Boar	an Affe	an Eagle
9	10	11	12
a Iack-daw	a Crow	a Fox	a Kite
13	14	15	16

4. Sixteen Aesopic beasts printed from an engraved plate for a bilingual edition of the fables. The book was intended as a help for any reader anxious to master Latin (or English) and the pictures were added 'to make it still more taking to Children and make the deeper impression of [the Fables] upon their Minds'. Numbers were placed at the head of each fable referring back to the numbered pictures.

This is a second edition of the *Fables* of 1703 which was published anonymously; the attribution to John Locke occurred only after his death.

his easy lucid style, did not make a full translation himself. The little illustrated specimen of 1703 which he either wrote or supervised was for scholastic purposes only. It had no life.

La Fontaine in France (and in translations in England), Gay (1727; second series 1738) in England, kept the fable, ostensibly or putatively Aesop's but with a great deal of wholly original invention added, well alive as a book for the general reader, and their versions were used by or adapted for young readers. But in 1722 a version was undertaken with a view to superseding all others and to providing children, in particular, with a complete, interesting and wholly innocuous rendering of a great classic, to be read with pleasure and for pleasure, with profit and for profit. It was the work of the Rev. Samuel Croxall.

It appeared in 1722, as *Fables of Aesop and Others. Newly done into English with an Application to each Fable. Illustrated with Cutts.* It was deliberately meant to oust L'Estrange, and becomes highly controversial at the very outset, when Croxall makes his apology. He agreed that before Sir Roger's time the translations were worthless, but he pointed out, quite truthfully, that L'Estrange neither fulfilled his own moral purpose nor was himself morally trustworthy. 'He was Pensioner to a Popish Prince . . . the Tool and Hireling of the Popish Faction.' Now – in 1722 – the Protestant line was firmly on the throne (even if its representative really did not like England); Croxall had written an Ode to George I on his accession. Such a man as L'Estrange was not a fit person to write books for 'the Children of Britain': 'They are born with free Blood in their Veins; and suck in Liberty with their very Milk . . . Let *L'Estrange*, with his slavish Doctrine, be banished to the barren Desarts of Arabia, to the Nurseries of *Turkey, Persia*, and *Morocco*.' He must certainly not be admitted to the august nursery of George, Baron Halifax, to whom Croxall's collection was dedicated: though, by the sycophant's own argument, such a wonderful boy could not have taken much harm. 'Very lately' – in his fifth year – the young nobleman had been 'capable of reading anything in the English tongue without the least hesitation.' It was an honour to present *Aesop* to such a prodigy, and to do so with propriety and no hint of profitable adulation:

Another Advantage [in this offering], My Lord, is That when I tell the World You are the most lovely and the most engaging Child that ever was born, I cannot be charged with offending in Point of Flattery. No one ever saw You but thought the same.

And this puts me in Mind that You are descended from a Race of Patrons . . .

Here was a child's book, with a vengeance.

In spite of his vagaries as a Press censor, L'Estrange was a better man than Croxall. He may have been a political tool, but he was not the complete toady. Moreover, he had shown a sense of humour, realism, and sympathy, which Croxall had not. Observe Croxall's uneasiness about the grape-lust of foxes. It would be wrong in him to let 'the most engaging child that ever was born' swallow an impossibility. Foxes do *not* eat grapes. Still, there the thing was in print, and Aesop had undoubtedly taken it for granted. Perhaps Aesop, like L'Estrange, was really writing for the nurseries of Turkey, Persia and Morocco. At any rate, the strange circumstance must be explained in the 'Application', which fills a page and a half in all: 'This Scene being laid in a foreign Country, where either the Appetites of Foxes or the Texture of Grapes may differ from those which are peculiar to these Islands, it makes the Fact not improbable.' *The*

Dictionary of National Biography calls that style 'naïve, clear, and forcible': what adjectives can be left for Caxton?

4

It is at this point that John Newbery joins Aesop's progress through English letters. His name is associated with several versions, though only one of them can be traced to his own lifetime; and that one is a great deal more Newbery than 'Aesop' – in fact, it is about as much Aesop as Jack in the *Pocket-Book* was the authentic giant-killer. It is a characteristic production. It was issued in Dutch flowered paper covers, from the *Bible and Sun* in 1757 under the title *Fables in Verse for the Improvement of the Young and the Old*, 'by Abraham Aesop, Esq.' It had many rough simple woodcuts and sold at 6d. bound, a price which remained through ten editions or so up to 1783. The preface, which draws heavily on Croxall, claims that the volume is useful and entertaining, and defends the use of simple tales on the authority of Addison, the Bible, Roman history, Boileau and La Fontaine. It is typical of Newbery that though he evidently knew Locke on Education, he does not here cite that valuable witness. It is also typical that while many of the fables are taken from Aesop – whose 'life' is given in stock form from earlier 'adult' editions – some are attributed to 'Woglog the great Giant', one of the publisher's favourite mock authors. In fact, Woglog's own life is described, and his humanity and moral tendencies exhibited in several arch little anecdotes. As one of these is concluded, Woglog, no doubt exhausted, 'stept into Mr *Leake's* [bookshop at Bath] to read one of Mr *Newbery's* little books. More anecdotes we have respecting Mr *Woglog's* life, but they must be deferred, till another edition of this work is published, which will be in a few days.' Woglog, in fact, bore much the same relationship to John Newbery as existed between Mr Snawley and the two little boys he left in charge of Mr Wackford Squeers. His fables are ordinary enough. Most of them have a 'moral', usually pompous, and a 'reflection', or rather crude satire upon the follies of the rich and great. Woglog was evidently a middle class giant.[3]

The other editions of Aesop with which the Newbery firms were involved show connections beyond St Paul's Churchyard. Somewhere round about 1780 Elizabeth Newbery issued a *Select Fables of Aesop and Others*, which may well have some link with a group of 'select fable' books published in Newcastle by T. Saint, a notable manufacturer of chapbooks, during the 1770s and 1780s. These are famous for containing some of the early wood engravings of Thomas and John Bewick, which, even in their 'prentice days, were in a different class from the ordinary coarse chapbook woodcut. The text too – an amalgam of Croxall and Dodsley (see p. 21) – was decently pulled together and the books appeared as a compact and synoptic whole, neither scrappy nor grandiose.

These *Select Fables*, however, should not be confused with both Newbery and

Bewick's fuller use of the ubiquitous Croxall. In 1770 we find F. Newbery joining the conger which issued the ninth edition of the 'official' Croxall sequence, and the book with its (probably) soft-metal relief engravings by Elisha Kirkall continued in E. Newbery's list down to the sixteenth edition of 1798. At the same time, though, the volume was of great interest to Thomas Bewick ('I was always extremely fond of that book', he recalled in his *Memoir*) and although he was clearly much indebted to Kirkall's pictures in the period of the *Select Fables*, his *Fables* of 1818 (published in Newcastle by his own firm) is his fullest acknowledgment of influence.[4] The text is mostly modified Croxall, with a drastic curtailment of the moral commentary, but the book is chiefly famed for Bewick's elegant re-engraving of the Kirkall originals – with the addition of a number of his own inimitable 'tale-pieces'. In such a garb Croxall really did supersede L'Estrange.

5

One other important version preceded Bewick's adornment of Croxall, and followed Newbery's 'Abraham Aesop'. Like those two enterprises, it was commercial in intention, and meant mainly for children. It too had a great vogue, and was produced by the best printer who had touched Aesop since Caxton. It was *Select Fables of Esop and other Fabulists . . . Birmingham. John Baskerville, for R. and J. Dodsley in Pall Mall.* 1761. It was cheap at 5*s.*, with Baskerville's fine type and a number of neat and pretty engravings. A preliminary *Essay on Fable* is signed by Robert Dodsley, who was responsible for the text itself. It was in three 'books', the third of which, it was claimed, was original.

Dodsley had already put forth for children his *Preceptor*, which lived up to its title, and his famous *Oeconomy of Human Life*. He was a versatile and eccentric man, but in fable-compilation he showed a decided conventionality. His *Essay* has the assured, sententious complacency of an eighteenth-century middle-class London blessed with secondary culture. One passage will suffice both for his manner of writing and his attitude of mind:

The style of Fable then must be simple and familiar; and it must *likewise* be correct and elegant. By the former, I would advise that it should not be loaded with figure and metaphor; that the disposition of words be natural; the turn of sentences, easy; and their construction unembarrassed. By elegance, I would exclude all coarse and provincial terms; all affected and puerile conceits; all obsolete and pedantic phrases. To this I would adjoin, as the word perhaps implies, a certain finishing polish, which gives a grace and spirit to the whole; and which, tho' it have always the *appearance* of nature, is almost ever the *effect* of art.

The beasts, in *his* Fables, must always use language suitable to their acknowledged character. The Lion must speak in a kingly manner, the Owl with 'a pomp of phrase' which 'the buffoon-monkey should avoid'. Nor did Dodsley avoid it.

5. As with the 'Locke', fable book (fig. 4), the engraved illustrations for 'Dodsley's Fables' are here grouped together on a single leaf with numbered references. Despite the simplicity of the pictures a debt may still be noticed to the motifs of the 'Barlow tradition', while the style of framed portraiture also proved influential later (see fig. 29).

But if this posture of make-believe had not been so strongly encouraged in the eighteenth century, and become common form in any *Aesop*, children might never have had any of the light-hearted prettinesses and animal stories of the next century at all. It is a most valuable asset in fiction that animals should have stock human characters; and L'Estrange, Croxall and Dodsley standardized those characters for juvenile consumption, having found a framework in the oldest artificial stories in the world, which came into our language along with printing itself.

Another stage of evolution also stood out clearly at this point. Fables, or *Aesop*, had certainly become an important commodity in the general book-market: Ogilby and Croxall had perceived that. But a specialist within that market saw what Newbery had also discovered in the course of business, and what publishers to this day appreciate just as acutely – that a good solid *children's* book is a very valuable property. Shenstone, author of *The Schoolmistress*, wrote to the Rev. Richard Graves soon after Dodsley's *Select Fables* were published, that 'a book of this kind, once established, becomes an absolute estate for many years; and brings in at least as certain and as regular returns'. Ogilby and his rivals for the patronage of the great and good had not envisaged that commercial fact so sanely, because they had been thinking in terms of library folios, not of hungry readers.

Thus, before George III's reign was half over, the Fable had passed, like an embryo, through the literary and social changes of its full growth. It had been something not far from folk-lore long before, had been regimented for schools and decked out for fashion. It had been Everyman's and now was Everychild's. All its supporters and well-wishers were at last ready for it together – the publisher, the author who could make a living out of it, the artist who could embellish it, and the large solid reading public who merely wished to enjoy it. Its later history, once it was a children's book, is but the record of the redecoration of a known model.

6

Apart from 'Aesop', popular literature in the Middle Ages included one great and almost universal work which contained a number of the elements of later English children's books and yet did not survive among them up to modern times in anything like its original form. It was the large and extraordinary collection of tales and fables known as *Gesta Romanorum*. It is dead now as a book, but it lived as one for children till the eighteenth century; and its contents in part have endured because of its tenacity.

It is necessary to give briefly the circumstances of its obscure origin. It was compiled in Latin by an unknown hand at an unknown date; possibly by an Englishman and probably about 1300. It consists of stories of all kinds drawn from many sources, a large number, far back, from Eastern tradition – for example, from the fables of 'Bidpai'. Each story has a 'moral', which was for generations considered to be at least as important as the tale. Knowledge of the tale, in fact, was almost taken for granted – which is more than many of the morals could have been. The collection differs widely in the manuscript versions; their pedigree need not be traced here. The Latin text was done into English by another unknown hand. The earliest known extant English manuscript is probably of the fifteenth century. But before 1400, in Western Europe generally, 'the Acts of the Romans' – the usual English title – was a universal, accepted and even authorized story-'book'.

The public for which the tales were apparently meant was not strictly a juvenile one. The chief English editors of the text virtually agree that the stories were collected and 'moralized' in order 'to furnish a series of entertaining tales to the preachers of the day or to monastic societies, accompanied by such allegorical forms of exposition as to convey, according to the taste of the age, information of a theological character or moral tendency'. The compilation, in fact, was meant for grown-up children, for ignorant or half-instructed folk who sought pleasant and profitable knowledge, usually, perhaps, in monastic surroundings, but also in the ordinary domestic life of cultivated households – 'after supper on bleak winter evenings by the fireside of rich men'.

It is not necessary to pursue the mutations of the text in detail. In effect, the stories could not be killed. The manner of telling could. Changes of detail came – inevitably and visibly – with changes of costume, custom and religious usage. The differences were no more than those which the first compiler had enforced upon his own material, when he endued classical Greek and Roman heroes with the garb and manners of early mediaeval knights. The monastic gown fell off, the story-teller remained. It was perhaps not quite the same process as took place in regard to *Aesop*. The text shrank rather than was elaborated, and, to some extent, the 'moral', such as it was, changed its character.

Consider the descent of one story in the collection, perhaps the most famous of them all. It began heaven knows (nor does it matter) where. It ends, for my purpose here, in a very celebrated children's book. For Englishmen and the world in general it has a larger immortality. It is the tale – no. XL in the standard version – which supports Shakespeare's *Merchant of Venice*. His plot, as everyone knows, contains two elements – the choice of the Three Caskets and the pound-of-flesh Bond motives. It is not certain beyond dispute whence Shakespeare drew those two ideas, but they both appear in *Gesta Romanorum*. The Casket plot is in de Worde's printed English text, the Bond plot not, though it appears in other versions. This, in summary, with the 'morals' – separate in the original – interpolated in brackets, is how it is presented.

Portia has no name, but is simply the daughter of Selestinus, 'a wise emperor in Rome'; 'Portia' must suffice for convenience here. She was loved by a knight who sought her hand, although he was sure 'the Emperor would not let him to have her, for he was unworthy thereto'. ('Dear friends, this Emperor is the Father of Heaven, our Lord Jesu Christ. The daughter, that is so fair, is the soul made to the similitude of God . . . The knight . . . is Every worldly man . . . the fleshly man.') Portia did not wholly repulse his suit, but demanded payment for her person, and they made a fantastic bargain on it. The knight went travelling to get the necessary money, and at last came 'to a great city, in the which were many merchants and many philosophers; among the which was master Virgil, the philosopher'. The knight visited 'a great merchant' ('*scilicet* the devil'), and borrowed from him on the guarantee that in default of repayment the merchant should 'draw away all the flesh of thy body from the bone, with a sharp sword'. ('In Holy Writ effusion of blood is not else but trespass in sinning.') The knight, uneasy, went to Virgil ('Virgil is pride of life'), who gave him some curious advice which enabled him to win his way with the princess – quite un-morally.

The facts at this stage are easier to follow than the reasons for them, or their lessons, or, for that matter, Virgil's exact spiritual significance in the affair – he was the enchanter-Virgil of the famous myth. Infatuation led the knight to forget his bond, and Portia eventually had to rescue him in the manner of the trial scene in *The Merchant of Venice* ('Us must take away the flesh, *scilicet* fleshly affections, so that no blood falls, *scilicet* no sin be in us'). Afterwards there was a recognition scene, as in Shakespeare, but without the device of the pledged rings. 'And he [the knight] wept; and after, he wedded her, and lived and died in the service of God, and yielded to God good souls.' The final moral is 'if we will thus allege [declare] against the devil, as the damsel did against the merchant, without doubt then shall the flesh and the spirit be married, to live in bliss, &c.'.

Shakespeare – it is impossible to resist the quotation – transmuted that marriage 'in bliss, etc.' into something to which, perhaps, even the compiler of the *Gesta Romanorum* could not well take exception:

> Look how the floor of heaven
> Is thick inlaid with patines of bright gold.
> There's not the smallest orb which thou beholdst
> But in his motion like an angel sings,
> Still quiring to the young-eyed cherubins;
> Such harmony is in immortal souls;
> But whilst this muddy vesture of decay
> Doth grossly close it in, we cannot hear it.

But this is how it reached children in the accepted standard version of Shakespeare in prose: 'So these tragical beginnings of this rich merchant's story were all forgotten in the unexpected good fortune which ensued; and there was leisure to laugh at the comical adventure of the rings, and the husbands that did not know their own wives.' In gratitude to Charles Lamb it is kindest not to comment on Mary.

That is the fate of only one of the tales. Others flicker up unexpectedly in children's books, poems and stories, like sudden flames from a seeming-dead coal; the anecdote of faithful Gelert, for example. The main text of the whole book, in various forms, remained in print stubbornly – in spite of print, so to speak. De Worde's text (1517?) was long used, whether it was reprinted or not. The chief later version, Richard Robinson's (originally issued in 1577, though no copy seems to have survived), was avowedly only a 'repolishing' of de Worde. It survived the Puritans in substance and purpose, but not in its religious trappings. Indeed, it flourished when the anti-Papists were strong. Hoole in 1660, in his *New Discovery*, speaks of the *Gesta* as 'so generally pleasing to our Country people'. (It is not clear whether he means rustics or fellow-countrymen.) There were editions in 1663, 1689, 1696, 1698, 1703, 1713, 1720 and 1722; for aught I know, more. Under the Georges it seems almost to have vanished as a complete work, but it turned up again in modern days in various forms, providing ingredients, neither ecclesiastically compounded nor moralized, for many story-books. There are various texts for scholars. For the younger or the more ignorant reader the tales survive with no visible relation whatever to the originals, and the very title is probably now known to few children.

That decadence, or maybe mutation, is due to the simple historical fact that the *Gesta* were themselves 'deeds' of a fantastical synthesis of history, myth and religion. Their basis is enduring. But once education passed from the Church's hands, the original purpose of the book declined. The greater part of the editions enumerated above are but dry disarticulated skeletons of a great pretypographic monster which once walked the old world full of power and life. Two of the versions show odd stages in the creature's desiccation.

The edition of 1703,[5] a rare book, was by 'B.P.', who claimed to have translated from a Latin original published in 1514 in Paris. It was issued by an almost unknown bookseller, T. Davis, of Red Lion Street, Whitechapel. The printer was R. Janeway, who, from the Stationers' Registers of the period, seems to have been a bookseller also, dealing in cheap books and chapbooks. Who 'B. P.' was is not known.* He wrote clearly and straightforwardly. He prefixes to each 'Deed' a didactic summary, and adds a moral subtly but not at all ironically varied from the monkish 'applications'. He is openly Protestant. He dwells on the wickedness of Sabbath breaking, the powerful grace of Baptism, and the inevitable doom of original sin without Baptism. He attacks the rich, and is at least as much concerned with the pains of hell as with the conversion of the soul by spiritual repentance. But he upholds the Church's authority valiantly. This appears in the tale of the Blind Man and the Lame Man:

> The *Lame* Man implies many Pious Persons of the *Clergy*, who through Poverty as [to the goods of this world] are not able to Improve *themselves*, or to do that *great Good* to these Rich and others, as by their *Holy Office*, and their Learned Skill in seeing into the abstrusest Points of Religion, if things were better with them, they are most largely *capable* of: And would to God this were effectually laid to Heart by all Persons concerned in the Payment of Tythes, or who have *Impropriations*, or in those Parishes where the Priests are forc'd to send *good People* on Collecting, or on Begging, from House to House for their Corporal Relief.

He urges that 'we apply ourselves more intently to the Holy Catholick Church', and mend our lives by the medicine of '*Confession, Contrition*, and *Satisfaction*'. He is in fact tolerant but not latitudinarian, standing between the Puritan acerbity and the Georgian smugness. In spite of the intrusion of doctrine, he tells the stories themselves straightforwardly, as if he were conscientiously trying to write them to give children profitable pleasure, which was his avowed aim.

The 1722 edition, by a no better known 'A.B.', says on its title-page[6] that
> The Story's pleasant, and the Moral good,
> If read with Care, and rightly understood.

---

*   He might just possibly be the 'B.P., Parish Clerk', who in 1709 issued through Benjamin Motte (the publisher of *Gulliver*) *The Parish-Clerk's Guide*, a handbook to congregational Church-Service-singing.

That was the reason for offering them to children, not any loyalty to a decaying classic. 'A.B.' was no stickler for a pure text. He addresses the reader thus:

Whether the following Stories were Originally collected from the Roman Records, or not, I think is of little Weight in the present Case; 'tis sufficient that the Design is Honest and Rational, and the Morals and Applications adapted intirely to the promoting of Virtue and the Love of God, and the Suppressing of Vice and Immorality.

He certainly went far from the usual text. The illustrations ('a new Set of Cuts') are interesting. They include the Ass trying to embrace his Master (allegedly 'Aesop'), Androcles, a snake being hanged ('Aesop'), and there is a story of a basilisk looking in a mirror with fatal results, which is a relic of the Bestiaries.

7

The Bestiaries are a genuine cousin of Fable, and they also fell, like the ingredients of *Gesta Romanorum*, into the Church's hands, or perhaps were compiled for devout purposes. They did not get so far as being printed for ordinary use, but they passed into men's minds and emerged in children's books very oddly. The standard texts are all in manuscript. Dr M. R. James, in his fine study of the whole subject (*The Bestiary*, Roxburghe Club, 1921), concludes that this extraordinary 'natural history' 'seems to have assumed its standard form (or *a* standard form) in England'. It was 'one of the leading picture-books of the twelfth and thirteenth centuries in this country'. It can be traced in substance, he holds with earlier students, to a Greek book known as *Physiologus* (which may well be no more than a personified title like the Victorian *The Entertaining Naturalist* or *The Juvenile Conchologist*). Possibly, as a collection, it originated in one of the ascetic communities of Egypt. But in many of its strange details it goes back to Pliny, and, beyond that, to Aristotle and Herodotus.

The same legends, or fragments of them, come into many early travel books regularly. This, for instance, is from 'Mandeville': 'In Araby . . . there are many camelions, that is a little beast, and he never eateth or drinketh, and he changeth his colour often, for sometime he is of one colour, and sometime of another, and he may change him into all colours that he will save black or red.'

The authorship of those Travels, and the author's own personality, are a welter of controversy. But this Bestiary–Mandeville scrap deserves quotation, for my extract is from a chapbook edition of 1705[7] – that is to say, from a booklet pretty certain to have been in the hands of English children in that century.

It is impossible to say, even within the limited scope of the *Bestiary*, whence all such scraps of misinformation derive. In our own day the difficulty has been strangely exemplified. *The Times*, in the course of April 1932, had a correspondence about the jealous virtue of Turkish storks, who killed a hen bird because a turkey chick was found among her own brood: the great newspaper's own Correspondent in Turkey had reported it. Dr M. R. James at once said it was in Horace Marryat's *Jutland and the Danish Isles* (*c.* 1860). Dr Paget

Toynbee adduced a similar tale from Vincent of Beauvais's sixteenth-century *Speculum Naturale*: Mr J. A. Herbert found something very like it in *Gesta Romanorum* itself, with a list of supporting sources. But the Correspondent stuck to his latest version. Another tale, used in *Peter Pan*, is that wolves flee if you look at them backwards between your legs: I have had this sent to me (as an editor) as an original Indian story, vouched for, but with a tiger for Sir James Barrie's wolves. Such things – the ostrich's head-hiding habit, for example, or the bear's custom of licking its cubs into shape, which *is* in the *Bestiary* – often become proverbial and unarguable. Sometimes they are justified even by professed teachers, or rather, modified with a rationalist scepticism which itself is a form of credulity, like Herodotus's own. Hoole, for instance, a pedagogue of some parts, insisted that the legendary rhinoceros *must* whet its teeth against a tree, in a standing posture, not sitting down, 'as the Latin hath it, which is impossible for such an huge beast to do'.

This delicious lore endured and crept into English nurseries in all manner of ways. Some is directly found in the *Bestiary* but reached children by other routes. The espidochelone, for example – a fish big enough to be mistaken for an island, and encamped upon – obviously swam into the books of infancy in an *Arabian Night*. Raspe fathered other yarns upon Munchausen. Some beasts we have lost altogether, like the eale or yale who could move his horns back and forth and independently; though he is said to be sculptured at Hampton Court.[8] Children are no longer made acquainted with the simple-minded generosity shown by the beaver when he is hard pressed by the hunter in quest of material for castor oil. On the other hand, the elephant and his castle live for many diverting reasons. He was first made known in England in the thirteenth century, by Matthew Paris of St Albans. He is famous in London today. And my own ancestors produced a fine 'moral game'[9] about him in 1822, when the elephant stood for Asia and the Gospel was pictured as entering the porches of his ears through the efforts of a black-coated missionary.

The remnants of the legends did not escape the Newbery firm. In 1770 Francis Newbery published *The Natural History of Birds. By T. Teltruth* (later *Telltruth*) – a real children's book, one of a Natural History series for home use. It contains among other matter some surprising information about the ostrich and the cock. The ostrich, the young reader is told, 'is the most greedy bird that is known, for it will devour leather, grass, bread, hair, or any thing else that is given him; however, he does not digest iron and stones as some have pretended, but voids them whole'. The cock also has interesting traits, for,

being a most lecherous bird, he doth suddenly grow old, and seldom liveth above ten years. It hath been delivered and received by ancients and moderns, with unanimous consent and approbation, that the lion is afraid of a cock, cannot endure the sight of him, yea is terrified by his very crowing; and divers reasons sought and assigned for this antipathy; whereas the thing itself is by experience found to be false.

'The thing itself', told as true, and illustrated, is to be found in an illuminated Bestiary in Cambridge University Library, where the cock ought to be a white

The COCK.

THE *common Cock* being fo well known, it will be but loft labour to beftow any words about it. It is fo courageous and high-fpirited a bird, that if of a good breed, it will rather die than yield; and being a moft 'it-cherous

6. The woodcut of a cock as rendered by 'T. Telltruth' (a), and a medieval representation of the cock's domination of a lion (b).

one. As for Newbery's text, 'T. Telltruth' has here appropriated – without acknowledgment – passages from Thomas Boreman's *Description of Three Hundred Animals* (1730). The borrowing is not altogether heinous, however, since by 1774 the book had come into the Newbery fold, John's nephew Francis publishing in that year a so-called eleventh edition (actually the thirteenth).

29

Popular speech preserves still some touches of the antique lore of these 'natural histories', not only in adages but even in beliefs shyly half-held. Books continue to appear about them. It took a vastly enlarged and familiar geographical world to kill them, and to sterilize a little of the wonder of man's own childhood. Mr T. Telltruth's figure is both an emblem and a notch in that process.

8

These three concurrent streams of what may be called 'natural' learning, fables, decayed history, fabulous monsters, together with the still unexpressed Fairy-Tale – all 'traditional' in their English form, as opposed to 'fictitious' – made up one part of the English mind, so far as it was influenced by reading-matter, in the period between Caxton and that almost rebirth of literature for which 'Tottel's Miscellany' (1557) affords a rough-and-ready date; up to that date, certainly. And after, for young people; for if there is one thing clear about children's books in England it is that before *Alice* – so late as all that – they were dominated by inhibitions as well as prohibitions. It has been well said that 'modern science, while reducing man to zero, has banished fear from his universe. In Shakespeare's limited cosmos fear met him at every turn.'* Moral fear also – visible most plainly in the history of fairy-tales, but afraid to show its face, and masked as superior knowledge – moral fear was present throughout. It was not ignored completely – and with success – till 1865. 'Morals' were tacked on to everything, or thrown into relief, lest harm should come from the simplicities of false fable and crude inaccurate science. Not sin but Evil itself was the foe. The dread of evil not as a mere temptation or lure but as an invasion, an unprovoked fury and an incalculable wound, restrained and restricted all movement in the world of children's books long after the monkish mysteries had gone into limbo along with their salutary moralizations. Right up to Lewis Carroll's day authors who composed books for children inhabited an universe as 'diminutive, compact, and tidy' as, in its more varied colours, Shakespeare's own – 'Hell lying beneath it and Chaos about it': 'a pretty little musical box'.

These foreign or larger-world legends, then, though they may seem childish now, were not childish even in Newbery's day. But by that time they had long become English, natural things in our island goldfish-globe. It is likely, indeed, that after the manner of native things they might have perished altogether, as knowledge broadened; or perhaps there would have been only one goldfish left, like *Gesta Romanorum*, with all the rest inside him. It is clear, at least, that but for the needs of ignorant persons and young children, much of the homelier aspects of ancient learning might have been hidden from us, if not altogether

---

* J. Dover Wilson, *The Essential Shakespeare*, Cambridge, 1932. The phrases quoted just afterwards are from the same stimulating work.

lost. Fortunately, as the fables and legends reached us, they met with a language which suited them, just as their fantastic inconsequence suited our racial temper: nonsense is our prerogative, and they had become excellent nonsense.

Nor was it only the speaking beast and the fabulous monster that were thus saved from the Dark Ages. 'Alle maner of fables ben found for to shewe al maner of folk what maner of thyng they ought to ensyewe and folowe.' There is a pattern of lost life likewise in the Middle Age Romances, which Caxton and his peers preserved for the English people – and for the children who are now almost their sole readers.

BRIEF BOOK LIST

For Caxton, Henryson, Brinsley, Ogilby, Aphra Behn, Hoole, L'Estrange, Dodsley, see *D.N.B.* and *C.H.E.L.*; for Bullokar and Croxall, *D.N.B.* The following works may be of use, as a starting point: further research leads to very specialized study.

Bewick's Select Fables [a reprint using the original woodblocks from the Saint edition of 1774?] with an introduction by Edwin Pearson (London, 1871). An edition was later issued privately (Edinburgh, 1879).

The Fables of Aesop. Selected, with an introduction by Joseph Jacobs (London, 1894 and 1926). Also a reprint of Caxton's edition of the *Fables*, 2 vols. (London, 1889), the first volume being an essay on 'The History of Aesopic Fable' by Jacobs.

Gesta Romanorum. Edited by Sir Frederic Madden for the Roxburghe Club (London, 1838); re-edited by S. J. H. Herrtage for the Early English Text Society (London, 1879); the great Berlin edition, ed. Oesterley (1872), is drawn upon in the latter. A convenient modern edition is in Routledge's Library of Early English Novelists (London, 1905).

The Bestiary. A Peterborough Psalter and Bestiary of the Fourteenth Century (London, 1921) and *The Bestiary*, being a reproduction of the manuscript in the University Library, Cambridge (London, 1928). Both edited for the Roxburghe Club by Dr M. R. James.

Supplement

A facsimile of Caxton's *History and Fables of Aesop* (1484), with an introduction by Edward Hodnett, was published to celebrate the quincentenary of printing in England (London, 1976) – an event which also drew forth an authoritative biography: *William Caxton*, by George D. Painter (London, 1976). The author occasionally notes, not without irony, the relationship between some of Caxton's publishing and a child audience.

Note also:

Hodnett, Edward. *Francis Barlow; first master of English book illustration* (London, 1978).

Quinnam, Barbara. *Fables, from Incunabula to Modern Picture Books. A selective bibliography* (Washington, 1966), which shows something of the continuing publication of fables in children's books and elsewhere.

CHAPTER III

The Legacy of the Middle Ages:
(ii) Romance and Manners

I

There can be no doubt whatever that the chief romances of the Middle Ages, in English prose of some sort, were read by children before John Newbery's time. The evidence is in *The Tatler* (no. 95: Nov. 15-17, 1709). Steele is describing a visit to his godson, aged eight:

I perceived him a very great historian in Aesop's Fables: but he frankly declared to me his mind, 'that he did not delight in that learning, because he did not believe they were true'; for which reason I found he had very much turned his studies for about a twelve-month past, into the lives and adventures of Don Bellianis of Greece, Guy of Warwick, the Seven Champions, and other historians of that age . . . He would tell you the mismanagements of John Hickathrift, find fault with the passionate temper in Bevis of Southampton, and loved Saint George for being the champion of England; and by this means had his thoughts insensibly moulded into the notions of discretion, virtue, and honour . . . [then] the mother told me that the little girl . . . was in her way a better scholar than he: 'Betty (says she) deals chiefly in fairies and sprights.'

Aesop's appearance has already been accounted for. The story of the fairy-tale comes later into this chronicle, for it had no printed past to speak of in 1709. The allusion is not clear, and we are not told what Betty's precise dealings were.[1] She may possibly have come upon *Nymphidia*, or Spenser, or browsed among the poets. But so far as present-day knowledge goes, she must otherwise have had commerce with sprites only through some book which has utterly perished, or else, which is more likely, through the kindly lips of a nursemaid.

The immediate point, however, is how the little boy came to read the romances, and what kind of edition he used. There was no children's version. When John Newbery started publishing much later, he issued no romances, though he had no scruples about letting children have fiction. Presumably, therefore, he had no convenient large text to work upon. Possibly, also, he could not lay hands upon one of those mean little chapbooks, bought for a few pence, which may just have been in existence in 1709. Steele's godson might conceivably have acquired some of these. Or he may have found some of the oldish 'quartos' of various kinds which no doubt were in the library of the country-house which Mr Bickerstaff was visiting. At any rate, there were, it is plain, a good many romances in print, within a child's reach, whether he was meant to use them or not. And they must have been well known, at least by name, to the polite readers of Steele and Addison's fashionable periodical. How did they reach that matter-of-course condition of existence?

32

The Mediaeval Romances first came into the English language by various processes which do not matter here. Some were definitely artificial productions; some, especially those which can be traced to Scandinavian origins, come very close to a basis in folk-lore. When they first appeared in England – in manuscript, before the invention of printing – they were already literature. Some were well on their way to become proverbial, and to furnish allusions, episodes and heroes known, by hearsay or oral tradition, to folk who could not even read. Some again, in their very earliest manuscript forms as well as in the *incunabula*, incorporated details, which were older than themselves, and, in a sense, not inherent in their subject. Dragons are as common in them as in the Bestiaries, and there is no lack of the magic which belongs to the darkness of the primitive mind: though it is often (as in the divine light coming from Havelok the Dane) given a semi-religious turn. But whatever their parentage and contents and literary form, they all had this in common, that even when they got into English print they were what they have ever since remained, wonder-tales for simple minds.

For their diffusion and popularity in England before Steele's godson could question them, we have two admirable documents, fifty-odd years apart. There are countless allusions in literature to particular tales or heroes, and a good many general condemnations of romance by the moralists from time to time. But these two pieces of evidence prove the actual circulation of specified legends in print in recognizable strata of society.

2

The earlier of them is a commercial fragment. It is part of the Day-book or Daily Ledger of John Dorne, an Anglo-Dutch bookseller who for one year at least, 1520, kept an exact list of his retail sales. The original document, in the library of Corpus Christi College, Oxford, was printed for the Oxford Historical Society in 1885, with notes that make clear what was actually sold. Dorne dealt in newly printed books (now naturally, all of the greatest rarity) of a general kind and evidently had a good trade outside strict academic circles. In his list, 'very common are the service-books, and the ballads, Christmas carols, and almanacks . . . the books actually "required for the Schools", here found, are surprisingly small.'*

Only a limited number of the many entries concern us here. Sales of *Aesop*, in Latin, and *Gesta Romanorum* (probably de Worde's edition) are recorded. With them occur 'Books of Courtesy' (like *Stans puer ad mensam*) and kindred works and Romances, including Ballads. The last category – Romances – is the most

---

* *Collectanea*, 1st series, ed. by C. R. L. Fletcher: the *Daybook* is annotated by Dr Falconer Madan. Henry Bradshaw in 1886 made some illuminating suggestions and comments. Some additional pages of the manuscript, discovered later, were printed in 1890 in the second volume of *Collectanea*, ed. by Dr Montagu Burrows.

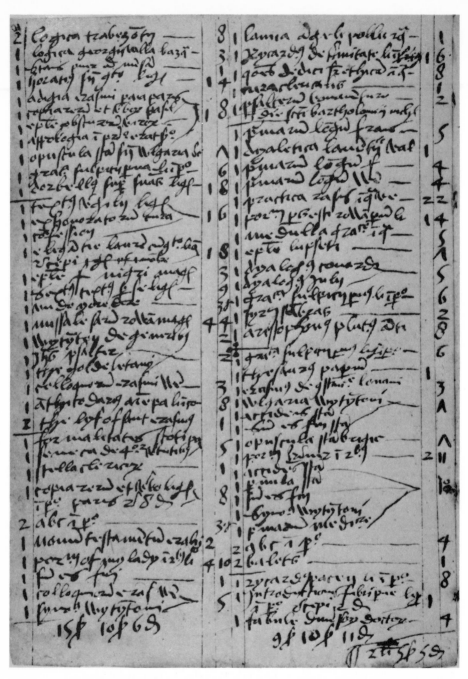

7. A page from John Dorne's 'Day-book', listing several grammars etc., an alphabet, 'balets', and the romance 'Syr Jsambras'.

numerous of these. The following works in it are mentioned as having actually been sold over Dorne's counter. Some of them appeared definitely as children's books two or more centuries later. (The titles are modernized.)

34

(*a*) *Robin Hood*. The hero of Sherwood Forest has become so familiar to every Englishman, young or old, that his entry into the nursery can be taken for granted as normal: that is to say as soon as books were printed for children, he leapt into them, as he had into the earliest popular literature.[2] There are scores of editions of his history, in prose and verse and drama, based upon sources which have been exhaustively discussed by many scholars.* He was known to the simplest folk as early as the 1370s, because Sloth, in *Piers Plowman*, was well – and discreditably – acquainted with rhymes about him. The edition sold by Dorne was probably the earliest printed version, the *Geste of Robyn Hode*, issued by de Worde (*c.* 1510). There were at least three printed versions before 1534, and about 1560 Copland reissued it with an early play on the subject, 'very proper in May-games'. Thereafter there were many texts of all kinds.

As for the veritable existence of Robin Hood and his meinie, it does not matter here. I see no reason to disbelieve that some such person did once exist – that somewhere in this country one particular rebel against slavish conditions (whether he were an outlawed noble or not) did make such an impress on his fellows that he outgrew his particular district. The legend itself can be shown to have been changed and enlarged from time to time: Maid Marian, for instance, is a late arrival in the greenwood company. But it is worth keeping, this story of a manly Arcadia:

> Hath not old custom made this life more sweet
> Than that of painted pomp? Are not these woods
> More free from peril than the envious court?

Children have accepted it, at any rate, and with it its doctrine of retributive justice, of plundering the wicked rich to help the deserving poor. Grammarians, in sixteenth-century schoolbooks, tried to enforce the translation of the Latin phrase, 'nihil ad rem' (nonsense), as equivalent to the English 'a Tale of Robin Hood'. They failed.

(*b*) '*Undo your door*.' This, by a piece of clever bibliography, was discovered to be the famous ballad of *The Squire of Low Degree*, well known to Shakespeare (*Henry V*, v, i), and found in one form or another, prose or verse, in modern children's books.

(*c*) *Sir Isumbras*. Copland printed an undated version of this (1565?), but I have found none for juvenile use.

(*d*) *The Four Sons of Aymon*. An English version of Part 1 of this Charlemagne *chanson de geste*, in a debased form, survived as *Renaud of Montaubon* (Aymon's eldest son), and this is found as an eighteenth-century chapbook (see Chapter V); that is, children probably read it then.

---

* Thomas and John Bewick illustrated Ritson's large collection of Robin Hood ballads, published in 1795 and an edition of this which could with propriety be put into the hands of young persons was published in 1820. Thomas had done an earlier *Robin Hood's Garland* for Saint, of Newcastle: I have not seen this.

(e) and (f) (sold together). *Bevis of Southampton* and *The Friar and the Boy*. *Bevis* is dealt with immediately. *The Friar and the Boy* survived as one of the nastiest chapbooks.

(g) *Sir Eglamour*: in like case to *Sir Isumbras*.

For the moment, leave Dorne's list, bearing in mind, however, that he links the eighteenth-century versions of *Aesop* and the *Gesta* commercially – in social intercourse, that is – with those of the first English printers.

3

The book-trade under Henry VIII was perhaps no great affair. Its rapid expansion appears in my second document, a record of his daughter's time, too happy not to be quoted even at the risk of irrelevance. It is a letter written in 1575 by Robert Laneham, a London mercer who was also a great book-lover, to his friend Humphrey Martin, describing the festivities held at Kenilworth, when Elizabeth was welcomed there in a splendid progress.* Laneham was immensely stirred by the pageant: 'Aware, keep back, make room now, here they come', he writes joyously. He becomes almost ecstatic over the notable figure of Captain Cox of Coventry:

An odd man, I promise you; by profession a mason, and that right skilful, very cunning in fence, and hardy as Gawain, for his tonsword [? long sword] hangs at his tables end. *Great oversight hath he in matters of story* . . . Besides this, in the field, a good marshal at musters; of very great credit and trust in the town here, for he has been chosen Ale-conner many a year, when his betters have stood by; and ever quitted himself with such estimation as yet to taste of a cup of nippitate [strong beer] his judgement will be taken above the best in the parish, be his nose never so red . . . [He] came marching on valiantly before, clean trussed, and gartered above the knee, all fresh in a velvet cap . . .flourishing with his tonsword.

Cox was a man a year or two older than Shakespeare, of Shakespeare's own county; and that passage is the pure raw material of Shakespeare's English scenes.

So were also the numerous books (well over fifty) owned by this magnificient figure from the prosperous Tudor trading class, for that is what Cox obviously was. After the words I have italicized above Laneham gives a list of the great man's library, a collection which America, or even England for all her native store, would be frenzied to possess in its entirety today. The good mercer is as greatly excited by Cox's knowledge as by his splendid person: he has, he writes, 'as fair a library for the sciences, and as many goodly monuments both in prose and poetry, and at afternoons can talk as much without book, as any inholder –

* Reprinted in 1871 by the Ballad Society, as *Captain Cox, his Ballads and Books: or Robert Laneham's Letter*, with notes by Dr F. J. Furnivall. [A facsimile of the "A" text (with corrections possibly deriving from the author) was published in the Scolar Press Facsimile Series, Menston, 1968.]

betwixt Brentford and Bagshot, what degree soever he be.' Among those books he knew so well were all the seven I have picked out from Dorne's traffickings; and with them others like *The Seven Wise Masters, Stans puer ad mensam, King Arthur's Book, Sir Gawain, Huon of Bordeaux, A Hundred Merry Tales* and *The Book of Riddles,*★ and ballads and almanacks and plays and interludes.

It would be possible to trace most of the volumes in substance back to de Worde at least, and many of them in manuscript beyond Caxton. But Cox's possession of them, his pride in them, Laneham's admiration of him for their sake – these are the important things in social history. The mixture would seem extraordinary if it were not 'silly sooth'. Here is a Coventry 'mason' owning and enjoying printed versions of the decayed Mediaeval Romance, of coarse crude vernacular things old on the lips of English peasants from time immemorial, of recent literature (Skelton's *Colin Clout*, for example), of the most famous of all the handbooks of conduct written for lads like Chaucer's Squire; and all this within a century or so of the invention of printing. The variety of the collection is remarkable enough. The wonderful thing is that people like Cox and Laneham, who would hardly have been able to read a hundred years before, even if there had been print to read, should be as familiar with it as an Extension student today is with a reference library.

4

Where, however, do children come into this picture? It is easy to say that as the books were in print and children were being more or less habitually taught to read, they read them. There is practically no evidence of a positive kind as to that. The relevance of these two lists lies in their coincidences, in the proof of a continuous and growing undercurrent of popular reading; and the relevance to the history of children's books is in the fact that one book known to both Dorne and Cox was also known to Steele's godson – the romance of *Bevis of Southampton*. That work (like a few others, but one example is enough) can be followed almost step by step from its first appearance in England to modern times. It can be taken as typical.

It is not at all certain where the legend of Bevis originated. It has even been claimed that he does not belong to Southampton at all, for the earliest known manuscript version appears to be a French one of the thirteenth century, and Antonne, in France, has been suggested as the knight's proper home. This hypothesis, however, is not strongly held. A printed French edition, in prose, dated conjecturally 1525 – *Le liure intitule Beufues de hantonne . . . imprime a Paris pour Phelippe le Noir* – is verbally very close to the earliest English prose

---

★ For these two last, cf. 'I had my good wit out of the *Hundred Merry Tales*' (Beatrice, in *Much Ado*, II, i) and 'You have not the *Book of Riddles* about you, have you?' (Master Slender, in *The Merry Wives*, I, i). But there is a stranger piece of Shakespeare lore yet to come from Dorne and Captain Cox.

editions, but those editions themselves differ in many details from the English manuscript texts, which are in verse, as indeed the Mediaeval Romances in general first were, because they were composed for song-recital in knightly halls.

The manuscripts and their variations, but for one significant point, need not be recorded here. Six have been printed by the Early English Text Society (1885–94), with exhaustive notes by Eugen Kölbing, who gives pride of place to the important Auchinleck manuscript.

The two earliest English printed versions have vanished, but for fragments: they were produced by Pynson and de Worde, and cannot be dated more nearly than that. The oldest complete printed text is William Copland's (n.d. – about 1565). The British Museum has the Garrick copy of this. It contains woodblocks of a crude type, some of which might be the ancestors of the still more rugged cuts that afterwards 'adorned' the chapbook editions, while others look like copies or imitations of blocks in European *incunabula*. The volume – in black letter throughout – is not an illustrious piece of printing.

Within the next two generations or so according to Hazlitt's *Hand-book* (1867), there were at least four undated English editions before one produced at Aberdeen in 1630. Three others are entered in the Stationers' Registers for 1558, 1560–1 and 1568–9, but if they were ever published (which did not necessarily follow upon official entry), they have disappeared: the fate of far more once-popular books than many readers imagined or now imagine, and also, even more vexatiously for historians of numberless children's books.* Other editions are dated 1640(?), 1662 (published by Andrew Crooke, who issued Ogilby's *Aesop*) and 1689. The full title of this last is worth quoting. It runs:

The Famous and Renowned History of Sir Bevis of Southampton, giving an Account of his Birth, Education, Heroick Exploits and Enterprises, his Fights with Giants, Monsters, Wild-Beasts and Armies, his Conquering Kings and Kingdoms, his Love and Marriage, Fortunes and Misfortunes, and many other Famous and Memorable Things and Actions, worthy of Wonder; With the Adventures of other Knights, Kings and Princes, exceeding pleasant and delightful to Read.

The title-page bears a woodblock of two knights on horseback. It was to do duty over and over again on the covers or in the text of chapbooks, and to stand not only for Sir Bevis, but for Sir Guy of Warwick, Parismus, St George, the Seven Champions, and many others of the knightly ghosts. The book itself is printed almost haphazard[3] in black letter mixed with ordinary roman type, as if old founts were being used up economically and the volume rushed out for a waiting market. In fact, *Bevis* is here caught in the very act and article of changing from a dignified old Romance into a cheap and ugly book for travelling hucksters, and so into a children's book, in which form it could be gradually rebeautified.

---

*   A similar mishap befell the equally popular romance of *Sir Guy Earl of Warwick*. Guy is in the *Gesta Romanorum*, in a rather sketchy form, and he had also much the same manuscript history as Bevis. Like Bevis too and St George, he was probably as well known in verbal allusion in Shakespeare's time as Sherlock Holmes today.

8. A woodcut of the battle between Bevis and Ascapart the Giant from W. Copland's edition of *Syr Beuys of Hampton* (1565?).

The title-page just quoted, grandiose though it is, is not a bad description of the romance itself, in any of its forms. Bevis as a child was sold by a wicked mother to the Saracens. He won favour with his ultimate lord, King Ermyn, and also with the king's daughter Josian. He was duly knighted, but his firm adherence to Christianity set Ermyn against him, and he became more or less a knight errant, and included among his enemies not only pagans wherever found, but a number of Christians of evil character, and a fine collection of other creatures – dragons, giants, lions and boars (which appear to have become hypertrophied during Europe's anarchy); several of each. He possessed prodigious strength, of course, increased upon occasion by the recurrent mad fury which Steele and his godson discussed gravely. He had also a notable steed, Arundel, and an almost invincible sword, Morglay. (The alleged sword was dug up many years ago in Arundel Park.) In the English version, he is said to have lived in the time of King Edgar, and to have been the son of a Sir Guy – late-born, which was the cause of his mother's hostility. (Sir Guy is sometimes represented as Guy of Warwick himself.) When after fighting erratically over half Europe and part of Asia, Bevis returned to England, he won a great battle at

39

London over the heathen, and his son married King Edgar's daughter. Local tradition later turned him into a gigantic warder of Arundel Castle, in Sussex, and pointed out as his grave a long barrow, found to be empty when it was opened.

There is obviously a wide field for fascinating conjecture in a wild narrative like that. It was hardly all pure invention, with its mixture of historical names, folk-lore, creatures out of the *Bestiary*, Saracens, and places in Eastern Europe where heaven knows how much fighting has taken place since the Roman Empire fell. But guesses at what tiny grain of fact is hidden in all the dust are probably useless, and certainly irrelevant here. What is interesting in the actual text of the legend is a famous quotation from it, which, when it was first spoken on the stage, must have been in some sort familiar to the audience, and which will live as long as English literature lasts. It comes in the account of Bevis's most outrageous feat.

His most relentless enemy was King Brademond of Damascus, a bitter follower of Mahound (Muhammed). Brademond by good luck captured him, and cast him into a deep loathsome dungeon. There he abode in the dark for the surprising period of seven years, with only 'a mess of wheat' each day for food. At the end of that time he found a cudgel, and almost simultaneously two dragons (two lions, by one account) emerged from the gloom and attacked him. He fell into one of his berserk rages – 'passionate temper', as Steele calls it – killed the dragons, broke his bonds and all bars and doors, and hacked and roared his way to freedom.

Such deeds are more or less common form in the old romances. What is still remembered is Bevis's long fast. It sticks in the memory today because of a couplet in *Lear* (III, iv). Edgar, in his feigned madness, raves half-irrelevantly:

> But mice, and rats, and such small Deare,
> Have bin Tom's food for seven long yeare.

That is an almost exact verbal quotation from Copeland's version of the romance, which, unlike later texts, is in verse throughout, with short incident-headings in prose:

> Rattes and myse and suche smal dere
> was his meate that seuen yere
> thus is beuis on the pryson grounde
> god bring him oute hole and sounde

The words are not so closely alike in any other text of the romance, though all offer something like them. The French prose version is bald, and allows Bevis a small daily ration, but mentions no 'deer': 'La ou estoit beufues emprisonne commanda le roy Brandimont quon luy donnast pour chacun jour ung quartier de pain et non plus.' There are no mice in the Auchinleck manuscript (early fourteenth century), which gives seven years as the length of confinement, and allows him wheat; but otherwise

> Now is Beuis at this petes grounde,
> God bringe him vp hol and sonde.

And the Early English Text Society knows no other food either. There is enough coincidence, in fact, to prove an originally identical text, but enough dissimilarity to show that Shakespeare either knew only Copland's version (in whatever edition – some may have perished) or had the words by rote from it or some lost original.

That is a small point, of greater interest to students of Shakespeare's text than, strictly speaking, to an historian of children's books. Its importance here is that the passage quoted is by no means solitary in Shakespeare. In *Lear* also occurs the famous passage (III, iv):

> Childe Rowland to the darke tower came,
> His word was still, – fie, foh, and fumme,
> I smell the blood of a British man.

(One quarto has the odd variant 'towne' for 'tower'.) You will find the story of *Child Rowland* in Joseph Jacobs's admirable children's book, *English Fairy Tales* (1890); and what child today does not know the giant who said 'Fie, foh, and fumme'? In *Much Ado* (I, i) you read the passage 'Like the old tale, my Lord, it is not so, nor 'twas not so, but indeed, God forbid it should be so.' That is from the old tale of *Mr Fox*, and you will find that story also in Mr Jacobs's book.

5

So Shakespeare and Captain Cox of Coventry knew already the tales which were to become familiar in English nurseries when books were specially written for them. They knew them, too, as part of a culture increasingly shared and diffused in print among ranks of society which had had a bare century of education. And these were not tales told, like *Aesop's Fables*, for a moral or educational purpose. They were the recreation of ordinary people. The stories had become popular by decay. Even in their first complete formulation they had shown only a wan ghost of the romantic chivalry which may at its best, if it ever had a best, have inspired them. The Middle Ages saw knights who had been the paladins of Christendom as the pillars of a vanishing or vanished social order, the age of chivalry. To the Elizabethans, it is probable, they were not much more than robust jokes. But in the nurseries of today they are once again heroes.

It is unnecessary to trace the story of the Romances further in detail. Their journey into an ordinary library is clear. Of *Bevis*, after 1689, there seem to have been several more or less pretentious editions up to 1711. Then he descended into the stockpot of the chapbook producers, whose strange activities are described below. He was to reappear in some pride in Victoria's reign, as a defender of English faith against American rationalism: but that also is for later treatment. It is enough that he was a battered but recognizable and obtainable romantic figure by the time a child could comment upon him in *The Tatler*; and to that state he had come by way of Shakespeare himself. Whether Shakespeare had read of him in a book, or absorbed him as he assimilated fairy-lore in Warwickshire, we shall never know for certain.

6

Thus the chivalry of the Middle Ages, coming back later into English literature itself by way of the romantic novel and poem, crept underground for a time, as it were, and took refuge in the nursery library. The manners and customs which were the background of mediaeval life had a different kind of hold upon children's books. The sway of ancient morals – mankind's own morals rather than those of one particular epoch – lived on for the young in the Fable. The social aspect of morals – behaviour and mental culture – survived in two forms of printed matter: Books of Courtesy and Schoolbooks.

The Romance writers had not troubled much about that passive side of life, except by implying that virtue (in an accomplished knight) usually conquered in the long run, and by insisting frequently in great detail, upon the punctilio of the armigerous. Books like *Stans puer ad mensam*, which, as has been said, occurs both in Dorne's *Daybook* and in Captain Cox's catalogue, were a natural product of such an attitude. They became, as soon as print was ready to be the vehicle of instruction, an honest safeguard against the hoggishness of mind and custom which their pages reveal as both extant and deplorable. Education, as such, was less necessary than decency: and decency did not include reading for pleasure.

But education did not include it either. Books meant for children (few enough in any case) before the seventeenth century contemplated two sorts of reader – those who could take a suitable place in good society, and those who would in one way or other serve the Church. Girls had not much future beyond the domestic arts, or wifehood and motherhood, or a nunnery. For boys, the alternatives are shown vividly enough by Chaucer. A well-born lad could become a squire, a lowly one a monk or a minor servant outside orders or vows: that is, if they received any education at all. The one 'carf biforn' his father at the table; the other, the 'litel clergeon', learnt the alphabet, and the gracious ritual of worship, and sang 'Ave Mary's' and the hymn 'Gentle mother of the Redeemer'; by which process, according to Dame Alison of Bath, Bishop Corbet of Oxford, and other authorities, all the native nonsense about fairies and so on, which children might mischievously pick up, was knocked out of their heads; or, according to Hobbes, aggravated.

Thus Books of Courtesy were not idle manuals of a polished life, in the first instance. They were books of 'nurture', guides to professional efficiency. John Russell wrote his work on the subject – *the* 'Boke of Nurture' (1460–70?), one of two bearing the same title – for practical purposes. He was walking in a forest, 'where sightes were fresche and gay', when he met a disconsolate lad deer-stalking with a bow. The youth's gloom arose because he wished to be a butler, pantler, chamberlain, or carver, and could find no master to take and train him, and knew nothing. In the face of that baulked desire – not unlike, in essence, the call of the towns to our young folk today – Russell felt impelled to set forth all the customs of good breeding which would fit an ambitious lad for court life, just as apprenticeship fitted a merchant's son for full guild membership, and all the prosperity and prestige which that meant.

The contents of such works, however, are irrelevant here: they are not really children's books at all.* They make no provision for reading in a child's upbringing, or in the building of his character. They put the mould before the character, and would have no divergence from it. Reading, in fact, was a danger, from one point of view, and useless from another. The words of a kind of hawbuck of about 1500 have an oddly modern ring. Richard Pace in a letter to Colet (printed in *The Babees Book*) tells how a rough country gentleman at a feast blurted out: 'Abeant in malam rem istae stultae literae, omnes docti sunt mendici, etiam Erasmus ille doctissimus (ut audio) pauper est . . . Studia vero literarum, rusticorum filiis sunt relinquenda.' (But the sons of rustics did not often get the legacy. When they did, they made good use of it – as, for instance, the Russells had at that very period.) It was manners, not learning, that society still demanded, even under the two first Tudors, except at the universities: the new knowledge bore spontaneous fruit a little later, under Elizabeth.

The moral danger was a different thing. The objection to light reading as a recreation was that it led to idleness and to false beliefs: that it was harmful as well as a waste of time. That is a curiously persistent doctrine. It appears in the earliest Books of Courtesy, and, changing into a kind of snobbishness which looked on culture as ungentlemanly, continued into their much later equivalents.

One of the earliest and most famous examples of such a standpoint is in the other *Boke of Nurture* ('for Men, Seruantes and Children') by Hugh Rhodes. Rhodes was a Devonshire worthy of Henry VIII's time. His treatise was first published in *c.* 1545, 'to teche vertew and connynge'. This is his warning to parents:

Take hede [your children] speake no wordes of villany, for it causeth much corruption to ingender in them, nor shew them muche familiaritye, and see that they use honest sportes and games. Marke well what vice they are specially inclined unto, and breake it betymes. Take them often with you to heare Gods word preached, and then enquire of them what they heard, and use them to reade in the Bible and other Godly Bokes, but especyally keepe them from reading of fayned fables, vayne fantasyes, and wanton stories, and songs of love, which bring much mischiefe to youth.

That is exactly what the Puritans were saying, more vehemently and with more visible excuse, a century later. But it is also almost exactly what Roger Ascham,

---

* Furnivall's edition of *The Babees Book* (1868) gives many texts. Mrs Field also quotes freely from them in the first half-dozen chapters of *The Child and His Book*.

the humane and tolerant master of Queen Elizabeth, had uttered at about the same time as Rhodes, in *The Scholemaster*.*

In our forefathers' time, when Papistry, as a standing pool, covered and overflowed all England, few books were read in our tongue, saving certain books of Chivalry, as they said, for pastime and pleasure, which, as some say, were made in monasteries by idle monks or wanton canons: as one for example, *Morte Arthure*: the whole pleasure of which book standeth in two special points, in open manslaughter and bold bawdry . . . Yet I know, when God's Bible was banished the Court, and *Morte Arthure* received into the Prince's chamber. What toys the daily reading of such a book may work in the will of a young gentleman or a young maid, that liveth wealthily and idly, wise men can judge and honest men do pity.

These dreadful works,[4] therefore, must have been available for young persons, though they may not have been meant for them. And it would be unfair to Rhodes and Ascham to suppose that they cried out, like the White Queen in *Alice*, before they felt the prick. The Romances must actually have been read by some at least of the adolescents of England: hence the alarm.

7

That then is the historical value, a negative one in a sense, of the Books of Courtesy in the history of children's books. They prove that society was for a long time opposed to the idea that the young should read anything like what we should call fiction – even 'juvenile' fiction, had it existed. The opposition became clamorously triumphant under the Puritans, as will be seen. But the Romances outlasted their earliest enemies, while Fables, as was plain from Scripture, were lawful weapons for moralists themselves to use. It may be worth while, however, to carry the story of courtesy a little further in order to emphasize the dislike, almost (I repeat) amounting to fear, which the exponents of good breeding constantly displayed towards the amenities of literature.

Stans puer ad mensam had been printed in an English edition by Caxton before 1479. De Worde issued at least three more editions in English and five in Latin. (The English version is ascribed to John Lydgate, the monk of Bury, Chaucer's devotee;† the Latin to Sulpitius.) There were a good many reprints in the sixteenth century, and probably it was one of these which Captain Cox owned, though by his day most of the social usages described in the book must have been virtually obsolete. It seems to have dropped out altogether after Elizabeth's

---

* Published posthumously in 1570. Ascham had said virtually the same thing in *Toxophilus* (1545). He complained too, that the shops in London were 'full of lewd and rude rhymes'. His learned editor, J. E. B. Mayor, quotes a ballad of 1561–2, directed specially against the 'fylthy wrytinge' which was on sale in those dangerous places.

† These words occur at the end of the Harleian manuscript:

> Of the writying, though ther be no date
> If ought be mysse – worde, sillable, or dede -
> Put all the defaute vpon John Lydegate.

The chief extant English manuscripts are dated approximately 1430 (Lambeth) and 1460 (Harleian).

reign. Schools and their books were making such works to a great extent unnecessary – at any rate, as detailed primers of behaviour. On the other hand, perhaps because the new-rich of the post-Dissolution period needed some social polish, more general treatises became popular.

Of these perhaps the best known was *The Gentleman's Calling* (1660),[5] the authorship of which is still in dispute. For younger people, Francis Osborne's *Advice to a Son* (1656; Part II, 1658) and Halifax the Trimmer's *Lady's New-Year's Gift, or, Advice to a Daughter* (1688), had a considerable and long vogue, though Osborne's book had the distinction of being condemned by the Vice-Chancellor of Oxford University as atheistical. His Part II contains a section headed 'Great libraries more for pomp than use' and in his pragmatic remarks on 'Studies' in Part I he says that 'Company', if good, 'is a better Refiner of the spirits than ordinary Bookes'. He almost ignores reading altogether, beyond generalizations like these.

So does Halifax, who wrote admirable English himself. He says nothing whatever about books as aids or enemies to refined conduct. But the daughter he addressed had a son who certainly had views on the subject – that most eminent of all polite moralists, Philip Dormer Stanhope, fourth Earl of Chesterfield, the author of the famous *Letters*, the 'patron' of Johnson. He gave both his (natural) son and his godson very deterrent advice about reading trivial stories for amusement. To his son he wrote in 1740

The reading of romances is a most frivolous occupation, and time merely thrown away. The old romances, written two or three hundred years ago, such as Amadis of Gaul, Orlando the Furious, and others, were stuft with enchantments, magicians, giants, and such sort of impossibilities; whereas, the more modern romances keep within the bounds of possibility but not of probability.[6]

The boy was then eight years old, and was reading Saint-Réal's *Dom Carlos: Nouvelle historique et galante*, a work of 1673, now deceased. To his godson in 1764 Chesterfield gave a warning against even simpler fiction:

J'aimerois . . . un livre amusant et instructif en même tems, plutôt qu'un livre frivole, et où il n'y a rien a apprendre. Par exemple les Fables de La Fontaine, les Comedies de Moliere, Puffendorf, etc., valent bien mieux, et vous divertiront bien plus que les contes d'Ouville ou de ma Mere L'Oye.

The *Contes de ma Mère l'Oye* are Perrault's Fairy-Tales. Chesterfield could not tolerate even fashionable fantasy, and he had a very clear idea of the distinction between fable and fiction, and their social value.

Newbery, on the other hand, had not, as the *Little Pretty Pocket-Book* showed. He and his successors produced several code-books of behaviour, however which ignored amusement almost entirely. One such work – issued by his rivals, Baldwin of London and Collins of Salisbury – though it contained *Beauty and the Beast* as a moral tale, warned the reader, 'Never read or look upon a Book in Company.' This was a magnificent survey of the proper conduct for all possible occasions, *The Polite Academy* (1762; in the tenth edition, published by Darton and Harvey and others *c.* 1800, the code was textually identical). Works with such titles as *The Juvenile Monitor* and *The Polite Preceptor* were common under George III; and Newbery himself edited a collection of *Letters upon the most common, as well as important, Occasions in Life* (1756), the preface to which states his comprehensive object – 'that there may be something said suitable to every circumstance in life'.

But that was only one branch of his children's-book business, the deportment section. It mattered little to a publisher, as a commercial man, that it conflicted theoretically with the work of his more original department which conveyed amusement without much stress on polished manners. Both kinds of book were vendible wares.

8

The fashionable antagonism to reading, naturally, did not endure to any serious extent when once social changes had made reading a habit – a 'circumstance in life'. Schoolbooks, not less naturally, became even more necessary in consequence of the same changes. They also had, in a way, to meet the competition of amusement disguising itself as instruction. The way to do so, obviously, was to pretend to be amusing themselves: to suggest the friend rather than the coercive schoolmaster. The matter was, in the earliest stages, simply a practical question. The ABC could not be learnt by mere rote always. It merged itself often in the nursery rhyme, and so was woven into the fabric of pleasant books: the *Little Pretty Pocket-Book*, for example. 'A was an Archer' appeared long before that.* 'A was an Apple Pie' (why?) is referred to in 1671 as if it were a commonly known rhyme. The first English alphabet printed in book form[7] – Petyt's, of *c.* 1538 – contained not only the ABC, but 'devout prayers' and the Ten Commandments: the Decalogue, significantly, was versified for little readers. It was not without good and kindly reason that a famous early-eighteenth-century bookshop bore the inviting sign of *The Great A and Bouncing B*.[8]

The Abcie's companions, the primer and the schoolbook proper, could never have quite the same chance of translation into happy fancifulness. Moreover, they changed with every development of educational theory and method, and so had no permanent fabric for decoration. They do not concern us here: they belong to a history of education. But they too had sometimes to hint that school had something to do with human nature. In the strange underwoods of such books are often to be found odd little treasures. You can see the schoolboy tricks of any and every age in some of the homely dialogues invented as exercises in Latin and English. For instance, under 'Formulae accusandi quempiam' – the phrase in *Pueriles Confabulatiunculae* for what is commonly known as sneaking – occur 'Fabulatur de re scurrili': 'Hic non detexit caput cum praeteriret magistratum': 'Vulsit me crinibus' – 'Please, sir, Johnny's pulling my hair'. You find also not quite dead superstitions: when anyone sneezes, for instance, you

---

* See below, Chapter IV.

must say, 'sit salvum', 'sit felix', or 'prosit' – or, as Chaucer records, 'Ben'cite'. You find traces of habits now modified so far as the young are concerned. When you have drinks together, the first drinker must say 'praebibo tibi totum poculum' (in Mr Jingle's words, 'no heeltaps'), or, if he is moderate, 'propino tibi dimidiatum cyathum'; and the other will reply 'accipio libenter' ('which, altering to the name of Sairey Gamp, I drinks with love and tenderness'). One sentence asks who among all men, are 'honestissimi': the immediate answer, without comment, is 'potatores'. You even get strange hints of the antiquity of timeworn phrases, like 'a tale of a tub', or (in *Paroemiologia Anglo-Latina*, by John Clarke, 1639) a translation of the Latin proverb 'flet victor, victus interiit' by the English 'he gets by *that*, as Dickons did by's distress'. The same work – 'more especially profitable for Scholars for the attaining elegancy, sublimity, and variety of the best expressions' – gives 'Jack and Jill [Sprat]' as the equivalent of 'palatum non omnibus idem': 'Jack will eat no fat, and Jill doth love no leane.'[9] Here is today's children's literature in embryo.

But if you find in these higgledy-piggledy repositories of linguistic lumber that kind of elusive yet enduring humanity, which has flashed whimsically in and out of obscure books, you will also discover something which makes the Puritan attitude to a good deal of seventeenth-century education very easily comprehensible. They had plenty to react against. These dialogues reveal frankly the coarse truth of English domestic life, with no sign of repugnance. It is necessary to quote a few sentences which children were expected to repeat: they might not be believed without quotation. In *Pueriles Confabulatiunculae*, which, among others, Brinsley edited – but it was respectably old then – one complaint by a boy against a schoolfellow is 'perminxit calceos meos'. Hoole re-editing the same work as *Children's Talke – English and Latin*, 1652, gives blunt English for some of the Latin sentences (in his text the words are spelt out in full): 'Where do foxes f—t? A little above their hams.' 'Why doth a dog, being to p—, hold up one leg? Lest he should bep— his stockings.' 'Ad tergendas nates in latrina – to wipe one's breech in the house-of-office.'

It would be possible, by devoting a lifetime to the task, to dig up in the vast arid deserts of grammar, especially of mediaeval grammar, enough material for a pretty solid reconstruction of school-life, and child-life generally, between, say, 1300 and 1650; and in the course of that labour, which I do not propose to undertake, there would be found many more fragments than I have quoted or could quote of folk-lore, fairy-tale, nursery rhyme, proverbial sayings, and so on, which, after the tumult of the Civil War was ended, gradually settled themselves into something like a whole. Much of that material, in its original form, or in a coherent shape, had vanished altogether from print – if it ever reached it – before Newbery's day. But the memory of it, rags and tatters of phrase and thought, lived on.

So likewise did the mode, and its survivals have coloured many much later reminiscences of alleged children's books. Amiable persons think of Mangnall's *Questions* and 'Little Arthur's England' almost as if they were the only things young people read a century or so ago; whereas they were nothing but domestic aids to class-room work. I can only give here, by way of record (and even that is really out of place), a list of a few eminent catechetical works. At least it entitles John Newbery to a small place in this by-way. He published *The Circle of the Sciences*, which he called 'a compendious library, whereby each Branch of Polite Learning is rendered extremely easy and instructive'. It was in dialogue form, chiefly, with some lapses. It consisted of seven volumes, each devoted to one subject, but before the definitive group was established in 1748 there were various experimental efforts, some of which were either abandoned or issued, finally, *hors série*.* The eventual make-up of subjects was: Arithmetic (first published 1746), Chronology (1748), Geography (1748), Grammar (1745), Logic (1748), Poetry (1746), and Rhetorick (1746). The volumes, separately, were rife for a good forty years, and were frequently pirated or imitated.

Now where did Newbery, a year after his commencement, when he was in the full flush of new enterprise, get those seven sciences for his bespoke 'Governesses of Great Britain and Ireland'? Poor wretches, valiant pioneers of agreeable knowledge for minds that could but chirrup 'a, b, ab', humdrum imitators of Newbery's (and Goldsmith's?) ideal Mistress Margery Two-Shoes teaching Miss Primrose Prettyface – they must grapple with logic, rhetoric, and all in a concatenation accordingly. Why?

The selection must be Newbery's own, with throwbacks now inexplicable. Maybe it was a long backward glance. The Trivium and Quadrivium of Scholasticism consisted of *Grammar, Dialectics, Rhetoric* – ultimately nos. I, V and III of Newbery's *Circle – and Music, Arithmetic* (no. II), *Geometry* and *Astronomy*. Locke, on the other hand, in a long passage which rather gives his own tentative ideas than sums up current practice, recommends (after the alphabet, reading, writing and elementary religious knowledge have been mastered) the study of a foreign language at first hand, and Latin, and *then* – poetry being discarded – grammar, arithmetic, geography, chronology, history and geometry, to be taken in an order which he discusses and leaves reasonably open. That is, he also chooses four of Newbery's seven sciences, but not the same four as the Scholastics used.

It is a strange mystery. But it is not for solution here. The later dialogue instruction–amusement books cannot receive even so much as this suggestion of pedigree-hunting. The day of less interesting catechisms dawned with the nineteenth century. In 1800 appeared *Historical and Miscellaneous Questions*, by Richmal Mangnall: they were being reprinted till at least 1869. William Pinnock (1782–1843) 'improved' (his own word) the *Questions* into his eighty-three *Catechisms*. 'The Rev. D. Blair' (Sir Richard Phillips) improved Pinnock. 'The Rev. T. Wilson' (the Rev. Samuel Clark) sought to improve upon the *soi-disant* Blair. In 1825, between 'Blair' and 'Wilson', there had quietly crept into

* [The complications in the publishing and numbering of the series, which also threatened to include criticism, history and philosophy, are fully explained in S. Roscoe's bibliography of Newbery.]

print at Thetford *262 Questions and Answers, or, The Children's Guide to Knowledge . . . By a Lady*. It was known from its second edition in the year 1828 up to its revision in 1875 as *The Child's Guide to Knowledge*: the Lady was a Miss Fanny Umphelby. A few years earlier, in 1823, was published *A History of England . . . With Conversations at the End of Each Chapter*, by 'Mrs Markham', Elizabeth Penrose; a work which, if one prefers an easy narrative to closely accurate history, is by no means uninteresting to this day. (There is, by the way, far more history than conversation.) And there were Mrs Marcet and her *Conversations*, and Mrs Mortimer with the *Peep of Day, Far Off, Near Home* and *Line upon Line*, and a score of other dialogue-makers who did not know, probably, that they were carrying on the work of Aldhelm and Aelfric. The 'catechism' was the subtlest and most lasting of all the spells cast by the Middle Ages upon English childhood. But the Middle Ages never invented a real children's book.

The long epoch summarized for convenience under that title, then, held children in mortmain. The Renaissance and the Reformation did little for juvenile literature. But before the Georgian middle-class became aware of itself and of its infants, and while the real enchantments of the older world were still invisible, because fairy-tales were not yet put into books, children, like the rest of England, had to be searched and examined by an Inquisition as strict as any that came out of Rome. New presbyter was for them old priest writ large and more formidable. Yet it was the greatest of all the Puritans who wrote the first work that claimed and deserved to be called an English children's book.

BRIEF BOOK LIST

For the whole subject of the Romances, see *C.H.E.L.* vol. I, and *N.C.B.E.L.* vol. I. A convenient modern text of some of them is provided in Messrs Routledge's reissue of Thoms's *Early English Prose Romances* (London, 1907).

For 'courtesy' and schools, any general history of education can be consulted: for the careers and works of the chief persons mentioned here, see *D.N.B.* and *C.H.E.L.* It is pleasant and relevant to remember that the main social conditions were excellently described by an eminent writer for children, to be treated hereafter – William Brighty Rands – in *Chaucer's England*, by 'Matthew Browne'. 2 vols. (London, 1869). See also Dr F. J. Furnivall's introduction to the present writer's *Tales of the Canterbury Pilgrims* (London, 1904). For special points see:

Bradshaw, Henry. *Collected Papers* (Cambridge, 1889), no. XVIII, ' The ABC as a schoolbook'.
Furnivall. F. J. ed. *The Babees Book*, for the Early English Text Society (London, 1868).
Hazlitt, W. Carew. *Schools, School Books and Schoolmasters* (London, 1888).
Watson, Foster. *The English Grammar Schools to 1660* (Cambridge, 1908).

Supplement

Little advance has been made since 1932 on the relationship between topics discussed in this chapter and children's books, but of great general interest are three volumes on *English Books and Readers* by H. S. Bennett: vol 1, 1475 to 1557, with a Handlist of publications by Wynkyn de Worde, 1492–1535, and a trial list of translations into English, 1475–1560 (Cambridge, 1952); vol. II, 1558 to 1603 (Cambridge, 1965); vol. III, 1603 to 1640 (Cambridge, 1970). Note also an attempt to place Robin Hood studies on to a more orderly footing:

Dobson, R. B. and Taylor, J. *Rymes of Robyn Hood; an introduction to the English outlaw* (London, 1978).

A Bibliography of Robin Hood by J. Harris Gable (Lincoln, Nebraska, 1939) offers little help to the student of children's books.

CHAPTER IV

The Puritans: 'Good Godly Books'

I

By far the greater part of the works for or about children which may for convenience be called 'Puritan' were written and published after the Restoration; most of them after the Act of Uniformity of 1662. Those which were written *for* children were as a rule conceived and executed with so strong a didactic and religious bias that to many they seem not be 'children's books' at all, in the sense here adopted. On the other hand, the authors meant them to fulfil that end – to give children pleasure and to make them happy: it was their idea of happiness which is foreign to that usually held today. If for that reason alone, it is necessary to look at the intention behind these often grim products; especially as they are often dismissed with an unfair lack of sympathy and in an unhistorical perspective. But they have also the further importance that the spirit in them, modified only in expression, informed the majority of real English children's books for at least a century and a half. It was the spirit of fear; the plainest, sternest, most inelastic ideal of training up a child in the way he should go – the way he *must* go, without regard to his nature or his environment or his equipment for this world. 'Be good, and let who may be clever': the Puritans were more openly honest in that doctrine than many who came after.

Their books for children, it is a commonplace to say, were based upon the plain dogmatic belief that a definitely revealed heaven and hell existed on every edge of this mortal life, and that conduct here on earth leads irrevocably (but for the mercy of God) to the one or the other. The authors wrote to the end that children might be saved from hell, with the implication that salvation is extremely difficult. That is how Bunyan and a few contemporaries, who wrote genuine 'children's books', took up their happy duty of composing works for the young. It is how (but much more gently) Isaac Watts took it up a generation later. The purpose is apparent in all early American children's books;[1] in the greater part of Mrs Sherwood's writings, often with emphasis. It is logically implicit in all 'moral tales', including the Lambs'; in 'Peter Parley's' instructive works; in the writings of partisans of the Establishment, like Mrs Trimmer, and even, later, Charles Kingsley. It is only not in the philosophical freedom of the Rousseauists, in the attempts at nonsense before and after Lear, in fairy-tales, and in books published after the appearance of *Alice's Adventures in Wonderland*.

The peculiar vehemence with which the seventeenth-century Puritans adopted this view has made both historical and spiritual sympathy with them difficult. Historically, they are often travestied, apart from mere vulgar exaggeration; psychologically, misunderstood. It is not necessary to bring in here the precise questions and events in politics and civic conduct which moulded their lives so strangely. But it is necessary to remember the reality of such things, and the reactions they would have upon any normal mind at any period. To get into touch with the Puritan outlook upon reading for children, consider the life and books of one who, after Bunyan, had the widest and longest popularity as the author of works read in English nurseries; read, and, sometimes, as they were meant to be, enjoyed; real children's books of one period in particular, and in the background of others.

2

The author is James Janeway. Take his works first. To start with, he said plainly that children were 'Brands of Hell' in any case: a perfectly natural consequence of the doctrine of Original Sin. They must be born again, because 'Hell is a terrible place, that's worse a thousand times than whipping'. (Whipping, it must be remembered, was as ordinary then as in the nineteenth-century school, and therefore a stronger sanction of the moral law had to be displayed.) But if they attained Heaven, 'they shall never be beat any more, they shall never be sick, or in pain any more'. The salvation from sickness deserves notice.

The full title of the book in which these words occur is *A Token for Children: being an Exact Account of the Conversion, Holy and Exemplary Lives, and Joyful Deaths of several young Children*. It was entered in the Stationers' Register on October 13, 1671 and was followed shortly after by a Second Part, both published unillustrated by Dorman Newman.* By 1720 the book was extended with 'Prayers and Graces, fitted for the use of Little Children' and was 'adorned with cuts'. These illustrations are not in the nature of horrific warnings (as in martyrologies), but are meant to be attractively, if austerely, moral. Thus a child is shown as praying for its parent, the appeal being not to the sense of pity for the grown-up, but to the joy in piety of the child. Similarly, three little creatures whip a top (a grave crime, often reprobated, the whirling top being a notable emblem), while a fourth prays. In another picture, a child thoughtfully, but without terror, contemplates a corpse in a coffin. The woodblocks were used several times over in the volume, without exact relevance. They were clearly expected to have aesthetic value. They may be contrasted, however, with the contemporary pictures in collections of Fables, which show a philosophy of design.

The text is of a piece. It insists on the (to us) gloomy joy, the triumphancy, of unflinching rectitude, and of constant fortitude in circumstances which were almost always discouraging. Nearly all the children who provided examples died

* [The earliest extant copy is in the Osborne Collection at Toronto; both parts dated 1672.]

young – it is really *ex hypothesi*, from the title; most of them of 'a decline', but some of the Plague. Nearly all, also, rebuked their companions, brothers, sisters, and even parents, for frivolity, and were bent on inculcating a right faith. One, aged eleven, tried to convert a Turk to Christianity by going to fetch his beer for him, and so winning his stubborn heart. Another had wider ideals. Before his death, he 'was not a little concerned for the whole Nation, and begged that God would pardon the Sins of this Land, and bring it nearer to himself.' In his Preface to Part I 'containing Directions to Children', Janeway includes one which asks for results: 'How art thou now affected, poor Child, in the reading of this Book? Have you shed ever a Tear since you begun reading?' There is no doubt that he really hoped they would weep; not, however, at the thought of the actual pains of Hell, but spontaneously from a conviction of sin; sin not committed but inherent. In all their lives, in all they did, thought, read, they must remember that they were, 'by Nature, Children of Wrath'.

It is only partly just to say that such works as this are not 'children's books'. It is true that they do not provide 'amusement', except unintentionally. But that is exactly why, at that time, they *were* 'children's books'. They *were* meant to give pleasure: the highest pleasure, that of studying and enjoying the Will of God. They were to be a natural happiness: no other happiness was conceivable. They were to be the recreation of leisure, not schoolbooks; nor did Janeway, or any other writer of the kind, separate the didactic or monitory–minatory element in them from the enjoyable. If his, Janeway's, persuasions were not alluring enough, others might be – 'get your Father to buy you Mr White's *Little Book for Little Children* (an adjuration changed in later editions to read Mr Jole's *Father's Blessing* and *A Guide to Heaven*)'.* There were plenty such books; and they were not all of the close-woven Janeway texture. They contain gleams of other matter.

They will receive brief mention shortly. Janeway was not only typical, but more eminent than they, and he was read with appreciation into the mid nineteenth century,† though by then the *Token* had long ceased to be the only kind of fare offered to children in the strictest Puritan circles. He wrote also another *Token*² – *A Token for Youth . . . to which is Added, An Account of God's Gracious Dealings with some Young Persons and Children . . . With Pictures, Poems, and Spiritual Songs, proper to the Subject.* (I have seen only an edition of 1709: there were undoubtedly earlier ones.) The 'young persons' here are not quite children, and the 'accounts' are more deliberately harrowing, more, so to speak, in the 'Foxe's Book of Martyrs' manner. The 'spiritual songs' are not by Janeway, but by Abraham Chear. The 'pictures' are of the highest interest to the historian of domestic manners; but relevance and decency forbid details here. It is evident, from various typographical features, as well as other testimony, that both *Tokens* had a very great vogue between about 1670 and 1720. Probably it

---

* [William Sloane has pointed out that *A Guide to Heaven* (1687) is a book for adult readers by Samuel Hardy.]

† [The Religious Tract Society still carried the *Token* in stock in 1875.]

9. A mother and her seven sons are brought before Antiochus Epiphanes: a tale recorded in *Maccabees* II. 7 and Josephus, finding its way thence into martyrologies. It reached the *Token for Youth* via Thomas White's *Little Book for Little Children* (1660). Later woodcuts depict the tortures.

was fostered by parental vigilance, to which Janeway appealed directly: 'Are the Souls of your Children of no Value? . . . They are not too little to die, they are not too little to go to Hell, they are not too little to serve their great Master, too little to go to Heaven.'

3

'Not too little to go to Hell' – he meant it, believed it, he, an ordained minister of Christ. What manner of life did he live, to be so without bowels, and yet to claim, as he did, to be 'one that dearly loves little Children'?

He could well be singled out, by those who like such a portrait, as a hard and unlovely fanatic, narrowly educated and of narrow mind. He was obviously nothing of the kind, even though Anthony Wood, a contemporary, wrote of him in the best Dickens manner, as being 'much resorted to by those of his persuasion, and admired for a forward and precious young man, especially by those of the female sex'. He was of what today would be good middle-class Church of England stock. He was born about 1636, being the fourth son of the curate of Lilley, Herts. He was a student of Christ Church, Oxford, took his B.A. degree there in 1659, and seems to have been preparing to follow his father's example and take orders. But he may not have been ordained. He appears to have been 'silenced' by the Act of Uniformity of 1662. He preached in London as a non-conformist during the Plague; a terror which we today cannot easily grasp. He was there during the Great Fire; and that is not easily *felt* in England today either. A chapel was built for him in or about 1672 at Rotherhithe – Lemuel Gulliver's Redriff. It was 'pulled down by the soldiers', but the people rebuilt it. The troopers would have assaulted him in the pulpit of the new house, but his friends saved him, and from a second attack also. On another occasion he was shot at: 'the bullet went through his hat, but inflicted no personal injury'. He died of tuberculosis in 1674, and was buried at St Mary's, Aldermanbury.

Of his brothers the record is not dissimilar. The eldest, William, went to Cambridge, and in all probability succeeded his father, then rector of Kelshall, Herts., but was ejected in 1662. John, the second son, was first at St Paul's School, then at Eton as a foundation scholar, and lastly at King's, Cambridge, 'of which he afterwards became a Fellow'. James wrote an account of his edifying death – also of consumption – in 1657, at the age of twenty-three. Abraham Janeway was the fifth son, and he died young – of consumption – after having tried in vain to preach regularly in London. Others were Andrew, a London merchant, and Joseph, the youngest, a conforming minister. 'All were consumptive, all died under the age of forty.'

In their social and educational setting, the brothers might have been an ordinary parsonage family today. Janeway the zealot was an average man who chose the most arduous and spiritual profession out of those open to him. There is no evidence that he originally made that choice with the intention of 'protesting' or 'dissenting'. Nor, when one looks at the facts of his short life, do the extremes of opinion which he betrayed seem unrelated to anything in his experience, or arbitrarily embraced. He wrote, in the *Tokens,* of early deaths. He died young: 'all were consumptive', and he saw also at first hand the ravages of the Plague in a not over-moral city. He dwelt upon the pangs of hell: had he not seen the Fire? Upon persecution: he suffered from it. Those things are extra-ordinary to us, and we do not know how they impinge upon the mind. To very many plain Englishmen in Janeway's day they were in the warp and woof of life; ordinary happenings, yet so close and menacing that the contact called forth cries which were not mere babble in a nightmare. Severity of doctrine came from practical experience, not panic.

Finally, apart from all temporal facts, it is impossible to deny to the greater Puritans, like Janeway and Bunyan, an almost mystical strength of faith. They spoke in literal terms, interpreted metaphors as realities, saw bodily sin and pain where minds of another cast would know only a spiritual emotion. Their sincerity, their overwrought courage, indistinguishable, sometimes, from a kind of fear, were in two worlds at once. They conceived of eternal punishment not merely as estrangement from God – the 'Night of the Soul' of the anchorites and mystics – but as active mental torment: 'All the wicked desires and tormenting passions of the mind will rage to the utmost, without having anything to please or gratify them.'* At the same time, they envisaged that damnation almost ecstatically for the physical body; or at least they pressed the physical metaphor fiercely home. It was a duty of relentless love to save their children from that comprehensive doom of soul and body. In that duty, there was no room to contemplate 'amusement'; nor, if a child were guided aright, would it be anything but sinful – that is, contrary to his higher nature – for him to expect it or tolerate it. But he must not be at 'school' all the time: 'if (like bows) we

* William Jole, *The Pious Man's Kallender* (1690?).

should always stand upon our bent, we would in a while prove stark slugs'. He must have leisure. These books were written for use by the young in leisure: they were the first of their kind in England to be so written. They were in that sense 'children's books'; and even in this further sense also, that their writers believed the reading of them would induce an emotion which *ought* to be pleasant or happy.

4

The nearest approach to that melancholy emotion afterwards offered to children was in the American imports into England of 1850–60, satirized by Kingsley as *Squeeky, The Pumplighter* and *The Narrow, Narrow World*. At its least lachrymose, it is not much worse than what Newbery hoped for – Tommy's strenuous effort 'to be a good Boy' and Polly's 'to be a good Girl'. Not much worse in essence, that is. In outward expression it could reach an almost incredible depth of rhapsodical nonsense:

> Or that by large and lavish grief
> While wooing heaven for death's relief
> In silent tears (tears without noise
> Are louder languaged than a voice)
> My heart might quite dissolve and melt
> Till in the swelling stream I felt
> My soul to make its vent, and fly
> Wafted to Heaven in one great sigh.

That is from *The Spiritual Bee* (Oxford, 1662: possibly by William Penn himself), a work highly recommended for children by Puritan writers.[3]

Equally prone to tears was a little boy who 'when hee dyed was in Coats, somewhat above eight years old'. He wept frequently, because 'hee feared he should go to hell yet he served God as well as he could'. He got his brother to keep a diary, which, with a horrible sad precocity, he bade 'that wee should not know of till his death-bed'. In it, for all the world like a recluse searching for the minutest sins, he jotted down his misdeeds:

1. Hee whetted his knife upon a Lords day.
2. Hee did not reprove one that hee heard swear.
3. Hee once omitted prayer to go to play.
4. Hee found his heart dead, and therefore omitted prayer.
5. Hee omitted prayer, because hee thought God was angry.
6. When his mother called him, hee answered *Yes*, and not *Forsooth*.

Perhaps the only justification for inducing such a habit by means of 'Tokens' and such-like is that the victims knew no other state and might have been unhappier if they had.

This record of sin is from the twelfth edition (1702) of a work very notable in its generation, and not to be denied the name of 'children's book', because that is in fact its title – *A Little Book for Little Children*. It was first published in 1660

– thus preceding Janeway by eleven years – and was by Thomas White, one of the ejected ministers described by Calamy. 'He seems not to have been a settled pastor, but a lecturer only, in the places [in London] where he preached. He was a general scholar, and was the noted Mr Chillingworth's amanuensis. He was much esteemed and often very kindly treated by Archbishop Sheldon'; so that he too was hardly the ranting Puritan of popular tradition. He died about 1672. He was not, however, I think, the author of another book bearing the same title, published between 1702 and 1712, 'by T.W.'*

This second *Little Book* is much more genuinely within the terms of my definition. Indeed, it is of authentic historical interest in that very connection, because in it, for the first time in print, appears that famous nursery poem which opens with the immortal

> A was an Archer and shot at a frog,

and closes with a line which perhaps only its proper students have kept in memory:

> Z was one Zeno the Great, but he's dead.

Two other alphabets illustrate the fact that a definition of 'children's books' was hovering not far off. The 'A was an Archer' rhyme is frankly meant to be (and is) enjoyable. Another set of letters is given some excellent little woodcuts, of a design which persisted in cheap schoolbooks for a century and more: they are accompanied by rhymes. B, thus, is

> Balls children love to play with now and then,

with a cut of a striped ball as still used: Y, heedless of the Janeway hatred of the pastime, makes reference to whipping tops:

> The Youth is subject with a Gigg to play.

But the third ABC is simply the letters displayed in a border shaped like a hornbook. Thus the three stages of evolution – education, pleasant education, instructive amusement – are all contained within two covers.

This little volume of light in the gloom also contains three frivolous rhymed riddles, and a poem of which at least the first couplet is well known, if the whole is not:

> I saw a Peacock with a fiery Tail,
> I saw a Blazing Star that dropt down Hail,
> I saw a Cloud begirt an Ivy round,
> I saw a sturdy Oak creep on the Ground,
> I saw a Pismire swallow up a Whale,
> I saw a Brackish Sea brim full of ale,
> I saw a Venice Glass sixteen Yards deep,
> I saw a Well full of Men's Tears that weep,
> I saw Men's Eyes all on a Flame of Fire,
> I saw a House big as the Moon and higher,
> I saw the Sun Red even at midnight,
> I saw the Man that saw this dreadful Sight.

---

* The British Museum Catalogue apparently thinks he was; the Museum volume contains both 'Little Books' bound together, but obviously not published in that form.

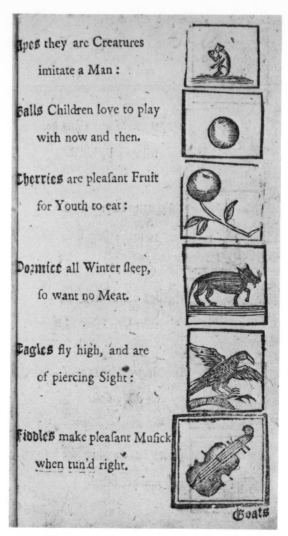

Apes they are Creatures
imitate a Man :

Balls Children love to play
with now and then.

Cherries are pleafant Fruit
for Youth to eat :

Dozmice all Winter fleep,
fo want no Meat.

Eagles fly high, and are
of piercing Sight :

Fiddles make pleafant Mufick
when tun'd right.

Goats

10. Part of T. W.'s 'plain and pleasant way' of appealing to children through a pictorial
alphabet in *A Little Book for Little Children* (*c.* 1702). The layout of the page may have
been influenced by an earlier, but still popular pleasure-book for young learners: J. A.
Comenius's *Orbis Sensualium Pictus*, first published in England in 1659. (It was designed
both as an introduction to the world through pictures and as a mode of teaching Latin. It
is famous throughout Europe as the first pictorial encyclopaedia.)

The use of boxed pictures with captions made an unusual page in the *Orbis Pictus*,
which was chiefly illustrated with single plates. As a way of presenting the alphabet,
however, it established a lay-out which continued through an immense series of 'reading
easy' books (including one illustrated by Bewick) and battledores.

(It is an exercise, far-fetched, in mispunctuation.) Altogether this *Little Book*,
unrelated as it seems to be to its surroundings, suggests the antiquity and the
complete obscurity of much that went to make what we can honestly recognize
as children's books. The matter was extant, even under a heavy layer of
'Tokens' of a different ideal.

Yet another 'T.W.' (i.e. Thomas Willis D.D.) increases the confusion. He wrote *The Key of Knowledg* [sic] . . . *designed for the Conduct of Children and Servants* (n.d. but probably 1682; issued by Thomas White's publisher). This, for the greater part of its length, is a warning against sin, but ends in a charming section called *Apples of Gold in Pictures of Silver*. This consists of some of the simpler didactic poems of Herbert, Donne, Crashaw, Cowley, and others of the Restoration period. The contrast is startling to anyone who believes the worst of the Puritans.

5

The many other writers for children in this period, with the one supreme exception, need not be surveyed in detail. They were, on the whole, of a recognizable pattern, with some personal idiosyncrasies. One of the most popular was Abraham Chear, whose poems got into many other writers' volumes. In them was contained a verse often quoted because of these lines:

> 'Tis pitty, such a pretty Maid
> As I, should go to Hell.

The work in which they appeared was *A Looking-Glass for Children* (1672). Apparently this at first contained only the recollections of Henry Jessey, an eminent Cambridge anti-paedobaptist and Hebrew scholar, who was persecuted and ejected often before his death in 1663. Chear added the poems and some elegies, and made the whole volume obituary in tone. Nothing is known of him except that he was 'a servant of the Lord . . . late of Plymouth' and wrote some of his poems 'whilst in bonds for the truth of Christ'. What is remarkable, historically, about the *Looking-Glass* is that J. Marshall of Gracechurch Street sold a fourth edition in 1708. Marshall's name, as will be seen in the next chapter, meant a large unsectarian popularity for any book he distributed.

At the end of this Marshall volume is advertised, as a work of like kidney – together with *The Pilgrim's Progress*, *The Heavenly Footman*, and Janeway's *Token** – Keach's *Instructions for Children*, which abridges some Janeway and quotes Chear's poem. Benjamin Keach may be called a professional. He may have had a genuine 'spiritual bee' in his bonnet, but he wrote too mechanically, too readily, and too catch-pennily, to be deemed an authentic voice. He aimed at the young in some of his copious works. *War with the Devil* (1673) was 'chiefly intended for the instruction of the younger sort'. It has an instructive frontispiece. 'The youth in his converted state Aetat. su. 16' is shown on the narrow way, in a stage-Puritan costume, being shot at by devils and enemies with guns. Opposite, he is displayed in full Cavalier dress going down a broad way to a flaming lake. Here at last is the real traditional black and white contrast.

---

* And the four last parts of *The Arabian Nights*, then only just translated from Galland's text!

Riddle XXXVII.

I Live and breath, yet neither drink nor eat ;
I can deceive no Creature of his Meat.
He that feeds high, and drinks that which is good,
May die as soon as I that take no Food.
My Cloathing's gay, a party-colour'd Coat.
Both Night and Day I wear, not worth a Groat.
The Colour's sure, yet changeth oft the Name ;
'Twill not endure and yet is still the same.
My Life's preserv'd by that which none can see :
Thou would'st be starv'd, if thou should'st feed like me.
G 4   The

11. The answer to this obscure and not very accurately worded riddle in R. B.'s *Winter Evening Entertainments* is 'A Camelion'. The spider appears to be irrelevant, but he comes into his own when the block is used again for Riddle XLIX, to which he is the answer. This economical employment of pictures is used throughout the book.

Even more of a market hack in this style was Nathaniel Crouch,[4] editor, writer and publisher: he used the initials R.B., which stood for the pseudonym Richard Burton – transformed into Robert Burton in posthumous reprints of his books. He did an *Esop* (advertised in 1695) and a *Youth's Divine Pastime . . . very Delightful for the Virtuous Imploying the Vacant Hours of Young Persons* (3rd edn, 1691). He spruced up Samuel Crossman's *Young Man's Monitor* of 1664 as *The Young Man's Calling* (1678), produced an unabashed reprint of George Wither's 1635 *Collection of Emblems*, without acknowledgment, and with a new title, *Delights for the Ingenious* (1684), and published some *Winter Evening Entertainments* (1687). This last was proclaimed to be

milk for children, wisdom for young men,
To teach them that they turn not babes again.

It consists of riddles and stories, with morals, and the 'milk', as well as being not very fresh, did not do much towards keeping readers young, for the stories are often broad as well as silly. Nevertheless, 'Richard Burton', a tradesman in piety, was in most of the lists of 'good godly' authors.

So was William Jole, mentioned already as recommended by Janeway. Little is known about him. He flourished *c.* 1660–1710, was a Master of Arts and minister of Sarrat, Herts., and wrote several pious tracts. His most famous work describes itself quite fairly – and proves its claim to be a children's book – by its full title: *The Father's Blessing Penn'd for the Instruction of his Children. Containing Godly and Delightful Verses, Riddles, Fables, Jests, Stories, Proverbs, Rules of Behaviour; and other useful Matters to allure Children to Read* (1674). There were several editions. A rhymed alphabet, under the letter O, can be quoted both for the author's lighter manner and for a hint of an early date:

> Q. What rare Outlandish Fruit was that of late
>   Which Heaven sent us to restore our State?
> A. Our Statesmen had the Scurvy deeply, sure
>   The Princely Orange was a sovereign cure.

A woodcut of an orange, in the same style as the blocks of 'T.W.'s' *Little Book*, accompanies this. The mixture suggested by the title was fully purveyed: the twopenny-worth (excellent value) contains nearly everything from the sternest piety to complete silliness. It was published at the *Ring* in Little Britain, the significance of which is made clear in the next chapter.*

6

These authors could certainly be assigned at sight to their period even if one did not know it. With some reservations, they may be said to show that the Puritans believed honestly that they were writing to give children pleasure – spiritual pleasure, or the spiritual health which should be pleasure – and that they took their conception of pleasure for granted, it being one held by few other epochs. Two writers, however, lie a little outside that generalization: one by his extreme attention to practical detail in his earnestness, the other because of an imaginative quality, a touch of freedom, which is unique in this region and period of sub-literature. They both seemed to see children as human beings, living identities, not merely salvageable little souls. They were George Fox and William Ronksley.

George Fox, however, wrote nothing specially *for* children. What is important is his deadly sincerity in wishing the least taint to be kept from them. His famous *Battle-Door* (Battledore) *for Teachers and Professers*, written with John

---

* Other blessings, advertised in this one as obtainable at George Conyers' sign, were 'An Electuary for the Gout, Dropsy, Rheumatism, Cancers, and Giddiness of the Head, price 1s. Also a Bottle of Drops for the Cholick, Giddiness, and French Disease.' Advertisements, then as now, serve to indicate a social atmosphere.

Stubs and Benjamin Furley (1660), with its vast catalogue of parallels from other tongues for the use of 'thou' instead of 'you', is lit up with an eager vivid watchfulness. He is on guard, but not passively: he is seeking to pin the conventional person, the careless mind, the casual next-person-he-meets, to a realization of what words mean. 'What a bad word is this, not fit to learn any child, to call any "fool"?' Why use harsh terms like 'knave' and 'rogue'? You cannot really mean them. You do not think what a mischievous slovenly phrase like 'in good *faith*' means. Be natural, be sincere. Not only on doctrinal grounds (which he does not press in this connection), but because of their un-truth, their defect in sincerity, 'prophane and old Wives Fables' for children are all condemned. Still more undesirable, naturally, are the schoolbooks of which examples have already been given; and Ogilby and Hoole, with their versions of *Aesop,* or other 'heathenish books in the Latine tongue', were all awry in aim. Simplicity ought to be a habit of mind, expressed in every word.

His outlook had its value, though not at that time its effect, as against the tormented logic and arbitrary creed of full Puritanism. It bore fruit for children a hundred and fifty years later, when Quakers like Priscilla Wakefield and Maria Hack were writing books for the young in the extremest simplicity of thought and manner.

William Ronksley also desired or appealed to simple natural impulses, and saw things plainly. I can discover nothing about him except that he (unless it was another person of the same name) wrote a grammar issued in 1681, and also *The Child's Weeks-work: or, a Little Book, so nicely suited to the Genius and Capacity of a Little Child . . . that it will infallibly Allure and Lead him on into a Way of Reading.* It was published in Little Britain in 1712, by George Conyers and J. Richardson. It consists chiefly of rhymes for every day in the week, written on a cumulative-syllable plan, but with no more forceful idea in the arrangement than that of giving continuous pleasure as the gateway of reading was thrown more widely open. Though it teaches, it is yet an indubitable 'children's book'.

It is with a curiously fresh and almost un-contemporary voice, as a rule, that Ronksley speaks. One feels that to him children *were* children, then as now, and that grown-ups cared for them. On Thursday morning, for instance, the child learns about birds, in words of one syllable:

> Hear you a lark?
> Tell me what clark
> Can match her: He that beats
> The next thorn-bush
> May raise a thrush
> Would put down all our wayts.

It has not the ease of Herrick, but it reaches back, faintly, from him to Shakespeare, and forward to Blake: indeed, there was practically nothing like it again for children until *Songs of Innocence* appeared. Yet on the same day of the week, on Thursday afternoon, the author sets the child to learn about a very different type of bird:

> Poor men, whose wives
> Have led loose lives,
> A bird comes once a year
> And twitts – this done,
> She's dumb and gone
> To dwell, we know not where.

Ronksley perhaps was not a Puritan at all. But his scholastic aim is plainly announced. Perhaps, though, the Puritans themselves were not so fierce as they seem. They feared God, in one sense; they feared man, in another; and reverence and dread, mingling, hardened into an unequalled gift for repression. But sometimes their eyes must have lit up with a gentler fire.

7

Bunyan, in respect of children's books, as in adult literature, is alone. It would be impertinent here to discuss *The Pilgrim's Progress,* or even *The Holy War,* which I confess to reading rapturously – as an adventure story – when I was a boy. Both have been in the hands and minds of children and their seniors ever since they were published. *The Pilgrim's Progress* has been translated into almost every known language – into very many not known in Europe in Bunyan's day. It has been 'adapted', 'edited', 'shortened', cut into 'scenes', made into little moral plays; has had the constant Scripture references cut out, to suit changed times, has even been put, very superfluously, into words of one syllable. In each and every form it is a children's book, however you frame definitions.

It is now well known that Bunyan also wrote a book which he meant for children; meant them to read for amusement and instruction, both equally, and, so far as instruction went, without absolute terror. He wants to persuade children, not frighten them, into righteousness, even if punishment, not unhappiness, is the wages of sin. No one had written an English book for the young quite like this before.

The work has had a strange history. All through the eighteenth century a very popular book for children and ignorant folk was *Divine Emblems, or Temporal Things Spiritualized,* by John Bunyan. The earliest copy bearing that title then known to bibliography was of the ninth edition, issued in 1724 by the chapbook merchant, John Marshall of Gracechurch Street. But no such work appeared in the seventeenth-century list of Bunyan's works. On the other hand, Bunyan in that list was credited with having written *A Book for Boys and Girls: or, Country Rhimes for Children,* which was not known to exist. Various conjectures were made, one, by Offor, very near the truth, which was that the first book had been revised and given a new title after Bunyan's death. A copy of *A Book for Boys and Girls* ('for N.P.[onder], and sold by the Booksellers in London. 1686') turned up from the United States in 1889. It had been in the Luttrell collection, sold to an American, and resold to the well-known London bookseller, the late Mr Henry Stevens, in 1889 – in which year it passed to the

British Museum.* This first edition, it may be said, is much better printed than any of its successors, and has no illustrations.

The fate of the book between 1686 and 1724 is perhaps still not fully known. A copy survives of a 'second' edition of 1701, with the sub-title changed to 'Temporal Things Spirtualized'; and a third was advertised in 1707 as 'ornamented with cuts'. In the 1701 edition the 'emblems' were cut down from seventy-four to forty-nine, and some introductory school-text-matter dropped – Bunyan, like Ronksley, evidently had one eye on the schools, in his first intention. No copy of any other edition before the ninth has been discovered. As *Divine Emblems* the book remained in ordinary print, for common use, till at least the middle of the nineteenth century.

Bunyan stated his purpose in the introductory lines to the Reader:

> The Title-page will shew, if there thou look,
> Who are the proper Subjects of this Book.
> They'r Boys and Girls of all Sorts and Degrees,
> From those of Age, to Children on the Knees.
> Thus comprehensive am I in my Notions;
> They tempt me to it by their childish Motions.
> We now have Boys with Beards, and girls that be
> Big as old Women, wanting Gravity . . .

And a little farther on

> I do't to shew them how each fingle-fangle,
> On which they doting are, their souls entangle,
> As with a web, a trap, a gin, or snare,
> And will destroy them, have they not a care.

He had the moral aim.

But he had also an eye for everyday things outside books and the Authorized Version. His plan was to take common objects, describe them with a rugged simplicity, and then say what lesson could be drawn from such emblems. His choice of subjects is extraordinarily confused, and his 'comparisons' are seldom what would be expected. At one moment the Lord's Prayer is versified. Another page gives 'Meditations upon an Egg'. An insect beloved by all other moralists is treated thus:

> *Upon the Bee.*
> The Bee goes out, and Honey home doth bring;
> And some who seek that Honey find a Sting.
> Now would'st thou have the Honey and be free
> From stinging; in the first place kill the Bee.
> *Comparison.*
> This Bee an Emblem truly is of Sin,
> Whose sweet unto a many Death hath been.
> Now would'st have sweet from Sin, and yet not die,
> Do thou it in the first place mortify.

---

* A second copy has since been discovered. For full details of the book's history, and particulars of the 'editorial' changes, with much other interesting matter, see Dr John Brown's Introduction to a facsimile reprint (Elliot Stock, 1890). The verses have also been reprinted in America, by the American Tract Society (New York, 1928: Introduction by E. S. Buchanan).

12.   Meditations Upon an Egg
The Egg's no Chick by falling from the Hen;
Nor man a Christian, till he's born agen . . .
The Hyppocrite, sin has him in Possession,
He is a rotten Egg under Profession.

The woodcut (a) to Emblem IV in the first known illustrated edition of *Divine Emblems* (1724), which clearly served as the model for a more elaborate reworking in 1793 (b). Because the original design was copied, with embellishments, directly on to the surface of the new block the subsequent printing naturally produces an image in reverse.

Herrick, Milton, Dr Watts all found lessons or metaphors in the bee. But Bunyan alone conceived of the insect as immoral.

That was his singular quality in these *Emblems*. He, who as the greatest and most direct of all allegory-writers had used complete simplicity, here almost tortures his mind to find a moral. His analogies are as devious and strained as those of the *Gesta Romanorum* – a suggestive parallel between Puritanism and extreme Catholicism. Yet he is always, however intricate his thought, an oddly plain Englishman. The little touches of homeliness are those of English peasant life, and he is almost John Bullish in his contempt for frippery. And he has at times a queer gentleness (not queer when one knows his life, but queer in so valiant a Puritan in print) which gives his very rough verse great charm. There is in the halting lines a soul at once violent and tender, rigid and loosely sinewy, trying to speak to those whose unformed minds it hardly believes it can understand.

That is a thing not to be forgotten in Puritanism – that its faith was an argument as well as an emotion. It becomes incomprehensible to us, perhaps even intolerable, when the argument asks too lofty, too perfect a standard in those to whom it is addressed. The impossibility of perfect goodness thus argued makes one forget the emotion which craves for it. The dual nature is strangely clear in this masterful little book. It is a quality to be searched, and understood, if possible, by intuition, not by cold analysis nor by careful historical retrospect. It is the secret spirit of all the Puritan books for children.

8

The mind of England in the seventeenth century was hammered to a surface something more like that which it wore in, say, 1860 than at any earlier time, except perhaps in that brief year or two which live for us in *The Canterbury Tales*. The nature of Englishmen maybe did not change much, but after 1688 they were much more apt to the national temper of amiable compromise. When the violent internal conflicts ceased, and even the formalities about them vanished – when, for instance, the statute about the combustion of heretics, already really dead, was repealed, and Habeas Corpus and the Bill of Rights expressed a desire to get on with the work of making a peaceable living – the tiny threads of ordinary existence began to have leisure to form a pattern. Trade broadened socially: the age of the Gilds was past, and even the Venturers had safely endured their first hazards. A catastrophe like the South Sea Bubble was directly national, not merely an infliction on certain classes percolating through to other classes indirectly.

It was at that stage of popular enlargement that children and their books stood a short generation before John Newbery took his chance. By about 1700 or so there were left for the nursery library a few shreds of Middle Age tradition which still possessed in them a spark of universal life; a great many prohibitions of undesirable things; some still dumb, tough, immortal memories – the Fairy-Tale and the Nursery Rhyme – which were at last to get into print in the coming intermediate generation; and the nucleus of a smooth machinery of book-distribution. It is therefore to the commercial side of literature that attention must next be directed, and to the wares which reviving trade brought to readers young and old. They had not been so purveyed before.

BRIEF BOOK LIST

For chief writers and their works, see *D.N.B.* and *C.H.E.L.*; for general purposes, any standard histories. The text above uses some special references (e.g. Dr F. A. Cox on Janeway in his 'History of the Janeway Family' which figures as a preface to his edition of *Heaven Upon Earth* (London, 1847), and Dr John Brown on Bunyan's *Divine Emblems* in the facsmile mentioned on p. 64.)

Most of the books quoted or mentioned are hard to date, being rare, though not as a rule valuable in the collector's sense[!] The known periods of their writers' lives are a near enough general guide to historical accuracy. For dates of publishers of the period, see *Notes and Queries*, vol. CLXI, 1931, no. 3 *et seq.*

Supplement

For much information on further reading consult William Sloane's *Children's Books in England and America in the Seventeenth Century* (New York, 1955). This includes a detailed essay on godly, and other, books and has a valuable descriptive checklist of books published between 1557 and 1710. There is also a photographic reprint of a weighty sixteen-page list of 'Good and Useful Books Proper to be Given to Young Persons': *The Young Christian's Library* (London, 1710).

An early edition of Janeway's *Token* (pt I, 1676; pt II, 1673) may now be consulted in a photographic reprint, with a slender introduction by Robert Miner (New York and London, 1977). It is in a composite volume which includes reprints of four American godly books.

A more helpfully supported reprint is that of the 1659 English edition of Comenius's *Orbis Pictus,* with an introduction by John E. Sadler (London, 1968). This almost coincided with an Australian facsimile of the 1672 edition, with an introduction by James Bowen (Sydney, 1967).

CHAPTER V

The Pedlar's Pack: 'The Running Stationers'

'Chapmen', of the tribe of Autolycus, were the travelling salesmen who, but for a few gipsy vans, have now practically vanished from the face of England. When print grew cheap, news-sheets, ballads, broadsides and inexpensive books and pamphlets were popular wares in the pedlar's pack. It is possible to make a direct connection at once between printed matter and the general state of ordinary English society, and between Puritan literature and the trade in cheap books, because at the end of the 1708 edition of Abraham Chear's *Looking-Glass for Children* (p. 61) there appears this announcement:[1]

The Confession of Faith, put forth by the Elders and Brethren of many Congregations of Christians Baptized upon Profession of their Faith in London and the Country . . . The Third Edition . . . and also The Catechisms agreeable to the Confession of Faith, owning Election and Final Perseverance, necessary for the Instruction of Youth in the Fundamentals of Religion: the Remainders of the Impressions of these Two Books, with the full and true Right of Printing them for the future, are Sold by us, *William Collings* and *Benjamin Keach*, to *John Marshall*, Bookseller, at the *Bible* in *Grace-Church-Street, London*. It is desired that all Persons that are desirous to promote such useful Books do apply themselves to him.

(That must be a very early use of the trade term 'remainder'.)[2] It is evident that Keach not only knew how to write books – neither of these, in all probability, is by him – but also the value of them as property. Moreover, he took them to the right market, for Marshall must have been in a pretty large way of business.

Marshall's surname is one that goes through the history of publishing with perpetual recurrences. It is borne by two well-known but unrelated London houses today.[3] It was borne also by two houses in 1708 – John Marshall's own, and the firm of Joseph and William Marshall, who were in business at the Bible in Newgate Street from 1679 to at least 1725. At the end of the century, another John Marshall was still in the City of London, first of all at the chapbook centre, Aldermary Churchyard, where he continued the business which his father, Richard Marshall (d. 1779), had run with Cluer Dicey. He became the first important 'specialist' rival to the Newbery firm, and from 1787 onward had premises also at 17 Queen Street, Cheapside. (Around 1806 he moved these to 140 Fleet Street, whence – after a period of inaction – he was to issue some very cheerful publications before his death in 1823.)

The John Marshall of 1708, in Gracechurch Street, not only dealt in such books as have been mentioned – 'Good godly books' and livelier works like the *Arabian Nights* – but in almost everything that a travelling hawker could require. His advertisement, after giving a list of popular books, announced that at the sign of the Bible in Gracechurch Street the trade

may be furnish'd with all sorts of Chapmen's Books, Broadsides or Half-Sheets, and Lottery Pictures, as Birds, Beasts, London Crys, etc., by the Gross or Dozen; also Labels for Chyrurgeons Chests, Venice-Treacle Directions and Rappers, Hungary Directions, Bills, Funeral Tickets, Affidavits for Burials in Woollen, Receipts for Land-Tax, etc., Wholesale or Retail, at the very lowest prices.

The reference to 'Birds, Beasts',[4] as evidently a well-known title, is the earliest I have come across, and I have found no book that really answers to it at that date. 'London Crys' is also an early mention: apparently an edition of *Habits and Cryes of the City of London* was printed in 1688 – A. W. Tuer reprinted a 1711 edition. Venice Treacle is no longer a common medicine, and it is not now a legal necessity to be buried – without a coffin, unless you were well-to-do – in a woollen winding sheet. But in 1708 everyone knew what such things meant, and that the chapman, the peripatetic village-shop, made provision for these ordinary facts of life.

Such wares do not concern us here. They were small domestic necessities which would certainly not be always in stock in any village, and possibly not in many towns. The significant thing is that books appeared so prominently in their company, and travelled with them all over the kingdom. Newspapers were rapidly growing in number, and were being produced at many provincial centres. Cheap books, under Anne, seem to have issued chiefly from London. But by the middle of the century a score of towns in the provinces did their own production for large local areas. As children's books – or works which children read – bulked large in the packs of the 'Running Stationers' – who were also called 'Flying' and 'Walking' – it may be well to trace the trade story a little farther before looking at the contents of the books themselves. It is a genuine chapter of minor social history.

2

The true chapbook, as a common vendible piece of reading-matter distinct from broadside ballads, almanacs and the like, really came into an embryonic existence in the seventeenth century, and grew up rapidly after the Star Chamber was abolished in 1641. A horde of political and religious pamphleteers fell upon the excited public as soon as they could do so with reasonable safety. In fact, as Milton, the greatest of all apologists for a free Press, complained, they 'well-nigh made all other books unsaleable'. But the other – non-controversial – books did appear. Thus there were editions of *Guy of Warwick* (in prose) in 1640 (licensed, if not published), 1681, 1685, 1695, 1703, to say nothing of one or two which bear no dates. *Bevis* has already been traced. *The Seven Champions of Christendom* – a more original work: it was by Richard Johnson, who was born in 1573 – appeared in known editions dated 1608, 1616, 1670, 1675, 1676, 1680, 1686, 1687, 1690, 1705; and there were several undated editions which probably belong to about 1650. The publisher–booksellers at that time chiefly interested in such books seem to have been Andrew Crooke (publisher of Ogilby and Hobbes), W. Thackeray of Duck Lane (both about 1650), and, a little later, two generations of Bates's (or perhaps husband and, later, widow) in Giltspur Street, close to Aldermary Churchyard and Little Britain, which were for a century and a half the chief London centres for cheap literature.

The Licensing Act of 1662 did not hinder this stream. It merely canalized it in the direction desired by Roger L'Estrange, though in some respects he was curiously tolerant. But when that Act expired in 1694, the strenuousness of controversy had abated, and fiction – the main substance of chapbook literature – had a more ample chance. The Copyright Acts – the first, 'An Act for the Encouragement of Learning', was passed in 1710 – made no difference to the increasing number of literary pirates, who 'encouraged learning' in a manner quite different from that intended by legislators influenced by authors and reputable booksellers. The day of the penny, twopenny and sixpenny chapbook had dawned, and by the middle of the eighteenth century the grimy little productions were everywhere.

The lowlier books, during the Commonwealth and Restoration period, were usually produced either as quartos almost of the familiar Shakespearean size and shape, or as plump little volumes about 4 by 2½ in. Both were bound in leather, sheepskin, or calf. The smaller volumes had very scant margins to the type, and the short crowded lines, in which 𝕭. 𝕷. (black letter) still survived alongside roman, made ugly pages. The rag paper used was as a rule good: a great deal better than anything now produced from woodpulp, or even than much made out of esparto grass. It must be remembered, in judging such works, that we can see very few of them now in anything like their 'mint' condition. That they exist at all is not far short of wonderful. Apart from trade calamities – fires, the accidents of rough travel, abrupt changes due to current events, even suppression – they suffered the fiercest form of attrition to which printed matter can be subjected – daily use by heedless persons, and, when they were the property of children, destructive persons. It is very rare to find a really popular book of even a century ago in a moderately good state of preservation. They *were* preserved, because they were not so numerous or so easily procured as to be thrown away lightly. But they became dog-eared, stained, frayed, broken-backed, and, if they were (as often) rebound, they were likely to be cut badly in the process. They were never then the honoured treasures of a fine library, as, with the wheel come full circle, they usually are today. But they were read and re-read and loved, and were the romance of life. They were the books of the people of England.

In the eighteenth century, as the mechanical side of cheap book-production progressed, leather, with its heavy solidity, was dropped for the more inexpensive volumes, and the length of the contents was reduced. It became easy, and more economical, to produce a mere sixteen, thirty-two, or occasionally sixty-four pages, in stiffish paper covers or, for cheap books like schoolbooks, that might see a lot of use, sheepskin; sixteen was then as now the most convenient unit for folding sheets for book form. The slim volumes were lighter and less bulky for the pack, and the sale larger, while the price – one penny to sixpence – was lower, though the difference in the retail price between leather and paper was not relatively so large as it was later: cloth binding was not invented till the 1820s. The cover, like the old title-pages, had as a rule a block printed upon it, or else a naturally graceful compost of 'printer's ornaments'. It was usually of a pale yellow colour; sometimes grey or even white. A smaller size – about 3 by 2 in. – was also introduced concurrently with the standard one. Finally, by about 1760, many were issued without a cover at all. They were just a sheet folded in sixteens or eights, with uncut unopened edges, rarely even stitched. You find them sometimes stitched thoughtfully, one would say almost tenderly, with ribbon or silk, by some owner-devotee: a child, as like as not.

Text apart, the illustrations are the most interesting feature: as perhaps they were to the first simple reader. From about 1700 or so the small woodblocks became ubiquitous: many still survive in public and private collections. Whether through loans or through direct copying and recutting, the same 'cuts' appear constantly in different books issued by different publishers. George, Guy, Bevis, giants, dying Christians, boars, dragons, fiddlers were interchangeable figures, and historical propriety, or fidelity to the detail of any one text, did not matter. The technique was of the simplest – just plain cutting with coarse deep lines: Bewick's graceful use of 'white line' appeared, of course, late in the eighteenth century, though all that was white line was not Bewick. Copper, so far as I know, was not used in these cheap books, at any rate not till very late in George III's reign, and by then steel had almost begun to be a simple vehicle of reproduction.

Very many of the cuts must have had an interesting lineage. But it cannot now be traced with any certainty. A rough guess would say that far back they were derived from the homely vigorous German, French or Flemish pictures that adorned the earliest *Aesops* and similar works. It looks as if the first illustrations in most English printed books of the fifteenth and early sixteenth centuries were inspired by, if not to a great extent copied from, those sources, and such printers as Caxton, De Worde and Pynson can well be seen as providing the models for the later stage-army of blocks for the true chapbook. They persisted in that decadence almost as long as chapbooks themselves.[5]

As regards the mechanism of the trade – its geographical distribution especially – it also is to some extent a matter of guesswork, the results being based mainly upon a scrutiny of imprints usually undated. Up to about 1750, chapbooks were probably manufactured almost solely in the capitals of the three kingdoms, with London, naturally, as the fountainhead. But the rise of the

middle-class traders into what Mrs Trimmer later called 'secondary opulence'
gave the country towns a wealth and security, and with those benefits an
activity, not based wholly upon the private interests of this or that territorial
magnate, powerful though he might be politically. The growth of the squire-
archy involved the growth of the tradesman. Culture, even of the chapbook
level, was more evenly diffused, and yet at the same time more localized.

In London John Marshall, already mentioned, and William and Cluer Dicey
(immigrants from Northampton, who were at work from about 1710 onwards),
were the chief producers. Possibly the earliest English rival to the metropolis
was Newcastle-on-Tyne, long a sturdy centre of minor literary culture. J. White
there 'furnished Country Chapmen with Sermons, Historys, etc.' He put forth
Jack and the Giants in 1711, if not earlier. But exact evidence of provincial
efforts at that stage is very difficult to find. Many chapbooks which from
internal evidence should belong – at any rate in their first state – to the reigns of
Anne, George I and George II bear no true imprint at all: they are simply 'for
the Booksellers', or 'for the Stationers', or even 'for the Running Stationers',
with no other birthmark.

By the middle of George III's long reign all that was altered. At Newcastle,
for instance, Saint was prominent; his best products are associated with Thomas
Bewick the engraver – one of them has already been mentioned (p. 20).
Another firm in the same town was that run by the Angus family for some fifty
years after the mid-1770s. At York, R. Spence in Thursday Market, and
Kendrew in Colliergate, had a very large trade. Salisbury, Cirencester, Derby,

THE

DEATH AND BURIAL

OF

COCK ROBIN;

AS

Taken from the original MANUSCRIPT, in
the Possession of

MASTER MEANWELL.

LICHFIELD :

Printed and Sold by M. MORGAN, and

A. MORGAN, *Stafford.*

a   b

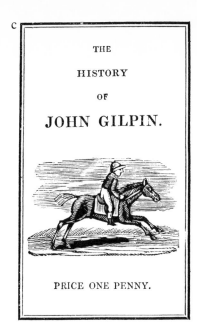

c

THE

HISTORY

OF

JOHN GILPIN.

PRICE ONE PENNY.

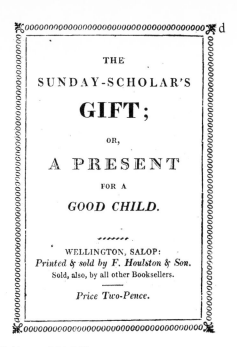

d

THE

SUNDAY-SCHOLAR'S

GIFT;

OR,

A PRESENT

FOR A

GOOD CHILD.

WELLINGTON, SALOP:
Printed & sold by F. Houlston & Son.
Sold, also, by all other Booksellers.

Price Two-Pence.

13.   (a) *The Death and Burial of Cock Robin* . . . Lichfield, *c.* 1795.
        (b) *The Death and Burial of Cock Robin.* Otley, *c.* 1825.
        (c) *The History of John Gilpin.* Derby, *c.* 1830.
        (d) *The Sunday-Scholar's Gift* . . . Wellington, 1817.

Three provincial chapbooks and a pseudo-chapbook for children. The first *Cock Robin*, issued without covers, is one among many chapbook examples using this rhyme, which fitted neatly into sixteen small pages. (A London edition, published by J. Evans, at about the same date, contains the 'drasty' version of *Little Robin Red Breast* noted below on p. 81.) The second *Cock Robin* is an example of a later edition of the rhyme, covered in yellow sugar-paper wrappers from the firm of W. Walker 'at the Wharfedale Stanhope Press', whence flowed many cheap children's books and chapbooks down to the present century.

John Gilpin is one of a series of penny books, also in sugar-paper wrappers, issued by Richardson of Derby *c.* 1830 and following a more stylish mode of production, which was also used by Evangelical publishers like Houlston of Wellington, who made Sunday School tracts and rewards look like chapbooks.

The Lichfield chapbook ends with an advertisement in which M. Morgan offers to supply 'Travellers . . . with all Sorts of Histories . . . Tom Thumb Play Books, Godly Books, Cock Robins, &c. &c.', and the Derby chapbook lists twenty-four companion works at a penny and mentions 'An excellent Assortment of halfpenny Books and Lotteries'.

Alnwick, Darlington, Durham and, later, Banbury are among the towns which under Farmer George had wholesale publishers of their own. It is not clear why they had this independence of even larger centres. Roads and garrisons and assizes, all agencies of gregariousness, no doubt had something to do with it. But that does not account for the comparative dearth of Third-Georgian material surviving with the imprint of places where much of it might have been expected – Bristol, for instance, Chester, Norwich, or even hale little literary towns like Woodbridge. However, with goods so perishable, the lack of evidence is no argument.

It was, then, by this form of printed matter, hardly known to serious students of imaginative literature, or to the history of the higher publishing trade, that the rather muddy mind of humbler England was penetrated throughout the Georgian era, and beyond it. In that rank mist, as many thought it, the hungry sheep looked up for at least a hundred years, and were fed with little else until Hannah More started the organized diffusion of tracts – the expression of fear as opposed to the habit of casual freedom. Even in this low stratum that warfare was always present, but with the odds on levity. 'Penny Merriments' were being sold alongside 'Penny Godlinesses' all through this period of obscure traffic. Quite late, in the epoch of better transport, T. Cheney,[6] the proprietor of a famous Banbury Series (stereotypes of which, if not the original plates, seem to be still extant), could advertise that 'Country Dealers, etc., may be supplied with a good Assortment of Histories, Godly Books, Patters, Children's Books, Collections, Songs, Old Sheet Ballads, etc., etc., on the lowest terms.' He ran the Banbury firm from 1808–20. And the like wares were still being sold when Victoria married Albert. Until that happened, disapproval and progress alike had little effect on them.

3

The trade, in fact, remained always in a kind of busy stagnation: a perpetual marketing of old stuff without change even in its appearance. It preserved, nevertheless, much that would else have been utterly lost to the nursery library. But it could pretend to no ideals except those of money-making and of versatility at a high commercial pressure. The history of two firms has been preserved for us in some detail, and is worth scrutiny, because it is, in its way, a flesh and blood narrative, not a dry skeleton. You see behind each firm a 'pleasing anxious being' trying, not unsuccessfully, to make a fortune out of the precarious trifles that amused shallow or immature minds. It is extremely likely that that being actually revised the texts he used.

The first business is that of Kendrew of York. The British Museum possesses a large number of his publications, together with some from his competitors, with catalogues, and circulars to customers, and manuscript notes by the final direct partner in the concern. The collection was made as a stock book or office copy for filing purposes. The notes are by James Hattersley Carr, grandson of the founder of the firm. 'My grandfather, Mr James Kendrew', he writes, 'commenced business about 1803 . . . He did an extensive business in [Songs], Pamphlets . . . Calenders [sic], and dying speeches of criminals, Primers, Battledores, ½ & 1d. Toy Books for children &c.' The woodcuts for these publications were done freshly in York itself, by 'Mr Carrall, a Celebrated Wood Cutter . . . His son carries on business [i.e. in the seventies] in Parliament

Street as a Shoemaker.' 'The Valentines and plates for Pamphlets were coloured, by hand, by my Mother and Aunts, in their leisure Hours when at home from school.'

James Kendrew was succeeded in 1841 by his son John Lofthouse Kendrew, who issued a polite notice of the change to all his customers, printed by himself. But in 1848 he disposed of the printing plant to Mr William Allerston, another citizen of York. His nephew, Carr, entered the business in 1869, and took it over on his uncle's death in 1874. It is not clear when he gave it up, but it is plain that for three-quarters of a century the concern was purely domestic and local in its internal economy. It is hardly less certain, from their number and frequent appearances, that the Kendrew publications went, in their small way, all over England. And their substance was not in the least degree local. It covered the whole range of general chapbook literature, and was kept up-to-date by additions like *The Victoria Primer, or First Book for Children*, by pamphlets on the Great Exhibition of 1851, by songs of all periods from the Stuart to the sentimental-Victorian, and even by broadside *facetiae* about 'bloomers' and negro minstrels.

Hardly less long-lived and still better known, even almost proverbial, was the firm of Catnach. 'Jemmy' Catnach's broadsides have not wholly passed from elderly memories and have become booty for collectors.

The business that bore his surname was founded by his father, John Catnach, who was born in 1769 at Burntisland, Fifeshire. He was probably apprenticed to a printer in Edinburgh. He set up in business on his own account at Berwick-on-Tweed, and in 1790 settled in England, at Alnwick. In 1807 he went into partnership there with Davison, a chemist – whose profession has more than once been connected with bookselling. In 1808, however, Catnach moved to Newcastle, and Davison continued issuing his own chapbooks independently at Alnwick: copies of them are still to be met with frequently. After about five years Catnach migrated farther south, to London itself, and set up in or near Wardour Street; for a short time only, for he died in 1813. His son James, who had previously been an 'improver' with Joseph Graham, another Alnwick printer, then came to town to take over the business, and moved to the site always connected with his name – Seven Dials. That neighbourhood still houses a well-known printing firm,[7] but 'Jemmy' had only one serious rival in his particular line – 'Johnny' Pitts, of 'the Toy and Marble Warehouse', 6 Great St Andrew Street, close by.

Jemmy Catnach was a voluminous printer. His chief trade was in ballads and broadsides. He was a combination of 'dealer' and printer. He bought up old blocks and founts of type promiscuously, and used them haphazard. He could vamp a plate on soft metal himself if need be and he had all the old Aldermary Churchyard recklessness in the use of his woodcuts. It is said – in Charles Hindley's *History of the Catnach Press* (1887), from which many of these facts are borrowed – that he had something like a modern newspaper's 'stop press' arrangements for public events. If a great man were dying, he would start a block of the funeral procession with one or two stock figures already cut, or cut

So sad a scene to view.
A heart of stone would melt, I wist,
And gave their last adieu!
With clay-cold lips the babes they kiss'd,

Of which He takes regard.
All actions are within His sight,
From God expect reward;
If you direct their steps aright,

5

4

Pisarius call'd his brother near,
    As on his bed he lay:
Remember, oh! my brother dear,
    Remember what I say?

This life I quit, and to your care
    My little babes commend:
Their youth in hopeful virtue rear;
    Their guardian, uncle, friend.

Their parents both you must supply,
    They do not know their loss,
And when you see the tear-swoln eye,
    For pity be not cross:

'Tis in your power (now alone)
    Their greatest friend to be;
To give them, when we're dead & gone,
    Or bliss, or misery.

To cover them with leaves.
But Robin Redbreast forms the plan,
No funeral rite receives;
These pretty babes from any man,

Till death did end their grief.
The woods, the briers, and thorns among,
Without the least relief,
These pretty babes thus wander'd long,

12

13

And now the heavy wrath of God
    Upon their uncle fell;
The furies haunt his curst abode,
    And peace bade him farewell.

His barns consum'd, his house was fired,
    His lands were barren made,
His cattle in the fields expired,
    And nothing with him staid.

For what he had receiv'd.
And vow'd that he would do his part,
Was not at all aggriev'd,
The other still more hard of heart,

He sorely did repent.
For though he undertook the deed,
Made one rogue's heart relent;
The pretty speeches which they said,

And work their lives decay.
To those who should their butchers be,
As they ride on the way,
They prate and prattle pleasantly,

On horseback for to ride:
It gave them both no small content,
Rejoicing with much pride;
Away the little babes were sent,

6

8

The trees are now felling in Blackberry Wood,
Where the ruffians did leave both the babes without food.

The Interesting Story

OF THE

CHILDREN IN THE WOOD,

AN

HISTORICAL BALLAD.

———

BANBURY:

Printed by J. G. Rusher.

14. An example of an unfolded, uncut Banbury chapbook from Rusher's later series.

ad hoc, and add at the last moment a crowd and the proper amount of ceremonial trappings.

He gave a good deal of attention to rough little productions for children. So far as I can discover he issued nothing original for them, but his selection of old material was as varied in scope as it was crude in presentation. His advertisement of these wares ran thus:

> Little Boys and Girls will find
> At Catnach's something to their mind,
> From great variety may choose,
> What will instruct them and amuse;
> The prettiest plates that you can find,
> To please at once the eye and mind,
> In all his little books appear,
> In natural beauty, shining clear,
> Instruction unto youth when given,
> Points the path from earth and heaven.
>   He sells by Wholesale and Retail,
>   To suit all moral tastes can't fail.

Like others, he desired children to have the best of both worlds. Among his offerings to them were *Nurse Lovechild's Legacy* (a borrowing from the eighteenth century), *The Butterfly's Ball* (rather worse than borrowed from Roscoe's charming poem of 1807), *The Easter Gift* (the antique 'A was an Archer' and other rhymes), and many similar pieces entirely suited to their purpose, not at all gross in taste, but far from shining clear in natural beauty so far as format went.

He retired in 1838 and died in 1841. The business became A. Ryle and Paul. (Annie Ryle was Catnach's married sister, Paul had been a boy in his office.) In 1845 the firm became Ryle and Co., and at some later date passed to W. S. Fortey, still at the same address – Monmouth Court, Seven Dials, where the business continued until 1882–3, when the court was pulled down to make room for the Charing Cross Road, and Fortey moved to Great St Andrew Street. Fortey's flimsy little books, with garish hand-coloured engravings, I have myself bought in almost new condition on London book-barrows, for a penny or two, in the present century. But the firm exists no longer.*

With Fortey, for all practical purposes, ended the English trade in chapbooks for children. It had had over a century and a half of strong, grubby life. Its place has been taken by the provision of equally cheap and ugly weekly journals and 'strip' monstrosities in the daily press.

---

* The Catnach Press had an influence outside its intrinsic merits. Its work possessed in spirit, though not in execution, something of the quality that has made boldly drawn woodcuts a joy to artists today. It is no secret that Claud Lovat Fraser's decorative designs, even on the large theatre scale, drew some inspiration from the simplicity of the Seven Dials productions. Fraser seized with delight upon a small collection I had years ago, got hold of Hindley's *Life*, and in 1913 designed among other things his *Flying Fame* booklets and rhyme sheets on those lines.

4

A brief note must be interpolated here on the kindred trade in Scotland, whence Catnach himself had set out. There is direct evidence that the publications of the north penetrated southern nurseries. Sarah Trimmer, born in 1741 at Ipswich, read and enjoyed *The Babes in the Wood*, when she was young, in an edition like the chapbook that she reviewed in 1802 that was published by Lumsden of Glasgow. In her riper wisdom, when she set up as *The Guardian of Education* (1802; see below, Chapter VII), she condemned this work unreservedly: it was 'absolutely unfit for the perusal of children'. It was an unhappy judgment even from her own point of view, which disliked the subject rather than the treatment of it; because in her excellent story, now known as *The Robins*, she had praised those identical Christmas-card birds for their piety and zeal in covering the Babes with leaves. If she had been excited by the chapbook manner rather than its substance, and had looked more closely at the Scottish products of her young days, she would have found a good deal more justification for her strictures.

The Scottish chapbooks were not in a general way very different from their English rivals, which indeed were imported into North Britain in great numbers. Aberdeen, Paisley, Edinburgh and Glasgow were the chief centres of distribution. But local heroes stood at least as good a chance as invaders, and of course dialect, if not essential, was an important feature. So was another characteristic, which I had better, for the sake of peace, describe in the words of a native enthusiast:

These carelessly got-up publications . . . possess one advantage over the sensational reading of the present-day penny journals, in that they represent the opinions and manners of those who read them, and, consequently, have a truthfulness and reality of which their London-manufactured substitutes are entirely destitute. The Chap-book is a mirror of rural opinions and manners; the Penny Sensational is only evidence of a vitiated popular taste.

That is from the anonymous preface to *John Cheap the Chapman's Library*. It shows a very proper spirit of nationalism. But it may be doubted whether even mid-Georgian London, or England in general would have stood such 'rural opinions and manners' as many of these works offer. They are far grosser than anything produced for the poor folk of England, and their grossness is nasty, not humorous. Anyone, however, who likes to look at the collection of *Scottish Merriments* bound up by 'Mr Ritson' in 1793, where will be found *Fun upon Fun* (Glasgow, 1786) and some of the many editions of *Lothian Tom* (1770 onwards) can form his own opinion.

Lothian Tom, like *The History of John Cheap the Chapman*, was probably the work of one Dougal Graham, 'Skellat Bellman of Glasgow'. His *Collected Writings* were privately printed in 1883, with an introduction by George Mac Gregor. Graham was a wandering soul who had been out in the '45, and his career has a mild picaresque interest. But only a fervid patriotism would desire to keep his writings alive.

Such works, like the English chapbooks, appeared cheek-by-jowl in the pedlar's tray with more moral tracts – in Scotland, pamphlets by or about John Knox, for example, or Alexander Peden – and alongside the cheap pictorial Bible. They deserve everything derogatory that has ever been said about chapbooks. The corresponding output in Ireland (in Dublin, chiefly) was largely English, and cleaner.

5

It has been advisable to dwell thus fully on this obscure commercial aspect of children's literature for three reasons. In the first place, the wide circulation of the chapbooks, which is evident from at least the reign of Anne onwards, created or indicated a very large public, which Newbery, whether he actually visualized it or not, captured. In the second place, both the virtues and the vices of these random catchpenny booklets were important. By way of service, they and they alone preserved much that escaped even Newbery but has passed indefeasibly into our nursery archives with the aid of his successors. By way of disservice at the moment, they presented their contents so inadequately, so unpleasingly, that they almost forced a reaction to better productions. They were in fact the provocative of the Moral Tale, which dominated children's literature in England for at least seventy years. And thirdly, they were actually read by children.

Of this last fact there can be no doubt at all. Mrs Trimmer is evidence for somewhere about 1750, even if we suppose that Steele's godson had long before got hold of better volumes than chapbooks, though it is unlikely that the Hickathrift saga existed in any but that form in 1709. An earlier date than 1750, however, is provided by a greater writer than Sarah Trimmer. My Uncle Toby read indubitable chapbooks, obviously cheap books, as a boy: 'When *Guy, Earl of Warwick*, and *Parismus and Parismenus*, and *Valentine and Orson*, and *The Seven Champions of England* [sic] were handed around the school, – were they not all purchased with my own pocket-money?' Sterne was born in 1713, which would date that experience in the twenties of his century. Sixty years later, in the *Microcosm* of 1787, Canning was devoting witty magniloquence to these same heroes, who by then were certainly only to be met within the flimsy covers of a chapbook.* Mr Spectator, Dr Johnson, William Wordsworth all knew stories which they can hardly have met in any other medium, except oral relation, which must never be overlooked but which does not account for many textual permanencies.

When it dawned on the moralists, in and after the Blue-Stocking Age, that chapbooks were low, they had a very wide hostile field to survey: nothing less than a universal library, which was at the same time a sub-history of English

---

* And not, in all probability, in anything published in that form by Newbery, as Canning carelessly suggested: 'Newbery' had become a symbol for children's books.

literature. The good godly books were in it, as has been said, both those meant for children and those above their heads. The lives of those who wrote them – Bunyan's, for instance – were likewise in it. Jumbled in the pack were things for half a dozen other types of mind: *Mother Shipton* (identified, more or less, as one Ursula Sontibles of Knaresborough), Cocker's *Spelling Book* (first published in the seventeenth century) and *Arithmetic* (1660), *Joe Miller's Jest Book* (Miller lived, less eminent in life than in name, about 1684–1738), *George Barnwell* (adapted from Lillo's play of 1731 and from the older facts), *Bampfylde Moore Carew* (the mid-eighteenth-century vagabond), *The Wandering Jew* (whose story in England goes back as far as Roger of Wendover, in the thirteenth century), *Fair Rosamund, Jane Shore, John* or *Tom Hickathrift*, several *Jacks* – housebuilders, giant-killers, climbers and others – *Dick Whittington*, various chapters of Arthurian legend, *Fortunatus, Friar Bacon, Friar Rush* ('full of pleasant mirth and delight for young people' as early as 1620), *The Friar and the Boy, Dr Faustus, Mother Bunch's Closet newly broke open* (advice to maidens and wives), *The Wise Men of Gotham* (attributed, with no certainty at all, to Andrew Boorde), *Dorastus and Fawnia* (based – in England – on Greene's *Pandosto*), *Don Quixote, Francis Drake* and later admirals, alphabets, *Robin Hood, Tom Thumb*, practically all the known Middle Age Romances, *Robinson Crusoe* and his shadow, *Philip Quarll*, Perrault's fairy-tales (usually singly), Aesop, Dr Watts's *Divine Songs*; anything and everything. The list could be trebled without repetition.

In short, the chapbook, from 1700 to 1840 or thereabouts, contained all the popular literature of four centuries in a reduced and degenerate form: most of it in a form rudely adapted for use by children and poorly educated country folk. Who the adapters were no one can guess. They did not always make texts we should now choose for high moral tone. For instance, Richard Marshall, round about 1770, printed *Cock Robin, a Pretty Gilded Toy for either Girl or Boy suited to Children of all Ages*, and probably *The Child's New Year's Gift*.* The former contains a popular 'nursery' rhyme which children now know only in a different and expurgated version, though the 'drasty' phrases were still in print at the start of the new century. The latter is adorned with blocks strictly faithful to an occasionally coarse text. But that is a question of contemporary manners, and outspokenness did not necessarily come from a nasty mind. What in the long run offended refined critics to the point of making them try to write better stuff was the mean format, the ill-cut and barely relevant illustrations, and the rambling, crazy-paved and ungrammatical text.

It is in the text, I think, that we must find, for what it is worth, something of the personality of the publishers themselves. There can be little doubt that either they, or, under their eye, unknown members of the painful army of hacks, were responsible for most of the words actually used in sentences which,

* [Attractive title-wordings of a kind not uncommon in the period, thanks to the influence of such as Newbery. It can also be noted that the British Museum copies of these chapbooks exist as unfolded sheets, like those uncut items mentioned at p. 71 above.]

varying little once they were established, appeared simultaneously in a dozen or more provincial towns. One quotation will be enough. The romance of *Valentine and Orson* was translated very early from the French, and probably printed and published by de Worde, though only fragments of the oldest edition remain (*c.* 1510). William Copland printed two later editions (*c.* 1555 and *c.* 1565), and thereafter dated versions appeared in 1637, 1649, 1664, 1667, 1680 (two), 1682, 1685, 1688, 1694, 1696, all more or less with the same text.* In the eighteenth century there were definitely chapbook editions which have been conjecturally dated 1710, 1750, 1790, and others later in 1816 (dated) and 1825(?). There may have been many more. At any rate, it was in print till the Georgian era drew to a close, and, if the number of editions is any guide, one of the most popular of all the Romances. Why, it is hard to say, for it is intricate and dull as a story. It was certainly a children's book from the eighteenth century onwards.

The Tudor prose translation was reasonably good and robust. But by 1750 or so Aldermary Churchyard had reduced it to this sort of thing:

> Soon after news came that a mighty fleet of Saracens were entering the harhour [*sic*]; whereupon Valentine judged it necessary to go thither, and oppose their landing, but it proved fatal; for in his fleet was the Emperor his father, who being clad in Saracen armour, Valentine, by mistake run him quite through the body with his spear; which when he knew, he was going to kill himself, had not his brother and the Green Knight prevented him; but getting an horse with an intent to lose his life, he rushed into the midst of the enemy, overthrew all that opposed him, till he came to the Giant Bandiser, who when he saw Valentine, encountered him so fiercely, that both fell to the ground; but Valentine recovering, gave him a stab which sent him to hell, to see his false prophet Mahomet.

In that condensed hotch-potch – it is a passage selected at random – you can see the quarter-educated mind at work: ignoring utterly the dramatic values, the αναγνώρισις which is the whole point of the story, the climax which gave it its universal appeal, and simply tumbling into bad print a collection of hasty words which made up, somehow, that saleable article – that best-seller, in fact – already well known as *Valentine and Orson*. The label was all that mattered to seller or buyer. Fortunately for the children of a later age, though that particular Romance has virtually perished of internal decay, many of the labels hid material which suffered only from a slight surface mould.

It is easy to condemn that huckstering trade and its products. Its crude straightforwardness can be defended as on the whole honest: it did not make its less pleasant wares the staple of its trade. And if the chapbooks do contain unseemly elements, and offer bad English, ugly print, and silly degenerate twaddle, they also, and they alone, found a home in print, among all the treasure and the rubbish they preserved, for two higher, more immortal things, the Fairy-Tale and the Nursery Rhyme.

* See Esdaile's *English Tales and Romances* (1912) and *Valentine and Orson*, by Arthur Dickson (New York: Columbia University Press, 1929).

BRIEF BOOK LIST

It would hardly be relevant here to give the sources of early editions of the books which eventually formed the chapmen's regular stock-in-trade. Some are indicated in other chapters. Many have been investigated not only by the more general bibliographical experts – e.g. in Esdaile's *A List of English Tales and Prose Romances* (London, 1912) – but also in the proceedings of 'Academies' like the Folk-Lore Society, the Early English Text Society, and so on. See *N.C.B.E.L.* The following works also pursue the subjects a little more comprehensively:

[Cheap, John.] *John Cheap the Chapman's Library: the Scottish chap literature of last [18th] century classified.* 3 vols. (Glasgow, 1877–8).
    John Cheap the Chapman. [A chapbook about a chapman's adventures.] (Edinburgh, 1785 and other dates: many editions).
Cunningham, Robert Hays. *Amusing Prose Chap-books* (London, 1889).
Fairley, John A. *Dougal Graham and the Chap-books by and attributed to him.* With a Bibliography (Glasgow, 1914). Also in vol. I of the Records of the Glasgow Bibliographical Society.
Fraser, John. *The Humorous Chap-books of Scotland* (New York and Glasgow, 1873). American title, 'Scottish Chap-books': title varies on wrapper and title-page.
Halliwell-Phillipps, J. O. [J. O. Halliwell] *Catalogue of Chapbooks.* Privately printed (London, 1849).
MacGregor, George. *The Collected Writings of Dougal Graham . . . with . . . a sketch of the chap literature of Scotland.* Privately printed, 2 vols. (Glasgow, 1883).
Villon Society. *Chapbook and Folklore Tracts.* 5 vols. Various editors, (London, 1885).
[British Museum Catalogue, under York, City of.] *A Collection of the Publications of J. Kendrew.*

The St Bride's Institute Library, London, contains a large number of chapbooks conveniently kept together. By a pleasant coincidence, the collection passed at one time through the hands of a famous writer for boys, Talbot Baines Reed. Harvard College Library also houses a large collection, listed in W. C. Lane's *Catalogue* (Cambridge, Mass., 1905).

A. W. Tuer's *1000 Quaint Cuts from Books of other Days* (Leadenhall Press, n.d.; with Introduction) shows that many of the chapbook blocks were extant in the 1890s, as does Edwin Pearson's *Banbury Chap Books and Nursery Toy Book Literature of the Eighteenth and Nineteenth Centuries* (London, 1890).

Supplement

Since 1932 there has been much enthusiastic publishing on the subject of chapbooks, but with little of the authority that is required. A summary of these writings, to 1971, is given in Victor Neuburg's *Chapbooks: a guide to reference material*, 2nd edn (London, 1972). The same author has also contributed a general guide: *Popular Literature . . . to the Year 1897* (Harmondsworth, 1977); a detailed study: 'The Diceys and the Chapbook Trade' in *The Library*, 5th ser. vol. XXIV, Sept. 1969, no. 3, pp. 219–31; and an introduction and bibliography for *The Penny Histories* (London, 1968), an account of chapbooks for children which includes seven photolithographic reprints of chapbooks, including an Aldermary *Guy of Warwick*.

Other topics discussed by Darton in the above chapter and not given bibliographical references elsewhere are treated in the following:

NEWCASTLE AND DISTRICT

Bland, D. S. *Chapbooks and Garlands in the Robert White Collection in the Library of King's College, Newcastle-upon-Tyne* (Newcastle, 1956).

Isaac, Peter G. C. *William Davison of Alnwick* (Oxford, 1968).

Thomson, Francis M. *Newcastle Chapbooks in Newcastle-upon-Tyne University Library* (Newcastle, 1969).

BANBURY

Cheney, C. R. 'Early Banbury Chap-books and Broadsides', *The Library*, 4th ser. vol. XIX, June 1938, no. 2, pp. 98–109.

GLASGOW

Roscoe, S. R. and Brimmell, R. A. *James Lumsden & Son of Glasgow; their juvenile books and chapbooks* [a bibliography] (Pinner, 1981).

MARSHALL AND PITTS

Shepard, Leslie. *John Pitts; ballad printer of Seven Dials, London 1765–1844* (Harrow, 1969).

VALENTINE AND ORSON

Elizabeth MacRae appends brief notes on the tale to a facsimile of a children's edition originally published by John Harris in 1822 in his 'Cabinet of Amusement and Instruction': *Valentine and Orson , . .* reproduced in 1971 for the Friends of the Osborne and Lillian H. Smith Collections (Toronto, 1971). This volume also includes colour reproductions not only of the book's illustrations but also of the artist's original water-colour designs.

CHAPTER VI

Fairy-Tale and Nursery Rhyme

I

The history of fairy-tales and nursery rhymes, in their progress towards becoming the true natural staple of the juvenile library, is a record of strong self-preservation under neglect and deliberate persecution. Even John Newbery, who took almost whatever he pleased to fulfil his vision of making children's books for real children, paid small heed to this material which lay ready to his hand. He may perhaps be said to have encouraged the Nursery Rhyme, though not as a rescuer nor as an original explorer; but he did practically nothing for the Fairy-Tale. That is, however, a social rather than a personal phenomenon. Such things as moon-leaping cows, Banbury cock-horses, booted cats, stirred but faint enthusiasm in the eighteenth-century middle-class mind. They were not yet 'commercial propositions'. They were not 'respectable', in the Georgian or original sense of that very English adjective. They were the imbecilities of the peasantry. They had not been honoured in print, but had only been told for generations by word of mouth in places where even a chapbook could hardly be read. They were frowned upon by moralists in the seventeenth century, and in the eighteenth – when they had got firmly into print – by the theorists of Rousseau's school. They had – in England – no noble descent nor aristocratic patrons. A little prince might indeed know them, as Mamillius did in *The Winter's Tale* (II, i); but only because to Shakespeare himself were revealed the secrets of his own country.

Of these two great traditional things, the Fairy-Tale was the earlier to attain print; and that rather singularly. It came into English juvenile society through being first presented at the French Court. But here it does not seem to have been forced to masquerade at all. It became a direct possession of children. Still, but for that warrant of aristocratic sanction, it might have remained in France, where its uncouth graces had become a pretence of rusticity. Bucolics and eclogues, on neo-classical models, were in fashion under Louis XIV, and the stories which peasants honestly told to their children were furbished up for a pastime of elegant salons. They were put forth in literary form by various writers, far the greatest of whom was Charles Perrault: greatest because he embellished least.

The title of his book was *Histoires ou Contes du temps passé; avec des Moralitéz*. It was published in Paris in 1697 (but 'La Belle au Bois Dormant' had already appeared in the February 1696 number of the *Mercure Galant*). The work was

In the illustration, a sign reads:

con les
De ma mere
Loye

15. (a) The earliest known version of five of Perrault's tales exists in a French manuscript: *Contes de ma Mere L Oye*, dated 1695. This was also furnished with seven gouache illustrations, as here, which were the models on which the first printed woodcuts were based.

(b) As occurred so often in the illustration of popular books, later publishers simply copied the established designs. The early English editions of Perrault thus contrive to follow the work of the original manuscript illustrator.

said to be by Perrault's son, P. Darmancour , whose name appears after the dedication to 'Mademoiselle' – Elizabeth Charlotte d'Orléans. The frontispiece, showing an old woman spinning with three children listening while she tells a tale, bears the famous inscription *Contes de ma Mère L'Oye* – 'Tales of Mother Goose'. The titles of the eight tales in the little volume, with their usual English equivalents, are:

La Belle au Bois Dormant – 'The Sleeping Beauty' (incorrectly).
La Petit Chaperon Rouge – 'Red Riding Hood'.
La Barbe Bleüe – 'Blue Beard'.
Le Maistre Chat, ou le Chat Botté – 'Puss-in-Boots'.
Les Fées – 'Diamonds and Toads'.
Cendrillon, ou la petite Pantoufle de Verre – 'Cinderella, or the Glass Slipper'.
Riquet à la Houppe – 'Riquet with the Tuft'.
Le Petit Poucet – 'Hop o' my Thumb'.

'Hop o' my Thumb' is not the same as our national Tom Thumb, and none of these tales in any form, so far as is known, had before then appeared in English. They were translated by Robert Samber, thirty years later, as *Histories, or Tales of Past Times. Told by Mother Goose* (1729), and have been naturalized citizens of the British nursery ever since.

They were said to have been told to the alleged young author by his peasant nurse; and there is no reason to suppose that untrue. But if essentially the *Contes* were folk-lore happily foisted into literature upon a Court occasion, and kept reasonably simple because simplicity of a sort was the rage, they were not allowed to appear unadorned. Even if, by the accident of the moment, they conquered severe critics, they had to apologize for their existence. They appeared with 'moralities'. 'What large teeth you have, grandmamma? . . .' The French version comments:

> tous les loups
> Ne sont pas de la mesme sorte . . .
> Mais hélas! qui ne sçait que ces Loups douceureux
> De tous les Loups sont les plus dangereux?

And England echoed faithfully, when the tales were translated –

> Wolves too sure there are
> Of every sort and every character.

All that can be said of such 'morals' is that they are not nearly so far-fetched as those appended to the *Gesta Romanorum*, and that children (as Mr Bickerstaff hinted in *The Tatler*) probably paid no attention to them. Perrault, however, had to be serious on the point. 'Ainsi sur ce conte on va moralisant', he says in the postscript to *Cinderella*; and in the Dedication he had written: 'ils renferment tous une Morale trés-sensée, et qui se découvre plus ou moins, selon le degré de pénétration de ceux qui les lisent.' The matter may be safely left to the reader, then or now.[1]

2

More than twenty years before the arrival of Mother Goose in England a different group of French tales was translated, and found favour in a variety of editions – coming to be known later in the eighteenth century as the tales of Mother Bunch. These were the *Contes de Fées* – invented fairy-tales, not re-told ones – by Marie Catherine La Mothe, Countess d'Aulnoy. Other English versions of her name are d'Anois, d'Alnois and d'Aulnois, and her husband's family name is also rendered de la Motte. Her marriage was not a happy one. She was of the family of de Berneville. She died in 1705, aged over fifty, celebrated as a wit as well as a writer.

A quotation from her, rather than Perrault, illustrates well the social or historical position of the fairy-tale as the French authors produced it. It comes from the first translation of her *Diverting Works* (1707). The story of *Graciosa and Percinet* is in Part IV of that collection, and it still survives in some modern

English fairy repositories:[2] it passed at once into chapbook editions. When the fairy prince Percinet took Graciosa to his palace,

Every thing was to be distinctly seen: In one place Shepherds and Shepherdesses curiously drest, and dancing to their Flutes and Bagpipes. In other places, by the sides of purling Fountains, she beheld the Country Swains courting their Mistresses, and heightening their Jollity with Feasting and Singing a thousand Roundelays and Catches.

That tale, like *The Yellow Dwarf, Goldylocks, The White Cat*, and a few others out of Mme d'Aulnoy's compilation, contained some scraps of far-distant folk-lore, and in so far as they did so they all have enduring life in French as well as in English. But in their original literary form they are three-quarters dead. In that form they had a double purpose. As Lady Ritchie (Thackeray's daughter) wrote: 'These special stories have fallen out of circulation, since the days when the French ladies and gentlemen all read fairy tales together, and the Order of the Terrace was instituted for Little Louis XV . . . It was not only children who liked fairy tales in those days; there was a general fashion in them.' The fashion is extinct, like many of the tales. *The White Cat*, that charming beast-spell fancy, has deserved its immortality. *The Yellow Dwarf*, not popular in books, gained the popular Victorian acclaim of becoming a 'fairy pantomime', in part by the aid of James Robinson Planché, who was at once a prolific play-journeyman and a diligent collector of folk-lore. Most of the other stories are in or on the edge of limbo.

But the vogue was powerful while it lasted. After it was spent, the more or less final encyclopaedia of fairy-invention, *Le Cabinet des Fées* (Amsterdam, Paris and Geneva, 1785–9), ran to forty-one volumes, including a great deal of rubbish which is hardly fairy-lore at all. Among its tales, however, is one of the true immortals, *Beauty and the Beast*,[3] the author of which never wrote anything quite on the same plane. The story is a good instance of the changeling process.

It is usual to attribute the tale to Mme Jeanne Marie le Prince de Beaumont, because the version which is most nearly reproduced in standard collections of fairy-tales is in the main hers. It is in any case not original in its elements. But the first 'popular' or fashionable presentation of the story is by Gabrielle Susanne Barbot de Gallon de Villeneuve, and is also hidden in the vast *Cabinet*. She died in 1755, and little is known of her. Her version, though excellent in many ways, is very long and goes into side-issues about the parentage of both Beauty and the Beast. It was meant rather for adult 'children', whereas Mme de Beaumont's text was well and truly aimed at the real inhabitant of the nursery. Mme de Beaumont is therefore, for the purposes of this book, the prepotent author of the well-loved story. 'Felix Summerly' (see below, Chapter XIII) followed her in substance: so did whoever wrote the version attributed to the Lambs (Chapter XI). It is quite true that, as M. de Lescure (*Le Monde Enchanté*, 1883) hints, she made it a moral tale. But the moral is there all the time, whoever tells the story, and it is not rendered in the least degree more insistent or menacing when it is shorn of fripperies.

désaltérez-vous, beau Fanfarinet et Souvenez-vous de m'en garder, car je meurs de faim et de soif

16. An elegant engraving on copper for a 'fashionably dressed' French fairy-tale *La Princesse Printanière*. Contrast the woodcut at fig. 15, typical of those supplied for editions of Perrault.

Mme de Beaumont, however, has another claim on English respect. She lived for many years in this country, was well known here, and was highly esteemed as an educational writer. She was born at Rouen in 1711, and died in France in

1780. She was married twice. The first union, like Mme d'Aulnoy's, was
unhappy, and was annulled. After the publication of a novel in 1748, she
crossed the Channel, and 's'est entièrement consacrée à l'éducation des enfants'.
She wrote a complete set of treatises on juvenile education, in dialogue form, in
successive instalments – *Magasins des Enfans, des Adolescens, des Pauvres*, and so
on. They covered, for their increasingly instructed readers, religion, morality,
history, geography, 'et quelques notions sur la physique élémentaire'. Their
life was long. As late as 1855, the editor of the *Nouvelle Biographie Générale*
could call her books 'les meilleurs peut-être que l'on puisse mettre entre les
mains des jeunes filles'. They had a great vogue in English translations. But no
one now puts the *Magasins* into young hands. Their author lives today by a tale
which she did not invent herself. Is there any child who has read it who has not
felt the authentic thrill at the Beast's roaring when Beauty's father picked the
rose, and not trembled with fear lest Beauty should not arrive in time to save the
poor hairy monster and turn him, by faithful love, once more (we knew it all
along) into an incomparable prince, and live with him happily ever after?

3

Such was the noble gift of France to our nursery library. It was supplemented –
from similar fashionable sources and at the same time – by the presentation of
one of the other ingredients in the *Blue Fairy Book* list – the *Arabian Nights*. The
sources and aetiology of that amazing compendium are no matter for discussion
here. The Eastern tales, already present in some sort in *Aesop*, and to a less
extent in details of the *Romances* and *Gesta Romanorum* – even in Chaucer's
Squire's Tale – spread over Western Europe in the eighteenth century like an
epidemic. The first serious European translator of them was the French
diplomat Antoine Galland, whose *Mille et une Nuits* appeared in twelve volumes
between 1704 and 1717. The English version now most often used or adapted
for juvenile purposes is the nineteenth-century text by Lane (1839–41, with
William Harvey's careful drawings). The *first* English translation, from such of
Galland's edition as had appeared, came out between 1705–8; no perfect copy
seems to be known. Three other partial editions came out by 1715, and the
chapmen got hold of the text at once (see p. 59), especially the stories of
Aladdin and *Sinbad*. The tales appeared in all sorts of miscellanies, including the
periodical essays, from that time onwards. The ramifications of the subject are
immense. All that need be done here is to accept the stories joyfully, and to note
the date of their appearance in English. It need hardly be said that a rigid
moralist would feel his hair standing on end at the thought of allowing even
adults to read freely an unexpurgated text of the *Thousand and One Nights*.

4

But what was England herself doing about her fairies, her native pucks and elves and sprites? Oberon and Titania may have worn a dazzling literary splendour, but they were surely plain native folk by birth. And there was a fairy-tale in Chaucer, told by Dame Alison of Bath, and something very like another one told by the Franklin. Did we have to wait for a French fashion before we could get our own fairy mythology into print?

Not exactly. But the story of the admission of our authentic folk-lore into the nursery is a very curious piece of social history. And it really does begin, so far as books are concerned, with Caxton, like the story of *Aesop*; for Caxton first printed Chaucer, and Chaucer is the true literary starting-point of the English fairy-tale, mainly because of what he made the Wife of Bath say on the subject.

She was the right person for folk-lore. It was obvious that a coarse old woman who would need a sixth husband when her fifth died, and would justify him because even octogamy (like punch) was nowhere spoken against in Scripture, would attack ecclesiastics roundly, and, most certainly of all, would tell an admirable fairy-tale both convincedly and convincingly, with, in its midst, the best definition of a gentleman in our language. She *knew* there ought to be fairies:

> In tholde dayes of the Kyng Arthour,
> Of which that Britons speken greet honour,
> Al was this land fulfild of fayerye.
> The elf-queene, with hir joly compaignye,
> Daunced ful ofte in many a grene mede,
> This was the olde opinion, as I rede;
> I speke of manye hundred yeres ago,
> But now kan no man se none elves mo.

The friars had driven them all away. But her hero lived in those old days, and saw the elf-queen's jolly company in the proper way – as properly five and a half centuries ago as now. He came upon them in his journey to find the answer to the riddle he must solve, or lose his head, to expiate a crime:

> The day was come, that homward moste he tourne,
> And in his wey it happed hym to ryde,
> In al his care, under a forest syde,
> Wher as he saugh upon a daunce go
> Of ladyes foure and twenty, and yet mo;
> Toward the whiche daunce he drow ful yerne,
> In hope that som wysdom sholde he lerne.
> But certeinly, er he cam fully there,
> Vanysshed was this daunce, he nyste where.
> No creature saugh he that bar lyf,
> Save on the grene he saugh sittynge a wyf –
> A fouler wight ther may no man devyse.

Two kinds of fairy are implicit in that vision and in the action of the tale, though it ended happily enough. There are the creatures like Titania herself, the beautiful sprites of a Midsummer Night's dance. And there is the grim old woman of that race which behaved spitefully at christenings, or put changelings into human cradles, or turned handsome princes into Beasts. They both run through our native fairy-lore; but the Titanias tend to become at times the artificial nymphs of Arcadia.

For over a century after Chaucer's day there was almost silence about the little people, except for a few chance allusions. Suddenly, however, as English literature itself blossomed in the astonishing English spring, books were once more 'al fulfild of fayerye'. The dramatists are full of both kinds, and serious controversialists found it useful to bring them in. Nashe knew them, in his *Terrors of the Night* (1594): 'the Robbin-good-fellowes, Elfes, Fairies, Hobgoblins of our latter age . . . did most of their merry Prankes in the Night'. Harsnet, from whom Shakespeare got spirits for *Lear*, put Robin among the Popish crew. Reginald Scot, in his sane and enjoyable *Discovery of Witchcraft* (1584), made a full catalogue:

bull-beggers, spirits, witches, urchens, elves, hags, fairies, satyrs, pans, fauns, sylens, kit-wi-the-canstick, tritons, centaurs, dwarfes, giants, imps, calcars, coniurors, nymphes, changlings, INCUBUS, Robin good-fellowe, the spoorne, the mare, the man-in-the-oke, the hell-waine, the fierdrake, the puckle, Tom-thombe, hob gobblin, Tom tumbler, boneles, and such other bugs.

And Shakespeare and Spenser had nothing whatever to learn on the subject.

Spenser's fairy family tree, however, deserves rather more mention, because, by reason of its carefulness, it suggests that literature gradually overlaid life, stifled Puck and his meynie, and would hardly let Oberon and Titania themselves earn a straightforward living. In the *Faerie Queene* the House of Oberon is alleged to have descended from one great original, Prometheus; and as a comment on that piece of learning it should be recalled that Titania in Ovid's *Metamorphoses* is a name-adjective for Diana, and means no more than one who has a strain of Titan blood.* Between Prometheus and Oberon there came, among others, Elfe, Elfin (ruler of India and America), and Elfinell, who overcame 'the wicked Gobbelines'. Spenser is in fact partly an inventor, partly an antiquary, partly a poetic interpreter, where fairies are concerned. His creations belong to the Arthurian cycle, to the *chansons de geste*, to mediaeval and classical literature, far more authentically than to the soil of England.

There are plenty of other pretty allusions from Elizabeth's time onwards: Drayton, Herrick, anyone who had a light fancy and a spark of native tradition could make a charming picture without much artifice. Meanwhile, however, as literature toyed with the subject, blunter people were turning some indigenous heroes into legendary persons who at any rate are in fairy-tales now, whatever we call the earlier records of their careers: Dick Whittington, for instance, one of the strangest of changelings.

Richard Whittington was undoubtedly a real person, a prosperous merchant, four times (last in 1419) 'Lord' Mayor of London, and high in the favour of

* But Oberon is also found in the old French Romance of *Huon of Bordeaux* (which became an English chapbook), and has been plausibly traced to an Indian origin.

Richard II. Moreover, he did marry Alice Fitzwarren. He died in 1423. But he never 'turned again' on Highgate Hill, where a stone formerly marked an event that did not take place. In one of the earliest versions of his story the stone had got no farther than 'Bun Hill' (Bunhill Fields?), and even in later chapbook versions it has only moved to Holloway. As for the valuable pussy-cat, she belongs to half the world: the folk-lore specialists have traced her among many nations. No one knows how or when she was tacked on to the romantic record of Whittington's successful business career. It is suspected that she got there out of an old ballad in the time of Elizabeth, in whose reign the first printed version of the tale may have appeared. But that occasion is not now known to exist. It is *The History of Sir Richard Whittington*, licensed to Thomas Pavier in 1605, when a play on the subject was also licensed. There are allusions to the story from about 1600 onwards. It is sometimes conjectured to have been the work of Richard Johnson, the obscure author of *The Seven Champions of Christendom* (two parts, 1596–7). At any rate, whether time eventually reveals earlier things or not, there was Dick in Elizabethan print, a true born Englishman accompanied by an Oriental cat, and sentimentalized into the virtuous apprentice. But there is nothing about Puck or Titania in his story. There is neither folk-lore of the soil nor fantasy of the Court. Dick, in fact, is a third partner, a third estate, in the fairy kingdom – a changeling carried from our world into Elfland, instead of the other way round.

Robin Hood, Jack of Newbury, possibly Tom Hickathrift and the Pindar of Wakefield are in like case; real, perhaps, but also legendary. It is as impossible to keep them out of fairyland as it is to deny the presence, in their worked-up and worked-out epics, of genuine folk-lore. Other old friends, like Tom Thumb and the Jacks, have small taint of reality, and are suspected, in some details, of foreign blood.

But none of them were in any real sense the inmates of children's *books* before 1700 or so; or, if they were, the books have disappeared. The chapmen gave them their true juvenile vogue in print. And long before 1700, as well as long after, they had to endure far more persecution and contempt than any other form of ancient lore which is now acceptable to the parents and guardians of young readers. Not even the fashionably dressed French invaders escaped that ordeal.

5

The fact is that in this matter of fairy-tales a pique began early. Almost anyone conscious of a moral sense disliked them heartily, said so loud, and got a hearing. The first literary record of such hatred is that already quoted – the Wife of Bath's assertion that the ecclesiastics drove the fairies out. It need not be accepted literally, especially as later witnesses said exactly the opposite. Hobbes, in a famous chapter of *Leviathan*, identified the fairy realm with the

Kingdom of Darkness, and that was the ecclesiastical dominion itself. On the other hand, his slightly senior contemporary, Richard Corbet, contended that the Church and fairyland were interrelated, but regretted the change that had come to both.

Corbet was certainly an authority on all sides of the question. As an Anglican prelate – he filled successively the sees of Oxford (1628) and Norwich (1632) – he could neither speak ill of religion (which was no uncongenial task to Hobbes) nor admit the claims of Rome. But he was robustly conservative about things he loved and, one would like to think, believed in: Puck, for instance. His famous poem *Farewell to the Fairies*[4] is still worth re-quoting:

> Lament, lament, old Abbeys,
>   The fairies' lost command;
> They did but change priests' babies
>   But some have changed your land;
> And all your children sprung from thence
>   Are now grown Puritans;
> Who live as changelings ever since,
>   For love of your demains.

It was not the bigotry of Holy Church which had banished Puck and his mischievous-kindly band, for they all

> Were of the old profession;
>   Their songs were Ave-Marys,
> Their dances were Procession.

However, if the old magic had almost vanished, Corbet's wise servant, William Churne, or Chourne, of Staffordshire (mentioned in the same song), had preserved a little of it in his 'noddle'. He saved the bishop from an evil manifestation of it on one occasion. Corbet and a friend, setting out on an *Iter Boreale*, as a poem of that name tells us, were hopelessly lost in the woods near Cole Orton. Churne sought to break the spell with magic:

> 'Turn your cloaks',
> Quoth he, 'for Puck is busy in these oaks.
> If ever we at Bosworth will be found
> Then turn your cloaks for this is Fayry-ground.'

but before they could adopt his advice a 'massy Forrester' arrived and, like the 'gentle keeper' he was, led them to Bosworth.

Obviously, therefore, the cheerful bishop could not bid farewell to rewards and fairies; he had too sound a sense of humour. It is, in fact, as a wise, reasonably righteous scholar humanely testifying to the reality of things that never existed, that Corbet is here so valuable a witness to our underlying faith in fairyland. He stands for the whimsical sanity of the average Englishman. It was a happy inspiration which led Rudyard Kipling to borrow from Corbet's most characteristic poem a title for his own restoration of Puck to the history of England.

There are many other derogatory allusions to the fairies in the century and a half after Corbet. The general Puritan discouragement of light reading of course covered them. So, in a negative way, did Newbery's matter-of-factness; Oliver Goldsmith, of all persons, proposed that Whittington should be deprived of his cat and recognized only as an example to industrious apprentices. Rousseau would have no such fantastic creatures, and Maria Edgeworth, though she knew too much about Ireland to deny fairies altogether, kept them strictly out of her books. The general opinion of the Blue-Stockings was against them, naturally, on the grounds of truth and reasonableness.

It was not, however, till the nineteenth century that a full attack, fierce and authoritative, was made. It came from Mrs Trimmer, like a good many other odd things in this survey. In 1802 she decided that England and Christianity – which meant, as Mr Thwackum had held, the form of religion maintained by the Established Church – were in grave danger from the Jacobinical tendencies of France, and especially from the doctrines of the Encyclopaedists. There was certainly no love lost between the parties concerned, but it may be doubted if the peril was so grave, or its ramifications so minute, as the good lady thought. 'Jacobin' was a term then as loosely used as 'pro-Boer', or 'German', or 'Bolshevik', or 'Socialist' in more recent times.

However, whatever the truth about the catastrophe she dreaded, Mrs Trimmer was not disposed to let it be fulfilled. She founded a magazine called *The Guardian of Education,* in which from month to month she inserted articles on moral subjects, reviewed books, and answered correspondents. Her main object was 'to contribute to the preservation of the young and innocent from the dangers which threaten them in the form of infantine and juvenile literature'. As, in the course of her labours to that end, she surveyed the world, and passed from the comparatively easy task of attacking Rousseau, Voltaire, Diderot, and any French or German writer on education – Germany being involved through the vileness of Basedow's 'Philanthropine' – she made some terrible discoveries about things she had once loved. Looking back, she well remembered, 'as the delight of our childish days, *Mother Goose's Fairy Tales; Esop* [*sic*] and Gay's *Fables; The Governess, or Little Female Academy,* by Mrs Fielding'. Still, the memory was not bitter – at first. Such books did not at once seem harmful. They were merely 'calculated to entertain the imagination, rather than to improve the heart, or cultivate the understanding'. It was not till one of her numerous correspondents fairly bristled that she realized her own undue leniency. *Cinderella,* wrote this lady, over the initials 'O.P.' 'is perhaps one of the most exceptionable books that was ever written for children . . . It paints some of the worst passions that can enter into the human breast, and of which [*sic*] little children should, if possible, be totally ignorant; such as envy, jealousy, a dislike to mothers-in-law and half-sisters, vanity, a love of dress, etc., etc.'

Poor Sarah Trimmer. In her first volume she had commended a book published by Newbery, a fairy-tale called *Robin Goodfellow,* as both entertaining and improving – though of course 'care should be taken to make children understand that fairies are imaginary beings'. And now, in view of a letter from one who (she had to admit) 'appears to be so good a judge of what children *ought* and *ought not* to read', she had to banish Cinderella. A little later an imitation of Sarah Fielding's *Governess*[5] was sacrificed: it is 'in some respects very exceptionable'. *Robinson Crusoe* must stay marooned: his history might lead to 'an early taste for a rambling life, and a desire of adventures'. All Mother Goose's and Mother Bunch's tales, henceforth, were 'only fit to fill the heads of children with confused notions of wonderful and supernatural events, brought about by the agency of imaginary beings'. But she refused to condemn dolls and toy teathings.

She represented the strait Church standpoint. She had two independent allies, outside her own circle. One was Robert Bloomfield, the unhappy author of *The Farmer's Boy*. In the intervals between struggling with the patronage of Capel Lofft and making Aeolian harps, he wrote a child's book called *The History of Little Davy's New Hat* (1815); it was published by my Quaker ancestors. Bloomfield compiled this artless little story because he had been brought up on *Jack the Giant-Killer*, and had learned to remark its 'abominable absurdities'.

The other was the redoubtable historian of *The Fairchild Family*. Mrs Sherwood 'edited' – entirely rewrote, in fact – the once-loved *Governess* of Sarah Fielding. 'Several' fairy-tales had formed part of the original work (which, in its description of Mrs Teachum, the governess, shows something of Henry Fielding's own humour). The editor 'admitted' one of them. 'But since fanciful productions of this sort can never be rendered generally useful, it has been thought proper to suppress the rest, substituting in their place such appropriate relations as seemed more likely to conduce to juvenile edification.' As a matter of fact, the fairy-tale 'admitted' is an entirely new one, about a Princess Rosalinda, who attained happiness by the aid of a Fairy Serena, a companion (seen in a mirror) named Soimême, and toys made by 'an old fairy called Content': characters certainly conducing to edification.*

The moral tale was then omnipresent, though Roscoe's *Butterfly's Ball*, Mrs Dorset's *Peacock 'at Home'*, Lamb's *Prince Dorus*, and similar pieces of levity stood up gallantly against numbers. The attack faded away. *The Guardian of Education* disappeared in 1806. And twenty years later (1823–6) Grimm's *Popular Stories* were translated into English. The war – in Great Britain – was apparently over. But it is a singular proof of the danger of being a fairy-tale[6] that the first and greatest illustrator of Grimm – George Cruikshank himself – in his later years, turned moralist and broke into the fairy-garden – 'a Whole Hog of unwieldy dimensions', as his friend Dickens was fain to call him. It was not,

---

* By some chance of oversight, or possibly through the loss of its prefatory leaf, this book has been selected by Mrs Amy Cruse as an example of Mrs Sherwood's own work, and, as that, typical of what was offered to children in the first quarter of the nineteenth century (*The Englishman and his Books in the Early Nineteenth Century*, 1930). Sarah Fielding's own original tale was published in 1749. Mrs Sherwood, in her version (1820), admits the fact, and preserves the main virtue – the general structure. The 'several' fairy-tales were really only two in number; one about 'the cruel Giant Barbarico, the Good Giant Benefico, and the pretty little Dwarf Mignon' (a semi-Arcadian story), and the other, with an Eastern colouring, about the Princess Hebe and the good fairy Sybella, who owe much of their character to the idealised creatures who people the *Cabinet des Fées*.

17. A cheerful scene at the end of the fairy-tale war. The etched title-page of the first English translation of 'Grimm's Fairy Tales'. (There were two issues of this first edition; the 'first issue' shown here has no diaeresis over the 'a' in 'Marchen' and the plates are printed uniformly in brown.)

however, so much enmity against the fairies as zeal in another cause that inspired him. He was, at that period of his life, a violent teetotaller, and he turned the tales into temperance tracts. When Cinderella was to be married, 'all the wine, beer, and spirits in the place [were] collected together, and piled upon the top of a rocky mount in the vicinity of the palace, and made a great bonfire of on the night of the wedding'. Even Mrs Trimmer's correspondent, with all her anxiety about 'mothers-in-law', never thought of that.

6

There was also, almost simultaneously with Cruikshank's personal outburst, a much more dangerous onslaught on all things fanciful. But it came from America, and was part of a general conflict of ideals rather than a show of special hostility to fairy-tales and nursery rhymes as such. It took the form of war between South Kensington and North America. Its proper place in these pages is in the chapter on the Early-Victorian era – Chapter XIII below. By that time it had become a recognized thing to invent new fairy-tales as well as edit old ones. The quarrel between rationalism and imagination may be left here for the moment.

The fear or dislike of fairy-tales, in fact, was not and is not dependent to a marked extent on the feeling of any one period. It is a habit of mind which has often been dominant in the history of children's books without much aid from contemporary circumstances. It is a manifestation, in England, of a deep-rooted sin-complex. It involves the belief that anything fantastic on the one hand, or anything primitive on the other, is inherently noxious, or at least so void of good as to be actively dangerous.

By the same reasoning in the same minds Nursery Rhymes should be abolished; and indeed 'Peter Parley' did suggest that in his New England campaign. 'You might as well try to catch a Bandersnatch.' They are as old as the hills where the first human mothers bore children. They are of parentage as uncertain as a piebald kitten. They overlap into the baby talk and the ancestral singing games of children themselves. They have often, literally, neither rhyme nor reason. They vary from one mother to another, one child to another, one street or village to another. They belong to all epochs and all nations, and there is (thank Heaven) no hope of ever identifying the true source of more than a handful of them.

It is a mistake to criticize them, or indeed to treat them as 'literature' at all. They are practical. In the Singing Games, the secret rites of children playing by themselves, we have in fact something like Nursery Rhymes in their rudimentary form. Mr Norman Douglas has shown, in a remarkable little collection of these solemn liturgies, how difficult it is both to collect them and to account for them: it is a matter of uniting the power of inspiring confidence in children with a minute and far-ranging scholarship. Scraps of one game turn up in another. Modern people intrude upon long-dead figures of romance. Who in Tynemouth now would ask seriously

> How many miles to Babylon?
> Three score and ten.
> Can I get there by candle-light?
> Yes, and back again.

But they *do* ask it there, and in London, and it is in half the nursery rhyme books ever printed. Here, again, is the 'official' (Lady Gomme's) version of another game, with a Tyneside variant:

> We are coming to take your land,
> We are the Rovers!
> We are coming to take your land
> Though you're the Guardian Soldiers.

Lady Gomme says the parties may be Roman and English soldiers. They are so on Tyneside:

> Have you any bread and wine? –
> We are the Romans.
> Have you any bread and wine? –
> We are the Roman soldiers.
>
> Yes, we have some bread and wine –
> We are the English.
> Yes, we have some bread and wine –
> We are the English soldiers.

Again 'Charlie Chaplin went to France', in another North Country game; while

> Mr Spence, he had no sense,
> He bought a fiddle for eighteenpence;
> And all the tune that he could play
> Was 'over the hills and far away',

was to me, as a London boy,

> Lottie Collins, she had no sense,
> She bought a piano for eighteenpence,
> And all she played on it all day
> Was 'Ta-ra-ra-ra-boom-de-ay' –

an exotic whirlwind song even now not forgotten.

What Mr Chaplin did in France was 'to teach the ladies how to dance':

> And this is the way he taught them –
> Heel, toe, over we go;
> Heel, toe, over we go;
> Right, left, turn about.

Did that come into the last thoughts of John Davidson, when he wrote his *Testament*?

> Deeds all done and songs all sung,
> While others chant in sun and rain,
> 'Heel and toe from dawn to dusk,
> Round the world and home again.'

Heaven knows what broken pride, what good cheer, what devious politics and baby prattle, fears, hopes, eternities of the human mind, are jumbled in this flotsam of the most private of all worlds, child's play. And may heaven keep its knowledge secret.

7

The Games, however, have been put into print mainly as vestiges of social use, rather than as an anthology for the users themselves. The Nursery Rhymes, equally old and mysterious, were collected and published as soon as children's books became a matter of commerce. But how they were collected, no one can tell; nor when.

The first collection traced as yet, meant for English children, appeared in 1744, the year Newbery opened his shop in London. But it was not published by him. Mary Cooper was responsible for it – the busy widow of Thomas Cooper, who had been active as a publisher and wholesaler of journals and pamphlets. Mrs Cooper was associated with publishing works by such as Richardson, Young and Fielding, having something of a line in *belles lettres*. It has been conjectured that she may have been the 'N(urse) Lovechild' who was author–editor of the book. Apart from that though, it comes to us from nowhere, almost out of the World of the Unborn, where, till then, the rhymes had been beating ineffectually against the gates of our Erewhon. Now they can never go back.

The only surviving copy of this little classic[7] – it is little, for in its 'cut' state it measures only 3 by 1¾ in. – is in the British Museum. It consists of one out of two volumes, the second, and before being re-bound [in 1938] it was in its original (?) very much darkened Dutch flowered paper boards. The frontispiece, in red ink, shows a boy in early eighteenth-century fashionable costume playing a flute, while two girls sing from books. On the back of this, almost like a cover design, is a vignette, semi-allegorical, of an ape in a feathered hat, carrying a standard, followed by a sort of Policinello with a box (possibly a musical instrument of some kind), and a stout figure blowing a trumpet. This looks French or Italian in design and conception. The title-page has a young miss and master in a curly scroll at the top, in red ink. The lettering underneath, also in red, runs: 'Tommy Thumb's Pretty Song Book. Voll. II. Sold by M Cooper, According to Act of Parliam [leaf cut off].' On the back of this, in black ink, is a picture of an ape fiddling, bearing a forked pennant on a pole, with a cross at one end; on a bench stands an unhappy cat (or perhaps bear?) with a cake (?) in one paw and in the other a scroll. This scroll is of peculiar interest. The three tiny lines of 'writing' on it are almost illegible to ordinary sight. The interpretation of them is very doubtful. I make them out as a rough scrawl (perhaps only half-meant to have verisimilitude) of the words 'C'nts d.m.o.' The 'C'nts' (Contes?) is rather conjectural, and the 'd' is only a dot. But the 'C' and 'ʋ' upstroke in 'contes' make that word likely. Is it a suggeston of 'Contes de M[ère] O[ie]'? but except that 'm.o.' is clear, it might be nonsense.

8 Sing a Song of Sixpence 	9 The Old Woman. 
Sing a Song of Sixpence, A bag full of Rye, Four and twenty Naughty boys, Bak'd in a Pye. GRANDE	There was an Old Woman, Liv'd under a Hill, And if fhe'int gone, She lives there ftill. RECITATIVE

18. A page opening (actual size, printed in black) from the oldest surviving nursery rhyme book. The alignment and placing of the letters would be impossible to achieve by conventional letterpress and – given Mary Cooper's penchant for the opera – may plausibly be assumed to have been stamped in with punches of a kind used in stamping the text on to engraved music plates (see note 7).

Mere guesswork. If it is true it proves only that Mother Goose in rhyme was in the market which she had already occupied with Perrault's prose. The significance of that is a little less vague when we reach the next book of the kind.

For the rest, this volume starts (on p. 5) with

> Lady Bird, Lady Bird,
> Fly away home,
> Your house is on fire,
> Your children will burn.

in black ink. At the foot of this page, like a signature imprint, is (in Portuguese) 'Replicao'. Page 6 gives the coarse version of 'Little Robin Red Breast' (see p. 81), and is in red. At the bottom is 'Pronto', and at the bottom of page 7 (red), 'Recitatio'; pages 8–9 have 'Grande Recitative'. These seem to be mock musical directions, and others appear spasmodically throughout. The facing pairs of pages are alternately red and black, and nearly all have a little picture atop. The contents are mostly old and dear friends: 'London Bridge is broken down', 'Hickere, Dickere, Dock', 'There was a little man, and he had a little gun', 'Oranges and Lemons', which if they should perish from the world would leave it a sadder place. Only two, apart from the robin, are nasty.

The last page (64) is headed 'Advertisement'. It has a picture of a child (see note 7) in a three-cornered hat and a skirt, with a drum near by. He holds an open book on which is written *The Child's Plaything* 1744. Beneath are the words:

The Childs Plaything
I recommend for Cheating
Children into Learning
Without any Beating.
          N. Lovechild.
Sold by M   Cooper.
Price one Shilling
THE END

The air of mystery that surrounds this unique volume can also be felt when looking at some of its immediate, and almost equally rare, successors.[8] There are, for instance, two books put out by S. Crowder of Paternoster Row, in partnership with Benjamin Collins of Salisbury: *The Famous Tommy Thumb's Little Story Book,* which included nine rhymes in its section of 'pretty stories that may be either sung or told', and *The Top Book of All for Little Masters and Misses* ('all wrote by Nurse Lovechild, Mother Goose, Jacky Nory, Tommy Thumb and other eminent Authors'), which also contains nine well-known rhymes and some other matter, including Dr Watts's 'Sluggard'. Both books are undated and must be assigned to about 1760 on the evidence of the picture of a 'new' George II shilling. Such a date would certainly give them priority over the otherwise far more important *Mother Goose's Melody; or Sonnets for the Cradle,* which has sometimes been dated *c.* 1765, but which was not advertised until 1780 and was in all probability first published then. One may be more certain than usual in such a judgment because the *Melody* was a Newbery book and was presumably subject to the customary Newbery publishing procedures – but no early editions are known and for the hard evidence of surviving copies one has to wait till 1791 and an example issued by Francis Power '(Grandson to the late Mr. J. Newbery)'. Attempts have been made, not convincingly, to connect Goldsmith with the collection – but whatever the validity of such claims the book still stands out as the richest and most sprightly one-volume collection of its time, and one that formed the basis for many future compilations both in Britain and America. (This is true too of another good collection made by Joseph Ritson the antiquary: *Gammer Gurton's Garland; or the Nursey Parnassus,* first published anonymously at Stockport in 1784, and much later helping to inspire the highly influential editions of *The Nursery Rhymes of England* made by James Orchard Halliwell (1842 onwards).)

And those are the five earliest appearances of the nursery rhyme in English print in England; late, but young and immortal. Snatches of them, as of folk-lore and fairy-tales, are in *Lear* and elsewhere, and some of them can be plausibly traced back to real political events as well as to far-distant literature. But no one knows who – publisher, student, or hack – 'went up and down gathering up limb by limb still as they could find them', and putting them together into one literary figure.

American bibliography, to which English literature owes much, has attempted to go a little further into the matter, though only tentatively, and even so not reaching an original editor, but merely discussing first appearances. An older

Mother Goose's Melody than the Power –Newbery version (which, as we have seen, may be considered extant in 1780 and quite certainly in 1791) has been claimed for America, for Thomas Fleet of Boston, who is said to have produced one in 1719. All that can be said is that the American experts themselves admit there is no evidence, and do not believe in the existence of such a book. The chief point in its favour is that Thomas Fleet printed a hundred primers in 1719, which is not strong enough proof technically, and that his wife was 'Elizabeth Goose, daughter of Elizabeth Vergoose', which is no evidence at all.

What is certain about America's handsome share in this branch of literature is that Isaiah Thomas of Worcester, Mass., produced a second edition of his own *Mother Goose's Melody* in 1794. It has been conjectured that his first edition was about 1786, and that he took it, as he took other books, from Newbery's lost original; and, indeed, the earliest surviving printing of the *Melody* is his: a fragmentary copy of what is probably that 1786 edition. He is said to have been the first to introduce music-type into the States. For that and for *Mother Goose*, wherever he found her, he deserved well of his country.

A connection, furthermore, between Mother Goose of the Nursery Rhymes and Mother Goose of the Fairy-Tales has also been conjectured: it is upheld chiefly by Mr Whitmore, of the United States, who edited a valued reprint of the *Melody*. There is little evidence for such a connection to be found in any clear facts. The hypothetical Mère L'Oie whom I have guessed at in *Tommy Thumb's Pretty Song Book*, even if she is really there, is about as much use as a witness as Gammer Gurton or Nurse Lovechild; less than Lovechild, perhaps, for that Nurse is obviously an invention, whereas Goose and Gurton are traditional beyond memory or known invention, even when they can be traced in sixteenth-century dramatic literature.

It is unlikely that any true parentage can ever be found for such dear and homely persons. Who first called a dog Tray or Jowler? Why are so many heroes named Jack? Perhaps it really was John Newbery himself who invented Mrs Lovechild, Tommy Trip and the Giant Woglog. Perhaps Dorothy Kilner or Lady Fenn actually did give a name to Mrs Teachwell. It does not matter much. These half-corporeal abstractions appeared in English print, and were admitted to the nursery openly, in the eighteenth century. That is the only indisputable fact.

BRIEF BOOK LIST

There is an immense amount of material available for the study of fairy-tales and nursery rhymes, particularly of their origins and general archaeology. Much of it is to be found in the Proceedings of special societies like the Folk-Lore Society or the files of journals like *Notes and Queries*. Minute research in those directions is not necessary here.

Some of the authors mentioned in the preceding chapter – Mrs Trimmer, Mrs Sherwood, the Grimms, for instance – are dealt with independently later. For both special and general works up to about 1922, see *C.H.E.L.* Addenda; and *N.C.B.E.L.* vol. II, for later references.

PERRAULT

Histories or Tales of Past Times . . . Ed. with an Introduction by J. Saxon Childers (London, 1925). Limited edition: reprint of the book believed to have been published in 1719, but now known to be 1799.

Vizetelly, E. A. *Bluebeard* . . . (London, 1902).

Cox, Marian Roalfe. *Cinderella; three hundred and forty five variants* . . . with an introduction by Andrew Lang (London, 1893).

FAIRY-TALES, GENERAL

Hartland, E. S. *The Science of Fairy Tales* (London, 1890).

Lang, Andrew. *The Blue Fairy Book* (London, 1889). [Introduction in large-paper edition only but reprinted in the revised edition of 1975.]

[Wheatley, H. B. ed.] *The History of Sir Richard Whittington, by T. H.* Villon Society, Chapbooks and Folklore Tracts, vol. v (London, 1885).

Yearsley, P. M. *The Folklore of Fairy Tale* (London, 1924).

ARABIAN NIGHTS

Conant, Martha Pike. *The Oriental Tale in England in the Eighteenth Century.* Columbia University Studies in Comparative Literature (New York, 1908).

Times Literary Supplement, 10 April 1930. List of early English translations.

SINGING GAMES

Douglas, George Norman. *London Street Games* (London, 1916; rev. edn 1931).

Gomme, Sir George Laurence. *A Dictionary of British Folklore.* 2 vols. (London, 1894–9).

Gomme, Alice Bertha (Lady Gomme). *The Traditional Games of England, Scotland and Ireland* . . . 2 vols. (London, 1894–8).

King, Madge and Robert. *Street Games of North Shields Children.* Limited edition (Tynemouth, 1926; reissued 1931).

MOTHER GOOSE, ETC.

The Original Mother Goose's Melody. With Introductory Notes by William H. Whitmore (Boston, 1891). Facsimile of Worcester, U.S.A., edn of 1785(?). [There was also a facsimile of *Mother Goose's Melody* (1791 edn) published, with an introduction by Colonel W. F. Prideaux (London, 1904).]

The Boyd Smith Mother Goose, with illustrations . . . from original drawings by E. Boyd Smith [and a wayward introduction by Lawrence Elmendorf] (London and New York, 1920).

Starrett, Vincent. *All About Mother Goose.* Privately printed (Appelican Press, U.S.A., 1930).

Welsh, Charles. *A Book of Nursery Rhymes* (London, 1901). 'Mother Goose's Melody' logically classified, with an Introduction.

Supplement

The 'immense amount of material', of which the above references were a selection, has since expanded yet further and taken on, in some quarters, the attributes of an arcane science. No guide can be given here, but for the student of children's books three major contributions to the subjects of Fairy-tale and Nursery Rhyme make an essential starting point. They are all by Iona and Peter Opie: *The Oxford Dictionary of Nursery Rhymes* (Oxford, 1951); *Three Centuries of Nursery Rhymes and Poetry for Children* (an annotated exhibition catalogue) (London, 1973; revised and expanded, 1977); and *The Classic Fairy Tales* (London, 1974). This volume includes an extensive list of 'Commentaries Consulted', and this may serve in the first instance to bring up to date information on the topics listed above.

CHAPTER VII

Interim: Between the Old and the New

I

Thus far, there appears to have been collected most of the material for composing English children's books, and a public was recognized as ready to read them. But there was no agency or person to bring them habitually together. At the date of Steele's conversation with his godson, a child could have read for pleasure fables, probably some decayed romances, possibly early editions of French fairy-tales and the *Arabian Nights*, and some odds and ends of native legend in chapbooks. He would very likely have come across the *Pilgrim's Progress* and *Divine Emblems*, but not necessarily, because they would still, if he were of gentle birth, have a certain Roundhead air about them. If he did get hold of them, he was probably introduced to Janeway as well. And that is all he could find for his leisure hours, unless he had recourse to schoolbooks, or manuals of conduct, or grown-up literature itself. What is more, only two of those possibilities had been created with him as their especial object – the fables (Ogilby's and L'Estrange's versions, not yet Croxall's, at that) and the Puritan volumes; and of those two, the shelf of good godly books alone represented a deliberate and *sustained* effort to invade and pervade his mind when it was left to its own resources. Everything else was haphazard.

John Newbery's adventure was still a whole generation away in the future. In that interval between 1709 and 1744 three books appeared which made a deep mark in children's literature, both by their merits and by the ideas for which they stood or came to be considered as standing. They were Isaac Watts's *Divine Songs Attempted in Easy Language for the Use of Children** (1715), Defoe's *Robinson Crusoe* (1719) and Swift's *Gulliver's Travels* (1726). *Robinson Crusoe* must be regarded as two kinds of book – an adventure story, and a romance which could serve the ends of a school of philosophic thought. As an adventure story it can for the present purpose be yoked with *Gulliver*; and it will be convenient to consider these two together as that first, before dealing with the professed children's book, Watts's *Songs*, on the one hand, or the importance of desert islands on the other.

---

*   This is the title by which the book was known for the first hundred years of its life. From 1812 onwards it was increasingly referred to as *Divine and Moral Songs*.

2

They were not written for children: technically, I suppose, they were not 'children's books'. Common sense says that they are now, and that whatever the authors meant, they always were. It ought to be enough to assert that they are, to children, straightforward stories told with such superb ease and simplicity, with such absorption of the writer in the subject, that the mere telling is their strength, the secret of their power over young minds. A child does not need to know the malice behind a great man's fall on to 'one of the King's cushions', in order to be interested in the sports of Lilliput. Nor does he really care very much about Robinson's beating of his breast and monarch-of-all-I-survey meditations. What matters is the solitary footmark and the boat so foolishly built that it could not be launched.

It would be interesting, no doubt, to pursue the psychological basis of that appeal: to analyse the idea of romance, and particularly that variety of it which, a foreign critic acutely and admiringly suggests, makes every Englishman an essential Robinson Crusoe.* It would be no less interesting to study, with *Gulliver* as a text, the love of seeing things turned topsy-turvy. *The World Turned Upside Down* was a common chapbook, and Ann and Jane Taylor, nearly a century after this date, wrote a popular children's version of it:† the idea has a permanent appeal, and the general satire of Lilliput and Brobdingnag, over and above the topical details, is universal enough for children's minds to grasp. But to discuss such matters would be to abandon history.

The significance of the two romances, in fact – for that is what they are in this connection – is that they are new inventions. Even adults were only just beginning to be dowered with novels – with new works of art in the form of a fictitious story; indeed, only *Pamela*, out of the great eighteenth-century group of fictions, appeared before Newbery came to London. But here, under George I, children were already reading recent 'fayned fables and vayne fantasyes' – for Crusoe and Gulliver got into summary chapbook versions very early.[1] The novel-reading habit reached the nursery almost before grown-ups had acquired it.

That is an exaggeration, obviously. But the facts which suggest it, the popularity among young readers of Defoe and Swift as mere story-tellers (and for that matter, the vogue of the *Arabian Nights*), show that whatever stern parents might think, fiction for children was inevitable; indeed, close at hand. *Goody Two-Shoes*, hereafter, would not be a complete surprise: it would only be a Lilliput copy of what full-grown people were being given in increasing profusion.

---

* Emil Cammaerts, *Discoveries in England* (1930). M. Cammaerts appreciates no less warmly our unique addiction to nonsense.

† [*Signor Topsy-Turvey's Wonderful Magic Lantern; or the world turned upside down*. Printed for Tabart and Co. (1810). It is a much more sophisticated text than the chapbooks – and hardly 'popular' since it only ran to one edition.]

3

But Miss Margery Meanwell had not yet arrived, even when Isaac Watts's poems for children were published. Watts was not 'phenomenal': he was in the course of nature, at least in the ideals he set forth. His intentions, put with the most amiable lucidity and good sense, deserve fairly full quotation. His book, as the popular short form of the title suggests, was in two parts – 'Divine' as well as 'Moral' songs. In the preface to the 'Divine' section he wrote:

Verse was at first designed for the service of God, though it hath been wretchedly abused since . . . and there are these four advantages in it: 1. There is a greater delight in the very learning of truths and duties this way. There is something so amusing and entertaining in rhymes and metre that will incline children to make this part of their business a diversion . . . 2. What is learnt in verse is longer retained in memory, and sooner recollected . . . 3. This will be a constant furniture, that they may have something to think upon when alone, and sing over to themselves. This may sometimes give their thoughts a divine turn, and raise a young meditation. Thus they will not be forced to seek relief for an emptiness of mind out of the loose and dangerous sonnets of the age . . . 4. These *Divine Songs* may be a pleasant and proper matter for their daily or weekly worship . . . You will find here nothing that savours of a party: the children of high and low degree, of the Church of England or Dissenters, baptized in infancy or not, may all join together in these songs. And as I have endeavoured to sink the language to the level of a child's understanding, and yet to keep it (if possible) above contempt; so I have designed to profit all (if possible) and offend none.

That is neither more nor less than a Puritan of the previous generation become delightfully gentle, tolerant and persuasive.

The *Moral Songs*, on the other hand, were by way of being a more worldly supplement to these religious exercises: 'a slight specimen', he writes, 'Such as I wish some happy and condescending genius would undertake for the use of children, and perform much better.' Ordinary life and the Proverbs of Solomon should provide the themes: 'The language and measures should be easy and flowing with cheerfulness, and without the solemnities of religion, or the sacred names of God and holy things; that children might find delight and profit together.' So too, as by the *Divine Songs*, they would be delivered 'from the Temptation of loving or learning . . . idle, wanton, or profane songs'. Here he was again in the direct Puritan succession of active protest against current vice. But the first song, ''Tis the voice of the sluggard', though moral enough, is livelier and more fluent than anything written by his predecessors. And indeed that freshness of thought and expression was what he deemed necessary. He wrote the *Songs* at the instigation of a friend and very much in the spirit which his brother Enoch had urged for the publication of his adult *Hymns*: 'to quicken and revive the dying devotion of the age'. Sternhold and Hopkins, a biographer suggests,[*] had become stale and unprofitable.

Watts undoubtedly wrote to give children pleasure; and he did give them pleasure, for much more than a century; and then it was found almost suddenly

---

[*]   Quoted in *Isaac Watts, his Life and Writings*, by E. Paxton Hood (1876).

that his point of view was obsolete, if not narrow, and much of his verse for children ridiculous.

It was not really through any inherent fault in himself or his work that he suffered this catastrophe. It was not entirely, nor even very markedly, because of a slight change in the general adult outlook upon child-life, though that was the ultimate reason. It was because those who praised him forced their opinion upon others and saw to it that it was not questioned by his readers. They made him a task, not a pleasure; and the principles of task-work changed, just as the national sense of humour changed. Very few poems can survive the ordeal of being recited by children in public, year in, year out, to the mortification of the reciters and the weariness of the audience. Dr Watts had the misfortune to write at least four 'moral songs' which for several generations were infant-school entertainment pieces. And the greatest of all writers for children, Lewis Carroll, took advantage of the fact, though now and then one suspects that his Alice really liked the poems before he made fun of them.

As, indeed, why should she not? Here is the best known of them, entire:

> Let Dogs delight to bark and bite,
>   For God has made them so;
> Let Bears and Lions growl and fight,
>   For 'tis their Nature too.
> But, Children, you should never let
>   Such angry quarrels rise;
> Your little Hands were never made
>   To tear each other's Eyes.
> Let Love thro' all your Actions run,
>   And all your Words be mild;
> Live like the blessed Virgin's Son,
>   That sweet and lovely Child.
> His Soul was gentle as a Lamb;
>   And as his Stature grew,
> He grew in Favour both with Man,
>   And God his Father too.
> Now Lord of all, he reigns above,
>   And from his heavenly Throne,
> He sees what Children dwell in Love,
>   And marks them for his own.

That may not be imaginative poetry of a high order. It was not meant to be. But at the risk of being thought a prig, I maintain that it is exceedingly good verse, and, for its intention, perfect. Or take the equally hackneyed lines about the bee:

> How skilfully she builds her Cell!
>   How neat she spreads the Wax!
> And labours hard to store it well
>   With the sweet Food she makes.
> In Works of Labour or of Skill
>   I would be busy too:
> For Satan finds some Mischief still
>   For idle Hands to do.

'That threadbare old tag', a cynic will say. But it was not a tag in 1715, and even if it were, how easy and pretty the lines really are – how much more natural and charming, for instance, than Bunyan's on the same subject. Could it be done better for its gentle purpose?

Not all the *Songs*, it is true, are on the same level of serene kindliness, though if ever a writer for young children was serene and kindly, Isaac Watts was. He had still some Calvinistic sternness, though he did not often emphasize it ferociously. He had also the national feeling of satisfaction at being born both British and Christian. There is a famous passage in Song no. VI, 'Praise for the Gospel':

> Lord, I ascribe it to Thy Grace,
>   And not to Chance, as others do,
> That I was born of Christian Race,
>   And not a Heathen, or a Jew.

It is not really very different in spirit, however, from the equally well-known modern hymn which fears we may break into

> Such boastings as the Gentiles use,
>   Or lesser breeds without the Law.

His life was quiet and equable. He was firm in his beliefs, and his amiability was never weakness. We should not today echo the whole of Dr Johnson's memorable eulogy; we might find it difficult to credit such fame, indeed:

Few men have left behind such purity of character, or such monuments of laborious piety. He has provided instruction for all ages, from those who are lisping their first lessons to the enlightened readers of Malebranche and Locke; he has left neither corporeal nor spiritual nature unexamined; he has taught the art of reasoning, and the science of the stars.

Watts had exactly the retiring modesty and simplicity which makes a sonorous epitaph, in a conventional mode, sound insincere.

He suffered also, not only from parody, but from overpraise as a theologian for the nursery. His very freedom from harsh dogmatism was almost a fault: he could not be pressed home severely. Mrs Trimmer, in a popular commentary on him in 1789, when she was active in her great work for Sunday Schools, thought he had missed his opportunity by being too easy to understand. She wished the *Songs* first to be learnt by heart, then recited in a Sunday class, and then explained, doctrine by doctrine, detail by detail; which she proceeded to do. Nearly forty years later, doctrine being still in debate, 'a Lady' (thought to be 'Mrs Cockle, a resident at Ipswich') had to be even more laborious in an *Explanation* of the *Hymns for Children* (1823). Why, it might be asked, did dogs delight, by nature, to bark and bite, if God had made all things good? Because their nature had been changed by the sin of man.

Doctrine and imaginative quality both apart, Watts's *Songs* had a twofold importance. In mere verse-technique, they were unprecedented for children; they were not seriously rivalled in that respect till Ann and Jane Taylor appeared in 1804. And, being by a Puritan, they were yet the denial and, in a social sense, the end of the Puritan aggressive, persecuting, frightened love of children. They made up a real children's book, even if they had a didactic aim. They must ever be a landmark, early but clear, in the intimate family history of the English child, who was at last beginning to be seen to be a little adventurous independent pilgrim, worth watching with love and care, and even with some regard for possible differences of character within his own category. That was a notable advance, carried much further by Newbery, but only made possible by the personal tolerance and calm strength of a man like the author of 'Our God, our help in ages past'.

4

There remains Robinson Crusoe, the man cut off from his fellows, as the unconscious emblem of a philosophy which directly affected English children's books; which indeed actually inspired some of the best of them in the pre-*Alice* epochs. At all times, theory, recognized as such, has come into such books far less intimately than might have been expected. Writers who in their own minds had formed, on purely educational grounds, an idea of what a child's book should be, were seldom carrying out consciously the precepts of this or that philosopher, though often enough they did so unconsciously. In England their principles were usually in part empirical, in part founded upon a mixture of religion and social usage. Still less often is 'political' theory (in the Aristotelean sense) to be found visibly at large in the English nursery library. But in the Hanoverian reigns both kinds of underlying principle were to be seen there openly, or were strongly suspected of being there; as when, for instance, Mrs Trimmer smelt the brimstone in fairy-tales.

During that period, writers for children were, educationally, disciples of either Locke or Rousseau. If they followed Locke, it was, as likely as not, without knowing it. That was inevitable, because with his acceptance of facts as the basis of theory, Locke was typically English, down to the smallest practical detail. Theories apart, too, the *Thoughts Concerning Education* are a microcosm of English domesticity. Locke knew exactly what strict but not unkind English mothers did – did till well within today's living memory – about diet for their children, about the hours of sleep, about clothes, 'the peristaltic motion of the guts', exercise, self-denial, and all the tremendous triviality of infant life. If tiny points like those appear in later books by the Kilners, Lady Fenn, Mrs Trimmer, and others, it is not because the writers thought Locke out, but because Locke knew their long-established habits beforehand.

Such a philosophy really trusts a good deal to nature, plus experience of nature; but not to nature as Rousseau understood it – not to natural freedom with universal reason in the background. Yet Robinson Crusoe could be, and was, envisaged as the natural man in both senses – as the resourceful, practical human being, who could not but argue God from his own experience, and also as the innocent rational being who would end by finding that God is nature plus reason. To these conceptions, usually muddled in the interpretation, must be added the old vision of the noble savage, which goes back beyond the age of Defoe and Pope.* 'Oh what a blessed thing, sir, to be in a state of natur!' – the children's writers under George II and George III almost anticipated Mr Squeers's ejaculation; and, like him, they found nature 'more easier conceived than described'.

Add to that chance of philosophizing over Robinson – which Rousseau himself seized ecstatically – the splendour of Defoe's matter-of-factness and the magic of the desert-island idea, and it is not hard to understand the enormous crop of imitiations which *Robinson Crusoe* produced – largest and most various in the field of children's books, and richest, though with Defoe's tale as the active stimulus, after the appearance of *Émile* in 1762. French bibliographers have coined a convenient term for them – *Robinsonnades* – which itself is significant; the mere catalogue of them fills a large painstaking German volume. They run right through the story of English children's books, and can conveniently be viewed here from their date of origin; it being remembered that there are three potential Crusoes, the lonely savage, the mariner of York, and the rational–natural man.

5

The savage, simple and more or less pure, lives from almost Defoe's time chiefly in the phrase 'Peter the Wild Boy', a rather misty person who became proverbial, especially in the allusive jargon of country-bred nurses. It was in 1724 that the unhappy real creature was discovered. He ultimately became a children's book, because when he was found in a wood near Hameln, Hanover (of which George I of England was then sovereign), he was only twelve, putatively. He was exhibited to the King, and farmed out to an agriculturist near Berkhamsted. To the end of his life, which occurred in 1785, he had learnt to speak no more than a few simple syllables, though he grew tame and healthy. He was visited by the eccentric Lord Monboddo so late as 1782, but does not seem to have afforded much useful information about a genuine state of semi-nature. He got into the chapbooks, and was often mentioned in instructive works for children.

Much the same happened to a later example, commemorated in a book from the general and educational publisher, Sir Richard Phillips: *An Historical Account of the Disovery and Education of a Savage Man . . . Caught in the Woods near Aveyron in 1798* [actually 1800]. He was said to be the tenth example of derelict humanity so found, and he was examined by the chief deaf and dumb

---

* The essayists' and poetasters' stock tale, *Inkle and Yarico*, has its roots in Ligon's *True and Exact History of the Barbados* (1657). The 'noble savage', entirely dissociated from desert islands, helped the Anti-Slavery movement later on, and this also was reflected in children's books.

specialists of the day, notably by Itard, a French expert who wrote the book which Phillips published in 1802. This 'savage man' should have been useful as a test of Rousseau, but, apart from Itard's book he seems to have caused little stir.[2] He does sometimes occur as a topic in children's magazines.

6

These poor 'monsters' (in the Georgian sense) had little enough romance to recommend them. The appeal to 'natural' man, whether reason was dragged in or not, was at bottom sentimental. It was more honest to treat desert islands simply as the home of self-reliant adventure. But that method of flattering Defoe did not become really common in children's books till the nineteenth century – mainly because until then the most enjoyable juvenile fiction still had a moral bias. However, there were a few early *Robinsonnades* which, like their great original, did not unduly stress the didactic elements. One of the best, popular for well over a century, dealt with *The Hermit: Or, the Unparalleled Sufferings and Surprising Adventures of Mr. Philip Quarll . . .* (Westminster, 1727). (As a boy, I read him in a late chapbook edition, and liked him better than Defoe's own Robinson: he was not so wordy.) This desert-islander was apparently made known in 1727, as 'an Englishman, who was lately discovered by Mr [Edward] Dorrington . . . upon an uninhabited island in the South-Sea': a very appropriate home for such bubbles. Quarll never existed, nor 'Dorrington', which was a pseudonym for Peter Longueville. There were many popular editions of the adventures, however, for over a century. Apparently the first landing of Quarll in America was in a Boston edition of 1795.

He was followed by a less realistic and much better fiction, which also, like *Robinson*, became a children's chapbook – Robert Paltock's *The Life and Adventures of Peter Wilkins, A Cornish Man . . .* by R. S., a passenger in the *Hector* (2 vols., 1751). Paltock's imaginative story is still in print on its merits.[3] It is usually very slightly expurgated for children's use, but innocent enough in spirit: and it is one of the earliest romances about flying.

A later maroon than Selkirk, but a genuine one, achieved only temporary fame. *The Life and Adventures of Henry Lanson* was published in London round about 1800 and advertised by Kendrew of York (see Chapter v) in a catalogue of books 'moral, useful and entertaining' (*c.* 1820), along with other works meant for children, like Watts's *Divine Songs*, or for young women going out to service like Mrs Sherwood's *Susan Gray*. Lanson's semi-fictitious adventures, which included the conversion of West Indian or Spanish Main savages to Christianity, are described as happening in 1774. He was the son of a Virginian planter.

7

Finally, we come to the Crusoe of *Émile*, the castaway philosophized for the young. But there is some obscurity about these famous desert-islanders. There were two of them of major importance, and the better-known one was augmented and variously translated. The first, *Robinson der Jüngere* was put forth at Hamburg in 1779. It was by Joachim Heinrich Campe. Campe avowed a debt to Rousseau as well as to Defoe. He himself translated the work into English, as *Robinson the Younger*, in 1781. The English version which held the market for a generation or more, however, was one published by Stockdale in 1788 in four volumes with twenty-two cuts, many of which are signed by John Bewick, and 1789 in one, as *The New Robinson Crusoe*. (Stockdale was the publisher of the advanced Rousseauist Thomas Day's *Sandford and Merton*.) It was avowedly meant for the leisure reading of the young. The editor or translator dwelt upon Rousseau as the source of inspiration, but was conscientious enough to point out some inconvenient details. For instance, 'Young Emilius is the child of Mr Rousseau's fancy, not the child of education'– and the more convincing parts of *Crusoe*, as of *Émile*, demand, he implies, a certain basis of education in the hero, so that the coltishness of Nature may be wisely directed. (That, indeed, was one of Rousseau's own difficulties.) Robinson, in fact, was not a Peter the Wild Boy: a blemish which robbed him of some merit as a philosophical type, but made the story more interesting. A great deal depends on the muskets and the wreckage.

But Campe was more logical than Rousseau, and more honest than Defoe. His Robinson was a straightforward castaway. He had no well-equipped wreck. He had no ebullient, exploring family of his own to instruct. Stranded upon the coast of South America, he 'had nothing but his head and his hands to depend on for his preservation'. Providence, it is true, endued him with turtles, bread-fruit and llamas. But he could not make fire, the essential invention of mankind, until a tree was struck by lightning and he preserved the flame. He appears in the 1788 frontispiece with a goat-skin, a home-made umbrella, a bow, a kind of spear, but he has no rifle.

And what was worse, he met his adventures not in the course of nature, but through defective education. His parents – English – from Exeter in Stockdale's edition, but from Hamburg in Campe's – allowed him to do what he pleased when he was young, and so in the end he ran away to sea, and even there deserted without leave. It was his lack of civilized habits and routine that brought him trouble: indulgence in natural leanings, until he reached his lowest prairie value on his 'island', invariably got him into difficulties. It is possible that Campe did not perceive this irony clearly, and probable that his publisher did not either. The 1788 edition advertises Thomas Day's *Little Jack* (a kind of tentative Robinson), *Sandford and Merton* and various Anglo-French works which are all 'in the movement' of Rousseau a little more accurately than *The New Robinson Crusoe* itself.

The 'new' Robinson is sometimes confused with its celebrated 'Swiss' rival, and their authors praised or blamed accordingly. Between the two came St Pierre's *Paul et Virginie* (Paris, 1787), translated under that title in 1795 by

Helen Maria Williams. That rather sickly romance is technically a *Robinson-nade*, but it was too adult and artificial ever to live sturdily in the English nursery library. The *real* Swiss family was born about a quarter of a century after Campe's book appeared – *Der Schweizerische Robinson*, published at Zurich in two parts in 1812 and 1813. It was originally written and illustrated for the enjoyment of a single family by Johann David Wyss, pastor and almoner of the Swiss troops in Berne. Little seems to be known about him and the manuscript was published by his son Johann Rudolf. But the book brings us curiously near a tide in our life and letters. The English translation was issued by William Godwin, then, for political reasons, trading under his wife's name, and also writing as 'Edward Baldwin', whose publications are advertised in this work of 1814. It has been suggested that Shelley had a hand in the version, which was made direct from the German. That very year he eloped to Italy with Mary Godwin. But it is mere conjecture.

The original English text is very much shorter than that to which the still numerous readers of the story are accustomed. It contained only two parts and a fraction of the French version done by Mme de Montholieu. This lady, as much as Wyss, is the author of the most familiar of the instructive adventures of Fritz, Franz, Ernest and Jack. She apparently got leave from Wyss's son to alter the end of the story, and expand it enormously, and her full text ran to five volumes, of which the authoritative version is probably that published from 1824 to 1826. Her great addition was the introduction of the donkey. At some later period, the boa constrictor, which swallowed the donkey so demonstrably that the poor beast's outline could be seen plainly before the huge serpent was despatched, the ostriches (the hansom cabs of the island, one might almost call them), bears, tame antelopes, and the succulent truffle also appeared. W. H. G. Kingston got hold of this in 1879 – 'the second portion, forming the second volume, has but recently come to hand' – and, though as an editor, assisted by members of his family, he telescoped his original and altered it considerably, it is to him that most English readers owe the fully articulated skeleton. But a text by Mrs H. B. Paull (*c.* 1877; and *c.* 1890 in the 'Chandos' Library) contains what is claimed as the unabridged version of Wyss-Montholieu in its completest form. There is also a full translation (1869–70) by W. H. Davenport Adams.*

It is no great matter for lamentation that the romance is so patched and imperfectly authenticated. Loving fidelity in youth to a particular text will, of course, render any other version unpalatable. But on literary and philosophical

---

* The above are the editions now most conveniently identified. The bibliography of the earliest ones is complicated. The book was first published in two volumes as *The Family Robinson Crusoe* (M. J. Godwin, 1814) and later in the same year it was re-issued as one. It ended with a note saying that a Continuation would be translated shortly, but 'though as a story it is at present incomplete, as an exercise for the improvement of knowledge and ingenuity for children, it is entirely fit for use'. The two-volume edition which followed was published in 1816 and a 'second edition' (really the third) in 1818. It was this last that adopted the now familiar title of *The Swiss Family Robinson*. The stock Victorian edition was that illustrated by John Gilbert and others and published by Routledge in 1882.

grounds, as the Victorian editors might have said, there is little to choose between the rivals. There is, indeed, not much more reason for ending the story than for beginning it. It will be remembered that the pastor Robinson (a well-known Swiss name?) lost his fortune in the Revolution of 1798, and set out, family and all, on a missionary enterprise to Otaheite. In due course they were wrecked, and it became clear to the well-informed parent that 'we are not far from the Equator, or at least between the tropics'. In fact, he was rather surprised at finding an animal which is 'a native of [North] America'. But as penguins, kangaroos and a whale were also discovered, nothing should have seemed wonderful. And a man who, in the desperate stress of escaping from the wreck in a storm, 'explained, as well as I could in a hurry, the principle of the lever', was not likely to boggle at mere facts of natural history. As for the family's being rescued and leaving the island, 'for all I know, they may be living still', as the fairy-tales used to say. They should rotate, not advance or grow-up. That is why no one can read *Émile* for pleasure.

It is difficult not to become almost ecstatic over one's wholly erroneous recollections of that compilation (regard it as one work, for the moment). I never knew, until I re-read one of the texts a year or two ago, that it was full of the most extravagantly laboured piety. I never realized that half the globe brought its fruits and creatures to grow naturally upon one tropical island. I certainly never heard of questions of text and authorship and continuations by other hands, and doctoring by editors. All I remembered was that a very large snake swallowed the donkey and was killed when comatose from repletion; that the family had a house in a tree; that they tamed and rode ostriches, made lassoes, built a boat, tapped the india-rubber tree, obtained coconuts by the well-known method of encouraging imitation in monkeys, and found a salt mine. That ought to be enough for anybody, though it by no means exhausts all the wonders of the island. And as *The Swiss Family Robinson* still appears regularly in every list of 'reprints' for children, it is also, obviously, enough for immortality. It is one of the great stories, piety and all. Truth and probability do not matter when you read it. Events do.

However, that was not the view of the next great *Robinsonnade*-maker, Captain Frederick Marryat, R.N. He had sailed many seas, seen many wonders, and could not but put a high value on accurate navigation. His children had read *The Swiss Family Robinson*, and asked him to add to it; a proof that those who went to it in uncritical good faith preferred its naïve versatility to its truth. 'The fault I find in it', wrote Marryat in the preface to the first edition of *Masterman Ready* (3 vols., 1841–2), 'is that it does not adhere to the probable, or even the possible.' He found its seamanship very faulty, and its geography irreconcileable with the known globe. He complied with his children's request for more, but his 'continuation' had to be an entirely new book, founded upon realities; in fact, as realistic as *Robinson Crusoe* itself, but more densely populated and more purposeful.

That is the drawback to a story of which one would else have expected much. In *Masterman Ready*, as in *The Children of the New Forest*, though that work is not quite relevant at this stage, Marryat made the – to us – mistake of putting a didactic ideal above straightforward story-telling. Ready, as Mr David Hannay points out, 'owes something to Mr Barlow' (the *Sandford and Merton* perfect tutor), and he does not lose his priggishness by being dressed as a tar. One cannot see Mr Midshipman Jack Easy listening to him for long. However, that is a criticism which belongs to a survey of the Victorian period, not to a chronicle of *Robinsonnades*. *Masterman Ready* is a declared member of that family, but, between them, the schoolmaster and the godly moralist in the author have almost suppressed the seafarer as well as the general philosopher.

Marryat reverted much more closely to the pure *Robinson Crusoe* model in a book published in the last year of his life, *The Little Savage* (Part I, 1848). He died before it was finished, and Part II (1849) is by his son. In the story, so far as Marryat's own share goes, a man and boy arrive on a desert island, with a few desirable properties. The man dies, and the boy, who like Robinson himself had a Bible, lived a life of curious self-reliant piety. He tamed a seal – a genuine possibility which has a truthful ring about it – and (for his own benefit) read the Gospel aloud to gannets; had Anatole France seen this when he described S. Mael among the penguins? The story breaks off with the appearance of a boat's crew from a ship, who put a woman ashore and rowed away. In spite of occasional didactic fervour, this is a much more vividly imagined tale than *Masterman Ready*. One feels that for once Marryat had in him something deeper than his honest seafaring experience and his buoyant but rather facile humour: a kind of mystical romantic spring struggling to be free from religious and social inhibitions. It is to me the most sincerely emotional of all the *Robinsonnades*.

The innumerable host of other imitators, adapters, developers might feel a little uneasy under cross-examination. Did they really, as pseudo-Crusoes, try to get right inside the goat-skin costume? It must be left for the student of literary psychology to pass a verdict on them when he has read (if he can) these works, which can only be tabulated here by name, and by well-known names at that: Agnes Strickland's *The Rival Crusoes* (1826); Ann Fraser Tytler's *Leila, or The Island* (1839); Jefferys Taylor's *The Young Islanders* (1842); Mayne Reid's *English Family Robinson* (1851); Catharine Traill's *Canadian Crusoes* (1852; edited by her sister Agnes Strickland); Percy St John's *Arctic Crusoe* (1854); Fenimore Cooper's *Mark's Reef, or, The Crater* (1847; published later that year in the U.S.A. as *The Crater; or, Vulcan's Peak*); Anne Bowman's *The Castaways* (1857) and *The Boy Voyagers* (1859); Jules Verne's *L'Île Mystérieuse* (1874: English title *The Mysterious Island*); W. H. G. Kingston's *Rival Crusoes* (1878); and many others. (I do not claim to have read them all myself.) The choice of site, period and atmosphere is unlimited.

8

This parenthesis has carried us a long way forward from the interval between the Puritans and John Newbery. But it has shown how fruitful, in the end, that interval was. Before 1744, nevertheless, children with imaginative minds still had to steal in order to satisfy their free desires. Nothing cheerfully original was offered to *them*, nor were there facilities for them to look for it. They somehow got what they liked. The moralist was still a heavy burden upon them – then and for a century and a half to come – and the practical openings for literary enjoyment were scant and usually illicit. Newbery made the facilities plain and adequate; it was his great service to children's literature; but he could hardly even scotch the moralist. His period and his business environment had not gone so far forward as that. It was all very well to cry 'Trade and Plumb-cake for ever, Huzza!' Everyone agreed with that, when you shouted it loudly enough. But what did Mr Locke say when he came to define 'plumb-cake', what did the Georgian parent practise in his own home? Here is a thought concerning digestive education:

For Breakfast and Supper, Milk, Milk-Pottage, Water-Gruel, Flummery, and twenty other Things, that we are wont to make in England, are very fit for Children: Only, in all these let Care be taken, that they be plain, and without much mixture, and very sparingly seasoned with Sugar, or rather none at all; especially all Spice, and other Things that may heat the Blood, are carefully to be avoided.

John Newbery could supply cake in plenty, but of 'plumbs' no great store, and no highly sugared delicacies. Some of his fare has been described already. It is time to look at the general contents of his shelves: his flummery, a dish now obsolete.

BRIEF BOOK LIST

For Isaac Watts, Swift, Defoe and the other principal authors, see *D.N.B.* and *C.H.E.L.* Some of the minor authors are here dealt with in later chapters. See also:

Stone, Wilbur Macey. *The Divine and Moral Songs of Isaac Watts.* An Essay thereon and a tentative List of Editions (New York, 1918). Limited edition, privately printed for *The Triptych.*

Ward, James. *Notes on a Unique Copy of Dr Isaac Watts's 'Divine Songs'.* Privately printed (Nottingham, 1902).

Cammaerts, Emil. *Discoveries in England* (London, 1930). Chapter I is on Robinson Crusoe, but the whole book is relevant in spirit.

Groth, Prof. John Henry. *The Swiss Family Robinson* (New York, 1929).

Ullrich, Hermann. *Robinson und Robinsonaden* (Weimar, 1898). Vol. VII of Literarhistorische Forschungen, 1897, etc.

Marryat's *Robinsonnades* appear in Michael Sadleir's *Excursions in Victorian bibliography* (1922) [which was later to develop into his splendid *XIX Century Fiction; a bibliographical record* (London, 1951)].

Supplement

Modern studies of Isaac Watts are noted by J. H. P. Pafford in his Introduction and Bibliographies to a photolithographic reprint of two editions of *Divine Songs* . . . (London, 1971), where he also comments on Stone's essay, above. The European interest in *Robinson und Robinsonaden* has continued unabated, with numerous works published in Germany, Scandinavia and Switzerland on the influence of Defoe's book on children's literature (see the listings in Ørvig *Catalogue* (1975), pp. 41–2). Of particular importance however is:

Dahl, Erhard. *Die Kürzungen des 'Robinson Crusoe' in England zwischen 1719 und 1819* . . . (Frankfurt, 1977), which establishes detailed connections between abridged editions and gives much information on the publishing background. One of the few assessments of the treatment of Gulliver as a children's book has also come from Germany: Heinz Kosok, *Lemuel Gullivers Deutsche Kinder; Weltliteratur als Jugendbuch* (Wuppertal, 1976).

CHAPTER VIII

John Newbery

I

John Newbery by extraction came of a bookselling family, for Ralph Newbery, of Fleet Street, who issued books between 1560 and his death in 1603, was his ancestor. But he himself was a farmer's son, born at Waltham St Lawrence, Berkshire, in 1713. As a boy he read as widely as he could, and, at the age of about sixteen, gave up agriculture as an occupation, and became assistant to William Carnan, printer, of Reading. Carnan died in 1737, and not long afterwards Newbery married his widow. By her he had three children, Mary, afterwards Mrs Power, John, who died young, and Francis, who succeeded his father.

William Carnan (who had a son Thomas) was editor of the *Reading Mercury*. His business was mainly concerned with newspaper printing, but included also books, medicines, haberdashery, founts of type and cutlery. Newbery's first appearance as a partner seems to be in an imprint of 1740, quoted by his biographer and ultimate descendant in the publishing business, Charles Welsh. In that year the young bookseller made a tour through England, partly to gain knowledge of trade conditions and opportunities, and partly, more or less, as a commercial traveller for his firm. The notes he made on this journey, quoted by Welsh, show the alertness and breadth of his mind as regards business, and a keen appreciation of the possible trade value of books. About the same time, also, he became associated with Benjamin Collins, an energetic bookseller in a large way of business at Salisbury, the original part-purchaser of *The Vicar of Wakefield*.

In 1744, or more probably at the end of 1743, as has been said, he moved to London, and at once began publishing on a larger scale. His move to the Bible and Sun, in St Paul's Churchyard, in 1745, showed him with a fair number of books already in his list, most of them, however, except the *Little Pretty Pocket-Book* and *The Circle of the Sciences*, meant either for schools or for adult readers. Very early also – in 1746 – he added to the stock of patent medicines, which he had brought from Reading, the valuable commerce in the celebrated Dr James's Fever Powder, recommendations of which (followed in the stories by wonderful cures) are fairly frequent in Newbery's children's books. The firm, in the course of its career, held the agency for over thirty such remedies. Francis, Newbery's son, was at first destined for a medical career, but until some time after his father's death was content to be the partner in charge of the Dr James side of the business, with a share in the publishing activities as well. He made a fortunate marriage with a beautiful wife, and in 1795 was Sheriff of Sussex. The secret of the Powder was covered by an agreement of 1749.*

Once well established in London, John Newbery, in the course of building up a business in sound periodicals, became acquainted with many literary men – to their mutual benefit. He got Dr Johnson and Goldsmith to write for him, and it seems fairly clear that Goldsmith was willing to do hack-work for him, and did it, though how much has been far too rashly guessed. He employed Smollett to edit *The British Magazine, or Monthly Repository*. His most industrious hireling was the unhappy Christopher Smart, who married one of his step-daughters. Two very able but less famous writers who probably worked for him were the brothers Griffith and Giles Jones.

It was in 1759 that Oliver Goldsmith, then living precariously in Green Arbour Court, a little square on the site of the present Holborn Viaduct Station, was visited by the vigorous tradesman whom his friend Johnson already knew well. He desired to secure Goldsmith for his new venture, *The Public Ledger* (1760). For the sum of a guinea apiece he obtained for that journal the delightful essays afterwards published by Newbery, Collins and two others as *The Citizen of the World* (1762). Goldsmith had already had work published in *The Literary Magazine*, in 1757 and 1758, a journal with which Newbery is said to have been involved. But this meeting of 1759 seems to have been the true beginning of an association which lasted till Newbery's death. Neither the two men nor English literature had cause to regret it.

At this same time, possibly by reason of common friendship, Goldsmith was brought acquainted with Smollett, then also, as has been said, in Newbery's employ. The vivacious bookseller may have been more of a centre of intercourse than biographers of the day, slightly contemptuous of the trade side of books, admit. The aid which he gave to Goldsmith, at any rate, is well known, and this is not the place to recount in detail the practical steps by which *The Vicar of Wakefield* (1766), *The Traveller* (1764), *She Stoops to Conquer* (1773), and less important works were produced in print by John Newbery and his successors. It should be mentioned, if it is necessary to do justice in detail to the publisher, that he was not at all sure of the success of *The Vicar of Wakefield*, that it did not sell particularly well in its author's lifetime, and that Goldsmith died owing money to his benefactor's heirs. But no one ever thought the worse of Goldsmith for his frailties, nor did Newbery take the least unfair advantage of them.

There is really only one 'children's' book which can with certainty be ascribed to this friendship, and that is for persons rather above nursery age – *An History of England, in a Series of Letters from a Nobleman to his Son* (1764). Goldsmith received £42 for this. It became a stock household work rather than a

---

* See an article in *The Times*, Dec. 24, 1929 on *Dr James of the Powder*, and correspondence in subsequent issues about its composition, including a letter on Jan. 8, 1930, from a Newbery descendant.

schoolbook, but need not be examined closely here: it was not written for amusement only. It went into countless editions, many of them with the text abridged or expanded. Not wholly dissimilar productions were the *Plutarch's Lives* (1762), which was only in part by Goldsmith; *The Wonders of Nature and Art,* a work possibly revised by him in 1768, or possibly 'edited' by him piratically for another publisher, as *The Beauties of Nature and Art Displayed* (1763–4); and *A New and Accurate System of Natural History* (1763–4),* which he revised and adorned with Introductions. There is no positive evidence that he really wrote any other entire work for Newbery. The tradition and the internal evidence for *Goddy Two-shoes* are strong, but no more.

2

All books published by John Newbery, and most of those issued by his firm in the next generation, are rare. Bibliographical details were got together by Welsh (*A Bookseller of the Last Century*) from copies seen, from advertisements in them of unseen copies from advertisements in the Press – Newbery recognized fully the worth of publicity – and from the firm's papers of all kinds. Even so, some editions escaped his keen notice, and almost any date here given might at any moment be falsified by a chance copy not yet collated, as indeed has happened to some entries in Welsh's fundamental list.[1] It is virtually certain that if the later firms published a 'third' or 'fourth' edition of a book not long after John Newbery's death, he himself prepared and even published the first one. Where comparisons can be made, they show no marked deviation of text.

The later firms must therefore be summarized briefly. John Newbery died in 1767. Immediately afterwards the story of his business becomes for a time a little confusing to the historian. A few books, as has been said, had been issued with the imprint of his first employer, William Carnan of Reading. Carnan left a son Thomas, who was evidently associated with John Newbery when he, Newbery, became controller of the firm and married Carnan's widow. This Thomas Carnan was one of John Newbery's heirs. So also was John's son Francis, and so was John's nephew Francis. For convenience I will label these two Francis (S) and Francis (N). Francis (S) alone inherited the medicine side of the business. The literary copyrights were mostly bequeathed to Thomas Carnan and the two Francis's. Francis (N), however, set up independently, at the corner of St Paul's Churchyard and what was then called Ludgate Street, the present Ludgate Hill. He died in 1780. From evidence such as the advertise-

---

* Goldsmith never wrote a *Natural History* as such, as his own entire work. The title 'Dr Goldsmith's Natural History' or 'Goldsmith's Animated Nature' on the back of a book will occasionally be found to cover (inaccurately) this Newbery work, but it usually stands for *An History of the Earth, and Animated Nature,* published posthumously in 1774 (8 vols.), by J. Nourse. Nourse had bought the rights in this from William Griffin, who had paid Goldsmith 800 guineas for it between 1769 and 1774. See *The Times Literary Supplement,* March 5, 1931.

ment given on p. 127 below there seems to have been considerable animosity between the two firms, compounded with some family wrangling in which step-son Carnan was prominent.

Francis (S) remained with Carnan, also in St Paul's Churchyard, for a few years, but eventually devoted himself entirely to the profitable medicine business. On Carnan's death, in 1788, most of the bookselling business passed to Elizabeth Newbery, the widow of Francis (N). She continued the famous name at the premises at the corner of St Paul's Churchyard afterwards occupied by her manager and successor, J. Harris, and subsequently by *his* successors, Grant and Griffith, a firm which later evolved into Griffith, Farran, Okeden and Welsh. Charles Welsh, the historian of the firm, to whose wide knowledge all writers on children's books owe a great debt, was a partner in the late nineteenth century.

During Newbery's lifetime the firm published between twenty and thirty children's books which fall more or less satisfactorily within my definition, though others, like *The Circle of the Sciences* and the three *Descriptions*[2] (1753) of St Paul's, the Tower and Westminster, purveyed palatable instruction rather than amusement. That range of production itself was an entirely new thing in the English book-trade, and justifies wholly the claim that John Newbery was the first genuine 'children's publisher'.[3] It justifies also the fine compliment America has paid to his memory – perhaps more treasured in the States than here – by establishing the annual Newbery Medal for the best children's book of each year.*

After John Newbery's death the Carnan, Power and Newbery firms maintained, and probably enhanced the value of, the established copyrights, and during the final decades of the century (particularly after the uniting of the firms under Elizabeth Newbery) the trade in children's books further expanded. Elizabeth, or her managers, Abraham Badcock and John Harris, were responsible for issuing several hundred new books or new editions of standard titles. Of the new books many had a strong moral or didactic flavour, and some fifty or so were largely written or edited by a single paid hack: Richard Johnson (alias the Rev. Cooper etc.). Perhaps his most notable contribution – and the most notable post-Johannine work – was *Juvenile Trials* (T. Carnan, 1772): Miss Barry, in her *Century*, gives a delightful account of it. It was Harris who consolidated the businesses and gave them new youth and long life; and by his time there were many competitors.

It would be tedious to describe in detail the whole batch of the first publications. The 'Abraham' *Aesop*, *The Lilliputian Magazine* – which, excep-

---

* The idea was originated by Frederic Melcher of the *Publishers' Weekly* in 1921 (first award 1922). John Newbery, it is quite safe to say, would certainly have got some reference either to the medal or to the prize book into his publications, if he had had foreknowledge. But he never heard of Chicago. [He never heard of the Pennsylvania Library Association either, but this worthy body was responsible in 1978 for erecting 'The John Newbery Memorial Plaque' on a building as near as could be gauged to the original premises of the Bible and Sun in St Paul's Churchyard.]

[62]

dead : This is the fierceſt
beaſt in the Tower ; her
name is *Nanny.*

Third, the young he
Tiger, nam'd *Dick,* ſon
of Will and Phillis; de-
ſcribed in pag. 44, 45.

Fourth, a *Porcupine* in
an iron cage. This is one
of the ſtrangeſt animals in
the world ; its back, ſides
and tail; are guarded with
ſtrong quills, each a foot
and half long, all pointed
as

[63]

PORCUPINE.

19. A porcupine in the Tower of London. A page-opening with woodcut reproduced in the
same dimensions as it appeared in Thomas Boreman's 'Gigantick History' *The Curiosities
in the Tower of London* (1741).

Although it is justifiable to call Newbery 'the first genuine children's publisher', it is
important to recognize the influence which such immediate precursors as Mary Cooper
and Thomas Boreman may have had on him.

tionally, appeared under T. Carnan's imprint in John Newbery's lifetime – the
Pocket-Book, The Circle of the Sciences, and others have been mentioned already.
From a few of the remainder some features may be selected for comment and as
evidence of John Newbery's mind: that is to say, of the mind of the English
social stratum he courted, for his commercial success itself proves that his
wooing was agreeable.

His first real children's book – meant for their amusement – after the *Little
Pretty Pocket-Book* was *The Lilliputian Magazine,* in some ways the most
revealing of all his publications. It was advertised for publication in monthly
numbers in 1751[4] and was issued as a volume in 1752: my own copy of that
date bore in it the inscriptions of three successive owners. The volume was
undated. The full title must be quoted:

The Lilliputian Magazine: or, the Young Gentleman and Lady's Golden Library. Being
an Attempt to mend the World, to render the Society of Man more Amiable, and to
Establish the Plainness, Simplicity, Virtue, and Wisdom of the *Golden Age,* so much
celebrated by the Poets and Historians . . . Printed for the Society, and Published by T.
Carnan at Mr Newbery's, the Bible and Sun, in St Paul's Church Yard.

It had an engraved title-page and clear little engravings in the text, and was
bound in Dutch-paper boards. The 'Society' for which it was printed was one

invented in the course of the book, and was alleged to have been founded on December 26, 1750.

The contents are various enough for any modern magazine. They include a sort of juvenile Androcles lion tale; an adventure of children among thieves; an adult (or nearly) 'History of Florella'; an account of the rise of learning in Lilliput; an anti-cock-fighting letter; 'jests' (thin, but more decent than those in the chapbooks); a song by 'Polly Newbery' and two songs with music; some riddles; the 'Adventures of Tommy Trip and his Dog Jouler'; the 'History of Master Peter Primrose' (who 'when he was but seven years old . . . by reading *The Circle of the Sciences*, had obtained some knowledge of men and things'); and a list of young subscribers, who included, among others, Isaac Hawkins Browne (then aged about 6; afterwards M.P. for Bridgnorth and the friend and benefactor of Mrs Sherwood's family), and several children in Maryland, U.S.A. (How did Newbery come by that priceless secret of a bookseller's success, a list of *good* addresses?)

The next volume which demands notice opens another small social vista. It was – and once more the title is instructive –

A Little Lottery-Book for Children: containing a *new* Method of *playing* them into a Knowledge of the Letters, Figures, &c. Embellished with above Fifty Cuts, and Published with the Approbation of the Court of *Common Sense*. London: Printed for all the Booksellers, and sold at the Bible and Sun, in St Paul's Church Yard. 1767. Price 3d. bound and gilt.

Copies do not indicate a series of editions, but the 'Advertisement' (preface) is dated February 16, 1756 – well within John Newbery's lifetime – and the book was first advertised in the *Gentleman's Magazine* of that year. He or a minion probably wrote it.

The title-page alone 'surprises by himself'. It is the complete Newbery and middle-class blend of trade, 'plumb-cake' and morality; or, more bluntly, pure catchpenny, for in the book itself there is nothing concerned with lotteries, except some sentences in the 'Advertisement' which speak of their evils, and the selection of subjects by hazard. Even if lotteries were evil, the 'Court of Common Sense' here authorized them, and merely, through 'Peter Prudence, Secretary', deplored their abuse and showed how to avoid it: 'We do order and strictly command all . . . Gamesters and Gamblers whatever . . . that the Stakes they play for be either Apples, Oranges, Raisins, or Gingerbread Nuts'. The 'Court of Common Sense' perhaps reflects the City of London Court of Common Council, then regarded more highly than now as an authority on civic and social conduct. The proviso about the stakes is characteristic. But it has not yet lost all relevance.*

* The best Palaeo-Georgian example of this human frame of mind which I have seen occurs in a 'moral game' of 1807. Such games were played like the popular modern 'race game' with dice – you advanced, retired, or suffered penalties according to the number thrown and the cubicle in which it landed you. This example, published by Wallis, a specialist in such things, stated in its rules that if dice were thought immoral, a 'totum' (teetotum or top with flat numbered sides) could be used instead. That is to say, you could gamble in essentials, or in soul, but be saved by the look of the external symbol or machine.

BOOKS *for the Instruction and Amusement of Children, which will make them wise and happy, printed and sold by I.* THOMAS, *in* Worcester, Massachusetts, *near the Court-House.*

THE BROTHER's GIFT ; or the naughty Girl reformed. Published for the Advantage of the rising Generation.

The SISTER's GIFT ; or the naughty Boy reformed.

The FATHER's GIFT ; or the Way to be wise and happy.

The MOTHER's GIFT ; or a Present for all little Children who wish to be good.

The FAIRING : Or, a golden Toy for Children of all Sizes and Denominations.

In which they may see all the Fun of the Fair, And at Home be as happy as if they were there.

The SUGAR-PLUMB ; or Sweet Amusement for Leisure Hours : Being an Entertaining and instructive Collection of Stories. Embellished with curious Cuts.

BOOKS Sold by I. THOMAS.

The HOLY BIBLE abridged ; or, the History of the Old and New Testament. Illustrated with Notes and adorned with Cuts. For the use of Children.

The History of little King PIPPIN ; with an Account of the melancholy Death of four naughty Boys, who were devoured by wild Beasts. And the wonderful Delivery of Master Harry Harmless, by a little white Horse.

A BAG of NUTS, ready cracked ; or instructive Fables, ingenious Riddles, and merry Conundrums. By the celebrated and facetious *Thomas Thumb,* Esq; Published for the Benefit of all little Masters and Misses who love reading as well as playing.

Nurse TRUELOVE's new Year's Gift ; or the Book of Books for Children. Adorned with Cuts : And designed for a Present to every little Boy who would become a great Man, and ride upon a fine Horse ; and to every little Girl, who would become a great Woman, and ride in a Governour's gilt Coach.

20. A typical Newbery advertisement for a typical selection of Newbery publications. It comes, however, from the final leaf of Isaiah Thomas's edition of *The History of Little Goody Twoshoes* (Worcester, Mass., 1787) and is a clear example of his complete adoption of the Newbery style for the American market.

But the book itself, in spite of this appeal to current fashion in its title, was original in little else. It was no more than an amusing and cheerful alphabet, with numerous small blocks. They look as if they were specially cut for this work – that was Newbery's way – though the subjects are those of earlier *abecedaria*: once more, a revision, a revival of old, amorphous material. Each had a letter alongside, and when the reader had learnt the letters by pricking them with a pin, 'it will be proper to give him a sett of the Squares, sold at the *Bible* and *Sun* in *St Paul's Church-Yard*.' Upon this it is proper to observe (i) that games – cricket, for instance – can be and are still played surreptitiously in school by small boys upon the same pin-prick system;[5] (ii) that the British Museum copy of the *Lottery Book* shows no sign of having been pricked at all; and (iii) that Locke (§150 of the *Thoughts Concerning Education*; §143 in the 1693 edition) recommended 'an ivory-ball like that of the Royal-Oak Lottery, with . . . twenty four or twenty five sides', lettered alphabetically: 'it being as good a sort of play to lay a stake who shall first throw an A or B, as who upon dice shall throw six or seven'. But 'this being a play amongst you, tempt him not to it, lest you make it business'. Common sense? At any rate, as the average English middle-class understood it then and (on the whole) understands it now.

A few more Newbery books contain smaller points, facets of his bright if tawdry mind. I am pretty sure he invented *Giles Gingerbread* (1764), though I have only seen it in an edition by Kendrew of York, where it is alleged to be the work of Tommy Trip. Little Giles desired earnestly to ride in his own coach, and deemed the best means to that end to be the art of reading. He therefore 'lived upon learning' – literally, for his father gave him every day a fresh gingerbread cake ('which he eat up') with the alphabet stamped upon it. A short poem upon an illiterate boy shows the disadvantages of dullness, and the booklet ends with Watts's poem of thanks for Christian parentage.

The Easter Gift (1764) lived long enough to be one of Catnach's wares. It is, in his version, simply an illustrated edition of 'A was an Archer'. Welsh had not seen a Newbery copy. *The Whitsuntide Gift* and *The Valentine's Gift* were probably published also in 1764 and the sub-title of the latter is worth notice: 'A Plan to enable Children of all Sizes and Denominations to behave with Honour, Integrity, and Humanity. Very necessary in a Trading Nation.' On the back of the title-page is a suggestive note, which provides some public evidence of family differences:

The Public are desired to observe, that F. Newbery, at the Corner of St Paul's Church Yard and Ludgate-Street, has not the least Concern in any of the late Mr John Newbery's Entertaining Books for Children; and, to prevent having paltry compilations obtruded on them, instead of Mr John Newbery's useful Publications, they are desired to be particularly careful to apply for them to T. Carnan and F. Newbery, Jun. (Successors to the late Mr John Newbery) at Number 65, near the Bar in St Paul's Church Yard.

After a rambling account of St Valentine and his day, a not less diffuse story tells of the presents a good little boy received on that anniversary. They were practically an entire set of Mr Newbery's juvenile publications. The narrative ambles on into some information (true or false) about animals (in which a horse is addressed 'in the language of the Houyhnhnms') and about birds. It is given by 'Old Zigzag', and among the birds the names Flapsy and Pecksy occur – Mrs Trimmer may have borrowed them a generation later for her *Robins*. There are ninety pages of this formless stuff, much of which is obviously concocted to allow the use of old woodblocks. The rest of the book (122 pages, plus a list of publications) consists of 'lessons from King Solomon', a fable, and some prayers. For a Newbery production, it is ill-printed. It was bound in paper boards with a printed pictorial design, and cost sixpence. Lumsden of Glasgow did a cheap version about 1810, which is textually the same up to page 72 of Newbery's edition, but then stops short.

The Fairing or, a Golden Toy for Children (1764?) I have not seen in a Newbery edition although several were published, and in 1781 'P. Charles, A. Allardice and J. Thomas, in French-gate' published a version with the same full title. The text is as incoherent as that of *The Valentine's Gift*, but it has the merit of including the stories of Dick Whittington and Puss in Boots. The blocks look as if they came out of an inferior chapbook stock.

3

A study of these works reveals much of the outlook of Newbery himself and of the society whose petty needs he visualized so successfully. It is a purely middle-class and purely English society, and mainly urban in temper – unusually so in that agricultural century. Its folk were timid about making mistakes or doing unsuitable things, yet confident and happy about their own judgments; very particular about details, and determined not to be 'put upon' over them, anxious to succeed reasonably, but distrustful of ambition; extremely conventional and unimaginative, not nearly so quick-minded as Newbery himself, yet possessed, like him, of the greatest tolerance and placable humour.

They are little books about little things. The publication by which Newbery's name is best known, however, is not far off being a great one. Its spaciousness lies in what its author unconsciously put into it, not in what he meant it to be. *Goody Two-Shoes* is an extraordinary picture of rural England painted by, so to speak, a sentimental democratic conservative. As a children's book, it is utterly dead, and but for its one-time repute would be forgotten. It had no virtue of survival in its ideas, in its events, in its characters, or in its style. But great and lovable men praised it and remembered it – through the mist of years. And it was almost the first piece of original English fiction deliberately written to amuse children only.

As for its fame and alleged charm, Lamb is witness enough. But in such matters Charles Lamb was not necessarily a trustworthy guide. He wrote to Coleridge:

21. The progress of Goody Two-Shoes through various paper-covered editions:
(a) An unusual pair of paper board covers with woodcut decorations and fleurons for a Carnan edition of 1783.

Goody Two Shoes is almost out of print. Mrs Barbauld's stuff has banished all the old classics of the nursery . . . Science has succeeded to Poetry no less in the little walks of children than with men–: Is there no possibility of averting this sore evil? Think what you would have been now, if instead of being fed with Tales and old wives fables in childhood, you had been crammed with Geography and Natural History!

He had in mind, in memory, I think, the old familiar faces we all know – the folk in books who were never there in reality: the Robinson without prayers, the Red Riding Hood without a moral, the Aesop with no prosaic doubts about a fox's greed for 'raisins'. The sad truth is that Mrs Barbauld's books contained as much semi-detective 'stuff' as 'science', and some of them were in poetical prose which Elia himself might have respected; while *Goody Two-Shoes* itself was utterly remote from the region of 'tales and old wives' fables'. It was the very foundation of the Moral Tale – of *Mrs Leicester's School,* for example – and of the unimaginative virtue-is-its-own-reward *and* virtue-pays-in-the-long-run type of

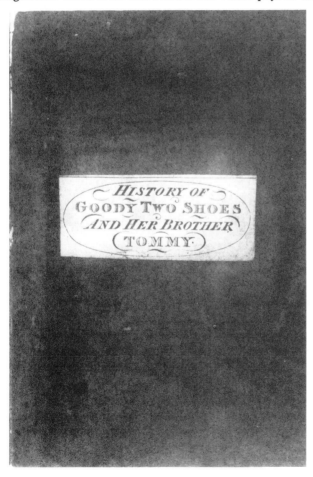

(b) A chapbook edition with plain paper wrappers and printed paper label, published *c.* 1810 by Lumsden of Glasgow, a firm noted for the elegance of their cheap books.

(c) A Victorian edition published by James Burns in 1845, with covers printed in three colours from wood blocks by Gregory, Collins and Reynolds – an early example of colour printing.

story which, in spirit, Lamb so thoroughly abhorred. It was to Coleridge he condemned that sort of thing, not to Godwin, for whom he himself wrote the same kind of stuff.

The book is not easily procured now, even in late editions or reprints. It really *is* dead, and no amount of sentiment can anyhow revive it, because it is not even a good readable story of its kind, whether Goldsmith wrote it or not. It is entirely of its period, and died with it, though, as is the wont of a popular children's book, once established, it loosed its grip very slowly. But more than most children's books it is an historical document. It must be summarized rather fully.

A unique copy of what is probably the first edition of 1765 is now in the library at the British Museum.[6] The title runs:

The History of Little Goody Two-Shoes; Otherwise called, Mrs Margery Two-Shoes. With the Means by which she acquired her Learning and Wisdom, and in consequence thereof her Estate; set forth at large for the Benefit of those,

> *Who from a State of Rags and Care,*
> *And having Shoes but half a Pair;*
> *Their Fortune and their Fame would fix,*
> *And gallop in a Coach and Six.*

See the Original Manuscript in the *Vatican* at *Rome*, and the Cuts by *Michael Angelo*. Illustrated with the Comments of our great modern Critics.

(d) A modern eight-page chapbook from Raphael Tuck's *Tiny Tuck* series, sold to be read in air raid shelters *c.* 1940!

All that in a little dumpy volume for sixpence. The dedication, 'To All Young Gentlemen and Ladies Who are good, or intend to be good', comes from 'their old Friend in St Paul's Church-Yard'. Since the year was 1765 Newbery had just come of age as a children's publisher in London, and might be pardoned for calling himself an 'old friend'.

The narrative is from the start native and topical. Margery's surname was Meanwell, and her father was a farmer of one of twelve farms in a manor, whose Lord was good: but he died, and one Sir Timothy Gripe had the estate, and let all twelve farms to Farmer Graspall 'as the Leases expired'. Mr Meanwell's was the last to fall in, and Sir Timothy tried to force him out by building a brick kiln and 'a Dog-kennel' in his orchard. Meanwell went to law and won, and had to repeat the remedy three times, till he could afford no more litigation and had to suffer the 'Nuisances'. He had, in fact, been forced into debt, and Sir Timothy turned him and his family – wife, Margery and her brother Tommy – 'out of doors, without any of the Necessaries of Life to support them'. A page or two earlier the editor had commented on the Gripe–Graspall régime:

Judge, oh kind, humane and courteous Reader, what a terrible Situation the poor must be in, when this covetous Man was perpetual Overseer, and every Thing for their Maintenance was drawn from his hard Heart and cruel Hand. But he was not only perpetual Overseer, but perpetual Churchwarden; and judge, oh ye Christians, what State the Church must be in when supported by a man without Religion or Virtue. He was also perpetual Surveyor of the Highways, and what Sort of Roads he kept up for the Convenience of Travellers, those best know who have had the Misfortune to be obliged to pass through that Parish. – Complaints indeed were made, but to what Purpose are Complaints, when brought against a Man, who can hunt, drink, and smoke with the Lord of the Manor, who is also the Justice of Peace?

Was that entirely fiction? It comes from the Introduction, which is typographically part of the main text. At its end the 'editor' makes the reader ask 'Do you intend this for Children, Mr Newbery?' Mr Newbery answers that 'this may come from another Hand', and is for 'Children of six Feet high', and is called for because of 'the unaccountable and diabolical Scheme which many Gentlemen now give into, of laying a Number of Farms into one, and very often of a whole Parish into one Farm; which in the End must reduce the common People to a State of Vassalage . . . and will in Time depopulate the Kingdom.' Did John Newbery write that, the farmer's boy of Berkshire, who liked better to produce books for little children than to plough, and sow, and reap, and mow, under Squire Gripe or Churchwarden Graspall? Or was it the chronicler of the *Deserted Village*:

> One only master grasps the whole domain,
> And half a tillage stints thy smiling plain . . .
> But a bold peasantry, their country's pride,
> When once destroy'd, can never be supplied.

Or was it yet another hand, that of Giles Jones,[7] who also wrote for Newbery, and had a grandson who was Principal Librarian of the British Museum? No one knows.

To return to Margery Meanwell, *soi-disante* Two-Shoes. Her father very shortly succumbed to a fever, 'in a Place where Dr James's Powder was not to be had', and her mother died a few days later of a broken heart. Margery and Tommy lived, after the manner of orphans, on hedge-berries and the kindness of the poor, until (the heading of Chapter II) 'how and about Mr Smith'. Smith was a kind of Parson Adams, who sent Tommy, properly clad, to sea, and gave Margery two shoes instead of the poor one left her after the eviction, and wished to take her into his family. But Graspall 'threatened to reduce his Tythes if he kept her', and Gripe ordered her to be sent back to her relations – who were 'rich and ashamed to own such a poor little ragged Girl' – so that she might not be 'harboured' in the parish; that is, be a charge upon it or even gain a 'settlement' in it, if she were left to her own resources.

At this point her career, as a practical matter, becomes obscure, for she was turned out, by order, yet managed to learn the alphabet from children going home from school, and set up as a 'trotting Tutoress' herself, and got paying pupils. (It is as vague as Peggotty or Little Nell and her grandfather setting off into the wide wide world, to live on air like the camelions of the *Bestiary*.) There are various moral incidents as a result, including one which is meant to convince the reader that 'the tales of Ghosts, Witches and Fairies are the Frolicks of a distempered Brain. No wise Man ever saw either of them'. (Alas for the *Robin Goodfellow* published by Newbery!) Finally, after overhearing thieves planning to rob Gripe's house, and so being enabled to return him good for evil, she became 'Principal of a Country College': in other words, of a dame-school rather like that in Shenstone's *Schoolmistress*.

Very much of Part II of the story, which begins at this point, is taken up with her progress as a teacher, and her special efforts to stop cruelty to animals; a welcome and constant feature throughout the history of real children's books, even when it was only introduced to enforce the *noblesse oblige* doctrine of the superiority of man to 'the brute creation'. One passage deserves quotation. The children buried a pet dormouse, with this

> *Epitaph on a* Dormouse, *really written by a little* Boy.
> I
> In Paper Case,
> Hard by this Place,
> Dead a poor Dormouse lies;
> And soon or late,
> Summoned by Fate,
> Each Prince, each Monarch dies.
> II
> Ye Sons of Verse,
> While I rehearse,
> Attend instructive Rhyme;
> No Sins had *Dor*
> To answer for;
> Repent of yours in Time.

Was that quite what would have been composed in one of those amateur academies which Goldsmith in *The Bee* condemned so roundly? And is it the work of John Newbery or one of his less-known hacks? Who *did* write it?

Margery went through some strange adventures, including an accusation of witchcraft. It is plain that the author, in writing this part of the book, had in mind the chapbooks about Fortunatus and Friar Bacon, and, to all appearances, was using the familiar names to make better stuff pass current. In due time Mrs Two-Shoes won a squire for her husband, and, at the wedding itself, there suddenly appeared 'a Gentleman richly dressed and bedizened with Lace' – who, of course, was Tommy Meanwell, returned from overseas laden with wealth. Margery lived in happy marriage for six years, when her husband died and she inherited his wealth. Severe misfortunes came upon Sir Timothy Gripe and Graspall, and she helped them; and she gave loaves and books and other useful presents to the poor, and especially 'so many Acres of Land' to be planted yearly with potatoes: and so died, mourned by all.

An Appendix, most of which only appears in later editions, drags in, with small relevance, a kind of fable about 'The Golden Dream' – in which everything turns to gold for an avaricious child, as for Midas – and the adventures of Tommy Meanwell, and an anecdote about a dog, and a list of the books 'usually read by the Scholars of Mrs Two-Shoes': that is to say, Newbery's own publications; and, last of all, a table of the medicines he sold, including Dr James's Fever Powders.

Was Lamb justified? Is it a book for children of his day or of our day? Is it not, unconsciously, a piece of serious English history? All the conditions of life so clear in it, or nearly all, are gone. It has an easy flow of narrative, but it bears little relation to anything children know, experience, or even learn in school now. Margery and her circle are not human beings: they are the vehicle of small, intense, and at the time very real social ideas. But no one can deny to *Goody Two-Shoes* the title of a genuine children's book.

4

Newbery had twenty-three years of well-won prosperity in London. It is impossible not to believe that, whoever he employed, his own personality really is in these books: and the best of his personality, at that, for except for such notable things as his interest in *The Vicar of Wakefield*, his activities, in original or quasi-original work, were nearly all directed towards children. He was enlightened enough, in a literary and aesthetic sense. He knew good work when he saw it. He improved the standard of cheap publication in every way. But I see him most clearly still as the two greatest of his friends and protégés portrayed him as the Jack Whirler of Johnson, and as the immortal figure of *The Vicar of Wakefield*. Dr Primrose, it will be remembered, lay sick at 'the Wells', and in want of money. His needs were supplied by a traveller, who stopped to take a cursory refreshment. This person was no other than the philanthropic bookseller in St Paul's Churchyard, who has written so many little books for children: he called himself their friend; but he was the friend of all mankind. He was no sooner alighted, but he was in haste to be gone; for he was ever on business of the utmost importance, and was at that time actually compiling materials for the history of one Mr Thomas Trip. I immediately recollected this good-natured man's red pimpled face; for he had published for me against the Deuterogamists of the age; and from him I borrowed a few pieces, to be paid at my return.

No publisher and no author need desire a more lasting monument; and perhaps the relations of few of them have deserved it in so generous measure. 'The friend of all mankind . . . To be paid at my return.' It never was.

5

If Newbery had – and took – the advantage of seeing what material for children's books had accumulated in the preceding two centuries and yet lay undeveloped, he was likewise fortunate in the economic and social conditions for his experiments. The publishing trade was becoming something like what we know today, though the publisher and bookseller, in the chief centres, were as often as not the same man – the producer and the distributor at once. The printer had been the predominant partner in the seventeenth century. The mechanical side of production was then the important thing, with censorship as a capricious deterrent against too great activity in any direction, and imperfect, troublous communications as a practical hindrance. By Newbery's time, however, the 'general reader' had come into existence. The Tonsons, Lintot, Cave, Longman, Cadell, and a little later the first John Murray, were all men of a different type from the printer–publishers of the Restoration period, and they had a changed, a wider, and a more generous-minded public for customers. Salesmen of printed matter had to realize this. Distribution, or what would now be called marketing, over and above mere hand-to-hand peddling, began to be a visible problem of the book business. Even a 'pretty gilded toy' for girls and boys needed a strategic mind to display it to the best advantage before the eyes of the Georgian modern world.

It is evident that either by instinct or by hard thinking (probably instinct) John Newbery perceived this. He grasped one great permanent truth of the publishing trade – that invasion of the market must be constant and continuous. It is useless to have an idea for a book or two and then stop. He comprehended also the further truth, that the publisher must not underrate his public for long if he wishes to achieve more than a temporary success. The number alone of John Newbery's juvenile books – as compared with the output of any other firm in his lifetime or for at least a decade after his death – is proof of this quality in his mental equipment.

But an even stronger testimony to his acumen and personality is to be found in his improvement in the format of his little books. They were all *his*. Even today, if you have but a slight experience of such wares as they changed through the ages, you can identify a Newbery 'juvenile' at sight. He set a standard in detail throughout. He often went to the expense of copperplate engravings. His engraved script title-pages, with their whorls and curly tails and serifs and intricate ampersands, if nothing great typographically, had a new charm all their own. Binding, again, was one of his most gracious gifts to the nursery library. The custom of issuing fully bound volumes still needs investigation, in spite of Mr Michael Sadleir's study of *The Evolution of Publishers' Binding Styles* (1930): there are too many examples of Newbery books in existence for them all to depend on individual retailers who bound up sheets at their own will. A number are in plain calf of no high quality. Some – before 1774, I think, but cannot be sure; 1774 is Mr Sadleir's date for Francis Newbery – are in half green vellum (backs)[8] on stout green paper boards. Still more, however, are in the charming gilt and flowered 'Dutch' paper; a thinnish layer of paper with floral patterns not unlike those of a Morris wall-paper, coloured in red, blue, green and gold. The design was either produced on a very stiff ground which was itself the whole binding, or mounted on the thinnest cardboard. The best quality was embossed or stamped, like a Lincrusta Walton wall-covering: the cheaper 'range' was coloured flat. All the colouring was, apparently, done by hand. When the covers were new, the effect was gay and delicious. The colours, by time and use, faded first to the mellowness of old chintz, and in extreme old age, to an almost dignified uniform mahogany brown, which, however, if the paper had been originally embossed, often retained the relief effect and looked like a carved pew-end. The paper is no longer made for ordinary purposes.*

Newbery himself did not live long enough to use the work of Thomas Bewick as an illustrator, for Bewick was only born in 1753. But, as has been said, his successors, in alliance with Saint of Newcastle, quickly became aware of the great wood-engraver's virtues and, more especially, those of his brother John Bewick. John Newbery, so far as can be judged by results, had old woodblocks copied and recut, but he evidently employed original artists as well. He was in fact the first major publisher to conceive of the illustrated book for children as a specially produced article, not a mausoleum of any blocks and types that were handy.

If you add to those technical improvements, trifling though they may seem, and trifling through they are taken singly, the robustness of character which runs through the very text of the books, whatever their absurdities, you get some measure of John Newbery as a benefactor of children. He is like the prevailing wind of southern England – the roughish, comfortable, yet not quite calculable fresh south-westerly breeze of spring and autumn. It is an open wind, with no real vice in it: it is neither a mean little draught nor hot air. There is a

---

*   Uncut pieces can now and then be picked up by lucky collectors; Claud Lovat Fraser gave me one. In *Pages and Pictures from Forgotten Children's Books* (1898–9) A. W. Tuer gave his readers a little specimen of the genuine paper, from a small stock he had. He also furnished – in that book and *Stories from Old-Fashioned Children's Books* (1899–1900) – a few trade details.

real difference between the gusts from the Bible and Sun and the few that came from different quarters.

6

Indeed these others were rare and infrequent, whatever their quality. There seems to be no record whatever of any other publication for children issued by the M. Lawrence who in 1715 put forth Isaac Watts's poems. Cooper of the nursery rhymes is not much better known in the infancy market. Cadell and others entered it only casually. Yet the trade was not wholly in Newbery's hands. Certain publications suggest that more children's books – real ones – were in existence under George II than has been suspected. They have vanished from record, to a great extent; perhaps, through the heavy mortality in these circles, vanished also as material paper and ink.

But such works, with their forgotten popularity, accentuate rather than diminish Newbery's eminence when they do appear. The market – the social environment, as I prefer to call it – had come into existence, and more than one vendor came forward with a desire to take advantage of it, and built a little booth, or sold a chance juvenile book at the corner of a general stall. But only Newbery, at first, set up a large permanent shop. It was not till the last quarter of the eighteenth century, as the Bible and Sun copyrights ran out or were sold (wholly or in part shares) by his heirs, that other publishers saw their full opportunity. They not only borrowed, legally or illegally, his ideas and his publications, but they found original authors of their own – or authors found them: it is difficult to say which. The most vigorous among the early newcomers was John Marshall.

Marshall, as has been suggested, is something of a mystery in the story of the publishing trade. So far I have been unable to prove any clear connection between the present man and others of the same surname before and after. All that can be said of this John Marshall is that he was in business in 1780 at no. 4 Aldermary Churchyard, London, in the heart of the chapbook manufacturing district: that in or about 1787 he had a shop at 17 Queen Street, Cheapside, moving in 1806, or perhaps a little earlier, to another at 140 Fleet Street, where he – or his firm under the same name – remained in business until at least 1828 (still retaining the Aldermary churchyard address as well); and that he published practically nothing but children's books – of a good type, not mere leaflets for the Running Stationers.

That last fact, with the evidence of his continuity drawn from dated imprints, is the striking point. Marshall's authors are really important in the history of children's books (most of them are dealt with in Chapter x below). He got into touch with them by steps not now to be traced, and he kept them and was responsible for nearly all their juvenile work. He started, perhaps, with

22. Not the least of John Marshall's contributions to the new, imaginative mode of publishing children's books lay in his exploitation of ideas related to the Locke–Cooper–Newbery play-approach to reading. Along with the games and puzzles that publishers were developing (see below pp. 150-1) he marketed a variety of boxed books and cards designed to appeal to children's liking for such things.

Here is shown his model book-case containing the sixteen little volumes of the *Infant's Library* (1800?) which included an alphabet book, books about games and pastimes and *A Short History of England*, which took the place of an index volume.

something of Newbery's impetuous anonymity and pseudonymity, and those who wrote for him disguised themselves after the fashion of the time. But they kept their identity, and were visible figures in the nursery adventure. The author, as well as the publisher, of children's books had arrived as a citizen of the republic of literature, with responsibilities, rights, and compatriots of his own tribe.
of literature, with responsibilities, rights, and compatriots of his own tribe.

Between 1780 and 1800 the publishers who gave special attention to this strong new branch of the book-trade grew numerous. Notable among them were Stockdale, of Piccadilly, the publisher of *Sandford and Merton;* Joseph Johnson (well known for his connection with Cowper), who issued Maria Edgeworth's *Parent's Assistant;* my own ancestors, who started in 1787; Dean and Munday, whom I mention later; Vernor and Hood, who often worked in association with Elizabeth Newbery in her later years; Baldwin Cradock and Joy, Taylor and Hessey, Lackington the resplendent; and the older general firms like Longman and Rivington had also departments for children's books. It was a wide gateway that John Newbery opened to the merchants of *Literae Juniores.*

BRIEF BOOK LIST

The standard work on Newbery is Charles Welsh's *Life*, already mentioned – *A Bookseller of the Last* [i.e. eighteenth] *Century* (London, 1885). See also his small monographs, *On Some of the Books for Children of the Last Century*, and *On Coloured Books for Children* (The Sette of Odd Volumes, privately printed Opuscula, nos. 11 and 13; London, 1886 and 1887). See also:

[E.] *Newbery's Catalogue of Instructive and Amusing Publications* (London, 1800).

Goody Two-Shoes. Facsimile reprint of 1766 edn, with Introduction by Charles Welsh (London, 1881).

A Pretty Book of Pictures for Little Masters and Misses. Reprint of 15th edn, with Bewick's illustrations. Saint, Newcastle, 1779. Introduction, etc. by Edwin Pearson (London, 1867).

Dobson, Henry Austin. *Eighteenth Century Vignettes*, 1st ser. (London, 1892). 'An Old London Bookseller'.

Newbery (Ralph, John and Francis) and John Harris are all in *D.N.B.*, treated by Charles Welsh. For Goldsmith and others, see *D.N.B.* and *C.H.E.L.* For Goldsmith-–Newbery and Goldsmith's children's books, add Iolo Aneurin Williams, *Seven Eighteenth Century Bibliographies* (London, 1924).

The Bewicks, Thomas and John, are a special branch of study in the history of engraving and book-illustration, and cannot be dealt with here. The most widely quoted reference book on their work is the Rev. Thomas Hugo's *Bewick Collector* (London, 1866; Supplement, 1868) but it should be used with caution. [An authoritative edition of Thomas Bewick's *Memoir* is that by Iain Bain (London, 1975).]

Supplement

S. Roscoe's work on Newbery, which supersedes much of Welsh, has already been referred to in the notes: *John Newbery and his Successors 1740–1814; a bibliography* (Wormley, 1973). A more discursive account of Newbery's activity may be found in M. F. Thwaite's introduction to a photographic reprint of *A Little Pretty Pocket-Book* (London, 1966), which also includes a short listing of John Newbery's children's publications. Of exceptional interest for a view of author–publisher relations in the post–J. Newbery firms see: M. J. P. Weedon, 'Richard Johnson and the Successors to John Newbery', an account and transcript of the Johnson Day-books in *The Library*, 5th ser. vol. IV, June 1949, no. 1, pp. 25–63. Several other reproductions of Newbery books have also been published, but without the detailed background given in Mrs Thwaite's edition of the *Pocket-Book*. See, for instance, [R. Johnson], *Juvenile Trials for Robbing Orchards . . .* (1786), introduced by Kathryn Dixon (Bern, 1973), and *The Fairing* (1768), introduced by Brian Alderson, with *The History of Little Goody Two-Shoes* (1765) introduced by Michael Platt (New York and London, 1977).

The only study of Thomas Boreman is a rather dated, privately issued booklet: Wilbur Macey Stone, *The Gigantick Histories of Thomas Boreman* (Portland, Maine, 1933). Some supplementary information does occur in Muir, *English Children's Books* (London, 1954) and a photolithographic reprint of the two volumes of *The Gigantick History of the Two Famous Giants* has been published, introduced by Michael Platt (New York and London, 1977).

CHAPTER IX

The Theorists: Thomas Day, the Edgeworths, and French Influence

I

Newbery was probably acquainted with the actual texts of Locke's *Thoughts Concerning Education*, though he might easily have quoted from them almost verbatim without knowing it. It might also, however, be argued plausibly that he admired and was familiar with Rousseau's writings too. In the preface to the *Little Pretty Pocket-Book*, so often quoted already, he advocates 'reasoning' as the only way to cure faults: certainly not complaisance – 'I would lay down this as a Maxim with him, that [a child] should never have anything he cryed for.' It looks as if that sentence must have been inspired by this passage: 'Si le besoin l'a fait parler, vous devez le savoir, et faire aussitôt ce qu'il demande; mais céder quelque chose à ses larmes, c'est l'exciter à en verser, c'est lui apprendre à douter de votre bonne volonté, et à croire que l'importunité peut plus sur vous que la bienveillance.' Unfortunately for those who see in such coincidences the contact between pioneer philosophy and the ordinary man, Newbery's sentence was in print eighteen years before the publication of Rousseau's *Émile*, from which the French quotation comes.

However, there can be no doubt whatever that in the period immediately after Newbery's death, the works of Rousseau had a very direct effect upon English books for children. Many writers acknowledged their debt to *Émile*. The Third-Georgian stories based upon it, however, enjoy under George V a strange death in life. They are as it were in cold storage. The best of them, Maria Edgeworth's, are highly esteemed by most critics and some children, and remain in print, though they are possibly not read so widely or so often as they deserve. But when they *are* read, it is not for their purpose. It is because they are really good *stories*, told in simple and delightful English, with frequent humour.

Such an unfair kind of survival can be readily understood and pardoned if one glances again at the supreme example of Miss Edgeworth's delicate didactic art. *The Purple Jar** is perhaps the most famous though not the 'best' of her tales. Why is it also one of the most unfailingly readable?

---

* The story first appeared in *The Parent's Assistant* (Part II; Vol. I, 1796) but is here quoted from its later re-issue in the series 'Early Lessons' Part III, *Rosamond Part I* (1801). The dates are a long time after Newbery's, but the philosophy is that of the period of his death, and the lives of Richard Lovell Edgeworth (1744–1817) and Thomas Day (1748–89) overlap his: Maria was born in the year of his death, 1767.

Rosamond, it will be remembered, was a nice, intelligibly thoughtless, intelligibly good little girl – own cousin in spirit to Alice of Wonderland, really, but not allowed to see wonders – who was to have a present given her by her logically minded mother. She craved the glowing purple jar in an apothecary's window. Today her imagination and colour-sense would probably lead to psychological study of her temperament. In the reign of George III the grown-ups thought in terms of daily working life. Rosamond's mother suggested a new pair of shoes instead, hoping that reason would prevail and indicate the joy, the practical value, of frugality. But her views were not adopted by her child, and, as a philosopher, she gave in, and, after saying in advance 'I told you so', left Nature to do her worst. The bright vessel, gaily bought, disappointed the poor little girl by containing nothing but coloured water and a smell. While she repented of her rash choice, her shoes wore out, and 'grew worse and worse, till at last she could neither run, dance, jump, nor walk in them'. Finally, her father would have taken her 'to a glass-house which she had long wished to see'. But that simple pleasure was denied her, for she was slipshod, and her worn shoe would no longer stay on her foot. Nature *had* done her worst, had taught her cruel lesson: the wraith of a purple jar, footwear fordone, no spectacle of a crystal palace: 'Rosamond coloured and retired. "Oh mamma", said she, as she took off her hat, "how I wish that I had chosen the shoes – They would have been of so much more use to me than that jar; however, I am sure – no, not quite sure – but, I hope, I shall be wiser another time." ' That paragraph is almost an epitome of Maria Edgeworth's books for children. You have read the story because of the excellence of the narrative: you wanted to see what would happen – you cannot help it, in spite of the oppressive certainty that a calamity with a vivid moral will befall the injudicious little girl. You hate the mother: she ought to have glass eyes and a wooden tail, like the new mother in Mrs W. K. Clifford's terrific *Anyhow Stories* of a century or so later. You know she is right, and you loathe rectitude accordingly. But then Rosamond should not be such a silly little fool. And besides, she ought to have been told the truth about the gleaming bottle; and surely she had more than one pair of shoes, and anyhow, are shoes – clothing which it is a parent's duty to provide – a present? In fact, everything is unsatisfactory from half a dozen points of view, though you simply cannot help reading the easily flowing story, with its occasional odd slyness of humour, its touches of dramatic vision (the jar itself is a property from a stage fairy-land), its simplicity so unforced; until, in the last sentence, you become aware (though you must have known it all the time) that Rosamond is a 'real live' child. 'I am sure – *no, not quite sure* . . .' Thank heaven she is not, after all, the horrid little prig her mother wished her to be. You actually become fond of her. But you continue to defeat the author's end by disliking the parents.

I do not propose to do Miss Edgeworth the injustice of further quotation. *The Purple Jar* contains her moral outlook, her 'values', more explicitly as well as implicitly than some of her other tales. Her Frank, perhaps, is a less human central figure than her Rosamond (both appear frequently), and to that extent a more cumbrous vehicle of purpose. Her single figures, like Susan, Hal Gresham, and others, are less weighted with protruding qualities; and her grown-up 'supers' are almost always delightful. But the moral outlook in her works, or at least in the best of them, is the entirely unessential part of them to us today. If you were set down to read *Simple Susan* or *The Basket Woman* or even *Lazy Lawrence*, without knowing beforehand that they had a didactic purpose, were based on a philosophic theory of child-nature, and were produced in circumstances which made their intention their most important feature – if you picked them up with a child's *tabula rasa* for your mind, in fact, you would go straight through them and be enchanted by the writer's skill as well as by her humanity.

But that is not at all what Miss Edgeworth meant. It is what she achieved because she is one of the most natural story-tellers who ever wrote English. She is also one of the most observant and the most easily eclectic. There might have been no limit to her success in the novel of domestic life – Mr E. V. Lucas has admirably called her 'the novelist of the nursery', for her children's tales – if it had not been for her dogmatic and all-pervasive father. But, as has also been pointed out, she might never have written at all without his philanthropic stimulus. He made her use children as the vehicle of progress. They were to grow in the delightful prairie of nature – though with monitors conveniently placed to see that nature was properly appreciated. They were to be little Émiles and Émilies, as Rousseau hoped; but Marmontel must be ready with *Moral Tales*. It is astonishing that with prepossessions and ideals so strongly and sincerely held Maria Edgeworth ever wrote anything that children could read save under duress or mental starvation (there was, at the time, a chance of that alternative). But she did, and her tales can still be accepted by simple hearts with unaffected pleasure. 'Love me and laugh at me as you have done many is the year', she wrote at the age of fifty-nine to her aunt. She was lovable all through her long, cheerful life; and if you sometimes laugh at her, you laugh with her a hundred times more often.

2

It is unnecessary to give full particulars of her life and books: a great deal has been written about both, and most of it is well worth reading. As compared with the most striking earlier figure in the field of children's books, John Newbery – or the stock author who may or may not have been Newbery, but at any rate carried out his ideas – she obviously possessed genius and he did not: not even if he himself wrote *Goody Two-Shoes*. But the essential difference lies in what I have just said – that she was thinking of real children, not of hypostatized moral qualities. With that human realism there went almost inevitably a sense of humour, which few business men possess, or possessed under George III.

Newbery, in so far as his mind genuinely visualized cousin Sue or Tommy Trip at all, was thinking in types, not in characters. He was flexible and acute enough in affairs. he chose and used his instruments – Christopher Smart, Smollett, Goldsmith – with a tolerant, wise shrewdness. But when it came to writing fiction, with something of a moral purpose to be kept up, he could only pose lay-figures.

Maria Edgeworth, on the other hand, had the essential humanity which Rousseau at his best inspired. She wanted her children to be natural; and if her conception of nature was Irish, full of exceptions and even failures, so much the better. Her characters never became abstractions: they had to work out their own salvation as human beings, not in a groove.

When one considers her social position as compared with John Newbery's, the difference of temperament more or less explains itself. He was a country farm-boy turned tradesman: an honourable thing to be. But such a man could not live easily in a world of accepted culture: he must have felt many awkward moments with men and women of greater elegance and education. He could never have drawn a Rosamond, because he probably was never familiarly acquainted with a nice little girl of her class. But she was natural to Miss Edgeworth of Edgeworthstown, the daughter of Richard Lovell Edgeworth, a volcanic squire as well as a magnificent gentleman. And Edgeworth had eighteen children who survived infancy.

That is not a snobbish differentiation. It is historically of social importance. It means that a new kind of writer for children is appearing: not a schoolmaster, or a moral fanatic, or a hack trying to make money, nor yet an eager sincere philanthropist who had a notion of making philanthropy pay its way. Except the Puritans – and Isaac Watts, if he be not called a Puritan – the writers of children's books hitherto, such as they were, had not been men of high culture or of a quickly established rank. Nor had they – again with some exceptions – been women, which is an important point, for by now we are in the heyday of the Blue-Stockings. It is that fact that makes Miss Edgeworth's social position significant. Education, as represented by attempts to amuse children out of school, was passing from the grasp, on the one hand, of the usher and the dame (Margery Two-Shoes grown up) and, on the other, of the nobility and gentry who had had their offspring privately trained for courtliness and good breeding, supplemented by a little useful knowledge. It was rapidly growing into a general domestic habit, like reading for pleasure itself.

That is one change that really came about in the underlying conception of children's books in the middle and later years of George III. They had become a marketable ware under George II. They became a minor social necessity and an expression of general social life under his grandson. Moreover, the fact was recognized by the writers themselves in the daily contacts of life. They knew one another, just as, for two centuries past, the greater writers had had knowledge of one another, as human beings; not merely as echoes of another voice in the

23. A unique trial engraving, possibly by Richard Lovell Edgeworth, for the trial printing of *Practical Education; or, the history of Harry and Lucy*, vol. II, Lichfield . . . 1780. The story was by Edgeworth's wife Honora, who died in that year, and some twenty years were to elapse before Harry and Lucy re-emerged in the series *Early Lessons* (1801–2), by Richard Lovell and his daughter Maria.

wilderness. Maria Edgeworth included in her list of friends and acquaintances such fellow-writers as Mme de Genlis, Mrs Barbauld, Dr Darwin, and later in life, Scott himself. In her circle at Lichfield – or rather, in the circle whence her father drew two of his four wives – moved Dr Butt, the father of Mrs Sherwood, who in her turn, like the Howitts and many other writers, was to meet and mingle with the 'rival' practitioners of her art. The children's author, in fact, was about to be established.

3

But the author with whose life and work the names of Edgeworth and Rousseau are for ever connected was Thomas Day. He and his young friend, the daughter of his contemporary and adviser, shared one philosophy. But whereas Maria Edgeworth was equable in her treatment of Rousseau's doctrine, Day was vehement both in his life and in his writings. His life is tolerably well known. His experiments in marriage, and in educating young females for marriage with himself, form the subject of essays every five years or so by 'prentice writers rediscovering old themes as new. It is enough to say that he tried to bring up a girl on uncontaminated Rousseau lines, with a view to providing himself with a perfect wife, and that, as human nature did not live up to his Garden of Eden principles, the attempt was unsuccessful. He married an heiress instead, and, being rich already, spent money on less fantastic social schemes. He had some hand in Maria Edgeworth's education, though (for he was a mass of contradictions) he was known to have pronounced 'an eloquent philippic against female authorship'. As for his sincerity in Rousseauism, he declared that if all the books in the world were to perish, 'the second book I should wish to save after the Bible would be Rousseau's Emilius'. *Sandford and Merton* (originally meant to be a short story) was his vivacious attempt to present *Émile* in the guise of fiction for English boys.

That great work – for it *is* a great work, in its queer little way – has been laughed at so often, and read as a whole so little in modern times, that some points in it deserve stress. The author, at first anonymous, wrote it because he found that there was a 'total want of proper books to be put into [very young children's] hands, while they are taught the elements of reading'. The only matter in what was provided which he thought suitable was stories from Plutarch and Xenophon, 'some part of *Robinson Crusoe*, and a few passages in the first volume of Mr Brooke's *Fool of Quality*'. Juvenile fiction – 'Mr Newbery's little books' – was inadequate, as Richard Edgeworth said. Fairy-tales were trumpery – 'fantastic visions', not at all 'useful'. The children's book-cupboard seemed almost as bare as Mother Hubbard's, of which, naturally, Day could take no cognizance.

He formed the idea, therefore, of collecting little stories likely to express judicious views of nature and reason, and connecting them together

so that every story might appear to rise naturally out of the subject, and might, for that reason, make the greater impression. To render the relation more interesting to those for whom it was intended, I have introduced two children as the actors, and have endeavoured to make them speak and behave according to the order of nature. As to the histories themselves, I have used the most unbounded licence; altering, curtailing, adding, and generally entirely changing the language, according to the particular views which actuated me in undertaking this work.

The 'two children', of course, were Harry Sandford and Tommy Merton, to whom were added bluff Farmer Sandford, rich Mr Merton, silly Mrs Merton, and the ineffable Barlow. As for their speaking and behaving 'according to the order of nature', it is a little difficult to be sure what Day really thought. There is a famous episode in which Harry threw a glass of wine and water into the face of the arrogant Master Mash. Master Mash, in modern slang, was 'asking for it', and few readers would deem Harry's action unnatural. But when, later on, those wicked boys persuaded Tommy to strike Harry, and call him coward, black-guard, and tell-tale, Harry showed a different nature: '"Master Tommy, Master Tommy, I never should have thought it possible you could have treated me in this unworthy manner": then covering his face with both his hands, he burst into an agony of crying.' It looks as if Day had not really thought out the discrepancies between natural, almost animal, impulses and reactions, and the sentimental 'Nature' of Arcadia and the eighteenth-century drama.

He comes into conflict with this difficulty more than once. Tommy, in Part III of the book, does not get a very satisfactory reply from Mr Barlow to his awkward questions (my italics) 'Are *all* the poor in this country better than the rich?' Newbery, obviously, had had no difficulty about it; they all were. But Mr Barlow had to hedge. And Tommy himself found Nature perplexing: 'Unfortunately for Tommy, his vivacity was greater than his reason, and his taste for imitation was continually leading him into some mischief or misfortune.' For instance, out of pure kindness, he offered bread to a sucking pig, whose lady mother disapproved and rolled him in the mud. It was disconcerting to be told that he must learn all about pig nature before indulging his own altruism again.

The story-teller in Day, with no sense of the ludicrous, but with a genuine desire to please, is at war with the propagandist very frequently. He probably expected this charge, for in his Preface he says:

I have only to add, that I hope nobody will consider this work as a treatise on education. I have unavoidably expressed some ideas upon this subject, and introduced a conversation not one word of which any child will understand; but all the rest of the book is intended to form and interest the minds of children; it is to them that I have written.

The 'ideas' are clearly those contained in pages 18–35 of Part I (first edition). Here Mr Barlow, after saying to Mr Merton that they need not discuss finance, because he came 'as a friend rather than a schoolmaster', expounds at great length his views on natural simplicity – the simplicity of the Christian faith, the simplicity desirable in daily life.

The First Part was published in 1783, the Second in 1786, the Third, with a frontispiece by Stothard, in 1789. It was immediately successful, and was translated into French by Berquin in four volumes in 1798, 'an VI de la République'. The stories which Day strung together were themselves old – Androcles the inevitable is there – but the framework of English country life is relatively fresh. It too, however, is conventional in conception. Not only were the poor good, and most of the rich idle, self-satisfied, and even wicked, but there appears a subordinate character, one Squire Chace, who must have been a close kinsman to Squire Gripe, the persecutor of the Two-Shoes household. Mr Barlow may have appeared a new creation at the time. But the good clergyman-tutor was a stock figure then or soon afterwards. None, however, except the later reincarnation in Mrs Sherwood's *Henry Milner* (1822) or the pastor in Catherine Sinclair's adult novel *Modern Society* (1837), has approached Barlow in complacent and devastating priggishness.*

---

* Day also wrote *The History of Little Jack* (in Stockdale's *Children's Miscellany*, 1788), and, with J. L. Bicknell, *The Dying Negro* (1773). Little Jack was a kind of Wild Boy, suckled by a goat; the Negro a Noble Savage.

Priggishness: from our point of view only. Day was writing with an ideal. It must be remembered – in respect not only of Day but of nearly all children's writers for fifty years after *Sandford and Merton* appeared – that neither writers nor readers expected anything but didacticism. To be good, very very good, not mundanely happy, was a spontaneous desire. Naughtiness aforethought, the enjoyment of mischief or even soulless levity, would have been utterly shocking to any normal child before about 1840.

And it is impossible to get away from the fact that a plain reader, given that now half-unintelligible prepossession, would find *Sandford and Merton* interesting. Like so many minor writers of the Georgian era, Day could tell a story, and the book is just as full of varied incident as *The Swiss Family Robinson*, if it lacks the exotic charm of desert-insularity. Even a contemner of smugness might feel a dreadful fascination in wondering what Tommy will be 'crimed' for next (the Army slang is useful). *Eric, or Little by Little*, seventy years later, had the same dual attraction. It draws the reader who is almost sodden with morality, and it amazes the irreverent continuously.

4

Apart from this deliberate propagation of Rousseau, the influence of France was pervasive through the moral tale, which had been fully developed on the Continent. It was based on educational theory, but not so definitely in detail on Rousseau's. The two chief purveyors of it, for English purposes, were Mme de Genlis and Arnaud Berquin.* Maria Edgeworth knew Mme de Genlis personally: Berquin probably translated *Sandford and Merton* into French, and was responsible for an odd *Petit Grandisson* [*sic*], an abridgement of Richardson for children (1787; done from a Dutch edition), put into English in book form in 1791.

The principal works of Mme de Genlis were *Le Théâtre d'Éducation* (1779–80, trans. 1781); *Adèle et Théodore, ou Lettres sur l'education* (1782, trans. 1783); and *Les Veillées du Château* (1784, trans. 1785). The 'castle' of which she wrote was in part a recollection of her own childhood in Burgundy, in part her school at the Convent of Belle Chasse, and in part the estate at St Leu of 'Égalité' Orléans, who made her the 'governor' of his sons. Perhaps she took too great pains over that employment to be a genius. Her life was versatile and varied, yet homely: full of energy and daily effort so honest that her stories show experience rather than imagination, and their very fidelity has deprived them of

---

* They are chosen here mainly as typical of the average. Mme d'Épinay, Rousseau's friend, was, naturally, in more direct succession from him: her *Conversations d'Émilie* (a female *Émile*) was published in English by Marshall, but does not seem to have had wide household use here, which is the true test of influence. Mme le Prince de Beaumont, in her very different way, was far more acceptable to the British family. She has dealt with already (p. 91) on account of *Beauty and the Beast*. There were a good many others, but they would take up too much space here.

long life. She was too sane to outlive her age. Her sanity included hostility to fairies: 'les dangereux *Contes de Fées*'. She had not Maria Edgeworth's humour or Day's lopsided force, and, her atmosphere being foreign, she remained, in England, a mere engine of moral amusement, not a comparatively long-lived and esteemed companion. But her repute was high and influential, especially among the Blue-Stockings. Her moral-romantic plays were constantly acted – their morality outweighed the theatrical taint – in English girls' schools like Miss Pinkerton's. The Victoria and Albert Museum, London, used to exhibit a fine toy-theatre set for the display of one of them.

Berquin (1749–91) won a stronger hold upon English affections, for the sweetness of his disposition shone in his simple writings, and for more than one generation survived our climate. 'Surnommé à juste titre l'Ami des Enfants', by his sympathies he brought something of Maria Edgeworth's easy realism into his characters; a gentle kindliness made them live, and though he borrowed his huge collection of stories – *L'Ami des Enfans* (1782–3, monthly) – from many sources, his personality, unobtrusive and simple, runs through most of his representations. The first English edition was published serially by Cadell & Elmsley – who advertised two numbers a month from November 15, 1783 onwards – and it was completed in twenty-four numbers. The format was small, and the numbers, when bound up two or three together, made dumpy little volumes. (Elmsley was also responsible for publishing the French edition in London: twenty-four volumes 'en petit format', 1783.)* Competition soon appeared, however, for in 1786 a completely new translation went on the market, initially from Stockdale in Piccadilly, but later from J. Bew and P. Geary (again twenty-four volumes, but all dated 1786). This was translated, and heavily edited, by the Rev. Mark Anthony Meilan, who rightly claimed it to be a freer, more English version of Berquin's work. (Later he followed it with a *Friend of Youth*, 'partly translated from M. Berquin and other French and German writers, and partly original, being written by the Editor himself' – twelve volumes, 1787–8 by T. Hookham, who also advertised a twenty-four volume *Children's Friend*.)

The really popular English version was a judicious selection made and translated by the Rev. W. D. Cooper (i.e. Richard Johnson) and published by Elizabeth Newbery, in 1787, under the title of *The Looking-Glass for the Mind; or, Intellectual Mirror*, with cuts by John Bewick. Welsh's reprint of this (1885) contains an admirable account of Berquin and his work. The *Looking-Glass* went into innumerable editions.

Apart from the demonstrable popularity of Berquin in England, two odd little details suggest something of the closeness of upper middle-class intercourse between England and France at this time. The first is a little touch, a faint breath on the *Looking-Glass*, which shows that John Newbery's genius for trade

---

*　This English production contained a fly-leaf giving a bibliography of the French versions.

was not lost to his heirs. A kind old woman helped a lost child, and questioned her about her motives for straying, the chief being terror: said she, 'I very well know that you young children are too apt to be fond of histories of haunted houses, of witches, ghosts, and apparitions, which tend only to fill you with idle fears and apprehensions, and make you afraid even of your own shadows.' But her apprehensions were at once removed when she learnt that all Annabella's story-books had been bought at the corner of St Paul's Churchyard.

The other is what might be called the pet-lamb *motif*. In *Sandford and Merton* Harry was conspicuous for his kindness to animals: 'If he walked in the fields, he was sure to gather green boughs for the sheep, who were so fond of him, that they followed him wherever he went.' In Berquin the devotee was even more persistent:

Nor was Baba insensible of the fondness of her little mistress, since she would follow her wherever she went, would come and eat out of her hand, skip and frisk round her, and would bleat most piteously, whenever Flora was obliged to leave her at home.

24. A wood engraving by John Bewick above the opening of an earnest tale, which incorporates an equally earnest puff.

THE BOOK OF NATURE.

My dear papa, said young Theophilus to his father, I cannot help pitying those poor little boys, whose parents are not in a condition to purchase them such a nice gilded library, as that with which you have supplied me from my good friend's at the corner of St. Paul's Church-yard. Surely, such unhappy boys must be very ignorant all their lives, for what can they learn without books?

I agree with you, replied his father, that you are happy in having so large a collection of books, and I am no less happy in seeing you make so good a use of them. There is, however,

Baba, however, repaid the services of her little mistress in a more substantial manner, than that of merely dancing about her; for she brought forth young lambs, those lambs grew up, and brought forth others; so that within the space of a few years, Flora had a very capital stock, that furnished the whole family with food and raiment. Such, my little readers, are the rewards which Providence bestows on acts of goodness, tenderness, and humanity.

Perhaps one should not look too closely into the details of agricultural economics. But the last sentence is pure Moral Tale, not Rousseau undiluted. And there seems to be ground here for a prior claim, by either France or England, upon the 'Mary had a little lamb' idea, which hitherto has been credited to America.

Translation was reciprocal, as has been suggested. And, educational zeal apart, it was necessary, for the Revolution brought many refugees to England, and they were received by the very class which was so readily devoting itself to the amusement and instruction of children. There was considerable intercourse with the Continent when the fury had abated and conditions permitted of travel. Both Miss Edgeworth and Mrs Sherwood record visits from or to the Pictets, a well-known Geneva family. Mrs Sherwood mingled with a biggish colony of *émigrés* at Reading, befriended by the celebrated Dr Valpy; and she went to a school kept by one of them, Mme St Quentin, who, when she removed to London, had many well-known pupils, among them Mary Russell Mitford and 'L. E. L.' This kind of international intercourse possibly affected the English middle ranks of society more equably and yet more lastingly than any other stratum.

5

One by-product deserves an aside in this connection. It was the incursion of the book-trade into the toy-trade: the frontiers of the two have been hard to delimit ever since. Newbery's *Lottery Book*, with its alphabet-pricking device, has already been mentioned; and the more elaborate developments of the horn-book and its final degeneration into the 'battledore' had tended to turn that instrument into a sort of educational toy.* But it seems likely that French influence brought the Moral Game, a form of instructive gambling, to the height of its vogue.

The Abbé Gaultier was probably the first to use it. He was born in Piedmont in about 1746, but settled in France in 1780, and devoted himself to education. During the Revolution he fled to London, where he founded a school for educating children of other French refugees, and owing to sudden desertion by his staff, hit upon the pupil–teacher system, thus anticipating Bell and

---

* The 'books' were made in fantastic shapes and embellished with designs other than alphabetical. Tuer in his standard work (*The History of the Horn-Book*, 1896) did not dwell on these extravagances. It is fair to his memory, however, to say that certain specimens of horn-book which have appeared since he wrote are of doubtful genuineness. *Caveat emptor.*

Lancaster, the virtual founders of the two chief English elementary education societies which anti-Jacobinism fostered. He wrote many educational books, which were widely pirated, and invented 'games' to go with them, and decorative charts for wall-pictures.

The idea was seized upon, and its poise reversed, by English print-sellers. They put the amusement first, whereas Gaultier was by way of being a serious psychologist. One of his 'games', in fact, was a print of our chief moral qualities. The English adapters as a rule got rid of the scholastic element, but retained the morality in order to excuse the game. They also coloured their sheets very gaily. *The New Game of Virtue Rewarded and Vice Punished* designed by T. Newton (1810) shows most engaging little symbolical scenes and figures: 'The Stocks', for instance, 'The House of Correction', 'Faith', 'Prudence', and so on. *The Magic Ring* (Champante and Whitrow, 1796) conducts one through fairyland in the same way. It need hardly be said that a totum-fall or a dice-throw on a virtuous number sent you forward ('take one counter and advance to the Arbour') and a vicious one back ('forfeit one and go to the House of Correction').

Apart from their school uses and their vogue as permissible pastimes, the substance of these games – their text-comments, and their plates (reduced or dissected) – was actually issued also, occasionally, in book form; and it would be difficult to say whether or not, in that form, they were true 'children's books'. They were also issued in card form, as in *The Elements of Astronomy and Geography* (1795), by the Abbé Paris; and these seem to have been handled somewhat in the manner of the later game of *Happy Families*. Such games are at any rate a distinct landmark in the history of the struggle between instruction and amusement.

A similar overlap between books and pastimes occurred in volumes with spaces for a movable head. These were produced rather later – in the period 1805–15, so far as copies seen can be dated. A single head with a long 'blind' tongue for its neck was to be stuck in slits in successive pages, showing Fanny or Henry, Frank Feignwell or Lauretta the Little Savoyard, in different costumes and attitudes, with appropriate letterpress. Naturally, such books were something of luxuries – I have seen copies with the prices 5s. and 6s., which was expensive for children's volumes under George III. And they were fragile. It is rare to find a specimen now with its peripatetic head intact, if it exists. Perhaps, also, they were soon thrown away, for a booklet of sixteen pages or so with only one performer, in fixed postures, must have grown dull in a short time. France and England both produced such things: I do not know which first. In London they were chiefly issued from Fuller's 'Temple of Fancy'.

6

To return to the moral urge in the 'amusing' printed page. It undoubtedly came from France, and the Edgeworths and the Berquin-translators said so. But it was soon acclimatized here, and appears with almost entire spontaneity in the works conveniently grouped as 'Aikin and Barbauld' – John Aikin, M.D. (1747–1822), his sister Anna Laetitia Barbauld (1743–1825), and his daughter Lucy, the biographer of them both. They were quiet folk in the middle ranks of society. John Aikin, their father, was a schoolmaster and a Doctor of Divinity – a Unitarian – and under him Anna had an education thorough enough to give her, had she wished it in later life, a personal position in the concentric circles of Blue-Stockings. She remained outside them, however, except by her work. She married a Dissenting minister, and they kept a school together at Palgrave in Suffolk. Apart from children's books, she edited Richardson's letters, wrote a good number of capable critical essays, made a well-known selection from the English essayists, and was the author of one lyric that has passed into the anthologies – *Life*, based on Hadrian's address to his soul:

> Life! We've been long together . . .
> Say not Good-night, but in some brighter clime
> Bid me Good-morning.

She had also the misfortune to be fiercely criticized by Coleridge and Lamb. But Lamb, as I have said, seems to have had a distorted memory in this regard, and perhaps allowed a half-Elizabethan contempt for her not very original adult work to colour his views of what she wrote for children. Besides, he disliked the intrusion of education – inconsistently. In any case, his views do not seem to have had any practical effect.

Her first two works were by herself alone, without the collaboration of her brother. They were *Lessons for Children from Two to Three Years Old* (1778)* and *Hymns in Prose for Children* (1781). Both were translated into French, and both were designed for the use of the 'Little Charles' of the dialogue in the *Lessons*, an adopted nephew. They have the same ideal, in one aspect held by Rousseau, in another wholly rejected by him: the belief that a child should steadily contemplate Nature, and the conviction that by so doing he will be led to contemplate the traditional God.

The *Hymns in Prose* make up a children's book like no other in our language. They are exactly what the title says. They were meant to be committed to memory and recited, and were written in 'measured' style for that very purpose. Moreover, Mrs Barbauld clearly had in mind a semi-liturgical use of them: 'Many of these Hymns are composed in alternative parts, which will give them something of the spirit of social worship.' Her object was to inspire devotional feeling early in life, and to 'connect religion with a variety of sensible objects'. The textual inspiration of the Hymns is obvious in such passages as this:

The sheep rest upon their soft fleeces, and their loud bleating is no more heard amongst the hills . . .

---

* [Extended in 1779 by three further volumes: *Lessons for Children of Three Years Old* (Parts I and II), and *Lessons for Children from Three to Four Years Old*.]

Darkness is spread over the skies, and darkness is upon the ground; every eye is shut, and every hand is still.

Who taketh care of all people when they are sunk in sleep; when they cannot defend themselves, nor see if danger approacheth?

But in less purposeful contexts the rhythm also is less derivative:

I saw the moon rising behind the trees: it was like a lamp of gold. The stars one after another appeared in the clear firmament. Presently I saw black clouds arise, and roll towards the south; the lightning streamed in thick flashes over the sky; the thunder growled at a distance; it came nearer, and I felt afraid, for it was loud and terrible.

Language like that, so simple, yet almost majestic, is worth giving to children, even if, as Miss Barry suggests, they do not appreciate it so fully as do their elders. Mrs Barbauld's masterly command of English has been rivalled by few other writers for children; possibly only by Mrs Sherwood. And if words alone sufficed, she would have achieved for all time her purpose of exciting wonder and delight in things seen. It is not surprising that on her death in 1825 Maria Edgeworth wrote: 'England has lost a great writer, and we a most sincere friend.' When *Lessons for Children* appeared, the Edgeworths had admired it 'exceedingly', and Mr Edgeworth had begun *Harry and Lucy* (nearly all Maria's, in the end) to carry on Mrs Barbauld's good work (see above, fig 23).

Evenings at Home (6 vols., 1792–6) was compiled in collaboration with her brother. It contains such an enormous mass of material that some of it could not but be as poor as some is exceedingly good. The best stories are still well worth reading. Miss Edgeworth praised it highly at the time. Mr E. V. Lucas comments upon the excellent detective work in *The Trial. Perseverance against Fortune* is even now a good piece of contemporary life, and exciting at that. It is only the manner and the visible purpose which cause much of the book to seem out of date; and those two qualities were inherent in almost anything then written for children.

Lucy Aikin did less for young readers, and her work in that direction is not memorable. But she compiled an anthology of *Poetry for Children* (1801) which contains, among other pieces – from Pope, Dryden, Mrs Barbauld, Otway, and many stock authors – the verses beginning '"You are old, father William", the young man cried', which are better known in Lewis Carroll's version than in Southey's original; this was possibly their earliest appearance as a 'selected piece' (they had been first published in the *Morning Post* on January 17, 1799). The volume also has in its 'Preface to Parents' a very interesting passage on the suitability of poetry for children:

Since dragons and fairies, giants and witches, have vanished from our nurseries before the wand of reason, it has been a prevailing maxim, that the young mind should be fed on mere prose and simple fact . . . [But] the magic of ryme is felt in the very cradle – the mother and the nurse employ it as a spell of soothing power.

That is almost a direct contradiction of what her aunt had said when she wrote *Hymns in Prose*. She had praised Isaac Watts for 'the condescension of his Muse, which was very able to take a loftier flight': 'But it may well be doubted, whether poetry *ought* to be lowered to the capacities of children, or whether they should not rather be kept from reading verse, till they are able to relish good verse: for the very essence of poetry is an elevation in thought and style above the common standard.' It is significant that Lucy Aikin's opinion was uttered only a year or two before Ann and Jane Taylor took up the neglected Watts tradition, expanded it, and gave it new life.

Mention of the Taylors, however, takes us outside the range of French influence as well as of conscious philosophy. The theorists had paved the way for the full-blown and home-grown Moral Tale.

BRIEF BOOK LIST

For the chief authors, see *D.N.B.* and *C.H.E.L.* See also *C.H.E.L.* on the Blue-Stockings. Add:

Maria Edgeworth: Chosen Letters. Introduction by F. V. Barry (London, 1931).

Paterson, Dr Alice. *The Edgeworths* (London, 1914).

Edgeworth, M. *The Most Unfortunate Day of My Life, and Other Stories* (London, 1932).

[A. Berquin.] *The Looking-Glass for the Mind.* Facsimile reprint of edition of 1792 with John Bewick's woodcuts. Introduction by Charles Welsh (London and New York, 1885).

Memoirs and Correspondence of Mme d'Epinay. Translated with Introduction by E. G. Allingham (London, 1930).

Dobson, Austin. *Four Frenchwomen* (London, 1890). With a chapter on Mme de Genlis.

Hansford, F. E. Articles in the *Schoolmaster*, May 5, July 2 and 16, Dec. 17, 1931.

Whiting, Mary Bradford. 'A Century-old Friendship; Unpublished Letters from Mrs Barbauld', *The London Mercury*, September 1932.

Paper Dolls and Other Cut-out Toys, from the Collection of Wilbur Macey Stone. (Account by owner. Exhibition held at Newark Museum, New Jersey, Dec. 1931–Feb. 1932.)

For a flippant treatment of Day, see Sir Francis Cowley Burnand's *New History of Sandford and Merton* (London, 1872), illustrated by Edward Linley Sambourne.

Supplement

Further works relating to topics discussed in this chapter are:

EDGEWORTH

Butler, M. *Maria Edgeworth: a Literary Biography* (Oxford, 1972).

Slade, B. C. *Maria Edgeworth 1767–1849; a bibliographical tribute* (London, 1937).

Two selections of letters have also been edited by Christina Colvin: *Letters from England 1813–1844* (Oxford, 1971); and *Maria Edgeworth in France and Switzerland* (Oxford, 1979).

DAY

Gignilliat, G. W. *The Author of Sandford and Merton . . .* (New York, 1932).

Scott, Sir S. H. *The Exemplary Mr Day 1748–1789* (London, 1935).

BARBAULD

Rodgers, Betsy. *Georgian Chronicle; Mrs Barbauld and her family* (London, 1958).

TOYS AND GAMES

Daiken, L. *Children's Toys throughout the Ages* (London, 1953).

Hannas, Linda. *The English Jigsaw Puzzle 1760–1890* (London, 1972). Contains much information on related book-publishing affairs.

Speaight, George. *The History of the English Toy Theatre*. 2nd edn (London, 1969). With extensive information on the publishing of juvenile drama.

Whitehouse, F. R. B. *Table Games of Georgian and Victorian Days* (London, 1951).

CHAPTER X

The Moral Tale: (i) Didactic

I

As supply and demand grew, children's books became much more definitely self-contained pieces of fiction – a recognized semi-artistic literary form, with philosophic purpose subordinated to the story, and moral atmosphere, rather than a particular moral axiom, the mainstay. The books so written had, on the whole, no marked categorical or sectarian bias. A few clear points of view were insisted upon specially, and to a certain degree different religious prepossessions were visible. You can nearly always recognize a child's book written by a Quaker, for instance, not from any idiosyncrasy of speech or definite religious outlook, but just because of its exceptional gentleness. At the other extreme are the very plain and even truculent dogmatic leanings of Mrs Sherwood and Mrs Trimmer.

Religion apart, several subjects do occur with some frequency. One is the slavery question. That had odd practical repercussions, not unlike some of today's reactions: 'Twenty-five thousand people in England have absolutely left off eating West India sugar, from the hope that when there is no longer any demand for sugar the slaves will not be so cruelly treated.' That has a modern ring. It is from Maria Edgeworth's *Letters*. Another topic was that of cruelty to animals, a subject upon which it is hard to come at any certainty. It is almost inconceivable that so many small boys spent so much time as is alleged in pulling the wings off flies, throwing at tethered cocks, and tormenting puppies and kittens: though it is true that England was a brutal country in that way. But whatever the truth, the children's authors were unanimous in protesting against such savagery. Finally, they were almost equally unanimous in reprobating belief in fairies, as has already been pointed out.

The weakness of the moral tale in its early stages was in construction. *Goody Two-Shoes* cannot be called strong in that regard, though it had a more or less continuous plot. In that respect it surpassed its only rival in the archaic stage of juvenile fiction, which, though all of a piece, was really only a collection of linked stories, like *Sandford and Merton*. This was Sarah Fielding's *The Governess; or, Little Female Academy*, already mentioned (p. 97). the author's name was not given, but it was described as by the author of *David Simple*, a grown-up piece of fiction about whose creator there is no doubt. Sarah had something of her great brother's power of drawing ordinary English character.

The book is really a collection of stories told to or by the pupils of a school kept by one Mrs Teachum, who sometimes is a formidable task-mistress, but now and then might have stepped out of the West Country chapters in *Tom Jones*. There is also a combat which in fury, though not in its more robust details, recalls an adventure of Molly Seagrim's. There were, as has been said, two fairy-tales in the volume, and these were the cause of Mrs Sherwood's monstrous recension of it.

Far longer lived, and if it were not for excessive stress upon the relative positions of mankind and the brute creation, almost deserving of immortality through the changing ages, was the story at first portentously entitled *Fabulous Histories. Designed for the Instruction of Children, respecting their Treatment of Animals.* It was by Mrs Trimmer. When it was first published – in 1786 – she was already known for good works, which perhaps is the reason why it was issued as a 'trade' book, undertaken by several firms, including Longman. Mrs Trimmer's later activities among the fairies have already been described, but a few words are needed about her vigorous and respectable life. She held great sway.

She was born Sarah Kirby, at Ipswich, on January 6, 1741. Her father was a man of good standing, an engraver and artist who specialized in architectural drawings. He was a close friend of Hogarth, Reynolds and Gainsborough. Gainsborough, in fact, asked to be buried by his side, and was, at Kew, where from 1759 Kirby had been Clerk of the Works to the Palace. The family had come to London in 1755. Here Sarah Kirby was introduced to Dr Johnson, and, to confirm a disputed quotation from *Paradise Lost* for his benefit, produced a Milton from her pocket; which so pleased the lexicographer that he gave her a copy of the *Rambler*.

In 1762 she married James Trimmer of Brentford, by whom she had six daughters and six sons, nine of whom, apparently, survived her. She lived the rest of her life, which ended on December 15, 1810, at Brentford. She took a strong interest in education, at any rate as soon as her family gave her experience of it; though she was not, as is asserted by a biographer, 'the only one of all our popular modern writers on education that had a mother's experience'. She watched closely the experiments of Robert Raikes with Sunday Schools, and in 1782 caused them to be started at Brentford, founding her Church School in the High Street in 1786. Between that date and about 1800 she produced a number of 'Series of Prints' (small books of copperplates) to illustrate sacred and profane history, and volumes of 'Lessons' to accompany them.* They were directly inspired by the success of Mrs Barbauld's *Lessons for Children*, according to the *Dictionary of National Biography;* but according to Mrs

---

* The dates are obscure. The earliest I have seen are 1786 (*Prints of Scripture History*), 1790 (*New Testament*), 1792 (*English History*), and 1797 (*Old Testament*). These dates, however, are from the plates themselves, not from the title-pages, which are later. There were thirty-two or sixty-four plates in each volume. They went into many editions and were also sold 'pasted on Boards for hanging up in Nurseries'.

Trimmer's dedicatory letter addressed to Mme de Genlis they were 'a humble imitation' of *Adèle et Théodore*.

In 1786 Queen Charlotte summoned her to Windsor for a consultation about Sunday Schools, and in that year she wrote a treatise on the subject, under the title of *The Œconomy of Charity*, as well as the *Fabulous Histories*. The next year she founded a 'school of industry' at Brentford, and thereafter devoted all her energies to similar works, especially, as will be seen, those connected with the Established Church.

The importance of Sarah Trimmer is that she *was* important. With fair but not overwhelming social advantages, and, in spite of the Johnson encounter, no peculiar intellectual eminence, she made herself, in respect of her writings for and about children, completely typical of the non-political, undoctrinaire English upper middle-class. She was much more the mirror of the average than Maria Edgeworth, and yet in practical affairs both more eager and more distinguished than her literary contemporaries, the Kilners, Priscilla Wakefield, Aikin, Barbauld and the Taylors; as a specialist in children, on firmer ground, at that time, than Lamb or Blake, Roscoe or Mrs Dorset. If you like, she was completely mediocre, though robins who bore the names of Dicky, Flapsy and Pecksy, and who looked on mankind as whimsically as Gulliver on the Brobdingnagians, ought to deprive her at least of the adverb. She was, as Calverley called her easily, *good*. She stood for all that solidity and stolidity which defeated Napoleon by not understanding him or realizing how huge was the menace of change. Stupid and intelligent at once; certain of all that was best in the past, yet blind to any decay; hardly aware, except by deprivations accepted in the plain course of duty and experience, that long life for all men is deciduous; severe (because she did not fully comprehend error), devout, and at the same time of great kindliness – she lived an honourable career without doubts of herself or hesitation about public conduct.

The views of such a woman deserve sane examination, even though her output of genuine children's books was in itself small. She regarded the title of her *Fabulous Histories* as significant – it was only known as *The History of the Robins* or *The Robins* much later. 'The sentiments and affections of a good Father and Mother and a Family of Children', she wrote in the preface, 'are *supposed* to be possessed by a *Nest of Redbreasts*.' But young readers should be

taught to consider them, not as containing the real conversations of Birds (for that it is impossible we should ever understand) but as a series of FABLES, intended to convey moral instruction applicable to themselves, at the same time that they excite compassion and tenderness for those interesting and delightful creatures, on which such wanton cruelties are frequently inflicted, and recommend *universal Benevolence*.

That accounts for the celebrated footnote when she lets a mocking-bird appear in an English garden: 'The Mock-Bird is properly a native of America, but is introduced here for the sake of the moral.' The moral is that you must sing 'a natural note', and not be a mimic.

Both she and the circles in which she moved were acutely conscious of the

superiority of man to the brute creation. They were sure Providence had
ordained the beasts – the domestic ones, at least – for our use and benefit, and
we could rightly kill and eat them. But we must not betray the trust given to us.
We must put lobsters and eels to death mercifully. We must destroy caterpillars
and snails, because 'they devour fruit and vegetables', but not butterflies and
moths (empirical natural history does not seem to have gone very far). But
sometimes, in spite of the neat hierarchy of life, doubts and difficulties crept in.
Animals' 'sufferings end with their lives, as they are not religious beings' (the
same argument was seriously advanced – not by such writers as Mrs Trimmer – in
favour of negro slavery). It was disturbing, however, if they showed abnormal
intelligence:

I have, said a Lady who was present, been for a long time accustomed to consider animals
as mere machines, actuated by the unerring hand of Providence, to do those things which
are necessary for the preservation of themselves and their offspring; but the sight of the
learned Pig, which has lately been shewn in London, has deranged these ideas, and I
know not what to think.*

Mrs Trimmer's humane common sense, however, soon settled that question.
Animals could not be trained to such tricks without grave cruelty, and it was
man who was to be blamed, not Providence questioned, for the Pig's unnatural
performance. Samuel Johnson could not have been saner or more forcible.

These speculations were made, these trivial solemn decisions reached, in all
sincerity. The Trimmers of that age honestly believed in man's pre-eminence in
a world-garden arranged by God and only untidy because of the first Fall. And
England being internally at peace and fairly prosperous – *they*, at any rate, lived
comfortably – they extended their faith to our social order. It also was planned
by the Great Architect, and must be accepted in those terms which Churchmen
today so justly repudiate. 'Be graciously pleased, O Heavenly Father', runs a
prayer in Mrs Trimmer's *Charity School Spelling Book Part II* (4th edn 1798),
'to give me . . . strength and cheerfulness to labour and do (my duty) in that
state of life which thy wisdom has seen fit to allot me.'

No wonder, then, that when France was in a state of turmoil and England full
of refugees, she was alarmed for the future of the State and concerned about its
heirs. From 1778 to 1789 she conducted *The Family Magazine*, 'designed to
counteract the pernicious tendency of immoral books'. Her fear of too-rapid
enlightenment was timely, for in that very year 1789 Andrew Bell invented the
Madras system of education, which was based largely on the use of monitors for
discipline and of sand-tracing instead of books and slates. His *Experiment in
Education* was reported in 1797. In 1798 Joseph Lancaster, a fervent but
rather ill-balanced Quaker, started a school in the Borough Road, London.
After reading the *Experiment* in 1800 he began to organize it on closely similar
principles, and published a treatise on *Improvements in Education* (Darton and
Harvey, 1803), which Mrs Trimmer attacked furiously in *A Comparative View*

* An account of this sagacious creature, with a picture, is contained in *A Present for a Little Boy*
(1798), written and illustrated by William Darton.

(1805). There was no commitment to Established religion in Lancaster's system, and his monitors, given their puny power in school, would become '*a ready instrument of sedition and rebellion*' (the italics are hers). In 1802–6 she had conducted her *Guardian of Education* to protect England from Jacobinism and Rousseauism – 'the greatest injury the youth of this nation ever received was from the introduction of Rousseau's system'; and now here was irreligion actually rampant in an organized set of schools – for Lancaster's supporters had built several, and, what was worse, good King George had blessed the ideal of education thus philanthropically put forward.

It was in the *Guardian of Education* that Mrs Trimmer printed a correspondent's bitter attack on Cinderella, as already recorded. Her effect upon English education, in spite of her exaggeration, was very considerable, even extraordinary. The two rival systems, Bell's and Lancaster's, were hotly debated all over the country, and the war between Bell and the Dragon, as a cartoonist labelled it, raged in all the magazines, even in the *Edinburgh Review* (October 1806), where it inspired in Sydney Smith some passages of invective not easily equalled. 'This uncandid and feeble lady', he called her, and wrote that she 'seems to suppose, because she has dedicated her mind to the subject, that her opinion must necessarily be valuable upon it; forgetting it to be barely possible, that her application may have made her more wrong, instead of more right.' She was, he said, 'a lady of respectable opinions, and very ordinary talents; defending what is right without judgment, and believing what is holy without charity'. That is severe enough in all conscience, though Mrs Trimmer had a pretty thick armour of rectitude. But George III read the criticism, and liked it so much that he had it read to him twice over: and *that—*.

However, the conflict bore fruit. Out of its early stages arose the two great societies – the National Society for Promoting the Education of the Children of the Poor in the Principles of the Established Church, and the British and Foreign School Society – upon whose work, fundamentally, the whole of our later elementary school system was based. Children's books had indirectly inspired the theorists, not *vice versa*. If Mrs Trimmer had never written *The Robins*, her advocacy of Bell would have been only the voice of an excited old lady at Brentford. Hers was no mean achievement.

There we must leave her, with the postscript that she died fighting. Her *Essay on Christian Education* contained these two indomitable sentiments: 'Formerly children's reading, whether for instruction or amusement, was confined to a very small number of volumes; of late years they have multiplied to an astonishing and alarming degree, and much mischief lies hid in many of them.' In fact, even schoolbooks and grammars were contaminated: 'In short, there is not a species of Books for Children and Youth, any more than for those of maturer years, which has not been made in some way or other an engine of mischief.' The *Essay* had been originally included in the *Guardian of Education*, but at the time of her death she was expanding it for issue in book form. It was published posthumously in 1812.

2

The transition from her to less pugnacious controversialists, but more voluminous writers for children, is easy, for some of the best of them went to the same
publisher, John Marshall, and in advertising their works – he had over a
hundred children's books in his list between 1780 and 1790 – he showed that
he shared Mrs Trimmer's opinions whole-heartedly:

Ladies, Gentlemen, and the Heads of Schools, are requested to observe, that the before-
mentioned Publications are *original*, and *not compiled*: as also, that they were written to
suit the various Ages for which they are offered; but on a more liberal Plan, and in a
different Style from the Generality of Works designed for young People: being entirely
divested of that prejudicial Nonsense (to young Minds) the Tales of Hobgoblins,
Witches, Fairies, Love, Gallantry, etc. with which such little Performances heretofore
abounded.

The authors chiefly covered by this handsome testimonial were 'M.P.', 'S.S.'
and 'Mrs Teachwell', the disguises respectively of Dorothy and Mary Ann
Kilner and Ellenor Fenn.

The two Kilners wrote a great number of books, most of which were very
popular. Mrs Trimmer read some of them in manuscript, and formed a close
friendship with Dorothy, whose *The Village School* (2 vols. 1s.; *c.* 1783) was
possibly composed to help the Brentford Sunday School project. The Kilners
themselves lived a very quiet life in Essex, at Maryland Point (now part of
London), a village whose initials Dorothy adopted as a pseudonym. She wrote
some purely didactic works on undistinguished lines, like *The First Principles of
Religion* (2 vols., 1780?), *Dialogues and Letters on Morality* (3 vols., 1781–7),
A Clear . . . Account of the Origin and Design of Christianity (1781), and *Letters
from a Mother to her Children* (2 vols., *c.* 1785). They have a rather strange
Puritan tone, which is absent from her fiction. Her best story for children, *The
Life and Perambulation of a Mouse* (2 vols., 1783–?4), begins with an easy
freshness hardly seen until *Alice* appeared eighty years or so later. The author is
supposed to be staying at a pleasant house called Meadow Hall, full of children:

After the more serious employment of reading each morning was concluded, we danced,
we sung, we played at blind-man's buff, battledore and shuttlecock, and many other
games equally diverting and innocent. And when tired of them, drew our seats round the
fire, whilst each one in turn told some merry story to divert the company.

She could not think of a tale for herself. Her own life had been so 'insipid':

'Then write mine, which may be more diverting', said a little squeaking voice, which
sounded as if close to me . . . You may be sure that I was much surprised to be so
addressed by such an animal; but ashamed of discovering any appearance of astonish-
ment, lest the Mouse should suppose it had frightened me, I answered with the utmost
composure, that I would write it willingly, if it would dictate it to me. 'O! that I will do',
replied the Mouse, 'if you will not hurt me.' – 'Not for the world', returned I; 'come,
therefore, and sit upon my table, that I may hear more distinctly what you have to relate.'
It instantly accepted my invitation, and with all the nimbleness of its species, ran up the
side of my chair, and jumped upon my table; when, getting into a box of wafers, it began
as follows . . .

The ensuing tale is on much the same lines as *The Robins*, but the moral is a little less emphatic.

Her *Little Stories for Little Folks* (c. 1781) and *History of a great many Little Boys and Girls, for the Amusement of all Good Children of four and five Years of Age* (1780?)[1] were long popular. *The Village School* was intended, among other things, to censure the vices of boarding schools, while *First Going to School, or, The Story of Tom Brown and his Sisters* (Tabart, 1804) contained some school scenes which are hardly flattering to the kind of establishment shown in the illustrations.

Her sister-in-law, Mary Ann Kilner, 'S.S.',* wrote fewer books but with a higher proportion of individual tales. One of her works deserves quotation as a piece of social life. It hints at some realities behind the smooth domestic 'interiors' which are usually the setting of the Moral Tale; nay, are even the moral itself. 'S.S.' wrote *A Course of Lectures for Sunday Evenings, containing Religious Advice to Young Persons* (Marshall, c. 1783). The Introduction, meant for the Young Persons, not for their parents, tells how the author went to stay with a certain family. You see the family in the frontispiece, a grave set tableau: two parents, two wax candlesticks, beautiful Chippendale furniture, and six children rapt. It is Sunday evening, and papa, as of wont, is reading to his descendants some 'serious truths which were contained in a very rational and well written discourse'. Alas! How frail is even the most aspiring human nature! 'The eldest daughter sat for some time listening with great earnestness; but by degrees, her eyes grew heavy, her head inclined alternatively on either side, till she fell into a profound sleep, interrupted only by involuntary starts when in danger of falling.' Nor could the other children keep alive the faculty of attention any better. So S.S. wrote *these* discourses, about which I can only say that they too are serious and rational and sensible.

These *Lectures* are signed S— S—, not S.S., which is the signature given them in Marshall's list. They are surely by Mary Ann Kilner – because Jemima Placid, in the story about her which is certainly by that writer, read

several books which she had bought at Mr *Marshall's*, and had already perused with much delight, particularly the *Course of Lectures for* Sunday *Evenings; The Village School* [by 'M.P.'] and *Perambulation(s) of a Mouse* [by 'M.P.'], 2 vols. each; together with the *First Principles of Religion* [by 'M.P.'], and the *Adventures of a Pincushion* [by 'S.S.'].

The art of the 'blurb' had not then progressed so far as now, or Marshall would not have put in that tell-tale trade detail, '2 vols. each': that is a publisher speaking, not an author.

Jemima Placid simply lived up to its sub-title – *The Advantage of Good-Nature, exemplified in a Variety of Familiar Incidents*. Jemima may perhaps have been a little bore in real life, with her perpetual acquiescence and rightness. But in writing about her, 'S.S.', like her sister-in-law, had a human touch. Some of the 'incidents' are both familiar and eternal – childish little facts truly observed.

* [S.S. = Spital Square, where Mary Ann Mazé lived for a while after marrying Dorothy Kilner's brother Thomas.]

Jemima in tribulation, for instance, consoled herself with a picture or drawing of a 'little horse', made by her brother. A lucky collector of old children's books and such-like will often come upon that very drawing. It is to be found in old family scrapbooks or waste-paper-books given to long-dead children, to keep Satan away from their idle hands. It shows a noble animal with a leg at each corner, as the ancient definition states it, and very often with two eyes in one profile. They all drew it, or a cow, or a dog; or inscribed their names over and over again with flourishes, or for pleasure wrote fragments of gnomic sayings originally inflicted upon them for instruction. Instruction *can* be amusement.

The Kilners had a popularity, in terms of continuous print, of more than forty years. Mary's most successful book was *The Adventures of a Pincushion* (*c.* 1780) which ran into numerous editions, and whose vogue probably led her to write a similar successor, *The Memoirs of a Peg-Top* (*c.* 1781). The Pincushion masterpiece – it is that, artistically – contains two passages which deserve to be quoted. The first, explanatory of motive, is Mary Ann Kilner apologizing, after the manner of her sex at that time, for being an author at all, and for the pretences used in what Mrs Trimmer more bluntly called a 'fabulous history'. She was not sure that she had not gone too far:

To exhibit their superiors in a ridiculous view, is not the proper method to engage the youthful mind to respect. To present their equals as the objects of contemptuous mirth, is by no means favourable to the interest of good-nature. And to treat the characters of their inferiors with levity, the Author thought was inconsistent with the sacred rights of humanity.

The second is a variant of 'handsome is as handsome does':

Charlotte was a very fair complexioned pretty girl; but you cannot imagine how ugly her ill-humour made her appear; nor how much more agreeable her sister looked, who was much browner, was pitted with the small pox, and a much plainer child.

If you contrast these extracts with the presumably honest passage about the effect of a 'rational discourse', you get not only the picture of a suavely ordered microcosm, but something of the human being who is depicting it – an observer who was not wholly lost in the moralist, any more than was her sister-in-law, the spontaneous chronicler of mice. The Kilners, unlike Mrs Trimmer, did not suffer from the importance of philanthropy.

3

Marshall's other early mainstay, Lady Fenn, was a childless and conscientious writer who possibly, by her obvious adaptation of her work to the market, had something of the professional moralist or even hack in her. She always used a pseudonym – 'Mrs Teachwell', 'Mrs Lovechild' and 'Solomon Lovechild', usually – or wrote anonymously. But she was well known in her district of East Dereham, Norfolk, as a propagating philanthropist and the wife of a most punctilious antiquary, John Fenn, the first editor of the *Paston Letters*. She herself was a Frere. Her children's books were written – and actually made by her, binding and all – for her nephews and nieces. She also set up Sunday Schools in her village and revived the cottage spinning industry: and she invented a *Game of Grammar*, not unlike those already described. She died in 1813, in her seventieth year. Most of her books appeared between 1780 and 1790.

In spite of writing to a kind of pattern, she showed a good deal of observation and humour. Both qualities are to be found in her *Juvenile Tatler* and its kindred *Fairy Spectator* (both 1789), with its moral Fairy Guardian. But the work by her which had the longest life and was most frequently pirated was the significantly named *Cobwebs to catch Flies; or, Dialogues in Short Sentences*, a near relation of Mrs Barbauld's *Lessons for Children*. The two volumes were possibly an experiment by the publisher, because the ostensibly first editions – undated, but reasonably attributed by the British Museum to 1783, from the dedication – vary remarkably. Volume I went up to words of six letters. Volume II comprehended words of from one to four syllables, in ascending order. That is, they were instructive. But the primary aim was amusement – cobwebs glittering in the sun. I once possessed a copy (undated) which in the eighteenth century was given to a child called Charlotte. It contained printer's directions in pencil, and the order of the pages and sheets was not quite that of the standardized version. The numerous blocks and 'printer's ornaments' also varied. One of the British Museum copies has a note in Volume II: *'The Printer thinks it but respectful to the Author, to acquaint Ladies and others, that his* inattention *occasioned the derangement of the Dialogues.'* It may be hazarded – though it is no more than conjecture – that Lady Fenn had a closer practical contact with Marshall over the arrangement of the text than his authors of more 'imaginative' works for the young. It is quite likely that my erratic copy may have been a set of proofs bound up – possibly by my piratical forebears.[2]

The idea is suggestive, at any rate, for when Marshall's pre-eminence, which lasted from about 1780 to 1800, was challenged by the rivals I have mentioned, the horde of minor moralists grew enormously. There is some evidence – as with the Lambs and the Taylors and Mrs Sherwood – that the publishers went out of their way to find writers. Two of them at least – William Darton and William Godwin – wrote books on their own account, and my ancestor went further: he drew and engraved the illustrations also, not very finely, it must be said, but adequately to his purpose if sales are any clue. It must be remembered that relatively to the population of the kingdom there was a large number of children's authors, though, on the other hand, a book once established had a more than seasonal life, whatever its merits. Editions, also, were not small;[3] fifteen hundred to two thousand was usually the first printing, and the majority of the works mentioned here went into three or four reprints, or were amalgamated with others and perpetuated in a new form. Beneath all this, so to speak, intellectual traffic, moreover, there went on the almost illicit trade in sordid chapbooks, then at its height.

4

Between about 1790 and 1820 there were at least a score of writers for children whose recognition by the public was sufficient, on economic grounds, to get them into print regularly. The stronger ones – those already mentioned and half a dozen yet to come – have escaped Time's scythe, though maybe they are only preserved for show in an old-fashioned garden. Those of less hardy growth are now little more than names, and must here have something like catalogue treatment. They were very much of a pattern. They were far better at telling a story than at constructing one. Their very themes made for feebleness of plot. They did not, till the end of the period, run to great length, a fact which upsets all comparison with modern books. Nor, except for an evidently increasing ease (fluency is the better word), did they differ greatly in their conception of what a Moral Tale should be. It should illustrate a particular platitude, and that was about all. Most of the heroes and heroines, or, if you will, villains or naughty children, were no more than those brats of the movable-head books: the same waxen face fitted into a succession of stiff bodies. Chronologically, except for a few trivial details, any year between 1790 to 1820 (with a slight bias to 1805–15) will fit most of their books, the dating of which is in fact very arbitrary.

The senior of them in order of publication may perhaps be Mrs Pilkington, who had experience as a governess to give her stories some sort of life. But she was also something of a theorist, because she translated Marmontel in 1799, having, the year before, imitated Mme de Genlis's *Tales of the Castle* with her own *Tales of the Cottage*. But she was also a professional writer. In 1795 she wrote to Messrs Cadell offering them a children's book; which, as they did not wish to consider it, was probably not published. She was evidently sought after before long, and found a home with the two firms of Vernor and Hood and Elizabeth Newbery, who seem to have been working together at the end of the century. They published her *Biography for Girls* in 1799 – although *Biography for Boys* in the same year was issued by Vernor and Hood alone. John Harris joined in later editions and was also joint publisher of books like *Marvellous Adventures; or, the Vicissitudes of a Cat* (1802). Mrs Pilkington was popular because of her moral sense. It is hard to find any individuality in her work, and she had none of the humour which one detects almost smothered in some of her contemporaries.

Nor can humour be attributed to a more voluminous writer, Mary Belson, afterwards Mary Elliott. She came late in this period, and reached into the twenties and *Tales for Boys, Tales for Girls* (both *c.* 1825) and *Tales of Truth* (1836) were still being reprinted in Victoria's reign. Some of her works – *Truth our Best Friend* (c. 1824) for example – were published in French as well as English. Her titles are nearly always significant: *Precept and Example* (c. 1810) – this contains publishers' puffs in the usual Newbery manner, but was produced like many of her books by William Darton; *Ill-Temper a Bad*

Playmate; *The Greedy Child Cured* – by eating poisonous berries, as in a famous Taylor poem; *Idle Ann, or The Dunce Reclaimed* (all *c.* 1824); *Industry and Idleness, a Pleasing and Instructive Tale for Good Little Girls* (1811).

The most exciting sub-title used by Mrs Elliott was that of *Confidential Memoirs; or, Adventures of a Parrot, a Greyhound, a Cat, and a Monkey* (1821). But it turns out to provide a very tame menagerie, hardly more lively than the Learned Pig. She also wrote *The Rambles of a Butterfly* (1819), and in her 'original poems', *The Rose* (1824), are some verses which are illustrated by a picture of boys carefully pulling a frog to pieces. The brute creation, in fact, receives a good deal of attention, as I have said – though it still *was* 'the brute creation'. Edward Augustus Kendall, in *Keeper's Travels in Search of his Master* (1798), certainly showed some dog-love, curiously in contrast with the dull solemnity of his other works (he translated Bernardin de Saint Pierre). But Elizabeth Sandham's cat, in *The Adventures of Poor Puss* (Harris, 1809; in two parts), is about as much like *felis catus* as the animal in the frontispiece to the book: which is hardly at all. (Miss Sandham was very popular. She also described, from an inverted human point of view, the careers of insects and birds, and wrote two school tales, and moral stories like *The Twin Sisters; or The Advantages of Religion* (Harris, 1805). In fact, as a Harris advertisement of 1812 says, she was 'the author of many approved works for young persons'.) Another such writer was 'Arabella Argus' (the name is impossible), who specialized in donkeys, in *The Adventures of a Donkey* (1815), and *Further Adventures of Jemmy Donkey; interspersed with biographical sketches of the Horse* (1821), from which it may be learnt that donkeys were then driven tandem, whatever the difficulty most people find in driving them singly. Miss or Mrs Argus, however, was an observer as well as a moralist. In *Ostentation and Liberality: a Tale* (1820, with plates dated 1821) she was the moralist. But in *The Juvenile Spectator* (1810) she was, in a small way, not unlike Mr Bickerstaff and his inventors – a commentator on juvenile humours, 'tempers, manners, and foibles'. Her method might have been more freely used: but the time had not yet come. Children in books were still cock-shies, good or evil qualities packed into little bodies to be praised or blamed by measure. And when animals were contrasted with them, as in these works, or in *The Dog of Knowledge* (anonymous: Harris, 1801), they too were often mere moral dummies.

But the writer of one un-natural history tale – *The Canary Bird* (Harris, 1817) – deserves mention for gifts she displayed outside the animal kingdom. Nothing seems to be known of Miss Alicia Catherine Mant except what is in her books. But in them she shows a very pleasant personality. She was didactic, but she tried with some success to be kind and amusing: Mr E. V. Lucas, quoting her in his *Old Fashioned Tales*, calls her work 'Ann-and-Jane-Taylorism translated into prose'. One of her stories, in *Tales for Ellen* (1825), is very similar to *The Purple Jar*; but the mother is not so cruelly logical as Rosamond's.

When she had reached her eighth year, . . . early as it might seem, Mrs Clavering had set aside a purse for the use of her little girl [Agnes], which she told her was all that would be expended for her amusements during the year, and she was anxious to see how far this arrangement might be a check on the boundless wishes of the little Agnes.

She certainly saw, for Agnes happily and naturally spent her money on toys for herself instead of on a present for a loved friend. She *wanted* those toys. She suffered when there was no money left for the present. But she did not undergo that odious economic retribution of being unable to go to see a glasshouse. The mother was kind and persuasive, not Nemesis. There is a world of difference in a lesson so gently conveyed.

Miss Mant also wrote *Ellen; or The Young Godmother* (1812), *The Cottage in the Chalk Pit* (1822) – both of which went into several editions – some other children's tales and one or two 'grown-up' stories like *Caroline Lismore: or, The Errors of Fashion* (1815). She had a virtue not common in nursery moralists of the day – she made her incidents frequent and almost dramatic. In the passage just quoted, however, she is reproducing contemporary child-life. When Lucy Butt (afterwards Mrs Cameron, Mrs Sherwood's sister) was eight or nine, her mother made her just such an allowance as was given to Agnes – 'for my clothes, as many guineas as I was years old' – and she was expected to manage and account for it.

A more prolific writer, long popular, though not always identified with her works, because they were often anonymous, was Mary Robson, afterwards Hughes (or Hughs; both spellings appear). Only by a comparison of a number of title-pages and advertisements is it possible to ascribe certainly to her many well-read books of 1811 to 1825. Two volumes of *Aunt Mary's Tales* ('for . . . Girls', 1811; and 'for . . . Boys', 1813), *The Ornaments Discovered* (1815), *The Alchemist* (1818), and *The Orphan Girl* (1819) are a few of them. She dedicated some to Miss Edgeworth, whose moral pattern she followed with some fidelity, but with very scant humour. I believe that so far as my own ancestors' books go, she compiled them by request, certainly with success. She wrote several juvenile pamphlets for the Christian Tract Society (founded in 1809) and in 1813 was made a life member of that undenominational body. Her works – like Mrs Barbauld's – appear in its lists and in those of several Unitarian associations. In 1818, a year after her marriage, she emigrated to the States with her husband, and, finding that the popularity of her books had preceded her, 'commenced a school for young ladies' at Philadelphia, which she conducted with wide repute till her retirement in 1839. A brief record of her life, written in the best Victorian style of florid complacency, appeared in Sarah Josepha Hale's *Woman's Record* (1855).

Mrs Trimmer was of the full Establishment in religious views; Mary Robson either non-committal or Unitarian; and Priscilla Wakefield, whose maiden name was Bell, was a Quaker, and of strong character at that, as an engraved portrait by Wageman, the theatrical artist, suggests. She wrote a dozen or more children's books between about 1795 and 1820, and also *Reflections on the Present Condition of the Female Sex* (J. Johnson 1798). Her *Introduction to*

Botany (E. Newbery, 1796; often found charmingly illustrated in colour) was for long an acceptable text-book. It was being reprinted as late as 1841. But her less pedagogic works were just as successful. She wrote little fiction, but strung together historical and similar stories under such titles as *Leisure Hours* (2 vols., 1794–6), *Juvenile Anecdotes* (2 vols., 1795–8); and *Domestic Recreation* (1805).

It is in *Juvenile Anecdotes* that there is recorded an illuminating piece of social usage. A parent, in her zeal for purity and reverence, was wont to examine every children's book in her nursery library very closely, and to cut bodily out of them 'as many leaves as contained passages likely to give false ideas, or to corrupt [children's] innocence'. 'Not an objectionable sentence escaped.' Her offspring were never suffered to pronounce

the sacred name of the Deity . . . but in the most reverential and serious manner making a solemn pause when it occurred, even in the Holy Scriptures; but, if it was ever introduced in other books, by way of exclamation, they passed it over, and mostly marked it as a word not to be repeated.

One of her sons, sent to school, was set to read 'a speech in one of Madame Genlis' Dramas'. He proceeded, but suddenly stopped and asked for a pencil. The master asked the reason. '"Do you not see, Sir," said the little boy, "that there is the awful name which I dare not repeat; and my mamma used always to draw a line through those words which she did not choose we should say."' The master was so struck that he adopted this practice in all his school-work. The doctrine is exactly that of George Fox.

I have traced over sixty editions of twelve of Mrs Wakefield's books between 1795 and 1818, some of them written while her husband, a farmer, was in some financial difficulty. Like him, as has been said, she was a Quaker, though they never wore the Quaker dress. As the quotation shows, she was thoroughly Quaker in mind; but her popularity was not confined to the Society of Friends, and personally she was fond of general society and decent amusement. She has a claim on greater history than that of nursery books, however, for she was the grandmother of that extraordinary man Edward Gibbon Wakefield, and was almost entirely responsible for his early upbringing. An entry in her diary for 1807 sounds prophetic: 'My thoughts much occupied with my little Edward, whom I tenderly love, but whose inflexible pertinacious temper makes me fear for his own happiness and of those connected with him.' History was to confirm that early view of one of the makers of Australia. But at least he proves that the atmosphere of the Moral Tale was not utterly stultifying and conservative. His grandmother's examples of it would not be read by any child now, but they have a characteristic sincerity and interest even yet for older readers.

Other writers of the period and manner must be passed over with the mere mention of their names and of the fact that they usually achieved more than one edition. Such are Mrs Pinchard of Taunton, who wrote *The Blind Child* (1791; 10th ed. 1814), *Dramatic Dialogues* (1792), *The Two Cousins* (1794) and *Family Affection* (1816); Mrs L. A. Marshall, author of *Henwick Tales* (1813); Isaac Day, *Scenes for the Young* (1807); E. Fenwick, Esther Copley (née

Hewlett), Mrs Hurry (née Mitchell), Elizabeth Helme (original, but also a translator of Campe), and some whose very names are hard to discover, though their books sold well. One such shy author was M. A. Hedge, who wrote anti-slavery tales – *Samboe; or, The African Boy* (1823; dedicated to William Wilberforce), and *Radama, or the Enlightened African; with Sketches of Madagascar* (1824).

5

The enlightened African leads fitly to the most intense moralist of them all, Martha Mary Butt, afterwards Mrs Sherwood; because, apart from her more particular dogmas, she spent a good deal of her useful and indefatigable life in trying – successfully – to bring the light of Christianity into dark places; particularly into India, where she went with her husband, a Captain in the 53rd Regiment. Her earlier works were planned, and many of them first written, in India between 1809 and 1813, and nearly all had a missionary tendency: *Little Henry and his Bearer* (1814 – by 1866 the publishers, Houlston, advertised that it had sold 'upwards of two hundred and fifty thousand copies'), *The Ayah and Lady* (1816?), *The Indian Pilgrim* (1818) and *The Infant's Progress* (1820?). These tales had an immense vogue in evangelical circles both in India, where they were translated into Hindustani, and in England.

That side of her character possibly was the best known even to her more general public. It was never much weakened. The fact is, however, that her life as a child, though strict after the fashion of the times, was by no means lacking in vivacity. But after her marriage she met and became imbued with views which tinged deeply her most popular books, and were so strongly expressed in them that no one today who does not feel some doctrinal faith faintly akin to what she believed from about 1812 to 1825 could read most of these works sympathetically, if at all. In India she came under the influence of the great missionary Henry Martyn. He changed her cast of mind. His evangelical zeal, passing into her, became for a time a Calvinism as rigid as any displayed by the Janeways or Whites of a century and a half before. 'All children are by nature evil, and while they have none but the natural evil principle to guide them, pious and prudent parents must check their naughty passions in any way that they have in their power, and force them into decent and proper behaviour and into what are called good habits'[4] was the belief she stated quite explicitly, and repeated many times, and quoted Scripture to support, throughout *The Fairchild Family*. Her doctrines, however, grew far gentler on her return to England, and in later work she used them with much less vehemence and frequency.

The Fairchild Family, a work teeming with personal force and vitality, was known to almost all English children up to about 1887,[5] and is not yet forgotten, if alive only by strong repute. It deserved its life, for it had certain elements of greatness. It was partly written at Meerut, in 1812 to 1813, just after Martyn left India for good. The first part was published in 1818, the third, and last, in 1847. During its vogue, and after, it was perhaps as widely read, as completely ridiculed, and as honestly condemned by child-lovers, as any English book ever written for children. It has deserved all three fates. It contains in its mass of minatory and exegetic detail two features not surpassed elsewhere. The prose Mrs Sherwood wielded was masterly; and no one ever described very simple childish pleasures – especially those of the table – with more obvious enjoyment in them. The meals eaten by the little Fairchilds, even if they teach lessons about greed, make the mouth water to this day. The buttered toast . . . alas, so prodigally wasted.

As for the prose, I must insist on a long quotation, partly because the profoundly sombre effect is cumulative, and partly because in such versions of the book as are now provided for children, this greatest passage in it is generally omitted – for moral reasons. Lucy, Emily, and Henry (all names of Mrs Sherwood's own children) had quarrelled over a doll. Lucy bit Emily and Emily scratched Lucy. Mr Fairchild overheard them saying that they did not love one another. He whipped their hands (Henry's as well) 'till they smarted again', repeated Dr Watts's views on bears and lions, and mentioned the first murder. Then he kissed them and forgave them, and they had the excellent family dinner; after which Mr Fairchild said to his wife (the italics are mine):

'I will take the children this evening to Blackwood, and shew them something there, which, I think, they will remember as long as they live: and I hope they will take warning from it, and pray more earnestly for new hearts, that they may love each other with perfect and heavenly love.'. . .

'What is there at Blackwood, Papa?' cried the children.

'Something very shocking', said Mrs Fairchild. 'There is one there', said Mr Fairchild, looking very grave, 'who hated his brother.'

'Will he hurt us, Papa?' said Henry.

'No', said Mr Fairchild; '*he cannot hurt you now.*'

When the children and John were ready, Mr Fairchild set out. They went down the lane nearly as far as the village; and then, crossing over a long field, they came to the side of a very thick wood.

'This is Blackwood', said Mr Fairchild, getting over the stile: 'the pathway is almost grown up; *nobody likes to come here now.*'

'What is here, Papa?' added the children 'is it very shocking? *We are afraid to go on.*'

'There is nothing here that will hurt you, my dear children', said Mr Fairchild. 'Am not I with you? and do you think I would lead my children into danger?'

'No, Papa', said the children; '*but Mamma said there was something very dreadful in this wood.*'

Then Lucy and Emily drew behind Mr Fairchild, and walked close together; and little Henry asked John to carry him. The wood was very thick and dark; and they walked on for half a mile, going down hill all the way. At last they saw, by the light through the trees, that they were come near to the end of the wood; and as they went further on, they saw an old garden wall; some parts of which being broken down, they could see beyond, a large brick house, which, from the fashion of it, seemed as if it might have stood there some hundred years, and now was fallen to ruin. The garden was overgrown with grass and weeds, the fruit-trees wanted pruning, and it was hardly to be seen where the walks had been. One of the old chimneys had fallen down, breaking through the roof of the house in one or two places; and the glass windows were broken near the place where the garden wall had fallen. Just between that and the wood stood a gibbet, on which the body of a man hung in irons: it had not yet fallen to pieces, although it had hung there some years. The body had on a blue coat, a silk handkerchief round the neck, with shoes and stockings, and every other part of the dress still entire: but the face of the corpse was so shocking, that the children could not look at it.

'Oh! Papa, Papa! what is that?' cried the children.

'That is a gibbet', said Mr Fairchild; 'and the man who hangs upon it is a murderer – one who first hated, and afterwards killed his brother! When people are found guilty of stealing, they are hanged upon a gallows, and taken down as soon as they are dead; but when a man commits a murder, he is hanged in irons upon a gibbet, till his body falls to pieces, that all who pass by may take warning by the example.'

Whilst Mr Fairchild was speaking, the wind blew strong and shook the body upon the gibbet, rattling the chains by which it hung.

'Oh! let us go, Papa!' said the children, pulling Mr Fairchild's coat.

'*Not yet*', *said Mr Fairchild*: 'I must tell you the history of that wretched man before we go from this place.'

And he did, *The Fairchild Family* being 'a Collection of Stories calculated to shew the Importance and Effects of a Religious Education', which this murderer had neglected.

No one can fairly say nowadays that that is fit reading for children, however naughty they were. Nor was it the sort of literature usually provided for them in 1818, or even under the Puritans. But the English is little short of majestic in its economy and plainness. The picture is appallingly vivid, and that sentence 'he cannot hurt you now' might, in a humbler way, come from the *Agamemnon* or *Lear*. And terrible though the episode is, Mrs Sherwood believed it to convey a holy lesson rightly needed. When the children had heard the murderer's story – how two brothers, 'when they first began to quarrel in their play, *as you did this morning,* did not foresee that death, and it is to be feared hell, would be the consequence of their quarrels' – they asked if they might kneel down and pray for new hearts, and did so. All hate, said Mr Fairchild, in giving his glad consent to this, must be taken from himself and all of us by the Holy Spirit of God, for even if he, Mr Fairchild, should take his 'natural heart' to heaven he would hate every angel above himself 'and even the glory of the Almighty God would be hateful to me'.

It is no use to argue with faith so completely unyielding; there is no basis of argument. Any criticism that could prevail against it would lead the victim into a black void of disbelief far more devastating than the torments of a soul that believes but knows itself short of perfection; and at that time Mrs Sherwood was unceasingly conscious of imperfection. She never lapsed into the ecstatic certainty of being saved while nearly all others were damned. She was far too human and humane for that. And her dramatic sense was seldom wholly in abeyance. But it must be admitted that she did sacrifice some sense of proportion to literal dogma in *The History of Henry Milner* (1822–37, in four parts: it was conceived in 1820). In that astounding tale she seems to have lost all the intimate touch with the daily realities of childhood, all the sharpness of familiar vision, which elsewhere gave even her most pietistic stories an oddly lifelike atmosphere. It is all about the Millennium.

She had a memory capacious, long, and minute; so that her books are all fragments of her life, with her later views on what it ought or ought not to have been as a framework of the events – not the events the framework of the views. If she desired to enforce a particular truth or error, she could always find her own practical example of it.

Her personal doings and reasoned principles, both revealed to us in full detail in her diary and in the formal Victorian autobiography edited by her daughter Mrs Kelly, are a sub-history of average English life throughout her period. She was the daughter of an attractive easy-going Staffordshire parson, George Butt, of a good minor-gentry family. The social circle of her first twenty years included the literary and well-educated folk who hovered, more or less, round Lichfield: Anna Seward, the Sneyds and Edgeworths, Erasmus Darwin, the Winningtons and Annesleys, Isaac Hawkins Browne, Dr Valpy of Reading (who introduced the Butts to many *émigrés*), Cyril Jackson of Christ Church, and many others of that intellectual middle-class which had produced the Blue Stockings and was itself a typical product of the Georgian era.

She received a good education at home, and afterwards, with her sister Lucy, went to a school at Reading Abbey (later moved to London) kept by a refugee, Mme St Quentin, who is described vividly both by herself and another pupil, Mary Russell Mitford. In 1803 she married her cousin Henry Sherwood, who had had adventures as a civilian in hostile France and had served with his regiment in the West Indies. For two years she followed the camp in England, under conditions barely imaginable in our lifetime. She went round the Cape to India (there is hardly a word of the European conflict in her diaries), met there the mission-field influences already mentioned and came back in 1816. None too well-off – for Captain Sherwood was now placed on half-pay – the Sherwoods settled near Worcester, and Mrs Sherwood engaged in writing regularly, and also took in pupils; and brought up her family in addition. She wrote, before her death on September 22, 1851 – *wrote* with her own hand almost entirely – over three hundred stories, tracts and similar publications, a diary more than half a million words long, and innumerable business and other letters.

In that fecundity, and in variety of experience, her career was very different from that of most contemporary writers for children. Yet it began and ended much as theirs did, and except for her particular shade of dogma it was the same in essence. She was a genuinely typical figure, running, by chance, in an unusual orbit.

In many of her smaller booklets – little story-tracts written chiefly for Houlston, her first publisher, of Shropshire, and for my predecessors – she had been associated with her sister Lucy, afterwards Mrs Cameron. On her return to England the publishers would send proofs of illustrations which they had in

25. A wood-engraved block prepared for *The Book of the United Kingdom* by 'Uncle John' (i.e. Samuel Clark), probably first published in 1839 for 1840. A year or two later, however, the picture was sent to Mrs Sherwood who used it with many others (including several from an earlier *Robinson Crusoe*) for her concocted tale *Think Before You Act*. In this the very typical Robin Hood group have become 'Spanish buccaneers'.

stock, and round these, with great ingenuity, the sisters wove tales moral in purpose but by no means uninteresting as narratives. Mrs Cameron, though slightly overshadowed by her sister, was a voluminous and popular writer. Her life, incorporating some autobiography, was written by her son Charles. *Margaret Whyte* and *The Two Lambs* were perhaps her best-known tales. She was consistently serious. As she grew older – like most writers for children, except Maria Edgeworth – she deprecated that frivolity of her own youth which she was equally apt to deplore in the rising generation. She viewed religious changes with apprehension, but seems never to have quite reached her sister's doctrinal inflexibility. The most striking thing in her life, in fact, was its tolerant religious atmosphere. She was staunchly Church of England, and when Catholic Emancipation came wrote 'Anti-Christ reigns over us once more'. She feared Lancaster's unsectarianism. She observed the Oxford Movement with some alarm. She urged her son not 'to visit the Oxford Tract People', though 'many of them mean well'. She saw, none the less, that the Tractarians might 'have been raised up to warn the Evangelical clergy of the danger they were likely to fall into, of mixing too much with the world'. Finally, Thomas Arnold of Rugby, J. H. Shorthouse and Pusey all recommended warmly her tract-stories for young children.

6

These two sisters, popular and eminent in their limited sphere, focus most of the development of the Moral Tale on its less imaginative side. Mrs Sherwood abhorred fairy-tales, as her treatment of Sarah Fielding's *Governess* shows. She reverted to extreme Puritanism. She was a magnificent story-teller. She was

173

what the Elizabethans called a 'good housekeeper'. Her sister would have no self-assertion in the lower orders, was a confirmed didacticist, an anti-Papist, and yet lived to half-condone as well as to be praised by the Tractarians. The average life was not taut at extremes.

One must, in judging the Moral Tale, forget what it is so easy to pick out afterwards, inaccurately, as typical – the noise made by the prophet in or near his own time. The propagandist appeared, certainly, or was heard, in the Edgeworths; and, very differently, in Mrs Sherwood's devotion to the poor Indian and Calvinism. But for the average English middle-class writer for children – the steady purveyors for the expanding market – there was no startling voice crying in a wilderness. The Pilkingtons, the Mants, the Elliotts, never knew what a wilderness was. There were firm principles behind what they wrote, but they were acceptances, not evangels. They sought to make no conversions to a bright new gospel, and they did not think out deeply their own prepossessions or the peculiarities of their enforced audience. They started and ended with what they had always taken for granted. They lived in a kind of abstract benevolence.

It often seems, in short, as if the real child were sometimes utterly overlooked by such writers, except as a *tabula rasa* for a heavy pen. And yet they were human, and now and then suddenly saw both weakness and sheer happiness not ungently. Maria Edgeworth gave Rosamond that illuminating little hesitation about her future goodness. Mrs Sherwood recorded that as a child, after standing in an iron collar with a backboard all day to do her lessons, she 'manifested her delight by . . . taking a run for half a mile through the woods'; and she must have understood very well the fearful joy of greediness. Mrs Trimmer was willing to tread on fairies, and insisted on 'really useful' toys; but she flatly refused to abolish dolls and doll's-house tea-things. She pictured, with hearty sympathy, a peasant's family enjoying themselves after the day's work, while the goodwife sang at her spinning-wheel,

and sweetened her harder labours. Her most favourite [songs] were, *The Berkshire Lady, Fair Rosamond, The Lamentations of Jane Shore,* and *Chevy Chace.* No song was ever sung by this fireside that had the least immorality in it, or that ridiculed anything that was religious: neither did anyone relate nonsensical stories about ghosts and apparitions.

But *The Guardian of Education* deplored that sort of song altogether. Many little chance touches like these hint that children were still children after all; and, what is better, that when it came down to life itself outside books, the moralists were well aware of the facts and did not try so hard as all that to get them altered.

Still, unless one reads very closely, their books cannot but give a certain impression of rigidity, of inhuman excellence, of making life not worth living in the attempt to live it worthily. Something a little different, a little more suggestive of greater changes to come, appears in the other aspect of the Moral Tale, in its expression (for the most part) in verse.

BRIEF BOOK LIST

For Mrs Trimmer, Priscilla Wakefield and Mrs Sherwood, see *D.N.B.* and *C.H.E.L.*;
for minor writers, works cited in *N.C.B.E.L.* and in text above. In general, add E. V.
Lucas, *Old Fashioned Tales* (London, 1905) and *Forgotten Tales of Long Ago* (London,
1906), and works cited in the General Book List, especially Miss Barry's 'Century'. The
following were omitted or have appeared since these lists were compiled:

'Anstey, F.' [F. Anstey Guthrie]. *The Last Load* (London, 1925). On *The Fairchild
Family* and *Henry Milner*: 'I doubt whether, with all its didactic piety, the most
secular-minded child can ever have found *The Fairchild Family* dull.'

Balfour, Clara Lucas. *A Sketch of Mrs Trimmer* (London, 1854).

[Cameron, George.] *The Life of Mrs Cameron* (London, 1862).

Cameron, the Ven. Archdeacon G. H. *John Cameron, Non-Juror*. Privately printed
(Oxford, 1919).

Darton, F. J. H. 'Bell and the Dragon', *Fortnightly Review*, May 1909, pp. 896–909.

Harrop, A. J. *The Amazing Career of Edward Gibbon Wakefield* (London, 1928).

Salmon, David. *The Practical Parts of Lancaster and Bell* (Cambridge, 1932).

Supplement

The work of Day, the Edgeworths and the moral writers receives general discussion as
part of a wider purpose in such books as Gillian Avery's *Childhood's Pattern* (see General
Book List). See also David Grylls, *Guardians and Angels; parents and children in nineteenth
century literature* (London, 1978). Narrower studies are:

Yarde, D. M. *The Life and Works of Sarah Trimmer* . . . (Hounslow, 1972). A pamphlet
which uses information drawn from an important work not mentioned above: *Some
Account of the Life and Writings of Mrs Trimmer* (London, 1814).

Jordan, Philip D. *The Juvenilia of Mary Belson Elliott*, with additions by Daniel C.
Haskell (New York, 1936).

Cutt, M. Nancy. *Mrs Sherwood and her Books for Children* (London, 1974), which
includes a list of Mrs Sherwood's books, categorized by publisher, and photographic
reprints of *The Little Woodman and his Dog Caesar* (12th edn, Wellington, 1828) and
the 'chapbook' *Soffrona and her Cat Muff* (Wellington, 1828).

Other reprints include:

'Mrs Teachwell' (Ellenor Fenn), *Fables in Monosyllables* (1783), introduced by
Catherine Shakura (New York and East Ardsley, 1970); and A. Berquin, *The
Looking-Glass for the Mind* (1794), introduced by Dana T. Herren (New York and
East Ardsley, 1969).

CHAPTER XI

The Moral Tale:
(ii) Persuasive; chiefly in verse

I

Between Isaac Watts's day and the early years of the nineteenth century, very little verse was written specially for children. The Newbery scrap about 'Three children sliding on the ice', whatever its origin, and the dormouse poem in *Goody Two-Shoes*, whatever *its* origin, were specks in a very small sea of adult condescensions. Nursery rhymes and rhymed alphabets, even if they were widely circulated in print, as to which the evidence is of a negative kind, were no more than traditional. Watts held a field which few people deemed worth tillage. It would be nearly true, but not quite, to say that between 1715 and 1804 no 'original poems for infant minds' were uttered.

Ann and Jane Taylor, who used those words as a title with good warrant, were in fact both the successors of Watts and the creators of the Moral Tale in verse. But in the interval there were three writers who stand out as separate figures. They made verse, respectively, for, at, and about children.

The earliest was John Marchant, Gent., who, from the little that can be gathered from his works, must have been a strange fellow. He published some sturdy and even violent anti-Papist books, and two very unusual volumes of verse for children – *Puerilia: or, Amusements for the Young* (1751) and *Lusus Juveniles: or, Youth's Recreation* (1753). The sub-title to *Puerilia*, which is a well-printed book with a folding copperplate frontispiece and an engraved title-page, runs 'Songs for Little Misses, Songs for Young Masters, Songs on Divine, Moral, and other Subjects', which sounds like a mixture of Watts and Newbery, but is no more than common form. The interesting feature of both works is what he calls 'other Subjects'. There was apparently no limit to what he deemed suitable, except that 'Fable conveys no other idea to the Mind than that of a mere Fiction', as he says in the Preface to *Lusus* and 'Tales, Novels, and Romances produce the same or the like Effect'. He ranges freely, otherwise. He describes in joyful, even luscious rhyme the pleasures of a harvest feast – the dancing, the good food, the lashings of drink, and that capacious song 'Here's a health to the Barley Mow'. Another poem (in the *Lusus*) is called 'Decoy-Ducks: or, the Pleasures of a Brothel'. He liked music (the frontispiece to the same book – which, incidentally, was published by Mary Cooper – shows an operatic performance); he knew that children played with toys, tops and kites – rather foolishly, he thought, but still they could get a lesson from them; and above all, he had a quick eye for country sights and vivid little peepshows. He *saw* a great deal – more than many children's authors before or since; and what he saw was usually – not always, as 'Decoy-Ducks' shows – 'Occurrences that happen within [children's] own little Sphere of Action'. But he had no true imagination. He was simply very much alive, very inquisitive, abruptly serious; as if he were immensely delighted with the bright surface of things and then suddenly remembered that he was a Puritan: an odd mixture, a little like Partridge in *Tom Jones*. So far as I can see, his books attracted little attention and were not reprinted.

Nathaniel Cotton, the second of these lonely figures, lived from 1705 to 1788, which, even had he not achieved it, would have been his proper span and sphere. He wrote *Visions in Verse, for the Entertainment and Instruction of Younger Minds* (1751). It went into many editions; Dodsley did a pretty one with a

HYMNS for CHILDREN. 73

Pray Remember the POOR.

I.

I Juſt came by the priſon door,
I gave a penny to the poor :
Papa did this good act approve,
And poor Mamma cry'd out for Love.

II.

Whene'er the poor comes to my gate,
Relief I will communicate;
And tell my Sire his ſons ſhall be
As charitably great as he.

H 3   PLENTEOUS

26. A fourth name that might be added to the three poets discussed here is that of John Newbery's afflicted son-in-law Christopher Smart. His *Hymns for the Amusement of Children* was first published by T. Carnan, probably in 1771, and stands mid-way between the conventional versifying of Cotton and the powerful originality of Blake.

frontispiece of cherub heads. It will be remembered that Dr Cotton was a capable and humane alienist who had Cowper among his patients. His verse has deserved less long recollection. It is bland and equable, and the *Visions* instruct 'Younger' minds excellently, within their professed range; as do some of his miscellaneous verses such as 'To Some Children Listening to a Lark':

> See, the lark prunes [or preens?] his active wings,
> Rises to heaven, and soars, and sings.
> His morning hymns, his mid-day lays,
> Are one continued song of praise . . .
> Shall birds instructive lessons teach,
> And we be deaf to what they preach?

There was nothing in such fancies to excite any particular emotion, good or evil. It is creditable to the author and his epoch that they were highly esteemed at the time. It would have been strange if they were not. That is their historical value today.

2

The third author is solitary and unique, in essence neither of his own period nor of any other, for genius is lonely. In that period, so far as children were concerned, he was little known. He transcended then and always all other poets whom children could read; but it is only in the last fifty years or so that his spirit has become a living spark in poetry meant for children. One can call his a new voice in 1789. It is still a new voice in 1932. Then and now its music is for those who are themselves the poets, the dreamers,

> World-losers and world-forsakers,
> On whom the pale moon gleams.

It has never become a detail of history, a mere emblem or witness from ordinary English life.

It is simplest to quote outright the first poem in William Blake's *Songs of Innocence*, for it can serve as a text for all that can be said of him in a record of real children's books. It is often quoted as 'The Piper', but that is not its title nor its strict connotation. The *Songs of Innocence* are usually treated as if they were songs for Innocents, whereas they are nothing of the kind. This is their

> INTRODUCTION
> Piping down the valleys wild
> Piping songs of pleasant glee
> On a cloud I saw a child.
> And he laughing said to me.
>
> Pipe a song about a Lamb:
> So I piped with merry chear,
> Piper pipe that song again –
> So I piped, he wept to hear.
>
> Drop thy pipe thy happy pipe
> Sing thy songs of happy chear.

So I sung the same again
While he wept with joy to hear

Piper sit thee down and write
In a book that all may read –
So he vanish'd from my sight.
And I pluck'd a hollow reed

And I made a rural pen,
And I stain'd the water clear,
And I wrote my happy songs,
Every child may joy to hear

(The punctuation is that of the engraved first edition. It is important. Line 8, for instance, is equivocal; a semi-colon or full-stop after 'piped' makes only one sense possible.) Blake, when he produced – literally produced : wrote, drew, engraved and put forth – his *Songs of Innocence* (1789, dated) and *Songs of Experience* (1794), was himself, in a spiritual sense, a child happy on a cloud, singing and desiring such songs as few but he could write. But he was also setting down what a child had thought, setting it down as an expression of human nature as he saw and had observed it – as innocent experience recorded, not as an offering to innocence; and the Introduction, to that extent, explains the very root of that experience, the immediate ecstasy of joy without shadow or reflection.

A great imaginative writer had, in fact, broken into this narrow library that others were toiling so laboriously to fill for children. Those others, the Edgeworths, the Watts's, the Taylors, the Lambs, the Trimmers (for they are all in the same gallery in this task), had their ideals, high, practical, long, severe, whatever you like to call them. But they never dreamt of knocking at the gate of heaven or playing among the tangled stars. At best they could only laugh a little and break a few weak chains of solemnity. They never saw the strange distance that is sometimes lifted up almost into sight beyond the clear clean horizon of sunset. They were never taken out of themselves. They always were themselves in a world of selves mutually communicable. Blake did not fit into their library, excellent though its accommodation was beginning to be. But today it is his spirit that its poets would like to recapture.

It is germane to the present purpose, however, to say only that at the stated time he brought these two books into the world, that he was received thus and thus, and that certain things were in his mind in the performance. As to his reception, whatever splendour we attribute to his genius now, under George III he was simply an obscure writer, painter and engraver: not the prophetic flame we see now standing out against a negligible background. Mrs Trimmer was better known and more widely read, as numbers go, than Blake or Lamb. Lamb had heard of her: there is no evidence that she had ever heard of Lamb. It should perhaps be unnecessary to say that kind of thing. But it is important to get the right local or temporary perspective. The plain fact is that when *Songs of Innocence* appeared, there was a large generation of young persons who had to have their faces washed, their bellies filled, and their minds garnished by a rough and ready habitual process rather than by a series of inspirations. The process ignored Blake for years to come. He was only a grubby old eccentric communing with God in a back garden, in a world where he, like everyone else, had to earn a living. A few intellectuals caught the flash of his curious eyes. But they too were eccentric, not of the general orbit.

Blake himself had to be aware of that fact, perforce. He did practical work which is curiously interwoven with the main thread of this record. Mary Wollstonecraft in 1788 wrote a children's book called *Original Stories from Real Life* (the text is more conveniently considered a little further on). It was published in that year by J. Johnson, and in 1791 he issued an edition with plates designed and engraved by William Blake. About the same time, Blake was doing hack-work of another kind for him – adapting some designs of Chodowiecki, the German illustrator, and engraving them for English use. These designs – with others probably not adapted by Blake – adorned the *Elements of Morality*, by Christian Gotthilf Salzmann, the German semi-Rousseauist, which Mary Wollstonecraft had just translated. In adapting the drawings, Blake naturally read the book, or rather the translation, which included Salzmann's own preface. Salzmann had dwelt, in a very modern manner, on the question of teaching children purity. We should, he said, 'speak to children of the organs of generation as freely as we speak of the other parts of the body, and explain to them the noble use which they were designed for, and how they may be injured.' Blake, as Mr Joseph Wicksteed points out, did what Salzmann could hardly hope to do with safety if even his less (as they then were) advanced views on other matters were to be printed at all. He wove the theme, the facts, of purity and human physical nature into the fabric of the *Songs of Innocence*. But he did the almost mechanical task of engraving another man's drawings in order to earn a living – to be able to do his own designs for the *Songs*.* It is a strange conjunction of the worldly and the spiritual: not less strange, and even ironical, when one remembers that a year after Blake did these engravings, Mary Wollstonecraft herself was, in the eyes of the world, going to the devil with Imlay in Paris, for the sake of the flesh; but, in her own sight, for the sake of freedom and the spirit.

3

These high thoughts had then no real place in the furniture of the nursery library. In the eighties and nineties of that century, and earlier, it was doubtful

---

* Mr Wicksteed pointed out Blake's familiarity with the Salzmann preface in *The Times Literary Supplement*, Feb. 18, 1932. He mentions there some of the dates of Blake's 'hack'-work. The first English edition of the *Elements of Morality* was in two volumes, dated 1790 on the title-page. The plates first appeared in the three-volume edition of 1791 and were dated from Oct. 1, 1790 to March 15, 1791. The sheets of this edition were re-issued by Johnson in 1792, 1799 and 1805 and, in a two-volume edition, by John Sharpe at the Juvenile Library, Piccadilly c.1815.

27. 'My Son! My Son!' An engraving by William Blake from *For Children*(1793). Only five copies are known of this extraordinary little book, and only twelve of its later expanded and re-worked successor *For the Sexes. The Gates of Paradise* (1818?). While in appearance it lies closer to an emblem book than to a book of illuminated verse like the *Songs*, the content and sequence of its images have a vibrancy and an imaginative potential that are the equivalent of that present in the poetry.

whether the verse form itself ought to be on the shelves. Isaac Watts and Mrs Barbauld were far from sure of its value to the young intelligence. Their eyes were holden by the period's strong sense of hard clear pattern, a pattern not of colour but of well-proportioned shapes fitting one another. By poetry they meant metre and scansion, which were the antithesis of prose: and poetry, by involving these artifices, was unnatural and difficult to children. They were underrating their own public, really. They spoke as grown-up patrons, aloof though affectionate, kindly but alien.

The book that awoke the nurseries of England, and those in charge of them – *Original Poems for Infant Minds*, 'by Several Young Persons' (1804; Vol. II, 1805) – might well have fallen under the same suspicion of condescendingness, if its preface were to be taken as literally as its authors seem to have expected. This introduction begins with a modest claim to a moral purpose, not very happily phrased:

If a hearty affection for that interesting little race, the race of children, is any recommendation, the writers of the following pages are well recommended; and if to have studied in some degree their capacites, habits, and wants, with a wish to adapt these simple verses to their real comprehensions, and probable improvement – if this has any further claim to the indulgence of the public, it is the last and only one they attempt to make.

'Piper, pipe that song again.' The several young persons heard the words, but in a different voice. The writers were Ann Taylor, aged twenty-two in 1804; Jane Taylor, aged twenty-one; Isaac Taylor (third of that name in the family), aged seventeen – these of the younger generation; their friend – was he? – Bernard Barton, aged twenty, possibly Isaac Taylor II, their father; and Adelaide O'Keeffe, aged twenty-eight, who apparently was foisted into the volume by the publishers. Though 'young persons', once grown-up were fully grown-up, the backward, downward glance, by writers of years so tender, at 'that interesting little race' is a trifle complacent. Were they really as mature as all that in 1804?

As a matter of fact, Ann Taylor herself had commenced author when she was only sixteen, so that perhaps there was some warrant for the adult attitude. But any fears that it would be dominant in the book are greatly allayed by the poems themselves. They were 'original', as no previous poems for the young had been, in that you can see the authors, as it were, talking lovingly and naturally to real flesh-and-blood middle-class children whom they knew: almost to themselves, indeed.

> It is not to tease you, and hurt you, my sweet,
>   But only for kindness and care,
> That I wash you, and dress you, and make you look neat,
>   And comb out your tanglesome hair.
> I don't mind the trouble, if you would not cry,
>   But pay me for all with a kiss;
> That's right, – take the towel and wipe your wet eye,
>   I thought you'd be good after this.

wrote Ann in 'Washing and Dressing'; and you feel sure that 'Mrs Taylor of Ongar' had been kissing Ann herself in just that simple family way not so many years before.

That is the revolution made by *Original Poems*, and its successors *Rhymes for the Nursery* (1806) and *Hymns for Infant Minds* (1810). They rendered the 'little race' natural, and the monitor's attitude to it also as natural as contemporary manners permitted. On the other hand, the *Original Poems* themselves, when they became tales in verse instead of comments on life or spontaneous little pictures of pleasant and beautiful things, as they sometimes were, lost much of their originality, and were no more than rhymed moralities. But they were that too with a difference. Miss Edgeworth had let foolishness or misconduct lead inevitably – by 'Nature' – to retributive justice. The other moral fabulists in prose had done the same, less dexterously, or had brought in the tutor or schoolmistress to point out the offence. The Taylors just made things happen. Meddlesome Matty spied the pretty snuff-box, and her idle hands mischievously opened it: 'she could do nothing else but sneeze', and so she broke her grandmother's spectacles. There is no real moral in that: the box might have been Pandora's, for all Matty knew, or a chest in King Solomon's mines, or have held a genie. The only lessons honestly conveyed is that you should never open any boxes at all. Equally untrue, didactically, is 'The Little Fisherman'. Harry, who *would* catch fishes (though Mrs Trimmer had given excellent reasons for proper use of the brute creation), was himself caught by the chin on a meat-hook – quite capriciously and un-morally, because he was doing what any prudent angler would have done, putting tomorrow's breakfast in the larder. The Taylors, in fact, invented the 'awful warning' school of poetry, which has led to a thousand cheerful parodies very remote from the authors' intentions.

However, in spite of their moral purpose, they never lost their humanity: they were still too close to childhood, and too happy a family, to become prigs when they started writing. And they had a sense of humour surpassed, among contemporary writers for children, only by Maria Edgeworth's. 'The Notorious Glutton':

> A duck, who had got such a habit of stuffing,
> That all the day long she was panting and puffing

is a timeless and jolly piece, in spite of Mrs Duck's unhappy end. The awful warnings, unlike Mrs Sherwood's in prose, are really quite cheerful. They had also a gift for legitimate pathos, as in 'The Last Dying Speech and Confession of Poor Puss', and for sheer unhesitating simplicity, as in 'Learning to go Alone' (from *Rhymes for the Nursery*):

> Come, my darling, come away,
> Take a pretty walk today;
> Run along, and never fear,
> I'll take care of baby dear;
> Up and down, with little feet,
> That's the way to walk my sweet.
>
> Now it is so very near,
> Soon she'll get to mamma dear,
> There she comes along at last,
> Here's my finger, hold it fast;
> Now one pretty little kiss,
> After such a walk as this.

You *must* like the Young Persons who could write in that style.

Some of their pieces, notoriously, have suffered, like Watts's, from the attrition of the school entertainment platform, or from the obloquy of easy parody. 'My Mother' is one, 'Twinkle, twinkle, little star' another, to meet that undeserved fate. But when it appeared, and for sixty years later, 'My Mother' was admired (as it was probably meant to be) for its moral tone as much as for the honest sentiment it expresses so fluently and yet so gracefully. It was by Ann. Augustus De Morgan, the mathematician, writing of it in *The Athenaeum* in the austere sixties, called it 'one of the most beautiful lyrics in the English language, or any other language', but thought that the 'bit of religion thrust in' spoilt it. He suggested that Tennyson should be asked 'in the name of all the children of England', to rewrite this verse:

> For God, who lives above the skies,
> Would look with vengeance in his eyes,
> If I should ever dare despise
>
>   My Mother.

He did not know that Ann – by then Mrs Gilbert – was still living, at the age of eighty-four. She at once agreed that she would no longer put the matter so straitly, and sent an alternative:

> For could our Father in the skies
> Look down with pleased or loving eyes,
> I ever I could dare despise
>
> My Mother.

'*Vengeance*', she wrote, 'is not a word I should now employ.'

That perhaps is the secret of the Taylors' freshness, which still lingers in the best of their children's verse, though the mode is nearly outworn. They were a large compact family, all alert. They wrote for and about real children – themselves – and did not press the moral issue for philosophical reasons, like Miss Edgeworth, or for theological, like Mrs Sherwood. The whole circle – in that generation Dissenters, in the next represented by Canon Isaac Taylor of *Words and Places* – could write, and most of them could also draw and engrave. They followed all these occupations in order to make a living, but they sought neither wealth nor fame. They did not go into public or literary circles to any great extent. They lived quietly in a middle-class fashion, serene and cheerful in the midst of tremendous happenings which are hardly hinted at in their writings. (But that silence is common to all domestic writers of the period.) What that meant in the way of circumscribed intercourse and mutual tolerance is best described in Ann's own words about their home at Lavenham, an old home of Pilgrim Fathers whose descendants occasionally try to transport its buildings to America today. The Taylors spent their early years there:

Nurseries at Lavenham, and at that time of day, I do not remember. The parlour and the best parlour were all that was known beside the kitchens, and thus parents and children formed happily but one circle . . . My father and mother were soon noted as good managers of their children; for little as either of them had experienced of a wise education themselves, they had formed a singularly strong resolve to train their young ones with the best judgement they could exercise, and not to suffer *humoured* children to disturb either themselves or their friends. There is scarcely an expression so fraught to my earliest recollection with ideas of disgrace and misery as that of a 'humoured child', and I should have felt truly ashamed to exhibit one of my own at my father's table.

('A child should never have anything he cried for': Newbery, Rousseau . . .) Their little world was repeated, probably, in almost every parish in England. Its difference from others lay in the fact that all its members were articulate and eager. 'It was', as E. V. Lucas has excellently said, 'almost impossible to be a Taylor and not write.'

His centenary edition of the *Original Poems* gives a crowded little picture of the family's life and writings. Of the non-Taylor contributors to that volume, Bernard Barton (1784–1849) is known for his friendship with Lamb, as well as by his own not very exciting work. Adelaide O'Keeffe (1776–1855) is the author of one of the best and best-known poems in the collection:

> The Dog will come when he is call'd,
> The Cat will walk away,

> The Monkey's cheek is very bald.
>   The Goat is fond of play.
> The Parrot is a prate-a-pace,
>   Yet knows not what she says;
> The noble Horse will win the race,
>   Or draw you in a chaise.

and deserves a few lines of comment. Her position is peculiar. She seems not to have been acquainted with the Taylors personally. There were thirty-four poems by her in the whole collection, and some of them, as compact narratives ('Idle Dicky and the Goat', for instance), are among the freshest. But she was neither a Quaker – like Barton and the publishers – nor at all in the same kind of social milieu as the amiable Taylor family. Her father was John O'Keeffe, the genial and for a time very successful Irish dramatist and song-writer, author of at least one song still known, 'The Friar of Orders Grey'. O'Keeffe, in spite of help from the Regent, finally declined in wealth and popularity, and Adélaïde – so she herself once spelt it – cared for him devotedly until his death in 1833. She lived with him first at Chichester, where they were 'much respected and esteemed', and afterwards at Southampton. She acted as his amanuensis and wrote for him the whole of his lively but untrustworthy *Recollections* (1826): her hand was nearly incapacitated by the strain. She managed his finances, and did her best to make money by writing herself. For her children's verses she received from my ancestors £100 in all: the Taylors, by her account got more, but she seems to have been treated not unfairly as regards actual cash. Her chief other books, all her own work, were *Original Poems calculated to Improve the Mind of Youth and Allure it to Virtue* (1808), *National Characters* (1818: verse), *Dudley* (1819: a novel), *A Trip to the Coast* (1819), *Zenobia, Queen of Palmyra* (1814), *Patriarchal Times* (1811) and *Poems for Young Children* (1849). Some of these were published by the Darton firms, but not all: she was therefore in some general demand. They were successful to a certain extent, but the Taylors remained in higher esteem as writers for children, while for her – as a pathetic inscription by her in one of her own copies of *Patriarchal Times* records – 'the Pen burned, and no Phoenix'. She is rather a melancholy and incongruous figure.

As for that lively family at Lavenham and Ongar, the Taylors themselves must here remain a representative assembly, and no more. Isaac the son wrote *The Natural History of Enthusiasm* and many other meritorious works: Isaac the father, *inter alia*, *Self-Cultivation Recommended; or, Hints to a Youth leaving School* (1817) and *Bunyan explained to a Child* (1824, followed by a second volume in 1825): his wife, *Reciprocal Duties of Parents and Children* (1818), *The Family Mansion: a Tale* (1819), and many other stories and didactic treatises, notably *Correspondence between a Mother and her Daughter at School* (1817), in which Jane collaborated as the daughter. Jane here and elsewhere showed a keen eye for kindly satire, and with a little greater freedom of circumstance might have stood near to Maria Edgeworth as a novelist for adults, if not, indeed, to Jane Austen herself. Ann wrote little independently. Another brother, Jefferys (1792–1853), too young to get into print in 1804, except possibly as the subject of one of the poems, produced *Aesop in Rhyme* (1820) already mentioned (see p. 9), *Ralph Richards the Miser* (1821), and several other 'instructive and amusing' little books. The most notable of these is an unusual Robinsonnade in which a whole boys' school is suborned into boarding a ship and meets with a lively series of adventures, almost entirely free of moralization: *The Young Islanders*(1842).

4

Original Poems had an enormous success. Its first volume of 1804 reached a second and third edition in 1805, and that year saw the appearance of volume II, which likewise ran to two more printings, 'with additions', before the end of the next year. There is no coincidence in the dating and edition-numbering of the two volumes, which were presumably often sold separately, until a 'new, revised' edition abandoned the sequence in 1835–6, by which time volume I seems to have been in its thirty-first edition and volume II in its twenty-seventh. The first one-volume edition, which was also the first to be illustrated with more than frontispieces, was that published by Virtue Bros. in 1865. Kate Greenaway did a famous set of illustrations in 1883. In 1925 Miss Edith Sitwell 'introduced' a selection under the title of one of the poems, *Meddlesome Matty*. I do not think they have ever been wholly out of print.

Naturally, both the originality and the success bred imitations almost at once, some of them deprecating comparison with the Taylors' work, though obviously inspired by it, others simply following the fashion without admitting it. The greater number do but accentuate the virtues of Ann and Jane in respect of rhythm, ease, and the one quality their title claimed, originality. One – *Rhymes and Pictures for the Nursery and School. By a Lady* (n.d.: type and illustrations of the period) – deserves quotation for that purpose. A little girl, as in so many poems and tales of that day, *would* eat forbidden fruit:

> They went on a little, but Anna complain'd
> 　Of pain in her stomach and head,
> And very soon follow'd most terrible pains,
> 　She shriek'd out with anguish and dread . . .
> She died from not doing what Ma had desired,
> 　And eating the fruit of the wood.

Not all the imitations were so remote as that.

Two other workers in this trim if narrow field survive today in a manner they can hardly have expected. One of them might scarcely be known as a writer for children but for her illustrious surname. The other lives, it is not too much to say, through the unholy mirth she has provoked in later generations. This was the redoubtable but mysterious Elizabeth Turner, about whom nothing, outside her books, seems to be known except that she lived at Whitchurch in Shropshire

28. Kate Greenaway's nursery interpretation of 'James and the Shoulder of Mutton', one of Adelaide O'Keeffe's contributions to *Original Poems for Infant Minds*, 1804. The scene shows an accident which is said actually to have happened to William Darton, the son of the book's first publisher.

and died in 1846. She wrote *The Daisy; or, Cautionary Stories in Verse. Adapted to the Ideas of Children from four to eight years old* (1807), *The Cowslip* (1811), *The Pink* (1823; edited, with additions, by Mary Howitt, in 1835), *The Blue-Bell* (1838) and *The Crocus* (1844). There were imitations by other writers.

No moralist was ever more straightforward than Elizabeth Turner. Right was right, wrong wrong, and wrong invited and received the rod, and no questions asked – or, at least, very seldom, and then only for good reason. One of her poems begins

> Mamma had order'd Ann, the maid,
> Miss Caroline to wash.

Miss Caroline had objected. The matter did not end with a kiss, as in *Original Poems*. The last line runs 'to whip her, there's no doubt'. In other pieces Nature was the agent of punishment. 'Jack Parker was a cruel boy', and teased animals:

> But all such boys, unless they mend,
> May come to an unhappy end;
> Like Jack who got a fractur'd skull,
> Whilst bellowing at a furious bull.

The rather ludicrous sight-rhyme in the last couplet is not up to the Turner level of metrical inevitability. It would be hard to find anything more defiantly rhythmical than some of the pieces: 'Truth the Best' from *The Crocus*, for instance:

> Yesterday Rebecca Mason,
>   In the parlour by herself,
> Broke a handsome china basin,
>   Placed upon the mantel shelf.
>
> Quite alarmed, she thought of going
>   Very quietly away,
> Not a single person knowing
>   Of her being there that day.
>
> But Rebecca recollected
>   She was taught deceit to shun;
> And the moment she reflected
>   Told her mother what was done;
>
> Who commended her behaviour,
> Loved her better, and forgave her.

It may be silly. It may lack humour – to such an extent that one very nearly suspects Elizabeth Turner of writing with her tongue in her cheek. But the martial beat of it is irresistible. And it could be bellowed, in the manner of Jack Parker, to half a dozen shoddy popular tunes in *Hymns Ancient and Modern*: perhaps Miss Turner even had a semi-liturgical use of it in her mind, as Mrs Barbauld, more legitimately, had for her *Hymns in Prose*.

But it is also so uncommonly like W. S. Gilbert's Archibald Grosvenor poems in *Patience* that the most sympathetic person may today feel uncertain about it. *Can* it be serious? Was Miss Turner in earnest? Or did she wink secretly? She also wrote this:

> 'Papa', said Eugene, 'is a daisy a book?
>   I thought it was only a flower;
> Just now I ran down in the meadow, and look,
>   I have found one all wet with a shower.
>
> 'A book would be spoil'd, you know, left in the rain;
>   And could not be read for the dirt;
> But a daisy all day in the wet may remain,
>   Without in the least being hurt.'
>
> 'You are right', said Papa, with a smile, 'but you'll find
>   The Daisy a book, my boy, too,
> Containing short tales for the juvenile mind,
>   And adapted for children live [*sic*] you.
>
> 'And call'd as it is by so humble a name,
>   This hint indirectly conveys:
> Like the flow'ret it spreads, unambitious of fame,
>   Nor intrudes upon critical gaze.'

That is the twenty-eighth blossom in *The Cowslip*, and it is nothing more or less than a recommendation of its predecessor, *The Daisy*, in a manner which John Newbery would have been proud to invent. How *could* she do it – she who had that mastery of technique, that epic 'rapidity', that concentration? The sternest moralists of her tribe never leapt so swiftly and surely as she from crime to doom: her cautionary tales fascinate one almost obscenely, like a murder-trial. But she checked herself in her stride to write a puff.

5

The other exceptional imitator of the Taylors was Sara Coleridge, the poet's charming daughter. She too suffered from lack of humour; but there is no doubt about her being in earnest. She said: 'The *Original Poems* give too many pictures of mental depravity, bodily torture, and of adult sorrow; and I think the sentiments – the tirades, for instance, against hunting, fishing, shooting – are morbid, and partially false.' That is honestly and plainly expressed, and many would share the opinion. But Sara Coleridge went a very odd way to substitute, in her *Pretty Lessons in Verse, for Good Children* (1834), 'nothing but what is bright and joyous' for the sentiments she thus deplored. A remarkable moral conclusion is reached in a poem called 'Disappointment'. A boy named Colin, mountaineering with old and young friends, carried with him an orange, on which he expected, rationally and even greedily, to slake his thirst in due course. He could not help playing with it, dancing about and tossing it up as he leapt over the rocks. Suddenly it jumped out of his hand and rolled far out of reach:

> For some little time he stood still as a stock,
>   His face wore a fixed vacant stare;
> But soon he recover'd this terrible shock,
> And turning away from the edge of the rock
>   Threw off his disconsolate air.
>
> With thoughts of the basket he solaced his heart,
>   From thence real comfort might come;
> For he in the sandwiches still had a part,
> He perhaps might come in for a slice of the tart,
>   And there was the pine-apple rum.
>
> Since pleasure is apt through our fingers to slip,
>   And fate we can never withstand;
> Whene'er the full cup is thus dashed from the lip,
> Before we have taken the very first sip,
>   'Tis well to keep temper in hand.

Pickwick did not begin to appear till three years later, so that the author cannot be accused of making Colin an amalgam of the Fat Boy and Mr Stiggins. But none of the didacticists she criticized ever thought of quite such a 'pretty lesson' as is afforded by the comfort of a picnic basket and pineapple rum if you carelessly lose an orange.

Her verses were for a time popular: they reached a fourth edition in 1845. But the Taylors, mental depravity and all, have outlived her in fact. She is of some historical importance because she is on the inner fringe of great literature.

She proves that the idea of the Moral Tale was at least known to the loftier minds of the day, and she serves to provide here a transition to her father's friends, Charles and Mary Lamb.

6

The Lambs' writings for children certainly lay, to a greater extent, well within the Moral Tale ring-fence. They were written for the market. On the other hand, the authors personally, like Blake and, in a less degree, Oliver Goldsmith, are apt to be a little one-sidedly viewed in this connection. Lamb, of all men, was least of any period, even when he was spinning his own epoch out of himself in delicately shot silk. England under George III contained him, but did not produce him – so far as Elia the man is concerned. If he lived today, he would not have to write or think differently to win the suffrages of the judicious (not that he ever sought them). But if he and his sister wrote their children's books today, they might very well not find an eager publisher. Neither would the Taylors, Mrs Trimmer, Mrs Elliott, the Kilners; and even Maria Edgeworth would probably have to adapt her genius to altered forms. You can see small gleams of timeless genius in the interstices of the Lambs' juvenile books, but they are rare glints in a drab not of their own creating.

It is very difficult to rid oneself of the confusion between affectionate appreciation of the writer for 'grown-ups' and a transferred uncritical affection for the same writer when he is not creating spontaneously. But love of Lamb as an essayist, and the inextricable love of himself and Mary as human figures, must not conceal the fact that their children's books neither were nor are of much value in the evolution of their kind. Except that one of the productions may have led some children to read Shakespeare, they inspired nothing, they showed no fresh point of view, they won no wide hearing as compared with workaday stuff by other writers with like aims and no claims on the adult intelligence. All their seven 'juveniles' (the coarse trade term is used on purpose) must be considered here simply as common objects by the wayside of social history, not museum pieces or personal treasures.

(They have, however – to step still further aside – this value: that they show, if it were necessary, that children's books were no longer a very minor by-product of general literature; and to that extent they direct to the special subject persons who might otherwise ignore it.)

The first of the series was Lamb's own – *The King and Queen of Hearts* (1805). It was not meant to be anything more than a trifle. The ancient rhyme – whose origin has been frequently discussed without much definite result – has not been ousted by this version which seems to have had no noticeable contemporary life. Nor had (whether Lamb wrote it or not) the same year's, now scarce, *Book explaining the Ranks and Dignities of British Society. Intended chiefly for the Instruction of Young Persons*. Tabart reissued this in 1809, but with coloured plates dated 1805; and that edition (reprinted in facsimile in 1924) is also scarce. Lamb, writing to Manning (then in the East) on January 2, 1810, said: 'I have published a little book for children on titles of honour.' He followed it up with a noble list of the titles which might be conferred on himself, and ended with a piece of almost sublime irreverence which the more timid editors of his *Letters* omit.[1] It is not at all certain, however, that this 1924 discovery is really Lamb's work.

Neither book has any importance now except to collectors of Eliana. *Tales from Shakespear. Designed for the Use of Young Persons* (2 vols., 1806, but dated 1807) is an altogether different matter. It was the first joint work of Charles and Mary, who received sixty guineas for it. The greater part was by Mary. Charles did *Lear, Macbeth, Timon, Romeo, Hamlet* and *Othello*, and probably some passages in other tales – 'groaning all the while, and saying he can make nothing of it'. The plates, which he did not like, were probably by Mulready.[2]

Lamb may have found the task-work – for it was that – a matter for groaning, and not everyone today, perhaps, would affirm with complete conviction that the *Tales* either represent Shakespeare accurately or provide all modern children with spontaneous pleasure. They are written 'down' rather obviously and are often laboured, though the example quoted above (p. 25) from Mary's work is something of an extreme. On the other hand, they have, even if they *were* groaned over, a kind of earnestness and faith which grows into charm and gradually fastens upon even a careless reader. Often one might well guess at the personalities behind them (and not guess wrongly) if one knew merely the period and not the authorship. The English, as language, is more than a means of expression; it is an expression in itself. And in one respect the *Tales* were unique. No one had hitherto attempted anything of the kind. The Lambs gave to children and simple folk something like a reality of the Elizabethan spirit which at that time they could not otherwise obtain. The presentation of Shakespeare on the stage was at its stagiest. A 'child', Master Betty, 'the infant Roscius', a male Ninetta Crummles, was not untypical of what other children might see if (by a rare privilege) they were taken to the theatre. A little later they might read the *Family Skakespeare* (1818) of Dr Bowdler,* who, as Swinburne (of all people) wrote, made it 'possible' to put the poet 'into the hands of intelligent and imaginative children'. For the rest, there were the *Beauties of Shakespeare* selected by 'the unfortunate Dr Dodd', and rhetorical passages embalmed in semi-educational anthologies like Enfield's *Speaker*. It was a great thing for the English nursery, in fact, that at that period of the romantic revival there was at hand for it the man who in 1808 exhibited *Specimens of English Dramatic Poets who lived about the time of Shakespeare*. The *Tales* have many defects, and they are not the finest Elia nor yet the best that Mary could do.

---

* [This was the first edition at the hands of Dr Thomas Bowdler. An earlier edition in four volumes had however been published at Bath in 1807. This date, coupled to the further facts that the edition consisted of twenty plays and was the work of Bowdler's sister Harriet, form a neat, if fortuitous parallel with the Lambs' *Tales*.]

They bear unmistakable traces of the period's morality and commerce (a Janus god), for that very reason. But they are also to some extent a revolt against the traffic in didactics. It was in 1802 that Lamb cursed Barbauld 'science' in the letter to Coleridge already quoted (p. 129). The *Tales from Shakespear*, undertaken four years later at the suggestion of his business friend Godwin, can be considered at least as his attempt at 'averting the sore possibility' of science's triumph. They provide a defence of poesy by a kind of nursery introduction to it in prose.

The next Lamb children's book was by Charles alone. In this too he gave a prose specimen of Elizabethan literature, for his *Adventures of Ulysses* (1808) is based on Chapman's translation, not on Homer. It was a vast advance on the dismal morality of Fénelon's *Telemachus*, then still very rife in translations for juvenile readers. Though Chapman, to unsophisticated minds, may appear a little tortuous or crabbed in his roughness, Lamb achieved the strange feat of getting some of the *Odyssey*'s glorious ease into what might almost be simple Elizabethan prose. There are a few slightly pedagogic asides here and there ('Ulysses, of whose strength or cunning the Cyclop seems to have had as little heed as of an infant's' – you should never explain the obvious), but the whole runs with a gracious Homeric speed and smoothness. There was a little disagreement with Godwin over slight details, but it came to nothing. In freedom of description Lamb went some distance from the continuation of Fénelon which he originally intended, and from the opinions he stated in his preface.

Ulysses is a refreshing oasis in the moral desert, but it does not seem to have caused much excitement. The next in the Lambs' list was an unassailably moral tale, or rather set of moral tales, of the approved substance, but a little more distinguished in manner than the ruck, and gentler in outlook. *Mrs Leicester's School* (dated 1809; at first anonymous) is nearly all by Mary Lamb. In this 'History of Several Young Ladies, Related by Themselves', three stories only – *Maria Howe, Susan Yates* (*First Time of Going to Church*), and *Arabella Hardy, or, The Sea Voyage* – are related by Charles himself, and they are more serious and meditative than most of the others, though they also contain Elian touches of fantasy. In Mary's work there is a weakish humour and a very real tenderness, with something of the same sudden vision here and there. The morality, throughout, is not rampant. Possibly that is one reason why, to be honest, the tales as a whole are dull. They are often too contemplative and also too flickering, with brief intuitions and withdrawals taking the place of experience and action. They had some contemporary success because they were near enough to the market standard; a ninth edition was called for by 1825. They have remained in print and in middling repute rather through the general love of their authors than by their own vitality.

To go for a moment out of chronological order, *Prince Dorus, or Flattery Put Out of Countenance* (1811), ought to be mentioned briefly, but only in justice to its author. It is neater than some of the 'nonsense' stories in rhyme, pseudo-nursery rhymes, which by then were epidemic, and to which I come later. It was reasonably moral in a crude fashion: the slight fashion of a stage pantomime, a mode which its plot might suit. But it has no historical and not much literary value unless it be as a variant telling of a tale by Mme le Prince de Beaumont, 'Le Prince Désir', which appeared in the *Magasin des Enfans* in 1756. Nor need *Beauty and the Beast* (1811) detain us, for it is disputably Elian. At that time there were plenty of cheap editions of the famous tale on the market.

The remaining work has a great deal of small significance (authorship apart), as much by what it fails to do as by what it succeeds in doing. It is fairly clear that *Poetry for Children* (1809) was published, probably at Mrs Godwin's instance, as a result of the Taylors' success. Lamb said the poems were written to order, by 'an old bachelor and an old maid'. They are a most curious and unequal mixture, perhaps what one might have expected when the old bachelor was a man of genius – but still an old bachelor – and the old maid that haunting figure whom we know, so closely yet so distantly, as Mary Lamb. It is stretching language very far to believe that Charles's 'Queen Oriana's Dream' is either good poetry or good children's verse; and many other arch pieces creak audibly in the mechanism, apart from the old bachelor and old maid point of view. Yet simplicity sometimes wins. The opening lines of 'Cleanliness' (attributed to Charles):

> Come my little Robert near –
> Fie! what filthy hands are here –
> Who, that e'er could understand
> The rare structure of a hand,
> With its branching fingers fine,
> Work itself of hands divine . . .

begin like Jane Taylor and run into something like Blake. When the poems are definitely of the moral type, they are overweighted by length, and they sometimes reveal a sense of humour more deeply asleep than Mrs Turner's. Practically none has the real intimacy which a child could draw into a friendly embrace and keep warm in memory. Few show the quick imaginative simplicity of wonder, to be grasped at one splendid leap, the quality that is in Blake, in *The Forsaken Merman*, in *Goblin Market*. They are poems about children (not, indeed, about moral dolls, which is something to be thankful for), or about what the authors would like children to be thinking in their moments of infant contemplativeness, with their mortal span just becoming visible in front of them; not poems *for* children, except in so far as a socio-commercial demand envisaged the child.

In its day the *Poetry* had no great vogue. In fact, it almost disappeared. It went out of print in England – the United States had an edition in 1812 – and seems to have survived, for a time, only fragmentarily, but suitably, in 'Mylius's Reading Books', compilations made for use at Christ's Hospital.

29. The most obvious difference between the 'superior' and the ordinary editions of 'Baldwin's (i.e. Godwin's) *Fables* of 1805 lay in their illustration. In the first (a) these were full-size head-pieces for each fable, while in the second (b) the same picture was engraved in much reduced form on a composite plate of twelve subjects. These plates were surely much influenced in their form – but not their content – by the Dodsley–Baskerville *Fables* of 1761 (see above, fig. 5).

7

Those books, as has been said, were written for the market. In a certain sense the merchant of them is really a more significant person than the prime producer, though he happens to have been also a producer himself. Godwin is the nucleus of many of the smaller 'movements' in children's literature at this point; or rather, he is the figure by whose aid other persons stand out in a rather confused picture.

He published all the Lambs' children's books except the *Ranks and Dignities*, if indeed that is to be scheduled here at all. But he did not do so under his own name; in fact, at first not even under his own surname. He used that of his manager, Thomas Hodgkins, because political as well as financial circumstances made the name of William Godwin a detriment to commerce, though he was certainly, if eccentric, the best business person of those concerned – himself, Hodgkins, and his second wife. Mrs Godwin herself – *veuve* Clairmont, much disliked by Lamb, also, by her first marriage, the mother of a daughter unhappily associated with Byron – became the titular head of the firm in 1808, when it was known (after starting in Hanway Street in 1805), in Skinner Street, Holborn Hill, as the City Juvenile Library. It is said, indeed, that she herself decided on publishing as a means of making badly needed money, and it is possible that she actually first suggested the ideas conveyed to and carried out by Lamb. It would be pleasant, to one who (like E. V. Lucas, Lamb's own best editor) has had some intimacy with the publishing trade, to know more about

the traffic in Skinner Street, but it is unnecessary. Lamb did not take to Godwin at first. His description of him to Manning in 1800, when the two had just come together, is not flattering – 'a middle-sized man, both in stature and in understanding'. But the business association was decent and tolerably harmonious.

The attribution of mediocrity, however, is not altogether fair to Godwin. Neither *Caleb Williams* (1794) nor *Political Justice* (1793) can now be adjudged a mediocre book. The adjective would be more justly applied to the forgotten works which Godwin himself wrote for children – *The Pantheon: Ancient History for Schools and Young People* (Hodgkins, 1806), for instance, or his histories of England (1806) and Rome (1809). His account of Mulready's early struggles – *The Looking-Glass* (Hodgkins, 1805) – was at least kindly intentioned. It was put forth as by 'Theophilus Marcliffe', a device like the use of Hodgkins's name. Another juvenile work which he wrote under the pseudonym of 'Edward Baldwin', with seventy-three illustrations almost certainly by the young Mulready (sometimes ascribed to Blake), was *Fables Ancient and Modern* (Hodgkins, 1805; also translated into French and published in 1806). This had a very considerable success. I have not seen a complete first edition, but it was from the outset issued in two forms – an ordinary edition in one volume, a 'superior' edition in two.* It had reached a ninth in 1821; the 'superior' attained at least a fourth (1815). 'Edward Baldwin', as a matter of fact, became quite an established educational writer for the benefit of the firm of M. J. Godwin. He prefixed to the 1809 edition of Mylius's *School Dictionary* – a well-received work – 'A New Guide to the English Tongue'; and this, like *The Pantheon* and Mylius's educational productions, was welcomed by the schools. (Mylius it was who preserved some of Lamb's *Poetry for Children* for us until it was rediscovered by R. H. Shepherd much later: Mrs Godwin issued his school anthology.)

But over and above such works, Godwin also wrote – and both the book and the fact are typical and not the expression of a man wholly 'middle-sized in understanding' – the *Memoirs* of his first wife; a courageous service to the reputation of a great woman, who is, as has already been suggested, of some importance in this record of lesser history.

Mary Wollstonecraft, in composing *Original Stories from Real Life; with Conversations, calculated to regulate the affections and form the mind to truth and goodness* (1788), was giving her own views of regulation, truth and goodness quite as much as following a philosophy of the time or of any particular thinker; though her translation of Salzmann has caused her to be identified to some extent with his general school or doctrine. The *Original Stories* are most determinedly original. Mary Godwin (as she became in law in 1797, having lived with Godwin after the Imlay catastrophe of 1796) is completely dogmatic in this very remarkable work, but also completely logical. In her outline, she farmed out two girls to a female super-Barlow. They were placed 'under the tuition of a woman of tenderness and discernment' – Mrs Mason; I suspect her, too, of glass eyes and a wooden tail.† Mrs Mason also 'kept her head clear': none clearer. She was quite sure, quite final, about all rights and wrongs – both of them, for she was no mere giver of negative verdicts. And Mary Godwin was convinced of her creation's truth to life, and of the general verisimilitude of her whole story. She claims in her preface that 'these conversations and tales are accommodated to the present state of society; which obliges the author to attempt to cure those faults by reason, which ought never to have taken root in the infant mind.' She had some warrant of experience, for she had been a school-teacher and governess before she became reader to Johnson the publisher. Her views were 'advanced', by the standard of 1788, before French or

---

* And in 1815 a cheap two-shilling one-volume version 'for universal accomodation'. Each form evidently was stocked and renewed according to demand.

† Getting on for fifty years after I met her first, I still cannot rid my mind of that fearful creation, whom I have mentioned before. The woman thus endowed with terror was an invention of Mrs W. K. Clifford, in her *Anyhow Stories* (1882).

German matter had been really widely disseminated in English nurseries. But in spite of her sternness, she – or Mrs Mason – gave her Mary and Caroline Mrs Trimmer's *Fabulous Histories* to read.

The disaster of Mary Godwin's death, her daughter's connection with Shelley, Mrs Clairmont's daughter's affair with Byron, Blake tinkering commercial stuff (excellent goods) for Johnson, Godwin generously aiding Mulready, Lamb excited about interference with an author, Godwin himself – they all seem things and persons in a queer dream when one thinks of the middle-class parlours with little girls falling asleep under a rational discourse by papa. The Moral Tale was the chronicle of solid quiet England, in staid homes remote from personal emotions or unstable ideals. Nor had it any contact with events that were shaking the nations, nor with the wonder and visions of beauty that were at that very time stirring in English poetry. The Georgian child knew nothing of such things. Even the fairies were in hiding. Or so it seemed in the years when Lamb himself could not do anything much more positive or new for the nursery than abuse the science-mongers.

BRIEF BOOK LIST

Biographical and bibliographical details, of a critical kind, lie outside the general scope of this volume, where the more eminent 'adult' writers like Blake, Lamb and the Godwins are concerned. They are in the province of special devotees of each author. For Blake the most convenient repository is Keynes's *Bibliography* (Grolier Club, New York, 1921); for Lamb, E. V. Lucas's *Life*, 5th edn (London, 1921) and vol. III (Children's Books) of the collected *Works* (London 1903–5). Some smaller and later references are given in the text above. The advertisements at the end of Godwin's *Fables* (edns of 1805, 1808, 1815) contain some Lamb bibliographical 'points' which may have been over-looked among *minutiae*. Godwin's *Looking-Glass* was reproduced in facsimile in 1885 (London and Derby) with an Introduction and amiably discursive notes by F. G. Stephens. E. V. Lucas edited the 1791 edition of Mary Wollstonecraft's *Original Stories* in 1906 (London). Other 'introduced' reprints not mentioned above are those of Elizabeth Turner (by Charles Welsh, 1883, and by G. K. Chesterton, 1927), and of Jane Taylor's *Prose and Poetry* (by F. V. Barry, 1925). For the writers themselves, see *D.N.B.* and *C.H.E.L.* 'F. Anstey's' *Mr Punch's Model Music-Hall Songs and Dramas* (London, 1892) is a joy to irreverent lovers of the Taylors and Mrs Turner: and there are plenty of other parodies.

Supplement

As for earlier and later chapters on poetry, a general debt must be noted to Iona and Peter Opie's *Three Centuries of Nursery Rhymes and Poetry for Children* (see General Book List), and also their notes to the *Oxford Book of Children's Verse* (London, 1973).

The large coverage in histories and bibliographies of the major authors discussed in this chapter has not lessened, but the following works may prove useful starting-points for readers concerned with children's books.

CHRISTOPHER SMART

Sherbo, A. *Christopher Smart; scholar of the university* (East Lansing, 1967). Arthur Sherbo has also examined separately some of Smart's work for Newbery etc. in 'Survival in Grub Street', *Bulletin of the NY Public Library*, March 1960; and there is a bibliographical discussion of some early editions of the *Hymns* in *The Library*, 5th ser. vol. X, December 1955, no. 4, pp. 280–2.

WILLIAM BLAKE

Bentley, G. E. Jr. *Blake Books; annotated catalogues of William Blake's writings* (Oxford, 1977). A wide-ranging account, which includes lists of secondary sources and later reprints of Blake's work, with often pained comments on editions of the *Songs* published for children.

Among more recent publications *Understanding Blake*, ed. Michael Phillips (Cambridge, 1978) includes penetrating essays on the songs and on *For Children*. A start has also been made on a bibliography of Blake's commercial engravings in *William Blake; book illustrator*, vols. I and II by Roger R. Easson and Robert N. Essick (Normal, Ill., 1972 and Memphis, Tenn., 1979).

THE TAYLOR FAMILY

Stewart, Christina Duff. *The Taylors of Ongar; an analytical bio-bibliography.* 2 vols. (New York and London, 1975).

WILLIAM GODWIN

Locke, Don. *A Fantasy of Reason; the life and thought of William Godwin* (London and Boston, 1979). Includes a chapter on M. J. Godwin and Co.

A detailed account of what we know of Godwin's publishing of the single stories from Lamb's *Tales* is: Foxon, David. 'The Chapbook Editions of the Lambs' "Tales from Shakespear"', *The Book Collector*, vol. VI, Spring 1957, no. I, pp. 41–53.

FACSIMILES ETC.

Of prime importance are the facsimiles of Blake's work undertaken by the Trianon Press in Paris for the William Blake Trust. They have produced a *Songs of Innocence* (1954), *Songs of Innocence and Experience* (1955) and both sets of *The Gates of Paradise* (3 vols., 1968), all with introductory information by Sir Geoffrey Keynes.

Other photolithographic reprints include: Nathaniel Cotton's *Visions in Verse* (3rd edn, 1752) introduced by Christina Budman (Bern, 1973) and Christopher Smart's *Hymns for the Amusement of Children* (3rd edn, 1775) introduced by Edmund Blunden (Oxford, 1947).

CHAPTER XII

Interim Again: the Dawn of Levity

I

The contrast between the opening generation of the nineteenth century and that of the eighteenth, in respect of children's books, is like turning from a world uneasily resting to a Vanity Fair rather excitedly awake. The Moral Tale was proceeding sombrely on its course, but all around it was a cheerful bustle. The traffic was only short-lived, like that of other Fairs. But plenty of folk were engaged in it. The flourishing state of the commerce in juvenile literature under the ageing George III and his son, first Regent and then King, is a vivid social phenomenon. The persons of interest are as much the traders as the customers and the authors.

On January 1, 1807, the year in which Lamb put forth *Tales from Shakespear*, the legatee of his beloved Newbery tradition, John Harris, published a longish poem[1] which began:

> Come take up your Hats, and away let us haste,
> To the Butterfly's Ball, and the Grasshopper's Feast.
> The Trumpeter Gad-Fly has summon'd the crew,
> And the Revels are now only waiting for you.

and after describing insect 'revels' which had not a trace of moral value, nor the least touch of archness, patronage, grown-up-ness, be-good-ness in the description of them, ended:

> Then Home let us hasten, while yet we can see,
> For no Watchman is waiting for you and for me.
> So said little Robert, and pacing along,
> His merry Companions returned in a Throng.

The last two lines (which actually did not appear until the 1808 edition of the book) are probably familiar even now. Lewis Carroll may have had both the poem and its easy rhythm in mind when he wrote "'O Looking-Glass creatures", quoth Alice, "draw near!"'.[2] But not even the kindly devastation of parody by Carroll himself could make *The Butterfly's Ball* lose one atom of its spontaneity and freshness.

It was written by a most respectable historian, William Roscoe (1753–1831), M.P. for Liverpool, and 'an accomplished botanist'. If he had been also an accomplished moral fabulist, he would no doubt have forced 'Little Robert' – his son, for whose private pleasure he wrote the poem – to know all about the

Loves of the Plants in the manner of Dr Erasmus Darwin. As he did not let his serious public occupations master his private life, he endures still, underided, as the accomplished minstrel of *The Butterfly's Ball*.

The thing was so happy, so fresh, so foreign to the continuity of any children's books yet known,[3] and was therefore so successful, that Harris himself immediately produced a crop of sequels, the first of which was, for a wonder, not at all inferior to its inspiration. It was *The Peacock 'at Home'* (1807; 29th edn 1819) by 'A Lady', who proved to be Mrs Dorset.

Mrs Dorset, born Catherine Ann Turner (1750?–1817?), was of good minor-gentry family. Not much is known of her own life outside her writings, except that she aided her sister in a temporarily popular compilation for children, *Conversations Introducing Poetry* (1804). The sister, Charlotte Smith (1749–1806), writing to support eight children, also produced a successful little *Rural Walks* (1795) and *Minor Morals* (1798), but won wider fame with her novels, especially *Emmeline, or the Orphan of the Castle* (1788) and *The Old Manor House* (1793): she was the friend of Cowper and Hayley. I recur to her later.

The Peacock 'at Home' and *The Butterfly's Ball* between them achieved a sale of 40,000 copies during their first year, according to Charles Welsh. They do not deserve oblivion yet, though they passed so quickly over the glass of current

30. After being in print for a year in a completely engraved edition (a), with illustrations after Mulready, *The Butterfly's Ball* was published in a revised edition on 25 January 1808 with a fresh set of engravings (b), printed separately from the text, which was now typeset and slightly altered and extended. The change was hardly for the better, as can be seen in these two contrasted engravings of the same scene: the one full of movement and caricature, the other stolid and fussy.

fashion that they may have suffered unduly in fame. Their imaginative qualities, perhaps, are not high, and they certainly serve no end which either Georgian morality or modern psychology could label educational. They are merely cheerful good fun of a simple kind; not bettered in that class. But it was a new class.

There was a whole small library of others. Harris himself put forth more than a dozen in the years 1807–8, with such titles as *The Elephant's Ball*, by W. B. (illustrated with singular and even ludicrous woodenness), *The Lion's Masquerade; a Sequel to the Peacock at Home* (still by 'A Lady'), *The Rose's Breakfast*, and *The Lobster's Voyage to the Brazils*. They all had a vogue, and Harris could justly boast in an advertisement that these 'little Productions . . . have been purchased with avidity, and read with satisfaction by persons in all ranks of life'. Other publishers joined in. One J. B. Batchelor published a *Lion's Parliament* (1808). Tabart published *The Tyger's Theatre* (1808), by S. J. Arnold, with a pretty folding frontispiece. The author claimed – probably rightly, if Harris's puff is to be believed – that this picture was 'invented and drawn' by Miss Caroline Spencer at nine years of age – who had been moved to it by her delight in *The Peacock at Home* etc., and whose work had consequently inspired Mr Arnold's verses. And Darton and Harvey published *The Wedding among the Flowers* (1808).

"Come take up your hats & away let us haste." *p.2*

Pub. Jan. 25. 1808. by J. Harris. corner St. Paul's Church Yd.

As to this last, its author gives frankly her reasons for writing it. *The Butterfly's Ball*, she revealed later in her life.

became so popular as to produce numerous imitations, much below the original, and my ambition being stirred, I entered the field pen in hand . . . completing the little poem in the evenings of a happy fortnight. Our good friend, Darton, rewarded the pleasant labour – pleasant enough without reward – with the munificent gift, as I thought it, of twelve guineas.

It was by Ann Taylor, and had a considerable success, though it was a little late in the day. It shows that the writing of Moral Tales in verse was at any rate not an exclusive passion.

The series no doubt owed some of its popularity to its format. An attractive square shape, about four inches every way, with large type and plenty of pictures, was a departure from the sober miniature-library get-up of the regular children's book. And the illustrations were not only plain but coloured.* The art of hand-tinting engravings suddenly became very popular. Lithography, discovered by Senefelder (1771–1834), was just coming into practical use, and was being employed even for children's books; though not so often as may sometimes be thought, for engraving on a soft copper surface has often a very close resemblance to the grain of prints from stone, or its modern substitute, rubber. *The Butterfly's Ball* books are all embellished with copperplates and the texts are often engraved on the plate too. The colour was put on by droves of children working together; so many put on the red patch, so many the blue, and the prints were passed on thus till the final gay thing was completed. Most of the colour-work thus done was not comparable in finish or delicacy with the very similar hand-coloured aquatints of a few years later. But it was surprisingly good in the better-class volumes, and the method continued long in use; my father saw it being employed by his father – that is, about 1855–60.† It was also used, in a much more rough-and-ready way, by Catnach and his successors (see Chapter v), who put on the hues in crude blobs without much regard to 'register'.

Around this period there was also a host of lowlier levities, conceived in the same amoral spirit, but executed with less literary and, as a rule, less artistic finish. These were collections of rhymed incidents strung together round one or more central figures, like Mother Hubbard and her Dog. (Her minor epic appeared in this form in 1805 – see note 3 – though apparently it had, in part at least, an earlier – unknown – origin.) The true nursery rhymes themselves were also reissued thus. The general plan was to give one verse and one incident and one picture on the same page; usually sixteen in all. Indeed, a famous 'sixteen' may serve as a general type. It is *The History of Sixteen Wonderful Old*

---

* Both forms were issued at once. But that is not to say that all coloured examples offered today to collectors are in their original state. Plain copies are not uncommon, and nothing is easier than for an unscrupulous person to turn an honest old black and white into a coloured specimen, by applying water-colour with an almost dry brush (as is done with 'old' fore-edge paintings). Detection is very difficult.

† [The firm of Dean and Son were still advertising 'Colouring for the trade' in 1860.]

Women (Harris, 1820). The coloured edition cost 1s. 6d. as did most; the plain ones were 1s. 0d. The quotation of a single stanza will show why it was notable:

> There was an Old Woman named Towl,
> Who went out to Sea with her Owl,
> But the Owl was Sea-sick,
> And scream'd for Physic;
> Which sadly annoy'd Mistress Towl.

That is said to be the first appearance of the verse form which Edward Lear made immortal a quarter of a century later, now known, for still unknown reasons, as the Limerick (but Lear commenced his verses after reading a Marshall imitation of the Harris book: *Anecdotes and Adventures of Fifteen Gentlemen*, 1821?). Even metrically, it was something of a breach with tradition, at any rate for the more demure kind of nursery.

Harris put forth a quantity of these trifles also. None has really endured. He had here, too, many rivals hot on his track, among others William Darton, Hailes (Sharpe originally; after 1809, apparently, Sharpe and Hailes, and then Hailes alone), Tabart, Richard Phillips, Wallis, A. K. Newman, and Dean and Munday. That so many firms should be in special competition – over and above the publishers of more august general literature – is certainly deserving of remark; and their activities, obscure now, but highly thought of then, warrant examination. They cover a lively field of English minor history.

2

My own publishing forebears can be dismissed with a few dates for the convenience of historians. William Darton junior was the eldest son of William Darton senior, who set up in business as a publisher in White Lion Alley, Birchin Lane in 1787, moving to Gracechurch Street in 1788: the father introduced Ann and Jane Taylor to English children. The son managed a separate but not hostile house on Holborn Hill from 1804, and members of the family joined one firm or another until the more or less direct line of succession ceased in 1928.* The Holborn Hill establishment issued most of the later work of Mrs Sherwood, much of William and Mary Howitt's, and, with or without authority, 'Peter Parley's'. They also took a hand in the light productions now under observation. But otherwise they need not recur here. Until 1837 all the Dartons were Quakers, and as such had a distinct business connection; not restricted, however.

Hailes kept 'the Juvenile Library at the London Museum', Piccadilly, an 'Egyptian' Hall. There really was a museum there, as well as a publisher's warehouse and shop. 'Purchasers to the Amount of Ten Shillings', says an advertisement of 1814, 'are allowed an Admission Ticket to the Museum, and

---

* [Such are the complications in the various imprints of the two firms that a summary of them has been consigned to Appendix 2.]

31. The proof that the *Anecdotes . . . of Fifteen Gentlemen* (a) influenced Edward Lear's
adoption of the Limerick is seen here in his own sketch (b) to the anonymous stanza first
published by John Marshall more than thirty years before the *Book of Nonsense*. It has
been suggested that the *Gentlemen* verses were by Richard Scrafton Sharpe and the
pictures by Robert Cruikshank.

Purchasers to the Amount of Twenty Shillings, a Ticket BOTH to the Pantherion
and to the Museum'.

That advertisement comes from a book which deserves mention by itself: it
will anticipate the next period of history. The work was *Sir Hornbook: or, Childe*

There was a sick man of Tobago
Lived long on Rice gruel and Sago.

Launcelot's Expedition. A Grammatico-Allegorical Ballad. On the title-page was a block of the publishers' house: their imprint is Sharpe and Hailes, and the date is given as 1814. The eight plates, however, are dated June 1, 1813. They are by Corbould; whether father or son there is no indication. No author's name is given, but the rhymes are by Thomas Love Peacock, at that time in the late twenties of his long life. Why he wrote a deft verse-exercise which serves to teach the parts of speech, grammar and accidence in a quietly facetious manner does not seem to be known. The printers were Whittingham and Rowland of Goswell Street and the plates are an early example of line-printing by lithography, with hand-colouring added. It is a rare volume.

The fate of the book is curious and as yet obscure. It was issued with illustrations both 'plain' and 'coloured', in the current mode, and had later editions in 1815 and 1818. But it seems to have vanished until Peacock's friend Henry Cole, leader in a great Early-Victorian English children's battle, as will be seen hereafter, rediscovered it and put it into his *Home Treasury*, which began to appear in 1843. Cole's friendship was one of Peacock's idiosyncrasies, for he began by hating the Great Exhibition of 1851 and eventually 'became fascinated with it', just as he did with the novels of Charles Dickens.

Cole's usual publisher, Joseph Cundall (also a meritorious book-designer[4] and amateur of the applied arts), produced a 'new' edition in 1843, which contained the eight plates very slightly redrawn – in fact, no more than retouched with some shading. This appeared in two versions, plain and coloured – not so daintily coloured as in Sharpe and Hailes's edition. In 1855 Chapman and Hall, giving their old Strand address on the cover, and their new Piccadilly one on the title-page, published another edition with the *Home Treasury* binding design on the paper wrappers, but with the addition in the centre of a family circle being read to in a stiff formal Home, and with only three plates, which were 'after' the originals, being entirely re-engraved by E. and G. Dalziel. This version was also plain (6*d*.) and coloured (1*s*.). The editions are a footnote to English domesticity.

Peacock's name never appeared at all in this spasmodic history; which is a reason for the bibliographical details, though they are also, as so often, evidence of some desire to test or discover the mind of the public. But the publication was apparently as capricious as one of the author's own novels.

To continue the trade-list, which has its human and social side. Tabart also kept a Juvenile Library – the 'Juvenile and School Library' – in the West End district (west and east were nearer in business temperament then than now). He was 'at the Corner of Grafton Street', New Bond Street. But he is an elusive person; probably attractive if one could catch him. He is constantly mixed up with Sir Richard Phillips, who had a Wilkesian career summarized in the *Dictionary of National Biography*. Tabart was at 157 New Bond Street as early as 1801, when he and Phillips (at 71 St Paul's Churchyard) issued a *Juvenile Plutarch* and other semi-educational works, like Mavor's, 'with a handsome allowance to schools'. By 1804 he could (still in conjunction with Phillips) advertise 'the established character of this shop', and beg the nobility and gentry not to open accounts of less than £2 in amount. Books he published or sold included works by Miss Sandham 'Dr Blair' (of 'Blair's Preceptor', long

32. Benjamin Tabart's shop at the corner of Grafton Street. In the left-hand window can be discerned some games-sheets, in the right some boxed 'miniature libraries'. It is to be hoped that the engraver rather than the sign-writer is responsible for the erroneous French.

popular), 'the Rev. J. Goldsmith', Joseph Taylor and E. Fenwick. Miss Fenwick I take to have been the 'E.F.' who wrote for Tabart in 1805 *Visits to the Juvenile Library*, an unblushing account of his shop and its contents, with a picture of its charming exterior. Another view of the premises was given in *Fortune's Football* (1806), an anonymous autobiography – meant for children – by Isaac Jehner or Jenner, the Anglo-German engraver. The plate, possibly by Jenner himself, shows a solitary customer looking in at a spacious small-paned curved window, with book-trays in front of it. Jenner was born in 1750, and this seems to be his last known work. How did Tabart come to know him so well as to get that pictorial advertisement?

In 1808 the publisher dedicated a *History of Domestic Quadrupeds* to Miss Emily Phillips. In 1809 he issued *The Dog of Knowledge* with no Phillips collaboration. He had already (1804) advertised *Cinderella, Blue Beard* and *Valentine and Orson* 'each with coloured representations of the scenes contained in the last spectacle at Drury Lane' – a significant announcement. In or about 1812 – between 1809 and then, by the dates of imprints and on plates – he moved to 12 Clifford Street, Bond Street. Here, he said, he would continue business 'on the approved plan under which it has been carried on so long'. Once more he implored customers not to ask for credit; but the purchaser of a guinea's-worth of books for cash would be given one half-crown volume (such as *Simple Stories in Verse*, which contains these details) for nothing. In 1816 he moved again, to 85 Piccadilly 'opposite the Green Park', but little is known of this final spell in trade.

Except in connection with fairy-tales – and there Phillips also recurs – I know no more of this lively and unconventional bibliopole. But it seems very likely that he *can* be caught. It is known that the publisher for whom George Borrow did hack-work was Phillips. He is given plenty of rope in Chapter xxx of *Lavengro*. In that work he had an intimate assistant, a 'pale shrivelled-looking man' called Taggart,[5] who took snuff constantly. Tabart?

Phillips himself had a stormy career in City politics. He was a children's author as well as publisher, and wrote also some affable topographical works – *A Morning's Walk from London to Kew* (1817) was one – which allowed him room for combative digression. But he was several people, under pseudonyms. He was no less a person than the above-mentioned Dr Blair and the Rev. J. Goldsmith. As Goldsmith – no connection with even an hypothetical Oliver, but a very useful disguise for the sale of hack-work – he composed a *Grammar of General Geography* (1803) and similar semi-school compilations which speedily became 'trade' books. As Blair, another venerable name in the history of didactics, he was the author not only of *The Governess's Register of the Good and Bad Conduct of the Several Pupils under her Care. . .* and *The Schoolmaster's Register* (both 1819), but of 'Blair's' *First, or Mother's Catechism*, which went into very many editions. He issued some older books of a stock type, and, in association with Tabart, a translation of some of Jauffret's dramas. His premises were first in St Paul's Churchyard and later at 7 Bridge Street, Blackfriars. He was certainly a cheap-literature pioneer, and very active.

John Wallis, and later his son Edward, had a Temple of the Muses, and specialized in the 'moral games' already described (p. 151). John began trading at 16 Ludgate Street in 1775 and by 1812, after several moves, he was near Mrs Godwin (yet another Juvenile Librarian) in Skinner Street, off Holborn Hill. The scene of the labours of those firms is described in a melancholy fashion in the Appendix to Stephens's edition of Godwin's *Looking-Glass* (p. 197). The buildings all disappeared to make way for Holborn Viaduct, but some parts of Saffron Hill still show a trace of what they looked like.

A. K. Newman offered his wares at the Minerva Press,[6] Leadenhall Street. A good many of his publications, however – and the best known of them at that – were not so much his as the productions of the old and famous house of Dean; at that time Dean and Munday in Threadneedle Street. The two firms issued jointly, among other things, several of the works of William Francis Sullivan, 'teacher of elocution and belles lettres', who was a little bit of a Rousseauist and more than a little of a social satirist. His *Mr Rightway and his Pupils* (which was published by William Darton Jr in 1816) might have rivalled *Sandford and Merton* if it had been more earnest and less jocosely topical. It is much too cheerful. But even though Sullivan was a cheerful author for Darton's list he was a stodgy one for Dean.

Newman and Dean were also associated over the well-known *Deborah Dent and her Donkey; The Life and History of A Apple-Pie,* 'who was cut to pieces and eaten by twenty-six young ladies and gentlemen with whom little folks ought to be acquainted'; and an *Original Poetry for Young Minds* (2nd edn 1819, with Preface dated 1815) by Miss Caroline Horwood, the title of which betrays its imitative purpose.

The firm of Dean is now the oldest in London which has always been continuously engaged in the provision of books especially for children. The first Dean married a daughter of Thomas Bailey, a printer, of Bishopsgate, whose sign was the famous AaB – 'Great A, little a, and a big bouncing B'; and there were other family ties between the Deans and the Baileys and Munday, an apprentice of the firm in the eighteenth century. As Dean and Bailey, Dean and Munday, Thomas Dean and Son, they were in premises in Threadneedle Street, Ludgate Hill and Fleet Street in succession; and the business continues today in Covent Garden.[7] The firm always specialized in coloured illustrations, and was connected with the early use of lithography for that purpose. It claims to have been the first to introduce cut-out figure-shapes for 'toy books', to say nothing of its modern invention of printing on untearable holland. It has certainly been in existence for a good two hundred years.*

At this period – 1800 to 1830 or so – Dean and Munday and Newman were putting forth a number of picture-rhyme books of the type just mentioned,

---

* I am indebted to my old friend Mr F. G. Green, of this firm, for many details, as well as for great generosity in respect of other information. I have also drawn upon A. W. Tuer's reprint (1887) of *Dame Wiggins of Lee* together with coloured parlour-game books: among them the celebrated *Gaping, Wide-Mouthed, Waddling Frog*, and the portentously named *Aldiborontiphos-kyphorniostikos*, an inconsequent farrago by Ralph Stennet. The most notable of all the rhymes, however, was *Dame Wiggins of Lee, and her Seven Wonderful Cats*, 'a humorous tale, written principally by a lady of ninety'. It appeared in 1823, under the joint names of Newman and Dean. It had sixteen illustrations, and verses in the easy-going Mother Hubbard metre. Apart from natural merits, it has retained its first fame because it was beloved, in his childhood, by one who himself composed an exceedingly good tale for children.

John Ruskin, in the intervals of alternately scolding and encouraging Kate Greenaway in her graceful work, had a sudden remembrance of *Dame Wiggins*, edited it, added new verses, got Miss Greenaway to draw additional pictures – very skilfully foreign to her usual manner – had the old ones recut (on wood), and induced his friend and publisher, George Allen of Orpington, to issue the result in 1885, saying, in a preface, 'I have the greatest pleasure in commending [the little book] to the indulgence of the Christmas fireside, because it relates nothing that is sad, and pourtrays nothing that is ugly.' He claimed to have added only four new stanzas, but there were six, so that the volume was not quite in the old format. However, the homely vigour of the original was preserved. There is no inherent reason why, between 1823 and 1885, this particular favourite should have been dethroned.

There was, however, a more general reason, and that was that profusion of output, hand in hand with greater mechanical ease of production, killed its own purpose. 'Colour books' deteriorated when Baxter's oil-process and the baser kind of chromolithography gave them a suicidal cheap popularity. Some of Baxter's earliest work was done for the juvenile market: indeed, a frontispiece to a late edition (n.d.) of Mary Elliott's *Tales for Boys* shows an attempt coming to grief, the whole thing being a collection of dingy brown and olive green blotches.

The results were not all bad. Hand-coloured lithography was used from time to time with entirely satisfactory results. For instance, Agnes Strickland's *Tales of the Schoolroom* (n.d., but an early work of hers) had an extremely delicate and charming frontispiece in this manner. Three copies I once had, otherwise identical, showed complete variation of colour in each, and exquisite finish into the bargain. The best-produced books even in the rather ugly period 1820–50 show a good standard of technique. But the worst deserved all the obloquy which Ruskin later on kept for the rival cheap productions of the sixties and seventies, which were embellished with lumpy mawkish woodcuts.

Whatever the standard, however, this was the first time in the history of English children's books that the illustrations were coequal with, if not more important than, the text. Not till the sixties did pictures have so full a share in a book's character. Why the period – from the *Old Mother Hubbard* of 1805 to the *Dame Wiggins* and other books of 1823 or so – should show this temporary efflorescence it is hard to say. The minor changes in things fashionable at the time were certainly extravagant in their way, and the Regency from 1810 to 1821 was prefaced by Dr Syntax and concluded by Tom and Jerry, in its minor adult literature, so that children's books were in the fashion. Some of their illustrations indeed are rather in the Rowlandson manner, but lack mastery of line and draughtsmanship. The liveliness continued into George IV's own day in the grown-up books, but declined in those for the younger public. It was strangely ephemeral.

The noticeable thing, however, in this scene of lightness is its superficiality. It was produced by cheerfulness rather than joy, on the one hand, and by archness rather than wit on the other. It is as clear as anything can be that *The Butterfly's Ball* was spontaneous, but that the huge success of its fashion was a mob-illusion. The later trivialities had even less enduring character. Nor can it be said upon any evidence that public events had much to do with the vogue. Trafalgar preceded Roscoe's poem by two years, Waterloo came in the middle of the boom; while in adult literature the romantic revival was at its height; but you would not guess that from children's books. On the other hand, George III went mad finally in 1810, and his son was neither as Regent nor as King an exhilarating figure to half his subjects.

3

In fact, it was not ugliness nor coarse technique nor decay which really overcame, in the higher nursery circles, the joy of the picture-and-rhyme book. It was a creeping paralysis of seriousness, which set in long before Victoria came to the throne. The Moral Tale was not dead; it is not dead now. It probably never will be dead in English until the United States cease altogether to speak that tongue. Its purveyors, also, as has been seen in the career of Ann Taylor, could reconcile cheerfulness with gravity. One of the *Butterfly's Ball* imitations was by Mrs B. Hoole,★ and might therefore seem an example of what inhuman judges would call two-facedness. Mrs B. Hoole was better known as Mrs Hofland, a most serious and industrious writer whom circumstances compelled to deny her better self and compose books that sold for a time and are now in limbo. Apart from this exercise in fantasy, they were all very Moral Tales, and had also a very large popularity.

She was a Miss Barbara Wreaks, born in 1770 at Sheffield. At the age of twenty-six she became the wife of a well-to-do merchant there, but he died in 1798, and his fortune soon afterwards vanished in a local commercial disaster. Ten years later Mrs Hoole married Thomas Christopher Hofland, a landscape painter of considerable repute and ability, but not a great practical economist: he provided material for his wife's *Son of a Genius: a Tale for the Use of Youth*

★ [*La Fete de la Rose; or the Dramatic Flowers*. A first edition was published in Sheffield by Montgomery and London by Longmans in 1809. Second and third editions appeared in 1810, printed at Knaresborough for a variety of booksellers, including Tabart.]

(1812). Before her second marriage she had set up a school at Harrogate, and her experiences there – she continued the enterprise after becoming Mrs Hofland – gave her realistic subjects for the children's books which she was soon obliged to write indefatigably for a living. She also wrote novels. But in her juvenile pieces – not meant for the youngest children of all – she catered for the market, and hardly showed a sign of the liveliness, courageous high spirits and broadmindedness which she certainly possessed in her private life – as, indeed, would be expected in a close friend of Mary Russell Mitford. Her output was great and continuous until her death, after a hard and well-spent life, in 1844. *The Son of a Genius* is her best-known children's book. She wrote a good Robinsonnade – *The Young Crusoe, or the Shipwrecked Boy* (n.d. [1828]). Hers too were *The History of an Officer's Widow* (a book Mrs Sherwood ought to have written if she could have got away from religion), *The Barbadoes Girl*, (3rd edn 1819) *Alfred Campbell, the Young Pilgrim* (1825 – a description of Eastern travel), *William and his Uncle Ben* (1826). But the full list is too long to quote. Some of them were undated, but as Harris or Newman published nearly all, they can safely be put between about 1805 and 1844. And that, it is to be feared, is what has happened to them. They have been left there, not because they were silly, or ultra-didactic, or wholly limited to transitory fashions and thoughts, but because they were the average marketable wares of what is now a past day. They were written as such wares, and the toiling author put almost nothing of her own attractive personality into them.

Much the same fate has befallen a writer about equally popular, though some of her vogue was probably due to her religious connection, the Society of Friends. Maria Hack was the elder sister of Lamb's friend, Bernard Barton: 'she was a sort of oracle to me',* he wrote, and he was deeply devoted to her. Her *Winter Evenings; or, Tales of Travellers* (4 vols., 1818) and *English Stories* (First and Second Series 1820; Third Series 1825) had a very large sale for a score or more years in Quaker circles, for 'schoolroom' use – amusement with instruction. In *Harry Beaufoy* (1821) she wrote fiction, and fiction with a purpose. Harry was according to the sub-title 'the Pupil of Nature', but not quite the Nature Rousseau dwelt upon. He was, in fact, a vehicle of Natural Theology – of Paley's *Evidences of Christianity*, so long popular at the University of Cambridge. He began by wondering why a watch goes, and deduced God from it. Religion apart, it is not an exhilarating story today, though it went into several editions. But one can understand and respect its motive. And there is no doubt about Mrs Hack's sincere and gentle personality. She recognized in her Preface to *Winter Evenings* that 'Stories of giants and castles do not accord with the taste of the present day', but she did not set about expelling them with abuse. She merely suggested, meekly, that 'Perhaps it may be doubted whether habituating children to seek amusement, almost exclusively, in fictitious narrative, has not a direct tendency to weaken the mental powers.' Her

---

* In E. V. Lucas, *Bernard Barton and his Friends* (1893).

antidotes to weakness have passed with herself, but they were never ridiculous or drastic.

Other authors, until the Moral Tale itself had changed its complexion, were neither so prolific nor so popular. The senior living writers – Mrs Sherwood, Mary Elliott, and one or two others – lasted on till Victoria's accession, and even later. Yet older ones, like Day and Maria Edgeworth, were reprinted, as indeed they still are. But between 1820 or 1830 there was a kind of small syncope or solemn pause in the general moral movement as expressed in juvenile fiction. The Early-Victorian favourites, like Agnes Strickland (1796–1874), Mary and William Howitt, Mrs Marcet (1769–1858), Harriet Martineau (1802–76), Miss Fraser Tytler (1782?–1857), had either not arrived or had only just begun to write, so that their most characteristic work belongs to a slightly later period. Except for a few volumes here and there which had a transient vogue – like *The Peasants of Chamouni* (2nd edn 1826), *Claudine; or Humility the Basis of all the Virtues,* by Maria Elizabeth Budden (1822), *Helen of the Glen* (1825?),* by the forgotten Robert Pollok (1798–1827), author of *The Course of Time* – practically no serious-minded work of fiction for the young by a new writer which appeared under George IV struck popular taste. There were a good many anthologies, and their contents are significant. Crofton Croker, for example, edited an annual called *The Christmas Box* (1828–9).† It was excellently printed at the Chiswick Press, with fine wood-cuts by W. H. Brooke, but the contributors were writers already known, like Maria Edgeworth, Mrs Hemans, and Allan Cunningham, or not fully established, like Mary Howitt. Mrs Hemans, indeed, was at large, and had become a sure candidate for recitation immortality. But her spirit, even in her *Hymns for Childhood* (Dublin, 1834), was not so much that of the Moral Tale in verse as of the writers who in a few years' time expressed a new view of child-life, the attitude which separated boys, girls and infants from one another.

4

We have reached, then, by somewhere about 1830, or even 1840, a period of apparent lack of central impulse. Fantasy had flamed up gaily and died down below general visibility. The Moral Tale had flourished reasonably, but was no longer rampant or aggressive. It was established just as peace seemed to be established at Waterloo. Only its best quality departed from it: its style. Its chief writers, whatever they had to say, whatever doctrine they urged, were, as a group, better at the task of English writing than any before or since who have

---

* [Alongside *Helen of the Glen* was published *Ralph Gemmell* and *The Persecuted Family* (all 1825?). These were collected as *Tales of the Covenanters* (Edinburgh 1833) and continued to be published at least until 1928.]

† [The lightness of editorial touch placed it ahead of its time, but it was probably too ambitious, as can be seen from its shifting imprints: W. Harrison Ainsworth in 1828, and John Ebers (London) and William Blackwood (Edinburgh) in 1829.]

made books for children. Almost any passage from Miss Edgeworth, Mrs Barbauld, Mrs Sherwood is a model of lucid ease of expression. You may dislike or disagree with what is said, but you could not say it better, and probably not in so few words. That was a gift possessed hardly at all by the next generation, or, if possessed, ignored.

Apart from style, however, the Moral Tale was beginning to change its soul. It was becoming the Matter-of-Fact Tale, with a strong sound unquestioned foundation of English (or, now, British) morality. When, after one false dawn, England rejoiced after Waterloo, writers for children, knowing themselves to be by then a special class of author, with a recognized position, must have felt a feeling of relief and almost freedom. The enemy without the gates, with his wicked subversive notions, was prostrate. Providence, as had really been expected, had been on England's side. The country teemed with old and new societies renewing or enlarging activities for good – societies for Suppressing Vice, for Educating the Children of the Poor, for distributing Tracts and Pure Literature, for this and that Reform, for all and sundry high aims. The machinery of book-distribution was large and efficient, the writers plentiful, the reading habit universal. The moralists could go forward with their good work for children, not so much, now, resisting evil as conquering it – and not in Britain only, but all over the world.

And forward they went. But they found, or the children's authors who supported them found, that at home so much had been done already in laying the foundations of moral excellence that what was wanted was not more light, but more facts to study by the light available. The fantasies of Roscoe and Dorset were past trifles, and the Moral Tale had been already supplied in sufficient quantities. What was needed was more plain (moral) knowledge of the now peaceful and (for Britain) vastly widened world; books about New Holland, India, China, the Polar Regions – even America, for as was observed by a super-Barlow in *Interesting Walks of Henry and His Tutor* (1827), 'Arts and sciences are turning the wildernesses of North America into a garden filled with all the goodly fruits of civilization.' Franklin had been adopted almost as an English author. Lindley Murray, of Pennsylvania, was living at York till his death in 1826, the accepted authority on our own English grammar. Dr John Carey, the author of the enormously popular *Learning Better than House or Land* (1808), had already visited Virginia, and seen that it was good.* The Howitts were about to approve of Ohio in a similar manner. The Diffusion of Useful Knowledge need not wait for a Brougham. All the habitable globe was an open Aladdin's cave for the English-speaking fact-collector.

And so one large section of writers for children tried to make it and keep it. Hence the enormous number of 'Questions', 'Catechisms' and 'Guides to Knowledge' which appeared under George IV. Under William IV their writers proliferated, and, reaching official recognition, produced in the next reign the

---

* Especially the 'rich apple-toddy, a mixture of rum, water, and sugar, enriched with the soft pulp of roasted apples, with or without nutmeg'. His visit took place in 1789.

type perfected in Mr Gradgrind. Large help arrived from America; and, by an odd irony, it was not from that romantic 'wilderness' of open spaces, but from the Teutonic factory of arts and sciences, that lighter air came to save us from asphyxiation by seriousness.

5

The history of the Fairy-Tale up to this stage has already been told: how it lay hidden from print in the minds and speech of common folk, how it came from France with some high support of fashion, how philosophy and common sense and religion fought and apparently prevailed against it; how it endured in mean forms of type. It was now at last to be taken with some seriousness.

As early as 1804 a really good attempt was made to digest simply the large annals of Fairyland. In that year, Benjamin Tabart produced his *Collection of Popular Stories for the Nursery; Newly Translated and Revised from the French, Italian and Old English Writers.* The stories, which included the whole of Perrault, were issued either in single booklets ('Lilliputian Folios') each with three hand-coloured engravings, priced 6*d.* each, or in a set of three parts, each of which could be sold separately. A fourth volume, containing Eastern stories, and 'Jack and the Beanstalk', was added in 1809, and thirty-five separate booklets seem to have been available (though some, like four devoted to *Gulliver's Travels,* did not get into the main collection). Later the stories appeared as a single compendium of twenty-six items – published by Phillips as *Popular Fairy Tales* 'collected and edited by Benjamin Tabart' (1818). In 1809 the *Dramas for Children* put out by the Godwin firm had advertised its author – probably Mrs Godwin – as also the 'Editor of Tabart's Popular Stories'. Godwin would certainly have approved of the venture, though, for in 1802 he had proclaimed that he was in favour of imagination for children, not knowledge: he wanted Perrault for them, and *The Seven Champions,* and so on: and he said so in a letter to William Cole. He may have had a hand in this collection, as well as his wife and Benjamin Tabart.

However, that is a mystery to me. The fat little volume of 1818 with its twenty-six hand-coloured engravings sold for 6*s.* bound and was cheap at the price. Its pages gave what might be called a plainish standard version of all the best stories: Beauty and the Beast, Aladdin, Tom Thumb, the two chief Jacks, and many others as well as Perrault, without a trace of novelty, invention, or research – just what every right-minded child in England should have expected in those pre-Grimm and pre-invention days. There was no Court frippery about the French *émigrés* (by then really naturalized in chapbooks) and no exotic floweriness in the Eastern stories; and there were no stuck-on morals. Mr Tabart (if it were he) claimed that an attempt was made 'to elevate the language and sentiments to a level with the refined manners of the present age'. But he was thoroughly workmanlike about it. He used a little of the simple grandilo-

CALGARY PUBLIC LIBRARY
BOYS' & GIRLS' DEPT.

quence of the chapbook style, but tightened up its inconsequent and breathless syntax, and did not fall into the terrible arch verbosity and explanatoriness which was to be used by many Victorians, Kingsley not least. It is in fact surprising to find that so complacent a claim to elegance and elevation had results so practical and mild.

I cannot discover whether the collection was commercially successful or not, but there is evidence that remainder sheets were being sold by Longmans in 1830. At any rate, except for a mere handful of stories not available in print at all in 1818, it contained everything that any good 'omnibus' fairy-book now holds, reasonably represented. Probably Phillips's trade and City connections gave it a fair vogue.

But it did not leave such a mark as was made by the most famous of all collections, new, under George IV, in form, but eternally old and young in substance. The brothers Jakob and Wilhelm Grimm, serious students of folklore (though the word was not then invented), had been for a number of years collecting the popular tales, as yet not written down, of the people of Cassel and Hesse. They copied many of the Märchen exactly as they were rehearsed to them, without any preparation or adornment, by the ordinary peasants who had handed them down orally from generation to generation and had never seen them in print, even if they could read it. The tales, even more than Perrault's, and even more than early British collections like those of Keightley, Campbell, and Crofton Croker, were in every way what their English title claims – *Popular Stories*.

They were published in Germany in two volumes (1812–15) and in an improved edition, with frontispieces by a third brother, Ludwig, in 1819. (A third volume of notes followed in 1822.) It is creditable to the English business man of letters that little time was lost in translating them, and that one of the best artists of the day – then in the prime of his long career – was chosen to adorn them. As *German Popular Stories*, illustrated by George Cruikshank, they were published in England in two volumes (1823–6) and have fortunately never been out of English print since.

Yet though 'Grimm' was popular at once, it was not really till twenty years or so later that the fairy-tale, and with it romance and fantasy in general, emerged unassailable. There was a curious numbness of imagination and also of impetus. The English people between Waterloo and Victoria's accession seem to have been like Mrs Gamp in regard to children's books – in a kind of 'walking swoon'; persisting in their perfunctory course, with recollections of old things, and aware of a world active all round them and acting upon them, indeed, but producing no promise of new inspiration or real wakefulness except in a sustained routine. It is difficult to square this rigid frame of mind with the movement of things in their greater world: with rick-burnings, Reform riots, machine-destroying, penal laws still savage, unemployment after the wars, and actual hunger. It may be that the middle-class was for the time veritably mediocre: not too poor, not too rich, and not at either extreme of politics in fear

33. The English edition of the Grimm tales published in 1823 was the first anywhere to be fully illustrated. The Brothers Grimm were so impressed with Cruikshank's etchings that they planned to use them in a subsequent German edition (but eventually turned to their brother Ludwig for the 'Kleine Ausgabe' of 1825). Cruikshank (a) has continued to be regarded as the finest interpreter, however, and this comparison of two drawings for the story of *Jorinde and Joringel* shows a famous modern English illustrator (b) refusing to compete.

or rage. Such a lymphatic state, if I am right in insisting upon children's books as essentially a middle-class product, would account for the drabness of this literature at that period. At any rate, the society which was in that condition showed no sign, in print for 'nursery' use, of possessing ideas or inspiration.

But such a judgment ignores what was beginning to break in upon the adult mind in regard to children – the discovery that *The* Child was *a* child, and, on top of that, that he was male and female, and was also different at five years of age and fourteen. It is difficult, naturally, to be certain always that a writer had a well-defined and precise reader as his object, and equally hard to be sure what object he actually hit. But hitherto the young readers had never been clearly defined. They were just 'children', and that meant anything from a baby lisping the alphabet to a young Miss or Master growing like the elder generation. Mere numbers now made sub-division inevitable. The population, increasing, included more children, while reform drew closer attention to them. There were more people ready to write books, more publishers ready to produce them, and more and better machinery – real, not metaphorical machinery – to put them on the more flexible market. The juvenile library was in some danger of being entirely commercialized; especially if its *ethos* could also be put under a classified regimen.

It is accordingly something of a new world which is to be explored after this halt and retrospect. But it was not yet really new on its spiritual side. The sense of fear, the inhibiting of joy, was still powerful, in spite of the outbreaks of levity, in spite of the acceptance of *Grimm*. Some of the writers knew that, though no one of weight said so effectively until the Victorian era. I have given instances of the ease with which, apparently, the stuffy atmosphere of repression could be blown away, even by Sherwoods and Trimmers. Here is the reverse picture, the reality that lay beneath the artificial Moral Tale when its recipients did not possess enough buoyancy. A boy, George, remarks that he would have liked to have lived with Robin Hood in Sherwood Forest:

Mrs TALBOT. I remember, George, when I was a girl, having an equal delight in wandering about woods and copses, but particularly among those beautiful beech woods, that shade some of the South Downs, where they descend to the weald. – And as I grew older, and became acquainted with the poets, I delighted to imagine myself engaged with a party of young friends, to act Milton's Masque of Comus, in a great wood that was not far from my then residence.

EMILY. But you never did so, Mamma?

MRS TALBOT. No – I should not have been allowed to have undertaken a part in any theatrical performance. It was merely one of those visions, in which I sometimes indulged myself. – At other times I used to fancy I could meet in those woods, with some of the Knights and Damsels that Spenser tells us of, in the Fairy Queen.

GEORGE. Did you really believe, then, that such persons existed?

MRS TALBOT. No . . . But tho' all these fairy visions have long since disappeared, a woody scene has still a thousand charms for me.

That is from Charlotte Smith's *Conversations Introducing Poetry* (1804). But Mrs Smith, poor lady, willy-nilly, was introducing the Moral Tale, not poetry. And it is quite certain, not only from this deliberate statement of repression, that she was aware of her loss; of unreality. In the same book she makes the mother tell her children, almost in so many words, not to be prigs: 'nothing offends more than pretence to knowledge, in a company which you know cannot possess it; and these [country] girls will never forgive you for telling them that they should say "viola tricolar" [*sic*] instead of "Leap-up-and-kiss-me", or "three-faces-under-an-hood".' She was by way of being a specialist in botany herself. There must have been a mortal struggle in her staid mind before she told that truth. The two quotations between them contain the whole psychology of the Moral Tale, and of much in the history of children's books all through.

BRIEF BOOK LIST

Nearly all the authors mentioned are in *D.N.B.* or *C.H.E.L.* Charles Welsh in 1883 reprinted not only *The Butterfly's Ball* but other 'Revels', with introductions. A. W. Tuer supplemented Ruskin's *Dame Wiggins* (1885) with a reprint of the original (London, 1887). Other references are given in the text; and most of the books mentioned at the end of the preceding chapters overlap this period. The most convenient edition of *Grimm* is still that translated by Margaret Hunt (*Grimm's Household Tales*, London, 1884), edited by Andrew Lang. For the general question of illustrated books of the period, see books by Martin Hardie, R. M. Burch and others in the General Book List (section II.4).

Supplement

Modern books noted in the Book List to Chapter XI also overlap here as does information in Mr and Mrs Opie's poetry catalogue. These two scholars have, however, provided an anthology specifically devoted to 'the dawn of levity': *A Nursery Companion* (Oxford, 1980), with a final section of notes on twenty-eight examples of the nursery books that appeared alongside *The Butterfly's Ball* and its imitations.

More thoroughly detailed background is given in:

Moon, Marjorie, *John Harris's Books for Youth 1801–1843* (Cambridge, 1976), a
　checklist which incorporates many quotations from contemporary reviews.

A great deal of work has been done on the activities of the Brothers Grimm, fostered in Germany especially through a Grimm Society and Museum at Kassel. So far as the English reception of the *Household Stories* is concerned the following references will provide initial help:

Briggs, Katharine M. 'The Influence of the Brothers Grimm' in *Brüder Grimm Gedenken*
　1963 (Marburg, 1963), pp. 511–24.
Hammond, Muriel. *Jacob and Wilhelm Grimm; the Fairy Tale Brothers* (London, 1968).
Michaelis-Jena, Ruth. *The Brothers Grimm* (London, 1970), and also:
'Edgar und John Edward Taylor, die ersten englischen Übersetzer der Kinder- und
　Hausmärchen' in *Brüder Grimm Gedenken II* (Marburg, 1975).

The most recent attempt at a complete translation is that by Ralph Manheim, *Grimm's Tales for Young and Old* (New York, 1977, London, 1978).

CHAPTER XIII

Two New Englands: 'Peter Parley' and 'Felix Summerly'

I

The first twenty-five years or so of Victoria's reign gave scope for the new matter-of-factness which came with the industrial era to compete and also to mingle with the high contemporary ideals of reform; and, in a manner nearly parallel, new conceptions of applied art, or domestic decoration, came into contact with native English humour. The result was a number of apparent contradictions, strikingly clear in children's books. A most suggestive and also eminent example of contrast is to be found in the work of Catherine Sinclair.

She was born in 1800, the fourth daughter of Sir John Sinclair, a Scots gentleman of good birth, characterized, according to the *Dictionary of National Biography*, by 'lack of humour and unbounded self-conceit'. He was the first President of the Board of Agriculture. The conceit did not descend to his daughter, but she sometimes discovered a lack of humour utterly opposed to her real store of it. She herself took an active part in public life, but she was more widely known for her novels than her philanthropy. She wrote half a dozen of them, the most successful being *Modern Accomplishments, or The March of Intellect* (1836) and (a sequel) *Modern Society, or The March of Intellect* (1837). Both sold well: 9000 of *Modern Society* on publication. Both were often reprinted, and were still being reissued in the late seventies, long after Miss Sinclair's death, which occurred in 1864. They do not now deserve, except to satisfy the curious, even that temporary exhumation which is given to the minor Victorian novelists from time to time.

Exactly why they had this vogue it is not easy to say. They are very wordy. They are professedly and aggressively moral. *Modern Society* is an 'attempt to contrast the happiness offered to us by our Maker with the happiness which we invent for ourselves'. It contains lively scenes which show that the author had a considerable gift for social observation and satire: it is hard not to suspect one character of being a laughable portrait of her own father. But what of her serious vein? There are two cousins, one serious, one light-minded, in the story, and an exceedingly virtuous minister. Eleanor (the minx) flippantly says that she won't reform till the weather does – nor indeed to modern eyes does she need it much.

'Miss Fitz-Patrick!' said Dr Murray, with mild but impressive earnestness. 'Pardon me if I estimate my professional privileges too highly; but believing as I do, that a sacred duty is imposed on me towards yourself, and seeing that hitherto no opportunity has been allowed me of discharging it, I venture to say a few words, trusting that they may be received as they are intended, in all sincerity and kindness. You are now in the morning of such a bright and prosperous existence, that . . .'

The 'few words' then run on for another page; and Dr Murray was, for him, brief at that particular reception of a house-party. He went to greater lengths several times in the book, and Miss Sinclair was obviously proud of him.

Yet the same hand in 1839 produced *Holiday House*, certainly the best original children's book written up to that time, and one of the jolliest and most hilarious of any period. There *is* a moral tone about it: Catherine Sinclair of North Britain, daughter of Sir John, could scarcely get right away from that. But nine times out of ten the morality comes in only to be flouted with the utmost goodwill. Of course that is not how the author put it. What she said, daringly enough at that time of day, was this:

The minds of young people are now manufactured like webs of linen, all alike, and nothing left to nature . . . While every effort is used to stuff the memory, like a cricket-ball, with well-known facts and ready-made opinions, no room is left for the vigour of natural feeling, the glow of natural genius, and the ardour of natural enthusiasm . . . In these pages the author has endeavoured to paint that species of noisy, frolicsome, mischievous children now almost extinct . . .

What she did was to invent a most charming and lenient old grandmother, a ferocious governess, Mrs Crabtree (very like Mary Wollstonecraft's Mrs Mason, but laughed at and 'ragged' endlessly by her young charges), and 'a nice funny uncle David'. There ought to be an Uncle David in every pious household. His parting counsel to the family (delivered quite irrelevantly) was: 'Now children! I have only one piece of serious, important advice to give you all, so attend to me! – Never crack nuts with your teeth.' In telling a story splendidly headed 'The Prodigious Cake', he insisted that his nephew Harry should learn and sing this anthem:

> I wish I were a brewer's horse,
> Five quarters of a year.
> I'd place my head where was my tail,
> And drink up all the beer.

Moreover, he invented a 'Nonsensical Story about Giants and Fairies' (all the Sinclairs were of gigantic stature), in which, though the names and events are very clearly didactic, the giant Snap-'em-up is described as being so tall that he had to climb a ladder to comb his own hair, a touch worthy of Lewis Carroll; and as for his habits: 'His dinners were most magnificent . . . For a side-dish his greatest favourite consisted of little boys, as fat as possible, fried, in crumbs of bread, with plenty of pepper and salt.' No wonder that E. V. Lucas speaks of *Holiday House* as containing 'the first example of modern nusery scepticism'. It contains more. It is the first example of real laughter and a free conscience. It sold well, and happily still does so.[1]

Miss Sinclair wrote one other children's book, *Charlie Seymour* (1832), rather more grown-up and sedate. But in actual circulation her greatest juvenile success came late in life, with her *Letters* (1861-4). These were amusing 'hieroglyphic' epistles, on the lines of the *Hieroglyphic Bible* of two generations or more before, with tiny, coloured pictures instead of many of the words. They were in imitation script, in coloured lithography, and when the first two appeared, at sixpence each (the coin itself being a 'hieroglyphic'), advertised as 'warranted to keep the noisiest child quiet for half an hour', the reviews were enthusiastic. Five thousand copies were sold in a fortnight, and according to the publisher the hundredth thousand reached by 1863. Nos. 3 and 4 attained 80,000 by 1863 and Nos. 5 and 6 100,000 by 1864. *All* Miss Sinclair's works – *Holiday House, Charlie Seymour* and the novels – were advertised on the paper wrappers.*

It is evident that she was a genuine 'best-seller'. It is likewise evident that she knew and understood real children, and that children liked her books, and that in her own mind – which was transparently honest, even naïve, whatever she wrote – she reconciled her staid primness in adult conduct with her complete abandonment of all constraint for the young. Many of the nursery moralists had known how to smile tolerantly, and Roscoe and his contemporaries had laughed outright. But Catherine Sinclair was the first to rollick.

2

The strangest antidote to hilarity was furnished not by native talent but by 'one of the most remarkable men in the country' – in the United States, that is. He deserves that phrase from *Martin Chuzzlewit*, for not only might he have walked straight out of its pages, but he was concerned in the very copyright questions which coloured, to some extent, Dickens's impressions of America.

Samuel Griswold Goodrich, of New England, 'the Original "Peter Parley" ', was born at Ridgefield, Connecticut, in 1793. His early surroundings, naturally, had a strong influence on his character, and their effect appears in his temperament in later life. His father was a Congregational Minster. Ridgefield was a township of some two thousand souls, chiefly engaged in agriculture. When Goodrich was a boy, memories of the American Revolution were still strong, and England was hated: but the excesses of the French Revolution were equally abhorrent. He grew up in an atmosphere of rather constricted but genuine piety, and of a local self-satisfaction which was both provincial in outlook and national in vehemence.

He received an average education of the time, first at a dame-school of an old-fashioned type, then at a larger establishment. His early reading, out of school,

---

*   [The letters appear to have been sold singly at 3*d*. or in a 'neat Hieroglyphic Illuminated Cover' containing two letters at 6*d*. The titles were [A Picture Letter], [Another Picture Letter], *A Bible Picture Letter, A Christmas Letter, A First of April Nonsense Letter* and *A Sunday Letter*. The British Museum also has bound in with the second pair of these, *Picture Proverbs*. All titles were four pages long.]

consisted of *The New England Primer* (with its strong Puritanism), *Goody Two-Shoes* and *Mother Goose's Rhymes*, up to his tenth year.

Somewhat later one of my companions lent me a volume containing the stories of Little Red Riding Hood, Puss in Boots, Blue Beard, Jack the Giantkiller, and some other of the tales of horror, commonly put into the hands of youth, as if for the express purpose of reconciling them to vice and crime. Some children, no doubt, have a ready appetite for these monstrosities, but to others they are revolting, until by repetition and familiarity, the taste is sufficiently degraded to relish them. At all events, they were shocking to me.

He believed them true, and was frightened by Red Riding Hood's wolf (he must have had an edition without the moral attached). He was hardly less horrified to find that they were untrue; and 'this general impression remained on my mind, that children's books were either full of nonesense, like "hie diddle diddle" in Mother Goose, or full of something very like lies, and those very shocking to the mind, like Little Red Riding Hood.' It is clear that he was, at that age, far more finely fibred and sensitive than his later work, done when a moral sense had been encouraged to distrust and suppress instinctive impressions, would lead one to expect.

It was perhaps that later wisdom, not the feelings of a boy, which really judged that 'much of the vice and crime in the world are to be imputed to these atrocious books'. In his *Recollections* he stressed this point at great length, and then proceeded to the books which, at the age of sixty-one, he said he *did* like at twelve. They were *Robinson Crusoe, Alphonso and Dalinda* (one of Mme de Genlis's *Tales of the Castle*), and Hannah More's *Moral Repository* – 'the first work that I read with real enthusiasm. That I devoured.' Much later in life he had the honour of visiting Hannah More – that 'elderly Phoenix', as a less reverent devotee called her – and it was at Barley Wood, in conversation with her over the delights of *The Shepherd of Salisbury Plain*,* that he 'first formed the conception of the Parley Tales'. Hannah More had a longer and stronger grip on English minor morals than any writer since Puritan days.

At eighteen Goodrich entered seriously upon the task of making a living. He had intimations of immortality even then – 'a vague idea of some sort of eminence' – and did not set his whole mind upon 'selling goods or making money'. 'I resolved to re-educate myself.' In 1818 he married, and became a partner in the publishing business of his friend George Sheldon, of Hartford, Connecticut. Thenceforward all his work was connected with books. In 1819 his firm produced an edition of Scott in eight volumes. He does not say whether he asked Scott's leave or not, but in view of later events the absence of such a statement – which he should have been proud to make – suggests that he did not. He also 'turned his attention' to children, and himself wrote 'a small arithmetic and half a dozen toy-books'.

In 1823 he visited Europe and saw Scott himself, and had his meeting with Hannah More. He seems to have had friendly relations with the book-trade – with William Blackwood, James Ballantyne, and the useful Lockhart. In 1826

* According to Mr Titmarsh, *The Washerwoman of Finchley Common*.

he removed to Boston, and in the following year produced his first 'Peter Parley' book – *Tales of Peter Parley about America*. A sequence of similar *Tales* followed, and from 1828 to 1832 he was working fourteen hours a day, and producing five or six volumes a year over and above his ordinary business routine.

There is no doubt whatever that he invented the ingenious and happy pseudonym 'Peter Parley', nor that he wrote an enormous number of books under it: he gives an immense list of those which he claimed as his own original work – though it is fair to say that some American authorities do not accept it *in toto*. There is no doubt, either, that the pseudonym was shamelessly borrowed by English authors and publishers; and this will be the most convenient place to give a tentative list of the pseudo-Parleys, before considering the merits of Goodrich's general quarrel with English habits or the character of the volumes themselves, which, whoever the author, were much of a muchness.

3

Six Parleys can be clearly identified in England. They were:

(i) William Martin (1801–67), a Suffolk man of Woodbridge, then a considerable minor literary centre. He began life as a draper's assistant, and ended it, it is said, in 'dissipated habits and loose morals'. Between those two extremes, he produced more and better Parley than any other rival; and he was livelier than Goodrich himself. A great deal of his work was done for my grandfather, but other firms produced his output as well. He certainly edited many numbers of *Peter Parley's Magazine*, which began monthly publication in 1839 under the imprint of Darton and Clark. As was customary with magazines, the monthly numbers were bound up as a gift book at Christmas (usually dated for the year ahead) and *Peter Parley's Annual; a Christmas and New Year's Present for Young People* began publishing with the date 1840. (In the early years the *Annual* carried on its title-page the name of its distributors, Simpkin, Marshall and Co.) Although the *Magazine* seems to have ceased publication in 1863, the *Annual* continued under various imprints until 1892.

But Martin had started independently already with *The Educational Magazine* (1835), short-lived and uninteresting, and *The Parlour Book* (1835?),* which had a large sale over a good many years. He certainly stole the American pseudonym, but he preserved his own identity. The last original works by him that I have been able to trace were (*a*) *The Hatchups of Me and My School-Fellows* (1858), a set of loosely connected short stories, said to be 'by Peter Parley, edited by William Martin, author of . . . "Parley's Annual"'; there is no pretence in this volume that it is the work of the American or 'original' Parley; it is definitely English fiction for boys: and (*b*) *Our Boyish Days, and How we Spent Them* (1861), 'by the Editor of *Peter Parley's Annual*', the preface, which states

---

*   The British Museum's conjectural date. By the imprint, the volume cannot be later than 1838. The first use of 'Peter Parley' in England was before 1832.

that 'cheerfulness is . . . my motto', being signed William Martin. It is a batch of short stories which 'will, I trust, however light they may be, convey to the young reader some useful and valuable lessons in a pleasant manner'.

Martin, in fact, was a very capable all-round hack, and but for his theft of Goodrich's pseudonym would have honourably deserved his market repute – for he won no more than that. But no Parley book, whether it succeeded in the market or not, was ever anything but a thing of its period, whoever wrote it.

(ii) George Mogridge (1787–1854) was a Proteus of the Early-Victorian Juvenile Library. He wrote as Old Humphrey (perhaps his best-known pseudonym), Peter Parley and Ephraim Holding. Most of his work was semi-evangelical, and he was popular enough to have a book made about his *Life, Character and Writings* (1856). He has been credited with composing *Sergeant Bell and his Raree-Show* (published in 1839 by Tegg), which has also been unwarrantably foisted on Dickens, but is mere Parleyism. As regards Parley books, he seems to have been an editor and rewriter of them for Tegg, though Tegg was afterwards said to be the author of his own publications in that vein. Mogridge was in some ways not unlike Goodrich himself, though the American would have deplored the comparison – he thought Mogridge a sanctimonious humbug. 'Old Humphrey' had been brought up on chapbook literature – *Friar Bacon*, *The Seven Champions* and *Tom Thumb* – and had come to appreciate the romances of chivalry, Bunyan, and 'emblems' like those of Quarles. One must take his sincerity at its face-value. In some 'friendly remarks' at the start of his *Sunday-School Illustrations* (written under the name of 'Ephraim Holding' [Edn rev. by Mary Mogridge 1863]) he wrote thus:

Had the morals of Aesop's Fables been published by themselves, and the fables been withheld, in all probability the former would scarcely have been read, much less remembered; but, as it is, they will probably be handed down to the end of time. I am sanguine enough to believe that my Illustrations may be the means of enabling you to remember some of my remarks for a longer period than they would otherwise be retained.

That was at least a modest view of the effect of 'the moral'. Mogridge, however, remains the most ghostly of all the Parleys.

The others – the proven ones – were all publishers: if they delegated the work to an unknown 'someone in the office', the responsibility is nevertheless theirs. The first and – to the authentic Parley – worst of them was (iii) Thomas Tegg (1776–1845), to whom, in spite of his conduct over copyright, fiercely denounced by Wordsworth and Carlyle, England owes something for his production of cheap literature for young and old. He also bestowed much of Mary Howitt's work on juvenile readers, to her entire satisfaction. But it was a dozen or more years before he secured her work, 'in the most straightforward satisfactory manner', that he used Goodrich in quite a different fashion.

In 1832 the true Parley learnt that 'a prominent publisher' – Tegg – was republishing *Parley's Tales* without leave (apparently from American editions). As he was then on a second visit to England, on account of his health, he confronted the pirate, and managed to get an 'agreement' out of him. Tegg had apparently issued a number of *Tales*, four being genuine Goodrich. Goodrich agreed to revise these four for English use, and to give Tegg the English licence to publish. For one about to be published – *Tales of Animals* – he was to have £10 for every 1000 copies *printed*, the first edition consisting of 4000. For all the rest, £5 on delivery of the revised copy, and £5 for every 1000 *printed* after the first edition, with a bonus of £5 on each 1000 after 4000 were *sold*: Tegg to have the right to decline 'unsuitable' *Tales* and Goodrich to take them elsewhere.

The years passed. Goodrich got no statement of sales, no payment. But he learnt that Tegg was selling Parleys freely – 'many thousand pounds of profit had been realised thereby'. Revisiting England in 1842 – the year of Dickens's American visit and *Notes* – he bearded the man Tegg, only to be laughed at. The agreement was not a valid document; only a 'note'. There was no legal liability. As to moral liability, Tegg said (1) he had not made the alleged profits; (2) the genuine Parley work was not 'adapted to his purpose'; (3) he – Tegg – had really made Parley's name in Great Britain, and had had to pay for suitable work to carry that name. In fact,

Sir, I do not owe you a farthing; neither justice nor law requires me to pay you any thing. Still, I am an old man, and have seen a good deal of life, and have learned to consider the feelings of others as well as my own. I will pay you £400, and we will be quits. If we can not do this, we can do nothing.

Law apart, in equity Tegg's pretensions were not so impudent as they seemed, on the face of it. Parley's manner *was* American, and 'Tales' about portions of the now large British Empire were really best left to a Briton. What Goodrich chiefly disliked in all the fabrications, Tegg's and others, was what he deemed to be the debasing of his pure style – which to modern eyes is not conspicuous – and the personal character given 'Parley', the Yankee from New England. He was made into a sort of genial stage British 'tar', with a wooden leg, and was even caused (not by Tegg) to express willingness to sing 'Rule Britannia' and vow loyalty to the young Queen.* Still, £400 was not an ungenerous offer. Goodrich accepted it. But Tegg was still selling 'Parleys' in 1847, and it was claimed for him after his death that he *was* Peter Parley.

(iv) A second early Parley-thief was Charles Tilt, of Fleet Street. Goodrich, so far as I can see, does not mention him by name (he is 'Mr T—'), but there was no surreptitiousness about his borrowings, though he does not seem to have made a long-standing habit of them. In 1838 he published *Peter Parley's Visit to London, during the Coronation of Queen Victoria*. It had a frontispiece and six plates in coloured lithograph, and was dedicated 'To the Good Little Boys of Great Britain', to whom Parley says: 'I have already told you about my voyages across the Atlantic.' But Goodrich never crossed it to see Queen Victoria

---

* There was also an Aunt Parley (in an *Annual* of 1840 published by Simpkins), and a Parley kinsman, 'Uncle' or 'Grandpa' Ben.

crowned: he was in America in 1838. He apparently took no steps about this affront.

Tilt seems to have done little else in the Parley line; partly, no doubt, because he had already an equivalent in the travel and natural history books of the prosaic and popular Englishman Thomas Bingley.* This particular *Visit* went into a second edition, and possibly more. Tilt had a large business. He had the credit of employing George Cruikshank.

(v) It is evident that Edward Lacey was one of the first in the English Parley field, though Goodrich did not mention him till late in life – in his autobiography, in fact, as a long past or long dead foe. He is looking back to the beginnings of piracy, and after singling out Martin as the worst of the freebooters, he continues:

Among these London counterfeiters, there was formerly a bookseller by the name of Lacey. He was what is called a Remainder Man – that is, he bought the unsold and unsaleable ends of editions, put them in gaudy bindings, and thus disposed of them. When he got possession of a defunct juvenile work, he galvanized it into life by putting Parley's name to it – as 'Grandfather's Tales, by Peter Parley', etc.

'Remaindering' is a legitimate practice, and renaming old material is not unknown in connection with it; but borrowing the pseudonym for alien substances was not fair. However, Goodrich had no remedy.

Lacey was in other respects an able and by no means disreputable publisher, who did a good many useful reprints. He also issued a pleasant *Juvenile Library* (*c.* 1834) consisting of seven little volumes, chiefly original, in a neat case.

(vi) The sixth English Parley was my great-uncle, Samuel Clark, from 1836 to 1843 partner in the publishing business of his brother-in-law, John Maw Darton. He gave up publishing to take Holy Orders and achieve some distinction as a theologian and educational expert, but he continued to undertake editorial work for the firm and his name appears in imprints up to 1847. He was a man of acute ability and great probity, and what he did – as 'the Rev. T. Wilson' – for Messrs Darton and Clark was not a strain on commercial honesty as things then were. He almost invariably posed as 'editor' only, unlike Martin, whom my grandfather used more flagrantly. The morality of literary 'ghosts' is hardly a question to be discussed here. Such wraiths were very numerous in the first Victorian period, but they are not yet extinct.

Parley had serious trouble with Darton over Martin, but remained, rather inexplicably, on good terms with him; most of the authentic English editions bore my surname; and so did a good many forgeries.

4

That was one aspect of the 'real Peter Parley's' vicissitudes in the English

---

* Who wrote *Tales about Birds* (2nd edn 1840), *inter alia*. Not to be confused with the Rev. William Bingley, of *Animal Biography* (2nd edn 1804), for whom see *D.N.B.*

EDWARD LACEY,

Wholesale and Retail

𝕻rintseller, 𝕻ublisher, and 𝕾tationer,

DEALER IN ANNUALS, BOOKS OF PRINTS,

REWARD-BOOKS, &c. &c.

76, ST. PAUL'S CHURCH-YARD, (Near Ludgate Hill,)

LONDON.

All Orders, of whatever magnitude, whether for home trade or exportation, will be executed with the utmost promptitude, and on the lowest possible terms. EDWARD LACEY *takes this opportunity of informing his friends in the trade, and the public generally, that, owing to his extremely small profits, and having reduced his Prices, so as to supply every Article considerably under the usual Charges, he is compelled to have no Credit Accounts whatever, and can do business for Ready Money only, but so low as cannot fail to give universal satisfaction.*

*** Prints, Books of Prints, Annuals, and Stationery Stock, in any quantity, BOUGHT OR EXCHANGED.

34. Following the style of John Harris as to illustration, and of Benjamin Tabart as to advertising copy, Goodrich's 'Counterfeiter' Edward Lacey woos his public.

nursery world. The grievance was not so small as it looks. In thirty years over 7,000,000 copies of some 116 *genuine* Parleys were sold. Probably no 'juvenile' author, purporting or appearing to be one person, has ever had so large a circulation of so many books in so short a period. Goodrich was worth pirating. The mere figures tell their own tale about the magnitude of the children's book-trade. The copyright question does not concern us here, but it was important in international intercourse and in subtle influence on the social amenities.*

---

* In the forties, between 40 and 50 per cent of all books published in America were English productions. That is Sampson Low's figure, and Goodrich admitted it. All the piracy was not this side of the Atlantic [nor all the double-dealing – see Dickens's furious letter to Thomas Hoad in 1842 on Goodrich's declared support for a free market in literary property.]

Goodrich had another significance for English children's books, a less worldly and personal importance. But before that is dealt with, some other points had better be exhibited. So far as the well-intentioned and undoubtedly injured visitor from New England was concerned, the piracies must be left in their forgotten past. Goodrich does not seem to have revisited England between 1842 and 1852, when he once more complained. He carried on his American business successfully, and was also for a time United States Consul in Paris. He retired in 1855, to live in New York, and died of heart failure on May 9, 1860. He was simple, kindly, industrious, and sincere.

A few words should be said about the format of these volumes. It is easily recognized and may be called characteristic. They were usually bound in cloth. Cloth binding was invented in the twenties – it is not quite certain in which year. Gold, according to Michael Sadleir, was first blocked upon it in 1832: it was evidently applied to children's books at once. For such volumes the favourite cloth was a bright red – but blue and green were used simultaneously – with a heavily floral design in gold on the back and a figure or small scene in gold in the middle of the front cover (sometimes on the back cover as well): 'rich', but not ostentatious, solid-looking like an English merchant, not Orientally garish nor yet finicking. The publishers affected as a rule a square shape of volume. The type was reasonably clear, but not beautiful. There were often coloured illustrations, usually by some temporarily popular artist, but unmistakably belonging to their period, and not, in most cases, eternal as works of art: nor, it is fair to say, expected to be. Baxter's process, modified, was used in several *Annuals*, and black and white pictures, generally fine-line woodcuts, but quite frequently steel engravings, were liberally inserted in the text. They are very interesting. Occasionally one meets a very ancient one indeed, dating almost from the late chapbook period at its best: if so, the text as a rule has obviously been written 'up ' to it. Others, likewise decorated with letterpress, not *vice versa*, were part of the large stock ordinarily kept by publishers of the time: a mountain range, a volcano, a lake, a storm at sea, and so on. The best were drawn specially, and in them can often be found good work. Sir John Gilbert, Harvey, Sam Williams did much of it. The 'prentice work of Charles Keene is not at all uncommon, and some are signed by George and Robert Cruikshank. But the next stage in the Victorian era made a revolution in all book illustration.

5

Goodrich was not alone as an American invader of the English nursery. Commercially, other authors from the States were not mixed up so closely as he was with international differences. But in 'spiritual' influence they stand out with some prominence in the early and middle periods of Victoria's reign. They appeared to English children in three characters – as writers transcending local atmosphere, as authors creating a fresh and acceptable local atmosphere, and as purveyors of reading-matter almost, but not quite, peculiar to a temporary culture.

The authors who are, so to speak, extra-territorial are four in number. The most evanescent, but for a time also the most universal, was Harriet Beecher Stowe. Strictly speaking, *Uncle Tom's Cabin* (1852) was not a children's book at all. But there can have been few mid-Victorian children who did not drop a spontaneous and, all things considered, a justifiable tear over its pages. The slavery question was deeply felt in England, and children, as has been said, had been familiarized with it already: the Ethiop, as a Man Friday, as a Noble Savage, and as the slave wrongfully oppressed, was a known figure. Mrs Stowe's great melodrama, strong over and above its topical appeal, was more popular with English young people than the books – *Queer Little People* and *The Daisy's First Winter* (both probably 1867)* – which she designed for that class of reader.

Equally universal, but more enduring, was another great book with a negro hero, the considerably later *Uncle Remus* (1881) and its sequels. It escapes geography and time not through the broad personality of its author, for Joel Chandler Harris was, and insisted upon being considered, 'provincial', but through the essence of its subject-matter. The Georgia negro spoke Aesop, and added his own African and American humour and circumstance: a detail which at first allots the *Remus* tales to rather older children in England than in America, because of the difficulty of the dialect, but in the end adds to their attraction. Many of the stories have become catchwords. Many have analogues in the long history of fable. They are both local and world-wide.

Nathaniel Hawthorne, on the other hand, had neither our common humanity nor our primeval lore as a basis of popularity for his children's books. His subject indeed was almost entirely delocalized. His *Wonder Book* (1852) and *Tanglewood Tales* (1853), anticipating Kingsley's treatment of the Greek legends,† are essentially timeless and raceless. They are in any good English juvenile library today on their merits as a great writer's excellent rendering of immortal stories.

The fourth of these authors, however, is universal just because of the depth and breadth of his American-ness. He was not the sort of writer one would have expected to come from the native country of a Samuel Goodrich; and yet even 'Old Peter Parley', as he loved to call himself mellowly, gave a hint of a freer personality, especially when, in describing his own boyhood, he told of people who might be models for the grown-up characters in the work of 'Mark Twain'.

---

* Here and hereabouts the dates are those of first English editions; but they are not guaranteed as correct at that. Exactness is impossible in regard to this minor international traffic. [In many cases the dates are exactly the same as those of American publication – indeed, some important books, like *Little Men* and *Huckleberry Finn*, were published in London before the U.S. editions appeared. Only where there is a wide discrepancy in dates have both been given.]

† [Not only anticipating, but prompting. It is reported that Kingsley began to write *The Heroes* (1856) because he found *Tanglewood Tales* 'distressingly vulgar'.]

Goodrich repressed 'nature', thinking it uncivilized. Clemens saw mankind in it. So it comes about that *Huckleberry Finn* (1884), with characters like Parley in it dressed up as deacons and farmers, is one of the greater books in the English language, in its kind; far better, to me, than even its fine predecessor *Tom Sawyer* (1876), which is a 'boy's book' pure and simple, of the best quality, but not capable of lifting the reader out of time and place. In the longer, fuller book, so skilfully put into the first person, the figure of Huck Finn himself, simple, resourceful, clean, indomitable, makes any character of a 'manly' boy drawn by lesser authors look like a stuffed dummy: even Tom Sawyer is only pretending to be alive alongside Huck and Jim. The scenery, the actual events, the whole atmosphere of the book are equally above criticism. They are attached to the Mississippi, but they are part of the world.

The authors who made domestic America, so to speak, part of the English nursery scene, at any rate for more than a moment or two, were few, and not on the same plane as these four. One of the earliest arrivals was Jacob Abbott (1803–79), a Congregational minister and teacher who wrote excellent tales about ordinary life in New York State. His *Young Christian* appeared here in 1833, and the *Rollo* books began in 1836. *Beechnut: a Franconia Story* does not seem to have come out till 1853: it is probably the best known of Abbott's works. He had, as E. V. Lucas says, 'a pleasant, leisurely, and very wise pen'. Yet he has never been dear to English readers, never known in the sense that half the middle-aged English people of fifty years ago, and later, would begin talking in affectionate reminiscence or kindly gentle derision (a good test, when one is grown-up) if they were mentioned. Probably his pen was too leisurely even for the young readers to whom, at that time of day, he was describing unfamiliar scenes. The 'wilderness' of America ought, for them, to have been more populous and exciting, and the very naturalness of his pictures left the sense of romance unsatisfied. That initial lack of enthusiasm in English circles accounts for much in the neglect of him, even though his books have been fairly often reprinted over here. A children's book once established has a long life; but if it is not successful at the outset, it can seldom gain solid acceptance. When Abbott first wrote, the English juvenile public was not ready for him, and later there were too many rivals. By the time *Rollo in Paris* (1854) appeared, England was wallowing in Parleys, and more deeply, if also more artificially, in numerous editions of *The Swiss Family Robinson*, which was a wide wide world in itself.

Louisa May Alcott was fortunate in coming much later, when domestic fiction, unpretentious and not aggressively moral, had already got a footing which her own work made sure. Miss Alcott served in the American Civil War as a nurse, and was a woman of varied experience and interests, but quiet, even dull, simplicity is the staple of *Little Women* (1868) and its sequels about the same characters. The comparative eventlessness of life and the evenness of the persons concerned give her stories a curious fascination which even boys – these were really 'girls' tales' – have acknowledged. They contain the fun of being ordinary, with a wealth of detail, and with no hint of abnormal perfection in any of the actors. The descriptions of food – American food, enticingly exotic to English readers who may not even have known what waffles are – made one as hungry as Mrs Sherwood's. Miss Alcott never became, so to speak, naturalized; but she was and has remained a permanent and well-loved guest.

Less permanent, perhaps, because more easily grown out of, were the decidedly sentimental works known collectively as the 'Elsie Books'. They were contemporary with the rather older *Little Women* series, beginning in 1867 with *Elsie Dinsmore* (London, 1873). Domestic and homely without being sloppy, and, in spite of the complete ordinariness of the life they depicted, without being monotonous, they had every chance of exhausting an inquisitive or lively young reader, because Elsie was pursued, in successive volumes, through her friendships, through girlhood, motherhood, kith and kin, widowhood, woman-hood, grandmotherhood, and even to new relations; and then, from 1876 (London, 1890), a Mildred supervened and set out on a similar career. The stories mount up to a chronicle unrivalled by the work of any other 'juvenile' writer. They were all devoured here as eagerly as in America. They prove the great virtue of naturalness and lack of affectation. Their author, Martha Finley (whose earliest books appeared under her middle name, Farquharson), was a born story-teller, and never strained a word or an incident, and that is all that can or need be said.

Since then, American authors have enjoyed in English juvenile circles a pleasant and unprejudiced popularity on their merits; Thomas Bailey Aldrich, Eugene Field, and Charles Dudley Warner. They came later in Victoria's reign, and have never been completely acclimatized. Probably the warmest memories of such work in the minds of English children linger round the magazine in which some of it greeted them – *St Nicholas*. It was 'conducted' in its heyday, from 1873 to nearly the end of the century, by Mary Mapes Dodge, the author of *Silver Skates* (1865). It had a considerable English readership and for a number of years the name of F. Warne of London shared the title-page with the American publisher.

But side by side with productions of general appeal of that kind there was growing up a school of American children's literature which was curiously akin, and yet, by its provinciality of manner, inferior, to the English output of what would now be called, in slang which cannot be improved upon, 'sob-stuff'. In 1851 appeared that astonishingly lachrymose work *The Wide, Wide World*, by 'Elizabeth Wetherell', the pseudonym of Susan Bogert Warner of New York City; her sister 'Amy Lothrop' (Anna Bartlett Warner) also wrote books of the same kind. It was followed in 1852 by *Queechy*. Both fictions perhaps still rouse not wholly respectful memories in middle-aged English readers. The chief things that could be said for them were, first, that tears were then in fashion in adult fiction – honest tears, like those shed by Thackeray over Dickens's Paul Dombey; and second – much later, by the Warners' biographer, in 1925 – that these works were 'of historical value, reproducing scenes in New York society and the neighbouring country nearly one hundred years ago.' (The district of *The Wide, Wide World* is Canaan, N.Y., and of *Queechy*, Lebanon Springs, in the same state.) As to that, one can only say that in 1825 New York society must have moved very slowly, for the events are interminably clogged with lamentations. The characters lived in a perpetual condition of self-reproach which must have hindered the most trivial duties: 'She did not let her mother see but very few tears, and those were quiet ones; though she drooped her head like a withered flower, and went about the house with an air of submissive sadness that tried her mother sorely.' No doubt it did. But it did not try young girl readers in 1851, and nor, presumably, did another lachrymose tale that also had a great success in England, *The Lamplighter* by Maria Suzanna Cummins (1854).

These productions were vastly popular both here and in the States. In later books – *Ellen Montgomery's Book* (1853), and, by far the best for 'children's' use, *Melbourne House* (1864) – Miss Wetherell came nearer to normal equanimity.

The Wetherells were followed by one whose feelings hiccoughed rather than wept; Sarah Payson Willis, sister of the notorious journalist N. P. Willis, who, incidentally, was a friend and colleague of Samuel Griswold Goodrich. She wrote as 'Fanny Fern', and English girls now fifty years old read much of her, for her vogue here was long. Some of her books in their English form were illustrated in sepia, with an added tint, which seems to have been one of the early experiments of Edmund Evans, the well-known engraver and colour-printer: that is to say, they were meant for a considerable and well-to-do public in this country. They contained many autobiographical fragments. Miss Willis led a life full of emotions, and put her experiences into semi-fiction like *Fern-Leaves from Fanny's Portfolio*. There are plenty of nice clammy death-bed scenes.

Later manifestations of the same overwrought sentiment can only be briefly mentioned, though they were popular enough in their day. They were not all mere exuberance. The 'Katy Books' – *What Katy Did* (1872), and many others – were good popular specimens, not seriously overdone in a general way. The author was Sarah Chauncey Woolsey, who wrote as 'Susan Coolidge'. A little later, the Rev. E. P. Roe, who managed to get a frigid mention by Matthew Arnold, produced novels like *Barriers Burned Away* (1873), which really suited the adolescent and the 'young person' – at any rate in Great Britain – rather than the adult. They were inspired by a fervent Christianity: 'even the lurid and destructive flames' of the great Chicago fire of 1871 'might reveal with greater vividness the need and value of Christian faith' – it is not distantly unlike the Puritan use of London's fire. But the supreme work, produced a dozen years later still, was Mrs Hodgson Burnett's *Little Lord Fauntleroy* (1886, but serialized in *St Nicholas* the year before). Mrs Burnett was English, but this appeared in America. It ran through England like a sickly fever. Nine editions were published in as many months, and the odious little prig in the lace collar is not dead yet.

6

These features – the contradictions of Miss Sinclair and the solidity of Parley – were symptoms. The quiet upheaval in children's books which this period – the Albert–Victorian, as it may be called with no derogatory intent – brought about can be seen almost symbolically in what happened to be an international as well as a philosophical clash of faiths. 'Peter Parley' had a panoplied fight with 'Felix Summerly'; New England with South Kensington.

It was in the forties that Goodrich, whose views on his own childhood's books have been quoted, made a most alarming discovery. England's young people were being warned against Peter Parley. They were being encouraged to read, not fairy-tales exactly, but old legends, and, what was worse, those dreadful inanities known as nursery rhymes. This is his record of the evil practices:

In England, at the period that the name of Parley was most current – both in the genuine as well as the false editions – the feeling against my juvenile works was so strong among the conservatives, that a formal attempt was made to put them down by reviving the old nursery books. In order to do this, a publisher in London reproduced these works, employing the best artists to illustrate them, and bringing them out in all the captivating luxuries of modern typography. A quaint, quiet, scholarly old gentleman, called Mr Felix Summerly – a dear lover of children – was invented to preside over the enterprise, to rap the knuckles of Peter Parley, and to woo back the erring generation of children to the good old orthodox rhymes and jingles of England.

He went on to denounce 'Hallowell's' collection of *Nursery Rhymes*: by which he meant either the Percy Society's *Nursery Rhymes of England* (1842, but much enlarged in later editions) or the independent volume by the same editor, J. O. Halliwell (afterwards Halliwell-Phillipps) – *Popular Rhymes and Nursery Tales* (1849). He set to work to invent some rival doggerel of his own, to show how easy it was to write such unprofitable rubbish, and then proceeded to attack *Jack the Giant-Killer*, English folk-tales, and romances in general, on grounds which had been gone over amply and often enough for a century past or more. In 1844 (*Peter Parley's Annual,* vol. v) he resented criticism of his own unimaginativeness as 'ill-natured'.

Now hear the other side which inspires that remark. It is from an announcement of 1843, proclaiming the issue (1843–7) of 'Felix Summerly's Home Treasury of Books, Pictures, Toys, etc., purposed to cultivate the Affections, Fancy, Imagination, and Taste of Children.' The prospectus was quite frank:

The character of most Children's Books published during the last quarter of a century, is fairly typified in the name of Peter Parley, which the writers of some hundreds of them have assumed. The books themselves have been addressed after a narrow fashion almost entirely to the cultivation of the understanding of children. The many tales sung or said from time immemorial, which appealed to the other and certainly not less important elements of a child's mind, its fancy, imagination, sympathies, affections, are almost all gone out of memory, and are scarcely to be obtained . . . As for the creation of a new fairy tale or touching ballad, such a thing is unheard of . . . The conductor of the proposed series . . . purposes . . . to produce a series of Works for children, the character of which may be briefly described as anti-Peter Parleyism . . . All will be illustrated, but not after the usual fashion of children's books, in which it seems to be assumed that the lowest kind of art is good enough to give first impressions to a child . . .

It was a pretty quarrel: the touchy New Englander, rightly aggrieved at being exploited without payment, and a trifle vexed by the fictitious physical appearance ascribed to him, coming over here with the best intentions and telling the Prince Consort's right-hand man that English children must not be allowed to degenerate through the use of their own national stories and rhymes; and being confronted with a determined and excellently managed re-presentation of those very relics of Old England.

Parley resigned himself to the hands of Providence and the esteem of the public. He did not see the distant result of the strife.

I have written openly, avowedly, to attract and please children; yet it has been my design at the same time to enlarge the circle of knowledge, to invigorate the understanding, to strengthen the moral nerve, to purify and exalt the imagination. Such have been my aims; how far I have succeeded, I must leave to the judgment of others.

They have judged. His books have perished. His publisher rushed out fifteen or twenty volumes of a *Holiday Library* in gay bindings, including work by the real Parley, by Martin, by Mary Howitt and Mrs Sherwood, to counteract the *Home Treasury*: but not one of them has any life now, whereas the stories chosen by 'Felix Summerly' are perpetually reissued in various forms.

The 'quaint, quiet, scholarly old gentleman' thus rather injudiciously challenged was Henry Cole, afterwards Sir Henry Cole, a modest benefactor whose work is much better known than his name or the events of his energetic life. He was born in 1808, so that his fullest activity should have been in play at Victoria's accession, and he would have been an honoured figure at her Jubilee: but he died in 1882. He served on the Record Commission, and, very influentially, on the Committee for the Great Exhibition of 1851. He was one of the founders of the Royal College of Music, the Albert Hall and the South Kensington Museum, and a trusted adviser of that firm idealist Prince Albert. Among his more intimate friends were Thackeray, John Stuart Mill, Thomas Love Peacock, George Grote and Charles Buller; he could not be accused of rigid doctrine with men so varied round him in his private life.

The *Home Treasury* produced by Cole under his not infelicitous pseudonym was in part undertaken for a practical personal need. 'My young children being rather numerous', he wrote, 'their wants induced me to publish.' His general aim, well directed at the large Victorian families, is contained in the prospectus just quoted. His publisher was Joseph Cundall, who issued both by himself and later in partnership with Addey a good many children's books distinguished by sound typography and illustration; for instance, *A Treasury of Pleasure Books for*

Young Children (1850), which he dedicated to his own family, and which he followed with *A Treasury of Pleasure Books for Young and Old* (1851), where he told them that he had no fear of their imitating the 'disgraceful' conduct of Puss in Boots or becoming robbers like Bold Robin Hood.

The *Home Treasury* proper was illustrated by well-known artists of the 'literal' school – J. C. Horsley, R.A., C. A. Cope, R.A., T. Webster, R.A., and Mulready, who thus late in life returned to the field of his 'prentice work. The volumes, squarish and handy in shape, with reasonably large type, of an antique face, on good paper, contrasted more than favourably with the meaner conventional print and stock steel and wood engravings of most of the English Parley books. But Goodrich did not see any virtue in such 'captivating luxuries'.

The subject-matter which so offended Parley was honest salvage of various kinds. A complete set of volumes is probably rare, and I have never seen one. Advertisements, however, indicate that the original series may have consisted of twelve or more booklets in stiff ornamented paper covers, with these titles:

1. Jack the Giant-Killer
2. Jack and the Beanstalk.
3. The Sleeping Beauty.
4. Little Red Riding Hood.
5. Cinderella.
6. Beauty and the Beast.
7. Chevy Chase.
8. The Sisters and Golden Locks, etc.
9. Grumble and Cheery, etc.
10. [Peacock's] Sir Hornbook.
11. Dick Whittington.
12. Bible Events (four series).

These were sold at 1s. plain, 2s. 6d. coloured. They were redistributed into four larger volumes at higher prices, thus:
1. Traditional Nursery Songs (not in the above). 2s. 6d.
2. Chevy Chase and Sir Hornbook etc. (nos. 7, 8, 9 and 10 above). 4s. 6d.
3. Traditional Fairy Tales (nos. 4, 6, and 2). 3s. 6d.
4. Popular Fairy Tales (nos. 1, 5, and 3). 3s. 6d.

and there were also longer single titles like *Reynard the Fox* (4s. 6d.) and a variety of 'educational toys' like a 'Tesselated Pastime' – a set of mosaic tiles in a box (6s.). The more expensive books were bound in cloth gilt. A further series, edited by 'Ambrose Merton' (that is to say W. J. Thoms, the founder of 'folklore') was *Gammer Gurton's Famous Histories*, and included *Guy*, *Bevis* and other romances, but I have only seen odd volumes and no full list.

They were issued at frequent intervals[2] from 1843 onwards, but the dates are capricious and sometimes absent. The whole series, with its well-planned scope and straightforward contents, represents the first really systematic attempt to give English children the wealth of their own literary inheritance, with no conditions as to its use, no disguise, no spoilt simplicity.

One other thing, still extant, if less esteemed now, was bequeathed by Sir Henry Cole to later generations. He produced the first English Christmas card. It was designed in 1845 by J. C. Horsley, and issued in 1846 from the *Home Treasury* offices. It shows a domestic dinner-party of parents and children. The table is festively lavish in the manner of the period, with plenty of wine, but no robins or holly.

35. Sir Bevis and Josyan leading Ascapart. Frederick Tayler's wood-engraving, contrasting both with the medieval woodcut for the same story (fig. 8) and with the more intense engravings of the mid-Victorian period.

Tayler's picture originally appeared in this version of *Sir Bevis* in 'Ambrose Merton's' *Gammer Gurton's Story Books*, published by Joseph Cundall in 1843(?). Here the illustrations were mostly printed in colours, but later the story was bound into various compendia where it was also hand-coloured or issued plain.

7

The verdict on Parley, as has been said, has been given by time, whose chariots were indeed now close. The betterment of book-illustration began in the late fifties, and *Alice* changed the whole ideal of children's literature in 1865. Goodrich and Cole stand out as protagonists, the writers who actually spoke the chief parts and put the two conflicting policies into set words. The contrast was not so sharp among the rank and file who did not come forward as leaders. In fact, the two ideals, fact and fancy, old and new, were often held by the same writers; of whom two in particular may be taken as typical. Their lives and their books include nearly every activity of average contemporary minor thought.

William Howitt (1792–1879) and Mary Botham (1799–1888) were both members of the Society of Friends, though when, in 1822, they were arranging for their first joint publication – a volume of poems issued in 1823 as *The Forest Minstrel* – they consulted first the printer Davidson, 'for we are not so orthodox as to employ the Friendly firm of Darton and Harvey'. Mary's family had been of stricter Quaker adherence than her husband's. Religious tuition was never given in it, and they never made Bible-reading a habit: they waited, both for self-expression and for resort to the Scriptures, until the Spirit definitely moved them. On the other hand, Mary's mother, as she sat spinning (like the goodwife in Mrs Trimmer's *Two Farmers*), would recite or sing poems to her children, 'both grave and gay' – like *Auld Robin Gray* and *The Derby Ram*. Her nurse also was 'familiar with ghosts, hobgoblins and fairies', and passed on her knowledge. Mary herself, however, singles out Mrs Trimmer's *Robins* as her favourite reading, and her sister Anne was devoted to *Hymns in Prose*. The date of their acquaintance with these works was about 1809, when Mary was ten.

She and her sister, living in the Trent district of Staffordshire, saw the same kind of country scenes as Mrs Sherwood and the Sneyds and Edgeworths – the bull-baiting, the poverty, the sleekness, the quiet ceremonial of visits exchanged, but more demurely in the limited Quaker connection. When they went to school at Croydon, near London, it was to learn for the first time the accomplishment of fancy-work. All their sewing hitherto had been domestic and useful. But they found in that training a certain superiority over their fellows: 'It was one of our characteristics that we could do whatever we had once seen done. We could hackle flax or spin a rope. We could drive a nail, put in a screw or draw it out. We knew the use of a glue-pot or how to paper a room.' Both she and her husband (they were married in 1821) were eminently practical in all they wrote, and both kept throughout their very real knowledge of country life. They never collected information merely from books, or advocated work or play on second-hand experience.

William, on the other hand, had at any rate the chance of a less limited outlook in his upbringing. His father was actually a Rousseauist; though the son wrote in after years, in regard to Rousseau's views on the value of learning a mechanical trade, that 'his sophisms have long fallen before common sense'. Yet the young Howitt was brought up at Heanor, between Derby and Mansfield, on local legends of Robin Hood and on strange stories of Byron at Newstead Abbey. He knew also the tale of his own descent from a famous London merchant, Sir William Hewet of London Bridge, whose apprentice Edward Osborne, in 1547, saved his master's daughter Anne from drowning, married her, and became the founder of the Dukedom of Leeds. That story Howitt afterwards used, and it has appeared over and over again in children's magazines ever since.

He also assimilated the realities of country life, both at Heanor and at Ackworth School, the famous Quaker foundation: 'Boyhood in the country!', he wrote in a fragment of autobiography. 'Paradise of opening existence! Up to the age of ten this life was all my own, and I revelled in it.'

It and the Ackworth experiences came out again in print in one of his best-known works, *The Boy's Country Book* (1839) – 'a real transcript of my youthful life'. If it were not that what is now called nature study has increased so vastly in its scope, that unpretentious compilation might well have remained a simple classic of its kind.

In some respects the life of the Howitts was ordinary. They were successful in selling their literary wares. They were devoid of vanity or pushfulness, but attained an excellent and secure position in a wide circle of friends – not all Friends, for their adherence to strict Quakerism waned early in their middle life. William Howitt was an ardent reformer within the Society, and, among other things, urged publicly – in *Tait's Edinburgh Magazine* for 1834 – that the traditional Quaker dress should be abandoned. They finally quitted the Society; and in 1882, three years after William's death, Mary became a Roman Catholic. Writing of a visit to a Unitarian chapel in 1844, she had said: 'if we lived in a

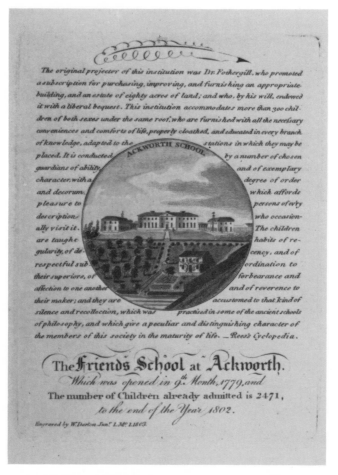

36. An engraving by William Darton Junior, printed on silk and possibly designed for a watch-case. It shows the school at which he and Howitt were educated.

village where there was a good clergyman, I should go to Church'. Not to a Puseyite one, she added. Yet 'I sometimes could almost wish that I were a good Catholic; for they, of all people, have faith.' She died in that faith on January 30, 1888.

Their social range was wide, wider indeed than that of any preceding writers for children, except Miss Edgeworth's, though such breadth itself was an example of the change of social circumstances. Their friends at different times included not only professional literary folk of similar standing to themselves – the S. C. Halls, Miss Jewsbury, 'L.E.L.', Alaric Watts and his wife, Mrs Hemans – but others of great diversity: Bernard Barton the Quaker, Charles Kean, Wordsworth, Tennyson, Joaquim Miller, Lady Burdett-Coutts, Moncure Conway, Augustus Hare, Octavia Hill, Louisa May Alcott, and the Pre-Raphaelites. They were in the regular circle of intellectual activity, not mere country cousins or lonely crusaders. They were interested in all liberal movements – in anti-slavery propaganda, in the Married Woman's Property Act, and in Church Disestablishment.

On the ecclesiastical question, indeed, William Howitt took a strong line, not only in his *Popular History of Priestcraft* (1833), but in service on important committees and delegations set up by Nonconformist bodies. But though religious differences were evident enough in England, they had but faint repercussions in children's books as compared with the noise of the Trimmer–Lancaster dispute. The Establishment did its own work for children without rancour or excitement. It laboured for faith rather than prestige, as is shown by a series planned for prize-givings and Sunday-reading: *The Juvenile Englishman's Library* (1845–9), edited at the start by the Rev. F. E. Paget (1806–82). It was an altogether more severe series than 'Summerly's' *Home Treasury* and Darton's *Holiday Library* but neat in appearance and illustrated with 'standard' wood-engravings of the time. It ran to twenty-two volumes altogether, and was designed to amuse and instruct, and at the same time to adhere to sound Church of England doctrine. Perhaps the most striking volume in that respect was the Rev. J. M. Neale's *Triumphs of the Cross*, which can hardly be thought fervidly dogmatic. Other interesting volumes were a good little semi-moral fairy-tale, by the editor, *The Hope of the Katzekopfs* (1844), frequently reprinted even in recent times, and a volume of three *Popular Tales* from the German, which included tales from Hauff and De la Motte Fouqué. The Hannah More rural tradition was kept up in two volumes of *Tales of the Village Children*. The whole series was clear in purpose and completely temperate in tone.

To return to the Howitts. Their interest was not confined to England. They visited some relatives in America, *Our Cousins in Ohio* (1849), a volume of some historical interest, being the result. They travelled widely in Europe. Above all, they translated foreign books. William Howitt did an English version of Chamisso's *Peter Schlemihl* (1843 – better known as *The Shadowless Man* – was it the inspiration of a famous detail in *Peter Pan*?). In 1842 Mary began to publish an English rendering of Frederica Bremer's Swedish novels, much to the benefit of piratical publishers in the United States, and also in 1846 – much to the benefit of the whole English-speaking world – Hans Andersen's fairy-tales, under the title of *Wonderful Stories for Children*: the first and greatest new ally of the Summerly army. The victory of fantasy was in sight.

8

Andersen had become a close personal friend of the Howitts, and, though they found him 'over-sensitive and egotistical', he himself was greatly pleased by the translation. But it 'did not pay the cost of printing'.

Possibly that was because the publishers – Dickens's publishers, Chapman and Hall – had to face three rival translations in the same year; Caroline Peachey's *Danish Fairy Legends and Tales* (Pickering) and Charles Boner's *A Danish Story Book* and *The Nightingale and Other Tales* (both published by Cundall – Cole's firm). But England was certainly ripe for the work, and it blended successfully for the first time and for all time the strains of fantasy and folk-lore. Andersen's tales contain both elements in a pure state. An admirable modern retranslation, by Dr M. R. James, gives conveniently the sources of the forty stories contained in it – the forty best-loved, I imagine, of the whole series.* Seven of them are genuine Danish folk-tales – 'old stories retold', little sophisticated in the retelling. The chief of them, perhaps, as folk-lore, is *The Wild Swans*. Most of the rest are near the same primitiveness, and are stated to have been heard by Andersen himself as a child. Among them are *The Tinder Box*, with those glorious dogs of progressive stature, and *Little Claus and Big Claus*, in which the attraction of the under-water world can never grow dim. But the ever-heroic *Tin Soldier*, and lily-leaf *Thumbelina* (*Tommelise* in some versions), are said to be entirely original, while *The Emperor's New Clothes*, which is not far off cynicism in its universal moral, is from a Spanish source. Andersen, in fact, was at once an involuntary collector of tradition, a poet, and an original genius; and 1846 recognized the fact.

The fairy-tale had at last come into its own. The story of its struggle without the aid of originality like Andersen's had culminated in such versions as Tabart's and in the immediate success of *Grimm*. But now there was added the recognition that it was lawful, and even praiseworthy, to invent and release fantasy, and to circulate folk-lore itself. Even the versatile Parley–Tegg departed from gradgrinding, and put forth a *Child's Fairy Library* in four series (1837–8), based upon an earlier French edition, with some of the woodcuts signed by Grandville. The forties and fifties saw many collections, partly translations of new work, partly collections of old. Hauff and De la Motte Foqué were introduced (Hauff's *Sultan Stork*, a mixture of several old elements, even now deserves to be better known, but has suffered from school

---

* [*Forty Stories* (1930). Later two further stories from Kristensen's collection of Danish folk-tales were added and the book has thus come to be titled *Forty-two Stories.*]

37. Alongside his *Juvenile Englishman's Library* the publisher James Burns issued several
similarly neat volumes in a *Cabinet Library for Youth*. The second book in the series was a
'new translation' of Andersen's *Tales for the Young*, which, as well as having 'Engravings
after the German' included this illustration by William Bell Scott, associate of the Pre-
Raphaelites.

As a translation of Andersen this stands early in the English sequence and demonstrates
as well as any the lamentable performance of Andersen translators before the 1930 edition
of M. R. James (and even his work must be seen as marking only a stage towards the
easier, more colloquial renderings by such as R. P. Keigwin).

use). In 1849 Anthony Montalba put together a volume of *Fairy Tales of All
Nations*, with illustrations, some of the best ever done for a children's book, by
Dick Doyle. A German collection, *The Old Story-Teller*, by Ludwig Bechstein,
was translated in 1854, and published by Addey, the successor of Joseph
Cundall. In 1857 Annie Keary translated the Norse *Tales of Asgard*; in 1858
James Robinson Planché, the dramatic expert, *Four and Twenty [French]
Fairy Tales*; in 1859 Sir George Dasent Asbjörnsen and Moe's *Popular Tales
from the Norse;* and so we had most of the tongues of Europe speaking to our
children. There were also new native voices in England, but they were heard in
greater volume later.

Finally in the next epoch, the post-*Alice* period, authority delivered itself *ex
cathedrâ* upon this matter of elves, sprites, trolls, hags, giants and all such other-
world folk. John Ruskin declared the national mind upon the subject in a
preface (1868) to John Camden Hotten's edition of *German Popular Stories*. A
child, he said pontifically,

should not need to choose between right and wrong. It should not be capable of wrong; it
should not conceive of wrong. Obedient, as bark to helm, not by sudden strain or effort,
but in the freedom of its bright course of constant life; true, with an undistinguished,
painless, unboastful truth, in a crystalline household world of truth; gentle, through
daily entreatings of gentleness, and honourable trusts, and pretty prides of child-

fellowship in offices of good; strong, not in bitter and doubtful contest with temptation, but in peace of heart, and armour of habitual right, from which temptation falls like thawing hail; self-commanding, not in sick restraint of mean appetites and covetous thoughts, but in vital joy of unluxurious life, and contentment in narrow possession, wisely esteemed.

Children so trained have no need of moral fairy tales . . .

The root-principle of the matter is in that pomp. It had been put a little more simply in the preface to the 1823 *Grimm*, in the suggestion that folk-lore is after all really child-lore. But Ruskin now exalted the fact into doctrine. His voice was thunderous in those days. Thus, nearly five centuries after the Wife of Bath had complained of the fairies' outlawry, the first Slade Professor of Fine Art at Oxford removed the ban.

9

The introduction of Andersen was the most considerable imaginative service which the Howitts did to the younger generation. They did not contribute appreciably to the output of adventure romance, which will be dealt with shortly; and sheer frivolity was alien to them. In fact, the sudden flash of levity which burst upon the world in the very year of the Andersen translations was a thing unrelated to its surroundings: as, perhaps, nonsense usually is.

It is true that the metre of Edward Lear's *Book of Nonsense* (n.d., 1846) had been anticipated, as has been shown; and nonsense of a sort had been fitted into it. But the *Fifteen Gentlemen* (p. 204) had been a conscious and jocular conception, almost arising, as it were, out of a desire to exploit an infectious rhythm; whereas in Lear's limericks the nonsense informs and is part of the rhythm, and both are filled with a completely un-self-conscious irresponsible ecstasy. 'How pleasant to know Mr Lear': no doubt Lord Derby's children thought so. At least they were intimate with the nonsense writer, rather than with the bearded artist who displayed in his water-colours the mind of a cultured but restrained poet. It may be true that in the limericks the repetition of the first-line end-word is a technical weakness; but it does not detract from the spontaneity. The man who could write the compressed epics

> There was an old man with a beard,
> Who said, 'It is just as I feared',

and

> There was an old man who said 'How
> Shall I flee from this horrible cow?'

knew the whole insane liberty of being absurd. Nor can his ridiculously child-like illustrations – which really *illustrate* – ever be separable from the verbal happiness. But as a matter of fact his nonsense is even more gloriously silly, more remote from anything approaching either facetiousness or fact, in other metres than the limerick. His invented words, only less admirable than Lewis Carroll's portmanteaux and coinages, some of which have actually become 'dictionary words', are delightful: 'runcible' is perhaps the best – everyone *must* know at once what a runcible cat with crimson whiskers is, though no one would dare to describe it more closely. The easy metrical complications of poems like *The Owl and the Pussy Cat* fit such a new language perfectly.

There is nothing to be said about work like Lear's except words of gratitude. It belonged to its period, certainly, in its sincerity. But it was not a clear product of evolution, and was too high above the more frivolous work of the time to produce anything but imitations: not descendants nor rivals.

About the same time, nevertheless, there did appear a kind of rival. But it is comparable only in also appealing to the sense of the ridiculous, and was hardly meant, in itself, to be preposterous. It was Heinrich Hoffmann's *Struwwelpeter* – in translations, *Shockheaded Peter*, or else *The English Struwwelpeter; or, Pretty Stories and Funny Pictures*. It apparently got here in 1848. It has probably never been received in England, except by those infants who could only just 'read' the 'funny pictures', as anything but splendidly hilarious. It is the Taylorian Awful Warning carried to the point where Awe topples over into helpless laughter. Much of it has become a semi-proverbial jest in English, a singular fate for a foreign book if it was composed seriously,[3] and in any case a very remarkable freak of acclimatization.

But with anything purposely or unconsciously beyond the range of orderly definition the Howitts had little contact. They regarded Andersen with a kind of severe tenderness rather than as a liberator of fancy. The same gracefully kind and gentle temperament, willing to be happy but unwilling to exult, is in their children's poetry. Admirable as it was in its sphere and period, it never passed the bounds so implied. Yet it is not by any means all prosaic, and certainly not so obvious as wear and tear has made much of it seem. Perhaps the most hackneyed of Mary's pieces – if 'hackneyed' can be taken to mean so familiar that its virtues have become invisible – is the notorious 'Spider and the Fly'. But look with a fresh and open mind at some of its lines:

> Come hither, hither, pretty Fly, with the pearl and silver wing;
> Your robes are green and purple – there's a crest upon your head;
> Your eyes are like the diamond bright, but mine are dull as lead . . .

That is not quite the work of a pedestrian recitation-monger. Her husband, too, though he wrote admirable recitation-pieces (if that black art must be practised at all by children), rose above mere rhymed playfulness in 'The wind one morning sprung up from sleep'. His lines have movement, something like a rush of real wind. Mary's charming fancy, *The Fairies of Caldon-Low*, is above even the charge of being a good entertainment item:

> Then take me on your knee, mother;
>   And listen, mother of mine.
> A hundred fairies danced last night,
>   And the harpers they were nine.
>
> And their harp-strings rung so merrily
>   To their dancing feet so small,

At length one day, so long she cried
That round her flowed the briny tide
First ankle deep, then higher still
It rose and 'gan the room to fill.
Next knee deep, then waist high the flood
Beyond high-water mark soon stood.

And as her tears still ceaseless flowed,
Across their flood you might have rowed:
But Susan lacking oar and boat,
Could neither stand, and scarcely float.
Thus 'midst the tears, her eyes that dim,
She floundered, all unused to swim,
And must have soon been drowned outright,
Had not her Ma, who saw her plight,
Now rescued her from out the wet,
And fished up Susan in a net.

38. Premonition of a more famous pool of tears. 'Naughty Susan' in the English edition of an
early *Struwwelpeter* imitation by Dr Julius Bähr, illustrated by Theodor Hosemann and
translated by Mme de Chatelain. Addey and Co., the publishers, were successors to
Cundall and Addey, who, a year previously, had published another such imitation: *A
Laughter Book for Little Folk*, n.d. [1851].

> But oh! the words of their talking
> Were merrier far than all.

It has gaiety and homeliness and a pretty rhythm, with but the barest hint of being written by one older than a child, yet by one who understood children and who had not forgotten the fairyland that was somewhere beneath her own demure Quaker childhood. It makes one understand why Mary Howitt translated Hans Andersen.

That was a note the Howitts seldom struck. They were in all their writings very much of the market-place: their wares were good, but not much more than what was expected. What matters, however, is that though they may have been manufactured for sale, they were honestly and naturally made. It would be unjust to decry either their sincerity or their valuable appropriateness. It would be equally unjust, though much easier, to disparage Mrs Hemans, who was to mid-nineteenth-century children very much what Cotton had been to those of a hundred years before. It would be not less easy, though much more dangerous, to belittle Macaulay, whose *Lays of Ancient Rome* (1842) appealed then, and do appeal now, to young minds. Macaulay's attitude, like his rushing metre, is rhetorical, and therefore seems artificial. But artificial is an adjective uncritically inhuman, especially in relation to swift narrative verse. The *Lays*, as George Saintsbury says admirably in the *Cambridge History of English Literature* (vol. XIII), belong to 'a class of verse which sets itself to give the public just that sort of poetry which it can well understand, and nothing more. In the better examples . . . there is no sacrifice of poetry itself.' That is equally true of William Howitt's *The Wind in a Frolic*, of *Hiawatha*, of Southey's *Inchcape Rock*, of Byron's *Sennacherib*, and of a dozen or more simple poems that have been rendered over-familiar just because the public does, quite rightly, like them. The mid-Victorian age got them together and put them into schoolbooks, or, worse still, collections of verse awarded as school prizes, until now they seem threadbare. There is no sting for our imagination left in them. But there was in the forties and fifties; a stimulus that inexperienced children can still feel if it is not repeated too mechanically.

10

There was one branch of juvenile literature which the Howitts might possibly have touched, but which they avoided, or rather treated in a negative fashion. They eschewed adventure, as has already been said. When they surveyed the outer world, they came near the Parley attitude. It was a place from which to learn lessons, to get reasonable inspiration; not the region in which boys should live dangerously and, at some risk of contamination, become rashly heroic. Yet in America, and gradually in England also, there was growing up the new school of adventurous fiction for young persons. In America, it may be said here in anticipation, it took the form of what is known as 'the dime novel', or more intimately, after its first robust publisher, the Beadle novel. In the United States the 'penny dreadfuls' attained their greatest notoriety as the work of Edward Sylvester Ellis (1840–1916), who wrote under various pseudonyms. His books were imported into England: they began to appear in the sixties. No one seems to know who wrote the English specimens, nor exactly when they emerged. But their germ was present, in a more reputable form, in the heyday of the Howitts.*

What had happened, in fact, was that 'boys' and 'girls' were perceived to be markedly different from 'children' and 'babies', and that though, where instruction – amusing instruction or instructive amusement – was concerned, much the same basic material might be used for all classes, even in language when once multiple syllables were mastered, the subject-matter and treatment of fancy or romance had to be graduated. Once juvenile fiction, shorn largely of instruction, got a hold, a new class of juvenile literature was bound to be developed. Hence the 'boy's book': that is, the boy's *tale*, not the boy's story-book nor the boyish book, but the whole synoptic literary composition the basis of which is fictitious romance.

The mass of works which took that form from the early fifties onwards is so great that very few writers can here be dealt with as individuals. They had 'arrived' as a class. It would be tedious and unnecessary to differentiate closely, for instance, between Ballantyne and Kingston, except in the matter of dates, plots and scenes; though that is not to say they were at all alike, personally, as writers. The important thing is the collection of characteristics they and others had in common. They had some main unity of idea.

It is clearest historically. The Robinsonnades, with their basis of mixed conceptions about savages and nature and desert islands and morality, had all the elements latent in them. The last notable one of them in the old tradition, for the juvenile library, was Marryat's *Masterman Ready* (3 vols., 1841–2). *Mr Midshipman Easy*, a novel and never meant to be anything else, had appeared five years before it, in 1836; and that was the real boys' book, in spite of objection which censors could take to a few details. Scott's novels, without even that hint of reproach, were being read by young and old. They had been compressed or adapted for 'children' very early, but, like his poetry, they were found to be excellent reading without any adaptation. James Fenimore Cooper (1789–1851) was quickly introduced into England from America. Mayne Reid, beginning to appear in the late forties, joined him.

But those were not really 'boys' ' authors, any more than Defoe had been. The writers who now gave boys excitement or romance instead of moral prattle *and were allowed to do so*, wrote for that very purpose. William Henry Giles Kingston's *Peter the Whaler* was published in 1851: his *Three Midshipmen* series

---

* I do not feel called upon to deal here, either in this chapter or in the next, with the question of their moral effect. Opinions about it, and about the kindred modern matter of exciting cinema films, are strongly held and diverse. The subject is briefly but fairly reviewed by an expert, Mr Berwick Sayers, in his *The Children's Library; a Practical Manual* (1909) and his *Manual of · Children's Libraries* (1932).

not till the seventies, when fiction for boys was a well-established commodity. He was paralleled in America by the German writer who had spent many years 'knocking about' in that land, Friedrich Gerstäcker, whose *The Little Whaler* was translated in 1857. Robert Michael Ballantyne, drawing upon first-hand experience more directly than some later rivals, produced *The Young Fur Traders* in 1856. They opened, between them, the door of contemporary romance, of life in books not drawn from the past, but close at hand and accessible in very truth to those who read about it. The wide world was made real and present, and yet was neither a schoolroom nor a forbidden Paradise.

And it was certainly not a place for tear-shedding and the terror of sin. The true novelty in these books was the absence, in the majority of them, of any appeal to a dogmatic religious belief, or any *open* theory of conduct or education. The belief and the theory were at last kept inside the authors' minds. The heroes are shown as praying, as trusting in God, as stout Britons with a sense of honour, honesty and duty; and the need of those qualities is always visible and sometimes made explicit (there are more pieces of 'pi-jaw' in Ballantyne than devout memory will readily now believe without reference to the original). But they are not the dominating, purposeful, obvious cause of the book's existence. There is all the difference in the world between the *Swiss Family Robinson*, with its prayer-intervals, and *Ungava* or Percy St John's *Arctic Crusoe* (1854). And there is an equal distance between both these kinds of adventure – fiction and the fare of solid facts offered by Peter Parley. The display of universal products, arts and industry in Paxton's great greenhouse in 1851 showed that facts were human in a broad sense: that behind the uses of shagreen, blubber, caoutchouc and other valuable commodities just coming within the daily reach of the fairly prosperous, lay the thrilling hardship of life endured by those who found and procured such goods in their raw state. The explorer was no longer a mere missionary of religion. His travels were such stuff as dreams are made on. The English boy, like Drake in Darien, could look upon the unknown seas and vow that he would sail in an English ship upon them.

But the moralists were not easily beaten or displaced. It is significant that the first title of Ballantyne's *Young Fur Traders* was *Snowflakes and Sunbeams*, which surely must have been invented with an eye to the preceptor. It is worthy of remark, also, that the last half of *The Little Savage* (2 vols., 1848–9), by Marryat's son, is infinitely more pietistic than the first, by Marryat himself. The first volume had not led one to expect that Marryat wished to repeat the deliberate didacticism of *Masterman Ready*; but the second does so, with emphasis, the Crusoe adventurous introversion being wholly subordinate to Christian uplift. Now the criticial reviews had just been praising unreservedly Marryat's *Children of the New Forest* (2 vols., 1847), which was the first book in his projected 'Juvenile Library', because it was so clearly meant to 'amuse, excite, inform, and instruct the youthful mind', or, in the sincere but smug words of its own prospectus as quoted by one reviewer '*to elevate the moral feelings*'. Adventure was not to be let loose without a licence.

The 'teachers' themselves, indeed, had seen the need of a brighter coat of fiction; with results that have not worn well. Has anyone now ever heard, familiarly, of Mrs J. B. Webb? She wrote *A Tale of the Vaudois* (1842, later published as *Julio Arnouf*, 1854), and *Naomi, or the Siege of Jerusalem*, which, published in 1841, was in an eleventh edition by 1853. Does any ardent imperialist now give children M. Fraser Tytler's *Tales of the Great and Brave* (1838 with a second series Edinburgh, 1843)?*

If it comes to that, does anyone now *really* read Harriet Martineau? If she is seized upon by the young for pleasure, it is not because of the economics in *The Playfellow* (4 vols., 1841). It contained *The Settlers at Home, Feats on the Fiord, The Peasant and the Prince* and *The Crofton Boys*; each is now usually reprinted separately, the third, so far as I can see, least often. (This collection had been preceded ten years before by *Five Years of Youth*, which is completely dead.) Three-quarters of *The Playfellow* perhaps survives, in a desiccated way. The difficulty in reading Harriet Martineau is her total lack of imagination rather than her insistent purpose: the purpose was there, but it never glowed – political economy is a tinsel fire for purposes of fiction. She did not succeed in bringing her characters to life. Capable though she was, and more, she had no sense of humour. Anyone who could state that

From my youth upwards I have felt that it was one of the duties of my life to write my autobiography . . . When my life became evidently a somewhat remarkable one, the obligation presented itself more strongly to my conscience: and when I made up my mind to interdict the publication of my private letters, the duty became unquestionable

ought to have been kept away from nurseries and schoolrooms the moment she grew out of them.

But the change from the older Moral Tale, in spite of a certain pompousness in the new model, was genuine. It lay in the recognition of a non-schoolroom atmosphere, in the acceptance of a comparatively innocent outside world where the home governess was not always round the corner. The books produced for it were honestly meant to be 'children's books' (or boys' and girls' books) within the fullest meaning of my original definition. They did not succeed in becoming so, however, except in a very limited sphere, and accordingly they are little more now than half-forgotten titles, though some of the authors' names endure not wholly dimmed. Only a few can be enumerated, like the works of Mrs Samuel Carter Hall (*The Hartopp Jubilee*; 1840?), the Rev. Bourne Hall Draper, the Rev. William Gresley, the Cowden Clarkes, Samuel Wilberforce (*Agathos*, 1840), Mrs Mackarness (Matilda Anne Planché) (*A Trap to Catch a Sunbeam*; 2nd edn. 1849; 10th edn. 1850), Sarah Crompton (*Tales that are True*, 1854), Agnes Strickland, who as early as 1822 had written a genuine Moral Tale of the old pattern, *The Moss-House*.

---

* The 'great and brave' were the Black Prince, Wallace, the Bruce, Joan of Arc, Coeur de Lion, Charles Edward the Young Pretender, Nelson and Napoleon. The volume had a Baxter frontispiece not chronicled in Martin Hardie's *English Coloured Books*. It was another Miss Fraser Tytler (Ann) who wrote *Leila, or The Island* (1839), a very pious Robinsonnade.

Younger folk to some extent shared in this emancipation, though the border-line between moral and tale, as also between 'child' and 'boy-or-girl', was often blurred. They were given the works of Mrs Mortimer (*The Peep of Day, Line upon Line, Reading without Tears*, and the more educational *Near Home* and *Far Off*), Mrs Leathley (*Chickseed without Chickweed*, of which over 250,000 copies were sold in the generation of children that began in the late fifties), and Mrs Jerram (née Holmes; *The Child's Own Story Book*; 3rd edn. 1843). Sometimes scraps of their writings are reprinted today: they have the strange life of domestic objects in a jumble sale. Nobody wants them; nobody destroys them.

I I

Such, then, was the general condition (with its dates here a little deranged for convenience of grouping) of English children's literature during Victoria's first twenty-five years. There are few single outstanding *books* to be observed in the period. Even *Holiday House* has not the eminence of Lear's *Nonsense* books, which are almost solitary in constituting a whole class. Yet between 1837 and 1862 the following elements in the juvenile library had been clearly stabilized: some had actually been discovered, or, chemically, 'isolated', for the first time, some have been dropped:

(i) A great deal of 'useful knowledge', which, being (naturally enough, in the course of time) no longer fully adequate as knowledge, has largely ceased to be useful. It never had a high imaginative value, because of its dehumanized form.

(ii) A considerable exchange of ideas, and of pictures of juvenile life, with America; the best of which was invigorating, the worst the reverse.

(iii) The 'boy's and girl's' book: original unbabyish stories, without explicit 'morals', ranging, for subjects, far outside English domestic circles: the beginnings of the higher juvenile fiction.

(iv) Fairy-tales as a permanent and honourable possession: native and naturalized folk-lore was recognized, *Grimm* glorified, from the previous generation's legacy, and original work added.

(v) The *Reliques* of our own literature, in a direct comprehensible form. These and the fairy-tales and the adventure-stories made up Romance for children: a new thing, unless they stole it – as they had hitherto.

(vi) Nonsense: the joy of being silly, inconsequent and innocently hilarious.

Against those gifts, except the last of them, must be set the absence of a dower from the higher imagination; for book romance is, at bottom, derivative, even if it inspires a loftier, freer fancy.

In mechanical presentation, the new juvenile library hardly equalled the freshness of its contents. Production was at a sombre level. Reaction from the wickedness of the Regency and George IV's reign had eclipsed the gaeity of engravings, as every print-collector knows, and affected books, even if Leech and Alken began to gallop cheerfully through Surtees. Most of the children's-book pictures from 1830 to 1860 were stodgy or sham-theatrical. The blue, red, green and gold bindings were often bright but not often beautiful. Except in its own home treasures, South Kensington had not had time to make grace and sweetness a middle-class decorative habit. That came in the next generation, after the manner of Movements.

On the negative side, the writers of the period rendered the chapbook, with its now glaring defects, obsolete. They almost – but certainly not quite – killed the Moral Tale, in the restricted sense of the term. They mitigated – indeed, turned to joy – the Awful Warning.

That was a very large contribution for one generation to make, even within the narrow confines of this subject. It formed a hoard upon which the sixties drew freely to make new treasures.

BRIEF BOOK LIST

From this period onwards books of reference are so numerous and ordinary facts so easily accessible that it is hardly necessary to refer the reader to many specific works. Some particular publications are mentioned in the text for special reasons. Nearly all the authors and artists are in *D.N.B.*, *C.H.E.L.* and *D.A.B.* Edward Lear, though included in *D.N.B.*, is not yet very satisfactorily shown to us – except by his own work. The two series of his *Letters* might be supplemented by the Introductions to *Queery Leary Nonsense*, ed. Lady Strachey (London, 1911), the selection in the *Augustan Books of Poetry* (London, 1927) and the miscellany, *A Book of Nonsense*, ed. Ernest Rhys (London, 1927), in the *Everyman* Series. See also the brief *Edward Lear*, issued in 1932 by Messrs Warne.

For some of the less-known American writers, readers may be able to consult the following works:

Abbott, Jacob. Introduction in the *Everyman* Series (the fullest in any English publication).

Roe, E. P. *Taken Alive, and other Stories* (New York, 1889). Autobiographical preface.

[Warner, Susan and Anna Bartlett.] *Letters and Memories*, by Olivia Egleston Phelps Stokes (London and New York, 1925).

[Willis, Sarah Payson.] *The Life and Beauties of Fanny Fern* (Philadelphia, 1855).

The pseudo-Parleys are in *D.N.B.* Add George Mogridge, *His Life, Character and Writings*, by the Rev. C. Williams (London, 1856).

Sir Henry Cole is summarized in *D.N.B.*, but his life can be best, if rather painfully, appreciated, in the collection of letters, speeches, prospectuses and the like, published in two volumes, in 1884, as *Fifty Years of Public Work*. A striking portrait of him has recently been inserted in the walls of the Victoria and Albert Museum, South Kensington. See *Fraser's Magazine* for 1846 for Thackeray's high appreciation of the *Home Treasury*, and the *Cornhill Magazine*, November 1932, 'Peter Parley and the Battle of the Children's Books' [by F.J.H.D.]

Two works of considerable use for this period (as well as for others) are E. V. Lucas's anthologies, *A Book of Verses for Children* (London, 1897) and *Another Book of Verses for Children* (London, 1907). A very charming and acute criticism of the English gift for nonsense and for poetry is to be found in Emil Cammaerts's *The Poetry of Nonsense* (London, 1925).

Supplement

More recent times have seen an even vaster increase in books on the topics dealt with in this and subsequent chapters. The following are some essential additions, many of which give guides to further exploration:

CUNDALL
McLean, Ruari. *Joseph Cundall; a Victorian Publisher. Notes on his life and a check-list of his books* (Pinner, 1976).
Summerfield, Geoffrey. 'The making of the Home Treasury' in *Children's Literature*, no. 8 (New Haven and London, 1979).

THE HOWITTS
Lee, A. *Laurels and Rosemary; the life of William and Mary Howitt* (Oxford, 1955).
Woodring, C. R. *Victorian Samplers; William and Mary Howitt* (Lawrence, Kansas, 1952).

ANDERSEN
Among many biographies in English the most fully documented is:
Bredsdorf, Elias. *Hans Christian Andersen . . . 1805–1875* (London, 1975).
A recent translation of the complete stories, with Andersen's notes, is:
The Complete Tales and Stories, translated by Erik Haugaard (New York and London, 1974).
For good retrospective information on Andersen, especially in relation to his English and American reputation see:
Library of Congress. *Catalog of the Jean Hersholt Collection* (Washington, 1954).
National Book League. *Catalogue of a Jubilee Exhibition* (London, 1955).
  Some indication of the immense range of primary and secondary sources on Andersen may be gleaned from the sale catalogue of the collection assembled by Dr Richard Klein, sold by Sotheby's, March 6–7, 1980.

LEAR
A 'full treatise' on Lear, mentioned by Harvey Darton in his 1932 text, is:
Field, W. B. Osgood. *Edward Lear on my Shelves*. Privately printed (Munich, 1933).
And two biographies have shown the man more 'satisfactorily':
Davidson, Angus. *Edward Lear: landscape painter and nonsense poet (1812–1888)* (London, 1938).
Noakes, Vivien. *Edward Lear; the life of a wanderer* (London, 1968). With a bibliography.

BALLANTYNE
Quayle, Eric. *R. M. Ballantyne; a bibliography of first editions* (London, 1968).
The same author has also written *Ballantyne the Brave; a Victorian writer and his family* (London, 1967).

For a full, categorized listing of American sources see first the guides to reference sources edited by Virginia Haviland (General Book List, section II.1). Nevertheless, there should be singled out here a study of 'Peter Parley':
Roselle, Daniel. *Samuel Griswold Goodrich, Creator of Peter Parley; a study of his life and work* (New York, 1968).
and two accounts which dwell upon the mid-Atlantic figure of Mrs Hodgson Burnett:
Laski, Marghanita. *Mrs Ewing, Mrs Molesworth and Mrs Hodgson Burnett* (London, 1950).
Thwaite, Ann. *Waiting for the Party; the Life of Frances Hodgson Burnett 1849–1924* (London, 1974).

CHAPTER XIV

The Sixties: 'Alice' and After

I

In the second period of Victoria's reign, which is that in which the domestic life of the Court was, to the majority of the people, the main loyal interest – when, in fact, Victoria was no longer the young Queen and had not become the Great Queen – those who wrote books for children were in a more assured social position than before. They were more nearly of the 'ruling' classes. They had a modest feeling of prerogative audience. They were more widely cultured, more experienced, less provincially minded or else less disdainful of the provinces.

Naturally, when they came to writing juvenile books, they did not produce violent revolutionaries: but they did not produce fossils either. 'Lewis Carroll', indeed, changed the whole cast of children's literature, but he founded, not followed, a gracious type. Much more clearly of the period than *Alice* was a work which preceded it by two years: Charles Kingsley's *The Water-Babies: a Fairy Tale for a Land-Baby*. Like other well-loved children's books, it is a story which is very likely more talked about by grown-up people today than re-read by them.

Kingsley was forty-four when he wrote it. He had already published, in 1856, *The Heroes*, which, excellent though it is, hardly needs comment here as an expression of a period, or of an author whose character is so well known. He had also produced *Westward Ho!* (1855) as a novel. But like a good many straightforward romances, that is now and was almost then a boy's book, though long as boys' books went. In *Glaucus, or The Wonders of the Shore* (also 1855), he had composed a sort of half-way work, a kind of simply written guide to the knowledge then visibly expanding before intelligent and marvelling eyes under the demonstrations of Hugh Miller, Philip Gosse and the not yet evolutionary Darwin. *Glaucus*, indeed, unimportant as it now is, shows the Kingsley whose zeal for learning was fully compatible with his zeal for Anglican Christianity. He could enthusiastically reconcile the new science with the old Creation cosmogony, and at that stage – for he had Darwin's *Coral Reefs* (1842) to support him, and *The Origin of Species* was not published till 1859 – did not fear that thinkers whom he respected held subversive views. But by 1863 – the date of *The Water-Babies* – things had begun to look different. There is a clear hint of uneasiness in the Fairy Bedonebyasyoudid's account of the History of the Doasyoulikes, with its mixture of science and economics, and its faintly derisive dislike of those who were easily tempted into infidelity (through God's prescience, according to Philip Gosse) by otherwise inexplicable fossils.

If he could have kept away from preaching, his generous enthusiasm for and real knowledge of science would have made the children for whom he wrote a little apter to comprehend the new doctrines, which he accepted as evidence for, not against, the Faith. In *The Water-Babies* year he wrote to F. D. Maurice – the inspiration of so many at that time by his personality, of so few now by his written words – that he was working hard at 'points of Natural Theology, by the strange light of Huxley, Darwin, and Lyell'. The shallower scientists, he claimed, 'find that now they have got rid of an interfering God – a master-magician, as I call it – they have to choose between the absolute empire of accident, and a living, immanent, ever-working God'. In the same letter, he anticipated and denied logical ultra-mechanicalism: 'You fancy that the axe uses the workman, I say that the workman uses the axe, and that though he can work rather better with a good tool than a bad one, the great point is, what sort of workman is he . . . Whereby you may perceive that I am not going astray into materialism as yet.' Curiously enough, in that very year Samuel Butler was satirizing the same view in the *Christchurch Press* (N.Z.), under the title *Darwin among the Machines*, the first draft of Chapters XXIII–XXIV of *Erewhon*.

But Kingsley did not dream of suggesting such an argument, either clearly reasoned or set forth in the similitude of a charming fiction, to children. Neither the doubtful axioms of science, nor even such metaphysics as Lewis Carroll played with, were for the young, in his eyes. He had, in fact, to keep up the patronizing attitude – to write 'down'; and once he started writing down, he could not but behave as a kind lecturer to a beloved but ignorant set of disciples. He had been unable to keep away from the pulpit even in *Westward Ho!*, though there he could find a certain amount of justification in the natural militant Protestantism of Hakluyt's heroes, great as well as humble.

In *The Water-Babies* that tendency is often distressingly clear. For instance, as Tom is washing and refreshing himself in a delightful stream, he believes that he hears the church bells ringing and thinks he would like to go to church, for he had never been inside one (that is a legitimate and at the time true use of social facts). He was afraid he would be late. 'The door will be shut, and I shall never be able to get in at all.' It was a natural and pathetic fear. But Kingsley the English vicar must step in:

Tom was mistaken: for in England the church doors are left open all service time, for everybody who likes to come in, Churchman or Dissenter; ay, even if he were a Turk or a Heathen; and if any man dared to turn him out, as long as he behaved quietly, the good old English law would punish that man, as he deserved, for ordering any peaceable person out of God's house, which belongs to all alike. But Tom did not know that, any more than he knew a great deal more which people ought to know.

It is an admirable sentiment, even if, perhaps, it was not universal in England at the time. But it is entirely out of place in a fairy-tale.

The fact is that when Kingsley wrote for children he posed, quite unconsciously. His profound sincerity deluded itself, and mistook enthusiasms for facts. The preface to *Madam How and Lady Why* (1870; it had previously appeared in *Good Words for the Young*) contains this passage:

MY DEAR BOYS, – When I was your age, there were no such children's books as there are now. Those which we had were few and dull, and the pictures in them ugly and mean . . . Now, among those very stupid old-fashioned boys' books was one which taught me [to use my eyes] . . . Its name was *Evenings at Home;* and in it was a story called 'Eyes and no Eyes'; a regular old-fashioned, prim, sententious story.

If you substitute 'hearty', or (in a derogatory sense) 'worthy', for 'prim' in the last sentence, it might be today's verdict on the 'old-fashioned' *Water-Babies* or Kingsley's popular-science books. He had, as he claimed, 'a certain artistic knack of utterance (nothing but a knack)'. But he was incapable of regulating it, or of keeping it merely 'artistic', or of seeing that his use of it was exactly the same as what he rejected.

Nor could he – it might fairly be asked, why should he? – exclude temporal things of small controversial or moral importance from his generous garrulity. It is not difficult to see, but it is annoying to be forced to do so, at whom he is hitting when Tom falls asleep because 'the fairies took him':

Some people think there are no fairies. Cousin Cramchild tells little folks so in his Conversations. Well, perhaps there are none – in Boston, U.S., where he was raised . . . And Aunt Agitate, in her Arguments on political economy, says there are none. Well, perhaps there are none – in her political economy. But it is a wide world, my little man – and thank heaven for it, for else, between crinolines and theories, some of us would get squashed.

Again, in *The Water-Babies*, when Pandora's box was opened (a tale unfolded with a tediousness which it is fortunate Lamb did not possess when he retold Greek stories), among the evils which escaped were monks, popes, wars, peacemongers, tight stays, bad wine, 'and, worst of all, Naughty Boys and Girls'. It is a mixture of the arch geniality of a governess and the prejudices of a hearty country parson.

He simply could not write without a moral purpose. By 1863 he was a public man, a novelist with propaganda, a leading Christian Socialist, known to the world outside his secluded Hampshire parish. He had a mission: he had always had one. He said so, and the obviousness of the fact spoils much of his fiction. He held that characters in books should talk naturally, so that they seemed real to the readers. But they must also talk so as to 'show more of their character' than in real life; and as a principle the author should 'take care that the general tone shall be such as never to make the reader forget the main purpose of the book'. The *envoi* of *The Water-Babies* betrays his self-consciousness:

> Hence, unbelieving Sadducees,
> And less believing Pharisees,
> With dull conventionalities;
> And leave a country muse at ease
> To play at leap-frog, if she please,
> With children and realities.

His unconventionality became itself almost a convention, as is also the posture of a middle-aged Victorian clergyman playing at leap-frog.

In that personal half-deception of its author by himself, *The Water-Babies* is a veritable document of social history. It is honest, forensic, and blind; truth and mimesis. Kingsley almost hypnotized himself, but remained sincere. Behind the bubbling dogmatist and the ardent reformer, there is a devout, unpolemical soul of fine imagination and pure simplicity: the soul of one who loved the very soil of England and all its folk – the branch-charmed Hampshire hangers, the little shy trout streams, the long hill shadows, the gentle English mist, and the old ancient habits that still had some virtue, some life to be quickened, even in their sleep of decay. It was that essential Englishman who wrote the song of the river:

> Clear and cool, clear and cool,
> By laughing shallow and dreaming pool

and the dame's regret, which we all feel at some time or other:

> When all the world is young, lad,
>   And all the trees are green;
> And every goose a swan, lad,
>   And every lass a queen;
> Then hey for boot and horse, lad,
>   And round the world away;
> Young blood must have its course, lad,
>   And every dog his day.
>
> When all the world is old, lad,
>   And all the trees are brown;
> And all the sport is stale, lad,
>   And all the wheels run down;
> Creep home, and take your place there,
>   The spent and maimed among:
> God grant you find one face there,
>   You loved when all was young.

Those little poems are both in *The Water-Babies*, but people who might scoff at the book find them in anthologies and like them, and do not read between their lines the sermons of an English Churchman struggling to be free from his own prepossessions.

2

'Lewis Carroll' was, at sight, a much odder figure than an effervescent country vicar. He was a reserved and slightly eremitical Oxford don whose special subjects were mathematics and logic. And no one who ever wrote for children is more completely assured of unacademic immortality. *The Water-Babies* is a very fine period piece, almost, indeed, a museum piece: the *Alices* will never be put in a museum, because they will neither die nor grow out of fashion.

The facts about Lewis Carroll's books are well known, and need only be summarized briefly. He was a coach and a lecturer at Christ Church when one afternoon he went on the Upper River at Oxford with the three little Liddells, daughters of the Dean, and was asked to tell them a tale.

> All in the golden afternoon
> Full leisurely we glide;
> For both our oars, with little skill,
> By little arms are plied,
> While little hands make vain pretence
> Our wanderings to guide.
>
> Ah, cruel Three! In such an hour,
> Beneath such dreamy weather,
> To beg a tale of breath too weak
> To stir the tiniest feather!
> Yet what can one poor voice avail
> Against three tongues together?
>
> Imperious Prima flashes forth
> Her edict 'to begin it':
> In gentler tones Secunda hopes
> 'There will be nonsense in it!'
> While Tertia interrupts the tale
> Not *more* than once a minute.
>
> Anon, to sudden silence won,
> In fancy they pursue
> The dream-child moving through a land
> Of wonders wild and new,
> In friendly chat with bird or beast –
> And half believe it true.

And that is almost the whole story. The 'wonders' were written in a book and illustrated by Dodgson himself: this version was reproduced in 1886 as *Alice's Adventures Under Ground*. The tale itself, as we know it, after some hesitation about the title, became *Alice's Adventures in Wonderland*, and was 'published', with Tenniel's superb illustrations, in July, 1865. Owing to defective printing – a matter about which Dodgson was very scrupulous – the majority of the first issue was withdrawn, which partly accounts for the comparative scarcity and high price of a genuine copy; but only partly, because such a welcome awaited the book as made the preservation, in a good 'state', of almost any early copy well-nigh impossible.[1]

Alice through the Looking-Glass – the full title is really *Through the Looking-Glass and what Alice found there* – appeared for Christmas 1871, dated 1872: that is, it only just escapes being technically a publication of the sixties. It is unfortuante for historical truth that the best appreciation of Alice and her creator, Walter de la Mare's *Lewis Carroll*, appeared in a volume of essays devoted wholly to the eighties.* It is, however, a mere mistake of popular ignorance to believe that the first *Alice* was (it is often implied) the work of an

---

*   [It was published separately as a book in 1932.]

elderly recluse – a 'remote and ineffectual don' – unbending for a few favoured children. It was written by a young man of thirty-three, with a wide circle of literary friends and no little zest for life.

Dodgson's other children's books have not the same spontaneity. *Sylvie and Bruno* (1889 and 1893), by the mere dates of its two parts, was the work of a changed man; perhaps, as Harry Furniss, its illustrator, said, of 'a spoilt child'. *The Hunting of the Snark* (1876), however, with the severe humour of Henry Holiday's drawings, has enough pure aimless nonsense for both children and adults to enjoy it, though it puzzles some readers, and mystified a few older ones, who deemed it a subtle allegory: one of them identified the Bellman with Gladstone, then at the height of power and fame.

Otherwise, except *Phantasmagoria* (1869; expanded in 1883 into *Rhyme? and Reason?*), which was little more than an exercise in facetious versifying, and *A Tangled Tale* (1885; originally in *The Monthly Packet* from 1880 onwards), a collection of ingenious mathematical problems in the form of fiction for young ladies, nearly all Dodgson's publications were of a professional character, with flippancy intruding here and there. That is to say, they were by the Rev. C. L. Dodgson, *ex Aede Christi Oxon.*, not by Lewis Carroll. He was punctilious about the difference between the two persons, though by all accounts Lewis Carroll crept into Dodgson's logic lectures, and certainly also into his *Symbolic Logic* (1896), where only the author of *Alice* could have produced such a fallacious minor premise as in

> A prudent man shuns hyaenas;
> No banker is imprudent.
> No banker fails to shun hyaenas.

He died on January 14, 1898. The centenary of his birth was lavishly celebrated in 1932.

None of the later works is on a par with the two *Alice* books, which themselves are an almost unique example of a precedent and sequel inseparably linked and absolutely equal in excellence. Every reader has his preferences for particular chapters. But those who think the Mad Hatter's tea-party the supreme joy of the first volume will be quite ready to put the Tweedledum and Tweedledee chapter in the second on a level with it. Those who agree with the Cheshire Cat that 'we're all mad here', or with the unanswerable truths of the tea-party nonsense, will accept with equal joy the version of Bishop Berkeley furnished by Tweedledum and Tweedledee at 'the *lovely* sight' of the Red King asleep. It is sometimes only by remembering that the one tale is about a pack of cards, and the other about a chess-problem, that a devoutly familiar reader can separate the different scenes and persons into their appropriate books. The whole twofold work is Wonderland, one and indivisible.

And the same criticism or argument for the foolishness of criticism – applies to the illustrations. They were not only the happiest achievement of John Tenniel in his long and honoured career, containing his freest draughtsmanship (never his strong point) and his most universal humour, but they were never unequal, and they cannot ever be dissociated from the text. Carroll and Tenniel, though not one name to the extent that Gilbert and Sullivan became fifteen years or so later, make one complete work of art – and the *Alices* are each a work of art, with a climax, a beginning, a middle and an end, as inevitable as in any greater fabric of the literary imagination, but entire and indivisible in the imagination of all affectionate readers.

The drawings do not 'date', except for the Victorian figure of Alice herself, and she only wears the wrong costume for today. The fact that Tenniel's work remained in copyright while Dodgson's text ran out of it has shown that clearly enough. The admirable living or recent artists who have re-illustrated the stories prove it. The best of them have made a charming modern flesh-and-blood Alice. But – as they would doubtless admit generously enough – they have not invented a new Gryphon, or a new Mock Turtle, White Rabbit, March Hare, Hatter, Caterpillar, Cheshire Cat, Red Queen, White Knight. These are

39. 'Splash! she was up to her chin in salt water'. Lewis Carroll's own drawing of the incident in the manuscript which he made for Alice Liddell (a), and Tenniel's polished version for the first published edition (b).

essentially, and must always so remain, the creation of the first artist and of the author whose fantasy provided the vivid details. A twentieth-century heroine merely accentuates that fact.

The collaboration was curious. Dodgson was not an easy man to work with: both Holiday and Harry Furniss were made aware that he believed in verbal rather than imaginative inspiration for an artist. He actually drew for Alice Liddell the picture of Wonderland Alice with the extensible neck, the White Rabbit, the animals in the pool of tears, Bill the Lizard, the Caterpillar, Father William, the Court Hearts (though they are very like those in Lamb's *King and Queen of Hearts*), the flamingo, the Gryphon and Mock Turtle, and some other details. Tenniel – introduced by Tom Taylor, of *Punch* – took these models and translated them from amateur homeliness into riper, more workmanlike copies so individual as to be almost fresh imaginings. The rest – and the *Looking-Glass* pictures – he seems to have more or less invented, but on the basis of the strict text and verbal conference.

The strange thing is that in spite of this joint originality some of the drawings look as if they had been based on other illustrations or things of the day, or even upon older sources. The Duchess is neither more nor less than Margaretta of Carinthia, the 'ugly Duchess' of Matsys. And if a forgotten picture-book of 1864, an anonymous *Rummical Rhymes*,* be exhumed, it will be found to contain much the same Duchess, and several other figures oddly like Tenniel's. There is here no suggestion of plagiarism. The artists of the day had much technique in common, as well as a slight general identity of conception. If less personally characteristic minor work by Tenniel, Linley Sambourne, C. H. Bennett, Stacy Marks, and even Dick Doyle, were assembled without identification, it would sometimes be hard to name the artist correctly. Sambourne, in the *New Sandford and Merton*, often uses Tenniel's rather rigid line with more of his own fluidity. And for comic characters they all had a certain repertory in the pantomime-stage of that Planché era. It remains true that the Duchess for all English children is the work of John Tenniel, not of Matsys, Old Father William a credible absurdity in a poem by Lewis Carroll, not a bore in Southey's *Old Man's Comforts*: just as Portia is from a play by Shakespeare and not from a tale in *Gesta Romanorum*. Tenniel, at least, never did better drawings. Indeed, he did not do much other book illustration in the narrow sense. When the decoration of *Sylvie and Bruno* was suggested to him, he declined it: he had somehow lost the faculty for such work; which, considering the completely different temper of the later book, is something to be thankful for. There is not a word in the *Alices*, nor a line of drawing, to be explained or regretted.

There is no need here to articulate, as it were a skeleton, the alleged dual personality of Dodgson. It can be done, with a reasonable amount of insight, by anyone who is able to guess at the mind of a bachelor specialist in a precise

---

* Published by Dean and Son. Mr Vaughan Knight communicated the point to Mr F. G. Green of the present firm, and he kindly passed it on to me. [The rhymes are by C. H. Ross and the illustrations signed J. V. B[arrett].]

subject, living in a period of accepted inhibitions, who suddenly, for a few glorious moments, sees quite clearly and lovingly all that mixture of credulity, acumen, and innocence which we call a child, and becomes ageless himself. 'What a wonderful dream it had been.' The real Lewis Carroll, the human being pacing Tom Quad in an obsolete uniform, is in the few pages of *Alice in Wonderland* which follows those words.

So much for the personality of Lewis Carroll and the history of his work. But *Alice*, an undeniably Sexagesimal and yet ageless product, was more than a flare of genius. It was the spiritual volcano of children's books, as the activities of John Newbery had been their commercial volcano. There had preceded it eminently, in the unconscious struggle for natural liberty, *The Butterfly's Ball*, *Holiday House* and Lear's *Nonsense*. But Roscoe produced only a temporary levity; Catherine Sinclair was not a little in awe of her tall surroundings; Lear 'loved to see little folks merry', and lay on his back kicking his heels in an ecstasy; whereas Lewis Carroll, *aetatis suae aᵒ* XXXIII, *socius Aedis Christi Oxon.*, was whole-heartedly forthright, straightforward, plain – any adjective that defines the negative of *arrière-pensée*. Except in the tiniest details of customary manners – the adjuration to curtsey, for instance, or Alice's compact vision of lessons as she fell down the rabbit-hole – there is not a back-hidden thought, an ulterior motive, in the *Alices* from beginning to end. The logic, the metaphysics, as well as the inhibitions, prohibitions, or what not, are in the text, it may be, but only if you happen to know, as a critic and rather tiresome historian, the facts of Charles Lutwidge Dodgson's academic career. They are no more overtly and truly there than a cap and gown in the boat near the *Trout* at Godstow, in which, his hearers reported, Dodgson would suddenly say, 'That's all till next time', as if he had heard Great Tom boom across Port Meadow like a threat.

The directness of such work was a revolution in its sphere. It was the coming to the surface, powerfully and permanently, the first unapologetic, undocumented appearance in print, for readers who sorely needed it, of liberty of thought in children's books. Henceforth fear had gone, and with it shy disquiet. There was to be in hours of pleasure no more dread about the moral value, the ponderable, measured quality and extent, of the pleasure itself. It was to be enjoyed and even promoted with neither forethought nor remorse.

It is true that fairy-tales themselves already provided this outlet from the cells of virtue. But so, for many children, perhaps for the majority, did *Sandford and Merton* or *The Swiss Family Robinson*. The readers then and always overlooked or skipped the explicit moral – and fairy-tales, it will be remembered, did have explicit morals. And most of the fairy-tales, also, had hitherto been traditional; even Andersen's had the heart of tradition. But the *Alices* were pure invention, with nothing in their elements which was humanly old or made familiar through generations of mankind; nothing, that is, which any prose-writer for children up to that time had dared to think immediately acceptable to such readers.

Yet they fell then and still fall into the category of 'fairy-tales'; and as Dodgson himself once thought of calling the Wonderland book *Alice's Hour in*

Elfland, that is perhaps justifiable, though neither fairy nor elf appears from one end to the other. There is simply magic, and even that is treated as just an extension of the natural – 'curiouser and curiouser'. The essence of the story is the translation of the ordinary into the extraordinary in a plausible way – not as a conjuring trick (a white rabbit out of a madman's hat, so to speak), but as an almost logical extension of properties inherent in this or that person or animal. The lizard, the dormouse, the caterpillar, the cat (grin or no grin) – they behave as they ought to behave if our simple faith could give them human speech and mien; and the inventions, the story-book or nursery-rhyme folk, are just as inevitable, once you grant them anthropoid life. The fault of the many imitators of Lewis Carroll – who are to this day a permanent plague to all editors and publishers of literature for children – is that they force the transition from one nature to the other; they invent, but they have not the logic.

3

Invention alone was not enough. But *Alice* led to a prodigious crop of inventions at once; and historically, in the natural course of evolution, the sixties and seventies were the due period of ripening. The older foreign tales, as has been seen, had been admitted and acclimatized, our own folk-lore exonerated from guilt, and the imitation of either was not an offence against good morals, even in strict circles. Andersen had shown that originality and poetic feeling could be blended with tradition; and the Prince Consort's helper, Henry Cole, had had the double inspiration of German domestic kindliness and the far-reaching romantic impulse that went back, in a general popular sense, to Scott, and beyond.

There had, it is true, been little jets of originality in the fairy sphere before *Alice* and *The Water-Babies*. One of the most singular, and also most enduring, appeared just as Victoria came to the throne. It was the immortal tale of *The Three Bears*. It came out in volume IV of Southey's *Doctor* (1834–47), and is so startlingly like a genuine folk-story, both in plot and in style, that many have conjectured it to be a real peasant heirloom, fathered by Southey without any birth-certificate.[2] Southey's contributions to the juvenile library, indeed, were peculiar: this genuine treasure, the *Life of Nelson* – not intended for that fate, but subjected to it by school prize-givers – several recitation-pieces similarly bedevilled, and a poem for Lewis Carroll to make eternally ridiculous.

It was only four years after Victoria's accession that John Ruskin wrote his *King of the Golden River* 'at the request of a very young lady,* and solely for her amusement, without any idea of publication'. It did not quite accord with his later proclamation about Grimm (pp. 241–2), for it has a very distinct moral in it. The story itself had the half-German atmosphere: it is of the legend-of-the-Rhine type, the scene being 'Stiria'; and Dick Doyle's spirited illustrations,

---

* Euphemia Gray, afterwards wife of Millais.

more solid and less elvish than was usual with him, make it attractive in a straightforward way. The interesting thing, however, is that Ruskin, if he deemed it worthy of publication, was shy of acknowledging it. From 1841 to 1851 it 'remained in the possession of a friend, to whose suggestion, and the passive assent of the Author', the publishers then were 'indebted for the opportunity of printing it' – anonymously.

A like reticence and a like Teutonic inspiration were to be seen in Paget's *Hope of the Katzekopfs* (1844; see p. 239). But here there was also a

Park's New Twelfth-Night Characters.

KING OF HEARTS.

1. When is a king not a king?

QUEEN OF HEARTS.

2. Why does her Majesty resemble St. Swithin?

DICKY DAGGERWOOD.

3. Why is a melancholy young lady the pleasantest of all companions?

MRS. DAGGERANDO.

4. What description of drinking glass is more droll than others?

LORD BANDASH.

5. Why should a thin man make a better barge than a fat man?

LADY BOW-WELL.

6. If a single burner be taken from a chandelier, why should it be brighter?

40. In his Prelude to *The Rose and the Ring* M. A. Titmarsh says that the 'pantomime' was in part inspired by his having drawn some Twelfth-Night characters, 'those funny painted pictures . . . with which our young ones are wont to recreate themselves' at Christmas. Here is shown (divided) the top line of a sheet of just such characters published by A. Park *c.* 1850. Alongside are King Valoroso XXIV and his Queen from Paflagonia, Mr Titmarsh's imitations.

consciousness of English tradition, for the author adopted the pseudonym of William Churne – the old Staffordshire fairy expert who had assisted Bishop Corbet. Mark Lemon, in *The Enchanted Doll* (1849) – which again gave Doyle scope for his cheerful fancy – tried to be old English too, but succeeded in being little more than a rather jocularly moral Londoner. Thackeray was infinitely more universal and also more English in *The Rose and the Ring* (Christmas 1854, dated 1855), even though Prince Giglio and Prince Bulbo (whom he depicted in some of the best illustrations he ever did for his own work) belonged to that Court of Pumpernickel which Mr Titmarsh loved to satirize. But he too felt constrained to a certain pretence, a definite assertion of conscious make-believe: he called the story 'a Fireside Pantomime', an accurate enough description. It is odd that until 1930 no one seems to have thought of the value of the tale as the fabric of opera for children – a real 'pantomime'.

The heralds of fairyland or fantasy, in fact, were still a little afraid of blowing authentic trumpets. Montalba, in the collection published in 1849 (see p. 241), had said out loud – 'very loud and clear', like Humpty-Dumpty – that we had 'cast off that pedantic folly' of thinking fairy-tales immoral. But he was only

an importer, not a manufacturer. Addey,[3] the partner and successor of 'Felix Summerly's' publisher, Cundall, in starting a delightful children's magazine, *The Charm*, in 1852, saw what was wanted:

We shall never omit to set apart a space for legends of those gentle creatures who dwell in the realms of Fairy Land. We cannot do better than borrow now and then from our friends in Germany; but we are promised many contributions by English writers celebrated for their talent in weaving Tales of Imagination.

He kept his word. But *The Charm* (1852–4) was short-lived; the prosperity of juvenile magazines, as will be seen shortly, did not then lie in that particular service to Imagination. Even a loved author who still survives to some extent, Frances Browne, was fain to repeat a familiar lament – 'Farewell, rewards and fairies'. In *Granny's Wonderful Chair and its Tales of Fairy Times* (1857) she wrote: 'the fairies dance no more. Some say it was the hum of schools – some think it was the din of factories that frightened them; but nobody has been known to have seen them for many a year, except, it is said, one Hans Christian Andersen, in Denmark . . .' But at least she herself could make others see them, as, *longo intervallo*, the Wife of Bath had somehow succeeded in doing. She had a little of Catherine Sinclair's gift of mixing inconsequence and naturalness in her style; and also, it must be said, a slight touch of her prim goodnatured moral outlook, for she gave her (or the Wonderful Chair's) characters didactic names. But the Chair *was* Wonderful, and that was a great thing. It is pleasant, as well as significant, to record that the book was first published by the lineal business successors of John Newbery, the firm of Griffith and Farran. The illustrations were by that versatile not-quite-genius, Kenny Meadows.

41. Forest Trumpeter. A wood engraving by 'a German artist' in *The Charm* annual (1854). One tiny example of a busy international trade in book illustrations that went on throughout the Victorian period.

4

It is possible, then, to comprehend why, Kingsley's own predilections apart, there is in *The Water-Babies* a heavy vein of morality and conventional condescension, as well as plenty of imagination; and yet also why it did not seem outrageous when Lewis Carroll did without open morality altogether. In the work of an eminent figure in Dodgson's own circle the contradictions are united, though a deeper shade is given to the fanciful element. George MacDonald was at once a poet, a mystic, a practical literary man, and a strong Puritan. He wrote, in a full life, *Phantastes*, a number of novels, *At the Back of the North Wind*, and many pieces of serious literary criticism; and he also succeeded Dr Norman Macleod as editor of *Good Words for the Young*. His writings for children focus many tendencies of his time.

He was present, so to speak, at the birth of *Alice*. His son, Dr Greville MacDonald (himself the author of some attractive fairy-tales), records that 'Uncle Dodgson' showed the first draft to the MacDonald family 'about 1862'. Mrs MacDonald read it aloud to her children from a version 'with pen-and-ink sketches by [Dodgson] himself, and minutely penned in printing characters'. So delighted was the audience that when she came to the end, the young Greville, 'being aged six, exclaimed that there ought to be sixty thousand words of it'. Elsewhere Dr Greville MacDonald amplifies the picture:

My little brothers and sisters and I used to climb into Lewis Carroll's arms or on to his knees as he lounged in a big chair, for him to tell us his quaint, delicious stories. He would draw charmingly ridiculous pictures too to illustrate them, and some of these I have still in my ragged old scrap-book. It was because I shouted so loud and clapped my fat hands so madly over *Alice's Adventures in Wonderland*, when my mother read it to us from the author's manuscript, that he first thought of publishing it. Was I not a good critic at six years old?*

It is said that Dr George MacDonald himself urged the publication. But if he delighted in Wonderland, it was not quite the identical country into which he entered with his own stories.

His contribution to the 'invented' 'fairy-tale' – the adjective and the noun both have to be scrutinized – was something which was not there before. More than any other prose story-teller for children at that period, he brought serious imagination into the fabric of his tales. *At the Back of the North Wind* (1871), *The Princess and the Goblin* (1872), and other *Princess* books remain in the mind like an intangible atmosphere long after their details have faded beyond recall. It was a new element; or rather, its deliberate presence was new, not its essence, because the same quality of visionary wonder and otherworldliness was

---

* Quoted in the Introduction to the *Everyman's Library* edition of *Alice* (1929), which contains some of Dodgson's drawings also. The 'children's' section of that *Library* (itself something of a landmark in popular culture) can be warmly commended to students of this subject as a convenient starting-point for fuller exploration. The fact that the volumes are 'popular' has not prevented their containing, in most instances, a scholarly preface which shows original research and assembles scattered facts not elsewhere collated [1932].

in Hans Andersen, aided by contact with folk-lore, and in folk-lore itself without any aid at all.

But as in Kingsley, and as not in Carroll, there was also in MacDonald an open, conscious and sincere purpose of improving the young mind, as well as of letting its fancy roam. *Ranald Bannerman's Boyhood* (1871) has its passages of wonder, but the passages of didacticism are just as frequent. Both it and *The North Wind* appeared first in *Good Words for the Young*, overlapping one another. Both were illustrated by Arthur Hughes. The first editor of that periodical, Dr Norman Macleod, having his hands already full with the senior publication, *Good Words* itself, had handed the younger one over – after a year, 1869–70 – to MacDonald, who said, 'I want to keep the magazine up to its good title'; and did, even raising it a little before he gave it up in 1872 and the name was changed. The Doctor of Divinity in him had the imaginative Scot well under control. It did not seem to him incongruous that two of his stories so different in texture should be interpreted by the same fine artist and appear almost simultaneously in the same journal.

Nor was it in truth incongruous, if one takes the trouble to see of how many varying strands the Victorian seriousness was knit. The juvenile magazines, in fact – which it needs no excuse to treat here as children's books, though books *v.* magazines is a debatable issue – contain the whole texture. They were, commercially, a market development concurrent with the progress of adult newspapers and periodicals, which were then reaching one of their stages of temporary domestic stability – becoming the institutions of a brief epoch. Aesthetically and morally, they were also discreetly of the period. It is necessary to look at the ideals put forward by the chief among them.

5

They were not novelties, even in execution, much less in conception. The term 'magazine' had been applied in the eighteenth century to juvenile publications which were (so far as can be discovered) not always issued periodically; that is to say, in the older sense, like the French *magasin*, of a repository or storehouse of a rather general kind (Mme le Prince de Beaumont's *Magasin des Enfans*, for example), just as today a children's annual may be called (in a looser way) *The Playbox* or *The Merry-go-round*. But there were a few which really were periodicals.

After Newbery's failed efforts with the *Lilliputian Magazine* in 1751 (see p. 124) there was a pause. Then Marshall made at least three attempts at such an enterprise, with *The Juvenile Magazine, The Children's Magazine, or Monthly Repository of Instruction and Delight*, and *The Picture Magazine; or, Monthly Exhibition for Young People*. The first was in twelve parts: I have not seen them in any separate form, but they apparently came out in only one year, 1788. As they contained correspondence, they must have had some sort of existence independently of their bound-up form. *The Children's Magazine* also I have not seen complete, but its four numbered volumes run from January 1799 to December 1800. In that year it was joined by *The Picture Magazine*, which consisted of a monthly set of eight pictures and was published up to some time in 1801. About the same time (1798) my ancestors issued *The Minor's Pocket Book* which ran as an annual for a dozen years or so, and introduced Ann and Jane Taylor to their first publishers. Others can be discovered, but none had long life or, so to speak, a serial soul. There were also productions, already mentioned, with names borrowed from the old grown-up periodicals, like *The Juvenile Spectator* and *The Juvenile Tatler*.

But the chief attempts at first were in connection with Sunday Schools, and were concerned with the particular needs of the growing educational societies, or else, like Mrs Trimmer's journals, with criticism of the fulfilment of them. The idea, in the main, was that of Hannah More's famous series of household tracts for grown-up children, *The Cheap Repository* (1795–8):[4] the supply, at frequent if not exactly regular intervals, of plainly didactic fiction which at once taught the most ingenuous, least subversive arts and softened the morals. Their substance, as provided for children, need not be discussed here. It reflected or digested what was more fully at large in the books properly so-called and similarly intended.

The earliest serial publications for the young which secured long and continuous life as genuine periodicals – not solely as aids to education nor as seed for wayside sowers – were probably *The Child's Companion, or Sunday Scholar's Reward*, born in 1824 and still surviving,* and *The Children's Friend*, which was founded in 1824 by the Rev. W. Carus Wilson, famous in Charlotte Brontë's early life and in *Jane Eyre* itself. This *Friend*, which finally expired in 1930, had a younger son or brother, *The Infant's Magazine*, and both were flourishing in the sixties. The aim, in fact, of such magazines as existed was really that of the Moral Tale. For example, *The Youth's Monthly Visitor* (no. 1, vol. 1, Feb. 1, 1822) protested against the 'cheap and ephemeral publications of the day', and proposed to 'attend to the solid improvement of the Youth of both sexes' by 'combining *instruction* with *rational amusement*' – by describing and expounding the sciences, in especial, but also by 'Moral Tales, Anecdotes, Poetical Extracts, etc. etc.' It was published monthly, and on issue in three-volume form (in 1823) was called *The Youth's Miscellany of Knowledge and Entertainment*. It corresponds exactly with the 'conversations', 'leisure hours' and one-piece books of the period. But in its life of (apparently) eighteen months it carried on a small puzzle section with answers in subsequent issues†

With a few such exceptions it was not, it seems, until the fifties that the magazine idea achieved in the juvenile world what ought honestly to be called a

---

* [As with many periodicals it changed its title from time to time. Its final metamorphosis in 1928 was to *Every Girl's Paper*, and it seems to have ceased publication altogether in 1932.]

† 'Apparently'; because it had better be owned at once that all early dates in this connection, and many later, are very untrustworthy.

firm commercial value – that is, a good, steady popularity with an average intelligent public. Indeed, one of the first original ventures in this mode failed, in all probability, just because it did not pay close enough regard to the general average, but was above it. It came from the 'Felix Summerly' camp in the form of the magazine already mentioned, *The Charm*. This ran from 1852 to 1854, and contained, among much that was solid but not stolid, a very good proportion of imaginative matter, and illustrations by such serious but not crude artists as Wehnert and Harrison Weir. But the time was not quite ripe for it.

The sort of thing *The Charm* was really intended (by anticipation) to offset was publications like *The Boys' and Girls' Companion for Leisure Hours* (no. 1, April 4, 1857), edited by John and Mary Bennett. They provided, as they claimed, 'tales of interest and moral purpose', and 'pastime that, while it entertains, cannot fail to instruct'. Equally moral, down to its very title, was *The Youth's Instructor*, which, after a nine months' run in 1858, was merged in the rather older, far livelier, and much longer-lived *Boy's Own Magazine* (1855–74), published by the well-known and almost omniscient Beetons. This, though it had no connection with it, was a practical forerunner of the famous *Boy's Own Paper*, for among its authors were W. H. G. Kingston, J. G. Edgar, J. G. Wood the naturalist, W. B. Rands, and Pycroft on cricket. It was also notable for offering really attractive prizes to readers – in 1858, fifty watches and pencil-cases, to the value of 150 guineas. (Among the winners, with an essay on Penny Postage, was Francis James Chavasse, afterwards Bishop of Liverpool.) In 1863, when it had a circulation of 40,000, it put up its price from 2*d.* to 6*d.* ('enlarged and improved'), and to compensate its less opulent readers produced a cheaper brother, *The Boy's Penny Magazine* (1863–7). It claimed, in doing so, that it was itself 'an old friend who amused them, inspirited them, and never suggested anything unworthy of an English gentleman'. The Beetons, in fact, were an active household just then. They concocted also from old and new material *The Boy's Yearly Book* (1864–8), and *Beeton's Annual; a Book for the Young* (1866), which included contributions by Mayne Reid, Clement Scott, W. H. Davenport Adams and Austin Dobson.

This was the beginning of what became, in the next generation, a flood of magazines. The early and middle sixties saw this first wave; there came a second ten years or so later. Two which first appeared in 1866 represent extremes of the general ideals.

The first was *Aunt Judy's Magazine* (no. 1, May, 1866), edited by Mrs Gatty. It took its title from the family nickname of her daughter Juliana Horatia, better known as Mrs Ewing. The magazine is still remembered with affection, like Mrs Ewing's own stories, some of which appeared in it. But it was more pietistic in tone than most memories, unrefreshed, would probably now believe. The editor herself said that in it 'parents need not fear an overflowing of mere amusement'. The first number, however, contained a rather surprising contribution; some verses beginning 'By the wide lake's margin I marked her lie' and ending 'For she was a water-rat!' They were signed C.S.C., initials that were to have a painful significance for at least one writer for children, Jean Ingelow. The second number of the magazine began to give reviews, the first being warm notices of *Alice in Wonderland* and Hans Andersen. Aunt Judy was on the side of the fairies as well as of the angels.

Clearly she was, so to speak, one of the family, remaining within the home. The aim of *The Boys of England* (no. 1, Nov. 24, 1866; edited by Charles Stevens) was, on the contrary, wholly undomestic. 'Our aim is to enthral you by wild and wonderful but healthy fiction.' Instruction and amusement were also to be provided, because all boys have or ought to have a proper curiosity about life and manners and things. The general policy was to be 'a hearty, free, and trusty companion'. And fourteen hundred prizes were to be given away. The price was one penny.

The fiction was certainly wild and wonderful. In the early pages of this magazine appears – I think for the first time – that rendering of the Strawberry Hill Gothic style of English in a staccato or even pizzicato manner which came to be the usual mode of the 'penny dreadful', and has affected journalism: the abolition of the colon and semi-colon, the insistence on short sentences, the paragraph of one or two sentences only. But at this stage it also involved the use of good coloured stage epithets. Here is a short passage from the chief serial story of the first year, a tale of pirates quite as bloodthirsty as Capt. Jas. Hook:

At this moment arose a general shout.
'Silence! Don Pablo is coming.'
Our hero started with a sickening qualm.
He turned hastily to behold the pirate chief, who at the moment entered the cavern, accompanied by four or five companions, Spaniards and Portuguese.
Despite his abhorrence of the leading villain's hellish character, Jack could not help feeling a thrill of admiration at his eminently dashing and handsome appearance.

Apparently that kind of thing was too strong for some watchful guardians, for in the 'Answers to Correspondents', which soon took up a great deal of space, the editor rebuffs vigorously a remonstrant 'Preceptor': 'Our tales and articles do not contain "sermons in disguise" which are always distasteful to boys, but a moral and healthy tone may be maintained in conjunction with the boldest fiction.' As he secured a rowing champion to write on his sport, and Lillywhite on cricket, the editor could make a plausible case for a general good tone in his magazine.

The whole question of excitement, low life, and crime in fiction had been under debate ever since *Jack Sheppard* and *Eugene Aram* appeared, and Thackeray wrote *Catherine* as a counterblast. Now, however, it had come down to boys and girls. Mrs Gatty had taken no part in such strife. Her life was too serene and her circumstances too far above what we should now call the underworld. But people more actively engaged in work in great cities did see the danger of Godless romance. The still-surviving *Chatterbox** was founded in 1866, at only a half-penny a week, because the Rev. J. Erskine Clarke of Derby

* [*Chatterbox* ceased publication in 1948; *The Prize* in 1931.]

– afterwards a London vicar and Honorary Canon of Rochester – hated to see errand boys of fourteen or so reading nothing but (as he called it outright) 'blood and thunder'. He had instituted,three years before, *The Children's Prize* (from 1875 entitled simply *The Prize*), so as to catch readers at a still younger age, and instil Christian principles into their minds from the first. His touch was not light, and the realities which, working in a poor parish, he had to meet daily came rather oppressively into both magazines, and were interpreted sometimes too painfully and clumsily by his wood-engravers. Ruskin attacked *The Prize* in *Fors Clavigera* (Letter L) for its complete un-beautifulness. It belonged, he said, to

the literature which cheap printing enables the pious to make Christmas presents of for a penny . . . full of beautiful sentiments, woodcuts and music . . . Splendid woodcuts, too, in the best Kensington style, and rigidly on the principles of high, and commercially remunerative, art, taught by Messrs Redgrave, Cole, and Company.

He obtained his copy from a young friend, Little Agnes – the daughter of a cottager – and he found in it a moral story about the coach-riding middle-classes, which he then dissected and found wholly inappropriate for readers of Agnes's station. He quoted a 'Christmas Carol' that accompanied the story, and really was dreadful doggerel, and he contrasted it unfavourably ('I consider good rhythm a moral quality') with *Dame Wiggins of Lee*. From there the prophet worked himself up to denounce the educational system which produced such things. The final consequence, he roared, could only be 'Ruin – inevitable and terrible, such as no nation has yet suffered . . . Yes – inevitable. England has to drink a cup which cannot pass from her – at the hands of the Lord, the cup of His fury; – surely the dregs of it, the wicked of the earth shall wring them and drink them out.' There can be no doubt that in 1874 (the date of this attack) children's books were a genuine phenomenon in social history.

Still, Erskine Clarke was thinking of them, really, in the same old terms of the Moral Tale, even though the exciting serial stories for which *Chatterbox* became noted were spiritually and even in fact very closely akin to those of *The Boys of England*. Ruskin was justified in the real gist of his criticism, which was that, especially for younger children, there was no lightheartedness, no joy, no freedom in these magazines. It is almost ironical that the title *Chatterbox* should cover heavy prosiness, whereas the *Good Words for the Young* of Drs Macleod and MacDonald were often very nearly flippant.

The magazine bearing that title, or variants of it, had a short life – 1869–77 – but it possessed always a marked character. Almost everything in it deserved to be considered as literature. It was the younger version of *Good Words* (1860–1906, with a change of title), which was the invention of Strahan the publisher, and his partner Isbister. Dr Norman Macleod (who was succeeded by his brother and biographer, Dr Donald Macleod), when asked to edit the senior magazine, at first hesitated, and then undertook the task with 'the conviction that a periodical was greatly required of the type sketched by Dr Arnold'. It was to be 'distinctively Christian'. But it was also to be open-minded. Himself a minister of the Scottish National Church, Macleod welcomed contributions to *Good Words* by Dean Stanley and Charles Kingsley, and was not affected by the criticism that 'young persons may be tempted to read the 'secular' articles on Sunday'. Both the letterpress and the illustrations were kept on a high and even austere level, without pedantry (as the standard of seriousness went then) and without easy facetiousness.

The first number of the first (i.e. 1869) volume of *Good Words for the Young* appeared on November 1, 1868, at sixpence. Contributors that year included Kingsley (*Madam How and Lady Why*), George MacDonald, 'Matthew Browne' (W.B. Rands), Mrs Craik, as 'the Author of *John Halifax, Gentleman*', and William Gilbert, the father of the dramatist. W. S. Gilbert himself, as 'Bab', illustrated his father's *King George's Middy** which was afterwards issued in book form (1869). The more serious artists included Arthur Hughes, G. J. Pinwell and Boyd Houghton, names high in the history of English book illustration. Dr Macleod himself was responsible for more definitely but not annoyingly didactic articles. In 1873 the title became *Good Things for the Young of all Ages* (and MacDonald gave up the editorship at the end of that year). Changes began to be made in the mode of issuing the magazine and in 1877 it perished, having made an honourable and lasting impression on children's literature in England. It was Victorian, but by not much more than an accident of time.

Two years after its birth it had had a rival for some part of the kingdom created or revealed by *The Charm* and *Aunt Judy*, and rather dragooned by *The Prize*. In 1871 appeared *Little Folks*, another gallant survivor today.† The most remarkable thing about its first volume was the feature announced on its title-page – 'Containing about 500 Pictures'. Among the early contributors were W.H.G. Kingston and Mrs Ewing, but it did not rely either upon names or upon the impression of strong, purposeful editing. It gave, as it intended, simplicity, great variety, plenty of illustrations, with a freedom and kindly naturalness which sought to 'amuse' its readers and at the same time 'to teach them to think and do a little for themselves'. It aimed at the younger ranks of the younger readers, and reached them, as it well deserved. Like those of its contemporaries which still live, it has to some extent changed its manner and, rather less, its scope: the readers themselves are not quite the same in disposition. But it kept, throughout, its purpose of being a magazine *for* children, not a volley at them. In some ways it was much nearer the old sense of 'magazine' than any other production of the day. The readers went to it for what they hoped to get.

In 1871 also began to appear a journal called *Our Young Folks' Weekly Budget*. But its chief importance came later, upon a particular occasion.

---

* [W. S. Gilbert had also illustrated his father's *The Magic Mirror; A Round of Tales for Young and Old*, which Strahan published in 1866.]

† [It ceased publication in 1933.]

CHATTERBOX.

PUBLISHED FOR THE PROPRIETORS BY W. WELLS GARDNER, IO PATERNOSTER ROW

"JOHN BULL JUNIOR."

The Magnet 1ᵈ Library

Splendid School Tale of Harry Wharton & Co.

Thrilling Detective Story of Stanley Dare, the Boy Detective

No. 152 | The Complete Story-Book for All | Vol. 5.

"My hat!" murmured Billy Bunter. "This is ripping! They can put it down to the cat in the morning."

42. Forty years on. The anonymous design for the cover of *Chatterbox* (1871), a magazine concerned to combat the influence of 'penny-dreadfuls' (a); and an early cover for the boys' story-paper *The Magnet* (1911), written for more than thirty years by 'Frank Richards', and featuring his most famous creation, Billy Bunter (b).

6

Here for the moment the magazines must be set aside. Their peculiar significance lay partly in their popularity and partly in their contents. They were the typical product of the Victorian – the real Victorian – home circle: that circle in which there were children with intense vigour of life in their chubby bodies, and movement in their formally draped limbs; not jointed dolls for moral marionette-shows. They still had to be guarded from silliness, but not from laughter; from recklessness and vice, but not from brave adventure. And they were allowed to possess and use imaginations.

But in one direction, in spite of fairy-tales, *Alice*, princesses and goblins and all manner of heroics, the young imagination had not been greatly enticed in the magazines. The standard of their poetry was pedestrian, if not low. It often deserved Ruskin's anger at its humdrum form – which was none too perfect even in its own class; and it was almost void of any but the most conventional fancy. The quality of books of verse as such was not much better. The William and Mary Howitt standard, not exactly sublime at its very best, was not always attained as an average. The simplicities of Jane Euphemia Browne's *Aunt Effie's Rhymes for Little Children* (1852; illustrated by 'Phiz'), Scott Gatty's *Aunt Judy's Song-Book* (1871; with the jolly 'Three Little Pigs') and William Allingham's slight verses, *The Fairies* (published as a picture book with illustrations by E. Gertrude Thomson, 1883)* were no more than they pretended to be – pretty, unaffected jingles.

But there were two particular exceptions to this mediocrity which were of more than routine interest. The obvious one is Christina Rossetti, who was not a predictable figure in the social procession. The other is that odd, versatile writer who seldom used his own name even when (if one can so interpret his self-cramped character) he was being his own self: William Brighty Rands, *alias* Matthew Browne, *alias* Henry Holbeach, *alias* Thomas Talker. The children's books by which he is best remembered are *Lilliput Levee* (1864; illustrated by Millais and Pinwell and reissued in an enlarged edition in 1867), *Lilliput Lectures* (1871) and *Lilliput Legends* (1872). These were all anonymous. It does not seem to be known why so prolific a writer preferred secrecy and disguise. He also wrote, much earlier, a Dickens-and-water Christmas fairy-tale, *The Frost upon the Pane* (1854), with his name attached to it, and edited sympathetically Robert Bloomfield's poems (1855), with a long signed introduction. As 'Matthew Browne', he surveyed *Chaucer's England* at large, in a work not yet superseded. He contributed to all sorts of magazines, from *The Contemporary Review* to *Good Words for the Young*, under both his own name and pseudonyms. He was born in 1823, of non-conformist parents; he preached often in a Dissenting congregation, and had some inclination to the ministry. Apparently his private life was not very regular. It was at least difficult

---

*   ['The Fairies' originally appeared as one of the poems in Allingham's *Day and Night Songs* (1854).]

financially, for he had to supplement his earnings as a House of Lords official shorthand reporter (a very efficient one) by miscellaneous journalism. He died in 1882.

It is in the three *Lilliput* books that his chief originality appears. He was, or seems, nearly always sincere in them, not as one writing for effect or condescending to children, though in *Lilliput Lectures* he defines and defends clearly what he means by 'writing down': his is the best argument that can be given for the faintly didactic manner which is sometimes needed, in all honesty, to bridge the gulf between old and young. His nonsense, however, has no pretence, and he often mixes it with a whimsical moral pathos which is entirely his own; as in the poem about the giant who was reformed by being given a custard three times as big as the moon. His direct pathos, as in 'The Ship that sailed into the Sun', has touches of great beauty, even when it is based on the lost-brother tradition of sentimentalism.

The fact is that he was not a genius untrammelled, nor a hack, and yet he had something of both in him, with a touch of mysticism added and an occasional burst of sheer fun. He is grievously unequal and uncertain. But there were always dreams in his best work, and reality in the dreams. He felt that he could not always express that reality. The verse preface to *Lilliput Legends* tells how he went to a country full of story-book folk: fairies, Columbines, Punch and Judy, and the rest. They welcomed him, and he discovered there a wistful happiness. He came back full of stories about the place, but found he could not write them. Then he told the stories to write themselves:

> So they did. And the telling of them is true;
> Though they carried off some of the things I knew,
> But which never a soul in Lilliput Land,
> Or in Arcady can understand,
> Or know. And little of them know I
> Or you, except that they make us cry.

There was always in his work something of that struggle to be sure he had really got inside the country of a child's mind. He succeeded not seldom. A certain amount of his writings remains in print. But a selection from all that is best and most spontaneous in them would have lasting value, for he often escaped from his period, even in his inequalities.

Christina Rossetti not merely escaped. She made her own period, like William Blake. *Goblin Market* (1862), the most magical and vivid of all poems put before children, was not a voice of the sixties nor of a revival in art, though the starry detail of the Pre-Raphaelites shines in almost every line of it. There are pictures on every page, pictures both felt and expressed. It is a personal experience translated into the universal speech of an imaginative mind.

How far, or how closely, the poem and the others in the same volume influenced or were influenced by the main current of literature need not be considered here. It is perhaps not fair to consider it as a children's poem at all really, for its companions, which include the ever-quoted 'Uphill', certainly have not that character. It needs, no doubt, some depth of human experience to appreciate it fully. Nevertheless, like Arnold's *Forsaken Merman*, which had appeared a dozen years before, it had its direct appeal to the young imagination: and the fact was recognized without delay, which is here the significant historical point. Ruskin disliked it, as a matter of course: it was full of 'quaintnesses and offences. Irregular measure . . . is the calamity of modern poetry'. He deplored, upon this text, the influence of Coleridge; but to many, even then, *The Ancient Mariner* was becoming the very thing for children, in spite of the gruesome passages here and there.

When Christina Rossetti really wrote for children, as in *Sing-Song* (1872), she succeeded without the least apparent effort. She caught both the artlessness and the inevitability of the nursery-rhyme form, and added to it her own serene and tender intuitions. The joyous nonsense is often near tears, the simple tears of humanity: and yet it is joy too. These might be, as indeed they have often become, verses spoken lovingly by a young mother – and at any period of history, but for the accident of language so deftly and easily used. They were fortunate in being accompanied by one hundred and twenty illustrations by Arthur Hughes, perhaps the lightest, most graceful and most sympathetic he ever drew. The poems suited him exquisitely, for he could show his almost lyrical sense of fun as well as his direct feeling for beauty. The pictures are the work of a draughtsman, a wit and a poet.

7

The illustrators of this period, indeed, are more truly characteristic, very often, than all but the best of the written work which they adorned. 'The Sixties', in the graphic-arts sense, perhaps began in 1857 with Moxon's edition of Tennyson, and neared their end with the death of Fred Walker in 1875. Those who worked chiefly in wood have been briefly mentioned here and there already; they were aided – partnered is not too strong a word – by the craft of cutters like Swain, Linton, the Whympers and the Dalziels. They illustrated much original work, and they sometimes deserved to divide the first credit of a fine book with the author. But they also drew for old classics whose direct 'explanatory' virtue appealed or was thought to appeal to children; and here they can be taken as representative of the period's general aesthetic ideals and artistic imagination. The volumes were meant, as a rule, for 'family' use, with a particular eye upon the young person. The most notable, perhaps, was the famous *Arabian Nights* produced in monthly parts by Dalziel Bros. (1864–5), to which most of the leading artists contributed.[5] Others were the Bible (*The Bible Gallery*, also in parts 1880–1), *The Pilgrim's Progress* (1863– the ill-fated Fred Barnard also did a very fine set of drawings for this independently in 1884, and C.H. Bennett a fairly unconventional one for which Kingsley, in 1859, wrote a preface), *The Parables of Our Lord* (1864), and many anthologies, especially, for

children, Coventry Patmore's *Children's Garland from the Best Poets* (1873)*,
and the well-known collection of *Little Songs for me to Sing* (1865), with
Millais's drawings and musical settings by Henry Leslie, later published in an
enlarged edition as *Leslie's Songs for Little Folks* (1873). In addition, as has been
said, the artists had plenty of scope in the magazines of higher quality.

The virtue of their work was its honesty. Its fantasy, even when it may seem
to an unsympathetic eye rather didactic or heavy, was obviously sincere.
Drawing in great detail upon wood, or for reproduction upon wood,[6] is an art
not to be lightly undertaken. It almost involves earnestness of emotion in
addition to well-thought-out technique and composition. The personal quality
in it can probably be contemplated best in a comparison with the chapbook
woodcuts and the copper engravings of the Stothard and Corbould school, or
the here germane 'family' productions of Alderman Boydell towards the end of
the eighteenth century. The chapbook artist was obviously (at his best) thinking
in direct solid images, in the simple facts which were the core of his particular
subject. The Third-Georgian 'inventors' and 'sculptors', to use the old technical
terms, were consciously graceful, almost theatrical, idealizing their scenes in a
pose of romantic-classical beauty. Even in their simplest children's books
Master Tommy and Miss Sukey are apt to look like near relations of the Infant
Roscius and Miss Ninetta Crummles, at any rate in posture and expression.

The men of the sixties were serious, even in their humour. They lived
laborious, concentrated and thorough lives mentally and physically. When they
wrote for children they often used hordes of long words and periphrases, and
beat out a subject to utter thinness in their anxiety to be completely just,
completely clear, exhaustive. When they drew they often toiled with equal pain
at filling the whole picture. That is probably more of a virtue than a fault in
books for younger children, even if it does not leave gaps to stimulate free
imagination. At any rate, it resulted in a solid unflinching life-likeness, which
the artists' often masterly draughtsmanship could turn into beauty upon
occasion.

Most of them produced their illustrations for children's books in the course of
more general activities. But three, in spite of other work, have come to be
regarded in a special degree as benefactors of the young – Randolph Caldecott,
Walter Crane and Kate Greenaway. They made the modern 'picture-book'.

Of the three, Caldecott had the most robust and, so to speak, humane
personality. The other two seem like artists first and ordinary people afterwards.
You always feel that Caldecott is not thinking of a picture, but of folk and
lovable dogs and horses and flesh-and-blood hybrids like his fellow-Englishmen.
When he illustrated the *Elegy on the Death of a Mad Dog* (one of his *Picture-
Books*, which began with *The Diverting History of John Gilpin* and *The House
that Jack Built* so late as 1878), he saw with Goldsmith's own humorous eyes:

> The dog and man at first were friends;
> But when a pique began,

---

* [It was originally published in 1862, but with only a frontispiece.]

The dog, to gain some private ends,
Went mad, and bit the man.

It is quite clear, from the pictures, that that is what did happen; from the persons drawn, it is inevitable. Those *must* have been the adventures of even so excellent a man, and of a capering dog to whose burial marched six black Cocker spaniels with long silky ears. You understand the man and the dog, and their feelings, and Goldsmith's feelings. Caldecott understood men and dogs too, and that was the secret: he *liked* them, as Goldsmith did.

His early death – he was only forty-two when he died in 1886 – was a great loss, and though to some extent (chiefly for 'grown-up' books) his place was filled by the no less lovable Hugh Thomson, no other artist quite united so easily as he for children the qualities of humour, draughtsmanship and intuitive interpretation. He did not become part of his authors to the same extent as, say, Tenniel in *Alice* or Hughes in *Sing-Song*. But he could identify himself as fully with new work – in the illustrations to Mrs Ewing's tales, for example – as with the old which he lifted out of the costume-piece atmosphere into reality. Pictures were like speech or writing to him: his natural talk.

That could hardly be said of Walter Crane, to whom graphic art was a mission of beauty rather than a working compromise between sympathetic comprehension and rare ideals. He revolted against the crude 'toy-books' of his earlier days, which usually contained either woodcuts clumsily coloured in the manner already described (p. 202) or Germanic lithographs and oleography whose shiny ugliness betrayed their utterly commercial origin. His own bent was classical, though he was much influenced by the colour-work of Japan; in later life he was an examiner for the National Art Training School at South Kensington. But if he objected to ugly work uglily reproduced, he also saw children's books as an outlet for 'the modern illustrator, who likes to revolt against "the despotism of the facts"', and to that extent was not always a true illustrator when he was ostensibly tied to a text. His *Grimm* (translated by Lucy Crane, his sister, 1882) was as much Crane-1880 as timeless-Grimm. On the other hand, he produced delightfully original grace in such works as *The Baby's Opera* (1877), and in some of the picture-books (*Old Mother Hubbard*, for example) published in the seventies, where he had not very heavy fetters of words to bind him. He was the minister, almost the slave, of a doctrine of decorative arts and crafts.

He – like Caldecott and Kate Greenaway – was fortunate in the colour-printer who produced his work, Edmund Evans. Crane went to him in 1863 or 1864, at the age of nineteen, and began working at toy-books in three colours. Evans's firm was extremely careful over all details of reproduction, and not only in three but in many colours reached a technical standard very uncommon at that date. Nearly all the children's books with coloured pictures by these three artists were produced by this still flourishing firm,[7] which deserves honoured remembrance for its work at that pioneer stage of the modern 'juvenile colour-book'.

Kate Greenaway, in a sense, was not an illustrator at all. She was an artist whose pictures comprised the soul of the book in which they appeared: the soul, that is, as she saw it. No one would have bought her version of *Little Ann and*

Other Poems (1882, for 1883) merely because they were by Ann and Jane Taylor and nicely got up; there were plenty of other good editions, containing far more poems, in print at the time. This edition was Kate Greenaway's, which was the reason for its existence and its sale. She even invented and made the public believe in the costumes the children wore; as the Taylor archives, full of

43. The discovery of the baby in *Lob Lie-by-the-Fire*, as seen by two pre-eminent masters of nineteenth-century illustration. Caldecott (a) did not care for Cruikshank's (b) designs, which he thought to be 'in his worst style', and later remarked, 'Don't ask me to explain why I do not like Cruikshank's illustrations to *Lob*. I should have to use violent language about a very clever man.'

accurate contemporary drawings, show, no such raiment was ever indued under George III. Truth did not matter. Nor did the fact that Miss Greenaway, in spite of her training at Heatherley's and the young Slade School, never fully learnt to draw; Ruskin's letters to her are full of thunders at the starfish or blobs by which she represented hands. Her light and gentle fancy made her text and her fidelity to it of secondary importance. The book she illustrated, whatever it was, was Kate Greenaway's: not more so, but only more happily so, if she had no author to follow, as in her own *Under the Window* (1878), and could live in her enchanting and enchanted private nursery world, sharing it with children in frocks she made for it, but loved whole-heartedly by children in the less beautiful actual patterns of 1873 to 1900.

It is a comforting and useful fact in social history to know that her graceful originality pleased largely and instantly. She was not an esoteric idol, nor an ardent leader of a school, nor a lonely pioneer working neglected in her lifetime and feverishly 'collected' after her death; though she is, in her small way, a steady 'collector's artist'. When *Under the Window* was published with Edmund Evans in the role of commercial impresario, he surprised the nominal publisher, Routledge, by printing a first edition of 20,000 copies. But this unexpectedly large run was still not enough and large reprints followed, as well as editions in French and German. The result was profitable for Miss Greenaway, who liked to contract for royalties on her books once their costs were covered. Her biographers report few books that did not meet such expenses. Even so, she remained unspoilt, modest and lovable.

There are many other honoured names in that fecund period. Much of the best work was done for adult books, or by artists more famous outside books. Some of those now less esteemed, because they seem to a later age to lack imagination or creative interpretation of a more than workaday kind, were then placed higher in the general juvenile esteem. Two at least deserve a glance – Harrison Weir and 'Alfred Crowquill', who were good examples of the strictly professional illustrator.

Weir (1824–1906) was on the staff of *The Illustrated London News*, which on its foundation in 1842 set a new fashion in English periodical journalism. He was a versatile and multifarious artist, but was best known to children as a depictor of animals. 'Illustrated by Harrison Weir' meant that you were sure of a cat or dog with every hair meticulously accurate (he was an expert in the living cat and dog, and founded the Cat Show), or a large horse's head, or even some exotic beast or bird, drawn with the most wearisome fidelity, and cut on wood to a millionth of an inch, or so it seemed. 'Crowquill', like Absolon, a lesser contemporary, was a sort of sub-Doyle, jolly, facetious in a simple way, skilled both in form and in composition. He was Alfred Henry Forrester (1804–72). He and his brother Charles Robert used the pseudonym jointly, the one drawing, the other writing, until Charles died, when Alfred continued as an artist alone.

A more nebulous figure personally, but an often bolder draughtsman, was

Ernest Griset, about whom little is known. He was born in France in 1844, but came to England early, and began to work for *Punch* in the sixties. He did not remain in close touch with the editor, Mark Lemon, however, but migrated to *Fun*, in which his drawings appear from 1870 on. He did an admirable *Aesop* (1869) and a *Reynard the Fox* (1872) – animals were his strong point – and many odd 'juvenile' drawings here and there, Apparently he went to America, but returned to die in London (in poverty, it is said) in 1907. His work was so individual that one would like to know more of him as a man.[8]

Throughout this period, from long before its visible beginning almost to its end, for he died and was buried in St Paul's Cathedral in 1878, at the age of eighty-six, there stalked the tall figure of George Cruikshank; a man sometimes like one of his own giants, sometimes like an odd character out of the works of his friend Charles Dickens, sometimes a romantic throwback in history to one of Harrison Ainsworth's sombrely fantastic periods. He had begun work when Thomas Bewick's pupils were making the rough-hewn woodblock a thing of beauty. He had drawn for copper, steel, stone and again for wood. He had illustrated, in many scenes imperishably, the first English *Grimm*. He had been a valued adjunct to half the Victorian novelists, as well as the friend, the rather testy friend, of literary folk for two long generations. He lived to anticipate Caldecott in doing pictures for Mrs Ewing's *Lob Lie-by-the-Fire* on its first appearance (1873; Caldecott's edition appeared in 1885). He could never quite (he never had need to) acquire the broad new technique – then broad and new, at any rate – of the woodcuts of the sixties. But when he died, 'line' and 'process' were about to supersede even that highly developed mode. A close record of his life and work would be a very long chapter in the history of English book-illustration as well as a comment on the evolution of children's books.

8

There were many minor authors in this rich period whose work still lives, sometimes capriciously, but on the whole in virtue of the characteristic sincerity of their day and their work. One of the chief is Jean Ingelow (1820–97). In her life she was shy and quiet. She enjoyed the friendship and acquaintance of Ruskin, Farrar, Arthur Helps, Frederick Locker-Lampson, Dean Stanley and Christina Rossetti, among others. But she mixed little in even the milder public literary circles. Her sphere was curiously like, and connected with, that of the demure earlier writers for children and their philanthropic friends. Her father was a Lincolnshire banker. Her mother, a strict Evangelical, was the intimate friend of Mrs Stock, the sister of Daniel Wilson, Bishop of Calcutta, Mrs Sherwood's friend in India. It was Mrs Stock who recorded that Jean Ingelow very early 'gave up the world', and was never taught dancing and never went to the theatre. In fact, she lived much the same life as the Taylors, whom she knew well. From the time – 1834 – when her family moved to Ipswich, she had a close friendship with Isaac Taylor of Stanford Rivers (the brother of Ann and Jane), and afterwards with his son Canon Isaac Taylor of *Words and Places*.

As a 'grown-up' poet, of fluent and gentle emotion, she had a wide popularity; and her best-known piece, *High Tide on the Coast of Lincolnshire* (for which Pinwell, Poynter and others made drawings cut on wood by the Dalziels, 1867), was not ephemeral. Her facility of verse was so marked and so acceptable to the general public that it lent itself to one of Calverley's most ruthless parodies:

> Boats were curtseying, rising, bowing,
>   (Boats in that climate are so polite),
> And sands were a ribbon of green endowing,
>   And O the sundazzle on bark and bight!

It is said to have wounded her grievously. But it hardly hurt her general reputation, for when Tennyson died in 1892, 'some representative [American] authors petitioned the Queen to make her Poet Laureate'. However, Alfred Austin won.

In the capacity of a singer to higher audiences, she achieved possibly no more than Mrs Hemans in the previous generation. She could write verse with ease and prettiness for children, and sometimes it had a country freshness in it. For example,

> When I sit on market-days amid the comers and the goers,
>   Oh! full oft I have a vision of the days without alloy
> And a ship comes up the river with a jolly gang of tow-ers,
>   And a 'pull'e haul'e, pull'e haul'e, yoy, heave, hoy!' . . .
>
> Then I hear the water washing, never golden waves were brighter,
>   And I hear the capstan creaking – 'tis a sound that cannot cloy.
> Bring her to, to ship her lading, brig or schooner, sloop or lighter,
>   With a 'pull'e haul'e, pull'e haul'e, yoy, heave, hoy!'

A child might well appreciate that, and fail to see that it is not really a sudden flash of experience seized and put into rapid words, but a slightly 'literary' recollection of things seen in her childhood at Boston, Lincolnshire, the home of the Pilgrim Fathers, where from her home she looked out on Boston Stump and Boston River.

The quotation is from one of the lyrics scattered up and down her best book, her children's story, *Mopsa the Fairy* (1869). That is pure artless fantasy. It was to her, as to all who in childhood loved that delicious book, the most natural thing in the world to put your hand into a nest in an old tree and find it full of young fairies. She had the gift of complete and almost too artless spontaneity. The greater part of her *Little Wonder Box* (1887) was almost as easily and ethereally matter-of-fact. This was, by a pretty chance, produced in a manner surviving from seventy years or so before. The *Box* really was a box, of cardboard with a small wallpaper-pattern binding. It contained six booklets of one, two or three stories (the first, *The Ouphe of the Wood*, is the best known), each bound in imitation Dutch paper, with woodcut illustrations by J.

Mahoney, Townley Green and others.* The detail is worth notice, because the attractive collection was published by John Newbery's last heirs, Griffith, Farran, Okeden and Welsh, 'West Corner, St Paul's Churchyard'; and among the books advertised at the end was some of the first work of 'E. Nesbit', the late Mrs Hubert Bland, afterwards Mrs Bland-Tucker, who was to write of more modern children than Jean Ingelow ever knew.

Jean Ingelow's first book was a collection of stories first published in *The Youth's Magazine* and using her pseudonym there in its title: *Tales of Orris* (Bath and London, 1860). This was followed by *Stories Told to a Child* (1865) and *A Sister's Bye-Hours* (1868), books of a plain character, slightly religious in tone and not over-strong in action; and there I must let her gentle title to a little weak fame rest.

She is really, in this history, a single-book author. But that book, *Mopsa*, in its formless simplicity, has a compacter character than the much more numerous stories of her well-recognized contemporaries. One of them, Mary Louisa Molesworth (1839–1921), carried on her tradition in that most charming tale *The Tapestry Room* (1879), in which the gateway to fairyland, as in *Mopsa*, is part of everyday life. Mrs Molesworth's many other books, however, dealt chiefly with un-fairy life, very naturally, lightly and pleasantly: the best perhaps were *Two Little Waifs* (1883), *Little Miss Peggy* (1887) and, most popular of all, *Carrots* (1876).† They really belong to a slightly later stage of evolution, but they are definitely linked with the sixties by the fact that Walter Crane illustrated them all.

Here, too, perhaps, should be mentioned a few authors whose hold on the longer nursery memory is a little uncertain, and whose writings of a miscellaneous kind prevent them from being considered as entirely children's authors. Such were Mrs W. K. Clifford, whose early book *Anyhow Stories* (1882) was so full of pity and terror. She wrote also in this period *Children Busy, Children Glad* (1881) and *Very Short Stories* (1886), both for the youngest tribe of readers‡ Mrs Craik's *Little Lame Prince* (1875) was of a type which tends to be more and more disregarded, and her *Children's Poetry* (1881) was of the even older Hemans-hymnal fashion. She had done a *Fairy Book* (1863), a version of the chief of the accepted fairy-tales, which was pleasing and unpretentious, but had nothing to make it stand out against rivals except the fact that it was 'by the Author of *John Halifax, Gentleman*'. Lord Brabourne provided several semi-folk-lore volumes, such as *Tales at Tea-Time* (1872) and *Higgledy-Piggledy*

---

*   [The stories, with these illustrations, were first published in 1872 by Henry S. King, as *The Little Wonder Horn*. It looks as though Griffith, Farran bought the stereotype plates and adapted them for this six-volume printing.]

†   [*Carrots* was her second book for children, flanked by *Tell Me a Story* (1875) and *The Cuckoo Clock* (1877), which, sixty-four years later was in the first batch of 'Puffin Story Books'. All three Molesworth titles were originally published under the pseudonym 'Ennis Graham'.]

‡   Her husband, Prof. W. K. Clifford, contributed some delightful nonsense to a volume by himself, Lady Pollock and Walter Herries Pollock – *The Little People, and Other Tales* (1874).

44. Griselda approaches the cuckoo clock. Drawing by Walter Crane, in 'sixtyish' mood, for Mrs Molesworth's story.

(1875), which do not deserve entire oblivion; the first was very well illustrated by William Brunton, much in the manner of Linley Sambourne's more broadly comic work; the second had pictures by Dicky Doyle.

Finally – or rather, early in the period – there was Mrs Gatty, accompanied and followed by her daughter. Margaret Gatty's literary work, as Mrs Ewing said, 'was essentially educational and domestic in its aim and its effects'. Her *Fairy Godmothers* (1851) were not merely like the godmothers of traditional fairy-tales in being the vehicle of definite morals; they invented the morals beforehand, and stressed them, with a good deal of verbiage. Of *Parables from Nature* (1855, First Series: four others at intervals), which has become a classic of its kind, it can only be said that it fulfils the purpose of its title with the greatest sweetness and lucidity. But at this stage in the history of children's books it is on the very edge of my original definition of 'books intended to give pleasure'. It is moral rather than tale: more parable than nature.

Juliana Horatia Ewing (1841–85), her daughter, is, I have suggested, more lovingly remembered than closely read today by those who (like myself) were brought up among her books. She appears now as having very clearly the limitations of her surroundings, which the sentence just quoted from her about her mother indicates. She lived as a girl in – '*well* in' – Church of England circles, though she was never affected by strong dogmatic views, nor obtruded them. Religion, however, was a prominent feature in many of her tales, and she had some of the contemporary preoccupation with death-beds. *Laetus Sorte Meâ*, sub-titled *The Story of a Short Life* (in *Aunt Judy's Magazine*, 1882, and in book form, 1885), indeed, is well in the Little Nell–Eric tradition. Even the end of so excellent a book as *Lob Lie-by-the-Fire* (1873) bows to that prevalent fashion. Her literary qualities, however, as a rule far outweighed her didactic excrescences. One might almost call the construction of her scenes theatrical, in fact, because she had a considerable gift of dramatic vision; as a girl in her home she had acted Miss Corner's popular plays for children, and often took part in private theatricals in later life. She contributed 'Hints for Private Theatricals' to *Aunt Judy's Magazine* in 1875–6. She had also been a young story-teller in her family circle.

Much of her life was spent in England. Her husband was a Major in the Army Pay Department, and she accompanied him to New Brunswick, where he was stationed from 1867 to 1869. But her ill-health, which eventually caused her early death, prevented her from going to the East with him later on. Her marriage gave her material for many scenes of military life in her books, and no doubt to some extent was responsible for that sense of Army discipline which is apparent in most of her characterization.

Her strength lay in variety of character-drawing and in a realism of detail which informed it. *Jackanapes* (*Aunt Judy*, 1879; book, 1884) and *Daddy Darwin's Dovecot* (*ibid.*, 1881; book, 1884) contain a whole gallery of 'real live' people, such as exactly suited her chief illustrator, Caldecott. They have not survived as types, because they were too natural, too little reinforced, to dominate one another or be singly the whole staple of a book. Equally easy and observant are the settings in which they move so briskly, especially the scenes of country life. If an intelligent and sympathetic person desired to know what life in such circumstances actually was, he could go safely to Mrs Ewing, just as, for society of a larger scope, he would go to Trollope. But that virtue in her books automatically reduces the breadth of her appeal to later generations, as compared with her popularity in her lifetime.

9

This period of concentrated activity, then, had shown a willingness to use most of the best of the available material, think about it, and trust innocence, on the whole, not to take much harm from a freer presentation of it. But it did not merely accept, develop, and demarcate ideas and modes existing in, say, 1861, the year of the Prince Consort's death. When, or as soon as, its writers realized fully the importance of the adolescent, as distinct from the baby, stage in the younger generation – when, in fact, philanthropy and the factory system both began to face the details of reality, from their different points of view – they set up a more definite image of Young England: the Public School Boy for males, the Woman in the Home for females. But at the outset they retained, or even reinforced, something of the old Puritan consciousness of war against active and strongly menacing evil, rather than trusted to their own serenity of faith. The balance was a little overweighted, once more, on the side of fear.

The quality the two chief Public School writers – Thomas Hughes and Frederic Farrar – desiderated in boys was summed up at the time and for more than a generation later in one word – 'manliness'. Manliness was to be exhibited at home in England, too, without excursions into the romantic past or perils in the waste spaces of the earth. The Sandford and Merton type of boy was clearly dead, but no youth had taken his place in the fiction of English boyhood. Arnold of Rugby, not long before his death in 1842, had seen the defect: 'Childishness in boys, even of good abilities, seems to me to be a growing fault, and I do not know to what to ascribe it, except to the great number of exciting books of amusement like *Pickwick* or *Nickleby*.' It is a curious ascription, especially in view of Ainsworth's great vogue. However, the great school tale produced by one of his illustrious pupils certainly did not make for childishness.

Tom Brown's School-Days was published in 1857, as 'By an Old Boy': the author's name was not given. It was the most eminent and, so far as I can see, the first book for boys about boys in which the characters were really a collection of young human beings, all alive and all different, at a genuine school. Even Arthur, whose figure (as that of a person in a story) is not so acceptable now as in 1857, was not a ventriloquist's dummy, quacking out sentiments demanded by his appearance and the performer. That, indeed, is a little odd, for Thomas Hughes (1822–96) said quite plainly: 'Why, my whole object in writing at all was to get a chance of preaching!'

The confession is the whole case for and against the book, the details of which need not be discussed here. Hughes's purpose *is* too apparent. Yet the glow of his memories of Rugby, his generous temper, his noble enthusiasm, and above all, his natural quick-eyed realism, almost hid the didactic element and certainly far more than made up for it. *Tom Brown's School-Days*, for all its social purpose, remains a human picture of what Arnold's hopes implied. A few of its details – the more sentimental and funereal ones – have lost all value and have become, to modern eyes, false. But it stands yet as a just panorama of school life, and, at that, an exceedingly fine piece of story-telling.

It caused reactions and counterblasts, though not till Victoria's reign was almost ended; and then they were really directed at first – if they had a conscious aim – against a work which appeared only one year later, in 1858: the much-derided and much-discussed *Eric, or Little by Little: a Tale of Roslyn School*, 'by Frederic W. Farrar, Fellow of Trinity College, Cambridge'. Nearly everything that can be said against maudlin sentimentalism, against sincere and pious self-delusion, can be and has been said against this astonishing book. Yet by 1903 it had attained a thirty-sixth edition. In 1905 the author's son could still solemnly write (after having said that Kipling's *Stalky and Co.* was 'a lively and amusing presentment of one side, the slangy side, of schoolboy life'*) that 'I dare venture to say that few boys, however much they may sneer at it in after years, have read 'Eric' for the first time without tears coming to their eyes.' Its sub-title has become a tag, suited to the provision of clues for crossword puzzles; and in 1931 it was seriously broadcast on the British wireless.

What the author thought of it, or hoped for it, is not a matter of doubt. He made a definite assertion in the preface to the first edition:

In all humility I claim for the story a higher merit than that of style – the merit of truthfulness. If the pictures here painted are not always such as it would have been most pleasant to contemplate, they owe the darker shades of their colouring not to fancy, but to life. To the best of my belief, the things here dealt with are not theories, but realities; not imaginations, but facts.

He feared those 'darker shades', in a way. When he was told that the story might injure the school depicted in it, he exclaimed: 'Absurd! but even if so, I am not to blame.' He thought honestly that the injury might come to King William's School, Isle of Man, because of the depravity he had revealed there (he had been a boy at the school); not, as other Old Boys feared, through ridicule.

The secret of his faith in the book as a true picture of schoolboy life is to be guessed to some extent from his own upbringing and career. He was born in 1831, educated at King William's School, and at King's College, London: he took a London B.A. in 1852. While there, like so many others, he came under the influence of F. D. Maurice. Before taking his London degree he entered Trinity, Cambridge, as a sizar, and took the Cambridge B.A. in 1854. He was subsequently a master at Harrow, and from 1871–6 Head of Marlborough. His eloquence and his 'adult' books, especially his *Life of Christ*, won him enormous popularity, and he ended his honourable ecclesiastical career as Dean of Canterbury. He died in 1903. His writings in general had the merits and the defects of the professions of orator, schoolmaster and preacher.

To such a development of strong but not deep character his early days must have tended. A passage from *Eric* is referred to by his son as being really autobiographical:[9]

There was nothing exotic or constrained in the growth of Eric's character. He was not one of your angelically good children at all, and knew none of the phrases of which infant prodigies are supposed to be so fond. He had not been taught any distinction between 'Sunday books' and 'week-day books', but no book had been put in his way that was not healthy and genuine in tone. He had not been told that he might use his Noah's ark on Sunday, because it was 'a Sunday plaything', while all other toys were on that day forbidden . . . So Eric grew up to love Sunday quite as well as any other day in the week, though, unlike your angelic children, he never professed to like it better. But to be truthful, to be honest, to be kind, to be brave, these had been taught him, and he never *quite* forgot the lesson.

Farrar learnt it under the care of two maiden aunts at Aylesbury, to whom he

---

* 'Didn't I "Eric" 'em splendidly?' *Stalky and Co.* (1899).

was committed after his birth in India. But in spite of those restrictions he grew up with 'a voracious appetite for books', long retained:

> To the end of his life he loved the occasional relaxation of a good novel, but the boon, or, shall we say the blight, of cheap literature had not yet descended upon the land, and the schoolboy of those days was at least saved, in spite of himself, from becoming the debauchee of shoddy fiction. Even such standard novels as those of Scott, Fenimore Cooper, and Captain Marryat, which, fortunately, were almost the only romances then available, circulated almost by stealth.

He was, in fact, not part of that larger world of general culture and free ideas into which his career afterwards took him. It is not difficult to understand why his pictures of that world are not of this world.

But it is equally easy to understand, and, upon the same grounds, to sympathize with, the force of the convictions thus limited. His school-world was indubitably real to him. And that fact gives his books – even the preposterous *Julian Home*, for which few Cambridge men have ever displayed enthusiasm – their strength. Farrar the orator was also Farrar the fanatical moralist, and, almost as a consequence, a natural story-teller. The scene of Russell's death in *Eric* is in the last degree lachrymose and lush. But the episode of the caning of the vile Brigson by the virtuous Mr Rose, while it can certainly be considered as super-Dotheboys-Hall stuff, or outrageous melodrama, is, like melodrama at its best, powerful drama as well. *Eric* has the fascination, today, of the amazing, even of the absurd, but also of an inherent excitement which nothing but the story-teller's own personality could arouse.

Eric and Tom Brown are not, in point of fact, comparable heroes, any more than their schools were actually comparable. But there was the same general social principle behind both books, a lofty one in conception, an ephemeral one if the mere ceremonial aspect is the only thing looked at. The surface 'values' have now changed so much that the substance sometimes seems to have become obsolete too. The schools and their stories are apt to be regarded as pleasant myths.

10

Not less remarkable, though different in expression was the change which simultaneously came upon books for girls – girls, not little girls, not even Alices. That class of reader, hitherto sparsely provided for when it grew out of short frocks – for between *Aunt Judy* and the milder sort of adult fiction there was a considerable gap – seems almost to have appeared suddenly, like a younger Minerva. Charlotte Mary Yonge (1823–1901) sprang up at the same moment to meet its needs, and to meet them sanely and copiously.

She was a staunch Churchwoman, and, apart from her writings, did much for the Church of England's work for women. Her early life was spent in John Keble's neighbourhood, and her family were landowners of the kind that would now be called Tory, but then stood for a liberal dignity and broadening tradition. She introduced a solid but sound romantic touch into tales like *The Heir of Redclyffe* (1853), and in stories like *The Daisy Chain* (1856) intensified the home interest until it became almost exciting. As a critic has said, in her books 'an unwonted element of chivalry was happily grafted on the realism of contemporary English domestic life'. She wrote over a hundred of them.* She had not a strong sense of humour, and the very truth and honesty of her work, faithfully reflecting as well as inspiring lofty contemporary ideals, have to some extent diminished its interest for a later generation – for even 'young persons' do not read story-books as literature or as social documents. She was, in fact, an excellent example of a high-principled English Victorian gentlewoman, in a fine sense.

There were rivals to her, of a sort. Mrs Henry Wood (1814–87) was perhaps the most powerful. It has been her fate to pass into the garish immortality of melodrama with *East Lynne* (3 vols., 1861); and perhaps that was almost too strong meat for the type of 'young person' into which, at that date, females were expected to develop suddenly after being 'children' much longer than their brothers. But *The Channings* and *Mrs Halliburton's Troubles* (both three-deckers, 1862) were 'safe', and so was the admirable magazine owned and edited by Mrs Wood, *The Argosy*. Other such writers, whose work reached into the Edwardian period without much deviation from the type of the seventies were Emma Jane Worboise, 'Edna Lyall' (Ada Ellen Bayly), 'A L(ady). O(f). E(ngland).' (Charlotte Maria Tucker), and 'Hesba Stretton' (Sarah Smith), the pietistic author of *Jessica's First Prayer* (1866) and *Alone in London* (1869); much of her work appeared in *The Sunday at Home*, a magazine for family use as varied as the Sabbatical Noah's Ark – and as discreet.

Charlotte Yonge, however, was the true corollary to Hughes as a writer for the adolescent and the younger young woman. She was never provincial, like some of the Americans, and never condescending, nor yet ardently polemical, a virtue which puts her in many ways above Kingsley. When it came to established or classical fiction, girls had the better of boys in being more likely (at a young age) to appreciate Jane Austen, or *Evelina*, or *Cranford*. But of stories for their intermediate stage between Alice-hood and womanhood there was not much really worth having except Miss Yonge.

II

The mid-Victorian period was astonishingly productive. Its fulness carried with it the social blemish of such wealth – the commercial standard. Books for the young were multiplied to a pattern, and the pattern tended to be the brightest,

* [To say nothing of editing her own magazine *The Monthly Packet* from 1851 to 1894, helped during the final few years by Christabel Coleridge. It was a packet 'of Evening Readings for Younger Members of the English Church', but was more varied and less solemn than those words suggest. Many of Charlotte Yonge's own novels were first serialized there.]

the most specious, rather than the most enduring or most finely wrought. But all the best characteristics of the preceding generation had been confirmed, and had been developed and enriched. Fiction was now by a long way predominant over fact, magic was not rebuked but at large, nonsense was free. Children could go back to the enchantments of the Middle Ages without being told that they were really the work of the Devil; to Aesop and traveller's tales with the knowledge that such fables were not true but were thoroughly worthy of belief and love; to folk-lore with open rapture in the rogueries of the Booted Cat and the decapitation of ogres, without any warnings about superstition or ignorance or unreality; to fun, without being told not to be silly. And, say what you will, *Holiday House, The Book of Nonsense, Alice, Tom Brown, Sing-Song, The Water-Babies, At the Back of the North Wind* were pure 'Victorian' products and nothing else. Not only did no other age invent them; no other age could have invented them.

BRIEF BOOK LIST

Practically all the authors here mentioned appear in *D.N.B.* and *C.H.E.L.*; many of the artists and engravers in Bryan's *Dictionary of Painters and Engravers*. Some special references are given in the text above. Addenda:
The Eighteen-Sixties. By Fellows of the Royal Society of Literature. Ed. by John Drinkwater (Cambridge, 1932).

'LEWIS CARROLL'
De la Mare, Walter. *Lewis Carroll* (London, 1932). Reprinted and revised from *The Eighteen-Eighties*, ed. by W. de la Mare (Cambridge, 1930).
Williams, Sidney Herbert and Madan, Falconer. *A Handbook of the Literature of the Rev. C. L. Dodgson (Lewis Carroll)* (Oxford, 1932).
  And many books and articles published for the centenary of Dodgson's birth, 1932.

JOHN RUSKIN
The King of the Golden River. Illustrated by Ferdinand Huszti Horvath. Introduction by Eugene A. Noble (London and New York, 1930). The story was reprinted in facsimile in 1907 and 1909.

MAGAZINES
See General Book List, Section I. 3. vi.

ILLUSTRATIONS
M. H. Spielmann and G. S. Layard's *Kate Greenaway* (London, 1905) and M. H. Spielmann and Walter Jerrold's *Hugh Thomson* (London, 1932) contain much about contemporary book-illustration.
See also Spielmann's *History of 'Punch'* (London, 1895).
Reid, Forrest. *Illustrators of the Sixties* (London, 1928).

THOMAS HUGHES
Reprints in 1911 and 1923 of *Tom Brown's School-Days* contain good introductions by William Dean Howells and Frank Sidgwick respectively.

Supplement

KINGSLEY AND HUGHES
As well as friendship these two men share a bibliography (of sorts):
Parrish, M. L. and Mann, B. K. *Charles Kingsley and Thomas Hughes: first editions in the library at Dormy House* (London, 1936).
and there is a good short-listing of manuscripts, books and editions of Hughes in:
Mack, Edward C. and Armytage, W. H. G. *Thomas Hughes* (London, 1952).

As for Kingsley, although *The Water Babies* has been the subject of essays by Colin Manlove in *Modern Fantasy: Five Studies* (Cambridge, 1975) and Q. D. Leavis in *Children's Literature in Education*, no. 23, Winter 1976, his writing for children is not widely discussed, even in two 'centenary' biographies:
Chitty, Susan. *The Beast and the Monk; a life of Charles Kingsley* (London, 1974).
Colloms, Brenda. *Charles Kingsley; the lion of Eversley* (London, 1975).

CARROLL
The *Handbook* on Carroll's writings compiled by S. H. Williams and Falconer Madan in 1932 has subsequently acquired several layers of editorial accretion and now exists in almost definitive form:
The Lewis Carroll Handbook . . . edited by Denis Crutch (Folkestone, 1979). The reader will find here helpful, authoritative and often entertaining treatment of primary and secondary sources on the Rev. C. L. Dodgson.

THACKERAY
His one children's book has had its reputation enhanced by the sumptuous publication of its original manuscript including the author's own tinted illustrations:
The Rose and the Ring, reproduced in facsimile from the manuscript in the Pierpont Morgan Library. With an introduction by Gordon N. Ray (New York, 1947).

MACDONALD
The mid twentieth century's preoccupation with fantasy (and the advocacy of C. S. Lewis) has led to a rise in interest in MacDonald's fairy stories, as in:
Wolff, Robert Lee. *The Golden Key; a study* . . . (New Haven, 1961).
Bibliographies are:
Bulloch, J. M. 'A Bibliography of George MacDonald', *Aberdeen University Library Bulletin*, vol. v, February 1925, no. 30, pp. 679–747. Shaberman, R. B. *George MacDonald's Books for Children; a bibliography of first editions* (London, 1979).

ROSSETTI
A biography with a bibliography of manuscript and printed sources is: Packer, Lona Mosk. *Christina Rossetti* (Cambridge, 1963).

Insight into the publishing background is given in the same author's editing of the *Rossetti–Macmillan Letters* (Cambridge, 1963).

MRS GATTY, MRS EWING AND MRS MOLESWORTH
As well as Marghanita Laski's study noted above (p. 251) see:
Avery, Gillian. *Mrs Ewing* (London, 1961). Bodley Head Monograph.
Green, Roger Lancelyn. *Mrs Molesworth* (London, 1961). Bodley Head Monograph.
Maxwell, Christabel. *Mrs Gatty and Mrs Ewing* (London, 1949).

YONGE
Charlotte Yonge was the subject of attention of a private Charlotte Yonge Society during

the 1960s, which led to the publication of:

A Chaplet for Charlotte Yonge, edited by Georgina Battiscombe and Marghanita Laski (London, 1965) Its thirteen papers are accompanied by detailed genealogical tables and a bibliography.

THE TRIO OF ILLUSTRATORS

The *Reminiscences* of Edmund Evans, who brought to prominence the work of Walter Crane, Randolph Caldecott and Kate Greenaway, were edited, with a check-list, by Ruari McLean (Oxford, 1967). Significant books on the three are:

Massé, Gertrude C. E. *First Editions of Books Illustrated by Walter Crane* (London, 1923).

Spencer, Isobel. *Walter Crane* (London, 1975). With full book lists, etc.

Engen, Rodney K. *Randolph Caldecott 'Lord of the Nursery'* (London, 1976). Including a book list.

Hutchins, Michael. *Yours Pictorially; illustrated letters of Randolph Caldecott* (London, 1976).

Thomson, Susan Ruth. *Kate Greenaway; a catalogue of the . . . collection . . . in Detroit Public Library* (Detroit, 1977).

MAGAZINES
See General Book List, section 1.3. vi.

CHAPTER XV

The Eighties and Today: Freedom

1

To treat the reign of Victoria as a self-contained epoch capable of being pigeon-holed with an adjective is an elementary historical error which, among other things, the development of children's books makes clear. But it is not really safer to divide the period into neat segments. Catherine Sinclair, Lear, Dodgson, *The Boy's Own Paper* stand out as figures whose dates can be used as sign-posts; but like good sign-posts they point both back and forth. If therefore 'the Eighties' is used as a label, or the third twenty years of the Queen's sovereignty is called, say, Jubilee-Victorian, it does not mean that the period was abrupt or new.

As a matter of fact, the children's book which *ought* to belong to that hypothetical era appeared much earlier. But its circumstances contradict its logical importance. It was written, by the most famous English author of the time, at the height of his fame, was published first in the United States, had no effect whatever at the moment, and is now far from highly esteemed. It is, indeed, of no great value to anyone, on its intrinsic merits. But it was curiously prophetic in spirit and in fact. It was *Holiday Romance*, by Charles Dickens, who got £1000 for it. It appeared first in an American juvenile magazine, *Our Young Folks*, in the months of January, March, April and May, 1868. Dickens was in America at the time, and his portrait appeared with the first of the four instalments.

Holiday Romance, though quite jolly in a slightly sophisticated way, has most of the faults of jocular artifice. The alleged narrators, aged six and a half to nine, speak too often with a voice and mind like those of Charles Dickens being playful in his fifty-sixth year. He pretends to take seriously, but laughs a little superciliously at, the tremendous trivialities of make-believe which are so real to childhood. The narrative also is not devoid of some vulgar crudeness. But it does contain the right sort of properties. A colonel who is also a pirate, a magic fishbone, discomfited schoolmasters, cannibal savages singing an excellent anthem:

> Choo a choo a choo tooth,
>   Muntch, muntch. Nycey!
> Choo a choo a choo tooth,
>   Muntch, muntch. Nyce!

and mothers rejoicing (obviously) in the names of Mrs Alicumpaine and Mrs Orange: these are strained and overdone in the actual 'romance', but they have the root of the matter in them. Their presence as objects of both ridicule and sympathy so early as 1868 is remarkable. It is waste of time to ridicule unknown things.

The pirates are the most useful of these pieces of furniture. In 1868, though it might not be suspected from what was supplied to them by austere adults, children really did know a good deal about piracy and bloodshed – on paper. Dickens's William Tinkling, Esq., aged eight, and Lieut.-Col. Robin Redforth, aged nine, might very well have been regular subscribers to *The Boys of England* (p. 271), so easy was the nonchalance of their desperate conduct. What is more, a still greater authority on frightfulness was about that very time engaged in his earliest investigations. James Barrie, in the preface to the first book-form edition of the play of *Peter Pan* (1928), has confessed that as a boy he was terribly addicted to 'penny dreadfuls'. He was born in 1860. At an early age, he says, he had not only read all the 'bloods' he could obtain surreptitiously, but he tried to write similar works. Fortunately for his soul, the 'high class magazine *Chatterbox*', founded in 1866, came his way, and he buried his pirate hoard, both original and acquired, in a field at Pathead farm.

Lawless adventure was the feat that haunted the advocates of manliness. As Satan was sometimes considered the hero of *Paradise Lost*, so the Pirate King might almost be given a romantic halo. If the manly and righteous hero were too tame, the author would be accused of writing a disguised sermon. If, on the other hand, excitement was achieved by a heightening or empurpling of the literary style, the charge of sensationalism would be preferred. 'Adult' romance itself was even then beginning to be thought a little too heavy in manner. It was therefore a new and joyful experience for readers to find real literature concerning itself with reckless ferocity, as happened when *Treasure Island* in 1882 and *King Solomon's Mines* in 1885 carried both fathers and sons clean away and stirred their blood without any qualms.

2

One of the books was an historical throw-back, the other a product of then modern exploration. But in essence they were alike, in that, as books read by boys, they were different from anything that had been composed before, and different, at that, in the way in which they rekindled genuine romance. They did not furbish lumber. They caught the sudden freshness which is the very heart of an adventure-story in a way previously unknown, except perhaps in that one brief moment when Friday's footmark startled Crusoe and all readers of his story. Here, in Treasure Island and Kukuanaland, was surprise upon surprise, each one sudden, but each one also natural, capable of rational and brave explanation when you knew all the facts.

The publication of *Treasure Island* is a matter of historical as well as personal importance. For one thing, it made Stevenson's reputation. In terms of the market, 'I was thirty-one; I was the head of a family; I had lost my health; I had never yet paid my way, never yet made two hundred pounds a year.' In terms of moral strength to the writer, it meant that though he circumscribed his art within a style ostensibly suited to Jim Hawkins, he thoroughly enjoyed being himself over a tale which made him a boy again.

He had always been a boy at heart. He had adored Mayne Reid, Fenimore Cooper, Jules Verne and Marryat, and had had a passion for maps. He knew now that other grown men wanted to remain young. He read his manuscript in the early stages to his father and his twelve-year-old stepson Lloyd Osbourne, and made the discovery that 'it seemed to me original as sin; it seemed to belong to me like my right eye. I had counted on one boy, I found I had two in my audience. My father caught fire at once.' That was the real secret: not that boys delighted in tales meant for men, like *Robinson Crusoe* and *Midshipman Easy*, but that men – Victorian men – were eager for tales meant for boys, like *Treasure Island*.

So far as the younger half of Stevenson's audience was concerned, there was everything in the story which romantic boyhood ought to expect: buried treasure, pirates, strange noises, seafaring, a resourceful but quite fallible young hero, and a 'smooth and formidable' villain who has passed into the gallery of immortals. On the other hand, there was also nearly everything which most boys even then were guarded against: plenty of blood, plenty of rum, and that grim song, 'Fifteen men on the dead man's chest'.* It was the very apotheosis of the 'penny dreadful' which the virtuous and healthy magazines had been founded to dethrone. Not even the heroic shrill splendour of the boy Jim's defiance: 'the laugh's on my side; I've had the top of this business from the first; I no more fear you than I fear a fly. Kill me, if you please, or spare me'; not even that courageous grasp of morality could hide the fact that the expedition was launched by greed and decorated with murder and treachery, and concluded by luck rather than righteousness.

The method of the tale's appearance has also its significance in social history. It was shown in manuscript to James Henderson, editor of the blood-and-thunderous magazine *Young Folks*. Henderson liked it and took it for serial purposes, but caused the title to be changed from *The Sea Cook* to *Treasure Island*. It ran in vols. XIX and XX, from October 1, 1881 to January 28, 1882; and it did not make much difference to the sales of the journal. *Young Folks* itself, however, had a history which is an epitome of contemporary children's literature. It was founded in January, 1871, as *Our Young Folks' Weekly Budget*. It lived till the year of Victoria's Diamond Jubilee. In that space of time it rechristened itself thus:

---

* Probably everyone knows that by a typographical error this has become more gruesome than it should be. The words should have capitals – Dead Man's Chest, the name of a small island in the pirate zone.

July, 1876. *Young Folks' Weekly Budget.*
July, 1879. *Young Folks.*
December, 1884. *Young Folks' Paper.*
July, 1891. *Old and Young.*
September, 1896. *Folks at Home.*

At the end of April, 1897, it perished. The sequence is a skeleton picture of the domestic magazine-reading habit. In like manner a magazine of different aims became successively *Sunday Reading for the Young, Sunday, Sunday and Everyday, Everyday with which is incorporated Sunday,* and *Everyday;* and so to death. Each title is a fresh phase of current opinion.

3

King Solomon's Mines had no such intimate connection as *Treasure Island* with current sub-journalism, nor was its author, in an esoteric sense, a literary man like Stevenson when he achieved fame. Unlike Stevenson, too, he had to keep his hero alive – with *Allan Quatermain* (1887) – and to investigate his previous exploits later on. (Taught by experience, no doubt, he gave *She* – 1887 also – the power of reincarnation.) To some extent also, Rider Haggard did not openly write his first successful book for the boy public. He perhaps saw the double chance, for the story was dedicated by Allan Quatermain 'to all the big and little boys who read it'. Affinity with Stevenson is clearly visible. The real theme of *King Solomon's Mines* is once more the lust for treasure; that is to say, the reader is quite certain all through that the diamonds will be found, and wants them to be found. But it was disguised by the device of Sir Henry Curtis's search for his brother, whom it is safe to say everyone forgets completely between the second chapter and the last. And it was mitigated by the casual way in which the precious stones are actually picked up. The book is 'purer', a stern moralist might say, than *Treasure Island.*

Both authors, again, employed the trick of emphasis on one or two abnormal characters. That was not a modern invention, though it has become a common modern practice. But it was powerfully used. Long John Silver, Pew the horrible blind beggar, Ben Gunn, Israel Hands, the three English diamond-seekers, Gagool, and (according to the reader's fancy) Umbopa or Twala, all stand out independently complete, without special aid from the plot of the stories; just as Alan Breck and Umslopogaas do in other fictions from the same sources. Stevenson and Haggard both realized consciously or unconsciously, the need of something more than adventure undertaken in an atmosphere of 'manliness'. The events must be swift and stirring, but that is not enough. The persons must be such as the reader, young or old, would either earnestly desire or earnestly hate to be himself, or else (like Capt. Good, R.N., or Ben Gunn) companionably eccentric. They must *not* be tailors' models of good and bad male bipeds. They must have marked idiosyncrasies. But equally they must not be grotesques, suddenly triumphant or cast down with no reason given but their exceptional physique or intellect or vileness. They must in short be probable impossibilities – a necessity of romance as well as of Aristotelean tragedy.

That was an entirely new note in fiction for the young, just as was the deliberate fusion of father and son into one reader. The scenes and properties of the two stories were not new. Stevenson admits his theft of the parrot, for instance, from Defoe. Haggard's eclipse of the moon had appeared elsewhere. Neither pirate treasure nor Ophir was a novelty in history, let alone romance, nor was the desire for them a Victorian inspiration. But it was a fresh thing to have them treated with so careless a rapture. There is a certain difference in the raptures themselves. Stevenson appealed to a past which had in his day only a literary reality. There were no buccaneers left in 1882, and, though he could easily have invented a treasure-hunt for that very year, his bent lay otherwise, and he preferred the revival of the past. But Haggard was dealing with something like a genuine possibility: indeed, it is a history lesson in itself to realize that the districts of Solomon's Mines and of Milosis (beyond Kenya; in *Allan Quatermain*) were sufficiently unexplored in 1885 for his stories to be wholly plausible. He gave English boys a better idea of the potential wonders of the Empire than could be had from any school-task. Stevenson, in a way, did the same kind of service in colouring history, but it had been performed more often and more laboriously before.

4

But geography and history were old frames for embroidery in fiction. Another possibility of romance was rapidly appearing. Science, except as a testimony to Providence, had hitherto been too grave a subject for general reading at leisure. It now began to get into fiction for the young; at first by reason of its visibly increasing application to the practical side of life, to transport or communications, which the railway era had found to be civilization. The scientific romance, in fact, at its inception, was not very much more than a highly coloured supplement to the Guides of Mr Bradshaw the Quaker, who had succeeded Mogg, who in turn had succeeded Paterson and Ogilby.

The first great purveyor of boys' scientific stories had been assimilated by Stevenson, as has been said, along with the American Wild West experts and the British Tar. Verne was born in 1828, but did not reach England in translations until he was well established in France. The earliest English version of any work of his which I have seen and can date is *Five Weeks in a Balloon*. This came out both as a book in 1870 and in *The Youth's Play-hour*, an undated magazine which does, however, at one point answer a correspondent's letter dated 1871.★

★ The illustrations were produced by 'graphotyping', an early (and excellent) mode of direct line reproduction, by which the artists's own drawing, traced and inked on a block of compressed chalk, was converted into a stereo printing block. The process was invented in America and

But the romance had first been published in France at the end of 1862, when it marked the beginning of a creative co-operation between Verne and the progressive publisher Pierre-Jules Hetzel (1814–86) who was to establish in 1864 the fortnightly *Magasin d'Éducation et de Récréation*. Many of Verne's stories first appeared as serials here, beginning with 'Les Anglais au Pole Nord', which featured in the earliest numbers and was followed by further serials in quick succession. At the same time Verne was writing books for Hetzel and the *Voyage au Centre de la Terre* appeared in 1864. These and such other favourites as *De la Terre à la Lune* (1865) appear to have got into English in the mid seventies, many in magazines like *The Boy's Own Paper*, and often a good time after their French birth.

The success of Verne's books with English boys is remarkable in several ways. Their novelty as scientific prophecy was obvious. A few isolated works – Paltock's *Peter Wilkins* (1751), for instance, or Lytton's *Coming Race* (1871) – no doubt fell into the hands of younger readers and stimulated their vision of a possible future. But Verne anticipated the anticipations of H. G. Wells in his variety and daring: submarines, aerial cruisers, the Pole reached – by an Englishman – transport immeasurably quickened, the moon visited – all these elements in his romances stood for happenings clearly not quite impossible when he first wrote, but not in the least realized as many of them have been since. He had, it is true, more vague imagination than basic scientific knowledge. But he had a gift of grandiose generalization and rapidity of motive which almost amounted to real insight, and was certainly inspiring not to boys alone.

It is odd, nevertheless, that his French manner of exploiting marvels appealed so strongly to Young England. The French habit in this mode of fiction, as in the kindred but more prosaic art of the detective tale, is to spring the wonder, the wonderful possibility, upon the reader as a surprising thing suddenly accomplished, without that plausibly linked clearness of cause and effect and commonplaceness which gives verisimilitude to, say, *The First Men in the Moon*, *The Moonstone*, or *The Speckled Band*. The English mind usually demands a certain minimum of explanation, or else a continuous tenseness of inquiry, rather than a succession of abrupt facts. But Verne's stories, with all their surface celerity, are often also quite British as well in deliberate movement and atmosphere. Moreover his chief heroes are Englishmen.

5

The popularity of these three writers for boys was not a symptom of merely spatial expansion of mind. It is true that the two Jubilees gave Englishmen

patented in Britain in 1865. (An early production was a *Divine Songs*, illustrated by Holman Hunt and others.) The publishers claimed that the process was 'less expensive and tedious than woodcutting'. *Youth's Play-hour* itself was admirably fresh and healthy, but apparently had only a brief life (1870–2).

visible evidence of the huge and apparently prosperous geographical destiny they had created for themselves. But they also conferred a sense of spiritual as well as terrestrial responsibility. If the words can now be treated respectfully, insularity was becoming imperialism. But at the same time, liberty was gradually being regarded as an habitual and very elastic right, instead of a severely observed duty. It was natural enough, therefore, in such an atmosphere, that the subjects and settings of stories for the heirs of this vast legacy should now be more spacious and unrestricted. Candid and generous though 'children's' books were becoming before 1880 or so, they had still been a little parochial.

The new temper was not confined to romance. It appears at its most versatile and best in the famous magazine in which much of Verne's work was first presented to English readers. In scope, as compared with then existing periodicals, it had a very strong claim to novelty.

The first number of *The Boy's Own Paper* appeared on January 18, 1879. When it celebrated fifty years of existence, a Prime Minister of Great Britain was a principal guest at the festivities. His presence as a speaker upon that occasion was unmistakable social history, and so was the tribute he paid to the beloved magazine of his boyhood. In the record of gratitude made by him and others at the ceremony was a long list of names which have become, in the fullest and best sense, household words. In volume I appeared Kingston's *From Powder-Monkey to Admiral*. Frank Buckland and a then unknown writer called Talbot Baines Reed were contributors. Volume II included Ballantyne, Jules Verne and 'Ascott Hope' (A. R. Hope Moncrieff). Other well-known names soon turned up, while many new names became well-known on their merits. The specialists included Captain Webb on swimming, W. G. Grace on cricket, Whymper, Maskelyne, J. G. Wood, and other experts after their kind.

The magazine was projected and produced by the Religious Tract Society. But that famous publishing firm was not so religious as to issue nothing but tracts. In *The Boy's Own Paper* its ideal was to combat evil by treating goodness as ordinary unemphasized decency and honesty, which knew and avoided vice spontaneously, and rejected it also with vigour, but without loud chords of moral triumph. The general editor of the firm's publications, Dr Macaulay, was at first in charge of the venture, but at the very outset he called in George Andrew Hutchison, who from 1879 to 1912 (he died in 1913) perhaps had a stronger indirect influence on English boyhood than any man of his time. He was an ideal editor: unobtrusive – many readers can never really have envisaged him as a person at all – thorough, determined without dogmatism, always alive and keen, and, not a necessary corollary, equably sane. Only those who know the inner workings of any sort of periodical can understand fully what such a character in the editor meant. It meant in practice that *The Boy's Own Paper*, whoever wrote for it and whatever its 'features' at any one moment, was *The Boy's Own Paper*, and nothing else; just as *The Times* was *The Times* and *The Spectator*, *The Spectator*. It was not a number of lively competing voices, and it was not a committee meeting of moralists.[1]

Its well-rounded policy amounted to a strong compost of varied manliness and naturalness. Manliness, in fact, became in the long run rather wearisome. Not every adventure-novelist can invent a Jim Hawkins (much less a John Silver) or an Allan Quatermain. And if the hero is not to become a twopence-coloured Jack Harkaway (the 'blood and thunder' hero invented by Bracebridge Hemyng, and appearing in *Boys of England* from 1871 onward), he is apt to be colourless – a mere peg for events. He too often had no imagination or temperament of his own, and was only a type, conducting himself fearlessly, resourcefully and modestly in moments of great practical danger – which were the true point of the stories. In England, of course, he was emphatically British, in the United States as emphatically American. The hero was the plain boy, who dislikes singularity, and eventually becomes a bore.

That was his ultimate fate from the creative point of view, so to speak. He passed into currency and had face-value; and the money so minted was very plentiful, until a new standard had to be set up: until the grown-up novel ousted the boys' book. *Treasure Island* and *King Solomon's Mines* were the first signs of that change, but they were also, at the moment of their first appearance, the very stimulus which the boys' book proper needed. They made it grow up into greater maturity, but in doing so gave it also the chance of growing clean out of boyhood.To put it contrariwise, they increased the youthward frontier of the novelist's kingdom.

6

The Boy's Own Paper, at the same time, enlarged – or perhaps one should say democratized – the range of the school story. This, so far as could then be seen (but the expectation was wrong), could not well 'grow up'. It could only become more generous, less the private chronicle of a prosperous oligarchy. The new or more generalized schoolboy in fiction was almost entirely the creation of *The Boy's Own Paper*, and, in it, of Talbot Baines Reed, whose importance has perhaps been obscured by affection. The first page of the first number of the *Paper* contained his first work, and till his early death in 1893 he was a regular and eagerly welcomed contributor.

The facts of his life are few and simple. He was not a Public School boy at all in the strict old conservative sense of the term. He was born in 1852, and educated at the City of London School – a day school, it should be remembered by those who loved *The Cock House at Fellsgarth* – under a great headmaster, Abbott. He had an interest in a well-known family type-founding firm, of which eventually he became manager and director. He was a high authority on typography, and first secretary of the Bibliographical Society, and a number of his collected books – including a good many old children's books – went to form part of the typographical library at St Bride's Institute, Fleet Street.

That is almost all that can be said about his personality, which in one sense, hardly appears even in his boy's stories. That is to say, they might have been written by anyone, for all the idiosyncrasy they show. But no one else did write them, and very few people have written schoolboy stories for schoolboys anything like so well. Such tales present an artist with almost every known creative obstacle, but Reed's books always are the work of an artist, whether consciously or not. He had the gift of conveying, without defining it, the esoteric sense of ritual which every school hides. A reader could say, 'We do not call that *this* at Harton but we think they do at Harrowby, and it's really quite "decent"', and accept the story as a picture of places not vitally unlike his own. That is one of the hardest and most delicate tasks for any writer about Public Schools, and Reed accomplished it without suspicion. Hughes was too early in history to experience such subtleties, and too great-hearted to have found them a difficulty had he known them. Farrar was too alien to the real Public School world. But Reed was aware of the secrets, and absorbed them without criticism or emphasis.

The school story, however, bore in its very subject the explosive contradiction which was to kill it, or at least to blow away its layer of older readers. That contradiction was that its gradual perfection as a story took away any truth it had in relation to schools. The various kinds of boy, the obvious masters, the school servant, the townee friend or enemy, became all too soon stock actors. There was a mechanization like that of the earlier stage, when Congreve and Sheridan became Foote and Colman, and worse. It had come upon adult literature also, as writers once thought revolutionary perceived in the nineties. *Jude the Obscure, Plain Tales from the Hills, The Heavenly Twins, The Woman who Did*, to jumble a few names, were all books of the Diamond Jubilee decade; and the difference between *Erewhon* (1872) and *Erewhon Revisited* (1901) is more than a difference in the years of one man's life.

But the schoolboy readers, or those who chose books for them, were not conscious of this change in the national intellect. They overlooked the significance of the sub-title of 'F. Anstey's' *Vice Versa* (1882) – 'A Lesson for Fathers'. A great part of that lesson was that many boys are by nature nasty little beasts (in the schoolboy sense), and that life in schools did not stand still, rooted in parental tradition. *Tom Brown* had become a lonely deserted rock in the distance. *Eric* was a kind of immovable moral jelly-fish left behind by the tide. Baines Reed and his imitators were the regular ripples in a smooth sea. No wonder that when *Stalky and Co.* appeared in 1899 there was an outcry. High – the highest – traditions seemed to be flouted and defiled by it. The academy represented – Westward Ho!, which there is reason to believe felt about the book much as King William's College felt about *Eric* – was said by unsympathetic persons not to be a Public School at all, but an inferior place for inferior people, who not only spoke the wrong language, as all 'foreigners' do, but had the wrong code of life. It was not easily perceived that the code itself was under scrutiny, and that 'Beetle' was not meant to fit in with Tom Brown and Eric.

The book had in time many repercussions. It was read as general fiction, not only as a story for and about boys. The truth of its picture, in detail, though a matter of interest to persons immediately concerned, is not here a question of importance. The significant thing is the absence of the old standards, on the one hand, and the merging of boy-and-man interests on the other. The masters are not stock types, any more than the pupils. Moral issues are largely ignored. The good or evil effect of the events described upon the characters is as irrelevant as the good or evil effect of the book upon the reader. The reader, in fact, was the reader of the average novel; and he was now son as well as father. The 'school story', for any 'young' public over about fourteen years of age was dead, the public having grown up.

Stalky and Co., in that respect, became a precedent in adult fiction. It was the first of a number of school-life novels for the full-grown reader; later on, perhaps, for the full-blown. In the twentieth century these became common. Retaliation for *Stalky* came and was in turn retaliated upon. H. A. Vachell's *The Hill* (1905), produced in the stock form of a (then) six-shilling novel for the regular circulating library public, provoked the counterblast of Arnold Lunn's *The Harrovians* (1913). Much later, in 1917, Alec Waugh's *The Loom of Youth*, written when its author himself was only just out of school, set a second supply going until it almost became a distinction for a public school not to have a novel all about itself under a thin disguise.*

7

The same kind of evolution took place in the adventure-story, though here, as has been said, the original impetus to a raising of the reader's age-level had come from the novelists who wrote for boys, Stevenson and Haggard (Stevenson's most deliberate piece of boy-fiction, *The Black Arrow* – 1888 – had no such twofold appeal as *Treasure Island* and *Kidnapped*). The type became a standard thing. It is no harsh criticism of writers like George Alfred Henty (1832–1902) to say that if you have read only two or three of the eighty-odd books he wrote for boys you know most of the rest, even if you like one first encountered – say, *Under Drake's Flag*, a particularly good example of honest, vigorous work – better than those you met later when you could recognize the formula. Henty's biographer, George Manville Fenn – an admirable performer himself, as anyone knows who remembers the joy of *Nat the Naturalist* – insists on Henty's avowed enthusiasm for 'manliness'; and the various artists who illustrated such books (Gordon Browne, for instance, the capable and versatile son of 'Phiz') usually drew a stock figure of a manly young Briton of seventeen or so who could never be mistaken for anything more flexible or temperamental. It was against that

---

* In 1931 there was yet another possible portent – *Early Closing*, a successful novel about a boy's school written by a young woman of twenty-three, Dorothy Mary Wynne Willson, who unhappily died in 1932.

very type that the 'heroes' of the later school-novels protested. They deemed it too bovine, as the manly young gentlemen had deemed the Erics too pious.*

The adventure-story had in fact become a piece of manufactured goods. Henty's own career – Westminster, Caius, the Army, special Correspondent for *The Standard* – ensured not only that it could be manufactured readily but that the goods were of thoroughly sound quality. At his death half the 'juvenile publishers' in London advertised A—, B—, Y—, Z—, as his successor, so clearly was the market specialized and stabilized. He had many followers, and books as good as his, on much the same lines, though with all the adornments of later science and discovery to vary the incidents, appear in great numbers to this day. It is unnecessary to particularize them, though some are more expertly compiled, more vivid, more ingenious, than others. Their popularity is largely a commercial matter. That is to say, those which look the most thrilling at a given scale of prices, and which also – this perhaps is even more important – look largest and most valuable for the money, sell in the greatest numbers. The standard of contents and of production is a financially competitive one.

That criticism, however, while it is meant to apply to the books, has probably a different social application now. They are read, on the testimony of those who ought to know – librarians, schoolmasters, and others whose duty it is to tempt the human boy to soar – by a younger class of reader. Books which thirty years ago would have appealed naturally to boys up to the age of sixteen are now demoded by them as babyish and left to boys of fourteen. The older lads read grown-up novels, partly, no doubt, because, by mechanical means, thought in general is more widely and more deeply diffused than ever before: the diffusion may not be more profoundly rooted, but it goes lower down; and partly because the technique and scope of the novel itself have become more 'popular'. There are a score of reasons for that. The slightest survey of the novel-format of today – price, print, binding, handiness – as compared with that of the three volume product of the seventies and eighties – will suggest plenty of arguments to the historian, the reformer, the moralist and the enthusiast. A comparison of the newspaper and periodical press at the same periods wil be still more illuminating. The student can adjust the balance of the change according to his predilections. It is not hard to see why boys began to read novels freely in the last decade of Victoria's reign, if you consider some of the novelists who then became generally acceptable – 'Seton Merriman', Stanley Weyman, 'Anthony Hope', Conan Doyle, H. G. Wells (as story-teller), to name only a few. *Treasure Island* and *King Solomon's Mines*, in fact, had made boys and men one class. Nor has the fusion been dissolved yet.

---

* [Curiously, Browne also illustrated *Eric*, with a set of drawings, many of which were in wash for reproduction by the new half-tone process. His approach gives a remarkable liveliness to both book and process and brings Farrar perceptibly nearer to Talbot Baines Reed.]

8

Books for girls underwent a similar process, though with a striking difference in some details. The old restriction of females to home interest cramped the range of their reading. They did not get a host of magazines specially provided for them. The home journals, like *The Leisure Hour* (started as early as 1852, and living till 1905), *The Quiver* (1861–1908), *Good Words* itself, and, a little later, the excellent *Atalanta* (1887–98), were deemed sufficient. My father in 1877 started a *Girl's Own Annual,* but I believe it ran only for two years. *The Girl's Own Paper* began to appear on January 3, 1880, under the auspices of *The Leisure Hour.* It contained the work of writers like Mrs Linnaeus Banks, Gordon Stables, F. E. Weatherly, Alice Corkran, and had a long and not undistinguished career. But it was a career of usefulness rather than of inspiration. It does not seem to have become an institution, to the young imagination, as *The Boy's Own Paper* was.

It is possible that one of the very features which gave *The Boy's Own Paper* that universal character was what a magazine for girls could not at that time contain – the school story. Once more general social history comes into this smaller record. The big girls' schools, about which magazine stories could be written, were only just beginning to exist – to exist in the sense of having a full and living tradition which was part of their natural atmosphere as well as of their routine. Girls had not become, in the school world, 'political animals' – they had not realized their little intimate City State which could enclose and condition half their adolescent life. There was to most of them no visible circumference of 'barbarians' outside their own civilization – no 'townees', 'louts', or whatever your own school slang called them esoterically: 'lesser breeds without the Law' they became after 1897. There was only a shy and almost incommunicable freemasonry of sex.

That is a state of things hard for males to realize at any time since Thomas Arnold's day, and not easy of comprehension to educated females for thirty years past. It takes at least one generation to establish an *ethos*, a community sense; and that number of years is about what, at the Diamond Jubilee, 'Higher' Education for girls had had in the way of bare existence. Miss Buss founded the 'North London Collegiate School for Ladies' (the first title) in 1850, in order 'to educate future mothers of families'. 'The Cheltenham Ladies College' started in 1853, and Miss Beale became headmistress in 1858. But Miss Buss's academy was a private venture till 1871, and the Girls' Public Day School Company was not formed till 1872, the year when Girton College was incorporated, with Miss Emily Davies as 'mistress'.

That is a very solid reason why worldlily exciting books for girls' reading, in any sense comparable to those lavishly provided for boys, could not even be written until the Great Queen was becoming an old woman. There was nothing for them to be written about, except religion, the domestic arts, Shakespeare and the musical glasses; and though those subjects can nearly all be made 'amusing', as in Charlotte Yonge's books, they tend to monotony. There was no intermediate scene of full or bright life, between the nursery and good works, between the home and the slightly dangerous neighbourhood of Mrs Henry Wood and Miss Braddon, except historical romance, which could be 'safely' presented to girls. As for oversea adventure, it was not so much undesirable or unsafe as inconceivable.

The long and short of it was that girls very often read better books than most boys – English literature – or else, more or less surreptitiously, the birthday and Christmas presents bestowed (usually haphazard, though not so heedlessly as now) upon their brothers. They had also the chance of minor fiction, like that of 'Edna Lyall', Annie Swan, Adeline Sergeant, Mrs Hungerford, L. T. Meade, to say nothing of the more intentionally domestic writers already mentioned (p. 289). Novels, in fact, were possibly more accessible to them than to the average schoolboy, because they were so much at home, and the circulating library, before fiction (other than the classics) was cheaply reprinted in great quantities, was widely pervasive: hence, in fact – cause or effect, as you wish – the alleged moral tyranny of the library proprietors.

The school-tale for girls appeared in increasing numbers in the twentieth century, and in the past decade, it is said, has been in considerable demand. There can be little doubt that, if it has not already done so, it will soon reach, like the corresponding type of fiction for boys, a rather lower age-level than that which it was intended originally to satisfy; and that the senior girl, like the senior boy, will prefer the adult novel, magazine (especially magazine) and newspaper to graded fiction. The change, or the shifting of the age-curve, is inevitable here too; and it is more obviously explicable in regard to girls because their general 'secondary' education has been a later development than that of boys. They too, however, have grown up more quickly than their mothers and grandmothers for other reasons than education alone. They too have read scores of newspapers, heard wireless, used telephones as a habit, driven cars, joined in war: all very obvious daily things, not one of which was obvious (cars and wireless not even invented) when *Treasure Island* and *King Solomon's Mines* rekindled the reality of romance, for girls as well as boys.

9

The upper division of children, then, began in the last quarter of Victoria's reign to experience rapid 'materialistic' growth. Its temper of mind, the sum of little reflections from daily life which grow into an habitual outlook, was perceptibly affected by the mutations of practical progress. Whether there was an equally profound spiritual metabolism at work it is probably not yet time to say. We are still too near the World War and its emetic effects to be confident as to which new thing is symptom, which essence, which mere accident; and in that War many children of the nineties perished.

But in the world of younger children something very like a change of mental outlook was also becoming visible. 'Children', as now distinct from 'boys' and 'girls', were clearly unbabyish: old-fashioned people said more precocious. The simplicities and unquestioned make-believe of folk-lore were no longer quite adequate: even the youngest horizon was not the nursery wall. Rudyard Kipling, though not so devastating in this sphere, is once more a valuable index to what was happening. *Stalky* had been preceded by the two *Jungle Books* (1894 and 1895).* Obviously animal study and human sociability for beasts was no new thing. The nurture of Mowgli had a legendary precedent in Roman history, and a vaguely historical one hinted at in the history of Peter the Wild Boy; while the philosophy of Uncle Remus now and then flickers up in gnomic comments on life. But the freshness of style, colour and vision was unmistakable. Even the occasional stridency of emphasis was a novel virtue. As for moral qualities, the Jungle Law was not an unfolding of the wonderful ways of Providence. It was what Life had reached by Social Evolution. Its results were a code of honour based on hard facts, with tooth and claw for its practical sanctions, but with a consciousness of responsibility which the Breed (white bipeds, preferably English) felt even more exaltedly. Courage, endurance, observation, good faith, dexterity, physical and mental fitness – all these were transmuted from routine virtues into an eager inspiration. The *Jungle Books* were not romance, not fiction, even; they were young life conscious of itself and its extraordinarily stimulating world. And, while 'boys', 'girls' and grown-ups could enjoy them, still younger readers could find them, after a little practice in the language (as *Uncle Remus* also had needed), enchanting fairy-tales. The two volumes were and are genuinely a modern children's book, with no predecessors in their kind.

Kim (1901, two years after *Stalky*) was more of a boys' and girls' book, in the new age-ratings, though, as it is the most serenely impersonal of all its author's longer stories, it is for all ages, like *Treasure Island* and *King Solomon's Mines*. But unlike them, it is almost epic, and it is also instinct with a maturer wisdom. It comes nearest, perhaps, of all modern books in the form of fiction, to an intimacy with the strange association of East and West in India: to the sympathetic sensitiveness of good Imperialism. But it is all about a boy.

Similarly, though not quite so gently, the two 'Puck' books – *Puck of Pook's Hill* (1906) and *Rewards and Fairies* (1910) – come very near to an intimacy with England itself; the England of Bishop Corbet and William Churne of Staffordshire, 'Merlin's Isle of Gramarye'. They are good history and good fiction, both of a kind not common in 1906. Contrast them with the allegorical scraps of history in *The Water-Babies* or with the historical fiction of Harrison Ainsworth, or of Kingsley himself. It is a different voice speaking – it would have to be that, obviously; but it is speaking almost to a different race. The children of the stories, whom one can accept readily enough as true young

---

* [Almost all the stories in Kipling's children's books appeared in magazines before being collected into volumes.]

contemporaries, are not like any that any earlier author had deliberately addressed; though you can conceive that Lewis Carroll really knew their language, and Catherine Sinclair a few words of it, and Stevenson a few more words, and that Shakespeare had heard both Autolycus and Mamilius using it to Puck.

And then in the crude avuncularity of the *Just So Stories* (1902), the same author is observed to be after all only a conventional 'Victorian' brought up to date, with rather more insight in his jocularity than his grandfathers would usually have shown, but still only pretending to be young, like them: a performer for the occasion.[2]

He is, at any rate, a writer who has influenced adult literature. In children's books he has been both symptomatic and an influence. His effect on the school story has been dealt with. The effect of the *Just So Stories* has probably been infinitesimal, beyond the crystallizing of some animal attributes. But the other

45. Kipling's own drawing of 'the cat that walked by himself', reproduced full-size from the Tauchnitz edition of *Just So Stories*, published at Leipzig in 1902, the same year as the first English edition.

five volumes all contain two elements which have grown strong in the younger juvenile literature of the last thirty years – the qualities of unlimited range for the imagination (very evident in *Kim* and in isolated scenes in the others), and of packed comprehensive thoughtfulness. Mowgli and Kim are thinking hard and vitally throughout; and Puck is thinking for those to whom he is showing all the majesty and littleness of England. The children's story has got right outside its own self, and yet has preserved its identity. The author and the reader are as nearly as possible the same person, but infinitely more capacious – more prehensile and assimilative perhaps – than ever before. Man and boy, woman and girl, can lawfully try, even hope, to comprehend anything and everything. Nature-study has become a kind of intimate romance, because man, the paragon of animals, *is* Nature. The brute creation has been elevated to companionship with flowers and the stars and ourselves. We learn very early now that

> in a moment clouds may be
> Dead, and instinct with deity.

Those words were written before the Diamond Jubilee, nevertheless.

10

In an odd way un-morality or 'materialism' – both terms are really far too harsh – stand out rather boldly in a by-product. The Moral Tale had overflowed into the Moral Game a hundred years before. In the nineties the moralless children's book had a parallel in the de-conventionalized toy. Naturalistic dolls had been invented before, especially those with mobile features. But now there came in poppets which had no connection with the stereotyped 'baby', nor yet with the established figures of the stage. New figures were invented, and grotesques copied from fictitious models. The first novelty of that kind, I think, was the Golliwog, given to the world in print in 1895 (with two 'g's' at the end of his name) by Florence and Bertha Upton, and hypostatized immediately afterwards. Other examples were the Teddy Bear and the Peter Rabbit. Later on less admirable images were set up from the facetious 'children's pages' of the daily newspapers.

Such book-toys, unlike the old Moral Games, do not set out to teach anything. It is not certain that they are even expected to be lovable, as dolls were. But that is their very significance. The kindergarten idea and Froebel's play-teaching had entered fully into education during the solid past century, but these products make it clear that instruction, however gentle, had not penetrated, as a consequence, the province of non-educational amusement. Golliwogs, though perhaps they hide the last wisp of Man Friday's ghost, have not a philosophy or a theory behind them. They are a document of the new freedom.

11

The fullest, most careless exhibition of that freedom, however, was neither in a toy nor a book, but in a play, *Peter Pan*, which for all its dramatic form has influenced the spirit of children's books, and the grown-up view of them, more powerfully than any other work except the *Alices* and Andersen's *Fairy Tales*.

It is legitimate, however, to call *Peter Pan* a book, even though it moved the theatre as much as the printed word. It originated in a book. The substance of James Matthew Barrie's play is in part in his desultory novel *The Little White Bird* (1902). The play was produced in England in 1904, and revived yearly thereafter. The relevant part of *The Little White Bird* came out separately as a book in 1906, entitled *Peter Pan in Kensington Gardens*, with striking and elaborate illustrations by Arthur Rackham. The text of the play (quite a different thing), with enchanting stage directions and a typical preface, was not published till 1928. But before then many 'adaptations' of its plot and incidents had been made, by permission, by other writers, and published as books; and Peter himself, with Wendy and some of their companions, had become almost as familiar proverbially as Alice. (Alice, by the way, though she must have had parents, was almost as silent about them as Peter about his: could that have been a possible situation before Victoria's reign, which is deemed so parental?)

The play was received with unbounded gladness. It was in no way like anything known before. Naturally today, after the lapse of a quarter of a century, the rapture which first greeted the new phenomenon has been slightly soiled. In 1904–6 Barrie was at the height of popularity, and some of the enthusiasm for anything he wrote was a little uncritical. Reaction, so far as there has been any, has not in the least diminished his claim to originality, but repetition has made some of even his freshest fancies appear sentimental or trivial, or both. It is necessary for those who are old enough to recall the performances – and the audiences – of 1904–5 to reassure themselves that they had truly seen a revolution (almost a revelation) in the presentation of imaginative ideas to children. So much of *Peter Pan* seems obvious now: so little of it was then.

When the play is considered in detail it becomes clear that one thing Barrie did was to remember a hundred small whimsies and scraps of dream and beloved traditional illusions which most of us have forgotten, though to us also they were once life itself. There is a precedent for almost everything in the romance: a precedent in the warm embers of memory rather than in fact. The dialogue and the stage-business both made the old fire glow again, with an unearthly vividness which they had never quite possessed when they were first lit. Probably the Never Land, for instance – a genuine Australian name – had come to Barrie, and to boys of many lustres before him, from some arid Parleyish book, or even from a talkative geography of about 1820 or so, when Australia was becoming exciting. The idea of dispersing wolves by looking through your legs at them is an old traveller's tale. Pirates we knew all about ever since Morgan sacked Panama or Drake took the *Cacafuego*. Lagoons were in books like Ballantyne's *Coral Island*, for which, in 1913, Barrie wrote an Introduction with the glorious beginning: 'To be born is to be wrecked on an island.' Peter crying cockadoodle-doo is Jim Hawkins in *Treasure Island* or, more artifically, Capt. Boldheart in Dickens's *Holiday Romance*. Flying is eminent in *Peter Wilkins*. Peter's elusive shadow is to be found in *Peter Schlemihl* (translated for children by William Howitt), as well as in *A Child's Garden of Verses*: indeed, Stevenson's poems contain almost in themselves alone enough raw material for the play. The crocodile might be a recollection of Waterton's travels. Red Indians are Fenimore Cooper. And so on. Barrie's preface (or rather 'Dedication') to the printed play shows the humorous windings of his mind at work.

Then again, some of the English sentiment was common form; perhaps too common in places. The ritual of going to bed, the anxiety about a dress tie, the mother-love (except a deplorable scene of Beautiful Mothers which I think appeared in only one season of the play's annual 'runs'), the song of birds at sunset – these had been in books, in poetry and in plays often enough before. There was little throughout that a well-read person could feel sure he had never read, seen, or heard before – by itself. The change – a transformation scene, in the theatre sense – wrought by Barrie was in uniting all the particular gleams of memory into one universal radiance. He made the old young as they watched his puppets: he made the young live the stage-play visibly, as they lived it in the secrecy of their minds by themselves. It was not acting that was taking place for an audience: it was the all-conquering reality of fairyland, with not an atom of afterthought or seriousness prepense.

It does not matter if today the whole crowd of spectators does not clap its hands at Peter's impassioned plea for faith in fairies. What matters historically is that Barrie made all but shrivelled pedagogues see the value, even the necessity, of that nonsensical creed. And the influence of his concrete presentation has travelled far beyond the stage. He was no entire innovator as, in a sense, Lewis Carroll was. But he had the almost sudden effect of one in the way in which *Peter Pan* surprised, stirred and enlightened that slow-moving, thorough-going organism, the English mind. We had thought of his ideas for ourselves, now and then, here and there. We knew children really had these fancies, and that they were beneficial, not harmful. But an inhibition, a social fog, a Baconian Idol, had prevented us from being clear-headed and kept us silent.

12

Peter Pan set a fashion, or stimulated new ideas, in more ways than one. It had a commercial effect on the book-trade which was eloquent of child glorification. The volume called *Peter Pan in Kensington Gardens* was produced in a style of lavishness not hitherto attempted in such a direction, except in its immediate predecessor *Rip Van Winkle* (1905). It was followed by others – by no means all for children – on a similar scale, and these expensive compilations, usually consisting of a previously published text with elaborate coloured illustrations by artists either well known or expected to be collectable, became regular 'Christmas gift-books' for several seasons.

The best of these works could be claimed as examples of the twentieth-century revival of fine book-production: of the harmonious union of all the parties to the creation of a printed book – the type-designer, the artist, the printer of type and pictures, the binder and, in a few instances, the author. The fact that the author was as a rule dead and no longer protected by copyright gave the performance one touch of virtuosity. And the further fact that within a few years the number of such books competitively produced exhausted the public purse – that is to say, exceeded the number of possible ordinary purchasers – suggests that both the publisher and the buyer had been a little sheep-like, and had not had true uplift in their souls. But the vogue had its sequel in better – and cheaper – books for children, in respect of fineness of production; in popularizing artistic work of a not wholly routine kind; in emphasizing the modern mechanical resources of the colour-printers, block-makers, and other artistic craftsmen. And it had its historical value as showing that, even if there was a good deal of the humbug of fashion in such temporary popularity, there was at least no obstacle to treating children as worthy of loveliness, not to say aesthetic luxury: on the contrary, the well-to-do classes almost forced their offspring into a surfeit.

The great advance in the mechanical processes of illustration, in fact – the effect of which was by no means only mechanical, because they gave the artist a range, an ease, a liberty, he had never even imagined before, in illustrating books within set forms – the great mechanical advance also changed to some extent the general public conception of children's books. Stories, as such, whatever the age of the reader aimed at, still had, and have, pictures of particular scenes or situations described in the text of the book, at fairly regular intervals: 'illustrations', that is to say, in the old sense. Since the sixties, these illustrations had often shared, almost to a moiety, the prestige of a book. But now, especially in books for younger readers, the facilities for reproduction were so varied that the pictures as often as not dominated the text – as in those very 'toy-books' which have just been mentioned. A child's book – for 'boys', 'girls' and 'babies' – now *must* have illustrations. If not, it is a grown-up book, or a schoolbook. (Of course the advantage of the improvements in boys' and girls' books about inventions, travel, science, and the like provision for the romance of knowledge, are obvious.) That is probably a gain, on the whole. Illustration certainly lights up, as its name enjoins, when it is well done. It also tends to make reading easy. Commercially, it aids the magazine and newspaper against the book. But though one may rejoice at relief from the drab past, it is by no means unarguable that, as Mr de la Mare has said, 'a good deal of the nursery literature of our own day is as silly, if not worse, as theirs was dismal'.

There was also, from *Peter Pan*, a further effect, so far as children were concerned – its result in the theatre, partly fashionable, but genuine in intention, because it implied faith, the financial risks of the stage being infinitely heavier than those of books. *Peter Pan* itself became a regular Christmas production, year by year; and the old-fashioned Victorian pantomime, along with the Harlequinade, being already moribund, for a number of reasons little relevant here, it was perceived that plays meant specially for children were a necessity – in fact, there eventually appeared a theatre specially for children. *Pinkie and the Fairies, Where the Rainbow Ends, Alice* adaptations, *Treasure Island* on stage may all be called in some sort the offspring of *Peter Pan*. They cannot be discussed in these pages, because they are not books, any more than toys are books. But their existence at this particular period is evidence of exactly the same spirit as was informing children's books at the same time. The fullest conception of that spirit can be gained by repeating a few words from an earlier quotation (p. 217):

MRS TALBOT. I should not have been allowed to have undertaken a part in any theatrical performance . . . At other times I used to fancy I could meet in those woods with some of the Knights and Damsels that Spenser tells us of . . .
   GEORGE. Did you really believe, then, that such persons existed?
   MRS TALBOT. No.

Exactly one hundred years after Charlotte Smith wrote that, Peter Pan cried for the first time to an electrified audience, in order that he might save the fairy Tinker Bell, '*Do* you believe?' and saved her by their rhapsodical faith.

13

But neither Kipling nor Barrie was a lonely magician, nor did either lack disciples. To select by name even half-a-dozen authors who wrote very much in the spirit of those eminent prophets – both before and after they prophesied – would be to enter upon an amount of contemporary criticism which would be unsuitable here. It is incontrovertible, whatever one thinks about details of this, that, or the other book, that Kipling and Barrie were, after Lewis Carroll – forty years after the first *Alice* – the most prominent revolutionaries in the history of modern children's books. That does not mean that they caused or intended a revolution: and it ignores one further aspect of the change that came as Victoria's reign grew old and yet older. But they were more clearly than other writers powerful in their sphere, individual voices in a murmuring crowd which had not, in 1897–1904, become a confused roar. At first they were not shouting with the largest crowd: it gathered round them; they are almost 'noises off' now.

There were other voices, not wholly theirs, but singing like songs in their way. There was, for example, Kenneth Grahame discovering another Wonderland in *The Wind in the Willows* (1908 – dramatized by A. A. Milne in 1929), after showing in *Pagan Papers* (1893), *The Golden Age* (1895) and *Dream Days*

(1898) that he knew how far aloof Olympus was from the serious reality of child existence. In writing about children, in the first three books, he revealed that he could still feel as a child himself, though as a writer he was serenely Olympian in style. In *The Wind in the Willows* he simply enjoyed himself, though he indulged the poet in him in two passages of the finest modern English prose.* Not very far from him, though a little more mundane, inclined to be a trifle half-critical, almost, of her own characters, was 'E. Nesbit', indicating that the Bastable family, in their series of domestic adventures, could be as irresponsible as the children in *Holiday House*, as ingenious as, though more pleasant than, *Stalky and Co.*, and sometimes as discreet as Alice herself. She introduced a more genuine ease of family humour into her stories than anyone since Catherine Sinclair. There were joyful mockers like Hilaire Belloc, turning un-morality into a kind of inverted moral laughter in *The Bad Child's Book of Beasts* (1896) and that work which echoes in its title – if nowhere else – the admonitory Elizabeth Turner: *Cautionary Tales for Children* (1907). There were a score of others all deserving of notice, all lasting in popular favour for a decade or more (a long period in these matters), and leading on to justly esteemed writers of the Neo-Georgian thirties whom it would be invidious to name. There was no shade of Free Thought for Infant Minds which the Edwardian era did not welcome and develop.

Free Thought, that is, in subject-matter, and in reflection about it. It is not so clear that even these comparative innovators used absolutely free imagination. All through the history of English children's books the higher imagination, that starts with almost direct sensation and expresses itself in direct, unassociated, 'complex'-free reaction, has been hard to descry. It is the essence of Blake. It is the greater part of Christina Rossetti. In a sense, it is the root of pure nonsense, England's supreme gift to literature; but nonsense generally implies a standard for its incongruities, and the free imagination has no standards.

It is in that direction, possibly, that the future vision of our children's books will turn. Because it has been so rarely sought, so little followed even in the early twentieth-century sunrise of liberty, the gleam of poetry for children in the period has here been left till the last. It is clear in a writer who now is judged by standards other than that Victorian acclaim which greeted his technique and his

---

* Just after these words were finally revised, I saw the news that Kenneth Grahame died suddenly, on July 6, 1932. The simple facts of his life were that he was born in Edinburgh in 1859, joined the staff of the Bank of England in 1878, was Secretary to the Bank from 1898 to 1908, was married in 1899, and had one son who died as an undergraduate at Oxford. *The Wind in the Willows* was begun for the pleasure of this boy. (To me it had one special interest, that it was one of the first books I ever reviewed – with so much joy that the notice had to be curbed and shortened.) In its first twenty years the book went into thirty editions, in spite of the lukewarm critics.

Grahame's personal character is graciously and movingly described in a letter to *The Times* (July 16, 1932) by Sir Arthur Quiller-Couch, who, as 'Q', the author of *Dead Man's Rock* (1887), *The Splendid Spur* (1889) and other novels for boy-men, apart from graver work, has been almost as near the affections of adventurous readers as Stevenson himself.

literary accomplishment – the author of *Treasure Island*, which itself we have now perceived to be more than a thundering good yarn.

A Child's Garden of Verses contains its warranty and a criticism of itself in its title. It *is* a garden, full of natural flowers growing from wind-borne seeds. It is a child's garden. Metrically, its verse is deliciously modulated for its purpose. But the title as a whole phrase has something of grown-up after-thinking invention in it; not perhaps an excuse, but a touch of conscious description. Yet it is true that 'every poem in *A Child's Garden of Verses* was a bit out of his own childhood'. There are few thoughts in that little 1885 volume of *Penny Whistles* (the first title used in a privately printed volume in 1883) that children have not felt, even though here and there the grown-up can be detected using his literary art to express them. There is even the good little moral infant in them:

> A child should always say what's true
> And speak when he is spoken to,
> And behave mannerly at table . . .

are lines that Ann and Jane Taylor could have written, and that R.L.S. may, in childhood, have conceived from some such adult inspiration.[3] But it was almost a whimsical grown-up who added the fourth-line afterthought:

> At least as far as he is able.

But while it needed more mature skill to produce the metre and phrasing of *Pirate Story*, *My Shadow*, *Escape at Bedtime* and *North-West Passage*, the substance is in the fabric of a child's mind – of the child who was always in Stevenson, who reappeared, as it were to order, in the *Moral Emblems* and Davos booklets compiled for and with the aid of the boy Lloyd Osbourne. There was nothing, it is true, about deep intimations of immortality such as, without being told by Wordsworth, we should have guessed from Blake that children often feel. Nothing also, of the frustrate child-bearing tenderness of some of the poems in *Sing-Song*. The child is always, more or less, in an ordinary English garden, not Paradise. But there was a great deal of what is behind *Peter Pan* – gladness and wonder, which the spoken word on the stage must almost always kill if it attempts anything more than the most tenuous explicitness.

The flowers in such a Garden are not exotic, not forced; neither are they made of wax or paper or linen with wire ribs. Ninety per cent of all verse written for children before the last quarter of the nineteenth century was poetry-substitute, manufactured in good faith, but in a deliberate purposeful way. It was not perceived that children were their own spontaneous poets – the makers of their own world of imagination, each after his quality: or conversely, that while poetry may vary in content according to the years of experience, experience in a worldly sense is not its essence, nor explanation to less perceptive persons a condition of its existence.

That has been perceived since. It was seen, not for the benefit of children, but about them, by Kenneth Grahame. Walter de la Mare, A. A. Milne, and others have observed it *for* children, and have written, as nearly as adult human beings can, such poetry as children themselves may use without words. But before Stevenson, save for a chance line or two, hardly a verse had been written as a child, given word-skill, might have written it; except by Blake, Christina Rossetti, and, at odd seconds, William Brighty Rands. Herrick, the simpler lyrists, the more thought-free picture-poems of Wordsworth, Shelley, Arnold – these were long considered 'grown-up'. It was left for the most serious of all grown-up epochs, the Victorian, to break down for good and all, in poetry as well as in prose, the high fence that for centuries shut in the imagination of mankind at the very stage of its periodic growth when it is most naturally fitted to be free.

'He told me his dreams......' ISAAC WATTS

APPENDIX 1

Some Additional Notes on Victorian and Edwardian Times

1

'The longer I live', wrote Robert Bloomfield in 1817, 'the more I am convinced of the importance of children's books'. In thus launching the second edition of *The History of Little Davy's New Hat* upon his public he asked too that he might be remembered, along with the exalted names of his betters, for helping to turn the literary scale 'in favour of your children and mine'.

The passage is significant for several reasons. To start with, it suggests the widening acceptance of children's books as an essential part of a child's upbringing – not a matter that could be taken for granted a generation earlier. Secondly, Bloomfield used it to justify a dedicated scrutiny by adults of the books published for the young. Furthermore, by naming those 'exalted betters', who include Dr Watts, Mrs Barbauld, Mrs Trimmer and Maria Edgeworth, 'the farmer's boy' aligns his untutored, 'secular' thinking about children's reading with that of writers who developed a mode of address *to* children out of their own theories about child education. The time had gone that saw children's books as an unfrequented preserve on the edge of literature, visited only by specialists of one sort or another. They are here becoming an in-take where all and sundry may choose to go and where the formulation of ready personal opinions will become a regular occupation. A new self-consciousness has burgeoned, and this breeds a new self-confidence. The stage is set for that diversity of performance which is to be such a feature of children's book production during the latter part of the nineteenth century.

2

The erratic growth of this self-confidence, and many of the outstanding productions that it engendered, have been charted in the foregoing pages. But such is the scale of activity, particularly in the years from *Alice* to the outbreak of the Great War, that it may be helpful to characterize events from a different, more distant standpoint in order to show where the idea of the importance of children's books led in the late nineteenth and early twentieth century.

Before doing so, however, it is necessary to stress the relationship between the expansion of production and the emergence of 'publishing' as an activity largely separate from 'bookselling'. For, while it is true that entrepreneurs like the Newberys and John Harris I, Marshall and Johnson are important for the way in which they developed children's 'lists', they did this only as part of their general trade activity and they did it on the small scale of men working within the restraints of hand-printing. With the arrival first of the iron press in 1800 and then, soon after, of mechanical power, a 'new technology' intruded upon an ancient industry. Developments in the associated trades of paper-making, type-founding and setting, and book-binding allowed an enormous expansion in edition-runs and in the number of new books and magazines that might be projected or printed. At the same time the mechanization of transport, which led to the increasing accessibility of provincial towns for companies based in London, placed new emphasis upon the skills of the salesman and confirmed that, so far as books were concerned, commercial success for 'publishers' would lie in their concentration on production and 'marketing' rather than in running retail establishments.

It is perhaps not altogether fanciful to see in the setting-up of the Religious Tract Society at the beginning of the nineteenth century an early example of this new style of publishing activity. It is true that the Society was founded and motivated by extra-trade considerations; nevertheless, by its very efficiency in employing printers and devising a distribution network it was behaving in a way that would be followed by commercial publishers later on. Moreover the sheer size of its publishing programme caused it to become itself a 'professional' publishing house as the century progressed, and to influence other religious organizations – most importantly the Society for Promoting Christian Know-ledge – so that they became business, as well as theological, competitors.

Certainly any survey of the Victorian trade in children's books cannot neglect the role of these societies, by virtue of their ubiquity as much as anything else. From publishing tracts they quickly progressed to publishing magazines and books – educational and general, in paper or in cloth – and by the second half of the century their products were everywhere. (In the second edition of Whitak-er's *Reference Catalogue of Current Literature* (1875) the R.T.S. section occupied forty closely printed pages, many in double-column or triple-column, showing a colossal range of goods: books, tracts, magazines, coloured pictures, illuminated tablets, etc., with the books ranging from the secularism of Kingston's *Captain Cook* to a multitude of series for Sunday Schools, Bible classes, temperance meetings, and so on. The SPCK's catalogue of general publications, i.e. excluding Bibles and tracts, was forty-two pages long and contained rather more strictly schoolroom material, including manuals of elementary science.)

Nor were these books all negligible in terms of their literary artistry or their effect on a child readership. It has already been pointed out that the S.P.C.K. published much of the work of that sensitive writer Juliana Horatia Ewing, and that the Religious Tract Society was the initiator of those two popular magazines the *Boy's* and the *Girl's Own Paper*, whose serials were often later turned into books, a notable example being the stories of Talbot Baines Reed. Also, however, it was responsible for several works which, from the quantity of their editions, must be accounted among the major best-sellers of the century. 'Hesba Stretton' – for all the epithet 'pietistic' on p. 289 above – produced in *Jessica's First Prayer* (1867; 1866 in *Sunday at Home*) a book which has been found in over forty different printings or series-bindings and to which Richard Altick, in his *English Common Reader*, assigns a sale of over 1,500,000 copies in 'unspecified space of time'. Later on Mrs O. F. Walton, with her *Peep Behind the Scenes* (R.T.S. 1877), jerked happily remembered tears from several generations of readers and presented the student of children's books with one of those examples of extraordinary survival. Just as the R.T.S. preserved for the nineteenth century editions of Janeway's *Token for Children* and Bunyan's *Divine Emblems*, so its relics in the twentieth century – the Lutterworth Press – have sustained into the 1980s children's editions of Mrs Walton's lachrymose

46. Mabel's First Lesson in Organ Grinding. (a) A woodcut frontispiece from an early edition of *Christie's Old Organ* (*c.* 1877) and (b) the same theme used in a four-colour half-tone for the cover of a large format picture-book version (*c.* 1900). Original size 10½ by 8 in.

Peep and her almost equally famous *Christie's Old Organ* (1874).

As organizations capable of calling upon funds and voluntary labour outside the normal constraints of commerce, the religious societies cannot stand as typical examples of this new nineteenth-century phenomenon: the publisher pure and simple. (Indeed, once such creatures had emerged they tended to resent the element of subsidy in the societies' business activities.) Nevertheless, the model they present of a house primarily concerned with the editing, production, wholesaling and advertising of products may stand as typical of the new function of the publisher in the age of machine printing. Through the first fifty years of the century the specialized attention given to the manufacture and national distribution of books led several famous 'booksellers' like Longman, Murray and Rivington to redefine themselves as 'publishers' as we now understand the word, and in the second fifty years the British book-trade took on the character which it preserved up to the arrival of another 'new technology' at the end of the twentieth century.

Needless to say, those engaged in the special activity of publishing, in the ebullient expansionist atmosphere of the times, found themselves called upon to develop special lines of business – an economic determinant of incalculable influence on the development of English children's literature. For not only did some firms see the great potential of a children's list, but the competition engendered by specialist publishing for children also encouraged a variety of talents. There was hospitality for every kind of work, from the derivative to the experimental, in both writing and illustration.

A firm like Macmillan's – watchful but alive to the authentic voices of the story-teller – could bring into a warehouse stocked with some of the most respectable academic and theological works of the age *Tom Brown's Schooldays* and *Alice's Adventures in Wonderland*, *The Water Babies* and the Cranes' *Grimm*; and throughout the period of his (immensely profitable) copyright they were to preserve a standard edition of that giant among children's book authors, Rudyard Kipling.

On the other hand – graduating not from Presbyterian rectitude, but from the grubby work of the remainder merchant – there came George Routledge. Almost as soon as he entered publishing proper in 1843 he began to build upon his awareness of the potential of a huge popular market and, along with his phenomenal *Railway Library* he published the first of his toy-book series and his reprints of children's classics. By 1875 he could issue a *Catalogue of a Thousand Juvenile Books*. Arranged by price, it began with Mrs Webb's *Naomi; or the last days of Jerusalem*, with steel plates, at 12s. 6d. and ended up with 'Nursery Literature' at a penny or twopence a title; and within this scale could be found representatives of the eighteenth century (*Sandford and Merton, Evenings at Home, The Parent's Assistant* – all with coloured illustrations at 3s. 6d. each) and of the exciting present: Walter Crane heading a list that was soon to include some of the most famous picture-books of the century. And alongside Routledge there were such lesser rivals in the toy-book trade as Ward, Lock and Nelson (but each with other specialities too like Australiana or evangelical works); there was Dean and Son, foremost for their amazing range of gimmickry – Flexible-Faced Story Books, Scenic Effect Books, Spring Projecting Picture Books, Transparent Dioramic Pages etc. (they were rivalled towards the end of the century by the prolific lithographic importations of the Bavarian firm of Nister); there was also Cassell's, growing rich on part-issues, magazines, and semi-educational publishing; and from 1865 onwards, Frederick Warne, the one time partner of George Routledge, then founder of his own house, and finally purchaser of many of the Routledge children's titles – except for some oddities like *Uncle Remus* and *Struwwelpeter* – when that firm relinquished them in favour of the severer task of publishing monographs on science and psychology. And beneath, or around, these giants there flourished, or staggered, or perished a host of lesser firms – Strahan, say, flaring briefly in the sixties and early seventies, or Fisher Unwin, managing almost single-handed an elegant little list at the turn of the century, or that attractive rogue Grant Richards, in the same period, issuing a bevy of lively 'modern' titles: *Uncle Lubin* (1902) by Heath Robinson, who made his mark as a writer and illustrator for children before he ever turned to comic inventions; *Only Toys!* (1903), a satiric domestic tale by 'F. Anstey'; and of course *The Dumpy Books*, hospitable to old classics like Elizabeth Turner's *Cautionary Stories* (1897), and new ones like Helen Bannerman's *Little Black Sambo* (1899).

3

Incontestably the vigour of British publishing in the nineteenth century was a central factor in the development of what was surely the most diverse children's literature in the world – despite the depressions of the 1870s and the 1880s and the bad times for bookselling that preceded the negotiation of the Net Book Agreement in 1900. At the same time this literature could not be created without an equally responsive market and – unlike the expansive activity in the mid twentieth century, which was so dependent on 'institutional buying' – the Victorian trade centred upon the home.

The multifarious magazines, which were such an important part of the foundations of the children's book industry, are the most obvious manifestation of the way in which the publishers focussed on a family audience (in this case, too, prompted by the Sabbatarian tradition of Sunday reading). Alongside these, though, there is plenty of evidence that the editorial policy of most publishers was based on a reckoning that books were bought to go into homes – note for instance the prevalence of terms like 'nursery literature', 'toy books', 'movables' etc.; the wording of advertising: 'for the family circle', 'for the fireside'; and the regular build-up of publishing through the autumn months to the near hysterical exploitation of 'the Christmas trade'.

It is a focus which is in part responsible for the distinctive appearance and context of many of the prestige books of the period. The prodigal variety of illustrated books and baroque bindings during the high-Victorian period clearly presupposes the drawing-room as the place where books shall be read, just as the vogue for ostentatious colour-plate books during the Edwardian period necessarily implies private rather than public ownership. To the stern critic who requires balance between what a text says and the way it is presented, there may be much to deplore – or at least discuss – in this emphasis on the visual, but there can be no doubt that the quest for some individual quality of attractiveness during this phase produced a vastly more stimulating book-environment than occurred in more constricted times. Technical necessity imposed limits on the eighteenth-century producer's enterprise; economic necessity and a dependence on libraries rather than homes has reduced the late twentieth century to an almost equivalent espousal of dull uniformity.

This is not, of course, to say that there was no market for children's books beyond that of the family. A full history of Victorian publishing would need to explore a complex set of relationships that developed between the producers of children's books and a variety of other customers – even leaving aside the exploitation of foreign and colonial markets. The gradual emergence of 'education for all' that led, through the growth of church-aided and other charity schools, to the 1870 Education Act is one feature in the new prospect that was opening up for children's books.* And the arrival on the statute book of the Public Libraries Act in 1850 is another. The evidence would suggest, however, that these institutions played nothing like the part where children's books are concerned that Mr Mudie and the circulating libraries did for adult books. Their day was to come in the twentieth century – chiefly after the end of our period and not without powerful influence from the other side of the Atlantic. For although the public library movement in Britain was, from the first, aware of its responsibilities towards children, it gives the impression of being very slow and circumspect in its methods. At a time when Anne Carroll Moore – not without the *Schwärmerei* typical of lady-librarians of her generation – was leading the movement to set up Children's Rooms in the public libraries of the United States,† English librarians were still much preoccupied with closed access systems and the need for youthful readers to wash their hands thoroughly.

But if the collections of 'trade' children's books in schools or public libraries were never much more than rudimentary in England at this time there was nevertheless one profoundly influential role that institutions played in the market, a role related not to their own provision of books but, once more, to 'books in the home'. This, of course, was the universal exploitation of 'the reward'.

Books as prizes for children have a history almost as long as the literature itself. (Did not Isaac Watts in 1715 commend to 'all that are concerned in the Education of Children' the idea that his *Divine Songs* might be given to children as a reward for their learning ten or twenty of the poems in it?) But it was the Victorians who built up a standard trade in prizes and who discovered in series published for that purpose a firm annual turnover that would permit more experimental publishing to be done. After more than a hundred years of neglect or destruction books in these prize series are legion – a random sampling from the shelves of second-hand dealers producing almost instantaneously:

*   Thomas Galpin, says Simon Nowell-Smith in *The House of Cassell* (1958), 'used to quote the current official figure of elementary school children as the Cassell constituency'.

†   Miss Moore was appointed head of the children's department at the Pratt Free Library, Brooklyn in 1896 and moved to her position of central influence at the New York Public Library in 1906.

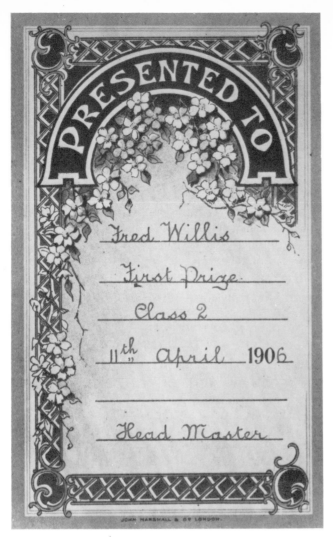

47. Lithographed prize label in pink, green and gilt. It appears in a copy of *Kilgorman; a story of Ireland in 1798* (1895), Talbot Baines Reed's last book.

1. Mrs Sherwood's *History of the Fairchild Family* in Nisbet's Pilgrim Series (*c.* 1890) with lists of other 'Select Series of Books Suitable for Presents and Prizes' like *The Chimes* (ten titles at 3*s.* 6*d.* each), *The Laurel* (ten titles at 2*s.* 6*d.* each), *The Sunshine* (nine titles at 2*s.* each) and so on.
2. E. Wetherell's *The Wide Wide World* 'Complete Edition': no. 10 of the ninety-one titles in Ward Lock's *Royal* series, with a catalogue of other 'Gift Books, Prizes and Rewards' (*c.* 1900).
3. Edward Garrett's *Equal to the Occasion* (*c.* 1905), published by the now little-known Edinburgh firm of Oliphant, Anderson and Ferrier, with a handsome *art nouveau* binding and a sixteen-page catalogue of 'Books for Gifts and Prizes to Young People' with 278 titles in it.

Alternative evidence, full of tiny insights into the lives of children in the past, comes from observation of the often amazingly ornate labels pasted into these books: 'to Harry Burnham for Good Conduct, Regularity and Diligence at Lessons', wrote J. Churchill, master of Bromley Boys' School, at 'Xmas 1901' in a copy of the anonymous *Baron and Squire* in Nisbet's *Boy's Holiday Library*; 'to Cadet J. Whalley for an Essay on Encouragement of Flower of Leigh', said the Order of the Sons of Temperance on an extraordinarily ugly label stuck in Talbot Baines Reed's *The Willoughby Captains* (1914); and – what an indomitable survivor – *Foxe's Book of Martyrs*, with eleven illustrations, given to Winnie Goldsworthy by the Barry Road Wesleyan Sunday School 'for regular attendance' in March 1900.

What this giving of rewards may have meant to families can perhaps be glimpsed in a bundle of books bought in 1978 at five pence a copy from a stall in Yorkshire, representing (probably only part of) the literature entering one household via the reward hand-outs of the Hawes Church Sunday School: *Ruth Willis; or, Living for Others* (S.P.C.K., 1877 – the dates are those of the award); *The New Boy at Merriton* by Julia Goddard (Blackie, 1885 – with a coloured frontispiece); *Wings and Stings* by A.L.O.E. (Nelson, 1887 – the book dated 1888); *Lena Graham* by Cecilia Selby Lowndes (Warne, 1887 – with sepia-tinted illustrations); *The Pearl of Contentment* by Madeline Leslie (Oliphant, Anderson, 1891 – with a horrid chromolitho frontispiece); Hans Christian Andersen, *The Jewish Maiden and Other Stories* (Ward, Lock, 1892 – excerpted from the publisher's complete edition, for the pages disconcertingly run from 478–531); and *Bravely Borne* by L C. Silke (R.T.S., 1896). Thus by zealous attendance at Sunday School and the learning of catechisms was a family's home library haphazardly put together.

4

Concomitant with the expansion of trade and the widening accessibility of children's books of all kinds it is only natural to find a like increase in their investigation by adults, and – in a slightly perverse sense – it is this which really marks the coming-of-age of children's literature. As with almost any activity that requires some degree of cerebration – whether cookery or chemistry – one can discern an evolution from localized, unco-ordinated activity, through stages of increasingly sophisticated experiment, towards a point where definitions become possible and the 'subject' emerges as capable of codified analysis. The middle decades of the nineteenth century were the years which saw children's literature emerging as a discrete 'subject' in this sense.*

To Mrs Trimmer, of course, belongs the credit for attempting the first systematic assessment of children's literature from a given critical standpoint. *The Guardian of Education*, in the brief time that she was able to labour at it

---

* This point is echoed by Darton and Sawyer in their Preface to *English Books* (1927) where they speak of book-collecting as having reached the stage when it has degenerated, or improved, into a scientific pursuit 'requiring accurate knowledge as well as affectionate appreciation'.

(1802–6), is remarkable for the care with which it elucidates a critical theory and the consistancy with which it applies it. That the theory now seems aberrant is not a matter so much for scorn as for a more balanced awareness of our own reigning dogmas. She was however a lone voice, as was remarked by the anonymous editor of *The Juvenile Review* (published by N. Hailes in 1817), who sought to bring her work up to date through two volumes of 'remarks on books' – one for children under eight and the other for children from eight to twelve. He – or more probably she – adopted a strong Trimmer-esque line, condemning, for instance, Tabart's delectable *Songs for the Nursery* for 'filling the mind with false ideas' and praising the Taylors' more morally instructive *Rhymes*.(The moral responsibilities of adults was the burden too of Robert Bloomfield's Preface noted at the start of this Appendix. If a children's book inculcates 'false principles, the pride of wealth, or . . . superstition, let them, for mercy's sake, use it for lighting the fire'.)

In those early decades of the century most comment on children's books seems to have been the result of brief spurts of critical activity of this kind (witness too for instance the lengthy round-up articles in magazines, where new books are assessed in the light of a more general commentary).* These are all examples of sporadic, highly personalized comment,[1] which are 'amateur' in the sense that they lack a continuing commitment to their subject.

The break-through came in 1869 with the appearance of three linked articles by Charlotte Yonge in *Macmillan's Magazine* (vol. xx, July–September). Miss Yonge had already established a central place for herself as a writer of children's books and as a commentator in her magazine *The Monthly Packet* (see above pp. 288–9), and in these three articles she emerged as the first truly engaged critic since Sarah Trimmer. In the modest compass allowed her by the form she chose to write in, she places contemporary fiction for children into historical perspective and knits into her descriptions a series of astute critical remarks. Her facts may not be all that one can desire (she places John Marshall in St Paul's Churchyard, and attributes *The Swiss Family Robinson* to 'Kampe'), but there is a positive force behind her arguments as she reveals herself as the first of a line of pragmatic critics that stretches forward to the present time. Indeed, she treads the tight-rope between literary criticism and populism with considerably more agility than some of her modern successors, and a number of her observations – on the prevalence and weakness of writing books for a particular class of reader, for instance – are as relevant to the present as they were to the past. She was to follow these articles later with an advisory book list of a kind much loved by children's book reviewers ever since: *What Books to Lend and What to Give*, published by the National Society's Repository in 1887. This society was the charitable one founded by Andrew Bell 'for educating children in the principles of the Established Church'.

---

* Examples of these are the anonymous article in the *London and Westminster Review*, vol XXXIII, 1840, pp. 137–62; and the famous article in the *Quarterly Review*, vol. LXXIV, 1844, pp. 1–26, assumed to be by Elizabeth Rigby.

From 1869 onwards the volume of discussion of children's books grew steadily year by year, so that the foundations were laid for a fuller understanding of both the facts of the matter and the vexed question of techniques – for the fluctuating emphases on instruction and amusement are always with us. The first (and for a long time only) lengthy historical account was Mrs E. M. Field's *The Child and his Book* (1891) and the first lengthy discussion of contemporary practice was Edward Salmon's *Juvenile Literature as it is* (1888) – and, while it is strange that neither of these writers persevered with their work, even though the first lived till 1941 and the second till 1955, these accounts point towards a time when children's books are to be accepted as a subject for adult curiosity[2] as legitimate as other forms of literature (and rather more demanding than their simple contents might suggest). Whether their authors would have accepted the need for world-wide conferences on children's books, or for the institutionalizing of the subject in university courses – in America, if not in Britain – is a matter for conjecture only.

5

Whatever the preoccupations of historians or critics, however, their activities occurred largely at the edges of the field of action. (Their most energetic intrusion into the centre was in children's books themselves: Jo weeping over *The Wide, Wide World* in an apple tree, Dan and Una bringing *Asgard* and Ballantyne and Macaulay into their adventures into the past; the Bastables forever commenting on the soppiness of *Ministering Children*, say, or the glories of Kipling.) Nevertheless the growth of critical awareness, like the growth of publishing activity itself, fostered an atmosphere which was conducive to self-expression – and there is no better evidence for the confidence which the creators of children's books had in their – relatively new – craft than the riches that accrued during the last years of the Victorian period and the first decade of the twentieth century.

Beatrix Potter could almost stand for everyone. As is well known, her first book, *The Tale of Peter Rabbit*, originated as a story told in a letter to a child. This fact, and the standard nursery device of 'bunnies' behaving like people, suggest to the unwary nothing more than the successful exploitation of a predictable cosiness. But the truth, of course, is different. There is first the determination of sheltered Miss Potter to convert her letter to a book and to publish it come what may – so that *Peter Rabbit* first appeared in a privately published edition of 250 copies (1901) before a publisher was persuaded of its potential. And this simply mirrors the determination of the story-teller's voice, not to follow the stereotyped tones of the standard bedtime story, but very consciously to control the pace and nuances of the prose.

For all its fame, *Peter Rabbit* is not the peak of Beatrix Potter's achievement and the shelf-full of tales she wrote between 1900 and 1918 contains more

48. '. . . put in a pie by Mrs. McGregor'. Four-colour half-tone of a picture by Beatrix Potter
for the first trade edition of *The Tale of Peter Rabbit* (a). Not only is the drawing poor, but
the content was deemed to be frightening and the illustration was soon withdrawn.
Nevertheless it made an unexpected reappearance in the first American edition of the
book (b), published in Philadelphia in 1904 (one of 'Altemus' Wee Books for Wee
Folks'). Warne's had failed to copyright *Peter Rabbit* in America, hence the changed
graphic style of the picture, and the appearance on the scene of the features of a very
badly proportioned Mr McGregor.

327

variety than its appearance of uniformity implies.* There were little anecdotes, like the two published as folding panoramas in a wallet, there were rhyme books and semi-traditional stories, and there were stirring adventures of a greater complexity than those of the early animal books. Her two masterpieces (if one can distinguish two from a number of contenders) are *The Roly-Poly Pudding* (1908) and *The Tale of Mr Tod* (1912), and in both of them may be seen the uncompromising story-teller, knowing that *her* way is the way that the story needs to go and that the childen will follow her. 'If it were not impertinent to lecture one's publishers', she wrote to Warne's of the latter book, '– you are a great deal too much afraid of the public; for whom I have never cared one tuppenny button . . . Most people, after one success, are so cringingly afraid of doing less well that they rub all the edge off their subsequent work.'

Her commitment to the work in hand here, and her refusal to be harried into easy popularity, are symbolic of the freedoms gained for the writers of children's books (including 'freedom of imagination' which Harvey Darton perhaps underestimates in his remarks on p. 313). These may be seen too in several remarkable works for older readers which are part of the legacy of this fruitful period to children nearly a hundred years later. Earliest is that extraordinary phenomenon, first published as a three-decker, *Bevis; the Story of a Boy,* by Richard Jefferies (1882). With its immediate predecessor, the more fanciful, not to say whimsical, *Wood Magic* (2 vols., 1881), it unites a near pantheism with the closely observed details of a boy's life in the country – Coate Farm, scene of Jefferies's own childhood, and now bordered on the one side by expanding Swindon and on the other by a motorway. It is not a book with any clear shape (like, say *Swallows and Amazons,* which is a distant descendant) and it lives through its several hundred pages by the sheer vigour of the author's perceptions. Whether Bevis and his friend Mark (modelled on Jefferies's brother, Harry) are building boats, fending for themselves on a desert island, or just beating a donkey, their inner and outer natures, their speech, their surroundings are portrayed with a dramatic flair and accuracy which, against all the odds, continues to draw the reader into the 'secondary world' of a long-past summer.

It is surely a book that influenced a writer from the next generation, whose early children's book *A Book of Discoveries* (1910) carries with it something of Jefferies' s own vigorous enjoyment of open-air action – plus something that he would never have dreamed of, a matily didactic adult. The book was published by Wells, Gardner, Darton and Co., with whom its author, John Masefield, seems to have been busily connected at the time, since 1910 also saw them publishing two stories set in the past: *Martin Hyde, The Duke's Messenger* (which Harvey Darton says was written in 1906–7)† and *Jim Davis* (serialized that year

---

* Originally the format was not so uniform. Not only did production details, especially bindings, differ, but there were also the 'panoramas' of *The Fierce Bad Rabbit* and *Miss Moppet* (both 1906), and the larger format stories: *The Pie and the Patty Pan* (1905), *The Roly-Roly Pudding* (1908), and *Ginger and Pickles* (1909).

† In *From Surtees to Sasoon,* p. 51.

in *Chatterbox* and published as a book in 1911). Of these historical stories for boys ('a difficult accomplishment'), Darton says that they are 'exciting without being an affront to the intelligence, and romantic without strain' – which judgment still stands. He might have added, however, that *Jim Davis* in particular makes an enhanced impact through the personality of its first-person narrator: a character with an eye (and ear) for circumstantial detail, and one, who, through the modulations of his story-telling, lifts the tale from being a mere smugglers yarn to one of human consequence.

This is a quality which derives not so much from the influential *Treasure Island* as from a book which has been seen as in the Stevenson tradition, but which possesses a more serious romantic – one could say nostalgic – element: *Moonfleet* by J. Meade Falkner (1898). By a quirk of misfortune this masterly historical novel was published by a company with an 'educational' rather than a 'children's' list, and for many years it had to struggle to make its way to readers in the guise of a text-book reserved for such occasions as 'reading around the class'. That this did not kill it, and that now, within sight of its centenary, it is being recognized as a children's book with a continuing power to move its readers is further witness to the resilience and craftsmanship of these turn-of-the-century children's books.

It would be possible to continue the list for some time, bringing in the sophisticated simplicities of William Nicholson's *Alphabet* (1898), or the simple sophistications of Frances Hodgson Burnett's *The Secret Garden* (1911).* Bearing in mind, though, how Masefield was eventually to convert his genius for romantic realism into those two superb fantasies *The Midnight Folk* (1927) and *The Box of Delights* (1935), and bearing in mind that it was the fantasy of such books as *The Rose and the Ring*, *The Water Babies*, and *Alice's Adventures in Wonderland* that led to 'freedom' for children's books, it is perhaps apt to conclude by noting that 1910 – the year of *Jim Davis et al.* – was also the year when Duckworth's published Walter de la Mare's *Three Mulla-Mulgars*.

Through various changes – of illustrator and of title (it is now *The Three Royal Monkeys*) – this haunting story has held its place in print to the present time – a new edition in paperback indeed being acclaimed in 1979. Like *Bevis* and like *Moonfleet* it may now make unusual demands on child readers who are not accustomed to sinking themselves into such profoundly imagined books. The journey of the monkeys through the icy jungle, the eccentric adventures, the games with language and the enigmatic purpose of the author all flow together to create a story outside the categories of most readers' expectations – but through the almost incantatory manner of de la Mare's story-telling the book assumes a persuasive reality:

At last, after fixing a lighted torch between the logs of each raft, the Mulgars began to get aboard. On the first, Ghibba and Thimble embarked, squatting the one in front and the

---

* When in 1960 the *Sunday Times* organized its exhibition 'The One Hundred Best Books for Children' (working closely with Kathleen Lines), the one hundredth item was *The Secret Garden* 'chosen by readers of the *Sunday Times* who voted overwhelmingly for its inclusion in the series'.

other astern, to keep their craft steady. With big torches smoking in the sunshine, they pushed off. Tugging on a long strand of Samarak which they had looped around the smooth branch of a Bōōbab, they warped themselves free. Soon well adrift, with water singing in their green twigs, they slid swiftly into the stream, shoving and pulling at their long poles, beating the green water to foam, as they neared the fork, to keep their dancing catamaran from drifting into the surge that would have toppled them over the cataract.

The rest of the travellers stood stock-still by the water-side, gazing beneath their hands after the green ship and its two sailors, dark and light, brandishing their poles. They followed along the bank as far as they could, standing lean in the evening beams, wheezing shrilly, '*Illaloothi, Illaloothi!*' as Moona and Mulla-Mulgar floated into the mouth of the cavern and vanished from sight.

Of such writing, literature for any reader need ask nothing more.

BRIEF BOOK LIST

At the end of his final chapter Darton commented that all its facts were 'matters of common knowledge and can easily be verified. The host of authors is so great and their work so near today that only a few of the more recent have been mentioned by name'. This broadly applies to the above Appendix too, and to the bibliographical information on the period that both chapters cover. *N.C.B.E.L.* vol. III (unhappily deficient in its updating) and the ever more sophisticated recording procedures of late-twentieth-century bibliography show the wealth of material that could have been included. Furthermore, such resources are now supplemented by the foundation of organizations like the Kipling, Henty and Beatrix Potter Societies which care for the reputations of their authors and encourage dedicated delving into the minutiae of their published works. Here nonetheless is a list of some preliminary information which has reference to the children's books of some of the authors in these two chapters. (Many standard general biographies etc. have been excluded. Studies of special aspects of children's books of the period, like Gillian Avery's *Childhood's Pattern*, or Nancy Cutt's *Ministering Angels*, are listed in the General Book List.)

BARRIE
Birkin, Andrew. *J. M. Barrie and the Lost Boys* (London, 1979).
Green, Roger Lancelyn. *J. M. Barrie* London, 1960; rev. 1968 (Bodley Head Monograph, abbreviated 'B.H.M.' below).

STEVENSON
Butts, Dennis *R. L. Stevenson* (London, 1966) B.H.M.
Darton remarked that 'the chief details about *Treasure Island* are conveniently contained in Vol. II of the "Tusitala" edition of Stevenson'. Also notable are the insights in Janet Adam Smith's fine edition of the *Collected Poems*, 2nd edn (London, 1971).

KIPLING
Green, Roger Lancelyn. *Kipling and the Children* (London, 1965).
Sutcliff, Rosemary. *Rudyard Kipling* (London, 1960; rev. 1968) B.H.M.
Much information about the publication of his children's books is given in Florence Livingston's *Bibliography* (New York, 1927, with a *Supplement*, 1938).

HENTY

Growing interest in 'boys' books' since 1950 and the formation of a Henty Society in 1977 have contributed to some ramifying investigations of the man and his books. An introduction to this can be found in John Cargill Thompson's *The Boys' Dumas* (Cheadle Hulme, 1975), which shows how *passé* is the *Life* by George Manville Fenn (1907) that was noted by Darton. A modern study is *Held Fast for England; GAH, Imperialist boys' writer* by Guy Arnold (London, 1980).

RACKHAM

Gettings, Fred. *Arthur Rackham* (London, 1975).

Hudson, Derek. *Arthur Rackham; his life and work* (London, 1960; re-issued 1973).
 With a check-list compiled by Bertram Rota, revised by Anthony Rota, 1973.

POTTER

Lane, Margaret. *The Tale of Beatrix Potter; a biography.* Rev edn. (London, 1968).

Linder, Leslie, *A History of the Writings of Beatrix Potter, including unpublished work* (London, 1971).

 The crowning work of an enthusiast who in 1966 published his decipherment of Beatrix Potter's coded *Journal*, who was responsible for several immensely popular exhibitions of her work, and whose own collection of Potter material is now lodged at the Victoria and Albert Museum and at the National Book League.

GRAHAME

Graham, Eleanor. *Kenneth Grahame* (London, 1963) B.H.M.

Grahame, Elspeth. *The First Whisper of 'The Wind in the Willows'* (London, 1944).

Green, Peter. *Kenneth Grahame; a biography* (London, 1959).

MASEFIELD

Fisher, Margery, *John Masefield* (London, 1963) B.H.M.

DE LA MARE

Clark, Leonard. *Walter De La Mare* (London, 1960; rev. 1968) B.H.M.

 The same author was responsible for compiling the *Checklist* of De La Mare's work for the National Book League exhibition of 1956. A close study of De La Mare's tinkering with the texts of his children's stories is Jane Gardner's 'W.D.L.M.'s Stories for Children; an analysis of variant texts', *Private Library*, 3rd ser. vol. 1, Autumn 1978, no. 3, pp. 101–18.

APPENDIX 2

An Outline of the Evolution of Two Publishers

TABLE 1. THE NEWBERY FIRMS AND SUCCESSORS

JOHN NEWBERY (1713–1767)

1740   Trading in Reading at the Bible and Crown in the Market Place.
1743(?) Moves to London to the Bible and Crown, near Devereux Court, without Temple Bar.
1745   Moves premises to the Bible and Sun, [no.65] St Paul's Churchyard.
1767   Death of J. N.
1768   The business, with most of J. N.'s titles, is continued at the same address by:
        Francis Newbery (J. N.'s son, 1743–1818) and Thomas Carnan (J. N.'s stepson and manager, 1733(?)–88) sometimes with the imprint 'Newbery & Co.'
1779   Francis Newbery withdraws from trade. The business continued by Thomas Carnan.
1788   Death of T. C. Copyrights and blocks of at least twenty-four children's books are bought by William Darton I of Gracechurch Street.
1789–93 Occasional publishing from the St Paul's Churchyard address by Francis Power, J.N.'s grandson.

THE NEWBERY–HARRIS SUCCESSION

1767	Francis Newbery (J.N.'s nephew, ?–1780) opens a shop 'at the corner of St Paul's Church Yard' [alternatively 20 Ludgate Street]. This Francis had been in business as a bookseller during J.N.'s lifetime, trading from the Crown, 15 Paternoster Row. Most of his publishing activity is concerned with introducing new titles, not exploiting J.N.'s stock which is in possession of the rival firm.	
1780	F.N. dies; the business is continued by his widow Elizabeth Newbery, née Bryant (?–1821). She publishes many books in association with the firm of Vernor and Hood, and may well have been dependent upon the activity of her managers, Abraham Badcock (?–1797) and John Harris (see below).	

1801–2	E.N. withdraws from the business which is taken over by John Harris I (1756–1846).	J[ohn] Harris
1819	J.H. I takes into partnership his son, John Harris II.	J. Harris & Son
1824	J.H. I retires, J.H. II continues.	J[ohn] Harris
1843	The business taken over by E. C. Grant (a shadowy figure who appears to have Army connections) and William Darling Griffith (1805–77), a trained bookseller.	Grant & Griffith
1856	Griffith takes Robert Farran as partner.	Griffith, Farran; or
1877	Death of Griffith. Farran alone, trading under Company imprint.	Griffith, Farran & Co.
1884	Farran joined by H.G.P. Okeden (1857?–?) and Charles Welsh (1850–1914).	Griffith, Farran, Okeden & Welsh or still Griffith, Farran & Co.
1888	Farran retires through ill health.	
1889	Death of Farran. At the end of the year, or right at the start of 1890, the firm ceases to act as retail booksellers and closes the shop at St. Paul's Churchyard, which is no longer associated with the trade. The Publishing Department (including fine binding of Bibles etc.) is now conducted from Newbery House, 39 Charing Cross Road.	
1893(?)	Management changes possibly occuring.	Griffith, Farran & Co.
1897	A Mr Browne takes a controlling interest. From this time on the publishing impulse fades and the last fugitive years of the firm appear to be increasingly devoted to selling stock rather than to implementing new enterprises.	Griffith, Farran, Browne & Co.
c.1900	Move to 35 Bow Street.	
1908	Move to Lovell's Court in Paternoster Row.	Griffith, Farran & Co.
1911	Move to 16 & 17 Paternoster Row, where the business closes in either 1911 or 1912.	

TABLE 2. THREE DARTON FIRMS

THE GRACECHURCH STREET DARTONS
William Darton I (1755–1819)

1787	W.D. I sets up independently as engraver, printer and stationer.	White Lion Alley Birchin Lane	William Darton, or W. Darton & Co.
1788	Moves premises.	55 Gracechurch Street	
1791	Commences partnership with Joseph Harvey (1764–1841). From this point on a 'rolling succession' of Dartons and Harveys manage the firm at the Gracechurch Street premises. They are: James Harvey (1778–1854), brother of Joseph (partner only in the printing business) Samuel Darton (1785–1840), third son of William I Robert Harvey (1805–67), son of Joseph Thomas Gates Darton (1810-87), son of Samuel		Darton & Harvey
1810	William I, Joseph Harvey, Samuel Darton partners.		Darton, Harvey & Darton
1819	Death of William I. Joseph Harvey and Samuel Darton continue.		Harvey & Darton
1834	Samuel Darton and Robert Harvey partners.		Darton & Harvey
1838	Robert Harvey and Thomas Gates Darton.		Harvey & Darton
1841	Robert Harvey alone.*		
1846	Business sold to Robert Yorke Clarke, but the Harvey & Darton imprint is still used occasionally.		
1852	Closure. Copyrights sold to Arthur Hall, Virtue & Co.		

* Samuel Darton died in 1840 but from 1843 to *c.*1855 his widow Ann published some books under her own imprint from the Crosby Hall Repository (Toys and Fancy Goods, 33 Bishopsgate Street Within).

THE HOLBORN HILL DARTONS
William Darton II (1781–1854), eldest son of William I

1804	W.D. II sets up independently as bookseller and publisher after serving apprenticeship to his father.	40 Holborn Hill	William Darton Junior
1806	Joined by Thomas Darton (*b.* 1783), second son of William I.		William & Thomas Darton
1808	Moves premises.	58 Holborn Hill	
1811	Thomas leaves partnership and, after trading briefly on his own at Great Surrey Street, disappears from view.		William Darton Junior
1819			William Darton
1830–1	William II takes into partnership his eldest son, John Maw Darton (1809–81).		William Darton & Son
1836	William II retires. Samuel Clark (1810–75) becomes partner.		Darton & Clark
*c.*1845	John Maw Darton alone.		Darton & Co.
1862	Frederick Hodge (former manager) becomes partner for about a year but imprint remains till 1866.		Darton & Hodge
[*c.*1863	Joseph William Darton (1843–1916), son of John Maw Darton and father of F. J. H. Darton, works for the publishing business of John Morgan. See opposite.]		
*c.*1866	Demolition of Holborn Hill. Temporary move.	175 Strand	
*c.*1867	Further move.	42 Paternoster Row	Darton & Co.
1876	Closure		

The Paternoster Buildings Dartons

Year	Event	Address	Imprint
1859	John Morgan publisher at 10 Paternoster Row (d. 1867).		
c.1863	Takes Joseph William Darton as manager (see previous page).		
1867	William Wells Gardner (1821–80) buys Morgan's business with J.W.D. as manager.	10 Paternoster Row	W. Wells Gardner
1869	J.W.D. becomes partner.		
1872	Moves premises.	2 Paternoster Buildings	
1880	W.W.G. dies. J.W.D. alone.		Wells Gardner Darton & Co.
c. 1890	Further premises opened at 44 Victoria Street, which is included in imprints from time to time.		
1893	Moves premises	3 Paternoster Buildings	
1904	Business becomes limited company with the following directors: J.W.D.; F.J.H.D.; Charles Clark Darton, second son of J.W.D.; F. G. Tanner (senior traveller) and C. A. Ashley (chief clerk).		Wells Gardner Darton & Co. Ltd
1908–9	Further premises added.	3 & 4 Paternoster Buildings	
1916	J.W.D. dies. His widow and daughter become directors.		
1928	Business taken over by Love & Malcomson of Redhill, who continued to publish under the imprint, from London until 1947, and from Redhill until c. 1960.		
1928–32	Charles Clark Darton continues as proprietor of *Chatterbox* under the imprint of The Chatterbox Co. Ltd, with Simpkin Marshall Ltd as publishing agent.	30–31 Paternoster Square	The Chatterbox Co. Ltd
1932–34		5 Ludgate Square	The Chatterbox Co. Ltd

Most of the information on these firms has been drawn from research into the family businesses undertaken by Lawrence Darton who has very kindly given the editor full access to his working papers.

APPENDIX 3

A Listing of Books by
F. J. Harvey Darton

A chronological list of books written or edited by Darton, including some of his contributions to other works.

The firm of Wells Gardner, Darton and Co. Ltd. is abbreviated in all entries to W.G.D.

1901   *The 'Midget' London.* W.G.D.

An anonymous work, but the G. C. Darton copy is inscribed by F.J.H.D. 'the first published work of the author, in original leather binding as issued . . . July 28, 1934'.

1901   *The Seven Champions of Christendom.* W.G.D.

Also in the *Midget Series* and possibly also by F.J.H.D.

1904   *Tales of the Canterbury Pilgrims,* retold from Chaucer and others. With an introduction by F. J. Furnivall. Illustrated by Hugh Thomson. W.G.D.

A cheap abridgment was published as *Pilgrim's Tales from 'Tales of the Canterbury Pilgrims',* 1908 (Children's Bookshelf Series).

1905   *Without Fear and Without Reproach; the adventures of the famous knight Bayard.* [Illustrated by John Jellicoe.] W.G.D.

1907   *The Merry Tales of the Wise Men of Gotham.* Illustrated by Gordon Browne. W.G.D.

1907   *A Wonder Book of Old Romance.* Illustrated by A. G. Walker. W.G.D.

Among the romances retold are 'Sir Gawain and the Green Knight', 'The Seven Wise Masters' and 'Guy of Warwick'. An eighth edition of the book was published in 1952.

A cheap abridgment was published as *Old English Stories from 'A Wonder Book of Old Romance',* 1909 (Children's Bookshelf Series).

1909   *A Wonder Book of Beasts.* Illustrated by Margaret Clayton. W.G.D.

A cheap abridgment was published as *Three Bears and other Wonder Tales of Beasts,* 1915 (Children's Bookshelf Series). See also *Reynard the Fox,* 1928 (below).

1909   *Ali Baba and the Forty Borough Councillors.* Published for Private Circulation from Toynbee Hall, Whitechapel.

1910   *The Life and Times of Mrs Sherwood (1775–1851); from the diaries of Captain and Mrs Sherwood.* Edited by F.J.H.D. W.G.D.

1913   *My Father's Son; a faithful record,* by W. W. Penn. Prepared for the press by John Harvey. Hodder and Stoughton.

A novel, with the dedication 'Conjugi Ter Dilectae Redactor'.

1913   *The Seven Champions of Christendom.* Illustrated by Norman Ault. W.G.D.

1914   *The London Museum . . .* Illustrated by L. Russell Conway. W.G.D. (The Treasure-House series).

1914 'Children's Books', Chapter XVI in vol. XI of the *Cambridge History of English Literature*. Cambridge University Press.

1914 'Illustrated and Juvenile Books' in the Catalogue of the British Section of the International Exhibition of the Book Industry. H.M.S.O.

1915 *Arnold Bennett*. Nisbet and Co. Ltd. (Writers of the Day Series.)
A new edition was published in 1924.

1916 *The Sea-Kings of England; stories of the Spanish Main retold from Hakluyt*. W.G.D.
Serialized in *Chatterbox* 1911–12.

1922 *The Marches of Wessex*. Nisbet and Co. Ltd. New edition 1936.

1923 *The Good Fairy; or, the adventures of Sir Richard Whittington, R. Crusoe Esqre, Master Jack Horner and others. A Play . . . with a particular description of a theatre contrived by Albert Rutherston . . .* W.G.D.
The play by F.G.H.D., 'The Theatre described' by A.R., who also provides in a pouch at the front of the book a large coloured poster of cut-out scenes and characters. Signed 'Underground & C. Lovat Fraser Concevit. 1921. Albert Rutherston Concevit & Fecit May 1922.' Printed at the Curwen Press. Lovat Fraser died in 1921.

1923 *The London Review; a moral pantomime . . . with a coloured representation of the characters and two scenes by Albert Rutherton . . . with directions for setting up a theatre*. W.G.D.
In series with the previous item but with two posters. One of these clearly links the two books to a publicity campaign for the London Underground by showing an Underground Station and lift.

1923 Preface to S.M.de Cervantes. *The History of Don Quixote*, reprinted by the Navarre Society.

1924 *The Golden Ass* in the translation of W. Adlington. Edited with an Introduction by F.J.H.D. for the Navarre Society.

1924 *A Parcel of Kent*. Nisbet and Co.

1926 *Vincent Crummles; his theatre and his times*. Arranged by F.J.H.D. with an historical introductory note and appendices from *Nicholas Nickleby* by Charles Dickens. W.G.D.
Limited to 400 copies 'with the Frontispiece coloured by hand in the antique manner'.

1927 *English Books 1475–1900; a signpost for collectors*. By Charles J. Sawyer and F.J.H.D. With one hundred illustrations. 2 vols. Published in the City of Westminster by Chas J. Sawyer Ltd . . . and in the United States from E. P. Dutton and Company.

1927 *When Crummles Played: being . . . Lillo's tragedy of 'The London Merchant'*. With an introduction and appendix by F.J.H.D. W.G.D.
The tragedy has a prologue by Nigel Playfair and an epilogue by A. P. Herbert. Parts of the Introduction are taken from *Vincent Crummles* (above).

1927–9 The Bankside Acting Edition of Shakespeare. Edited by F.J.H.D. W.G.D.
Sixteen Volumes were published: *As You Like It; Comedy of Errors; Coriolanus; Hamlet; Henry V; Julius Caesar; King John; King Lear; Macbeth; Merchant of Venice; Midsummer Night's Dream; Much Ado about Nothing; Richard II; Taming of the Shrew; The Tempest; Twelfth Night*.

1928 Introduction to Lord Lytton [i.e. Edward Bulwer-Lytton], *The Coming Race; and The Haunted and the Haunters*. Oxford University Press (Worlds Classic Series).

1928 *Reynard the Fox*, adapted from Caxton by E.L. and F.J.H.D. Illustrated by Margaret Clayton. W.G.D.

'The version here given is based on a longer one (itself very freely adapted from Caxton) which my late wife and I made for *A Wonder Book of Beasts*.' F.J.H.D.

1928   *J. M. Barrie*. Nisbet and Co. (Writers of the Day Series).

1929   *When —. A record of transition*. By the late J. L. Pole. With a foreword by Peter Grimstone. Chapman and Hall.
F.J.H.D.'s second pseudonymous novel.

1930   *Dickens v. Barabbas, Forster Intervening*. A study based upon some hitherto unpublished letters. With facsimiles. [Published by] Chas J. Sawyer, Grafton House . . .
An introductory note signed C.J.S. and F.J.H.D. explains that this study of Dickens's relationships with his publishers was intended for *English Books* (above) but, despite the expansion of that work to two volumes, there was still not room for it. Limited to 200 copies. Reprinted New York 1972.

1930   *The Surprising Adventures of Baron Munchausen*, reprinted from the earliest complete edition . . . Edited with an introduction and appendix by F.J.H.D. for the Navarre Society.

1931   *Essays of the Year 1930–1931*. The Argonaut Press.
There is a compiler's note signed by F.J.H.D. (which was not present in the one preceding volume for 1929–30). Darton also edited collections for 1931–2, and 1933–4. The first of these includes an anonymous essay on 'Early Poetry for Children' (pp. 191–206) which may be by F.J.H.D.

1931   *From Surtees to Sassoon; some English contrasts (1838–1928)*. Morley and Mitchell Kennerley Jr.

1931   *Modern Book Illustration in Great Britain and America*. London, 1931.
Winter number of *The Studio*.

1932   *Children's Books in England; five centuries of social life*. Cambridge University Press. Second edn 1958.

1933   *Dickens: Positively the First Appearance; a centenary review with a bibliography of 'Sketches by Boz'*. The Argonaut Press.

1933   *A Posie of Gilloflowers*, by Humfry Gifford, Gent. Edited with an introduction by F.J.H.D. Hawthornden Press.

1935   *English Fabric; a study of village life*. George Newnes Ltd.

1936   *Alibi Pilgrimage*. Newnes.
In the Canning Case of 1753–4 a group of gipsies were accused of abducting a servant-girl, but claimed that they could not have done so because they were on the road to London from Dorset. F.J.H.D. here retraces their journey to prove that they were right and thereby reveals 'the glory of this long walk' little changed from the reign of George II to that of Edward VIII.

APPENDIX 4

F. J. Harvey Darton: 'The Youth of a Children's Magazine'

In the Cornhill for May 1932 Harvey Darton published these recollections of his years as an editor of children's magazines. Since the magazine in question was still in existence he felt that 'it would be improper' to advertise it against its rivals by dwelling on its well-established fame, and he concealed the title. But there seems now little harm in revealing that *The — Magazine* was *Chatterbox* and that 'Mr Osborne' was its first editor, the Rev. J. Erskine Clarke. The essay is included here for the insight that it gives into both its subject and its author.

THE YOUTH OF A CHILDREN'S MAGAZINE.

AN EDITORIAL RETROSPECT*

Until a few months ago, the offices in which I edited children's magazines for thirty years were always to be found in the same small recondite Square in the City of London. The Square is a kind of rectilinear maze, such as I liked to contrive on paper when I was a boy. It can be reached only by narrow one-way traffic lanes and half-secret footpaths under archways. When you attain what should be its midst, you find a square within the Square. The central space was open till about seventy years ago, when it was a sub-market to Smithfield, for the meat trade. This accounts for a public-house in one corner and two others in the connecting by-ways, for today's commerce in the Square includes only two industries, each of the greatest quiet discretion – the book trade and the display of linoleum. But in the early sixties came the interior block, exactly proportioned to the outer, but itself sub-divided into four little squares by rectangular cross-passages, each with a built-over archway. It is as elusive as Todgers's and as neat as a Chinese nest of boxes.

It is impossible, for economic reasons, either to build huge new offices in such an inaccessible spot or (the better alternative) to afforest it. It retains always, therefore, something of its semi-domestic Victorian atmosphere: a compromise between continuous quiet efficiency and mere adhesion. It is the obvious natural home of children's magazines of the staider sort, and there *The — Magazine*, among many rivals, was cradled and grew to its present maturity.

Upon such a Square, an hour or so after offices are normally closed, there falls a

---

* The magazines of which I write are still in existence. It would be improper of me to advertise them against their many rivals by dwelling on their well-established fame. It would be equally improper to suggest that my own retirement involves any breach of continuity. I have therefore given fictitious names throughout. 'The trade' and a few readers will probably recognise certain facts, but without, I hope, thinking the worse of my late products or of myself.

339

gentlemanly peace, as of a suburban drawing-room about 3 p.m. on Sundays. 'The very
city seems asleep.' The postman slamming the pillar-box door, the faint cackle of women
with pails, the shuffle of a vast City policeman testing locks, have each an echo all the
more distinct after the roarings of huddled contorted traffic throughout the working day.
A mellowness slides into the soul. I felt that my sometimes absurd labours were really
benign, if not important, as, after staying late one spring evening a year or two ago, I
clanged a heavy door behind me and almost ran into a man who was peering about oddly.
'Aren't the offices of *The — Magazine* here?' he asked. He was soberly well-dressed, in a
rather countrified fashion. 'I've come twelve thousand miles to see them.'

I revealed my guilt as editor, and, to cut the story of a long and friendly encounter
short, learnt that he had been brought up on my senior magazine, and cherished
memories of the serial stories loved by him before he emigrated to New Zealand in the
late seventies, and had firmly resolved to visit, upon his first return to 'home', the actual
nursery of this dear and (he was kind enough to say) beneficial joy. We parted good
friends, and several months later I received a most amiable letter from his son, the editor
of a well-known Dominion newspaper.

Somewhere about the same time the creator of *Peter Pan* laid bare his soul. Years ago
that soul was a dreadful place. Its tabernacle had read dozens of penny dreadfuls, and,
still worse, had written imitations of them. But *The — Magazine* purged him. Vice fled.
He buried the lot, originals and copies, in the back garden. Yet what my New Zealand
friend, as honest and ingenuous a man as I ever met, had loved in this same magazine was
a long story called 'The Gold Diggers of Redville' – something like it, anyhow; a tale of
the Californian gold rush, nearly as rapid as a film of today. What is more perplexing, I
have learnt that a well-known nature writer was sustained and inspired by Us (I speak
editorially) to high adventure; that an equally well-known playwright, in a successful
comedy acted by all amateurs, pilloried *The — Magazine* as 'stuff for kids'; and that a
new and rising novelist of this very year thought that so recently as 1913 We produced
nothing but mawkish sentiment of two kinds – *Eric, or Little by Little*, in the upper class,
'daddy-dear-do-keep-off-the-drink' in the lower: deathbeds, anyway as formerly displayed in 1660 and 1860 for the betterment of evil brats.

The fact is, *The — Magazine* had become a household word; and a household word is
often a wholesale lie. No children's magazine, and very few children's books, ever really
existed on this earth. They lived only in a Platonic ideal reality in the heavens, and every
inhabitant of the Den saw and still sees only such a projection of them as his enslaved
adult mind can comprehend. I myself, though an editor ought to be at least the peer of a
Platonic guardian, have fallen to this pathetic fallacy. I simply adored, years ago, *The
Swiss Family Robinson;* especially the passage about the donkey visible inside the
serpent. But I never knew till about 1925, when I examined the work for trade purposes,
that it was stiff with prayers and piety. 'The One remains, the Many change and pass';
and, oddly enough, the residue in children's literature is usually the last thing upon
which an author prided himself or for which he had a hopeful purpose.

Solid old goodwill; preconceptions not to be disturbed; a sane and honest ideal to be
maintained; new conditions of thought and of practical mechanism – that was the
inheritance into which I stepped when, about 1901, I became editor of *The — Magazine*
and a twin production meant for younger readers. The Victorian era had just ended, as
years go. A turning-point had come for many magazines founded in the eighteen-sixties
at the heyday of the wood-block. They had to change as vivaciously as the fashions in
dress changed. Their conductors heard a new language being spoken, a little like their
own, but not the same; just as maybe Shakespeare's folk might recognise vaguely our
clipped version of their broader speech. The aims of *The — Magazine*, among others, had
become almost shadowy, the ghost of an ancient cause now won or lost, but at any rate no
longer inspiring. Where were we? Even our outward fabric was changing. The Bluecoat

School had just been turned into a kind of Aladdin's palace and wafted to Horsham. The Old Bailey was to be broken down. What would happen to our Square and its coeval enterprises? Had we passed our climacteric? Why did we exist?

Why indeed? Perhaps few remembered the truth. The old name, itself wearing an obsolescent air, stood now for affectionate memory, not for policy. But Barrie was right. The journal had set out heavy with purpose. In 1866, an able vicar in the provinces, much devoted to work among his younger parishioners, felt the need of healthy literature to combat blood-and-thunder, which, like many reformers then and now, he deemed a menace to juvenile civilization. He resolved to meet the want himself. He collected a few friends to provide him with literary matter – he had a ready-enough pen himself; and he got into touch – how, I do not know, and it really is an odd mystery – with a very competent London engraver and blockmaker, a Mr James. Both were tolerably well-to-do, and between them they put up several thousand pounds. It is certain that Mr James had no particular religious motive. But he was a good honest business man, and so, for that matter, was Mr Osborne, the Yorkshire vicar; and they conspired amicably and efficiently enough.

But an engraver in London and an editorial clergyman a long way off could not do all the work. Mr James could look after the practical side of the illustrations, but a working manager was needed to deal with artists, paper-makers, binders, advertising agents, even the wretched tribe of authors. For this purpose Mr James discovered an odd but capable man, a Mr Mullins, who, as if to add to the magazine's religious breadth, was a Roman Catholic. He was an engineer by profession, of a roving type; and I am told that when he received Mr James's offer, he had just landed in Liverpool in some financial straits, after adventures in South America suitable to that period of history. With him came his assistant, Mr Butcher, a confidential factotum who was always something of a mystery. He is still living, in retirement, and I will only say of him that, alongside some unimportant defects, he possessed a most extraordinary memory and a remarkable sense of what the peculiar public of *The — Magazine* would like. It is not unfair to support this opinion. In my own time, it was one of his duties to enter the titles of our illustrations in a register. We were then strong on what I might call moral or artistic 'close-ups'. We had a series of 'Bible Characters', among them Queen Candace of Ethiopia. The artist's writing was not very clear, and this rather nebulous monarch appeared in our books as 'Queen Canaan of Utopia' – queen of at least two fortunate worlds. Another series included a reproduction of Franz Hals's 'Laughing Cavalier'. This was recorded as 'Fancy Hats', a title so happy that I was sorely tempted to adopt it as the 'motto', or lettering under the published picture. On the other hand, if Mr Butcher provided diversion of this kind, he could have told me, twenty years after, in what month of what year Queen Canaan first astonished our public, without ever looking it up; and not less unerringly he would point out that such-and-such an anecdote, deemed new in 1910, had appeared in our pages in almost the same words in 1879.

His particular religion was not discovered to me; but he was Conservative in politics. Nor did I ask the religious beliefs of our printer, though I can say with sincerity that he was a man of good, simple and devout life, and that, as his was one of the earliest 'Union houses', he knew what labour problems were. His old-established firm printed our magazines for over sixty years without a break, except for a short interval when their premises were burnt down and the printers of *Punch* kindly came to the rescue – for by that time, a dozen years after its inception, *The — Magazine* in its humbler way had become an institution like *Punch* itself. Mr S— was as enthusiastic a reader of the paper as those for whom he printed it. He died after a few years, but his son, who passed away in 1930 at a great age, was equally devoted. He indeed was a distinguished and lovable gentleman, utterly wrapped up in his ancient profession, very sensitive of its honour. He had a shy, nervous manner that seemed sometimes almost irritability, but was in reality a delicate enthusiasm. He communicated his zeal and courtesy to his men, who all through took a pride in their work, as good printers do. They would bring us the damp sheets, 'made ready', to be passed before printing, with a mixture of anxiety and affection in their air which no machine-setter can ever quite display (until a few years ago the magazine was always hand-set). 'Too much ink there, but that block don't print up proper without you ink it well. The black's too heavy for it – the ink almost pulls the surface off the paper. Would you have it back, please, to be gone over before we print for the vols.?' To them the monthly issue was routine; but 'the vols.' – the annual volumes – were a typographical trust.

Finally, even in those days of simpler distributive methods, the publishing had to be in the hands of a competent organization. The founders discovered a man who issued a good many pious tracts, and booklets not out of keeping with their ideals. I never knew him. But I gather that he was not really fond of *The — Magazine*. He was a Dissenter, harmless but convinced; and though Mr Osborne's Anglicanism for children was not in the least militant, the old village church and the good vicar certainly did turn up pretty frequently. When, therefore, about 1870, the energetic junior partner in another firm bid for the publishing, he secured it. He not only came into close contact with the management, but he brought yet another point of view into the general outlook, for he came of old Quaker stock, and was an ardent Churchman, inclining to High, but not fanatically.

With such allies and officers, then, Mr Osborne was to lead his crusade to rescue tempted adolescence – the boy and girl of fourteen or so, especially those who had to make their own living. The first weekly number of *The — Magazine* appeared on December 1, 1866, at the price of one halfpenny. It was also issued monthly, at threepence, as from January 1, 1867; and in the autumn of 1867, in good time for the Christmas-book trade which Dickens and Thackeray had established as a matter of business routine, the first annual volume appeared, and was immediately and hurriedly reprinted. Within a year or two it had acquired a large oversea market, especially in the United States. It is significant of a general social change that in recent years America has lost much of the children's-magazine and Christmas-volume habit. The newspapers on the one hand, the host of cheap new books on the other, have deprived the publication-day of juvenile periodicals of nearly all its old excitement and innocent warmth.

That first volume, now very rare, would surprise the grandfathers who today look back to it, as I have said, with memory only of what struck their imagination. In spite of the mixture of interests in the band of producers, Mr Osborne dominated the magazine. He went beyond his explicit ideal of supplying good stuff to oust bad by the strength of mere excellence. What he was really anxious about was not so much the making of young criminals as the possible diminution of young Christians. He was ready and able to provide plenty of healthy, robust adventure, such as my New Zealand *revenant* had loved. But when it came to the seething pot of print, he flavoured the excitement – I fear 'larded' is nearly the right word – with an intolerable deal of aggressive piety; so that *The — Magazine* could almost (not quite, I think, for I was forbidden it myself) be read in the sombre peace, the devout restraint, of the mid-Victorian Sunday.

Mr Osborne's editing of the text was masterly; nay, masterful. Few contributors were allowed a signature, few even initials.* The editor himself took – usurped – all responsibility of every kind, even of authorship. He *did* edit. W. E. Henley was not more savage nor more painstaking. If a story contained a good idea with poor trimmings, Mr Osborne cut the trimmings away bodily, or re-wrote them. To make his views prevail, he added as well as took away. A famous Civil Service legend tells how a high official of the Home Office, checking the draft of the King's Speech one year,

---

* After the first few months, though Mr Osborne's original associates were naturally favoured, the magazine depended almost entirely upon chance contributions from outside. It has done so ever since. It never had any literary staff.

wrote on it the minute, 'Some reference to A. G. should come in about here.' He ought to have been the first editor of *The — Magazine*. It is not for me, in these discreet pages, to interpret the symbol '.A.G.': I will only say that in the nineteenth century our volume contained most strepitant morals.

Contributors had no say in the matter. The point as well as the length of their MSS. lay entirely in the editor's hands, and he was a ruthless surgeon. He was marvellously ingenious in hiding the wounds, but I think many a writer must have deemed his baby a changeling when he saw it in print – which was only after publication, for no proofs were sent; in fact, acceptance or rejection was often not notified. Yet there were, I gather, few unanswerable complaints. Besant and *The Author* were not yet heard of. Mr Osborne's moral standpoint was widely held, and writers who shared it were quick to find their market. And, almost *ex hypothesi*, the editor of a children's magazine is in a peculiar position of trust and vigilance. Certainly I cannot defend my predecessor's practices unreservedly. But frankly, after reading many thousands of 'juvenile' MSS. – unprinted – and observing the kind of people who compose about ninety per cent of them, I am charitable enough to understand Mr Osborne's holy ferocity and very nearly to excuse it. There is much to be said for Herod's abrupt manner of dealing with the songs of innocence.

Such vigilance, naturally, led to unconscious humour. It is all very well to justify the ways of God to man. It is no doubt true, also, in a philosophical sense, that virtue is its own reward. But if you took our pages from 1867 to 1897 as evidence, you found some singular phenomena adduced in support of such views. It is clear, for instance, that London contained an abnormal number of shivering crossing-sweepers and errand boys toiling to 'win a crust'. Day in, day out, they just won it. To that end, they did good deeds with the self-effacing persistence of a Boy Scout, and even less conspicuously, for they had no uniform. Bare feet, open-necked shirts, and rags – through which a spotlessly clean elbow *had* to be displayed by the artist – were much in vogue at that date, and, unfortunately, excited little attention. But in the end the crumb was added to the crust (I wonder why crusts were thought so nasty). Sooner or later a manly bearing or the very exceptional quality of honesty in a poor child caught the eye of a long-lost uncle or of a peppery old philanthropist with a soft (even sodden) heart and a full purse. And then you realised that in *The — Magazine*, at any rate, virtue was never its own sole reward.

The maintenance of a code at once so strait and so fluid involved great care over details, especially those of expression and even of spelling. Oaths, naturally, could not be admitted – hardly hinted at, except in the form of a 'string', or 'stream', 'rapped out' with no more definiteness than those stock phrases imply; and even that vague latitude was only conceded to very wicked persons, like drunkards, poachers, or exceptionally flashy young clerks engaged in embezzlement. This caution went to extremes, and banished words like 'hang', 'dash', and 'blow' (W. S. Gilbert knew it); while 'rotten' and 'what rot' were much too coarse for insertion. What, in those dim days, when 'awful' nearly was an awful thing to say, would have been thought of our schoolboy 'putrid' and 'stinking'? And, if slang was harmful, how much the more noxious might not contractions be? Suppose the apostrophe slipped out of 'he'll,' or even of 'can't?' The resultant word in the one case was wicked; in the other – well, it might recoil on the Editor. But that was not such an absurd fear as it seems, because *The — Magazine* was used as a 'reader' in schools, and 'she'll', 'we're' were real stumbling-blocks in sight-reading. 'He'll', however, remained anathema on moral grounds. Not ten years ago I had a letter myself – from a moral-sense American – protesting against its very appearance (misprinted, of course) in a children's magazine. Our language may have been stilted, but it was never bad.

Other inhibitions and prohibitions had a basis broader than strict morality. Ghost stories were excluded altogether. When my turn came, I tried the insertion of one or two which depended on a forewarned sheet-and-turnip practical joke. Even so, in my young days as an editor, I felt bound to put in a mild warning about the danger of such feigned terrors. And I soon learnt the risk, for I received several complaints that nervous children had been seriously upset by what I deemed mild fun. I went back to Mr Osborne's hard-and-fast rule. I never broke another he had set up – to debar murder entirely. I am as fond of fictitious corpses as any man; as I am, in an Elian sense, of the artificial comedy of the eighteenth century. But I think they may well be left to problem-solvers and to those who have a tincture of the more humane letters, which readers of children's magazines have not. Such journals have no need to meddle with what is 'news value' at the Old Bailey.

Fairy-tales also Mr Osborne ostracised, ostensibly (in the Puritan spirit) because they were impossible, but quite as much, he told me, because of the difficulty of keeping up the standard of such work, if you once admitted modern specimens. Every garrulous governess who ever lived thinks she can write a fairy-tale; and she cannot. Experience converted me inflexibly to this half of Mr Osborne's policy. It is a question of editorial self-defence, as avoiding being preached to death by wild curates is to the episcopacy.

So passed the sixties and the seventies, the Gladstonian eighties and the Yellerbocky nineties; and with the death of the great Queen who had overshadowed our lives in a way people under forty today cannot comprehend, Mr (by then Canon) Osborne laid down his blue pencil. He died, full of years and honour, in 1920, after the jubilee of his creation had been celebrated in its pages by the revelation of his features – *cut in wood* from a painting by a not undistinguished artist. I think that was the last new wood-block we used.

I was inexperienced enough – though Mr Mullins, Mr Butcher, and the printer and publisher were there to help me – when I succeeded him in 1901, but not so impatient as to begin to let off fireworks in the parlour as soon as Victoria was buried. Sudden transformation, abrupt modernisation, would be as dangerous and useless financially as blowing up our Square to build skyscrapers. Inevitability had to be gradual. And, practical efficiency apart, a magazine so blandly benevolent could not get rid of all its old contributors at one swoop. Most of the authors and artists were still living in the thought of the seventies, at latest, and must go; but they could not be kicked downstairs in a crowd.

The authors were not difficult to treat considerately. I could always say, for it was always true, from 1901 to 1931, that there was far too much unused material on hand for me to accept many new MSS. For some time to come; a time which was like the jam in *Alice* – never today. With one or two lingering exceptions, the writers had not met Canon Osborne personally, and I could make sure they would never meet me. They lived in different parts of the country, and did not know one another. I hope, therefore, they never guessed that I was telling them all alike, with fell purpose, the same story of repletion. At that time the free-lance world had not such a good intelligence system as today.

They are all dead now, and anyhow I was not openly cruel to their loyal efforts. They were only out of date — Not that my secret purge made much difference, for a good time to come. The schoolmaster in Rutland who every month used to submit about a hundred moral or facetious or moral-facetious anecdotes merely made his period two months instead of one, and I on my part accepted only five instead of twenty. (Juvenile magazines suffer from a permanent *bulimy* or ox-hunger for short 'fill-ups.') The chemist and druggist of Nether Wallop found more often than before that his little articles on 'Curious Birds' Nests' or 'How Pins are Made' had 'recently been anticipated by another contributor'. The short-story writer who had for so many years produced sobs about angel-faces and model-schoolboys was met with a slight change in the type, which got only 500 words into a column instead of 600 – and she could not cut her emotions down even to that extent, as I had expected. So they faded, with goodwill on both sides. Euthanasy.

I filled their place from the deathless host of free-lances. It was quite simple. It was necessary only to do without emphasis on the moral, and to be firm about certain exclusions – cripples, for instance, and garrets, frank manly faces and the general 'Eric' paraphernalia. There was no need to substitute for them dripping bowie-knives or triumphant low schoolboy cunning. I encouraged a few casual novices who showed signs of having read something later than Goldsmith's *Animated Nature*, Belzoni's *Travels*, and 'Peter Parley'. I asked one or two to look out for odds and ends in the Edwardian daily papers, rather than in the very back files of *The Gentleman's Magazine*, and to suggest subjects for illustration which they could themselves 'write up'. For the longer serials I even ventured to approach agents, though I asked for nothing definite. I did, indeed, think of persuading some obviously promising young authors to try their hand at the R. L. Stevenson business; and they did so, and their efforts, published a little later in book form, are now 'collectors' books'. But neither their growing fame nor the intrinsic worth of their tales made a difference of a dozen copies in our sales. We were established: our name was our advertisement. What had to be done was to wear sober new clothes, not the fashions of the day before yesterday nor the expected extravagances of tomorrow.

The real obstacle to progress was the illustrations. Most of the artists and engravers were wont to hold almost daily traffic with the manager, and it was convenient that I should enter into this, as I worked at the office and not at home. Thus, instead of doing as Mr Osborne had, and marking a proof or MS. 'Full page: page 3'; 'Half page: '*She turned abruptly*': N.B. her sleeve must be torn'; 'Full page: '*the dog leapt at him*'; tell Mr X — to make it a real terrier, not a woolly bear', or words to those effects, and sending it on to Mr Mullins to 'give out', I used to meet the artists in the flesh, and go into critical details, and discuss them also with the block-makers.

Their ghosts seem to stand before me to this day: meagre wraiths who knew not that they were even then dead. Heaven knows, they might long ago have set out briskly for a gleaming horizon, free, careless draughtsmen who thought their pencil could make vivid all the kaleidoscope of life. But there was nothing gay or Bohemian about them now. The end of their dream, their period, was settling upon them, and they were waking to know it in their old age. Only one of those I met survives today, and he, through his cheerful adaptability and stout North Country heart, has won a modest ease in retirement. The rest are as forgotten as their work, which seemed so apposite, almost so fresh, sixty years back.

Yet even in their twilight they had a kind of forlorn shrivelled grandeur. They were not the Millais's, the Boyd Houghtons, the Pinwells of the Victorian woodcut era, nor had they Dalziels or Swains now to reproduce their work. But they possessed the sincerity and thoroughness of that epoch. They lacked only imagination: they were void even of complacency. They offered instead a kind of doglike pains-taking, a simple fidelity such as they were wont to put into their innumerable drawings of pet animals. Some of them, it struck my young imperfect sympathy, had an almost Landseer appeal in their very look and mien. I remember well old Mr Slender, who could draw with an infinite fineness every hair on a monkey's coat or a kitten's tail. He had desiccated the free splendour of Bewick's woodcutting, and used the mere sawdust of his own contemporaries. But he came into our office, with his long Du Maurier moustache white but still luxuriant, as if Don Quixote had been his ancestor and Captain Costigan (I fear) no very distant kinsman.

And Mr Francis. He was the dirtiest artist I ever met. Not that his person was either untidy or unpleasant. In fact, I am not sure that 'dirty' is a just epithet. He simply didn't wash himself clean. It is an idle fancy, but somehow I associated this with his great failing as a draughtsman – his complete inability to draw noses. He was one of our 'figure-subject' artists, and, except that he portrayed the last fashion but three, and of a lower-middle-class stratum at that, he was trustworthy– save for noses. His children picking blackberries or finding a thrush's nest (stock situations) always wore boot-buttons in the middle of their faces, after the manner of politicians in some modern caricatures. It occurred to me that he spent so much time over the other details – the foliage, the distant kine, the spire lit by the westering ray – that, just as he forgot to wash his face, so he overlooked the noses, and put them in as a hasty piece of last-minute routine. It did not matter, once I had observed his weakness. He drew only in wash upon wood, so that a direction to the skilled engraver readily brought some modelling into the round blobs of putty. Woodcutting had its practical convenience; and he died before the wood-block vanished entirely from cheap popular magazines. He always offered a picture as 'a priddy liddle thing I'd like to show you'. His works, or their like, still lurk, in colour, in Parish Almanacs, or, in black and white, in one or two Parish Magazine 'centres'.

I could recall others, like Mr Layne, who drew burglars (apprehended, of course, by unselfish Katie who had stayed at home), Philip Sidneys, drummer-boys, Old London, Good but not Clever Wilfrids, dying ducks in thunderstorms, with equal versatility, speed, and lumpiness – poor man, he needed the money badly for internal use; or Mr Speedwell, who had illustrated some of the minor Mid-Victorian novelists, and even in 1900 or so could be trusted to produce knights and ladies and horsemen in the Sir John Gilbert manner, but less gallantly; or a few who acquired the new technique of drawing for direct 'line' reproduction and half tone, and then, after adapting themselves, were found not to draw well or spiritedly enough – they, whose spirit was numb. But it was the engravers who made me conscious of the altered world; that magazine world whose seismic changes between 1860 and 1900 I had not experienced, as they had, by close ordeal.

I came into a queer intimacy with them. They were the last survivors of the *Illustrated London News* foundation.* Our Mr James was dead, and though I could pick up a good deal from Mr Mullins and the publisher and the printer, I could not pretend to argue with the engravers on technical points. Pretend I did, however, and since they had much at stake in those changing times, they helped me generously and threw in pretences of their own – as, that I knew better than they did, or that their faint hint had been my original suggestion. They were glad, too, after climbing our steep stairs, to sit down and talk about old and new times and how (most valuable to me) so-and-so had got his effects. I absorbed the atmosphere, and it soon became easy for me to say, for instance, to gentle old Mr Stacey, who grew more and more like Father Christmas every day, 'Could you take out the 'stops' there?' or '*Enter* that, I think, Mr. Stacey'; so that his still deft and steady hand could take out in a trice some infinitesimal coarseness which in printing would turn fine shades into a motley of small blots. I was sorry when one day his daughter came shyly with a half-finished block which he would never complete, and asked if we could possibly pay full price for it; and yet glad, for if he had lived, before long we should have had to be paying him no price at all, or so rarely that it would come to the same thing.

I felt less compassionate towards Mr Poins. He was almost a joke – a kind of Falstaff turned conjurer – and valiantly he accepted the character. He had something of Chaucer's Pardoner in him, too, in his india-rubber versatility. He was certainly the cleverest engraver I ever met, in the highly skilled journeyman way. What is more, he had learnt the new methods, and while he would cut as many wood-blocks as he could secure, he attached himself securely to a modern engraver, and took up the delicate work of 'touching' the automatically etched zincos. That is a refinement little practised in

---

* One at least in actual fact, I believe; but I use that honoured name generically, as a matter of history, and without diminishing my respect for a magazine today younger than ever. The *News* not only made history but lives it.

England now, though I believe the better American magazines still use it. Poins was a genius at it. He always carried a few tools in a pocket-case, and in the twinkling of an eye, while I looked on at the conjuring trick, he would transform a dull blotch into a thing of nicely graduated values.

That, indeed, is the right word. His eyes did twinkle. He was a very large man, with a red face and a slightly waxed moustache. If he twirled the moustache and his small bright eyes shone wickedly, as he drew himself up with conscious pomp, it meant he was in a condition to perform miracles – upon his own work, which now and then he hustled through shamelessly, or upon another wood-engraver's block, or upon a mere mechanical piece of metal. When it was done, he would take a flat pull of it on our small hand-press, and lay it before me without a word; swaying a little, but otherwise grave, erect, and huge as a retired City policeman. He knew he was a master of craft and cunning, and he was proud of it. And that was all the pride there was in him, for after a glance at the proof I invariably laughed, and he joined in. We recognised, somehow, the absurdity of so gifted a man being so utterly past ambition or even ordinary common sense. He was large-mindedly heedless about money, though he took care to get it. If you told him his account was incorrect, he accepted your word. If he wanted cash, he said so. If you asked a small technical favour and suggested he should charge for it, as often as not he would refuse payment. He rectified his own lapses with a hilarious mixture of equanimity and gusto.

I never knew his exact age. He had been working for *The — Magazine* at least thirty years when I met him. Mr Mullins's henchman told me of his encounters with Mr James in the early days. Mr James was a little irascible, but he knew his man. If Poins sent in a baddish piece of work, James would summon him, and make certain arrangements. The engraver would be asked to wait a few minutes. An emmisary would pass outward with a parcel as if upon an errand: 'Come and have one round the corner, Mr Poins, while you're waiting.' Ten minutes later Poins came back ready for any sleight of hand. The only time this method failed, I was told, was once just before Easter. James and Poins were each in a hurry, because both were in some preposterous military costume of that 'Riflemen, form' epoch, and anxious to get away for manoeuvres. James also was a very big man. They confronted one another, and swelled and swelled like a pair of turkey-cocks. Poins slightly the redder. Luckily someone else came in, and they both saw that they were being and looking ridiculous.

That redoubtable engraver never drank to excess. He belonged in soul to the age which lived 'well' and produced the less crapulous jokes in *The Pink 'Un*. Perhaps there was a little more of respectable solidity in the alleged viciousness of his times than in the corresponding quality today. At least he earned his money by his skill – and earned it before he spent it.

All that kind of thing vanished during my thirty years of editorship. It did not survive the War, in outward appearance. All the Victorians had disappeared from our pages well before 1914, except one or two who could adapt themselves reasonably. I had taken over in 1901 traditions and customs at which it is now easy to laugh. I used, I hope, the spirit of them, but modified the letter, slowly but thoroughly. If I look back at, say, the volume for 1906, I find it utterly different from that of 1931; but 1926 is equally different from either. And yet readers and contributors always write about it as if it never changed.

I am not going to describe how the slow evolution has come about. It started in 1866 and it is going on in 1932; so that my New Zealander did not find ruins round St Paul's, like Macaulay's. Unless a children's magazine has a complete and drastic revolution – which, in the world of periodicals, sooner or later means death – it must always change without seeming to do so. Its public is perpetually undergoing, in mass, the metabolism of the human body, which renews itself every seven years; or the man-controlled destiny of a Kentish ash-copse, cut back and regrown likewise every seven years. That period, oddly enough, is just about the duration of one generation of child-readers.

So *The – Magazine*, in the first nine of such cycles of its life, has had to revive its tissues ceaselessly, sacrificing this or that limb, dropping this outworn feature, growing that novel one for a fresh set of circumstances; so that it has produced, as it were, one new young body about the time when Edward VII died, as it had when Victoria died; and another when the War ended; and still another – when? Now; when I realise that editors also must be cut down that the forest may live.

Editor's Notes

I An Introductory Survey

1. *Statistics.* Darton was here probably relying on the annual book-production figures given in the trade press. The *Publishers Circular* for 1930, for instance, showed that there were 1,479 new children's books and 3,922 works of fiction published out of a total of 15,393 books, including reprints. Children's books continued to occupy a dominant position, and fifty years later, in the figures for 1980, they numbered 3,485 to 5,145 works of fiction (global total for the year 48,158). One must gloomily add that in this year children's books were also exceeded by books on Political Science and Economy (4,269).

2. *A Little Pretty Pocket-Book.* Much work has been done on John Newbery's publications since 1932 and the chief sources of new information are listed at the end of Chapter VIII. Details will be found there of a complete facsimile of the *Pocket-Book*, with editorial notes, against which Darton's text has been checked. The history of the Newbery house is tabulated in Appendix 2.

3. *still in every nursery library.* Comparison of the *Pocket-Book* with a bumper book of 1977, *The Wonder Book of Stories and Poems* edited by Eric Duthie, yields one item in common: a reprinting of the fable of 'The Husbandman and the Stork'. Newbery's verse text is the superior version.

II The Legacy of the Middle Ages: (i) Fables

1. *John Ogilby.* The complex publishing history of Ogilby and Barlow's various fable books is discerningly analysed by Edward Hodnett in his *Francis Barlow* (see chapter Book List). He is less than enthusiastic about the 'unoriginal and unprepossessing' contributions of Stoop.

2. *apocolocyntosis.* Lit. 'turning into a pumpkin'.

3. *middle-class giant* In his 1932 edition Darton ran into some confusions over the complicated genealogy of eighteenth-century editions of Aesop. Rather than attempt an annotated clarification I have rewritten all his p. 22 on the subject of Newbery and Bewick, incorporating his own observations where possible.

4. *acknowledgment of influence.* Notes on Bewick's various essays in fable illustration appear in S. Roscoe's *Thomas Bewick; a bibliography raisonné* (London, 1953); and a close analysis of Kirkall's work as an engraver – with a strong case for his being the Croxall illustrator – is given by Edward Hodnett in his 'Elisha Kirkall *c.* 1682–1742' in the *Book Collector*, vol. XXV, Summer 1976, no. 2, pp. 195–209.

5. *the edition of 1703.* This is *Gesta Romanorum or, Forty-five Histories Originally (as 'tis said) Collected from the Roman Records. With Applications, or Morals for Suppressing Vice and Encouraging Virtue and the Love of GOD* . . . Darton probably consulted the British Museum copy (vol. I only).

6. *title-page.* 'Fifty Eight Remarkable Histories'. The title-page otherwise is very similar to that of 1703.

7. *a chapbook edition of 1705.* In fact a 140-page edition designed for popular consumption, rather than, strictly, a chapbook: *The Voyages and Travels of Sir John Mandevile, Knight*, printed for R. Chiswell etc. (1705). It is said to be a new edition of a text produced by the same publisher in 1696.

8. *Hampton Court.* The sculpture at Hampton Court is one of ten beasts originally carved for Henry VIII and restored early in the twentieth century. For the coronation of Queen Elizabeth II in 1953 another set of ten beasts was modelled and cast in plaster by James Woodford and these stood guard outside the Annexe of Westminster Abbey. Later a book was published about them: *The Queen's Beasts,*

described by H. Stanford Landon, and illustrated in colour by Edward Bawden and Cecil Keeling. At least one child of the fifties loved to pore over these boldly stylized compositions rolling his tongue round 'the falcon of the Plantagenets' and 'the black bull of Clarence'. James Woodford's beasts can now also be seen at Hampton Court.

9. *a fine moral game.* Presumably 'The Noble Game of Elephant and Castle; or, Travelling in Asia', a copy of which is in the Osborne Collection at Toronto, with an eighty-four page 'explanation, or key'. A variety of similar games are on permanent exhibition at the Museum of Childhood at Bethnal Green.

III The Legacy of the Middle Ages: (ii) Romance and Manners

1. *Betty's precise dealings were.* As Darton notes on p. 89, the tales of Mme D'Aulnoy do contain 'some scraps of far-distant folk-lore' and it is not impossible that Betty would have met fairies in these pages, since by 1709 the best-known stories had been translated: *Tales of the Fairys* (1699), and as the fourth part of her *Diverting Works* (1707).

2. *popular literature.* As with that other English folk hero, King Arthur, texts about Robin Hood were certainly read by children from manuscript times onward, but it is hard to establish when these heroes became the subjects of books *only* for children. It is possible that the earliest such version is *The History of Robin Hood*, with three elegant engravings, published by Tabart as one of his 'popular stories' in 1804, unless the *Entertaining and Remarkable History . . .* Printed by assignment of T. Carnan (Roscoe J102A) is a preceding example. As for a *Robin Hood's Garland* done by Bewick before 1795, the evidence is scanty. No copy is known.

3. *printed almost haphazard.* This is not quite fair to the *Bevis* printed for W. Thackeray of Duck Lane in 1689, which is probably the book that Darton is referring to (the British Museum copy is bound up in a volume which also includes the 1705 Mandeville mentioned on p. 27). In fact the narrative of the *Bevis* is set uniformly in black letter, with Roman being used for all proper nouns and dialogue and – with this procedure reversed for the preface – the chapter summaries and running heads. The seventy-eight-page book has clearly been printed in a hurry, but it has a rugged orderliness about it which is not displeasing. Among books advertised on the last leaf are popular titles like *The Seven Champions, The History of Fortunatus* and *Robin Hood's Garland,* with a note 'At the aforementioned places, any Country-Chapmen or others, may be furnished with all sorts of small Books, Broadsides and Ballads at very reasonable Rates.'

4. *dreadful works.* In their *Rymes of Robyn Hood* (see p. 50) Dobson and Taylor quote another notable condemnation which happens to bracket texts already discussed by Darton. William Tyndale, in 1528, attacks those who allow the laity to read 'Robin Hood and Bevis of Hampton . . . with a thousand histories . . . as filthy as the heart can think, to corrupt the minds of youth withal'.

5. *The Gentleman's Calling.* Published as 'By the author of "The Whole Duty of Man"' – one of the most popular devotional books ever printed (1658). In an article in the *Library*, vol. VI, June 1951, no. 1, Paul Elmen clarifies the case for the author being Richard Allestree.

6. *but not of probability.* This is the standard translation given of a letter originally written in French: 'enfin c'est une lecture trés frivole que celle des Romans, et l'on y perd tout le temps qu'on y donne. Les vieux Romans qu'on ecrivoit il y a cent ou deux cent ans comme Amadis de Gaule, Roland le Furieux, et autres, étoient farci d'enchantements, de magiciens, de geans, et de ces sortes de sottes impossibilités; au lieu que les Romans plus modernes se tiennent au possible, mais pas au vraisemblable.'

7. *alphabet printed in book form.* It is true that in 1520 John Dorne was listing numerous ABC's 'in papiro' at 1*d.* and 'in pergameno' at 2*d.* but Madan suggests that these were probably single leaves.

8. *Great A and Bouncing B.* I have not traced such a bookshop. Possibly Darton is confusing the sign with that of Thomas Bailey which he mentions on p. 208, possibly he was recalling Canning's jest in the *Microcosm* of June 11, 1787 about the 'Bouncing B in Shoe Lane'.

9. *Jill doth love no leane.* The phrase appears twice in the *Paroemiologia* and when it is set against 'marinam auditionem fluviali abluit sermone' it is followed by its proper conclusion: 'Yet betwixt them both they lick the dishes cleane.'

IV   The Puritans: 'Good Godly Books'

1. *all early American children's books.* According to d'Alté Welch in his *Bibliography of American Children's Books* . . . (see General Book List, section 1. 3. i) the earliest children's books published in New England were either sermons or piracies of Puritan books first published in Old England (the earliest seems to be Janeway's *Token* (Boston, 1700)), but there were also some courtesy books (e.g. *The School of Good Manners* (New London, 1715), based on the English *School of Manners* by J. Garretson, 4th edn (London, 1701)). Perhaps the first 'storybook' 'not patterned after an English work' was *The History of the Holy Jesus*, 3rd edn (Boston, 1746), and it was not long after the appearance of this that a greater number of secular books began to be published – many based upon the work of Newbery and other English publishers.

2. *wrote also another Token.* This is not so. The book described here is said on the title-page to be by 'J.J.' but much of its text consists of excerpts, or very close paraphrases, of Thomas White's *Little Book* and the two parts of Janeway's own *Token* (plus of course the poems by Chear). The 1709 edition was published by Benjamin Harris of Gracechurch Street – a volatile character – who spent some time in New England where he was probably involved with the editing and publishing of the *New England Primer* round about 1686. He had a shop there 'over against the Old Meeting House' and it is worth noting that the 1700 Janeway *Token* mentioned in the previous note came from that address. It is not clear whence Darton got the evidence for the 'undoubted' earlier editions of the *Token for Youth* nor for its 'great vogue'. The 1709 edition is the only one traceable, although a book of that title was advertised by John Marshall (also of Gracechurch Street) in his edition of Chear's *Looking Glass* (1708).

3. *Puritan writers.* Nicholas Horsman's *The Spiritual Bee* was 'a great companion' of Sarah Howley, the nine-year-old heroine of Janeway's first example in the *Token*. In small extenuation of the verses (which are far less controlled than the main part of the *Bee*) one should note that they were printed at the end of the book 'that the remaining pages might not be left vacant and naked'.

4. *Nathaniel Crouch.* John Dunton noted that 'he has melted down the best of our English Histories into Twelve-penny Books, which are filled with wonders, rarities and curiosities', and that he 'endeavours to fit his material to the capacity of his Readers' (*Secret History*, 1818 edn). It is a claim borne out many years later by no less a commentator than Dr Johnson who, towards the end of his life, wrote to the bookseller Charles Dilly asking him to procure 'a set of books; . . . called *Burton's Books* . . . very proper to allure backward Readers' an early use of the term much employed in post-1944 educational debates).

v   The Pedlar's Pack: 'The Running Stationers'

1. *announcement.* Not traced in any copy of the *Looking-Glass.* Mr and Mrs Opie, however, have an 'Advertisement', much as Darton gives here, in their eighth edition of Bunyan's *Heavenly Footman,* printed for John Marshall (1724). They have kindly allowed me to amend Darton's quote by reference to this volume.

2. *'remainder'.* The O.E.D., in a not very authoritative definition (which does not include use of the term as a verb), gives the earliest date as 1873. It was certainly a term commonly used in the later eighteenth century, but 1709 does seem to be remarkable.

3. *London houses today* Darton presumably meant the small publisher Horace Marshall and the technical publishers Percival Marshall, but there was also the ancient wholesaling house of Simpkin Marshall, and the Evangelical firm of Marshall, Morgan and Scott. Only the latter remains in 1980, as part of the Pentos Group of companies, which includes Ward, Lock and Co.

    To Darton's catalogue of chapbook Marshalls one should add the John Marshall of Gateshead and Newcastle-upon-Tyne, who printed and published huge quantities of booklets and song-sheets between 1800 and 1831. There is also the Richard Marshall who appeared in Darton's 1932 and 1958 editions in a footnote on p. 71: 'John Ashton (*Chapbooks* . . .) states that John Marshall was preceded in Aldermary Churchyard, as early as 1720, by R. Marshall . . .' This is puzzling. There is no such statement in Ashton's *Chapbooks* and one must assume that Darton was thinking of another reference, perhaps that in Charles Gerring's *Notes on Printers and Booksellers* (1900) where, on p. 110, Gerring cites a catalogue issued in 1764 by Cluer Dicey and Richard Marshall 'at the Printing Office in Aldermary Church-Yard'. There is a lot of evidence for the co-operation, or partnership, between these two firms, but none for R. Marshall being active as far back as 1720.

4. *'Birds, Beasts'.* The Pierpont Morgan Library has an illustrated French incunable: *Les Dictz des Oiseaux et des Bestes,* published at Châlons-sur-Marne *c.* 1493, which bears witness to the long-standing popularity of birds and beasts in the complex tradition of moralized fables and bestiaries. (See the Morgan exhibition catalogue of 1976, noted in section 1.7 of the General Book List.) Everything points to the subject as a natural one for card-games, using 'Lottery Pictures', in the eighteenth century, and hence leading on to the 'Lottery Books' and educational card-games of a later period.

5. *chapbooks themselves.* This paragraph has been amended by reference chiefly to Edward Hodnett's *English Woodcuts 1480–1535* (rev. edn., Oxford, The Bibliographical Society, 1973). Despite the necessary limitations which Dr Hodnett imposes upon himself for preparing this masterly catalogue it is possible to draw some conclusions about Continental influences on English illustration at this early period, and to foresee future uses for (especially) the non-religious illustrations. (For instance, De Worde's 'Friar and Boy', Hodnett no. 876, presents motifs clearly continued in an illustration for an Aldermary chapbook shown in Ashton, p. 238.)

6. *T. Cheney* was the son of the founder of a firm chronicled in *John Cheney and his Descendants; Printers in Banbury since 1767* (Banbury, 1936). This includes as an Appendix an inventory of the chapbooks and broadsides in stock *c.* 1815, with romances like *Valentine and Orson,* godly books like *Youth's Looking Glass,* fairy-tales like *Sleeping Beauty,* and nursery rhymes like *Simple Simon, The House that Jack Built,* and *Tom Thumb's Plaything.* Nothing is said, however, about stereotype plates still being extant, and from the scarcity of Cheney chapbooks today this seems unlikely. Possibly Darton is thinking of plates made by another Banbury firm of chapbook publishers: J. G. Rusher who put out two long series of children's chapbooks: sixteen titles (*c.* 1820), issued in coloured sugar-paper wrappers, and

eighteen titles (*c.* 1835), with covers printed on part of the sheet (see fig. 14). Many examples of these two series are to be found today, either in collections or in auctioneers' or booksellers' catalogues.

7. *well-known printing firm.* This might have been Harrison and Sons Ltd, printers 'by appointment', who were at 44–7 St Martin's Lane. Hazell's were at 52 Long Acre and 160 Shaftesbury Avenue.

VI Fairy-Tale and Nursery Rhyme

1. *then or now.* Here followed two paragraphs on the translation of Perrault into English which have now been overtaken by events. Indeed, at the end of them Harvey Darton warned of the perils of 'over-certain bibliography' and 'the horrid fate of old children's books'. The bibliographer in him would therefore have been delighted when Iona and Peter Opie announced in their *Oxford Dictionary of Nursery Rhymes* (1951, pp. 39–40) that a once-disputed first translation of Perrault into English was truly the first. This is the *Histories* noted on p. 88, translated by Robert Samber and printed for J. Pote and R. Montagu in 1729, a text which itself – or in a re-working by one G. M. – dominated English editions of Perrault throughout much of the following two centuries.

2. *fairy repositories.* The chief 'fairy repository' in which *Graciosa* was to be found, albeit abbreviated, in 1932 was *The Red Fairy Book*, edited by Andrew Lang (1890). In the 1980s it continues in print in that version in a new edition of Lang's work (1976). Several other tales by Mme D'Aulnoy are also preserved with varying completeness, in Lang's *Colour Fairy Books*, while Iona and Peter Opie assign classic status to *The Yellow Dwarf* by including it in their edition of *The Classic Fairy Tales* (see p. 105). From their notes to the tale it would seem that it was well established in pantomime repertory from the early nineteenth century onwards.

3. *Beauty and the Beast.* First published by Mme de Beaumont not in the *Cabinet* but as a story, *La Belle et la Bête*, which lightens the didactic burden of the *Magasin des Enfans* (London, 1756) mentioned by Darton on p. 91. It was first translated with the rest of the *Magasin* in 1761.

4. *'Farewell to the Fairies'.* As given in Corbet's *Poëtica Stromata* of 1648, this carries the title *A Proper New Ballad Intituled The Faeryes Farewell: Or God-A-Mercy Will. To be Sung or Whiseled to the Tune of the Meddow Brow by the Learned; by the Unlearned to the Tune of Fortune.*

5. *an imitation of Sarah Fielding's Governess.* This anonymous work *The Governess; or, Evening Amusements at a Boarding School* was published by Vernor and Hood in 1800. It includes Oriental tales of a moral nature, but Mrs Trimmer is unlikely to have enjoyed the references to Mecca and Medina, or to chewing opium.

6. *the danger of being a fairy-tale.* Newer didacticisms that have had currency in the decades since 1940 have also sought to harness fairy-tales to their objects – thus feminist and conservationist versions – but these have rarely been carried through with the panache of Cruikshank. 'Fear and dislike' of fairy-tales (p. 99) has also manifested itself in political attacks on the genre as 'anti-working-class' etc.

7. *this little classic.* In their catalogue *Three Centuries of Nursery Rhymes and Poetry for Children* (see p. 105) Iona and Peter Opie argue plausibly for this 'Voll II' indeed being the sequel to 'Vol I' now lost – probably the *Tommy Thumb's Song Book* which M. Cooper advertised in *The London Evening Post*, March 17–22, 1744. Equally plausibly this volume may be seen as being identical with an American book of the same title, published by Isaiah Thomas, at Worcester, Massachusetts in 1788. (The Opies exhibited a 1794 edition of the same book.)

In discussing the make-up of the volume, Darton confessed himself unsure of its method of production. In fact, it would appear that the whole book was printed from copper plates with the little pictures engraved and the letters stamped (see the present editor's 'Tommy Thumb's Pretty Song Book' in *The Private Library*, 3rd ser. vol. III, Spring 1980, no. 1, pp. 16–18.

Two other comments are perhaps justifiable on this tiny but monumental work. The first relates to Darton's conjecture on its relationship to *Mother Goose* – a link which can be modestly supported by noting the appearance in both books of the phrase 'Raw Head and Bloody Bones' as applied to ogres. The second comment relates to the picture in the concluding advertisement for the *Child's New Plaything* which was published in 1743. The figure is in fact a miniature version of the one appearing as frontispiece to the *Plaything*, and must be assumed to be His Highness Prince George.

8. *rare successors*. Fuller bibliographical information is now available than when Darton wrote of eighteenth-century nursery rhyme books (much of it in works by Iona and Peter Opie). In consequence considerable redrafting of this paragraph has been necessary.

VII   Interim: Between the Old and the New

1. *chapbook versions very early*. Here – and elsewhere, both in Darton and other commentators – assertions are made about the rapid conversion of popular works into chapbooks, but these assertions are too rarely supported by bibliographical evidence. (In the case of Watts's *Divine Songs*, which is often said to have early become a chapbook, J. H. P. Pafford has shown that it was issued only by its official publisher during the period of its copyright.) A detailed study of *Robinson Crusoe* by Erhard Dahl (see p. 119) shows an early dissemination of 'pirated' abridgements of the book, especially by the firms of Bettesworth and Hitch, but the arrival of 'summary chapbooks' was much later, and this kind of evolution holds good for *Gulliver's Travels* too. Teerink's *Bibliography* of Swift (Philadelphia, 1963) lists early abridgements and serializations (e.g. in the *Penny London Post* of 1826), but the first chapbook edition noted is an Aldermary Churchyard one conjecturally dated in the 1750s.

2. *caused little stir*. During the 1970s interest in 'the wild boy of Aveyron' was stimulated through Truffaut's film *L'Enfant Sauvage* (1970). At least two books discussed the matter in detail: Harlan Lane's *Wild Boy of Aveyron* (Cambridge, Mass., 1976) and Roger Shattuck's *The Forbidden Experiment* (1980).

3. *on its merits*. The most remarkable edition of *Peter Wilkins* in print in 1932 was a thick quarto volume with illustrations in line and colour by Edward Bawden (1928).

4. *L'Île Mystérieuse*. The adaptability of desert islands to the needs of modern novelists can be seen in such adult works as Michael Tournier's *Vendredi* (1967) and William Golding's *The Lord of the Flies* (1954). There is an unexamined relationship between the group Crusoe theme of the latter and Jules Verne's *Deux Ans de Vacances* (1888), translated by Olga Marx and published for a youthful readership as *A Long Vacation* (1967).

VIII   John Newbery

1. *Welsh's fundamental list*. S. Roscoe's *Bibliography* of the Newbery firms (see p. 139) now supersedes much of Welsh and should be consulted on the many intractable problems that arise in tracing and dating eighteenth-century children's books. Darton's chapter on Newbery has been corrected and in places re-worded in

consultation with Roscoe's book – but his general approach via Welsh has necessarily had to stand.

2. *the three Descriptions.* Roscoe lists these J.N. publications among his adult books (by David Henry, no. A219). The four volumes for children known as *The Curiosities of London and Westminster* were first published by F.N. (nephew) in 1770.

3. *the first genuine 'children's publisher'.* There were precursors, but of these, very little is known of the motives behind Mary Cooper's brief incursion into books for small children (see p. 101) and very little about the 'Gigantick Histories' of Thomas Boreman which he published at his stall 'near the Two Giants in Guildhall'. There were ten of these volumes: *The Gigantick History of the Two Famous Giants and Other Curiosities in Guildhall* (2 vols., 1740); *Curiosities in the Tower of London* (2 vols., 1741); *The History and Description of the Famous Cathedral of St Paul's* (2 vols., 1740); *Westminster Abbey* (3 vols., 1742–3) and *The History of Cajanus the Swedish Giant* (1742), and what is significant about them is that – like Mary Cooper's books – they display moments of light-heartedness which are one of the hallmarks of Newbery's best manner but which are appearing a year or two in advance of him. The lightness of touch (not to say levity), which shows in the 'editing' of *Tommy Thumb's Pretty Song Book*, are paralleled in Boreman's slightly earlier work by such things as the diminutive size (and the mockery made of it), the use of specially cut illustrations, the Dutch floral binding and a certain avuncularity of tone (not least the amusing little subscription lists at the start of each volume which included in the first publication 'Giant Corineus, 100 Books' and 'Giant Gogmagog 100 Books'). As has been noted above (p. 29) John Newbery knew and used one of Boreman's few other known publications, the *Description of Three Hundred Animals* (1730), and it is surely incontestable that he incorporated wholesale into his own publishing the ideas and the feeling for entertainment present in the few books of these predecessors (indeed Boreman can also be found in *Cajanus* advertising his own bookstall). As Darton rightly insists on p. 135, Newbery's genius lay in the consistent exploitation of these ideas in a practical commerical fashion. (Why Mary Cooper did not compete with him in the twenty years before her death in 1763 is inexplicable; Boreman probably died in 1743 and therefore was beyond competition.)

As a brief example of the way Boreman sought to wed charm to his didactic intentions we give below the verses with which he prefaced the first volume of his *Curiosities:*

> To the AUTHOR
> Of the
> CURIOSITIES
> In the
> Tower of London.
>
> Too rigid precepts
>   often fail,
> Where short amusing
>   tales prevail.
> That author, doubtless,
>   aims aright,
> Who joins instruction
>   with delight
> Tom Thumb shall now
>   be thrown away,
> And Jack, who did
>   the Giants slay;
> Such ill concerted,
>   artless lyes,

Our British Youth
   shall now despise:
In thy Gigantick works
   they'll find
Something to please,
   and form the mind.

Thy happy talent,
   Friend, pursue,
In thy own way
   search London thro':
Conduct thy Lilli-
   putians round,
Where any curious
   things are found.
What treasures in
   the Tow'r are laid,
And here –
   as in a glass display'd.
To Gresham College
   next repair,
And shew the works
   of Nature there.
Or, on the Abbey
   cast thy eye,
Where British Bards
   and Heroes lie
Obscur'd in ever-
   lasting night,
Who, living, were
   the world's delight.

Thence may thy LITTLE
   READERS learn,
That grandeur's vain,
   of no concern;
Since Death,
   with his impartial sling,
Wounds both the beggar
   and the king.

   Go on –
May all thy Volumes
   please!
Be fill'd with lectures
   such as these!
Meet with reception
   from all hands,
And live as long
   As Guildhall stands!

I am

thy affectionate friend,
   and well-wisher,
      A.Z.

4. *in monthly numbers in 1751*. None is extant, but the full background to this important experiment has been set out by Mrs Jill Grey in her 'The Lilliputian Magazine – a Pioneering Periodical?', *Journal of Librarianship*, vol. II, April 1970, no. 2, pp. 107–15.

5. *pin-prick system*. Lady Gomme in her *Traditional Games . . .* (1894), vol. I, p. 95, reports a game popular at least to the mid nineteenth century in which pins were poked randomly into the reverse side of leaves where pictures were present in schoolbooks. A rhyme accompanied:

> Dab a prin in my lottery-book;
> Dab ane, dab twa, dab a' your prins awa'.

6. *British Museum*. See the article by R. J. Roberts on 'The 1765 edition of Goody Two-Shoes', *British Museum Quarterly*, vol. XXIX, Summer 1965, pp. 67–70.

7. *Giles Jones*. A note of the evidence for Giles Jones being the author of *Goody Two-Shoes* is given in volume II of the *Catalogue* of the Osborne Collection (1975), p. 889.

8. *green vellum (backs)*. In a discussion of bindings (including Dutch paper) Roscoe argues cogently for 1768 as the date when Newbery and Carnan introduced 'the vellum manner'. *Bibliography*, pp. 393–6.

x   **The Moral Tale: (i) Didactic**

1. *(1780?)*. The exact dating of many early books published by John Marshall is not easy and an illustration of this is provided by *The History of a great many Little Boys and Girls*. This can fairly certainly be ascribed to 1780 since an early copy of the book exists with a four-page advertisement that lists only one other book by Dorothy Kilner: the first volume only of the *Five Principles of Religion*. This was published with a Dedication dated January 14, 1780, and since the second volume was added later, with a further dedication dated August 17, 1780, it may be conjectured that *The History* with its advertisements was published in between these two volumes. Arguments of this kind need to be adduced for many books of the period, hence the rash of (?)'s and *circas* in this chapter.

2. *forebears*. The 'erratic copy' may have been a set of proofs, in view of the pencilled 'directions', but other copies of the 1783(?) edition have the printer's apology. The book seems to have been treated in a generally cavalier fashion. At one stage a damaged engraving for the 'Country Walk' story in volume II was changed. Copies of later editions exist with sheets bound up from different printings and, consequently, with mistakes in pagination.

3. *editions . . . were not small*. Darton cites no evidence but his figures are probably fairly accurate. A contemporary summary of editions and print numbers in a manuscript volume kept by the Darton firm shows two thousand to be a reasonable figure for many first printings – especially when it is remembered that by the first decade of the nineteenth century the iron press was permitting more rapid work in print shops than ever before. (As a matter of interest, many children's novels by new authors in the glutted 1970s were not printed in hardback editions of more than three thousand copies.)

4. *good habits*. This quotation not traced. It may come from the extensive Sherwood manuscripts which Darton worked on for his edition of the *Life and Times of Mrs Sherwood*.

5. *known to almost all. . . to 1887*. A difficult conjecture to substantiate. However, judging from the number of references to the book by writers brought up in Victorian times, and by the book's presence in lists of rewards and classics, it could be said that it was well-known to children of Anglican homes and probably was known by them up to 1920. Two notable abridged texts appeared in 1902 (ed.

Mary E. Palgrave and illustrated in *art nouveau* style by Florence Rudland) and 1913 (ed. Lady Strachey, illustrated by Sybil Tawse); there were also two popular excerpts in T. C. Jack's *Grandmother's Favourites* series (both 1908).

XI   The Moral Tale: (ii) Persuasive; chiefly in verse

1. *editors of his Letters omit.* A new and exhaustively annotated edition of *The Letters of Charles and Mary Lamb* has been under way since 1975 under the editorship of Edwin W. Marrs, Jr, and where possible quotations have been checked against this text. The 'irreverence' in the letter to Manning of January 2, 1810 supposes the author to follow various 'accessions of dignity' from Mr C. Lamb to Pope Innocent, 'higher than which is nothing but the Lamb of God' (vol. III, Ithaca and London, 1978, p. 35). Marrs confirms the general doubt that Lamb had anything to do with the Phillips–Tabart *Ranks and Dignities.*
2. *probably by Mulready.* Darton added here E. V. Lucas's remark that it was customary to assign the engraving of Mulready's drawings to Blake. Modern analysis of the technique of the engraving does not support this view, nor can Blake have been in any way responsible for the quite different illustrations, from several hands, that were made for the now exceedingly rare issue of the *Tales* as individual, paper-covered sixpenny booklets.

XII   Interim Again: the Dawn of Levity

1. *John Harris published a longish poem.* Harris's was the first edition of the *Butterfly's Ball* in book form and he took the text from a printing that appeared at the end of November 1806 in the *Gentleman's Magazine,* a journal in which he had shares. However, Valerie Alderson has found a printing in the *Ladies Monthly Museum* (Sharpe, Vernor and Hood) for November 1806, and considers that, on the evidence of dates within the magazines, this was the earlier appearance. The poem here differs in points of detail from the *G.M.* version, and there is a note that a musical rendering of the verses had been given at the annual dinner of the New Musical Fund, the words set by Sir George Smart. If a programme of this entertainment ever comes to light it may yield an even earlier edition of the poem.
2. *'O Looking-Glass creatures . . . draw near'.* The rhythm of this line supports Darton's suggestion, but the rest of Alice's poem shows it to be a parody of *Bonnie Dundee.*
3. *children's books yet known.* Increased knowledge of the publishing activities of the period require this statement to be modified. Without disputing the freshness of Harris's presentation of Roscoe's poem – and the verve with which he exploited the sequels – one should point out that Harris had already carried through one major exercise with a group of engraved books in this format. Sarah Catherine Martin's *Comic Adventures of Old Mother Hubbard and her Dog* (1805) with its *Continuation* (1806), and *Dame Trot and her Cat* (1806) with its *Continuation* (also 1806). Furthermore a competitor such as Benjamin Tabart was not slow to work the vein himself with such adventures as *A True History of a Little Old Woman Who Found a Silver Penny* (1806) and his beautiful *Songs for the Nursery* (an 1808 edition has plates dated 1806). The appearance of so many examples before *The Butterfly's Ball* testifies to a widespread new mood in children's book publishing which that volume caught. (For a summary of the murky background to the invention of *Old Mother Hubbard,* see the *Oxford Dictionary of Nursery Rhymes,* no. 365.)
4. *book-designer.* Darton here wrote that Cundall was an 'engraver' but I can find no evidence for this (although his publishing monogram was very similar to that used

by John Gilbert and he did write a brief history of wood-engraving published in 1895). See McLean's study listed on p. 251.

5. *Taggart.* In Knapp's critical edition of *Lavengro* (1901) it is noted that the manuscript read 'Bartlett' and not 'Taggart' – which possibly adds further evidence that the figure was 'Ta-bart'.

6. *the Minerva Press.* Drawing in part upon A. W. Tuer's essay on 'The Old Minerva Press' in *The Bookworm* (1888), Dorothy Blakey explains in her bibliography of the Press, published for the Bibliographical Society in 1933, that A. K. Newman was not really a children's book publisher in his own right. He might take, say, a thousand run-on copies of a Dean and Munday book and give it his own title-page, or he might take a smaller number and share the imprint, but the entrepreneurial and editorial zeal was largely that of the originators, Dean and Munday.

7. *today in Covent Garden.* i.e. 1932. Dean and Son later moved back to Ludgate Hill, but in 1980 were to be found in Southwark Street with a list that still included board books, pop-up books and doll-dressing books. Independence had gone, however, the firm having become part of the Hamlyn Publishing Group.

XIII Two New Englands: 'Peter Parley' and 'Felix Summerly'

1. *still does so.* In 1980 it is still in print in one edition, with an introduction by a modern writer for children, Barbara Willard (Hamish Hamilton Reprints Series, 1972; the series includes Farrar's *Eric* and Talbot Baines Reed's *Fifth Form at St Dominic's*).

2. *issued at frequent intervals.* The publishing details of Cundall's activities, especially with regard to these various series, is complicated to a degree which makes it difficult briefly to qualify Darton's text here. Lists (and problems) are set out in Ruari McLean's *Joseph Cundall* (see p. 251).

3. *if it was composed seriously.* The background to Hoffman's kindly, and humorous (if not satirical) intentions in composing *Struwwelpeter* is given in a chapter in Bettina Hürlimann's *Three Centuries of Children's Books in Europe* (see p. 369). Like the Grimms, 'Struwwelpeter–Hoffmann' has now become the subject of a museum – in his home town of Frankfurt am Main where a large collection of Hoffmann translations and imitations is being assembled.

XIV The Sixties, *Alice* and After

1. *well-nigh impossible.* The facts behind the publication of *Alice* in 1865 are given in Williams and Madan's *Handbook* (see p. 289). Briefly: two thousand copies were printed. Of these, forty-eight were sent out as gifts or retained by Dodgson before publication. When the decision was made to withdraw the book these were recalled and they form the pool of '1865 English Alices' of which only eighteen copies, plus a set of proof sheets, survive. The 1,952 remaining copies of this printing were not destroyed, but were sent to America either as bound copies with a new, tipped-in title page (New York, Appleton, 1866 – 1,000 copies) or as sheets with an American-printed title page (952 copies). The first 'official' edition of *Alice* was published in England in November 1866.

2. *birth-certificate.* Following this Darton wrote: 'But there seems to be no doubt that Southey invented and wrote it himself; a remarkable anachronism'. Events have proved him wrong however, for a version of *The Story of the Three Bears* was independently composed in 1831 (six years before Southey's story) by Eleanor Mure of Cecil Lodge, Hertfordshire. This metrical telling of the tale, illustrated

with watercolours, has many features in common with Southey's version, and suggests an earlier, perhaps traditional source.

The manuscript is now in the Osborne Collection of Early Children's Books in Toronto who issued privately a facsimile in 1967. A trade edition followed in the same year: Eleanor Mure, *The Story of the Three Bears* (London, 1967).

3. *Addey*. The Addey-Cundall relationship was complex, but not unfruitful. Ruari McLean has sought to untangle it in his *Joseph Cundall*, p. 75.

4. *The Cheap Repository*. An account and list of the Cheap Repository Tracts, with comments on John Marshall's ambiguous publishing role, is given by G. H. Spinney, 'Cheap Repository Tracts: Hazard and Marshall Edition', *Library*, 4th ser. vol. xx, Dec. 1939, no. 4, pp. 295–340.

5. *the leading artists contributed*. They were: Thomas Dalziel, Arthur Boyd Houghton, J. E. Millais, G. J. Pinwell, J. Tenniel and J. D. Watson. The *Bible Gallery* called upon some eighteen illustrators, including Burne Jones and Holman Hunt. The hundred illustrations for the 1863 *Pilgrim's Progress* were all by Thomas Dalziel and the 1864 *Parables* was by Millais. A modern reproduction of this volume includes a good introductory account by Mary Lutyens of the artist's dilatory behaviour in preparing his illustrations (*The Parables of Our Lord*, New York and London, 1975).

6. *for reproduction upon wood*. Darton here alluded to an invention by Walter Roberts of a process for photographing artist's drawings on to the surface of woodblocks – thus obviating a problem that always faced the engraver: the production of a reverse image. The arrival of this photographic transfer process is not clearly documented, however, and it seems to have been introduced only very gradually after about 1866. (See Paul Fildes, 'Phototransfer of Drawings in Wood-block Engraving', *Journal of the Printing Historical Society*, vol. v, 1969, pp. 87–98.)

7. *still flourishing firm*. Edmund Evans and Co continued as a separate business until the 1960s, when it merged with the firm of W. P. Griffiths, who themselves ceased trading in 1971. At that time many of the original blocks used in printing the famous picture-books were still in the printer's stock and they were subsequently dispersed privately. 'Original Woodblocks', engraved from Caldecott drawings, was the subject of a California bookseller's catalogue in 1972; other blocks from a private collection appeared in a fine Caldecott exhibition at Manchester City Art Gallery at the end of 1977.

8. *more of him as a man*. The 1970s saw a revival of interest in this talented and original draughtsman. An exhibition of his work was held at the Victoria and Albert Museum, which possesses original material, and this led to a short article by its organizer Lionel Lambourne: 'Anthropomorphic Quirks', *Country Life*, 6 January 1977, and to a book *Griset's Grotesques* (1979).

9. *autobiographical*. Farrar's biography of his father (1904) includes the first three lines of this quotation and the last two. I have not found an edition of the biography, or of *Eric*, that brings in the central section, although it sounds authentic enough.

xv   The Eighties and Today: Freedom

1. *committee meeting of moralists*. But there were active moralists on the Religious Tract Society's Joint Sub-Committee controlling publications, and part of Hutchison's editorial skill lay in circumventing their objections. See an article on the policies and financing of the magazine by Patrick Dunae: 'Boy's Own Paper: Origins and Editorial Policies', *The Private Library*, 2nd ser. vol. ix Winter 1976, No. 4, pp. 122–58. Other evidence appears in Stanley Morison's *Talbot Baines Reed; Author, Bibliographer, Typefounder* (Cambridge, privately printed, 1960). There is

also an informal account of the early years of the *Girl's Own Paper:* Wendy Forrester's *Great-Grandmama's Weekly* (Guildford, 1980.)

2. *a performer for the occasion.* For once the present editor wishes to register strong dissent from one of his author's critical summaries. Despite their very personal 'jocularity' the *Just So Stories* seem to me to be almost perfect examples of story-telling converted into print. And Kipling's own illustrations ought never to be dropped or replaced (as has happened in some particularly insensitive modern picture-book versions).

3. *adult inspiration.* Janet Adam Smith records that Stevenson as a child owned a copy of Isaac Watts's *Divine Songs* and this could be seen as influencing both *A Child's Garden* and the gently satirical *Moral Emblems.* The book is preserved at the Huntly House Museum in Edinburgh and proves to be an edition published by Tilt in 1832, illustrated after Stothard. It originally belonged to R.L.S.'s grandmother.

Appendix 1 Some Additional Notes on Victorian and Edwardian Times

1. *comment.* An anthology of nineteenth-century writing about children's books provides many varied examples: *A Peculiar Gift,* edited by Lance Salway (1976).

2. *adult curiosity.* A further example of increased activity lies in the idea of putting children's books on public exhibition. The frustrated plans for the 1914 Leipzig Fair, in which Harvey Darton was himself involved, is a case in point. Before this, however, had occurred perhaps the first ever special exhibition of early children's books, at Malvern Public Library in 1911. It is commemorated by a catalogue issued many years later: *Children's Books* (Hereford, 1976), compiled at the age of ninety-eight by F. C. Morgan, the organizer of the original display.

General Book List

At the end of his 'Introductory Survey', (Chapter I) Darton added a brief book list of general works used in the compilation of *Children's Books in England*, and this was given a supplement by Kathleen Lines in the second edition. The following much expanded list includes all the books listed by Darton (marked with an asterisk) along with his brief descriptive notes, and adds many more, including most of the general works mentioned by Kathleen Lines.

In compiling this larger list I have attempted to group the material in a systematic series of categories. This may make it more easily digestible for the reader and may at the same time be helpful to those who wish to gain specific information on the subject of children's books of the past. (As is noted in the appropriate sections, however, references to publications in some categories have not been included here, since they are to be found in the Brief Book List at the end of each chapter.)

It should be stressed that the inclusion of material in these lists is not necessarily an endorsement of its adequacy.* While I have excluded meretricious works, double or treble checking of the remaining titles may often be necessary before bibliographical certainty is achieved – or, alternatively, the certainty of uncertainty.

The list is organized in the following way:

SECTION I. SOURCES DIRECTLY ABOUT CHILDREN'S BOOKS THEMSELVES
1. General Bibliographies
2. Trade Bibliographies
3. Bibliographies on Specific Topics
    i. Limited National Bibliographies
    ii. Authors
    iii. Single Books
    iv. Publishers
    v. Genres
    vi. Magazines
    vii. Illustrated Books
4. General Location Lists
5. Specific Location Lists
6. Catalogues of Collections
    i. National Libraries (general)
    ii. National Libraries (special collections)
    iii. Special Collections in Individual Libraries
7. Exhibition Catalogues
8. Sale Catalogues
    i. Booksellers' Catalogues
    ii. Auction Catalogues

SECTION II. SOURCES ON THE DISCUSSION OF CHILDREN'S BOOKS
1. General Bibliographies
2. Bibliographies on Special Aspects
3. General Histories and Studies
    i. Published before 1933
    ii. Published after 1933

---

* See the paper 'Bibliography and Children's Books: The Present Position' in *The Library*, 5th ser. XXXII, Sept. 1977, no. 3.

1 Sources directly about children's books themselves

1 General Bibliographies

Watson, George, ed. *The New Cambridge Bibliography of English Literature*, vol. II, 1660–1800 (Cambridge University Press, 1971).

> Includes a section on Children's Books (primary and secondary sources) compiled by Iona and Peter Opie; also extensive listings of related background material (e.g. on the book trade), with the children's books of major authors also included in the appropriate author section.
>
> This pattern of treatment is followed in vol. III (1800–1900), where the special section is compiled by R. L. Green, and in vol. IV (1900–50, edited by I. R. Willison), where the compiler is B. Alderson.

2 Trade Bibliographies

Low, Sampson, comp. *The English Catalogue of Books Published from January 1835 to January 1863* (London, 1864).

> First of a series of cumulations primarily drawn from lists appearing fortnightly in the *Publisher's Circular*. Five further volumes carry the catalogue to 1900.
>
> A preliminary volume covering the years 1801–36 was edited by R. A. Peddie and Quintin Waddington (London, 1914).

The Reference Catalogue of Current Literature (London, 1874).

> First of a series (still continuing) attempting to show all English books in print at a given date. Up to 1936 the Catalogues were made up of bound, indexed sets of publishers' catalogues. The work is a supplementary publication from the publishers of the periodical *The Bookseller* (1858–), whose monthly issues throughout the nineteenth century are a mine of information on trade activity.

3 Bibliographies on Specific Topics

i Limited National Bibliographies

Pollard, A. W. and Redgrave, G. R., comps. *A Short-Title Catalogue of Books Printed in England, Scotland & Ireland . . . 1475–1640* (London, 1926).

> A second edition, revised and enlarged by W. A. Jackson, F. S. Ferguson and Katharine F. Pantzer is nearing completion. Its volume II, covering letters I–Z, was published London, 1976 (preceding volume I).
>
> A continuation of *S.T.C.* to 1700 by D. G. Wing was published in three volumes, New York, 1945; and a massive project is now being undertaken by the British Library and others to prepare a short-title catalogue of eighteenth-century English books. This is bound to yield much more information on the incunabula of children's literature.

Welch, d'Alté A. *A Bibliography of American Children's Books Published Prior to 1821* (Worcester, Mass. 1972).

> Contains many references to related European publications. These are even more extensively detailed in the first edition of the Bibliography, published in six parts

in the *Proceedings* of the American Antiquarian Society between April 1963 and October 1967.

ii Authors

Bibliographies of individual authors (e.g. Slade on Edgeworth, or Duff Stewart on the Taylor family) are given in the chapter Book Lists, or in *N.C.B.E.L.*

iii Single books

Editions of individual works (e.g. Jill Grey's edition of Sarah Fielding's *The Governess*) may sometimes include a detailed publishing history. Some such editions have been noted in the chapter Book Lists or the Editor's Notes.

iv Publishers

The key role played by publishers in the field of children's literature gives special value to such bibliographies as those by S. Roscoe of the Newbery firms and M. Moon of John Harris, noted in the appropriate chapter Book Lists.

v Genres

Bibliographical entry to categories of publishing such as courtesy books or poetry for children is indicated in the chapter Book Lists.

vi Magazines

Egoff, Sheila A. *Children's Periodicals of the Nineteenth Century; a survey and bibliography* (London, 1951).

Indispensable, but badly in need of revision.

Lofts, W. O. G. and Adley, D. J. *Old Boys Books; a complete catalogue* [London] 1969).

Acknowledging much help received from the editors of the small, specialist publications: *The Collectors' Digest*, ed. Herbert Leckenby, and *The Story Paper Collector*, ed. William H. Gander.

Wolff, M. *et al. The Waterloo Directory of Victorian Periodicals; Phase I* (Waterloo, Ontario, 1976).

Includes children's periodicals, but, as Phase I of a long-term project, its facts about them have not always been checked in detail.

vii Illustrated books

As Harvey Darton suggests on p.139 this is a specialist area of study. (It is also one where bibliographical control is singularly uneven.) In this and later sections only a few important items have been listed. Further guidance may initially be sought in the columns of *N.C.B.E.L.* (section 1.1 above).

Houfe, Simon *The Dictionary of British Book Illustrators and Caricaturists 1800–1914, with introductory chapters on the rise and progress of the art* (Woodbridge, 1978).

Brief biographical accounts of artists, with short-title listings of their chief illustrated books.

Mahony, Bertha E. *et al. Illustrators of Children's Books 1744–1945* (Boston, 1947).

The bibliographical section is compiled by Louise Payson Latimer. This is a pioneer work and therefore of uncertain reliability. Three sequels published in 1958, 1968 and 1978 must also be used with caution.

Sketchley, R. E. D. *English Book Illustration of Today; appreciations of living English illustrators with lists of their books* (London, 1903).

The sections on children's books have been reprinted in the anthology by Salway (section II.3.ii).

4 General Location Lists

Field, Carolyn W. *Subject Collections in Children's Literature* (New York and London, 1969).
>An indexed analysis of collections mainly in the United States.

Salway, L., ed. *Special Collections of Children's Literature; a guide to collections in libraries . . . in London and the Home Counties* (London, 1972).

5 Specific Location Lists

>The rarity of many children's books has led bibliographers such as Grey, Moon, Roscoe and Welch to include location notes in their works, an aid which is rapidly coming to be seen as essential. One summary of a group of special collections is notable for its provision of location data:

Higson, C. W. J., ed. *Sources for the History of Education; a list of material (including school books) contained in the Libraries of the Institutes and Schools of Education, together with works from the Libraries of the Universities of Nottingham and Reading* (London, 1967).
>Children's books published before 1870 are included. A *Supplement* with Appendixes of additional locations and amendments was published in 1976.

6 Catalogues of Collections

i National Libraries (general)

British Museum. *General Catalogue of Printed Books to 1955* Compact edition. 27 vols. (New York, 1967).
>A micro-text edition with two sets of supplements carrying the dates forward to 1970.
>
>A full-size printing of the catalogue up to 1975: *British Library Catalogue of Printed Books*, is currently in progress (London, 1979–).

ii National Libraries (special collections)

Library of Congress. *Children's Books in the Rare Book Division*. 2 vols. (Washington, 1976).

Victoria and Albert Museum. The children's book collection at the National Art Library at the Victoria and Albert Museum is analysed in sheaf and card catalogues housed in the library.

iii Special Collections in Individual Libraries

[Aubrey, Doris] *The Wandsworth Collection of Early Children's Books* (Wandsworth, 1972).

Boggis, Doreen H. *Catalogue of the Hockliffe Collection of Early Children's Books* (Bedford, 1969).

[Darton, F. J. H.] *A Note on Old Children's Books (The Harvey Darton Collection)* [n.d.].
>Xerographic facsimile of the typescript catalogue prepared by F. J. H. D. before the sale of his books. The collection now stands in the Teachers College of the University of Columbia, New York. A typescript *Index* is separately issued.

Good, David. *A Catalogue of the Spencer Collection of Early Children's Books and Chapbooks . . .* (Preston, 1967). The notes owe much to those in the Osborne Catalogue (below).

Kilpatrick, P. J. W. *Catalogue of the Edward Clark Library; with typographical notes by Harry Carter and an essay on the printing of illustrations by Frank P. Restall*. 2 vols. (Edinburgh, 1976).

London Borough of Hammersmith. *Early Children's Books; a catalogue of the collection* . . . (Hammersmith, 1965).

Rosenbach, A. S. W. *Early American Children's Books; with bibliographical descriptions of the books in his private collection* (Portland, Maine, 1933).
> Arranged chronologically 1682–1836.

St John, Judith comp. *The Osborne Collection of Early Children's books 1566–1910; a catalogue* (Toronto, 1958). The first major attempt to catalogue in detail a large and varied collection of early English children's books. A second volume was published in 1975, and a third, devoted to periodicals and penny dreadfuls, is in preparation.

7 Exhibition Catalogues

> Appendix 1 notes the growth of adult curiosity about children's books of the past. This has tended to express itself through exhibitions and the annotation of exhibition catalogues, and these may supply information about otherwise obscure books.
>
> The following selection is arranged chronologically to show the variety of themes and approaches that have been presented. It may also emphasize the central importance of Percy Muir's *Children's Books of Yesterday* exhibition at the National Book League, an event which did much to stimulate the 'boom' in interest in early children's books since the Second World War.
>
> Alongside these general catalogues could also be placed many that celebrate the work of particular authors or illustrators. Some, such as the catalogue of the Beatrix Potter Centenary Exhibition held at the National Book League in 1966, or the 'Companion-Guide' to the 'Alice' Exhibition at Longleat in 1973, record events which prompted wide-spread or renewed public interest in their subjects.

Morgan, F. C. ed. *Children's Books Published before 1830, exhibited at Malvern Public Library in 1911* (Hereford, 1976).
> Probably the first large-scale exhibition of early children's books ever held in England. This catalogue is compiled from notes made at the end of the exhibition and is by the organiser of the event who, in 1976, was ninety-eight years old.

*H.M. Stationery Office. *Catalogue of the British Section of the International Exhibition of the Book Industry and Graphic Arts* (Leipzig, 1914).
> A section of this Exhibition – which was cut short in August, 1914 – was devoted to children's books, which were catalogued with an introduction. The books, lent from private and other collections, were honourably preserved in Germany from 1914 to 1918 and returned safely after the war.
> [The section 'Illustrated and Juvenile Books' is by F. J. H. D.]

*Fulham Public Libraries. *Catalogue of an Exhibition of Children's Books of Long Ago* [Dec. 1931–Jan. 1932], with a foreword by F. E. Hansford (London, [1931]).
> [Books for this exhibition by W. C. Cater subsequently formed the core of the Hammersmith Collection (Section 1.6.iii).]

Muir, Percy H. *Children's Books of Yesterday; a catalogue of an exhibition* . . . (London, 1946).
> An *Index* was separately published (London, 1977).

Osborne, Edgar. *From Morality and Instruction to Beatrix Potter; an Exhibition* . . . (Eastbourne, 1949).
> Held at the Towner Art Gallery, Eastbourne from 23 May to 12 June this exhibition marked the 'last public appearance' in England of Edgar Osborne's collection of children's books before it was shipped to Toronto. Reprinted in the privately published *A Token for Friends; being a memoir of Edgar Osborne* . . . (Toronto, 1979).

Hadfield, John, comp. *The Festival of Britain Exhibition of Books, arranged by the National Book League* . . . (London, 1951).

> Following a section on Nursery Rhymes and a modern panoramic peepshow, items 38–102 of the exhibition formed a 'Children's Corner'. On the selection of favourites for this section the Advisory Panel write that it 'took longer than that of any other, and was fought over until the last moment with unceasing gallantry and tenacity'.

Pierpont Morgan Library. *Children's Literature; books and manuscripts, an exhibition* . . . (New York, 1954). Compiled by Herbert Cahoon.

British Museum. *An Exhibition of Early Children's Books* (London, 1968).

> In order to show the continuity of traditions 'a number of specially selected modern children's books' were available on open shelves for visitors to the Exhibition to consult and compare. A hand-list of these was also issued.

[Whalley, I. and Hobbs, A.] *'What the Children Like'; a selection of children's books, toys and games from the Renier Collection* [London, 1970].

> An exhibition at the Victoria and Albert Museum from December 1970–February 1971 celebrating the gift to the Museum of children's books and related material by Mr and Mrs F. G. Renier.

Alderson, Brian. *Looking at Picture Books 1973; an exhibition* . . . (London, 1973).

> Like the British Museum exhibition of 1968 (above) this display at the National Book League was designed to show parallels between past and present. It also tried to substantiate a critical view of its subject.

Opie, Iona and Peter. *Three Centuries of Nursery Rhymes and Poetry for Children.* 2nd edn (Oxford and New York, 1977).

> Originally published as the catalogue of a National Book League exhibition in 1973, here revised, expanded and given detailed indexes in order to enhance its usefulness as a reference work.

[Whalley, I.] *Victorian Children's Books; selected from the Library of the Victoria and Albert Museum* (London, 1973).

> Arranged for the Europalia 73 Exhibition in Brussels.

Pierpont Morgan Library. *Early Children's Books and their Illustration* (New York, 1975). Compiled by Gerald Gottlieb.

Ray, Gordon N. *The Illustrator and the Book in England from 1790 to 1914* (New York and London, 1976).

Kloet, Christine A. *After Alice; a hundred years of children's reading in Britain* (London, 1977).

8 Sale Catalogues

> A like pointer to adult interest, and a like source for bibliographical information, occurs in material engendered by the rapid growth of children's books as objects of interest to collectors.

i Booksellers' Catalogues

> Two important items may be seen as standing at the start of a fashion which during the 1970s became almost a mania:

*Gumuchian et Cie. *Les Livres de l'Enfance du XVe au XIXe Siècle.* Prèface de Paul Gavrault. 2 vols. (Paris, [1930]).

> Bibliographical catalogue of a bookseller's huge international collection, with many illustrations.

Schatzki, Walter *Old and Rare Children's Books* . . . (New York, [1941]).

> Walter Schatzki's 'Reminiscences' were published in *Phaedrus*, Vol. II Fall,

1978. They bear witness to the enthusiasm for English children's books among American collectors and booksellers. Catalogues produced by the latter – such as the four *Chapbook Miscellanies* from Justin G. Schiller Ltd (1970) – may achieve the status of bibliographical reference works in their own right.

ii *Auction Catalogues*

The first major sale of children's books at Sotheby's to which a detailed catalogue was devoted was that of February 27, 1967. From that time on the London sale-rooms have held children's book sales with increasing frequency. The high point was undoubtedly the disposal of 'A Highly Important Collection' which took place in six sales between July 1974 and October 1977. The Collection was that of Edgar Oppenheimer, the foundation of which had been the books brought together by Percy Muir for *Children's Books of Yesterday* in 1946.

II Sources on the discussion of children's books

1 General Bibliographies

Crouch, M. H. *Books about Children's Literature*. Rev. edn (London, 1966).
  A pamphlet, as also is the more recent *Background to Children's Books* by Colin Ray, rev. edn (London, 1977).
Haviland, V. ed. *Children's Literature; a guide to reference sources* (Washington, 1966).
  Organized in subject categories and includes periodical articles. Supplements with addenda and new material have been published (Washington, 1972 and 1977).
Ørvig, Mary and Törnqvist, Lena. *The Swedish Institute for Children's Books: Catalogue of the Reference Collection: Acquisitions 1967–1973* (Stockholm, 1975).
  An international reference collection, including historical material, arranged alphabetically and with a key-word register in Swedish and English.
Pellowski, Anne *The World of Children's Literature* (New York, 1968).
  A country-by-country listing of secondary source material, including historical studies.
    Extensive references to secondary sources are also to be found in the volumes of *N.C.B.E.L.* (section 1.1). See also the bibliographies in the monographs by Hürlimann, Muir and Thwaite below.

2 Bibliographies on Special Aspects

Where bibliographies of books about individual subjects exist (e.g. Neuburg, *Chap Books*, 1972) or are given in other works (e.g. Opie, *The Classic Fairy Tales*, 1974), they are noted in the chapter Book Lists.

3 General Histories and Studies

i *Published before 1933*

*Andreae, Gesiena. *The Dawn of Juvenile Literature in England* (Amsterdam, 1925).
*Barry, Florence Valentine. *A Century of Children's Books* (London, 1922).
  Covers approximately the Georgian era.
*Field, E. M. *The Child and his Book; some account of the history and progress of children's literature in England*. 2nd edn (London, 1892).
  First published a year earlier. See Darton's comment on p.VII.
Hazard, Paul. *Les Livres, les Enfants et les Hommes* (Paris, 1932).

Translated by Marguerite Mitchell as *Books, Children and Men* (Boston, 1944). With the book by B. Hürlimann below, this represents one of the few attempts at a comparative discussion of (mostly European) children's books.

*Moses, Montrose J. *Children's Books and Reading* (New York, 1907).
Much bibliographical information as well as history, not only American.

Salmon, Edward. *Juvenile Literature as it is* (London, 1888).
Although primarily about books of the period, it shows awareness of the historical background.

*Sawyer, Charles J. and Darton, F. J. H. *English Books 1475–1900*, 2 vols. (London, 1927).
Vol. I, Chapter VIII, 'The People's Books' (i.e. chapbooks) and vol. II, Chapter IV, 'Nursery Treasures'. Mainly rare books.

ii Published after 1933

Avery, Gillian. *Childhood's Pattern; a study of the heroes and heroines of children's fiction 1770–1950* (London, 1975).
Based on a previous work: *Nineteenth Century Children*, which included two chapters on fairy tales by Angela Bull.

Cadogan, Mary and Craig, Patricia. *You're a Brick, Angela! a new look at girls' fiction from 1839 to 1975* (London, 1976).

Cutt, Margaret Nancy. *Ministering Angels; a study of nineteenth century Evangelical writing for children* (Wormley, 1979).
Includes short-title listings of books by A.L.O.E., Maria Charlesworth, 'Hesba Stretton' and Mrs O. F. Walton.

Green, Roger Lancelyn. *Tellers of Tales; children's books and their authors from 1800 to 1968*. Rev. edn (London, 1969).
Includes a chronological table and lists of titles by the authors discussed. When originally published in 1946 it was planned as a book for children.

Hürlimann, Bettina. *Europäische Kinderbücher in drei Jahrhunderten*. 2nd edn (Zürich, 1963).
Translated and edited by Brian Alderson as *Three Centuries of Children's Books in Europe* (London, 1967).

Kiefer, M. *American Children Through their Books 1700–1835* (Philadelphia, 1938).

Muir, Percy. *English Children's Books 1600–1900* (London, 1954).

Sale, Roger. *Fairy Tales and After, from Snow White to E. B. White* (Cambridge, Mass. and London, 1978).
An attempt at an 'adult' critical reading of children's books including folk tales and 'classics'.

Salway, Lance, ed. *A Peculiar Gift; nineteenth century writings on books for children* (London, 1976).
An anthology arranged in broad topics with editorial introductions, and biographical and explanatory notes.

Smith, Lillian H. *The Unreluctant Years; a critical approach to children's literature* (Chicago, 1953).
Less pretentious in its aims than Sale's book above, and with a deeper sympathy for historical factors.

Thwaite, Mary F. *From Primer to Pleasure in Children's Reading; an introduction to the history of children's books in England*. 2nd edn (London, 1972).
First published simply as *From Primer to Pleasure* (1963). Contains a chronological list 1479–1798 and a systematic bibliographical commentary on secondary sources.

Townsend, John Rowe. *Written for Children; an outline of English-language children's literature.* 2nd edn (London, 1974).

> First published in a briefer, racier version in 1965.

Turner, E. S. *Boys Will Be Boys; the story of Sweeney Todd, Deadwood Dick, Sexton Blake, Billy Bunter, Dick Barton et al.* with an introduction by Capt. C. B. Fry (London, 1948).

Whalley, Joyce Irene. *Cobwebs to Catch Flies; illustrated books for the nursery and schoolroom 1700–1900* (London, 1974).

4 Some General Works on Illustration and Book Production

Bland, David. *A History of Book Illustration.* 2nd ed (London, 1969)

Bland, David. *The Illustration of Books.* 3rd ed (London, 1962).

Burch, R. M. *Colour Printing and Colour Printers* (London, 1910).

Hardie, Martin. *English Colour Books* (London, 1906).

McLean, Ruari. *Victorian Book Design and Colour Printing* 2nd edn (London, 1972).

> Originally published in smaller format, 1963.

McLean, Ruari. *Victorian Publishers' Bookbindings in Cloth and Leather* (London, 1974).

Maré, Eric de. *The Victorian Woodblock Illustrators* (London, 1980).

Muir, Percy. *Victorian Illustrated Books* (London, 1971).

Reid, Forrest. *Illustrators of the Eighteen-Sixties; an illustrated survey of the work of fifty-eight British artists* (New York, 1975).

> Photographic reprint of a book originally published as *Illustrators of the Sixties* (London 1928).

Salaman, Malcolm C. *Modern Book Illustrators and their Work* (London, 1914).

> One of a series of special issues of *The Studio.* Later additions were:
> Salaman, Malcolm C. *British Book Illustration Yesterday and Today* (London 1923);
> and Darton, F. J. H. *Modern Book Illustration in Great Britain and America* (London, 1931).

Smith, Janet Adam. *Children's Illustrated Books* (London, 1949).

Thorpe, J. H. *English Illustration; the nineties* (London, 1935).

Wakeman, Geoffrey. *Victorian Book Illustration; the technical revolution* (Newton Abbot, 1973).

White, Gleeson. *English Illustration 'The Sixties': 1855–70* (London, 1897).

5 Biographical Compendia

> Some biographies of individuals are noted in the chapter Book Lists, and fuller listings for important authors may be found in the volumes of *N.C.B.E.L.* In addition several reference works should be noted (if not recommended) for their efforts to fill the need for a biographical dictionary of the authors and illustrators of children's books:

Doyle, Brian. *The Who's Who of Children's Literature* (London, 1968).

Kirkpatrick, D. L., ed. *Twentieth Century Children's Writers.* with a preface by Naomi Lewis (London, 1978).

> With an appendix on twenty-three influential nineteenth-century writers. Contains extensive title-lists.

Lofts, W. O. G. and Adley, D. J. *The Men Behind Boys' Fiction* (London, 1970).

> Notable for the affectionate attention which it gives to humble and obscure writers.

6 Periodicals Dealing with Children's Books

Children's Literature. Annual ([U.S.A.] 1972–).

> An annual collection of essays emanating in part from the Modern Language Association Seminar (later Group) on Children's Literature. It has had several changes of designation and place of publication. No. 8 (1979) is from New Haven and London.

Children's Literature in Education. Four p.a.

> Occasionally carries articles on historical aspects. Between 1970 and 1974 frequency of publication was only three p.a.

Phaedrus; an international journal of children's literature research. Two p.a. (Marblehead, Mass. 1973–).

> Originally subtitled 'A newsletter of children's literature research' and published from Madison, N. J. Includes reviews and notes on periodical articles etc. published eleswhere.

Signal; approaches to children's books. Three p.a. (Stroud, 1970–).

> Note also the increasing frequency with which the history of children's books may be discussed in other specialist journals such as the *Book Collector*, and the proliferation of societies such as the Children's Books History Society or the Lewis Carroll Society, whose newsletters and other publications may be a source of specialist information.
>
> Some guidance to articles published in periodicals may be gained from the classified entries in *Children's Literature Abstracts*, four p.a. (Birmingham, 1973–). An index for the years 1973–9 was issued in 1980.

7 Miscellaneous Related Works

Altick, Richard D. *The English Common Reader; a social history of the mass reading public 1800–1900* (Chicago, 1957).

*Babenroth, A. Charles. *English Childhood; Wordsworth's treatment of childhood in the light of English poetry from Prior to Crabbe* (New York, 1922).

> Chapters III, IV and V.

Coveney, Peter. *The Image of Childhood; the individual and society: a study of the theme in English literature.* Rev. edn (Harmondsworth 1967).

> First published as *Poor Monkey* (London, 1957).

*Newton, A. Edward. *This Book-Collecting Game* (Boston, 1928).

> Chapters II and IV.

*Sayers, W. C. Berwick. *A Manual of Children's Libraries* (London, 1932).

> Chapters I and II, with bibliographical details *passim* in other chapters.

Sources of Illustrations

Title-page. Medallion from a proof sheet of sixteen small pictures printed in 1804 by William Darton.

1   [John Newbery?] *A Little Pretty Pocket-Book* . . . London: printed for J. Newbery at the Bible and Sun . . . 1767. Taken from the facsimile of this book published by Oxford University Press, 1966 (original in British Library).

2   [John Newbery?] *The Twelfth-Day-Gift: or the Grand Exhibition. Containing a curious collection of pieces in prose and verse* . . . Second edition. London: printed for Carnan and Newbery . . . 1770.

3a   *Aesop's Fables* . . . illustrated with one hundred and ten sculptures by Francis Barlow. And are sold at his house The Golden Eagle in New-Street, near Shoo-Lane, 1665. [Etched title page. The letterpress title-page is dated 1666.]

3b   *Fables of Aesop and Others. Newly done into English* . . . [by Samuel Croxall D.D.] London: printed for J. Tonson, and J. Watts 1722.

3c   Aesop. *Select Fables, in Three Parts* . . . a new edition. Newcastle: printed by and for T. Saint, 1784. Taken from the reprint with original blocks, ed. E. Pearson, London, 1871.

3d   *Aesop's Fables.* A new edition with proverbs and applications, with over one hundred illustrations. Paisley: Alexander Gardner, publisher by appointment to the late Queen Victoria.

4   John Locke. *Aesop's Fables in English and Latin, interlineary, for the benefit of those who not having a Master, would learn either of these Tongues.* The Second Edition, with Sculptures. London: printed for A. Bettesworth, at the Red-Lyon in Pater-Noster Row, 1723.

5   *Select Fables of Esop and Other Fabulists. In three books.* By R. Dodsley. New edition. For J. Dodsley, London, 1776.

6a   'T. Telltruth'. *Natural History of Birds*, embellished with curious cuts. London: for Francis Newbery . . . 1778.

6b   The Bestiary being a reproduction in full of the manuscript ii.4.26 in the University Library, Cambridge. Ed. M. R. James for the Roxburghe Club, 1928.

7   Manuscript day-book kept by the Oxford bookseller John Dorne in 1520.

8   *Syr Beuys of Hampton.* London: W. Copland [1565?].

9   J. J. *A Token for Youth* . . . London: printed and sold by Benj. Harris at the Golden Boar's Head in Grace-church Street. 1709.

10   T. W. *A Little Book for Little Children; wherein are set down, in a plain and pleasant way, directions for spelling and other remarkable matters.* Adorn'd with cuts. London: printed for George Conyers . . . [1702?].

11   'Robert Burton'. *Winter Evening Entertainments; in two parts. Containing I. Ten pleasant and delightful relations of many rare and notable accidents and occurrences . . . II. Fifty ingenious riddles* . . . The whole enlivened with above threescore pictures . . . Excellently accommodated to the fancies of old or young . . . The sixth edition. London: printed for A. Bettesworth and C. Hitch . . . 1737. [Part II has a separate title-page claiming it to be the fifth edition. The book is continuously paged.]

12a   John Bunyan. *Divine Emblems: or, temporal things spiritualized, fitted for the use of boys and girls.* Adorned with cuts . . . The Ninth Edition. London: printed by S. Negus for John Marshall, at the Bible in Gracechurch Street. 1724.

12b   John Bunyan. *Divine Emblems* . . . London: printed for C. Dilly, in the Poultry, and sold by Darton and Harvey, Gracechurch-Street. 1793.

13a *The Death and Burial of Cock Robin* . . . Lichfield. Printed and Sold by M. Morgan, and A. Morgan, Stafford.

13b *The Death and Burial of Cock Robin* . . . Otley. Printed by W. Walker, at the Wharfedale Stanhope Press.

13c *The History of John Gilpin*. Derby: printed by and for Thomas Richardson, Friar-Gate.

13d *The Sunday-Scholar's Gift; or a present for a good child*. A new edition. Wellington, Salop: printed by and for F. Houlston & Son. And sold by G. and S. Robinson, Paternoster-Row, London, and all other Booksellers. 1817.

14 *The Interesting Story of the Children in the Wood. An historical ballad*. Banbury: J. G. Rusher [*c.* 1835].

15a 'P. P.' [i.e. Charles Perrault]. *Contes de ma Mere LOye*. 1695. Manuscript containing five stories, with seven gouache illustrations.

15b M. [i.e. Monsieur] Perrault. *Histories, or Tales of Passed Times With Morals* . . . Englished by R. S. Gent. The second edition corrected. London: R. Montagu & J. Pote, 1737.

16 'La Princesse Printaniére' in *Le Cabinet des Fées* . . . Tome Second. Amsterdam, et se trouve à Paris, Rue et Hotel Serpante, 1785.

17 M.M. [i.e. Messieurs] Grimm. *German Popular Stories* . . . [translated by Edgar Taylor and illustrated by George Cruikshank]. London, C. Baldwyn, 1823.

18 Nurse Lovechild. *Tommy Thumb's Pretty Song Book*. Voll. II. Sold by M. Cooper. 1744.

19 *Curiosities in the Tower of London*. Vol. I. The Second Edition. Printed for Tho. Boreman, Bookseller, near the two giants in Guildhall, London, 1741 [Price Four pence].

20 *The History of Little Goody Twoshoes* . . . The first Worcester edition. Printed at Worcester, Massachusetts. By Isaiah Thomas . . . 1787. Taken from a facsimile published by G. K. Hall & Co., Boston, Mass., 1969 (original in Library of Congress).

21a *The History of Little Goody Two-Shoes* . . . London: printed for T. Carnan, successor to Mr J. Newbery, in St Paul's Church-Yard. 1783.

21b *The History of Goody Two Shoes* . . . Embellish'd with elegant engravings. Glasgow, published by J. Lumsden & Son, & sold by Stoddart & Craggs, Hull [1810?].

21c *The Renowned History of Goody Two-Shoes* . . . A new edition with five original designs. London: James Burns, 1845.

21d *The Story of Goody Two Shoes*. Raphael Tuck [*c.* 1940] (Tiny Tuck Series).

22 *The Infant's Library*. Sixteen volumes. London, John Marshall, Aldermary Church Yard [1800?]. With a wooden cabinet painted to resemble a book-case.

23 Honora Edgeworth. *Practical Education; or, the history of Harry and Lucy*. Vol. II. Lichfield . . . 1780.

24 [Richard Johnson]. *The Blossoms of Morality; intended for the amusement and instruction of young ladies and gentlemen*. By the editor of 'The Looking-Glass for the Mind'. With forty-seven cuts, designed and engraved by I. Bewick. The Eighth Edition. London: printed for J. Harris et al. 1828. First published with these illustrations, 1796.

25 Mrs Sherwood. *Think Before You Act*. Sixth Edition. London: Darton & Hodge [*c.* 1865]. First published with these illustrations *c.* 1841.

26 Christopher Smart. *Hymns for the Amusement of Children*. Dublin, 1772. Taken from the facsimile published by Scolar Press Ltd, London, 1973 (original in British Library).

27   [William Blake]. *For Children The Gates of Paradise.* Published by W. Blake No. 13 Hercules Buildings Lambeth and J. Johnson St Pauls Church Yard 1793. Taken from the facsimile published by the Trianon Press, Paris, 1968 (original in Library of Congress).

28   Jane and Ann Taylor. *Little Ann and Other Poems.* Illustrated by Kate Greenaway. Printed in colours by Edmund Evans. London: George Routledge & Sons [1883].

29a   'Edward Baldwin' [i.e. William Godwin]. *Fables Ancient and Modern, adapted for the use of children from three to eight years of age.* Two volumes. London: T. Hodgkins at the Juvenile Library . . . 1805. [The 'superior' edition.]

29b   Standard edition of the above. Tenth Edition. London: printed for M. J. Godwin and Co. at the French and English Juvenile and School Library . . . 1824.

30a   [William Roscoe]. *The Butterfly's Ball, and the Grasshopper's Feast.* London: printed for J. Harris, corner of St Paul's Church Yard. Jany. 1st 1807.

30b   Mr Roscoe. *The Butterfly's Ball and the Grasshopper's Feast.* London: printed for J. Harris, successor to E. Newbery, at the Original Juvenile Library, corner of St Paul's Church-Yard, 1808. Taken from the reprint published by Griffith & Farran, 1883 (original in California University Library).

31a   [R. S. Sharpe?]. *Anecdotes and Adventures of Fifteen Gentlemen.* Embellished with fifteen laughable engravings. London: printed and sold by John Marshall [*c.* 1822].

31b   'The Old Man of Tobago'. Holograph drawing by Edward Lear, reproduced in *Lear in the Original*; drawings and limericks . . . for his 'Book of Nonsense', now first printed in facsimile . . . with an introduction and notes by Herman W. Liebert. New York & London, 1875.

32   E[liza] F[enwick]. *Visits to the Juvenile Library; or knowledge proved to be the source of happiness.* London: printed . . . for Tabart and Co. 1805.

33a   See above, fig. 17.

33b   Original pen drawing by Edward Ardizzone, prepared as one of his illustrations for *The Secret Shoemakers and Other Stories* [retold by] James Reeves. London, 1966.

34   Advertisement at the end of *Friendship's Gift: a forget me not for the young.* London: Edward Lacey, 76 St Paul's Church Yard [*c.* 1840].

35   'Ambrose Merton' [i.e. W. J. Thoms]. *The Gallant History of Bevis of Southampton.* [London] Joseph Cundall [1843?] (Gammer Gurton's Story Books No. 4).

36   Engraving by William Darton Junior, 1803.

37   Hans Christian Andersen. *Tales for the Young.* A new translation. London: James Burns, 1847 (Burns' Cabinet Library for Youth).

38   Dr Julius Bähr. *Naughty Boys and Girls.* Translated by Mme. de Chatelain. Illustrated by Theodor Hosemann. London: Addey & Co. [1852].

39a   ['Lewis Carroll' (i.e. Charles Lutwidge Dodgson)]. Manuscript of *Alice's Adventures Under Ground.* Taken from a facsimile, published Macmillan, London, 1886 (original in British Library).

39b   'Lewis Carroll'. *Alice's Adventures in Wonderland.* With forty-two illustrations by John Tenniel. London, 1866. Taken from a reprint, London, 1971.

40a   *Park's Twelfth-Night Characters.* A pleasure game. London: A. Park [*c.* 1850]. [Wallet title.]

40b & c   'Mr M. A. Titmarsh' [i.e. W. M. Thackeray]. *The Rose and the Ring; or, the history of Prince Giglio and Prince Bulbo. A Fire-side pantomime for great and small children.* London: Smith, Elder & Co., 1855.

41   *The Charm. A book for boys and girls.* Illustrated with above sixty engravings. Third Series. London: Addey & Co. . . . 1855. [An annual formed from the parts of the monthly magazine.]

42a [The Rev. J. Erskine Clarke ed.] *Chatterbox*. Part x. October, 1871. Published for the proprietors by W. Wells Gardner.

42b ['Frank Richards' (i.e. Charles Hamilton)]. *The Magnet Library. The Complete Story-Book for All*. Vol. 5. No. 152 [1911].

43a Juliana Horatia Ewing. *Lob Lie-By-The-Fire; or, the luck of Lingborough*. Illustrated by Randolph Caldecott. Engraved and printed by Edmund Evans. London and Brighton, Society for Promoting Christian Knowledge . . . [1885].

43b Juliana Horatia Ewing. *Lob Lie-By-The-Fire, or the luck of Lingborough. And other tales*. With illustrations by George Cruikshank. London, George Bell and Sons, 1874.

44 Mrs Molesworth. *The Cuckoo Clock*. Illustrated by Walter Crane. London: Macmillan & Co., 1877.

45 Rudyard Kipling. *Just-So Stories for Little Children*. Illustrated by the author. Leipzig, B. Tauchnitz, 1902.

46a [Mrs O. F. Walton]. *Christie's Old Organ; or, 'Home sweet home'* . . . London. The Religious Tract Society . . . [*c*. 1877].B

46b Mrs O. F. Walton. *Christie's Old Organ*. London. The Religious Tract Society [*c*. 1900].

47 Talbot Baines Reed. *Kilgorman; a story of Ireland in 1798*. London . . . T. Nelson and Sons, 1895.

48a Beatrix Potter. *The Tale of Peter Rabbit*. London, Frederick Warne and Co. [1902].

48b Beatrix Potter. *The Tale of Peter Rabbit*. Thirty-one illustrations. Philadelphia, Henry Altemus Company, 1904 (Altemus' Wee Books for Wee Folks).

p. 315 Walter De La Mare. *Peacock Pie. A book of rhymes*. With illustrations by W. Heath Robinson. London, Constable & Co. Ltd. [1916]. [The quotation is, of course, from the first of Dr Watts's Moral Songs.]

p. 331 Andrew Lang ed. *The Nursery Rhyme Book*. Illustrated by L. Leslie Brooke. London, Frederick Warne and Co., 1897.

p. 361 Joseph Jacobs comp. *More English Fairy Tales*. Illustrated by John D. Batten. London, David Nutt, 1894.

ACKNOWLEDGMENTS

Thanks are due to the following for permission to reproduce the illustrations listed below from their collections.

1, 3a, 3c, 4, 5, 6b, 12a, 16, 26, 27, 30b, 33a, 39b, 41, 42a, 42b, 43a, Cambridge University Library; 2, 3b, 6a, 8, 9, 10, 11, 18, 30a, 38, 43b, The British Library; 3d, Dr Mary Hobbs; 7, The President and Fellows of Corpus Christi College (MSS. 131, fol. 10ʳ); 12b, 13a, 13b, 13c, 13d, 14, 17, 20, 21c, 24, 25, 28, 29b, 34, 37, 40a, 40b, 40c, 44, 45, 46a, 46b, 47, 48a, 48b, tailpieces, Brian Alderson; 15a, Trustees of the Pierpont Morgan Library; 15b, 29a, Victoria and Albert Museum; 19, Birmingham Reference Library, the Parker Collection of early children's books and games; 21a, Justin Schiller of Justin G. Schiller Ltd, New York; 21b, 31a, 32, 35, Osborne Collection of Early Children's Books, Toronto Public Library; 21d, Raphael Tuck and Ronald Bayman; 22, David Chambers; 23, Christina Colvin; 31b, Oxford University Press and H. P. Kraus, New York; 33b, Abelard-Schuman Ltd, London; 36, Lawrence Darton.

Index

This index is modelled on that for the 1932 edition of *Children's Books in England* and follows the practice there of including many minor references, and of giving page references broadly in the order of their significance. Very often authors or titles mentioned in the book are so obscure that any note of them is worth recording. Less attention, however, has been paid to indexing authors and titles in the Book Lists and in the General Bibliography. These have usually only been included where an annotation is present or where reference to the works in question will fill out information directly related to children's books. Most illustrations have been indexed as 'illus. fig.' with the page number in parentheses, but where only the information in the caption is referred to this appears as 'fig.'.